Lecture Notes in Computer Science 7871

Commenced Publication in 1973
Founding and Former Series Editors:
Gerhard Goos, Juris Hartmanis, and Jan van Leeuwen

Editorial Board

Guillaume Brat   Neha Rungta
Arnaud Venet (Eds.)

NASA
Formal Methods

5th International Symposium, NFM 2013
Moffett Field, CA, USA, May 14-16, 2013
Proceedings

 Springer

Volume Editors

Guillaume Brat
NASA Ames Research Center
M/S 269-2
Moffett Field, CA 94035-0001, USA
E-mail: guillaume.p.brat@nasa.gov

Neha Rungta
Stinger Ghaffarian Technologies Inc.
NASA Ames Research Center
M/S 269-2
Moffett Field, CA 94035-0001, USA
E-mail: neha.s.rungta@nasa.gov

Arnaud Venet
Carnegie Mellon University
NASA Ames Research Center
M/S 269-2
Moffett Field, CA 94035-0001, USA
E-mail: arnaud.j.venet@nasa.gov

ISSN 0302-9743   e-ISSN 1611-3349
ISBN 978-3-642-38087-7   e-ISBN 978-3-642-38088-4
DOI 10.1007/978-3-642-38088-4
Springer Heidelberg Dordrecht London New York

Library of Congress Control Number: 2013936402

CR Subject Classification (1998): D.2.4, D.2, D.3, F.3, D.1, D.4.1

LNCS Sublibrary: SL 2 – Programming and Software Engineering

Typesetting: Camera-ready by author, data conversion by Scientific Publishing Services, Chennai, India

Printed on acid-free paper

Springer is part of Springer Science+Business Media (www.springer.com)

Preface

The NASA Formal Methods Symposium is a forum for theoreticians and practitioners from academia, industry, and government, with the goals of identifying challenges and providing solutions to achieving assurance in mission- and safety-critical systems. Within NASA, for example, such systems include autonomous robots, separation assurance algorithms for aircraft, next-generation air transportation (NextGen), and autonomous rendezvous and docking for spacecraft. Moreover, emerging paradigms such as code generation and safety cases are bringing with them new challenges and opportunities. The focus of the symposium is on formal techniques, their theory, current capabilities and limitations, as well as their application to aerospace, robotics, and other safety-critical systems.

The NASA Formal Methods Symposium is an annual event that was created to highlight the state of the art in formal methods, both in theory and practice. This volume contains the papers presented at NFM 2013, the 5th NASA Formal Methods Symposium held during May 14–16, 2013, in Moffett Field. Previous symposia were held in Norfolk, VA (LNCS 7226), Pasadena, CA (LNCS 6617), Washington, DC, and Moffett Field, CA. There were two categories of papers solicited in the call for papers of the symposium. The first category consists of regular papers describing fully developed work and complete results or case studies, and the second category consists of short papers describing tools, experience reports, and work in progress or preliminary results. The NFM 2013 Symposium received 99 submissions: 75 regular papers and 24 short papers. Each submission underwent a rigorous review process and received at least three reviews; most submissions, however, received four reviews. After a lengthy discussion phase, a total of 37 papers were accepted to be included in the proceedings out of which 28 are regular papers and 9 are short papers.

In addition to the refereed papers, the symposium features three keynotes and two invited talks. The keynotes were presented by Kenneth McMillan from Microsoft Research on "The Importance of Generalization in Automated Proof," John Rushby from SRI International on "The Challenge of High-Assurance Software," and Alex Aiken from Stanford University on "Using Learning Techniques in Invariant Inference." In addition to keynotes, the symposium featured two invited talks by Rajeev Joshi from the Jet Propulsion Laboratory on "Managing Data for Curiosity, Fun and Profit" and Michael DeWalt from FAA on "Certification Challenges when Using Formal Methods, Including Needs and Issues."

The Organizing Committee would like to thank NASA for sponsoring the symposium, the members of the NFM Steering Committee for providing valuable advice and support, and the members of the Program Committee and the external reviewers for their dedication in reviewing submissions and helping shape a strong program for NFM 2013. We are grateful to the authors for choosing to submit their work to NFM 2013 and the invited speakers for sharing their work and insights. Special thanks go to Lester Barrows whose picture of the shuttle flying over Hangar One was used in the NFM publicity poster. Finally, organizing this symposium and putting together the proceedings was greatly facilitated by the use of EasyChair.

March 2013

Guillaume Brat
Neha Rungta
Arnaud Venet

Organization

Program Committee

Julia Badger	NASA, USA
Thomas Ball	Microsoft Research, USA
Guillaume Brat	NASA Ames Research Center, CA, USA
Ricky Butler	NASA Langley Research Center, USA
Patrice Chalin	Kansas State University, USA
Darren Cofer	Rockwell Collins, USA
Radhia Cousot	CNRS / École normale supérieure, France
Leonardo De Moura	Microsoft Research, USA
Ewen Denney	SGT/NASA Ames, USA
Ben Di Vito	NASA Langley Research Center, USA
Jim Disbrow	NASA Dryden Flight Center, USA
Gilles Dowek	INRIA, France
Matt Dwyer	University of Nebraska, USA
Eric Feron	Georgia Institute of Technology, USA
Jean-Christophe Filliatre	CNRS, France
Kathleen Fisher	Tufts University, USA
Pierre-Loic Garoche	ONERA
Eric Goubault	CEA/Saclay, France
Orna Grumberg	Technion - Israel Institute of Technology, Israel
Klaus Havelund	Jet Propulsion Laboratory, California Institute of Technology, USA
Gerard Holzmann	JPL, USA
Joe Hurd	Galois, Inc.
Ranjit Jhala	University of California, San Diego, USA
Hadas Kress-Gazit	Cornell University, USA
Daniel Kroening	Oxford University, UK
Tiziana Margaria	University of Potsdam, Germany
Célia Martinie	IHCS-IRIT, University Paul Sabatier - Toulouse III, France
Eric Mercer	Brigham Young University, USA
Paul Miner	NASA, USA
Cesar Munoz	National Aeronautics and Space Administration, USA
Natasha Neogi	National Institute of Aerospace, USA
Ganesh Pai	SGT / NASA Ames Research Center, USA
Corina Pasareanu	CMU/NASA Ames Research Center, USA
Charles Pecheur	UC Louvain, Beligum

Suzette Person   University of Nebraska-Lincoln, USA
Franco Raimondi   Middlesex University, UK
John Regehr   University of Utah, USA
Kristin Yvonne Rozier   NASA Ames Research Center, USA
Neha Rungta   NASA Ames Research Center, CA, USA
Sriram Sankaranarayanan   University of Colorado, Boulder, USA
Stephen F. Siegel   University of Delaware, USA
Radu Siminiceanu   National Institute of Aerospace, USA
Henny Sipma   Kestrel Technologies
Sarah Thompson   NASA Ames Research Center, USA
Cesare Tinelli   The University of Iowa, USA
Oksana Tkachuk   Fujitsu Laboratories of America
Helmut Veith   Vienna University of Technology, Austria
Arnaud Venet   NASA Ames Research Center, USA
Willem Visser   Stellenbosch University, South Africa
Michael Whalen   University of Minnesota, USA
Virginie Wiels   ONERA / DTIM
Reinhard Wilhelm   Saarland University, Germany

Additional Reviewers

Backes, John   Konnov, Igor
Barrett, Stephen   Kupferman, Orna
Bogomolov, Sergiy   Larson, Brian
Boniol, Frédéric   Le Gall, Tristan
Bouissou, Olivier   LIN, Shang-Wei
Brain, Martin   Melquiond, Guillaume
Browne, Anca   Mimram, Samuel
Chen, Xin   Monniaux, David
Combéfis, Sébastien   Narayanaswamy, Ganesh
Esna Ashari, Alireza   Narkawicz, Anthony
Fowler, Kim   Naujokat, Stefan
Ghorbal, Khalil   Neubauer, Johannes
Giesl, Juergen   Nimal, Vincent
Gladisch, Christoph   Paskevich, Andrei
Godefroid, Patrice   Passmore, Grant
Goodloe, Alwyn   Putot, Sylvie
Hahn, Ernst Moritz   Reisig, Wolfgang
Harrison, John   Reynolds, Andrew
Heindel, Tobias   Rinetzky, Noam
Hoenicke, Jochen   Rojas, José Miguel
Jackson, Paul   Rozier, Eric
Jobredeaux, Romain   Schrammel, Peter
Komuravelli, Anvesh   Schumann, Johann

Sharma, Subodh
Shoham, Sharon
Siegel, Stephen F.
Sinn, Moritz
Sinnig, Daniel
Slind, Konrad
Sosnovich, Adi
Tautschnig, Michael

Thoma, Daniel
Vizel, Yakir
Védrine, Franck
Wang, Tim
Wang, Timothy
Widder, Josef
Wies, Thomas
Zuleger, Florian

The Challenge of High-Assurance Software*

John Rushby

Computer Science Laboratory
SRI International
333 Ravenswood Avenue
Menlo Park, CA 94025 USA

It is difficult to build complex systems that (almost) never go (badly) wrong, yet this is what we expect of airplanes and pacemakers and the phone system. In essence, we have to anticipate everything that could fail or go wrong, develop countermeasures, and then provide compelling evidence that we have done all this correctly.

I outline some of the intellectual challenges in construction of suitable evidence, particularly as applied to software. I introduce the idea of "possibly perfect" software and its associated "probability of perfection" and describe how this relates to correctness and reliability. I sketch some approaches to estimating a probability of perfection and touch on alternative proposals such as those based on "eliminative induction."

I then describe epistemic and logic uncertainties in high-assurance software and speculate on the relation between these and the notion of resilience.

Much of this material is based on joint work with Bev Littlewood and others at City University UK, some of which is described a recent paper [1].

Reference

1. Littlewood, B., Rushby, J.: Reasoning about the reliability of diverse two-channel systems in which one channel is "possibly perfect". IEEE Transactions on Software Engineering 38, 1178–1194 (2012)

---

* This work was supported by NASA contract NNA10DE79C and by DARPA under contract FA8750-12-C-0284 with AFRL. The content is solely the responsibility of the author and does not necessarily represent the official views of NASA or DARPA.

Using Learning Techniques in Invariant Inference

Alex Aiken

Stanford University

Arguably the hardest problem in automatic program verification is designing appropriate techniques for discovering loop invariants (or, more generally, recursive procedures). Certainly, if invariants are known, the rest of the verification problem becomes easier. This talk presents a family of invariant inference techniques based on using test cases to generate an underapproximation of program behavior and then using machine learning algorithms to generalize the underapproximation to an invariant. These techniques are simpler, much more efficient, and appear to be more robust than previous approaches to the problem. If time permits, some open problems will also be discussed.

The Importance of Generalization in Automated Proof

Kenneth L. McMillan[1] and Aws Albarghouthi[2]

[1]Microsoft Research
[2]University of Toronto

Generalization from cases is a widely used strategy in automated deduction. That is, in proving a theorem, we consider a variety of special cases. From the proof of a special case, we derive a fact that covers this case, and hopefully a large space of additional cases. The canonical example of this approach is conflict learning in a Boolean satisfiability (SAT) solver. In such a solver, we select a special case by deciding the values of certain Boolean variables. If we obtain a refutation of this case using a simple proof system called unit resolution, then we derive a new fact from this proof (a conflict clause) that rules out our particular set of decisions. This generalization can be viewed as a logical interpolant derived from the proof. Many other types of provers, including SAT module theories (SMT) solvers and model checkers for hardware and software, use similar strategies to focus deduction on relevant facts.

The difficulty with generalization is that there are so many possible generalizations we can make of any given case. Different proofs and proof systems will produce different generalizations, and many can typically be derived from the same proof. A relevant generalization may result in rapid convergence of the overall proof, while an irrelevant one may lead to explosion of the proof search, or even divergence (for example, in the case of inductive proofs).

Some weak heuristics have emerged to aid in this decision. For example, in a SAT solver, one seeks a generalization that is locally useful in guiding the model search (the selection of the next case). In other problems (such as SMT), we prefer stronger to weaker deductions. In inductive proofs (for example in model checkers) we may prefer simpler generalizations as more likely to avoid a divergence of inductive hypotheses.

These tactics suffer from a common weakness, however. They try to generalize from a single case, a highly under-constrained problem. A less myopic approach would be to revise one's generalizations in consideration of additional cases, as one would do in empirical reasoning. As additional cases are encountered, we might search for the simplest deduction that covers all or a large subset of the cases. A requirement of simplicity can force us to discover the underlying trend or pattern in the cases (that is, to avoid "over-fitting" the data).

Does the benefit of reconsidering past generalizations outweigh the cost? We will consider a simple approach that can infer common generalizations of multiple cases in linear arithmetic. This provides a means of inferring inductive invariants of numeric programs that is more robust than existing techniques. Moreover, there are problems on which modern SMT solvers suffer from an explosion of cases due to a failure to generalize effectively. On such problems, a structured approach that clusters similar cases can produce exponential speed-up.

The idea of generalizing from the proof of a single case may seem an extreme point of view, yet most modern approaches to decision problems and model checking problem rely on it in some way. Stepping back from this position, we might ask what can be done to help our reasoning tools see the bigger picture, what heuristics are needed, and what the costs and benefits might be.

Managing Data for Curiosity, Fun and Profit

Rajeev Joshi

Jet Propulsion Laboratory,
California Institute of Technology,
Pasadena, CA
`rajeev.joshi@jpl.nasa.gov`

Abstract. Since its dramatic landing on Mars on the night of Aug 5, 2012, the Curiosity Rover has been busy exploring Gale crater, looking for evidence of past habitable environments. To accomplish its ambitious scientific goal, Curosity is armed with a suite of sophisticated instruments, including cameras capable of 720p high definition stereo video, a gigawatt laser, a radiation detector, a weather monitoring station, and a sample delivery system that can drill into rocks and deliver the resulting powder to instruments that can determine its chemical composition.

As a result, Curiosity is a rover capable of gathering large amounts of both scientific data (with results of experiments commanded by the science team) and engineering data (with critical information about rover health). This data volume is too large to be sent directly to Earth via Curiosity's high-gain antenna (whose bandwidth is measured in hundreds of bits per second). Instead, most of the data acquired by the rover must be relayed to Earth via two orbiting spacecraft. Curiosity achieves this by autonomously engaging in "communication windows" with the orbiters, often by waking itself up in the middle of the night to avail itself of a passing overflight.

The asynchronous nature of relay communications necessitates on-board software for reliably storing data captured by multiple scientific experiments, for processing requests from Earth to reprioritize, retransmit and delete data, and for autonomously selecting, retrieving and packaging data for orbiters in time for communication windows. These functions are implemented in rover flight software by a collection of modules called the *data management subsystem*, which includes filesystems for volatile (RAM) and non-volatile (flash) memory, an on-the-fly compression engine, and a mini-database for cataloging and retrieving data.

In this talk, we describe the challenges involved in designing and implementing Curiosity's data management subsystem, and the important role played by formal methods in the design and testing of this software. We also discuss ongoing work on building tools based on formal methods for analyzing spacecraft telemetry for early anomaly detection during mission operations.

Certification Challenges When Using Formal Methods, Including Needs and Issues

Mike DeWalt

Federal Aviation Administration

The application of formal methods to aviation is a promising field. RTCA and EUROCAE have produced a supplement to DO-178C which provides guidelines on evaluating projects that implement formal methods. Formal methods require an extensive use of mathematics and complex tools. Obtaining confidence in these tools through qualification and reviewing formal methods proposals requires a skill set which has not been incubated within the FAA. This presentation will detail the issues and challenges of using formal methods in a civil certification environment.

Table of Contents

Session 4: Static Analysis

Session 5: Symbolic Execution

Session 6: Requirements and Specifications

Session 7: Probabilistic and Statistical Analysis

Session 8: Theorem Proving

Short Papers

Improved State Space Reductions for LTL Model Checking of C and C++ Programs*

Petr Ročkai**, Jiří Barnat, and Luboš Brim

Faculty of Informatics, Masaryk University
Brno, Czech Republic
{xrockai,barnat,brim}@fi.muni.cz

Abstract. In this paper, we present substantial improvements in efficiency of explicit-state LTL model checking of C & C++ programs, building on [2], including improvements to state representation and to state space reduction techniques. The improved state representation allows to easily exploit symmetries in heap configurations of the program, especially in programs with interleaved heap allocations. Finally, we present a major improvement through a semi-dynamic proviso for partial-order reduction, based on eager local searches constrained through control-flow loop detection.

1 Introduction

In [2] we have presented an approach to explicit-state LTL model checking of C and C++ programs that make use of POSIX thread APIs for shared-memory parallelism / multi-threading. While the initial implementation already showed promise, it also had multiple shortcomings. We have presented a reduction technique (τ-reduction) that allowed us to successfully model-check small examples, on a scale that would enable model checking of moderately complex unit tests. Nevertheless, the overall performance was unsatisfactory for day-to-day use, due to large state spaces and inefficient interpretation.

The basic approach we follow is to use a C or a C++ compiler with an LLVM-based back-end, such as Clang or GCC/dragonegg to produce, possibly optimised, LLVM bitcode file [17,18]. Using a modified LLVM interpreter, we then load the bitcode into our parallel LTL model checker DiVinE [3]. We have designed a set of traps that let us create and manage threads, atomicity and a dynamic heap, and on top of these traps, we built a POSIX-compatible thread API.

One of the key advantages of model checking over more traditional verification methods is that it will account for arbitrary thread interleaving, a phenomenon that is very hard to capture in both testing and theorem proving or symbolic

---

* This work has been partially supported by the Czech Science Foundation grant No. GAP202/11/0312.
** Petr Ročkai has been partially supported by Red Hat, Inc. and is a holder of Brno PhD Talent financial aid provided by Brno City Municipality.

G. Brat, N. Rungta, and A. Venet (Eds.): NFM 2013, LNCS 7871, pp. 1–15, 2013.
© Springer-Verlag Berlin Heidelberg 2013

model checking. At the same time, unexpected interleavings are a major source of bugs in multi-threaded programs and thus it is extremely desirable to have a tool to help with verification of such programs. Finally, the requirement to deal with an exponential number of interleavings is one of the main problems in implementing a feasible model checker. In addition to systematic exploration of thread interleavings, many model checkers include checking for more elaborate properties than simple safety statements: in case of DiVinE, this entails full LTL$_{-X}$ specification [4].

In our original approach, the proposed τ-reduction allowed us to somewhat restrict thread interleaving without impairing the faithfulness of the model checking process, yielding manageable state spaces for small programs or moderate unit tests. As outlined above, though, this reduction is still not strong enough to facilitate seamless, practical use of a model checker as an integral part of programming effort.

In this paper we identify two major causes of state space inflation in parallel programs and propose more efficient solutions. The first is control flow interleaving, which we discuss in Section 2, the second is memory heap layout, detailed in Section 3. We also take a closer look at the implementation of the interpreter and model checker in Section 5, and finally, we evaluate the new implementation in Section 6, with focus on the reductions described in this paper.

The main contribution of this paper is the combined strength of the newly suggested state space reductions. Using the proposed methods, model checking with DiVinE no longer suffers from the very fine-grained nature of LLVM bitcode. Consequently, regular programming languages, such as C or C++, may be directly used as the modelling language for the model checker, without a prohibitive impact on the size of the state space. The net effect is that the expensive and expert task of manually creating accurate system models can be skipped, turning model checking into a much more accessible method of software verification.

2   Control Flow

The graph induced by a single execution of a deterministic program is a linear sequence of states, with no branching: each state has (at most) one successor. Each "edge" of this induced graph represents a single instruction and each node corresponds to a snapshot of the machine state visible to the program (registers and mapped memory). In a sequential program, this "trace" is identical every time the program is executed with a given input. Without loss of generality, we can assume that input (and any interaction with the environment) is part of the program[1] (an assumption which is actually true in many interesting cases, notably various automated test cases, whether unit, functional or integration).

Generally, a trace that only has single instruction on each edge is more detailed than is useful. A chain of states can be collapsed if they are not relevant for

---

[1] There are other ways to efficiently deal with open-ended inputs and interactivity, most notably symbolic methods. We will discuss these in Section 8 on future work.

analysis, forming a compound edge which represents an arbitrary instruction block. This technique is known as path compression [24,15].

However, while any single execution may yield a sequential trace, in parallel programs, the trace may be different every time the program is executed, due to non-determinism inherent in how instructions are scheduled by individual CPUs or cores, and a time-sharing, asynchronous nature of the entire system. This non-determinism is reflected in explicit-state model checkers by introducing branching into the execution trace (which is called a state space in this context), thereby encoding all possible interleavings. In any given state, the system makes a non-deterministic choice on which thread is executed next, creating a single successor state for each active thread. The number of states in the state space is exponential in the number of different threads.

While there are cases where different interleavings produce different end results, there are also many cases where the exact ordering of instructions is irrelevant: different interleavings will yield the same end state. Such confluent executions are redundant and only one of each equivalent set needs to be explored. This idea is at the heart of a class of techniques known as partial-order reductions [20].

In a state space (as opposed to a trace), path reduction can only straightforwardly apply to trace-like sequences of states, where each state has exactly one successor. However, such sub-traces do not naturally occur in state spaces of multi-threaded programs, since almost all states will have multiple successors caused by interleaving. Nevertheless, when a partial order reduction is applied, we choose a single execution among a set of many possible, replacing a diamond-like structure with a trace-like structure. This new trace-like structure is in turn amenable to path reduction, further reducing the number of intermediate states.

Both these reductions can be approximated statically, and one example of such an approximation is the τ-reduction [2]. While its static nature makes τ-reduction extremely simple and easy to implement, it also somewhat limits its effectiveness. In this paper, we introduce a more efficient, semi-dynamic approximation.

2.1 τ+reduction

A simple way to approximate both partial order reduction and path compression is to keep a single thread running as long as cycle and observability criteria are met. In τ-reduction, the observability criterion states that an instruction is observable iff it affects content of shared memory: this approach is inherited without change by τ+reduction. The difference lies in the cycle check. In τ-reduction, any branching (jumping) instruction is treated as possibly closing a control flow cycle, forcing an intermediate state to be generated. However, if we defer the cycle check, we can do much better. Especially in optimised code, branching easily dominates memory access, and the static proviso becomes a major source of inefficiency. In lieu of a simple static check for a branching instruction, we can dynamically detect control-flow loops at successor generation time.

The control location of a thread is kept using a "program counter", a 4-byte integer value that uniquely identifies a specific instruction. Clearly, any actual loop in the program will traverse a single control location twice – hence, it will also encounter the same program counter value. With this in mind, we keep a set of program counter values that we traversed while looking for a successor. Only when an actual control flow loop closes, we interrupt the execution and generate a new state. Each time a successor is generated, the visited set is cleared.

While this is still an approximation, since the (unobservable) loop may finish in finite number of iterations, it is very cheap to compute. Keeping track of full system configurations – an approach that would achieve a better reduction for data-dependent loops with no memory access – would be much more computationally expensive. We reckon that tracking the comparably minuscule program counter value is a viable compromise.

From the model checking perspective, τ+reduction deals with successor states and state spaces, replacing diamonds and chains with one-step transitions. This view is useful for arguing correctness and when thinking in terms of systematic exploration. However, from the point of view of a single execution trace or from the point of view of the program being executed, this view is less appropriate. Therefore, we formulate an alternative, equivalent view of the reduction in terms of interleaving (also called interruption) points.

We define an interleaving point as a place "in-between" two instructions in the program text, where a context-switch (rescheduling) of threads (from the point of view of the program) might happen. When building an unreduced state space, an interleaving point is inserted between each pair of instructions. This intuitively captures what happens in a real CPU, whether a single core time-sharing multiple threads, or an actual multi-core unit. However, as outlined above, not all interleavings cause observable differences in behaviour of the program. τ-reductions then act by removing some of these interleaving points. τ-reduction simply inserts an interleaving point right before each **store** and each branching instruction, statically.

On the other hand, τ+reduction, as a semi-dynamic technique, acts on the program as it is being executed. First, interleaving points are inserted before all **store** instructions, just as with τ-reduction. Then, more are created and removed on the fly: whenever a thread closes a control flow loop, an interleaving point is inserted just before the first instruction that would have been repeated. After the re-scheduling happens, this interleaving point is then dropped again, since a non-looping execution might pass through it at other times. Apart from technical requirement of the model checker that each step is finite, these loop-related interleaving points are intuitively required to avoid delaying other threads indefinitely.

3   Heap

Most non-trivial programs nowadays use dynamic memory, also called a "heap". This memory is allocated on demand using function calls (usually **malloc** and its variants and `free`) provided by the runtime. The heap allows transparent re-use of memory that is no longer needed, without the requirement to allocate and de-allocate in first in / last out order like with the C stack.

We can consider a heap to be an oriented graph, with nodes representing individual objects and arrows representing pointers. A heap object is a result of a single allocation, it is internally always contiguous, but there is no guarantee on the actual layout of multiple objects in memory. In addition to pointers originating inside heap objects, there may be pointers in stack frames and registers pointing into heap objects (these are known as "root" pointers). While the exact heap layout is irrelevant with regards to program behaviour (bar pointer manipulation or indexing bugs), it affects the actual bit-level representation of a program state.

3.1   Heap Symmetry

This introduces a degree of symmetry into the state space of a program, where multiple distinct states may only differ in heap layout. Since the behaviour of the program is not affected by this difference, we obtain multiple mirror copies of a subset of the state space. This can be extremely wasteful, and is most pronounced when multiple threads are using the heap (which is a common case). Whenever allocations can become interleaved, two symmetric successor states arise, differing only in the ordering of the two heap objects in the physical address space. It is very desirable to detect and exploit this symmetry to reduce the state space.

There are two main ways to implement symmetry reduction. One is based on a modified state comparison function, which detects symmetric situations and makes any two symmetric states equal. The major downside of this approach is that it precludes use of hash tables – the structure of choice in explicit-state model checking. The other option is canonisation: a technique where each state is transformed to obtain a canonic representative of each symmetry class. This way, all symmetric states are represented by the same bit vector, and standard equality and hashing can be used.

On the flip side, detecting symmetric heap configurations is much easier than constructing a canonic representative. This is especially true for programs with explicit (manual) memory management. In some programming languages[2], the heap is subject to automatic garbage collection, and while LLVM has optional garbage collection support, it is not used when compiling C or C++ programs. If exact collection is used [16], all pointers must be tracked by the runtime, especially if using a copying (or more generally, moving) collector. If this information is available, it can be used to implement heap canonisation. In fact, a slightly modified single-generation copying garbage collector will produce a canonic heap layout after every collection cycle.

Opposite to languages with automatic memory management, languages like C and C++ require memory to be explicitly `free`-d to allow memory re-use

---

[2] Or, more exactly, programs, since garbage collection can be implemented for specific programs even in languages without intrinsic garbage collection support.

and avoid resource leaks. However, this also means that the C runtime puts very little constraint on how pointers can be manipulated, since correct memory management is the responsibility of the program, not the system. Unfortunately, this makes it impossible to retrofit garbage collection (and analogically, heap canonisation) to these languages while retaining full generality. In theory, it is legal for a C program to save pointers to a file and read them back later for further use, or to store them bit-flipped in memory or even xor'd together as in a xor-linked list. Such obscured pointers are however extremely rare in actual programs, and we can make them illegal. Basically, addition is the only reasonable operation to do on an (integer-casted) pointer value; an error can be raised when attempting any other manipulation. In most circumstances, a non-additive operation on a pointer would indicate a bug in the program.

Finally, in a controlled environment (i.e. when each instruction can be freely instrumented), obscured pointers are the only major obstacle in implementing heap canonisation. Therefore, restricting those, it becomes possible to fully track heap pointers throughout the program, and based on this information, compute a canonic heap representation, adjusting all pointers accordingly. The actual layout we chose is based on DFS pre-order, with root pointers forming the initial search stack, global variables first, then deepest frame of the first thread and traversing stacks upwards first, then threads from the lowest thread-id to the highest.

3.2   Tracking Pointers

Hence, the remaining problem to solve is exact pointer tracking. While approximate solutions for C and C++ exist, these so-called *conservative* approaches [16] cannot be used for implementing heap reorganisation. A conservative collector will, in a nutshell, treat any bit-pattern as a pointer as long as it corresponds to a valid memory location. Since in a typical program, the heap size is much smaller than the address space and the heap is usually located near its end, this only introduces a small amount of harmless error for a mark&sweep collector, where in the worst case, some garbage is retained. However, a conservative collector must not alter pointers, since it could accidentally alter an integral value that has no relation to the heap, simply having the same bit pattern as a valid pointer.

This means that for successfully tracking pointers, we must use a tagging scheme, where an integer can never be constructed to resemble a pointer and vice versa. On one hand, shrinking pointers by one or two tag bits is not a problem – the address space of the model checker itself is a limiting factor, not the size of a pointer. On the other, it is not feasible to shrink integral types, as this would wreak havoc with established semantics of integer arithmetic[3]. Hence, we cannot easily prevent an integer from mimicking a bit pattern of a pointer. An alternative is to keep tagging information out of band, in a separate image of

---

[3] This scheme has been adopted in early garbage-collected runtimes, like that of LISP, where all scalars would reserve tagging bits and integer size would not match the machine word size. However, this approach is not feasible in low-level languages.

the address space. This is possible since we can instrument any and all memory access with updates to this tag space at the interpreter level.

All the tracked pointers are created in heap allocations, and their pointer status is preserved throughout their lifetime. We use a special pointer representation, where the heap object and offset into that object are kept apart and manipulated separately. This prevents pointers from overflowing into a neighbouring heap object (this would be a programming error, and must be detected) and makes pointer arithmetic safe and supported. Since programs may not make any assumptions about the bit content of heap pointers, they cannot be legally hijacked for integer constants. Therefore, we can safely rewrite the tracked pointers, without the risk of accidentally altering integral values, or missing actual valid pointers.

Finally, a simple yet efficient optimisation can further reduce the tracking overhead: since we can require and enforce alignment constraints on pointer values, any pointer value will start at a 4-divisible address, thus only requiring a single tracking bit per 4 bytes of memory.

4   Store Visibility

The availability of exact pointer tracking (coming from the implementation of heap symmetry reduction) offers an opportunity to further improve on τ+reduction. In its general form, τ+reduction operates mainly on the notion of "observability": an instruction's effect is a cause for an interleaving point whenever this effect might have been observed by another thread. The main source of observability is writing to (shared) memory: in the thread-based programming model, all memory is implicitly available to all threads. However, it should be noted that in order for a thread to observe a memory write, it must be in possession of a pointer to that memory location.

Therefore, if a memory location has been allocated from the heap by a thread, but the pointer to this heap object is never provided to another thread, this memory location is essentially private to the allocating thread (this most importantly affects **alloca**-obtained memory, see also Section 5.1, although private heap-allocated structures are common as well). Since the layout of heap objects cannot be effectively predicted by the program being verified, it cannot "construct" pointers to objects out of thin air, and they must be explicitly shared by the allocating thread.

Since writes to such "private" heap objects cannot be observed by other threads, we can mark the corresponding **store** instructions as unobservable for the purposes of τ+reduction, again substantially improving its already very good efficiency.

In order to effectively identify the relevant **store** instructions, we trace the root set excluding the currently executing thread. If the heap object that is being written to is not encountered in this manner, then the write is invisible, since no other thread can read the corresponding memory location. Since we use tracing, this remains true after any combination of **load**s or pointer manipulation.

The only action that would make the `store` observable would be a different `store` *in the same thread*, writing a pointer to the relevant object into a preexisting, already shared memory location. However, since this must happen in the same thread, the change caused by first in such a sequence of `store`s can never be observed, and the later `store` will properly cause an interruption point to be inserted.

5   Implementation

In addition to the new reductions detailed in previous two sections, we have implemented a completely new LLVM bitcode interpreter since [2]. The interpreter itself is a component very important for both robustness and performance of the model checking solution. The previous version of the interpreter was based on the code provided by LLVM itself, with a number of modifications to hook it into the model checking framework. However, this approach had a few disadvantages. First, the interpreter was never built for performance: registers were implemented as arbitrary-precision integers with large space overhead and register files as red-black trees, with cache performance suffering as a consequence.

An explicit-state model checker based on a virtual machine (like our LLVM interpreter), needs to be able to take snapshots of the machine's entire state in order to be able to explore the configuration graph (the state space). These snapshots should be compact and ideally stored as continuous, hashable blocks of memory. In the original interpreter, the states needed to be unpacked into internal data structures and repacked every time a new snapshot was made. On the other hand, the current version takes a different approach, using the compact state representation directly to execute instructions, avoiding expensive unpack/repack operations. Moreover, since most of the data required by the interpreter is packed close together in memory, its cache performance has improved substantially.

5.1   Machine State Vector

A running program on a contemporary commodity computer normally has access to a number of resources. The most important, apart from the CPU itself, is a bulk of random access memory that is traditionally divided into text (program), data, stack and heap. Most systems today, with only a handful of specialised exceptions, do not allow the text of a running program to be modified. In DiVinE, we treat it as constant. Apart from the program text, part of the data region of memory is constant and never modified by the program. This usually entails message strings and numeric constants used in the program. These two sections (text and constant data) are stored only once for each instance of the interpreter. The remainder is stored as a compact *machine state vector*, with layout illustrated by Figure 1.

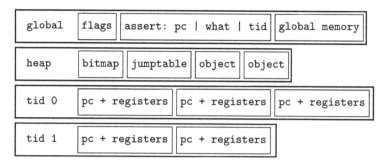

Fig. 1. A state vector with 2 threads, global data and an assertion violation

Out of the items in a machine state vector, the register stack needs special attention. Real machines (as opposed to virtual) have a limited set of registers, but a (comparatively) unlimited amount of memory. The "stack" in a C program consists of mapped memory and is used for many purposes: saving registers across function calls, storing return addresses and return values, and storing "automatic" local variables. All of this is organised into frames, and each frame on the C stack corresponds to a single entry into a C function.

Contrary to this, the LLVM virtual machine has an unlimited register file. When generating actual executable code, these virtual registers are allocated to machine registers and code for managing register spills (into the C stack) is inserted. However, at the level of LLVM instructions, access to the C stack is provided through the `alloca` instruction and is needed because values stored in registers have no address, and therefore cannot be passed by reference[4].

In our interpreter, we have a structure analogous to C frames, but our frames are not located in memory: they only contain register values and are not address-able (from the point of view of the code being executed). Since LLVM gives no guarantees about layout of memory coming from multiple `alloca` instructions, we allocate `alloca` memory from heap, which in our case is managed automat-ically. Therefore pointers to `alloca` memory go out of scope when their owner function returns and the heap memory is freed.[5]

5.2   Library Substitution and Masking

Moreover, an important aspect of the software model checking enterprise is API compatibility. In previous versions, we provided a relatively ad-hoc implemen-tation of POSIX threading API, spread over the interpreter itself, but partially implemented in a C header file to be included in user code. Our new approach

---

[4] Moreover, until recently, LLVM registers could not hold non-scalar values and those had to be stored in `alloca` or heap memory.

[5] A future revision of the interpreter will release the memory when its owning frame disappears, preventing programs to invoke undefined behaviour. The current version will fail to raise an error in this scenario, since the allocated memory is not specifically bound to its frame.

makes a much cleaner separation between "system space" (the interpreter itself and whatever built-in functions – traps – it provides) and "user space" (the user code to be checked and any libraries it links, some possibly provided by DiVinE as replacements for system libraries). Moreover, the separation within user-space is improved as well, since the implementation details of the DiVinE-provided library substitutions no longer leak into the user-supplied code, but are instead linked in at the LLVM level.

Essentially, DiVinE supplies replacements or partial replacements of system libraries, like `libc` and `libpthread`. These replacements are slated to become "drop-in" replacements for their system counterparts, shielding the program under verification from the uncontrolled outside environment. Eventually, such substitution libraries could provide I/O facilities implemented using non-deterministic choice. While this is in principle possible today, a purely-explicit-state representation is ill-suited for verifying programs with significant input-induced branching, especially on large domains.

The user/system-space separation is facilitated by a new technique, implemented through three new traps: `__divine_interrupt_mask`, `__divine_interrupt_unmask` and `__divine_interrupt`. These traps expose a low-level interface to atomicity control, making user-space implementation of library functionality much more feasible. When interrupt masking is in effect, the running thread must not be interrupted by any other thread, until after the masking is lifted. Moreover, the masking is bound to stack frames, which means that there is no danger of leaking the masking into user code, since a `ret` instruction to an originally unmasked function will automatically cause an unmask.

The advantage of explicit atomicity control is twofold: first, it makes library implementation much easier by avoiding the usual pitfalls of writing thread-safe code. Second, it substantially reduces the model checking overhead, since atomicized code is much cheaper to execute, as no intermediate states need to be created. This effect is exponential, since every interleaving point in a library function essentially multiplies the number of states stored during its execution.

5.3 Traps

Apart from the three traps mentioned in previous section, there is a trap, `__divine_choice` which implements non-deterministic choice, and a small set of traps falling into three categories:

1. memory management:
    - `__divine_malloc` – obtain fresh memory from the heap,
    - `__divine_free` – force invalidation of all pointers to an area of memory,
2. thread management:
    - `__divine_new_thread` – create a new thread, with a supplied function as an entry point and a pointer-sized argument
    - `__divine_get_tid` – obtain an identifier of the calling thread,

Table 1. Number of reachable states in different models under various reductions. The C++ models apparently expose a bug in the old version of the interpreter, hence the numbers are not available. OOM means that the model checker ran out of available memory (16GB).

model	old interpreter		new with heap reduction			
	∅	τ	∅	τ	τ+	all
peters.c, -O0	OOM	1316162	294193	2181	596	212
peters.c, -O1	148301	11877	33227	491	286	278
peters.c, -O2	89702	6035	21122	443	268	260
pe.bug.c, -O0	OOM	1106757	235272	1617	735	281
pe.bug.c, -O1	221681	19053	49691	613	440	432
pe.bug.c, -O2	188064	14155	43536	613	440	432
fifo.cpp, -O0	fails	fails	559364	22126	1723	108
fifo.cpp, -O1	fails	fails	104642	3926	43	26
fifo.cpp, -O2	fails	fails	83898	2660	148	143
ring.cpp, -O0	fails	fails	2502517	75498	13075	935
ring.cpp, -O1	fails	fails	713743	14157	1461	1405
ring.cpp, -O2	fails	fails	1439424	22735	2121	2065
global.c, -O0	3517	997	451	84	65	26
global.c, -O1	915	179	316	54	30	30
global.c, -O2	887	160	316	54	30	30

3. and property specification:
   - __divine_assert – ensure that a value is non-zero
   - __divine_ap – insert an atomic proposition for LTL model checking.

These traps are generally not meant to be used directly in user code, since they have no counterparts in standard system libraries. Instead, they can be used in support code (whether supplied by DiVinE or by the user), which is then linked into the executable before verification. Linking to a different version of the support code (normally, this would entail standard system libraries) will then yield an executable program, directly derived from the verified bitcode file.

5.4 POSIX Threads

We have implemented a substantial subset of the POSIX threading API, including thread management (creation, joining, detaching), mutual exclusion ("fast" and recursive mutexes), condition signalling and thread-local storage. To achieve smooth interoperability, DiVinE provides a compile --llvm subcommand, which invokes clang to produce bitcode for verification Since currently DiVinE provides its own pthread.h (the interface is not binary-compatible to glibc pthreads – some pthread types are shorter in the DiVinE implementation), divine compile --llvm will provide the correct #include paths and link the program with substitution libraries. This makes producing a verification-ready bitcode file a very easy, single-step operation.

6 Evaluation

To evaluate the actual improvements coming from the proposed reductions, we have taken a small number of example multi-threaded C and C++ programs

Table 2. Counterexample lengths for various reductions. The shorter "new, τ" counterexamples are due to better `pthreads` implementation based on masking.

	`pe.bug.c, -O0`	`pe.bug.c, -O1`	`global.c, -O0`	`global.c, -O1`
old, τ	172 -- 193	77	59	n/a
new, τ	54	37	21	19
new, $\tau+$	40	31	18	16
new, τ, store	26	20	12	12
new, $\tau+$, store	12	12	9	9

and compared state space sizes (see Table 1) using different options, starting with the old interpreter with no reductions, and with τ-reduction (this was the state of the art at the time of [2]). With the new interpreter, we have made 4 measurements, using heap reduction only, heap and τ-reduction, heap and $\tau+$reduction and finally all reductions including `store` visibility. We have used the following example programs:

- `peterson.c`: a C implementation of Peterson's mutual exclusion,
- `peterson.bug.c`: the same, but with a bug,
- `fifo.cpp`: lock-free first-in, first-out inter-thread queue,
- `ring.cpp`: a lock-free inter-thread ring buffer,
- `global.c`: a race condition when incrementing a shared variable.

While the increased complexity of reductions has non-negligible impact on throughput in terms of states visited per second, this deterioration is much slower than the drop in overall state count. Taking `peterson.c` with `-O1` on a Intel Core 2 Duo P8600 @ 2.4GHz, the throughput ranged from 2650 states/s with no reductions to 780 states/s with all reductions (3.5-fold loss in performance, compared to 530-fold reduction, for 150-fold gain in overall verification speed).

6.1   Counterexamples

A side benefit of the reductions is manifested in counterexample traces. Since the model checker produces a trace consisting of individual states, its length is inversely proportional to length of individual steps. This effect is especially due to the more aggressive $\tau+$reduction[6] and due to introduction of masking in pthread support code. A τ-reduced counterexample trace for the buggy version `peterson.c` spanned several pages, and was very tedious to follow for a human. The $\tau+$reduced version is much shorter and substantially more transparent to users. To put this in a more objective perspective, we have taken 3 sample counterexamples from each of the "buggy" models and summarised the numbers in Table 2.

7   Related Work

Model checking of programs at the level of the source code has been so far pursued in two major research directions. In the first branch, automated code

---

[6] Symmetric states are very unlikely to appear in a single counterexample, so the contribution of symmetry reduction to this effect is negligible.

extractors were used to replace the error-prone process of manual modelling. Tools such as Feaver [11] or Bandera [8] were introduced to extract C or Java code, respectively, into models to be used as an input for a model checker. The SLAM Toolkit [1] applies the CEGAR approach [6] on top of Boolean programs extracted automatically from a C program source file.

In the other branch, techniques allowing direct analyses of the program source files were examined. Pioneered by VeriSoft [10], model checkers begun to be able to accept C program files as input. While VeriSoft is a state-less model checker, SATABS [7] is a tool performing CEGAR verification of multi-threaded ANSI C programs. Other model checking tools capable of analyzing C programs went into the direction of bounded model checking. While CBMC [5], or F-Soft [14] tools were limited to analysis of sequential programs, TCBMC [21] introduced a bounded model checking approach for POSIX-thread C programs with two threads.

An obvious disadvantage of an interpreter that should be able to read all possible constructs of a high-level programming language such as C or C++, is its structural complexity. Consequently, the model checking tools that directly interpret some high-level programming language, are typically limited to just a subset of it. A possible solution to the problem is to build the tool on top of an intermediate representation language. Recently, the intermediate representation as defined in the LLVM project [17] became rather popular in this respect. Regarding model checking, there are, however, only two tools built on top of the LLVM project. These are, to our best knowledge, the LLBMC tool [19] and DiVinE [2], the former offering SMT-based bounded model checking and the latter enumerative LTL model checking of LLVM bitcode, respectively. Besides LLVM bitcode, Java intermediate representation is used heavily for analysis of Java programs, see Java PathFinder [23].

The key problem of model checking is the state space explosion. When speaking of model checking of the LLVM bitcode, the problem is even more painful as the input language of the model checker is very fine-grained. In this paper we opted to fight this problem using a combination of symmetry [22,13] and partial order reduction [20].

The problem of unnecessary state space explosion in explicit state model checking due to dynamically allocated entities has been observed and studied before. Symmetry reduction has been applied to model checking of object-based programs that manipulate dynamically created objects. In particular, linear-time heuristic to define canonical representative of a symmetry equivalence class has been presented in [12].

An approach to dynamic partial order reduction somewhat related to our own has been implemented in the VeriSoft state-less model checker [9]. This approach was based on initially exploring an arbitrary interleaving of the various concurrent processes/threads, and dynamically tracking interactions between these to identify backtracking points where alternative paths in the state space need to be explored.

8   Conclusions and Future Work

In our previous work, we have established a baseline which allowed verification of simple C and C++ programs. Most importantly, these programs required no modifications (compared to their form intended for normal execution), in order to be verified.

In this paper, we introduced techniques that significantly move the boundary on feasible verification of such programs. The property-preserving reductions make verification of real-world, multi-threaded C and C++ programs possible and compelling. While we focus on safety verification, in form of assertion statements, invalid memory access or mutex-safety – properties that are easily accessible to everyday programmers without specific verification knowledge – we also provide first-class LTL verification for more expert treatment of mission-critical systems.

There are multiple extensions planned in future revisions. A major class of programs is currently mostly unsuitable for our current approach to verification: open systems with data inputs over non-trivial domains will quickly cause the state space to explode beyond verification capacity of current hardware. Therefore, a semi-symbolic approach for such open-ended programs is required, and at the same time would break a new ground for model checking: programs that employ both multi-threading and data processing are currently out of reach for both explicit-state and symbolic-state tools.

Apart from this, most of the planned future work consists of improvements in the implementation and increasing the coverage of library substitutions to further reduce overhead in verifying new programs. Case-studies from verifying real-world multi-threaded applications are forthcoming as well.

References

1. Ball, T., Bounimova, E., Kumar, R., Levin, V.: SLAM2: Static driver verification with under 4% false alarms. In: Formal Methods in Computer-Aided Design (FMCAD 2010), pp. 35–42. IEEE (2010)
2. Barnat, J., Brim, L., Ročkai, P.: Towards LTL Model Checking of Unmodified Thread-Based C & C++ Programs. In: Goodloe, A.E., Person, S. (eds.) NFM 2012. LNCS, vol. 7226, pp. 252–266. Springer, Heidelberg (2012)
3. Barnat, J., Brim, L., Češka, M., Ročkai, P.: DiVinE: Parallel Distributed Model Checker (Tool paper). In: Parallel and Distributed Methods in Verification and High Performance Computational Systems Biology (HiBi/PDMC 2010), pp. 4–7. IEEE (2010)
4. Clarke, E., Grumberg, O., Peled, D.: Model Checking. MIT Press (1999)
5. Clarke, E., Kroning, D., Lerda, F.: A Tool for Checking ANSI-C Programs. In: Jensen, K., Podelski, A. (eds.) TACAS 2004. LNCS, vol. 2988, pp. 168–176. Springer, Heidelberg (2004)
6. Clarke, E.M., Fehnker, A., Han, Z., Krogh, B.H., Ouaknine, J., Stursberg, O., Theobald, M.: Abstraction and Counterexample-Guided Refinement in Model Checking of Hybrid Systems. Int. J. Found. Comput. Sci. 14(4), 583–604 (2003)

7. Clarke, E., Kroning, D., Sharygina, N., Yorav, K.: SATABS: SAT-Based Predicate Abstraction for ANSI-C. In: Halbwachs, N., Zuck, L.D. (eds.) TACAS 2005. LNCS, vol. 3440, pp. 570–574. Springer, Heidelberg (2005)
8. Corbett, J.C., Dwyer, M.B., Hatcliff, J., Laubach, S., Pasareanu, C.S., Robby, Zheng, H.: Bandera: Extracting finite-state models from Java source code. In: International Conference on Software Engineering (ICSE 2000), pp. 439–448. ACM (2000)
9. Flanagan, C., Godefroid, P.: Dynamic partial-order reduction for model checking software. SIGPLAN Not. 40(1), 110–121 (2005)
10. Godefroid, P.: Software model checking: The verisoft approach. Formal Methods in System Design 26(2), 77–101 (2005)
11. Holzmann, G.J., Smith, M.H.: A practical method for verifying event-driven software. In: International Conference on Software Engineering (ICSE 1999), pp. 597–607. ACM (1999)
12. Iosif, R.: Exploiting Heap Symmetries in Explicit-State Model Checking of Software. In: 16th IEEE International Conference on Automated Software Engineering (ASE 2001), pp. 254–261. IEEE Computer Society (2001)
13. Norris Ip, C., Dill, D.L.: Efficient Verification of Symmetric Concurrent Systems. In: IEEE International Conference on Computer Design: VLSI in Computers and Processors, pp. 230–234. IEEE Computer Society (1993)
14. Ivančić, F., Yang, Z., Ganai, M.K., Gupta, A., Shlyakhter, I., Ashar, P.: F-SOFT: Software Verification Platform. In: Etessami, K., Rajamani, S.K. (eds.) CAV 2005. LNCS, vol. 3576, pp. 301–306. Springer, Heidelberg (2005)
15. Jhala, R., Majumdar, R.: Path slicing. In: Proceedings of the ACM SIGPLAN Conference on Programming Language Design and Implementation (PLDI 2005), pp. 38–47. ACM Press (2005)
16. Jones, R., Lins, R.D.: Garbage Collection: Algorithms for Automatic Dynamic Memory Management. Wiley (1996)
17. Lattner, C., Adve, V.: LLVM: A Compilation Framework for Lifelong Program Analysis & Transformation. In: International Symposium on Code Generation and Optimization (CGO), Palo Alto, California (Marh 2004)
18. http://www.llvm.org/ (December 2012)
19. Merz, F., Falke, S., Sinz, C.: LLBMC: Bounded Model Checking of C and C++ Programs Using a Compiler IR. In: Joshi, R., Müller, P., Podelski, A. (eds.) VSTTE 2012. LNCS, vol. 7152, pp. 146–161. Springer, Heidelberg (2012)
20. Peled, D.: All from One, One for All: on Model Checking Using Representatives. In: Courcoubetis, C. (ed.) CAV 1993. LNCS, vol. 697, pp. 409–423. Springer, Heidelberg (1993)
21. Rabinovitz, I., Grumberg, O.: Bounded Model Checking of Concurrent Programs. In: Etessami, K., Rajamani, S.K. (eds.) CAV 2005. LNCS, vol. 3576, pp. 82–97. Springer, Heidelberg (2005)
22. Prasad Sistla, A., Godefroid, P.: Symmetry and reduced symmetry in model checking. ACM Trans. Program. Lang. Syst. 26(4), 702–734 (2004)
23. Visser, W., Havelund, K., Brat, G.P., Park, S.: Model Checking Programs. In: ASE, pp. 3–12 (2000)
24. Yorav, K., Grumberg, O.: Static analysis for state-space reductions preserving temporal logics. Formal Methods in System Design 25(1), 67–96 (2004)

Regular Model Checking Using
Solver Technologies and Automata Learning*

Daniel Neider and Nils Jansen

RWTH Aachen University, Germany

Abstract. *Regular Model Checking* is a popular verification technique where large and even infinite sets of program configurations can be encoded symbolically by finite automata. Thereby, the handling of regular sets of *initial* and *bad configurations* often imposes a serious restriction in practical applications. We present two new algorithms both utilizing modern *solver technologies* and *automata learning*. The first one works in a CEGAR-like fashion by iteratively refining an abstraction of the reachable state space using counterexamples, while the second one is based on Angluin's prominent learning algorithm. We show the feasibility and competitiveness of our approaches on different benchmarks and compare them to other established tools.

1 Introduction

Model Checking is a prominent technique designed for the verification of safety-critical systems [1,2]. Combined with the feature of *counterexample* generation, this may not only help to show the defectiveness of a system but also to identify and correct its errors. Classic model checking is based on a rigorous exploration of state spaces, which leads to serious problems considering the large size of models for real world scenarios. Hence, for large or even *infinite* systems, feasible abstraction techniques or finite representations are needed.

One natural approach to overcome this problem is to encode states of a system, e. g., configurations of a program, as finite words and symbolically describe such systems by regular languages. *Regular Model Checking* [3] refers to a technique where the set of the program's *initial configurations* is given as a regular set while the program's transitions are defined in terms of a *finite state transducer*. Additionally, a regular set of *bad configurations* is considered that describes configurations of the program that must not occur during the program's execution. Although the regular sets and the transducer need to be devised manually from the system in question, Regular Model Checking has been applied to many practical examples with infinite state-spaces [4,5,6]. In [4], the authors also describe for some examples how a concrete system can be transformed into a Regular Model Checking instance.

---

* This work was partly supported by the German Research Council (DFG)as part of the research project CEBug (AB 461/1-1).

G. Brat, N. Rungta, and A. Venet (Eds.): NFM 2013, LNCS 7871, pp. 16–31, 2013.

Tools for Regular Model Checking such as T(O)RMC [5], FASTER [6], and
LEVER [7] compute regular sets that either encode the exact set of reachable
configurations or overapproximate them. If such a set having an empty intersection with the bad configurations is identified, it is called a *proof* and serves as
a witness that the program is correct. Note, that the problem of Regular Model
Checking is undecidable in general. Thus, corresponding tools are necessarily
based on *semi-algorithms*, i.e., algorithms that are not guaranteed to terminate
on every input, but find a solution if one exists. Nonetheless, there is a large
number of practical applications where good results are achieved (see, e.g., [5]
and [6]).

A major drawback of all of these tools is that the computations are very
expensive if the automata defining the sets of initial and bad configurations
become large. Take, for instance, tools such as T(O)RMC and FASTER. They start
with a DFA for the initial configurations, successively iterate the transducer, and
then apply *widening* or *acceleration* to extrapolate infinite behavior. However,
if the initial DFA is large, the performance of these approaches is often poor.

In this paper, we overcome this problem by combining advantages of state-of-
the-art SAT and SMT solvers with automata learning techniques. Intuitively, our
approach is a combination of two existing methods. The first is a SAT and SMT-
based method for Regular Model Checking, which has recently been introduced
in [8]. The second is an automata learning technique as described, e.g., in [9,10].

The fundamental idea of our approach is to abstract from the exact sets of
initial and bad configurations by sampling them. More precisely, our approach
works by generating a proof from a sample $S = (S_+, S_-)$ containing finite (and
small) approximations of the sets of initial and bad configurations. Using the
sample sets, we compute a DFA that is consistent with these sets and *inductive*,
i.e., closed, with respect to the transducer by means of SAT or SMT solvers
(cf. Section 3). The resulting DFA contains at least the configurations reachable
from S_+ via the transitions defined by the transducer and does not contain any
configurations in S_-. If all original initial configurations and no bad configurations are contained, the DFA is a proof. If this is not the case, the respective
approximation has to be refined and the process is iterated.

We propose two algorithms here that differ in the strategy to sample and refine
sets of program configurations. Both are based on the popular learning framework introduced by Angluin [11], in which a regular language is learned in interaction with a so-called teacher that possesses knowledge about the language in
question. The first algorithm (cf. Section 4.2) straightforwardly follows the idea
of the CEGAR framework [12]: if the abstraction of either the initial or the bad
configurations is too coarse to compute a satisfactory proof, a counterexample is
given by the teacher and the abstraction is refined accordingly. The second one
(cf. Section 4.3) follows a more elaborated procedure based on Angluin's learning
algorithm [11], where additional queries ask whether individual configurations
belong to a proof. These queries refine the abstraction further and remove the
need of generating a new automaton at every step. Before we present our learning
algorithms, Section 4.1 describes how an appropriate teacher can be built.

Our approach has several advantages. First, the canonical usage of established learning algorithms offers an effective way to sample and refine the abstraction of the program. Second, our technique is applicable even if the sets of initial and bad configurations are no longer regular—as long as an appropriate teacher can be constructed (e.g., for visibly or deterministic context free languages). Finally, learning algorithms typically produce small results, which highly increases the practical applicability of our approach. We demonstrate the latter claim in Section 5 by comparing a prototype of our approach to established tools.

2   Preliminaries

Finite Automata and Transducers. An *alphabet* Σ is a finite, non-empty set. A *word* $w = a_0 \ldots a_n$ is a finite sequence of symbols $a_i \in \Sigma$ for $i = 0, \ldots, n$; in particular, the *empty word* ε is the empty sequence. The *concatenation* of two words $u = a_0 \ldots a_n$ and $v = b_0 \ldots b_m$ is the word $u \cdot v = uv = a_0 \ldots a_n b_0 \ldots b_m$. If $u = vw$ for $u, v, w \in \Sigma^*$, we call v a *prefix* and w a *suffix* of u.

The set Σ^* is the set of all (finite) words over the alphabet Σ. A subset $L \subseteq \Sigma^*$ is called a *language*. For a language $L \subseteq \Sigma^*$, let the set of all prefixes of words in L be $Pref(L) = \{u \in \Sigma^* \mid \exists v \in \Sigma^* \colon uv \in L\}$.

A *(nondeterministic) finite automaton (NFA)* is a tuple $\mathcal{A} = (Q, \Sigma, q_0, \Delta, F)$ consisting of a finite, non-empty set Q of states, an input alphabet Σ, an initial state $q_0 \in Q$, a transition relation $\Delta \subseteq Q \times \Sigma \times Q$, and a set $F \subseteq Q$ of final states. A *run* of an NFA $\mathcal{A}$ on a word $u = a_0 \ldots a_n$ from a state $q \in Q$ is a sequence $\rho = q_0 \ldots q_{n+1}$ such that $q_0 = q$ and $(q_i, a_i, q_{i+1}) \in \Delta$ for $i = 0, \ldots, n$; as abbreviation we write $\mathcal{A} \colon q_0 \xrightarrow{u} q_{n+1}$. A word u is *accepted* by $\mathcal{A}$ if $\mathcal{A} \colon q_0 \xrightarrow{u} q$ with $q \in F$. The language $L(\mathcal{A}) = \{u \in \Sigma^* \mid \mathcal{A} \colon q_0 \xrightarrow{u} q, q \in F\}$ is the language of all words accepted by $\mathcal{A}$. A language L is called *regular* if there exists an NFA $\mathcal{A}$ such that $L = L(\mathcal{A})$. To measure the "complexity" of NFAs, we define the *size* of an NFA as $|Q|$, i.e., the number of its states.

A *deterministic finite automaton (DFA)* is an NFA where for all $p \in Q$ and $a \in \Sigma$ there exists a unique $q \in Q$ with $(p, a, q) \in \Delta$. In the case of DFAs, we substitute the transition relation Δ with a transition function $\delta \colon Q \times \Sigma \to Q$.

A *(finite-state) transducer* $\mathcal{T}$ is a special NFA working over the alphabet $(\Sigma \cup \{\varepsilon\}) \times (\Sigma \cup \{\varepsilon\})$ with transitions of the form $(p, (a, b), q)$, $(p, (a, \varepsilon), q)$, and $(p, (\varepsilon, b), q)$. A transducer reads pairs of words and moves from state p to state q on reading $(u, v) \in \Sigma^* \times \Sigma^*$, denoted by $\mathcal{T} \colon p \xrightarrow{(u,q)} q$, if a sequence of transitions exists whose labels yield the pair (u, v) when concatenated componentwise. Rather than a regular language, a transducer accepts (or defines) a relation $R(\mathcal{T}) \subseteq \Sigma^* \times \Sigma^*$ where $R(\mathcal{T}) = \{(u, v) \mid \mathcal{T} \colon q_0 \xrightarrow{(u,v)} q, q \in F\}$. A relation $R \subseteq \Sigma^* \times \Sigma^*$ is called *rational* if there exists a transducer $\mathcal{T}$ such that $R = R(\mathcal{T})$.

For a relation $R \subseteq \Sigma^* \times \Sigma^*$ let R^* denote the reflexive and transitive closure of R. Moreover, for a language $L \subseteq \Sigma^*$ let $R(L)$ be the image of L under R defined by $R(L) = \{v \in \Sigma^* \mid \exists u \in L \colon (u, v) \in R\}$. Finally, if $R(L) \subseteq L$ holds, we call L a *regular invariant* or *inductive (with respect to R)*. Analogously, if $R(L(\mathcal{A})) \subseteq L(\mathcal{A})$ for some NFA (or DFA) $\mathcal{A}$, we call $\mathcal{A}$ inductive.

Regular Model Checking. In Regular Model Checking, a program $\mathcal{P} = (I, T)$ consists of a regular set $I \subseteq \Sigma^*$ of *initial configurations* over an a priori fixed alphabet Σ and a rational relation $T \subseteq \Sigma^* \times \Sigma^*$ defining the *transitions*. Regular Model Checking now asks whether there exists a path along the transitions from some initial configuration into a given regular set $B \subseteq \Sigma^*$ of *bad configurations*, which must never be reached. In other words, we are interested in answering the decision problem "Given a program $\mathcal{P} = (I, T)$ and a regular set $B \subseteq \Sigma^*$. Does $T^*(I) \cap B = \emptyset$ hold?". If the intersection is non-empty, we know that the program is erroneous. Note that Regular Model Checking is undecidable in general as rational relations are powerful enough to encode computations of Turing machines. Thus, the algorithms presented here are necessarily semi-algorithms.

A well-established approach to solve the Regular Model Checking problem used, e.g., by T(O)RMC [5] or LEVER [7] is to compute so-called *proofs*. Formally, a proof is a regular set $P \subseteq \Sigma^*$ such that $I \subseteq P$, $B \cap P = \emptyset$, and $T(P) \subseteq P$; for convenience, we also call an NFA (or DFA) $\mathcal{A}$ a proof if $L(\mathcal{A})$ is a proof. Note that any proof contains at least the set of reachable configurations and is, therefore, sufficient to prove a program correct. The advantage of computing a proof rather than the set of reachable configurations is that a proof might exists even if the set of reachable states itself is not regular.

Logics. In the remainder of this paper, we use both the propositional logic over Boolean variables and the quantifier-free logic over the integers with uninterpreted functions. *Formulas*, denoted by φ or—if the free variables are of interest—$\varphi(x_1, \ldots, x_n)$, are defined in the usual way. Moreover, a *model* of a formula $\varphi(x_1, \ldots, x_n)$ is a mapping $\mathfrak{M} \colon \{x_1, \ldots, x_n\} \to D_1 \times \ldots \times D_n$ that assigns to each variable x_i a value from the domain D_i of x_i such that φ evaluates to $\mathtt{true}$. Moreover, if φ contains uninterpreted functions, then the model has to provide an interpretation of these functions. If $\mathfrak{M}$ is a model of φ, we write $\mathfrak{M} \models \varphi$.

Formulas defined in propositional logic can be solved by SAT solvers, and formulas defined in quantifier-free logic over the integers with uninterpreted functions can be solved by SAT-modulo-theories solvers (SMT), which is a generalization of the classical propositional satisfiability problem (SAT). Compared to SAT problems, in an SMT formula atomic propositions may be replaced by atoms of a given theory, in our case *uninterpreted functions*. Several tools for solving SAT and SMT formulae are available, e.g., GLUCOSER and Z3, respectively.

3   Inferring Inductive DFAs from Finite Samples

In this section, we present a solver-based approach to compute inductive DFAs from a finite sample of initial and bad configurations of a program. Remember that the procedure of our Regular Model Checking approach works roughly as follows: we provide a procedure to compute a DFA that is consistent with a finite sample and inductive with respect to a given transducer. Starting with an empty sample, we use automata learning techniques to extend the sample, and compute a consistent and inductive DFA after each extension. This process continues until enough information has been learned and the computed DFA is a proof.

Our solver-based approach is a novel combination of techniques presented in [13] and [8], which both work in a slightly different setting. For the reader's convenience, however, we recap some principles of these techniques here.

Let us first fix the definitions of samples and consistency, which we already used informally above. A *sample* is a pair $S = (S_+, S_-)$ consisting of two disjoint and finite sets $S_+, S_- \subseteq \Sigma^*$ over the same alphabet Σ. Intuitively, the set S_+ contains words that have to be accepted by an automaton whereas the set S_- contains such words that have to be rejected. A NFA (or DFA) $\mathcal{A}$ is said to be *consistent* with a sample S if it accepts all words in S_+ and rejects all words in S_-, i.e., if $S_+ \subseteq L(\mathcal{A})$ and $S_- \cap L(\mathcal{A}) = \emptyset$.

In the following, let a sample S and a transducer $\mathcal{T}$ over a common alphabet Σ be given. We compute a consistent and inductive DFA by constructing (and solving) logical formulas $\varphi_n^{S,\mathcal{T}}$ that depend on the sample S, the transducer $\mathcal{T}$, and a natural number $n > 0$. A formula $\varphi_n^{S,\mathcal{T}}$ will have the following properties:

- $\varphi_n^{S,\mathcal{T}}$ is satisfiable if and only if there exists a DFA $\mathcal{A}$ with n states such that $\mathcal{A}$ is consistent with S and inductive with respect to $\mathcal{T}$.
- If $\mathfrak{M} \models \varphi_n^{S,\mathcal{T}}$, then we can use $\mathfrak{M}$ to derive a DFA $\mathcal{A}_\mathfrak{M}$ that is consistent with S and inductive with respect to $\mathcal{T}$.

Using these properties, a straightforward algorithm to find a DFA consistent with S and inductive with respect to $\mathcal{T}$ is depicted in Algorithm 1. The idea is to increase the value of n until $\varphi_n^{S,\mathcal{T}}$ becomes satisfiable. If a consistent and inductive DFA exists, the process terminates eventually, and $\mathcal{A}_\mathfrak{M}$ is such a DFA. However, such a DFA does not always exist, e.g., in the simple case that a configuration in S_- is reachable via the transitions from configurations in S_+.

Algorithm 1. Computing minimal consistent and inductive DFAs

Input: a sample S and a transducer $\mathcal{T}$ over a common alphabet Σ.

$n := 0$;
repeat
  $n := n + 1$;
  Construct and solve $\varphi_n^{S,\mathcal{T}}$;
until $\varphi_n^{S,\mathcal{T}}$ *is satisfiable (with model $\mathfrak{M}$)*;
Construct and **return** $\mathcal{A}_\mathfrak{M}$;

Note that Algorithm 1 does not only compute a DFA that is consistent with S and inductive with respect to $\mathcal{T}$ but a smallest such DFA in terms of the number of states. Although this fact is not important here, it will be crucial for proving the termination of the algorithms we will present in Section 4. Also note that a binary search is a more efficient way to find the minimal value for n such that $\varphi_n^{S,\mathcal{T}}$ is satisfiable. Let us sum up by stating the main result of this section.

Theorem 1. *Let a sample S and a transducer $\mathcal{T}$ over a common alphabet Σ be given. If a DFA consistent with S and inductive with respect to $\mathcal{T}$ exists, say with k states, then Algorithm 1 terminates after at most k steps. Moreover, $\mathcal{A}_{\mathfrak{M}}$ is a smallest DFA that is consistent with S and inductive with respect to $\mathcal{T}$.*

Proof (of Theorem 1). The proof is straightforward and relies on the fact that $\varphi_n^{S,\mathcal{T}}$ has indeed the desired properties (cf. Lemma 3 on page 23). Let a sample S and a transducer $\mathcal{T}$ be given. Suppose that a DFA consistent with S and inductive with respect to $\mathcal{T}$ exists, say with k states. Then, the formula $\varphi_n^{S,\mathcal{T}}$ is satisfiable for all $n \geq k$. Moreover, if $\mathfrak{M} \models \varphi_n^{S,\mathcal{T}}$, then $\mathcal{A}_{\mathfrak{M}}$ is a DFA with n states that is consistent with S and inductive with respect to $\mathcal{T}$. Since we increase n by one in every iteration, we eventually find the smallest value for which $\varphi_n^{S,\mathcal{T}}$ is satisfiable (after at most k steps) and, hence, a smallest DFA.   □

In the remainder of this section, we will implement the formula $\varphi_n^{S,\mathcal{T}}$ in two different logics: propositional Boolean logic, and the quantifier free fragment of Presburger arithmetic with uninterpreted functions. We will present the implementation in propositional Boolean logic in detail, but only sketch the implementation in Presburger arithmetic as the general idea is similar.

Finally, note that the application of SAT and SMT solvers in this setting is justified as already the special case of finding a minimal DFA that is consistent with a sample is computationally hard—in this case, the transducer defines the identity relation. To be more precise, Gold [14] showed that the corresponding decision problem "Given a sample S and a natural number k. Does a DFA with k states consistent with S exist?" is NP-complete. Moreover, there exist highly-optimized logic solvers that can solve even large problems efficiently.

SAT-based Approach. Next, we present a formula in propositional Boolean logic that encodes a DFA with a fixed number $n > 1$ of states that is consistent with a given sample $S = (S_+, S_-)$ and inductive with respect to a transducer $\mathcal{T} = (Q^{\mathcal{T}}, (\Sigma \cup \{\varepsilon\})^2, q_0^{\mathcal{T}}, \Delta^{\mathcal{T}}, F^{\mathcal{T}})$. The state set of the resulting DFA will be $Q = \{q_0, \dots, q_{n-1}\}$ with initial state q_0. To encode a DFA, we make a simple observation: if we fix the set of states, the initial state (e.g., as above), and the input alphabet Σ, then every DFA is uniquely determined by its transition function δ and final states F. Our encoding exploits this fact and uses Boolean variables $d_{p,a,q}$ and f_q with $p, q \in Q$ and $a \in \Sigma$. Their meaning is that if $d_{p,a,q}$ is **true**, then $\delta(p, a) = q$. Analogously, if f_q is **true**, then it means that $q \in F$. Note that this idea is used in [13], although not stated in this explicit form.

To make sure that the variables $d_{p,a,q}$ in fact encode a transition function of a DFA, we impose the following constraints.

$$\neg d_{p,a,q} \vee \neg d_{p,a,q'} \qquad p, q, q' \in Q,\ q \neq q',\ a \in \Sigma \qquad (1)$$

$$\bigvee_{q \in Q} d_{p,a,q} \qquad p \in Q,\ a \in \Sigma \qquad (2)$$

Constraints of type (1) make sure that the variables $d_{p,a,q}$ encode a deterministic function whereas constraints of type (2) enforce the function to be complete.

Now, let $\varphi_n^{\mathrm{DFA}}(\overline{d}, \overline{f})$ be the conjunction of these constraints where $\overline{d}$ is the vector of all variables $d_{p,a,q}$ and $\overline{f}$ is the vector of all variables f_q. From a model $\mathfrak{M} \models \varphi_n^{\mathrm{DFA}}(\overline{d}, \overline{f})$, we can derive a DFA $\mathcal{A}_{\mathfrak{M}} = (\{q_0, \dots, q_{n-1}\}, \Sigma, q_0, \delta, F)$ in a straightforward manner: we set $\delta(p, a) = q$ for the unique q such that $\mathfrak{M}(d_{p,a,q}) = \mathtt{true}$ and $q \in F$ if and only if $\mathfrak{M}(f_q) = \mathtt{true}$.

To guarantee that $\mathcal{A}_{\mathfrak{M}}$ is consistent with $\mathcal{S}$ and inductive with respect to $\mathcal{T}$, we impose further constraints on the formula φ_n^{DFA}. We do so by introducing two auxiliary formulas $\varphi_n^{\mathcal{S}}$ as well as $\varphi_n^{\mathcal{T}}$, whose meaning is the following:

- If $\mathfrak{M} \models \varphi_n^{\mathrm{DFA}} \wedge \varphi_n^{\mathcal{S}}$, then $S_+ \subseteq L(\mathcal{A}_{\mathfrak{M}})$ and $S_- \cap L(\mathcal{A}_{\mathfrak{M}}) = \emptyset$.
- If $\mathfrak{M} \models \varphi_n^{\mathrm{DFA}} \wedge \varphi_n^{\mathcal{T}}$, then $R(\mathcal{T})(L(\mathcal{A}_{\mathfrak{M}})) \subseteq L(\mathcal{A}_{\mathfrak{M}})$.

It is not hard to see that if $\mathfrak{M} \models \varphi_n^{\mathrm{DFA}} \wedge \varphi_n^{\mathcal{S}} \wedge \varphi_n^{\mathcal{T}}$, then $\mathcal{A}_{\mathfrak{M}}$ is consistent with $\mathcal{S}$ and inductive with respect to $\mathcal{T}$. When presenting both formulas in the following, we will describe their influence on the resulting DFA $\mathcal{A}_{\mathfrak{M}}$ rather than on the variables $d_{p,a,q}$ and f_q. We thereby implicitly assume that the formulas are satisfiable.

Let us begin by describing the formula $\varphi_n^{\mathcal{S}}$, which originally was proposed by Heule and Verwer [13]. The general idea is to consider runs of the DFA $\mathcal{A}_{\mathfrak{M}}$ on words from $\mathcal{S}$ and their prefixes. To this end, we introduce auxiliary variables $x_{u,q}$ for $u \in \mathit{Pref}(S_+ \cup S_-)$ and $q \in Q$. The meaning of these variables is that if $\mathcal{A}_{\mathfrak{M}}$ reaches state q after reading a word $u \in \mathit{Pref}(S_+ \cup S_-)$, then $x_{u,q}$ is set to $\mathtt{true}$. To establish this, we use the following constraints.

$$x_{\varepsilon, q_0} \tag{3}$$

$$(x_{u,p} \wedge d_{p,a,q}) \to x_{ua,q} \qquad ua \in \mathit{Pref}(S_+ \cup S_-),\ a \in \Sigma,\ p, q \in Q \tag{4}$$

$$x_{u,q} \to f_q \qquad u \in S_+,\ q \in Q \tag{5}$$

$$x_{u,q} \to \neg f_q \qquad u \in S_-,\ q \in Q \tag{6}$$

Constraint (3) ensures that the variable x_{ε, q_0} is set to $\mathtt{true}$ since $\mathcal{A} \colon q_0 \xrightarrow{\varepsilon} q_0$ holds by definition for every DFA $\mathcal{A}$. Constraints of type (4) describe how the run of $\mathcal{A}_{\mathfrak{M}}$ on some input develops: if $\mathcal{A}_{\mathfrak{M}}$ reaches state p after reading u and $\delta(p, a) = q$, then $\mathcal{A}_{\mathfrak{M}}$ will reach state q after reading ua. Constraints of type (5) and (6) assure that words from S_+ and S_- are accepted and rejected, respectively.

Let $\varphi_n^{\mathcal{S}}(\overline{d}, \overline{f}, \overline{x})$ be the conjunction of constraints (3) to (6) where $\overline{d}$ and $\overline{f}$ are as above and $\overline{x}$ is the vector of all variables $x_{u,q}$. Then, we obtain the following.

Lemma 1 (Consistency with $\mathcal{S}$, [13]). *Let $\mathcal{S} = (S_+, S_-)$ be a sample and $\mathfrak{M} \models \varphi_n^{\mathrm{DFA}}(\overline{d}, \overline{f}) \wedge \varphi_n^{\mathcal{S}}(\overline{d}, \overline{f}, \overline{x})$ for some $n \in \mathbb{N}$. Then, $\mathcal{A}_{\mathfrak{M}}$ is consistent with $\mathcal{S}$, i.e., $S_+ \subseteq L(\mathcal{A}_{\mathfrak{M}})$ and $S_- \cap L(\mathcal{A}_{\mathfrak{M}}) = \emptyset$.*

Lemma 1 can be proved by an induction over the length of the words from the sample. For further details we refer to [13].

The formula $\varphi_n^{\mathcal{T}}$ has recently been introduced also in the context of Regular Model Checking [8]. The basic idea is to keep track of the parallel behavior of the transducer $\mathcal{T}$ and the DFA $\mathcal{A}_{\mathfrak{M}}$. More precisely, we need to establish that if a pair (u,v) of words is accepted by $\mathcal{T}$ and $u \in L(\mathcal{A}_{\mathfrak{M}})$, then $v \in L(\mathcal{A}_{\mathfrak{M}})$ holds, too. To this end, we introduce new auxiliary variables $y_{q,q',q''}$ with $q, q'' \in Q$ and $q' \in Q^{\mathcal{T}}$. Their meaning is that $\mathcal{T}: q_0^{\mathcal{T}} \xrightarrow{(u,v)} q'$, $\mathcal{A}_{\mathfrak{M}}: q_0 \xrightarrow{u} q$, and $\mathcal{A}_{\mathfrak{M}}: q_0 \xrightarrow{v} q''$, then $y_{q,q',q''}$ is set to $\mathtt{true}$. The condition stated intuitively above can then be expressed using the following constraints.

$$y_{q_0,q_0^{\mathcal{T}},q_0} \tag{7}$$

$$(y_{p,p',p''} \wedge d_{p,a,q} \wedge d_{p'',b,q''}) \rightarrow y_{q,q',q''} \qquad \begin{aligned} &(p',(a,b),q') \in \Delta^{\mathcal{T}},\ a,b \in \Sigma, \\ &p,p'',q,q'' \in Q,\ p',q' \in Q^{\mathcal{T}} \end{aligned} \tag{8}$$

$$(y_{p,p',p''} \wedge d_{p,a,q}) \rightarrow y_{q,q',p''} \qquad \begin{aligned} &(p',(a,\varepsilon),q') \in \Delta^{\mathcal{T}},\ a \in \Sigma, \\ &p,p'',q \in Q,\ p',q' \in Q^{\mathcal{T}} \end{aligned} \tag{9}$$

$$(y_{p,p',p''} \wedge d_{p'',b,q''}) \rightarrow y_{p,q',q''} \qquad \begin{aligned} &(p',(\varepsilon,b),q') \in \Delta^{\mathcal{T}},\ b \in \Sigma, \\ &p,q,q'' \in Q,\ p',q' \in Q^{\mathcal{T}} \end{aligned} \tag{10}$$

$$(y_{q,q',q''} \wedge f_q) \rightarrow f_{q''} \qquad q,q'' \in Q,\ q' \in F^{\mathcal{T}} \tag{11}$$

Constraint (7) makes sure that $y_{q_0,q_0^{\mathcal{T}},q_0}$ is set to $\mathtt{true}$ since $\mathcal{T}: q_0^{\mathcal{T}} \xrightarrow{\varepsilon} q_0^{\mathcal{T}}$ and $\mathcal{A}_{\mathfrak{M}}: q_0 \xrightarrow{\varepsilon} q_0$ holds by definition of runs. Moreover, constraints of the types (8) to (10) describe how the parallel behavior of $\mathcal{T}$ and $\mathcal{A}_{\mathfrak{M}}$ develops depending on the type of $\mathcal{T}$'s transitions. This is done in a similar manner as the constraints (4) of the formula $\varphi_n^{\mathcal{S}}$. Finally, constraints of type (11) state that if (u,v) is accepted by $\mathcal{T}$ and u is accepted by $\mathcal{A}_{\mathfrak{M}}$, then v has to be accepted by $\mathcal{A}_{\mathfrak{M}}$, too.

Let $\varphi_n^{\mathcal{T}}(\overline{d},\overline{f},\overline{y})$ be the conjunction of constraints (7) to (11) where $\overline{d}$ and $\overline{f}$ are as above and $\overline{y}$ is the vector of all variables $y_{q,q'q,''}$. Then, we obtain the following lemma.

Lemma 2 (Inductivity with respect to $\mathcal{T}$, [8]). *Let $\mathcal{T}$ be a finite state transducer and $\mathfrak{M} \models \varphi_n^{DFA}(\overline{d},\overline{f}) \wedge \varphi_n^{\mathcal{T}}(\overline{d},\overline{f},\overline{y})$ for some $n \in \mathbb{N}$. Then, $\mathcal{A}_{\mathfrak{M}}$ is inductive with respect to $\mathcal{T}$, i.e., $R(\mathcal{T})(L(\mathcal{A}_{\mathfrak{M}})) \subseteq L(\mathcal{A}_{\mathfrak{M}})$.*

The proof of Lemma 2 uses an induction similar to the proof of Lemma 1. This time, however, the induction is over the number of $\mathcal{T}$'s transition used on a run. We refer to [8] further details. Let us now sum up.

Lemma 3. *Let S be a sample and $\mathcal{T}$ a transducer over a common alphabet Σ, $n \in \mathbb{N}$, and*

$$\varphi_n^{\mathcal{S},\mathcal{T}}(\overline{d},\overline{f},\overline{x},\overline{y}) = \varphi_n^{DFA}(\overline{d},\overline{f}) \wedge \varphi_n^{\mathcal{S}}(\overline{d},\overline{f},\overline{x}) \wedge \varphi_n^{\mathcal{T}}(\overline{d},\overline{f},\overline{y}).$$

Then, $\varphi_n^{\mathcal{S},\mathcal{T}}(\overline{d},\overline{f},\overline{x},\overline{y})$ is satisfiable if and only if there exists a DFA with n states that is consistent with S and inductive with respect to $\mathcal{T}$.

Proof (of Lemma 3). The direction from left to right is a straightforward application of Lemma 1 and Lemma 2. Let $\varphi_n^{\mathcal{S},\mathcal{T}}$ be satisfiable and $\mathfrak{M} \models \varphi_n^{\mathcal{S},\mathcal{T}}$. Then, $\mathcal{A}_{\mathfrak{M}}$ is a DFA with n states, consistent with S, and inductive with respect to $\mathcal{T}$.

For the reverse direction, suppose that there exists a DFA $\mathcal{A} = (Q, \Sigma, q_0, \delta, F)$ with n states that is consistent with $\mathcal{S}$ and inductive with respect to $\mathcal{T}$. Based on $\mathcal{A}$, we can find a model $\mathfrak{M}$ for the formula $\varphi_n^{\mathcal{S}, \mathcal{T}}(\overline{d}, \overline{f}, \overline{x}, \overline{y})$: let $\mathfrak{M}(d_{p,a,q}) = \texttt{true}$ if and only if $\delta(p, a) = q$ and $\mathfrak{M}(f_q) = \texttt{true}$ if and only if $q \in F$. The values of $\mathfrak{M}(x_{u,q})$ and $\mathfrak{M}(y_{q,q',q''})$ can then be derived accordingly.   □

Finally, note that $\varphi_n^{\mathcal{S}, \mathcal{T}}$ can easily be turned into conjunctive normal form for a SAT solver. In total, the formula comprises $\mathcal{O}(n^2|\Sigma| + n|Pref(S_+ \cup S_-)| + n^2|Q^{\mathcal{T}}|)$ variables and $\mathcal{O}(n^3|\Sigma| + n^2|Pref(S_+ \cup S_-)| + n^4|\Delta^{\mathcal{T}}| + n^2|F^{\mathcal{T}}|)$ clauses.

SMT-based Approach. We now sketch the the implementation of $\varphi_n^{\mathcal{S}, \mathcal{T}}$ in SMT logic. To this end, we assume without loss of generality that all automata have a special format: the set of states is $Q = \{0, \ldots, n-1\}$, $q_0 = 0$, and the input alphabet is $\Sigma = \{0, \ldots, m-1\}$.

Our approach is to encode the automaton directly into the formula utilizing two uninterpreted functions $d\colon \mathbb{N} \times \mathbb{N} \to \mathbb{N}$ and $f\colon \mathbb{N} \to \{0, 1\}$ where d represents the transitions and f the final states. Moreover, we use two additional uninterpreted functions $x\colon \mathbb{N} \to \mathbb{N}$ and $y\colon \mathbb{N} \times \mathbb{N} \times \mathbb{N} \to \{0, 1\}$, which have the same meaning as the variables $x_{u,q}$ and $y_{q,q'q,''}$ in the SAT-based approach.

Uninterpreted functions allow us to formulate constraints 3 to 11 of the previous section in a convenient manner. Constraints 8, for instance, can be expressed as $y(i, i', i'') \to y(d(i, a), j', d(i'', b))$ where $i, i'' \in Q$, $i', j' \in Q^{\mathcal{T}}$, and $(i', (a, b), j') \in \Delta^{\mathcal{T}}$. As the SMT implementation is analogous to the implementation in Boolean propositional logic, we skip the details here and refer to [8] for a more detailed description. However, let us mention that $\varphi_n^{\mathcal{S}, \mathcal{T}}$ comprises $\mathcal{O}(n|\Sigma| + |Pref(S_+ \cup S_-)| + n^2(|\Delta^{\mathcal{T}}| + |F^{\mathcal{T}}|))$ constraints.

4   Learning-Based Regular Model Checking

This section presents two algorithms based on algorithmic learning and solver technologies (introduced in the previous section) to compute proofs in Regular Model Checking. In contrast to most existing approaches, our idea is to learn a proof rather than to compute one in a constructive manner.

The learning framework we use was originally introduced by Angluin [11]. In this setting, a *learner* learns a regular *target language* $L \subseteq \Sigma^*$ over an a priori fixed alphabet Σ in interaction with a *teacher*. To do so, the learner can pose two different types of queries: *membership* and *equivalence queries*. On a membership query, the learner queries whether a word $w \in \Sigma^*$ belongs to the target language. The teacher answer either $w \in L$ or $w \notin L$. On an equivalence query, the learner conjectures a regular language, typically given as a DFA $\mathcal{A}$, and the teacher checks if $L(\mathcal{A}) = L$. If this is the case, he returns "yes". Otherwise, he returns a counterexample $w \in L(\mathcal{A}) \Leftrightarrow w \notin L$ as a witness that $L(\mathcal{A})$ and L are different.

Clearly, in our setting we cannot build a teacher that can answer arbitrary membership queries as this would mean to already solve the Regular Model Checking problem. Moreover, answering equivalence queries is possible, but there seems to be no way of finding counterexamples. Thus, we move to a slightly different learning scenario in which answering queries is possible: we allow the teacher to answer "don't know", denoted by ?, to membership queries, and we will only conjecture DFAs on equivalence queries that are inductive with respect to the transducer. This way, the teacher only needs to check whether the proposed conjecture classifies the initial and bad configurations correctly.

Employing learning techniques in an Angluin-like learning scenario is in general a two-step process. First, we need to construct a teacher that is able to answer membership and equivalence queries (cf. Section 4.1). Second, we have to develop a learning algorithm that learns from this teacher. For the latter task, we will present two algorithms. The first (cf. Section 4.2) follows the principles of the successful CEGAR approach [12]. The second (cf. Section 4.3) is based on Angluin's prominent algorithm for learning regular languages [11].

Both algorithms share the same fundamental idea. The learner supposes that the teacher knows a proof and asks the teacher if configurations belong to the proof or not. The problem is, that the teacher does not know a proof. However, he can clearly answer queries if the configuration in question belongs to the set of initial or bad configurations. If this is not the case, he simply returns "don't know". Once a learner has gathered enough information, he conjectures an inductive DFA consistent with the information obtained so far. To answer this equivalence query, the teacher only needs to check whether the conjecture classifies the initial and bad configurations correctly since we assume any conjecture to be inductive. If the check fails, the teacher can easily find a counterexample.

A similar scenario called *learning from inexperienced teachers* was investigated in [9] and subsequently in [10]. In [10], also the general idea of a CEGAR-style and Angluin-style learner have been discussed. Note, however, that the inexperienced teacher setting is simpler and does not involve computing inductive automata.

4.1   An Inexperienced Teacher for Regular Model Checking

Implementing a teacher for our setting is simple. On a membership query $w \in \Sigma^*$, the teacher returns "yes" if $w \in I$, "no" if $w \in B$, and "?" in any other case.

On an equivalence query with an DFA $\mathcal{A}$, the teacher checks whether $I \subseteq L(\mathcal{A})$ and $B \cap L(\mathcal{A}) = \emptyset$ holds and returns "yes" if so. If this is not the case, he returns a counterexample $w \in I$ and $w \notin L(\mathcal{A})$, or $w \in B \cap L(\mathcal{A})$. Note that this check is in fact enough to ensure that $\mathcal{A}$ is a proof since we assume that every conjecture provided on an equivalence query is inductive with respect to the transducer $\mathcal{T}$. Furthermore, note that all these checks are decidable for regular languages.

4.2   The CEGAR-Style Learner

The CEGAR-style learner (sketched as Algorithm 2) maintains a sample $\mathcal{S} = (S_+, S_-)$ as finite abstraction of the (potentially infinite) sets of initial and bad configurations. In every iteration, the learner computes a minimal DFA $\mathcal{A}$ consistent with $\mathcal{S}$ and inductive with respect to $\mathcal{T}$ using one of the techniques introduced in Section 3 in a black-box fashion. The DFA $\mathcal{A}$ is then conjectured on an equivalence query. If the teacher replies "yes", the process terminates.

If the teacher returns a counterexample w, we refine our abstraction. As a counterexample either satisfies $w \in I$ and $w \notin L(\mathcal{A})$, or $w \in B \cap L(\mathcal{A})$, we add w to S_+ in the first case and w to S_- in the latter case. This excludes a spurious behavior of further conjectures on w. Then, we continue with the next iteration.

Algorithm 2. The CEGAR-style learner

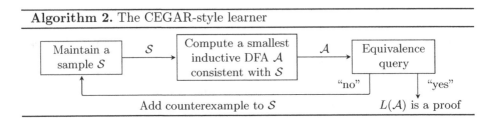

Algorithm 2 follows the CEGAR approach in the following sense. The DFA $\mathcal{A}$ produced from the sample in every iteration is an abstraction of the reachable part of the program. In the beginning, the sample contains only a few words and our algorithm will produce very coarse abstractions. An equivalence check with the abstraction reveals if a proof has been found. If this is not the case, counterexamples are used to refine the abstraction until a proof can be identified.

We can now state the main result of this section.

Theorem 2. *Let $P = (I, T)$ be a program and B a regular set of bad configurations with $B \cap I = \emptyset$. If a proof that $\mathcal{P}$ is correct with respect to B exists, Algorithm 2 terminates and returns a (smallest) proof.*

Proof (of Theorem 2). Due to the nature of equivalence queries, we know that the result of Algorithm 2 is in fact a proof once the algorithm terminates. Thus, it is enough to prove the termination of Algorithm 2 if a proof exists.

To this end, suppose that a proof exists, say with k states. We observe that Algorithm 2 never conjectures the same DFA twice and that the size of the conjectures increases monotonically. This can be seen as follows. Assume that the conjecture $\mathcal{A}_i$ of iteration i has n_i states and the conjecture $\mathcal{A}_{i+1}$ of iteration $i+1$ has $n_{i+1} < n_i$ states. Since the sample of iteration $i+1$ results from the one of iteration i by adding one word to S_+ or S_-, $\mathcal{A}_{i+1}$ is necessarily consistent with the sample of iteration i, but has fewer states than $\mathcal{A}_i$. This is a contradiction to the fact that we only produce minimal DFAs.

A second observation is that every proof is consistent with the samples produced by Algorithm 2 as the sample contains only counterexamples for which the teacher told us their classification; in particular, this holds for any smallest proof. Moreover, since Algorithm 1 always returns a smallest consistent and inductive DFA, it will eventually find a smallest proof as a solution once S_+ and S_- are large enough to rule out any smaller consistent and inductive DFA—regardless of the concrete choice of elements in S_+ and S_-.   □

4.3   The Angluin-Style Learner

Our Angluin-style learning algorithm is an extension of the CEGAR-style learner. Like Angluin's algorithm, it accelerates the learning process by additionally posing membership queries to gather further information before constructing a conjecture. Our general idea is to lift well-established querying techniques provided by Angluin's algorithm to our setting. Hence, when presenting the Angluin-style learner below, we assume a basic understanding of Angluin's algorithm [11].

Our Angluin-style learner, sketched as Algorithm 3, is an adaptation of a learning algorithm proposed by Grinchtein, Leucker, and Piterman [9]. The learner maintains a prefix-closed set $R \subseteq \Sigma^*$ and a set $S \subseteq \Sigma^*$ of words. Moreover, the learner organizes the learned data in a so-called *table* $T: (R \cup R \cdot \Sigma) \cdot S \to \{0, 1, ?\}$, which it fills by posing membership queries; the value of $T(u)$ is the answer to a membership query on u. The words from R are candidates for identifying states of a conjecture, and the words from S are used to distinguish such states. Using this intuition, we define two words $r, r' \in R \cup R \cdot \Sigma$ to be *equivalent* (i.e., to potentially represent the same state), denoted by $r \approx r'$, if they cannot be distinguished by words from S, i.e., $T(rs) \neq?$ and $T(r's) \neq?$ implies $T(rs) = T(r's)$ for all $s \in S$. In other words, r and r' are equivalent, if the ?-entries in the table can be resolved in such a way that $T(rs) = T(r's)$ holds for all $s \in S$.

Algorithm 3. The Angluin-style learner

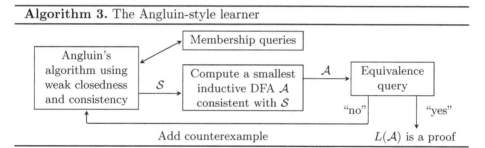

Our Angluin-style learner works like Angluin's algorithm, which makes the table closed and consistent in every iteration. Since we need to handle ?-entries, we switch to a weak notion of closedness and consistency as introduced in [9]:

- A table T is *weakly closed* if for $r \in R$ and $a \in \Sigma$ there exists an $r' \in R$ such that $ra \approx r'$. If this is not satisfied, the algorithm adds ra to R.
- A table T is *weakly consistent* if $r \approx r'$ implies $ra \approx r'a$ for $r, r' \in R$, $a \in \Sigma$. If T is not weakly consistent, then there exists an $s \in S$ such that $T(ras) \neq?$, $T(r'as) \neq?$, and $T(ras) \neq T(r'as)$, and the algorithm adds as to S.

Once T is weakly closed and weakly consistent, the Angluin-style learner turns the table into a sample $S = (S_+, S_-)$ where $S_+ = \{rs \mid r \in R, s \in S, T(rs) = 1\}$ and $S_- = \{rs \mid r \in R, s \in S, T(rs) = 0\}$. Then, it applies one of the approaches of Section 3 as a black-box to derive a smallest DFA $\mathcal{A}$ consistent with S and inductive with respect to T and submits $\mathcal{A}$ to an equivalence query. If the teacher replies "yes", the learning terminates. Otherwise, the algorithm adds the returned counterexample and all of its prefixes to R and continues with the next iteration.

The following theorem states the correctness of Algorithm 3. The proof is similar to the proof of Theorem 2 and, hence, skipped here.

Theorem 3. *Let $P = (I, T)$ be a program and B a regular set of bad configurations with $B \cap I = \emptyset$. If a proof that $\mathcal{P}$ is correct with respect to B exists, Algorithm 3 terminates and returns a (smallest) proof.*

5   Related Work and Experiments

Related Work. We are aware of three established tools for Regular Model Checking: T(O)RMC, FASTER, and LEVER. T(O)RMC iterates the given transducer and tries to identify differences between the iterations. These differences are extrapolated using *widening*, which approximates the limit of an infinite iteration of the transducer. The drawback of this method is that the bad configurations are not taken into account during the computation. If the the result is not disjoint to the bad configurations, the process has to be restarted with additional user input, which requires expert knowledge about the problem at hand. Moreover, T(O)RMC requires DFAs as input whereas our approach also works with NFAs, which can be exponentially smaller than equivalent DFAs.

FASTER computes the *exact* set of reachable configurations using *acceleration*, i.e., by computating in-the-limit effects of iterating cycles. This might lead to non-termination if the set of reachable configurations is not regular. In contrast, our learners always find a proof if one exists. Moreover, FASTER is originally designed for *integer linear systems* over Presburger formulas, which are internally translated into a Regular Model Checking problem. Thus, we can compare our approaches only on examples that are expressible as integer linear systems.

The LEVER tool uses Angluin's learning algorithm to learn proofs. The main difference from our approach lies in the fact that LEVER does not learn a proof directly, but a set of configurations that is augmented with distance information. These distance information encode how often the transducer has to be applied to reach a given configuration. The problem here is that these augmented sets are often not regular although a proof exists. Then, in contrast to our approaches, LEVER is not guaranteed to terminate. Unfortunately, LEVER is no longer publicly available, and, hence, were not able to compare it to our approaches.

Experiments. To assess the performance of our learning algorithms, we implemented a C++ prototype of both the CEGAR-style and the Angluin-style learner. The implementation uses the `libalf` automaton learning library as well as the GLUCOSER SAT solver and the Z3 SMT solver. We used two different benchmarks suits: integer linear systems and examples in which the size of the DFAs specifying initial and bad configurations were successively enlarged. For all experiments, we used a PC with an Intel Q9550 CPU and 4GB of RAM (at most 500MB were ever used) running Linux.

The first benchmark suit contains integer linear systems available at the FASTER and T(O)RMC websites. Table 1 shows results for FASTER, T(O)RMC[1], our CEGAR-style approach (CEGAR), and our Angluin-style approach(Angluin) on a simple petri net, the *Berkeley cache coherence protocol*, the *Synapse cache coherence protocol*, a lift protocol, the M.E.S.I. Cache Coherence Protocol and several more. Due to space constraints, we can provide only a selection of our results. However, all experiments showed the same qualitative results. Table 1 shows the running times in seconds. FASTER performs best on these examples, with the exception of petri net, where we had to pick FASTER-specific parameters by hand. On most examples, T(O)RMC is outperformed by the other tools.

Table 1. Results for integer linear systems

Experiment	Angluin		CEGAR		T(O)RMC	FASTER
	Glucoser	Z3	Glucoser	Z3		
petri net	0.12	0.15	0.11	0.11	0.02	1.13
berkeley	0.62	0.92	1.29	1.45	4.23	0.03
synapse	0.04	0.07	0.06	0.16	0.19	0.03
lift	0.01	0.01	0.01	0.02	5.54	0.15
mesi	0.58	2.64	1.55	6.24	5.52	0.04

The second benchmark suite demonstrates the advantages of our tool when confronted with large automata for initial and bad configurations. The suite contains examples of a modulo-counter and the well-known token ring protocol where we successively increased the size of the input automata. Table 2 shows the results together with the sizes of both initial and bad automata. In these experiments, we also compared ourselves to the mere SAT-based approach of [8]. "TO" indicates a timeout after 300 seconds and "–" indicates that the experiment could not be performed as we were not able to generate new benchmarks. We observe that T(O)RMC is clearly outperfomed by the CEGAR-style learner on the token-ring benchmark, but the solver-only method is the fastest. The best algorithm for the modulo-counter is the Angluin-style learner using GLUCOSER.

In total, we observe two things. First, our experiments show that we can handle problem instances specified for tools such as T(O)RMC and FASTER with competitive running times. Second, we observe that there is no superior algorithm. In particular, there are examples where the CEGAR-style outperforms the Angluin-style learner and vice versa, but both clearly beat T(O)RMC and the solver-only approach on the second benchmark suite. For the benchmarks at hand the implementations using the GLUCOSER SAT solver were always slightly faster than the one using the Z3 SMT solver. Note, however, that this might be different for larger instances as the size of the generated formulas grows faster for SAT than for SMT formulas. Moreover, note that our implementation is only an early prototype whereas T(O)RMC and FASTER are highly optimized tools.

---

[1] Please note that the 64-bit version of T(O)RMC did not work properly. The 32-bit version partly worked but suffered from severe memory access violation and leaks. For some benchmarks, T(O)RMC crashed and we were not able to obtain a result. Furthermore, it was not possible to generate new benchmarks for T(O)RMC.

Table 2. Results for Modulo counter and Token-ring

Experiment	Size	Angluin		CEGAR		Solver only T(o)RMC	
	init / bad	Glucoser	Z3	Glucoser	Z3	Glucoser	
Token-ring	50 / 3	1.23	1.52	0.07	0.14	0.02	0.31
	150 / 3	132.70	137.74	0.95	1.11	0.04	6.78
	250 / 3	TO	TO	4.13	3.43	0.04	31.57
	350 / 3	TO	TO	11.02	13.53	0.04	89.66
	450 / 3	TO	TO	24.65	24.90	0.04	203.36
Modulo counter	14 / 125	0.29	0.41	0.75	1.03	0.24	–
	14 / 156	0.58	0.99	1.75	2.09	0.29	–
	34 / 187	1.13	3.52	4.04	6.48	1.29	–
	34 / 218	2.49	20.42	6.45	47.84	27.49	–
	82 / 249	21.27	100.48	45.23	178.59	TO	–

6   Conclusion and Future Work

We presented two new algorithms for Regular Model Checking that combine off-the-shelf SAT and SMT solver technologies with automata learning. Our prototype implementation turned out to be competitive to FASTER and T(o)RMC, especially for large input automata. Moreover, our approaches work out-of-the-box, do not require expert knowledge, and always find a proof if one exist.

As future work we would like to investigate the applicability of nonregular sets of initial and bad configurations that still allow answering membership and equivalence queries, e.g., visibly or deterministic context-free languages. Another interesting field of further research is to use nondeterministic rather than deterministic automata as representation of proofs. This will increase the size of the formula $\varphi_n^{S,\mathcal{T}}$ on the one hand, but might yield an exponentially smaller result on the other hand. Furthermore, we will consider an incremental SAT approach, where clauses learnt during the solving process are reused in order to avoid complete restarts of the solver.

References

1. Clarke Jr., E.M., Grumberg, O., Peled, D.A.: Model Checking. The MIT Press (1999)
2. Baier, C., Katoen, J.P.: Principles of Model Checking. The MIT Press (2008)
3. Bouajjani, A., Jonsson, B., Nilsson, M., Touili, T.: Regular model checking. In: Emerson, E.A., Sistla, A.P. (eds.) CAV 2000. LNCS, vol. 1855, pp. 403–418. Springer, Heidelberg (2000)
4. Wolper, P., Boigelot, B.: Verifying systems with infinite but regular state spaces. In: Vardi, M.Y. (ed.) CAV 1998. LNCS, vol. 1427, pp. 88–97. Springer, Heidelberg (1998)
5. Legay, A.: T(O)RMC: A tool for (ω)-regular model checking. In: Gupta, A., Malik, S. (eds.) CAV 2008. LNCS, vol. 5123, pp. 548–551. Springer, Heidelberg (2008)

6. Bardin, S., Finkel, A., Leroux, J.: FASTer acceleration of counter automata in practice. In: Jensen, K., Podelski, A. (eds.) TACAS 2004. LNCS, vol. 2988, pp. 576–590. Springer, Heidelberg (2004)
7. Vardhan, A., Viswanathan, M.: LEVER: A tool for learning based verification. In: Ball, T., Jones, R.B. (eds.) CAV 2006. LNCS, vol. 4144, pp. 471–474. Springer, Heidelberg (2006)
8. Neider, D.: Computing minimal separating DFAs and regular invariants using SAT and SMT solvers. In: Chakraborty, S., Mukund, M. (eds.) ATVA 2012. LNCS, vol. 7561, pp. 354–369. Springer, Heidelberg (2012)
9. Grinchtein, O., Leucker, M., Piterman, N.: Inferring network invariants automatically. In: Furbach, U., Shankar, N. (eds.) IJCAR 2006. LNCS (LNAI), vol. 4130, pp. 483–497. Springer, Heidelberg (2006)
10. Leucker, M., Neider, D.: Learning minimal deterministic automata from inexperienced teachers. In: Margaria, T., Steffen, B. (eds.) ISoLA 2012, Part I. LNCS, vol. 7609, pp. 524–538. Springer, Heidelberg (2012)
11. Angluin, D.: Learning regular sets from queries and counterexamples. Inf. Comput. 75(2), 87–106 (1987)
12. Clarke, E., Grumberg, O., Jha, S., Lu, Y., Veith, H.: Counterexample-guided abstraction refinement. In: Emerson, E.A., Sistla, A.P. (eds.) CAV 2000. LNCS, vol. 1855, pp. 154–169. Springer, Heidelberg (2000)
13. Heule, M.J.H., Verwer, S.: Exact DFA identification using SAT solvers. In: Sempere, J.M., García, P. (eds.) ICGI 2010. LNCS, vol. 6339, pp. 66–79. Springer, Heidelberg (2010)
14. Gold, E.M.: Complexity of automaton identification from given data. Information and Control 37(3), 302–320 (1978)

Improved on-the-Fly Livelock Detection
Combining Partial Order Reduction and Parallelism for DFS$_{\text{FIFO}}$

Alfons Laarman[1] and David Faragó[2]

[1] Formal Methods and Tools, University of Twente, The Netherlands
`a.w.laarman@cs.utwente.nl`
[2] Logic and Formal Methods, Karlsruhe Institute of Technology, Germany
`farago@kit.edu`

Abstract. Until recently, the preferred method of livelock detection was via LTL model checking, which imposes complex constraints on partial order reduction (POR), limiting its performance and parallelization. The introduction of the DFS$_{\text{FIFO}}$ algorithm by Faragó et al. showed that livelocks can theoretically be detected faster, simpler, and with stronger POR.

For the first time, we implement DFS$_{\text{FIFO}}$ and compare it to the LTL approach by experiments on four established case studies. They show the improvements over the LTL approach: DFS$_{\text{FIFO}}$ is up to 3.2 times faster, and it makes POR up to 5 times better than with SPIN's NDFS.

Additionally, we propose a parallel version of DFS$_{\text{FIFO}}$, which demonstrates the efficient combination of parallelization and POR. We prove parallel DFS$_{\text{FIFO}}$ correct and show why it provides stronger guarantees on parallel scalability and POR compared to LTL-based methods. Experimentally, we establish almost ideal linear parallel scalability and POR close to the POR for safety checks: easily an order of magnitude better than for LTL.

1 Introduction

Context. In the *automata-theoretic* approach to *model checking* [27], the behavior of a system-under-verification is modeled, along with a property that it is expected to adhere to, in some concise specification language. This model $\mathcal{M}$ is then unfolded to yield a *state space* automaton $\mathcal{A}_{\mathcal{M}}$ (cf. Def. 1). *Safety properties*, e.g. *deadlocks* and *invariants*, can be checked directly on the states in $\mathcal{A}_{\mathcal{M}}$ as they represent all configurations of $\mathcal{M}$. This check can be done during the unfolding, *on-the-fly*, saving resources when a property violation is detected early on.

For more complicated properties, like *liveness properties* [1], $\mathcal{A}_{\mathcal{M}}$ is interpreted as an ω-automaton whose language $\mathcal{L}(\mathcal{A}_{\mathcal{M}})$ represents all infinite executions of the system. A property φ, expressed in linear temporal logic (LTL), is likewise translated to a Büchi or ω-automaton $\mathcal{A}_{\neg\varphi}$ representing all *undesired* infinite executions. The intersected language $\mathcal{L}(\mathcal{A}_{\mathcal{M}}) \cap \mathcal{L}(\mathcal{A}_{\neg\varphi})$ now consists of all counterexample traces, and is empty if and only if the system is correct with respect to the property. The emptiness check is reduced to the graph problem of

G. Brat, N. Rungta, and A. Venet (Eds.): NFM 2013, LNCS 7871, pp. 32–47, 2013.

finding cycles with designated accepting states in the *cross product* $\mathcal{A}_\mathcal{M} \otimes \mathcal{A}_{\neg\varphi}$ (cf. Sec. 2). The nested depth-first search (NDFS) algorithm [6] solves it in time linear to the size of the product and on-the-fly as well.

Motivation. The model checking approach is limited by the so-called *state space explosion* problem [1], which states that $\mathcal{A}_\mathcal{M}$ is exponential in the components of the system, and $\mathcal{A}_{\neg\varphi}$ exponential in the size of φ. Luckily, several remedies exist to this problem: patience, specialization and state space reduction techniques.

State space reduction via *partial order reduction* (POR) prunes $\mathcal{A}_\mathcal{M}$ by avoiding irrelevant interleavings of local components in $\mathcal{M}$ [16,26]: only a sufficient subset of successors, the *ample set*, is considered in each state (cf. Sec. 2). For safety properties, the ample set can be computed locally on each state. For liveness properties, however, an additional condition, the *cycle proviso*, is needed to avoid the so-called *ignoring problem* [9]. POR can yield exponential reductions.

Patience also pays of exponentially as Moore's law stipulates that the number of transistors available in CPUs and memory doubles every 18 months [22]. Due to this effect, model checking capabilities have increased from handling a few thousand states to covering billions of states recently (this paper and [5]). While this trend happily continues to increase memory sizes, it recently stopped benefitting the sequential performance of CPUs because physical limitations were reached. Instead, the available parallelism on the chips is rapidly increasing. So, for runtime to benefit from Moore's law, we must parallelize our algorithms.

Specialization towards certain subclasses of liveness properties, finally, can also help to solve them more efficiently. For instance, a limitation to the *CTL* and the *weak-LTL* fragments was shown to be efficiently parallelizable [25,3]. *In this paper, we limit the discourse to livelock properties*, an important subclass (used in about half of the case studies of [1] and a third of [24]) that investigates starvation, occurring if an infinite run does not make *progress* infinitely often. The definition of progress is up to the system designer and could for instance refer to an increase of a counter or access to a shared resource. The SPIN model checker allows the user to specify progress statements inside the specification of the model [12], which are then represented in the model by the state label 'progress' and referenced by the predefined *progress* LTL property [15]. Until 1996, SPIN used a specific livelock verification algorithm. Section 6 of [15] states that it was replaced by LTL model checking due to its incompatibility with POR.

Problem. LTL model checking can likely not be parallelized efficiently. The current state-of-the-art reveals that parallel cycle detection algorithms either raise the worst-case complexity to L^2 [3] or to $L \cdot P$ [8], where L is the size of the LTL cross product and P the number of processors. Moreover, its additional constraints on POR severely limit its reduction capabilities, even if implemented with great care (see models allocation, cs and p2p in Table 1 in the appendix of [9]). Last but not least, these constraints also limit the parallelization of POR [2].

---

[1] PROMELA database: http://www.albertolluch.com/research/promelamodels.

We want to investigate whether better results can be obtained for livelocks, for which recently an efficient algorithm was proposed by Faragó et al. [11]: DFS$_{\text{FIFO}}$. In theory, it has additional advantages over the LTL approach:

1. It uses the progress labels in the model directly without the definition of an LTL property; avoiding the calculation of a larger cross product.
2. It requires only one pass over the state space, while the NDFS algorithm, typically used for liveness properties, requires two.
3. It eliminates the need for the expensive cycle proviso with POR. Not only is the cycle proviso a highly limiting factor in state space reduction [9], it also complicates the parallelization of the problem [2].
4. It finds the shortest counterexample with respect to progress.

But DFS$_{\text{FIFO}}$ is yet to be implemented and evaluated experimentally, so its practical performance is unknown. Additionally, a few hypotheses stand unproven:

1. The algorithm's strategy to delay progress as much as possible, may also be a good heuristic for finding livelocks early, making it more on-the-fly.
2. Its POR performance might be close to that of safety checks, because the cycle proviso is no longer required [11], and the visibility proviso (see Table 1) is also positively influenced by the postponing of progress.
3. The use of *progress transitions* instead of *progress states* is possible, semantically more accurate, and can yield better partial order reductions.

Furthermore, no parallelization exists for the DFS$_{\text{FIFO}}$ algorithm.

Contributions. We implemented the DFS$_{\text{FIFO}}$ algorithm in the LTSMIN [21,5], with both progress states and transitions. For the latter, we extended theory, algorithms, proofs, models and implementation. We compare the runtime and POR performance to that of LTL approaches using NDFS. For DFS$_{\text{FIFO}}$, we also investigate the effect of using progress transitions instead of states on POR.

Additionally, we present a parallel livelock algorithm based on DFS$_{\text{FIFO}}$, together with a proof of correctness. While the algorithm builds on previous efficient parallelizations of the NDFS algorithm [8,17,19], we show that it has stronger guarantees for parallel scalability due to the nature of the underlying DFS$_{\text{FIFO}}$ algorithm. At the same time, it retains all the benefits of the original DFS$_{\text{FIFO}}$ algorithm. This entails the redundancy of the cycle proviso, hence allowing for parallel POR with almost the same reductions as for safety checks.

Our experiments confirm the theoretical expectations: using DFS$_{\text{FIFO}}$ on four case studies, we observed up to 3.2 times faster runtimes than with the use of an LTL property and the NDFS algorithm, even compared to measurements with the SPIN model checker. But we also confirm all hypotheses of Faragó et al.: the algorithm is more on-the-fly, and POR performance is closer to that of safety checks than the LTL approach, making it up to 5 times more effective than POR in SPIN. Our parallel version of the algorithm can work with POR and features the expected linear scalability. Its combination with POR easily outperforms other parallel approaches [3].

Overview. In Sec. 2, we recapitulate the intricacies of livelock detection via LTL and via non-progress detection, as well as POR. In Sec. 3, we introduce DFS$_{\text{FIFO}}$

for progress transitions with greater detail and formality than in [11], as well as its combination with POR. Thereafter, in Sec. 4, we provide a parallel version of DFS$_{\text{FIFO}}$ with a proof of correctness, implementation considerations, and an analysis on its scalability. Sec. 5 presents the experimental evaluation, comparing DFS$_{\text{FIFO}}$'s (POR) performance and scalability against the (parallel) LTL algorithms in SPIN [13,15], DiViNE [2,3], and LTSMIN [5,21]. We conclude in Sec. 6.

2   Preliminaries

Model Checking of Safety Properties. Explicit-state model checking algorithms construct $\mathcal{A}_{\mathcal{M}}$ on-the-fly starting from the initial state s_0, and recursively applying the next-state function *post* to discover all reachable states $\mathcal{R}_{\mathcal{M}}$. This only requires storing states (no transitions). As soon as a counterexample is discovered, the exploration can terminate early, saving resources. To reason about these algorithms, it is however easier to consider $\mathcal{A}_{\mathcal{M}}$ structurally as a graph.

Definition 1 (State Space Automaton). *An automaton is a quintuple* $\mathcal{A}_{\mathcal{M}} = (\mathcal{S}_{\mathcal{M}}, s_0, \Sigma, \mathcal{T}_{\mathcal{M}}, L)$, *with* $\mathcal{S}_{\mathcal{M}}$ *a finite set of states,* $s_0 \in \mathcal{S}_{\mathcal{M}}$ *an initial state,* Σ *a finite set of action labels,* $\mathcal{T}_{\mathcal{M}}: \mathcal{S}_{\mathcal{M}} \times \Sigma \to \mathcal{S}_{\mathcal{M}}$ *the transition relation, and* $L: \mathcal{S}_{\mathcal{M}} \to 2^{AP}$ *a state labeling function, over a set of atomic propositions* AP.

We also use the recursive application of the transition relation $\mathcal{T}: s \xrightarrow{\pi}{}^+ s'$ *iff* π *is a path in* $\mathcal{A}_{\mathcal{M}}$ *from* s *to* s', *or* $s \xrightarrow{\pi}{}^* s'$ *if possibly* $s = s'$. *We treat a path* π *dually as a sequence of states and a sequence of actions, depending on the context. We omit the subscript* $\mathcal{M}$ *whenever it is clear from the context.*

Now, we can define: the reachable states $\mathcal{R}_{\mathcal{M}} = \{s \in \mathcal{S}_{\mathcal{M}} \mid s_0 \to^* s\}$, the function $post: \mathcal{S}_{\mathcal{M}} \to 2^{\Sigma}$, such that $post(s) = \{\alpha \in \Sigma \mid \exists s' \in \mathcal{S}_{\mathcal{M}} : (s, \alpha, s') \in \mathcal{T}_{\mathcal{M}}\}$ and $\alpha(s)$ as the unique next-state for s, α if $\alpha \in post(s)$, i.e. the state t with $(s, \alpha, t) \in \mathcal{T}_{\mathcal{M}}$. Note that a state $s \in \mathcal{S}$ comprises the variable valuations and process counters in $\mathcal{M}$. Hence, we can use any proposition over these values as an atomic proposition representing a state label. For example, we may write progress $\equiv$ Peterson0 $= CS$ to have progress $\in L(s)$ iff s represents a state where process instance 0 of Peterson is in its critical section CS. Or we can write error $\equiv N > 1$ to express the mutual exclusion property, with N the number of processes in CS. These state labels can then be used to check safety properties using *reachability*, e.g., an *invariant* '$\neg error$' to check mutual exclusion in $\mathcal{M}$.

LTL Model Checking. For an LTL property, the property φ is transformed to an ω-automaton $\mathcal{A}_{\neg\varphi}$ as detailed in [27]. Structurally, the ω-automaton extends a normal automaton (Def. 1) with dedicated accepting states (see Def. 2). Semantically, these accepting states mark those cycles that are part of the ω-regular language $\mathcal{L}(\mathcal{A}_{\neg\varphi})$ as defined in Def. 3.

To check correctness of $\mathcal{M}$ with respect to a property φ, the *cross product* of $\mathcal{A}_{\neg\varphi}$ with the state space $\mathcal{A}_{\mathcal{M}}$ is calculated: $\mathcal{A}_{\mathcal{M} \times \varphi} = \mathcal{A}_{\mathcal{M}} \otimes \mathcal{A}_{\neg\varphi}$. The states of $\mathcal{S}_{\mathcal{M} \times \varphi}$ are formed by tuples (s, s') with $s \in \mathcal{S}_{\mathcal{M}}$ and $s' \in \mathcal{S}_{\neg\varphi}$, with $(s, s') \in \mathcal{F}$ iff $s' \in \mathcal{F}_{\neg\varphi}$. Hence, the number of possible states $|\mathcal{S}_{\mathcal{M} \times \varphi}|$ equals $|\mathcal{S}_{\mathcal{M}}| \cdot |\mathcal{S}_{\neg\varphi}|$, whereas the number of reachable states $|\mathcal{R}_{\mathcal{M} \times \varphi}|$ may be smaller. The transitions in $\mathcal{T}_{\mathcal{M} \times \varphi}$ are formed by synchronizing the transition labels of $\mathcal{A}_{\neg \varphi}$ with the state labels in $\mathcal{A}_{\mathcal{M}}$. For an exact definition of $\mathcal{T}_{\mathcal{M} \times \varphi}$, we refer to [1].

Definition 2 (Accepting states). *The set of accepting states* $\mathcal{F}$ *corresponds to those states with a label* **accept** $\in AP$: $\mathcal{F} = \{s \in \mathcal{S} \mid$ **accept** $\in L(s)\}$.

Definition 3 (Accepting run). *A lasso-formed path* $s_0 \xrightarrow{v}{}^* s \xrightarrow{w}{}^+ s$ *in* $\mathcal{A}$, *with* $s \in \mathcal{F}$, *constitutes an accepting run, part of the language of* $\mathcal{A}$: $vw^\omega \in \mathcal{L}(\mathcal{A})$.

As explained in Sec. 1, the whole procedure of finding counterexamples to φ for $\mathcal{M}$ is now reduced to the graph problem of finding *accepting runs* in $\mathcal{A}_{\mathcal{M} \times \varphi}$. This can be solved by the nested depth-first search (NDFS) algorithm, which does at most two explorations of all states $\mathcal{R}_{\mathcal{M} \times \varphi}$. Since $\mathcal{A}_{\mathcal{M} \times \varphi}$ can be constructed on-the-fly, NDFS saves resources when a counterexample is found early on.

Livelock Detection. *Livelocks* form a specific, but important subset of the liveness properties and can be expressed as the *progress* LTL property: $\Box \Diamond$**progress**, which states that on each infinite run, *progress* needs to be encountered infinitely often. As the LTL approach synchronizes the state labels of $\mathcal{A}_{\mathcal{M}}$ (see Def. 3), it requires that progress is defined on states as in Def. 4.

Definition 4 (Progress states). *The set of progress states* $\mathcal{S}^{\mathcal{P}}$ *corresponds to those states with a state label* **progress** $\in AP$: $\mathcal{S}^{\mathcal{P}} = \{s \in \mathcal{S} \mid$ **progress** $\in L(s)\}$.

Definition 5 (Non-progress cycle). *A reachable cycle* π *in* $\mathcal{A}_{\mathcal{M}}$ *is a non-progress cycle (**NPcycle**) iff it contains no progress* $\mathcal{P}$.
We define $\mathcal{NP}$ *as a set of states:* $\mathcal{NP} = \{s \in \mathcal{S}_{\mathcal{M}} \mid \exists \pi : s \xrightarrow{\pi}{}^+ s \land \pi \cap \mathcal{P} = \emptyset\}$.

Theorem 1. *Under* $\mathcal{P} = \mathcal{S}^{\mathcal{P}}$, $\mathcal{A}_{\mathcal{M}}$ *contains a **NPcycle** iff the crossproduct with the progress property* $\mathcal{A}_{\mathcal{M} \times \Box \Diamond \text{progress}}$ *contains an accepting cycle.*

Livelocks can however also be detected directly on $\mathcal{A}_{\mathcal{M}}$ if we consider for a moment that a counterexample to a livelock is formed by an infinite run that lacks progress $\mathcal{P}$, with $\mathcal{P} = \mathcal{S}^{\mathcal{P}}$. By proving absence of such *non-progress* cycles (Def. 5), we do essentially the same as via the progress LTL property, as Th. 1 shows (see [15] for the proof and details). This insight led to the proposal of dedicates algorithms in [15,11] (cf. DFS$_{\text{FIFO}}$ in Sec. 3), requiring $|\mathcal{R}_{\mathcal{M}}|$ time units to prove livelock freedom. The automaton $\mathcal{A}_{\neg \Box \Diamond \text{progress}}$ consists of exactly two states [15], hence $|\mathcal{R}_{\mathcal{M}}| \cdot 2 \leq |\mathcal{R}_{\mathcal{M} \times \varphi}|$. This, combined with the revisits of the NDFS algorithm, *makes the LTL approach up to 4 times as costly as* DFS$_{\text{FIFO}}$.

Partial Order Reduction. To achieve the reduction as discussed in the introduction, POR replaces the *post* with an *ample* function, which computes a sufficient subset of *post* to explore only relevant interleavings w.r.t the property [16].

For deadlock detection, *ample* only needs to fulfill the *emptiness proviso* and *dependency proviso* (Table 1). The provisos can be deduced locally from s,

Table 1. POR provisos for the LTL model checking of $\mathcal{M}$ with a property φ

C0	*emptiness*	$ample(s) = \emptyset \Leftrightarrow post(s) = \emptyset$
C1	*dependency*	No action $\alpha \notin ample(s)$ that is dependent on another $\beta \in ample(s)$, i.e. $(\alpha, \beta) \in D$, can be executed in the original $\mathcal{A}_{\mathcal{M}}$ after reaching the state s and before some action in $ample(s)$ is executed.
C2	*visibility*	$ample(s) \neq post(s) \implies \forall \alpha \in ample(s) : \alpha$ is *invisible*, which means that α does not change a state label referred to by φ.
C3	*cycle*	For a cycle π in $\mathcal{A}_{\mathcal{M}}$, $\exists s \in \pi : post(s) = ample(s)$.
C3'	*cycle (impl.)*	$ample(s) \neq post(s) \Rightarrow \nexists \alpha \in ample(s)$ s.t. $\alpha(s)$ is on the DFS stack.

$post(s)$, and dependency relations $D \subseteq \Sigma_{\mathcal{M}} \times \Sigma_{\mathcal{M}}$ that can be statically overestimated from $\mathcal{M}$, e.g. $(\alpha, \beta) \in D$ if α writes to those variables that β uses as guard [23]. For a precise definition of D consult [16,26].

In general, the model checking of an LTL property (or invariant) φ requires two additional provisos to hold: the *visibility proviso* ensures that traces included in $\mathcal{A}_{\neg \varphi}$ are not pruned from $\mathcal{A}_{\mathcal{M}}$, the *cycle proviso* prevents the so-called *ignoring problem* [9]. The strong variant **C3** (stronger than A4 in [1, Sec. 8.2.2]) is already hard to enforce, so often an even stronger condition, e.g. **C3'**, is implemented. While visibility can still be checked locally, the cycle proviso is a global property, that complicates parallelization [2]. Moreover, the NDFS algorithm revisits states, which might cause different ample sets for the same states, because the procedure is non-deterministic [15]. To avoid any resulting redundant explorations, additional bookkeeping is needed to ensure a deterministic ample set.

3   Progress Transitions and DFS$_{\text{FIFO}}$ for Non-progress

In the current section, we refine the definition of progress to include transitions. We then present a new version of DFS$_{\text{FIFO}}$, an efficient algorithm for non-progress detection by Faragó et al. [11], which supports this broader definition. We also discuss implementation considerations and the combination with POR.

Progress Transitions. As argued in [11], progress is more naturally defined on transitions (Def. 6) than on states. After all, the action itself, e.g. the increase of a counter in $\mathcal{M}$, constitutes the actual progress. This becomes clear considering the semantical difference between progress transitions and progress states for livelock detection: The figure on the right shows an automaton with $\mathcal{S}^{\mathcal{P}} = \{s_1\}$ and $\mathcal{T}^{\mathcal{P}} = \{(s_2, \alpha, s_1)\}$. Thus the cycle $s_2 \leftrightarrow s_3$ exhibits only *fake progress* when progress states are used ($\mathcal{P} = \mathcal{S}^{\mathcal{P}}$): the action performing the progress, α, is never taken. With progress transitions ($\mathcal{P} = \mathcal{T}^{\mathcal{P}}$), only $s_2 \leftrightarrow s_3$ can be detected as **NPcycle**. While fake progress cycles could be hidden by enforcing strong (A-)fairness [1], Spin's weak (A-)fairness [12] is insufficient [11]. But enforcing any kind of fairness is costly [1].

Definition 6 (Progress transitions/actions). *We define progress transitions as:* $\mathcal{T}^{\mathcal{P}} = \{(s, \alpha, s') \in \mathcal{T} \mid \alpha \in \Sigma^{\mathcal{P}}\}$, *with* $\Sigma^{\mathcal{P}} \subseteq \Sigma$ *a set of progress actions.*

Algorithm 1. DFS$_{\text{FIFO}}$ for progress transitions and progress states

1: **procedure** $dfs\text{-}fifo(s_0)$
2:    $F := \{s_0\}$ ▷*Frontier queue*
3:    $V := \emptyset$ ▷*Visited set*
4:    $S := \emptyset$ ▷*Stack*
5:    **repeat**
6:        $s := $ **some** $s \in F$
7:        **if** $s \notin V$ **then**
8:            $dfs(s)$
9:        $F := F \setminus \{s\}$
10:   **until** $F = \emptyset$
11:   **report progress ensured**

12: **procedure** $dfs(s)$
13:    $S := S \cup \{s\}$
14:    **for all** $t := \alpha(s)$ s.t. $\alpha \in post(s)$ **do**
15:        **if** $t \in S \wedge \alpha, t \notin \mathcal{P}$ **then**
16:            **report NPcycle**
17:        **if** $t \notin V$ **then**
18:            **if** $\alpha, t \notin \mathcal{P}$ **then**
19:                $dfs(t)$
20:            **else if** $t \notin F$ **then**
21:                $F := F \cup \{t\}$
22:    $V := V \cup \{s\}$
23:    $S := S \setminus \{s\}$

Theorem 2. DFS$_{\text{FIFO}}$ *ensures:* $\mathcal{R} \cap \mathcal{NP} \neq \emptyset \Leftrightarrow dfs\text{-}fifo(s_0) = $ ***report NPcycle***

DFS$_{\text{FIFO}}$. Alg. 1 shows an adaptation of DFS$_{\text{FIFO}}$ that supports the definition of progress on both states and transitions (actions), so $\mathcal{P} = \mathcal{S}^{\mathcal{P}} \cup \Sigma^{\mathcal{P}}$. Intuitively, the algorithm works by delaying progress as long as possible using a BFS and searching for **NPcycles** in between progress using a DFS. The correctness of this adapted algorithm follows from Th. 2, which is implied by Th. 4 with $P = 1$.

The FIFO queue F holds progress states, or immediate successors of progress transitions (which we will collectively refer to as after-progress states), with the exception of the initial state s_0. The outer *dfs-fifo* loop handles all after-progress states in breadth-first order. The *dfs* procedure, starting from a state in F then explores states up to progress, storing visited states in the set V (l.22), and after-progress states in F (l.21). The stack of this search is maintained in a set S (l.13 and l.23) to detect cycles at l.16. All states $t \in S$ and their connecting transitions are non-progress by l.18, except for possibly the starting state from F. $\overset{\text{next page}}{\longrightarrow}$ The cycle-closing transition $s \overset{\alpha}{\rightarrow} t$ might also be a progress transition. Therefore, l.15 performs an additional check $\alpha, t \notin \mathcal{P}$. Furthermore, an after-progress state $s \notin \mathcal{S}^{\mathcal{P}}$ added to F, might be reached later via a non-progress path and added to V. Hence, we discard visited states in *dfs-fifo* at l.7.

Implementation. An efficient implementation of Alg. 1 stores F and V in one hash table (using a bit to distinguish the two) for fast inclusion checks, while F is also maintained as a queue F^q. S can be stored in a separate hash table as $|S| \ll |\mathcal{R}|$. Counterexamples can be reconstructed if for each state a pointer to one of its predecessors is stored [20]. Faragó et al. showed two alternatives [11], which are also compatible with lossy hashing [4].

Table 2. POR visibility provisos for DFS$_{\text{FIFO}}$

C2$^{\mathcal{S}}$	$ample(s) \neq post(s) \implies s \notin \mathcal{S}^{\mathcal{P}}$
C2$^{\mathcal{T}}$	$ample(s) \neq post(s) \implies \forall \alpha \in ample(s) : \alpha \notin \Sigma^{\mathcal{P}}$

Combination with POR. While the four-fold performance increase of DFS$_{FIFO}$ compared to LTL (Sec. 2) is a modest gain, the algorithm provides even more potential as it relaxes conditions on POR, which, after all, might yield exponential gains. In contrast to the LTL method using NDFS, DFS$_{FIFO}$ does not revisit states, simplifying the *ample* implementation. Moreover, Lemma 1 shows that DFS$_{FIFO}$ does not require the cycle proviso using a visibility proviso from Table 2.

Lemma 1. *Under $\mathcal{P} = \mathcal{S}^{\mathcal{P}}$, $\mathbf{C2}^{\mathcal{S}}$ implies $\mathbf{C3}$. Under $\mathcal{P} = \Sigma^{\mathcal{P}}$, $\mathbf{C2}^{\mathcal{T}}$ implies $\mathbf{C3}$.*

Proof. If DFS$_{FIFO}$ with POR traverses a cycle C which makes progress, i.e. $\exists s \in C: s \in \mathcal{S}^{\mathcal{P}} \vee ample(s) \cap C \cap \Sigma^{\mathcal{P}} \neq \emptyset$, $\mathbf{C2}^{\mathcal{S}} / \mathbf{C2}^{\mathcal{T}}$ guarantees full expansion of s, thus fulfilling $\mathbf{C3}$. If DFS$_{FIFO}$ traverses a **NPcycle**, it terminates at l.16. $\square$

Theorem 3. *Th. 2 still holds for DFS$_{FIFO}$ with $\mathbf{C0}$, $\mathbf{C1}$, $\mathbf{C2}^{\mathcal{S}} / \mathbf{C2}^{\mathcal{T}}$.*

Proof. Lemma 1 shows that if the $\mathbf{C0}$, $\mathbf{C1}$ and $\mathbf{C2}^{\mathcal{S}} / \mathbf{C2}^{\mathcal{T}}$ hold, so does $\mathbf{C3}$. Furthermore, $\mathbf{C0}$, $\mathbf{C1}$ and $\mathbf{C2}^{\mathcal{S}} / \mathbf{C2}^{\mathcal{T}}$ are independent of the path leading to s, so $ample(s)$ with DFS$_{FIFO}$ retains stutter equivalence related to progress [14, p.6]. Therefore, the reduced state space has a **NPcycle** iff the original has one. $\square$

4   A Parallel Livelock Algorithm Based on DFS$_{FIFO}$

Alg. 2 presents a parallel version of DFS$_{FIFO}$. The algorithm does not differ much from Alg. 1: the *dfs* procedure remains largely the same, and only *dfs-fifo* is split into parallel *fifo* procedures handling states from the FIFO queue F concurrently. The technique to parallelize the $dfs(s, i)$ calls is based on successful multi-core NDFS algorithms [17,19,8]. Each worker thread $i \in 1..P$ uses a local stack S_i, while V and F are shared (below, we show how an efficient implementation can partially localize F). The stacks may overlap (see l.2 and l.9), but eventually diverge because we use a randomized next-state function: $post_i$ (see l.15).

Proof of Correctness. Th. 4 proves correctness of Alg. 2. We show that the propositions below hold after initialization of Alg. 2, and inductively that they

---

Algorithm 2. Parallel DFS$_{FIFO}$ (PDFS$_{FIFO}$)

1: **procedure** *dfs-fifo*(s_0, P)	13: **procedure** *dfs*(s, i)
2: $F := \{s_0\}$ ▷*Frontier queue*	14: $S_i := S_i \cup \{s\}$
3: $V := \emptyset$ ▷*Visited set*	15: **for all** $t := \alpha(s)$ s.t. $\alpha \in post_i(s)$ **do**
4: $S_i := \emptyset$ for all $i \in 1..P$ ▷*Stacks*	16: **if** $t \in S_i \wedge \alpha, t \notin \mathcal{P}$ **then**
5: $fifo(1) \parallel \ldots \parallel fifo(P)$	17: **report NPcycle**
6: **report progress ensured**	18: **if** $t \notin V$ **then**
7: **procedure** *fifo*(i)	19: **if** $\alpha, t \notin \mathcal{P}$ **then**
8: **while** $F \neq \emptyset$ **do**	20: $dfs(t, i)$
9: $s :=$ **some** $s \in F$	21: **else if** $t \notin F$ **then**
10: **if** $s \notin V$ **then**	22: $F := F \cup \{t\}$
11: $dfs(s, i)$	23: $V := V \cup \{s\}$
12: $F := F \setminus \{s\}$	24: $S_i := S_i \setminus \{s\}$

are maintained by execution of each statement in the algorithm, considering only the lines that influence the proposition. Rather than restricting progress to either transitions or states, we prove the algorithm correct under $\mathcal{P} = \mathcal{S}^{\mathcal{P}} \cup \mathcal{T}^{\mathcal{P}}$. Hence, the dual interpretation of paths (see Def. 1) is used now and then. Note that a call to **report** terminates the algorithm and the callee does not return.

Lemma 2. *Upon return of $dfs(s, i)$, s is visited: $s \in V$.*

Proof. 1.23 of $dfs(s, i)$ adds s to V. □

Lemma 3. *Invariantly, all direct successors of a visited state v are visited or in F: $\forall v \in V, \alpha \in post(v) : \alpha(v) \in V \cup F$.*

Proof. After initialization, the invariant holds trivially, as V is empty. V is only modified at 1.23, where s is added after all its immediate successors t are considered at 1.16–22: If $t \in V \cup F$, we are done. Otherwise, $dfs(s, i)$ terminates at 1.17 or t is added to V at 1.20 (Lemma 2) or to F at 1.22. States are removed from F at 1.12, but only after being added to V at 1.11 (Lemma 2). □

Corollary 1. *Lemma 3 holds also for a state $v \notin V$ in $dfs(v, i)$ just before 1.23.*

Lemma 4. *Invariantly, all paths from a visited state v to a state $f \in F \setminus V$ contain progress: $\forall \pi, v \in V, f \in F \setminus V : v \xrightarrow{\pi} f \implies \mathcal{P} \cap \pi \neq \emptyset$.*

Proof. After initialization of the sets V and F, the lemma is trivially true. These sets are modified at 1.12, 1.22, and 1.23 (omitting the trivial case):

1.22 Let i be the first worker thread to add a state t to F in $dfs(s, i)$ at 1.22. If some other worker j adds t to V, the invariant holds trivially, so we consider $t \notin V$. By 1.19, all paths $v \rightarrow^* s \rightarrow t$ contain progress. By contradiction, we show that all other paths that do not contain s also contain progress: Assume that there is a $v \in V$ such that $v \xrightarrow{\pi}{}^+ t$ and $\mathcal{P} \cap \pi = \emptyset$. By induction on the length of the path π and Lemma 3, we obtain either $t \in V$, a contradiction, $t \in F \setminus V$, contradicting the assumption that worker i is first, or another $f \neq t$ with $f \in F \setminus V$, for which the induction hypothesis holds.

1.23 Assume towards a contradiction that i is the first worker thread to add a state s to V at 1.23 of $dfs(s, i)$. So, we have $s \notin V$ before 1.23. By Cor. 1, for all immediate successors t of s, i.e. for all $t = \alpha(s)$ such that $\alpha \in post(s)$, we have $t \in V$ or $t \in F \setminus V$. In the first case, since $s \neq t$, the induction hypothesis holds for t. In the second case, if $t = s$, the invariant trivially holds after 1.23, and if $t \neq s$, we have $\alpha, t \in \mathcal{P}$, since otherwise $t \in V$ by 1.19 and 1.20 (Lemma 2). Thus the invariant holds for all paths $s \rightarrow^+ f$. □

Remark 1. Note that a state $s \in F$ might at any time be also added to V by some other worker thread in two cases: (1) $s \notin \mathcal{S}^{\mathcal{P}}$, i.e. it was reached via a progress transition (see 1.19), but is reachable via some other non-progress path, or (2) another worker thread j takes s from F at 1.9 and completes $dfs(s, j)$.

Lemma 5. *Invariantly, visited states do not lie on **NPcycles**: $V \cap \mathcal{NP} = \emptyset$.*

Proof. Initially, $V = \emptyset$ and the lemma holds trivially. Let i be the first worker thread to add s to V in $dfs(s, i)$ at l.23. So we have $s \in V$ just after l.23 of $dfs(s, i)$. Assume towards a contradiction that $s \in \mathcal{NP}$. Then there is a **NPcycle** $s \to t \to^+ s$ with $s \neq t$ since otherwise l.17 would have reported a **NPcycle**. Now by Lemma 3, $t \in V \cup F$. By the induction hypothesis, $t \notin V$, so $t \in F \setminus V$. Lemma 4 contradicts $s \to t$ making no progress.   □

Lemma 6. *Upon return of dfs-fifo, all reachable states are visited:* $\mathcal{R} \subseteq V$.

Proof. After $dfs\text{-}fifo(s_0, P)$, $F = \emptyset$ by l.8. By l.2, l.11 and Lemma 2, $s_0 \in V$. So by Lemma 3, $\mathcal{R} \subseteq V$.   □

Lemma 7. *dfs-fifo terminates and reports an **NPcycle** or **progress ensured**.*

Proof. Upon return of a call $dfs(s, i)$ for some $s \in F$ at l.11, s has been added to V (Lemma 2), removed from F at l.12, and will never be added to F again. Hence the set V grows monotonically, but is bounded, and eventually $F = \emptyset$. Thus eventually all dfs calls terminate, and $dfs\text{-}fifo(s_0, P)$ terminates too.   □

Lemma 8. *Invariantly, the states in S_i form a path without progress except for the first state:* $S_i = \emptyset$ *or* $S_i = \pi \cap \mathcal{S}$ *for some* $s \xrightarrow{\pi}^* s'$ *and* $\pi \cap \mathcal{P} \subseteq \{s_1\}$.
Proof. By induction over the recursive $dfs(s, i)$ calls, we obtain π. At l.20, we have $\alpha, t \notin \mathcal{P}$, but at l.11 we may have $s \in \mathcal{S}^{\mathcal{P}}$ (by l.19 and l.22).   □

Theorem 4. PDFS$_{\text{FIFO}}$ *ensures:* $\mathcal{R} \cap \mathcal{NP} \neq \emptyset \Leftrightarrow dfs\text{-}fifo(s_0, P) = $ ***report NPcycle***

Proof. We split the equivalence into two cases:
$\Leftarrow$: We have a cycle: $s \xrightarrow{\alpha} t \xrightarrow{\pi} s$ s.t. $(\{\alpha\} \cup \pi) \cap \mathcal{P} = \emptyset$ by l.16 and Lemma 8.
$\Rightarrow$: Assume that $dfs\text{-}fifo(s_0, P) \neq$ **NPcycle** $\land \mathcal{R} \cap \mathcal{NP} \neq \emptyset$. However, at l.6, $\mathcal{R} \subseteq V$ by Lemma 6 and Lemma 7, hence $\mathcal{R} \cap \mathcal{NP} = \emptyset$ by Lemma 5.   □

Implementation. For a scaling implementation, the hash table storing F and V (see Sec. 3) is maintained in shared memory using a lockless design [20,18]. Storing also the queue F^q in shared memory, however, would seriously impede scalability due to contention (recall that F is maintained as both hash table and queue F^q). Our more efficient implementation splits F^q into P local queues F_i^q, such that $F \subseteq \bigcup_{i \in 1..P} F_i^q$ (Remark 1 explains the $\subseteq$).

To implement load balancing, one could relax the constraint at l.21 to $s \notin F^q$, so that after-progress states end up on multiple local queues. Provided that $\mathcal{A}_\mathcal{M}$ is connected enough, which it usually is in model checking, this would provide good work distribution already. On the other hand, the total size of all queues F_i^q would grow proportional to P, wasting a lot of memory on many cores.

```
1: procedure fifo(i)
2:     F_i^q := {s_0}
3:     while steal(F_i^q) do
4:         F_i^q := F_i^q \ {s}
5:         if s ∉ V then
6:             dfs(s, i)
```

Therefore, we instead opted to add explicit load balancing via work stealing. The code on the left illustrates this. Iff the local queue F_i^q is empty, the *steal* function grabs states from another random queue F_j^q and adds them to F_i^q, returning false iff it detects termination. Inspection of Lemma 3 and Lemma 7 shows that removing s from F is not necessary.

The proofs show that correctness of PDFS$_{FIFO}$ does not require F to be in strict FIFO order (as l.9 does not enforce any order). To optimize for scalability, we enforce a strict BFS order via synchronizations[2] between the BFS levels only optionally[3]. As trade-off, counterexamples are no longer guaranteed to be the shortest with respect to progress, and the size of F may increase (see Remark 1).

Analysis of Scalability. Experiments with multi-core NDFS [8] demonstrated that these parallelization techniques make the state-of-the-art for LTL model checking. Because of the BFS nature of DFS$_{FIFO}$, we can expect even better speedups. More-over, in [17], additional synchronization was needed to prevent workers from *early backtracking*; a situation in which two workers exclude a third from part of the state space. The figure on the right illustrates this: Worker 1 can visit s, v, t and u, and then halt. Worker 2 can visit s, u, t and v and backtrack over v. If now Worker 1 resumes and backtracks over u, both v and u are in V. A third worker will be excluded from visiting t, which might lead to a large part of the state space. Lemma 3 shows that this is impossible for PDFS$_{FIFO}$ as the successors of visited states are either visited or in F (treated in efficient parallel BFS), but never do successors lie solely on the stack S_i (as in CNDFS).

5   Experimental Evaluation

In the current section, we benchmark the performance of DFS$_{FIFO}$, and its combi-nation with POR, using both progress states and progress transitions. We com-pare the results against the LTL approach with progress property using, inter alia, SPIN [12]. We also investigate the scalability of PDFS$_{FIFO}$, and compare the results against the multi-core NDFS algorithm CNDFS, the state-of-the-art for parallel LTL [8,5], and the piggyback algorithm in SPIN (PB). Finally, we in-vestigate the combination of PDFS$_{FIFO}$ and POR, and compare the results with OWCTY [3], which uses a topological sort to implement paralel LTL and POR [2].

We implemented PDFS$_{FIFO}$ (*Alg. 2 with work stealing and both strict[3]/non-strict BFS order*) in LTSMIN [21] 2.0.[4] LTSMIN has a frontend for PROMELA, called SPINS [12], and one for the DVE language, allowing fair comparison [21,5] against SPIN 6.2.3 and DiVinE 2.5.2 [3]. To ensure similar state counts, we turned off control-flow optimizations in SPINS/SPIN, because SPIN has a more powerful optimizer, which can be, but is not yet implemented in SPINS. Only the GIOP model (described below) still yields a larger state count in SPINS/LTSMIN than in SPIN. We still include it as it nicely features the benefits of DFS$_{FIFO}$ over NDFS.

We benchmarked on a 48-core machine (a four-way AMD Opteron 6168) with 128GB of main memory, and considered 4 publicly available[1] PROMELA models with progress labels, and adapted SPINS to interpret the labels as either progress states, as in SPIN, or progress transitions. leader$_t$ is the efficient leader election

---

[2] Parallel BFS algorithms, with and without synchronization, are described in [7].

[3] The command line option --strict turns on strict PDFS$_{FIFO}$ in LTSMIN.

[4] LTSMIN is open source, available at: http://fmt.cs.utwente.nl/tools/ltsmin.

Table 3. Runtimes (sec) of (sequential) DFS, DFS$_{FIFO}$, NDFS in SPIN and LTSMIN

			LTSMIN				SPIN		
	$|\mathcal{R}|$	$|\mathcal{R}_{LTL}|$	T_{DFS}	$T_{DFS_{FIFO}}$	T_{NDFS}	$|\mathcal{R}|$	$|\mathcal{R}_{LTL}|$	T_{DFS}	T_{NDFS}
leader$_t$	4.5E7	198%	153.7	233.2	753.6	4.5E7	198%	304.0	1,390.0
garp	1.2E8	150%	377.1	591.2	969.2	1.2E8	146%	1,370.0	2,050.0
giop	2.7E9	oom	21,301.4	43,154.3	oom	8.4E7	181%	1,780.0	4,830.0
i-prot	1.4E7	140%	28.4	41.4	70.6	1.4E7	145%	63.3	103.0

protocol $\mathcal{A}_{timing}$ [10]. The *Group Address Registration Protocol (GARP)* is a datalink-level multicast protocol for a bridged LAN. *General Inter-Orb Protocol* (GIOP) models service oriented architectures. The model *i-Protocol* represents the GNU implementation of this protocol. We use a different leader election protocol (leader$_{DKR}$) from [24] for comparison against DIVINE. For all these models, the livelock property holds under $\mathcal{P} = \mathcal{S}^{\mathcal{P}}$ and $\mathcal{P} = \mathcal{T}^{\mathcal{P}}$.[5]

Performance. In theory, DFS$_{FIFO}$ can be up to four times as fast as using the progress LTL formula and NDFS. To verify this, we compare DFS$_{FIFO}$ to NDFS in LTSMIN and SPIN. In LTSMIN, we used the command line: prom2lts-mc --state=tree -s28 --strategy=[dfsfifo/ndfs] [model], which replaces the shared table (for F and V) by a *tree* table for state compression [18]. In SPIN, we used compression as well (*collapse* [12]): cc -O2 -DNP -DNOFAIR -DNOREDUCE -DNOBOUNDCHECK -DCOLLAPSE -o pan pan.c, and pan -m100000 -l -w28, avoiding table resizes and overhead. In both tools, we also ran DFS reachability with similar commands. We write *oom* for runs that overflow the main memory.

Table 3 shows the results: As expected, $|\mathcal{R}_{LTL}|$ is 1.5 to 2 times larger than $|\mathcal{R}|$ for both SPIN and LTSMIN; GIOP fits in memory for DFS$_{FIFO}$ but the LTL cross-product overflows (NDFS). T_{NDFS} is about 1.5 to 4 times larger than T_{DFS} for SPIN, 2 to 5 times larger for LTSMIN (cf. Section 2). $T_{DFS_{FIFO}}$ is 1.5 to 2 times larger than T_{DFS}, likely caused by its set inclusion tests on S and F. T_{NDFS} is 1.6 to 3.2 times larger than $T_{DFS_{FIFO}}$.

Parallel Scalability. To compare the parallel algorithms in LTSMIN, we use the options --threads=P --strategy=[dfsfifo/cndfs], where P is the number of worker threads. In SPIN, we use -DBFS_PAR, which also turns on lossy state hashing [13], and run the pan binary with an option -uP. This turns on a parallel, linear-time, but incomplete, cycle detection algorithm called piggyback (PB) [13]. It might also be unsound due its combination with lossy hashing [4]. Fig. 1 shows the obtained speedups: As expected, reachability [20] and PDFS$_{FIFO}$ scale almost ideally, while CNDFS exhibits sub-linear scalability, even though it is the fastest parallel LTL solution [8]. PB also scales sub-linearly. Since LTSMIN sequentially competes with SPIN (Table 4, except for GIOP), scalability can be compared.

Parallel Memory Use. We expected few state duplication in F on local queues (see Remark 1). To verify this, we measured the total size of all local queues and hash tables using counters for strict[3] and non-strict PDFS$_{FIFO}$, and CNDFS. Table 4 shows $Q_P = \sum_{i \in 1..P} |F_i^q| + |S_i|$ averaged over 5 runs: Non-strict PDFS$_{FIFO}$ shows

---

[5] Models that we modified are available at http://doiop.com/leader4DFSFIFO.

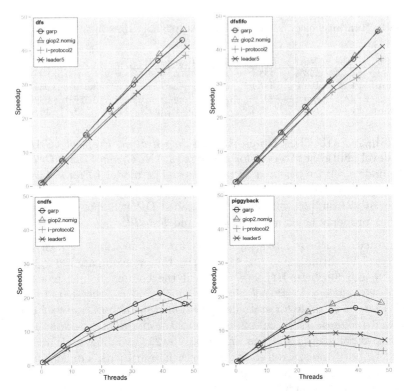

Fig. 1. Speedups of DFS, PDFS$_{FIFO}$ and CNDFS in LTSMIN, and piggyback in SPIN

Table 4. Runtimes (sec) / queue sizes of the parallel algorithms: DFS, PDFS$_{FIFO}$ and CNDFS in LTSMIN, and PB in SPIN

	DFS		PDFS$_{FIFO}$		CNDFS		PB		PDFS$_{FIFO}^{strict}$		PDFS$_{FIFO}^{non\text{-}strict}$		CNDFS	
	T_1	T_{48}	T_1	T_{48}	T_1	T_{48}	T_1	T_{min}	Q_1	Q_{48}	Q_1	Q_{48}	Q_1	Q_{48}
leader$_t$	153.7	3.8	233.2	5.7	925.7	51.4	228.0	25.9	1.0E6	1.2E6	1.2E6	1.4E6	2.7E6	3.6E7
garp	377.1	8.8	591.2	13.1	1061.0	58.6	1180.0	70.9	1.9E7	2.0E7	1.9E7	5.3E6	5.5E6	6.5E7
giop	2.1E4	463.3	4.3E4	9.7E2	oom	oom	1.2E3	57.8	1.1E9	8.4E8	1.1E9	8.4E8	oom	oom
i-prot	28.4	0.7	41.4	1.1	75.9	3.7	86.2	17.7	1.0E6	1.1E6	1.0E6	1.3E6	8.3E5	1.0E7

little difference from the strict variant, and Q_{48} is at most 20% larger than Q_1 for all PDFS$_{FIFO}$. Due to the randomness of the parallel runs, we even have $Q_{48} < Q_1$ in many cases. Revisits occurred at most 2.6% using 48 cores. In the case of CNDFS, the combined stacks typically grow because of the larger DFS searches. Accordingly, we found that PDFS$_{FIFO}$'s *total memory use with 48 cores* was between 87% and 125% compared to sequential DFS. In the worst case, PDFS$_{FIFO}$ (with tree compression) used 52% of the memory use of PB (collapse compression and lossy hashing) [18,5] – GIOP excluded as its state counts differ.

POR Performance. LTSMIN's POR implementation (option --por) is based on stubborn sets [26], described in [23], and is competitive to SPIN's [5]. We extended it with the alternative provisos for DFS$_{FIFO}$: $\mathbf{C2}^S$ and $\mathbf{C2}^T$. Table 5 shows the

Table 5. POR (%) for $\text{DFS}^{\mathcal{T}}_{\text{FIFO}}$, $\text{DFS}^{\mathcal{S}}_{\text{FIFO}}$, DFS and NDFS in SPIN and LTSMIN

	LTSMIN				SPIN	
	DFS	$\text{DFS}^{\mathcal{T}}_{\text{FIFO}}$	$\text{DFS}^{\mathcal{S}}_{\text{FIFO}}$	NDFS	DFS	$\text{NDFS}^{\text{SPIN}}$
leader_t	0.32%	0.49%	99.99%	99.99%	0.03%	1.15%
garp	1.90%	2.18%	4.29%	16.92%	10.56%	12.73%
giop	1.86%	1.86%	3.77%	oom	1.60%	2.42%
i-prot	16.14%	31.83%	100.00%	100.00%	24.01%	41.37%

Table 6. POR and speedups for leader_{DKR} using $\text{PDFS}_{\text{FIFO}}$, CNDFS and OWCTY

N	Alg.	$|\mathcal{R}|$	$|\mathcal{T}|$	T_1	T_{48}	U	$|\mathcal{R}^{\text{POR}}|$	$|\mathcal{T}^{\text{POR}}|$	T_1^{POR}	T_{48}^{POR}	U^{POR}
9	CNDFS	3.6E7	2.3E8	502.6	12.0	41.8	27.9%	0.1%	211.8	n/a	n/a
9	$\text{PDFS}_{\text{FIFO}}$	3.6E7	2.3E8	583.6	14.3	40.8	1.5%	0.0%	12.9	3.6	3.5
9	OWCTY	3.6E7	2.3E8	498.7	51.9	9.6	12.6%	0.0%	578.4	35.7	16.2
10	CNDFS	2.4E8	1.7E9	30'	90.7	30'	19.3%	5.4%	1102.7	n/a	n/a
10	$\text{PDFS}_{\text{FIFO}}$	2.4E8	1.7E9	30'	109.3	30'	0.7%	0.1%	35.0	2.5	14.0
10	OWCTY	2.4E8	1.7E9	30'	663.1	30'	8.7%	2.2%	30'	156.3	30'
11	$\text{PDFS}_{\text{FIFO}}$	30'	30'	30'	30'	30'	5.1E6	7.1E6	109.8	5.3	20.7
11	OWCTY	30'	30'	30'	30'	30'	9.3E7	1.7E8	30'	1036.5	30'
12	$\text{PDFS}_{\text{FIFO}}$	30'	30'	30'	30'	30'	1.6E7	2.2E7	369.1	11.2	33.0
13	$\text{PDFS}_{\text{FIFO}}$	30'	30'	30'	30'	30'	6.6E7	9.2E7	1640.5	38.1	43.0
14	$\text{PDFS}_{\text{FIFO}}$	30'	30'	30'	30'	30'	2.0E8	2.9E8	30'	120.3	30'
15	$\text{PDFS}_{\text{FIFO}}$	30'	30'	30'	30'	30'	8.4E8	1.2E9	30'	527.5	30'

relative number of states, using the different algorithms in both tools: For all models, both LTSMIN and SPIN are able to obtain reductions of multiple orders of magnitude using their DFS algorithms. We also observe that much of this benefit disappears when using the NDFS LTL algorithm due to the cycle proviso, although SPIN often performs much better than LTSMIN in this respect. Also DFS_{FIFO} with progress states (column $\text{DFS}^{\mathcal{S}}_{\text{FIFO}}$), performs poorly: apparently, the $\text{C2}^{\mathcal{S}}$ proviso is so restrictive that many states are fully expanded. But DFS_{FIFO} with progress transitions (column $\text{DFS}^{\mathcal{T}}_{\text{FIFO}}$) retains DFS's impressive POR with at most a factor 2 difference.

Scalability of Parallelism and POR. We created multiple instances of the leader_{DKR} models by varying the number of nodes N and expressed the progress LTL property in DIVINE. We start DIVINE's state-of-the-art parallel LTL-POR algorithm, OWCTY, by: divine owcty [model] -wP -i30 -p. With the options described above, we turned on POR in LTSMIN and ran $\text{PDFS}_{\text{FIFO}}$, and CNDFS, for comparison. We limited each run to half an hour (30' indicates a timeout). Piggyback reported contradictory memory usage and far fewer states (e.g. <1%) compared to DFS with POR, although it must meet more provisos. Thus we did not compare against piggyback and suspect a bug.

Table 6 shows that $\text{PDFS}_{\text{FIFO}}$ and POR complement each other rather well: Without POR (left half of the table) the almost ideal speedup ($U = \frac{T_1}{T_{48}} = 40.8$) allows to explore one model more: $N \leq 10$ instead of only $N = 9$. When enabling POR (right half of the table), we see again multiple orders of magnitude reductions, while parallel scalability reduces to $U = 3.5$ for $N = 9$, because of the small size of the reduced state space ($|\mathcal{R}^{\text{POR}}|$). When increasing the model size to $N = 13$ the speedup grows again to an almost ideal level ($U = 43$). With POR, the parallelism allows us to explore two more models within half an hour, i.e., $N \leq 15$. While OWCTY and NDFS also show this effect, it is less pronounced due to their cycle proviso, allowing $N \leq 11$ for OWCTY and $N \leq 9$ for NDFS.

As livelocks are disjoint from the class of weak LTL properties, OWCTY could become non-linear [3], but it required only one iteration for leader $_{DKR}$.

As PDFS$_{FIFO}$ revisits states, the random next-state function could theoretically weaken POR (as for NDFS, see Sec. 2). But for all our 5 models, this did not occur.

On-the-Fly Performance. We created a leader election protocol with early (*shallow*) and another with late (*deep*) injected **NPcycles** (see [5], [10]).

	CNDFS		PDFS$^{\mathcal{T}}_{FIFO}$		CNDFS		PDFS$^{\mathcal{T}}_{FIFO}$	
	T_1	T_{48}	T_1	T_{48}	C_1	C_{48}	C_1	C_{48}
shallow	~~30'~~	7	12	4	~~30'~~	16	16	16
deep	$16\binom{once}{30'}$	2	~~30'~~	451	577	499	~~30'~~	51

The table on the right shows the average runtime in seconds (T) and counterexample length (C) over five runs. Since PDFS$_{FIFO}$ finds shortest counterexamples[3], it outperforms CNDFS for *shallow* (more relevant in practice) and pays a penalty for *deep*. Both algorithms benefit greatly from massive parallelism (see also [19]).

6   Conclusions

We showed, in theory and in practice, that model checking livelocks, an important subset of liveness properties, can be made more efficient by specializing on it. For our PDFS$_{FIFO}$ implementation with progress transitions, POR becomes significantly stronger (cf. Table 5), parallelization has linear speedup (cf. Fig. 1), and both can be combined efficiently (cf. Table 6).

Acknowledgements. We thank colleagues Mark Timmer, Mads Chr. Olesen, Christoph Scheben and Tom van Dijk for their useful comments on this paper.

References

1. Baier, C., Katoen, J.-P.: Principles of Model Checking. The MIT Press (2008)
2. Barnat, J., Brim, L., Rockai, P.: Parallel Partial Order Reduction with Topological Sort Proviso. In: SEFM, pp. 222–231. IEEE Computer Society (2010)
3. Barnat, J., Brim, L., Ročkai, P.: A Time-Optimal On-the-Fly Parallel Algorithm for Model Checking of Weak LTL Properties. In: Breitman, K., Cavalcanti, A. (eds.) ICFEM 2009. LNCS, vol. 5885, pp. 407–425. Springer, Heidelberg (2009)
4. Barnat, J., Havlíček, J., Ročkai, P.: Distributed LTL Model Checking with Hash Compaction. In: PASM/PDMC. ENTCS. Elsevier (2012)
5. van der Berg, F., Laarman, A.: SpinS: Extending LTSmin with Promela through SpinJa. In: PASM/PDMC. ENTCS. Elsevier (2012)
6. Courcoubetis, C., Vardi, M., Wolper, P., Yannakakis, M.: Memory-Efficient Algorithms for the Verification of Temporal Properties. FMSD 1(2), 275–288 (1992)
7. Dalsgaard, A.E., Laarman, A., Larsen, K.G., Olesen, M.C., van de Pol, J.: Multi-Core Reachability for Timed Automata. In: Jurdziński, M., Ničković, D. (eds.) FORMATS 2012. LNCS, vol. 7595, pp. 91–106. Springer, Heidelberg (2012)
8. Evangelista, S., Laarman, A., Petrucci, L., van de Pol, J.: Improved multi-core nested depth-first search. In: Chakraborty, S., Mukund, M. (eds.) ATVA 2012. LNCS, vol. 7561, pp. 269–283. Springer, Heidelberg (2012)

9. Evangelista, S., Pajault, C.: Solving the Ignoring Problem for Partial Order Reduction. STTF 12, 155–170 (2010)
10. Faragó, D.: Model Checking of Randomized Leader Election Algorithms. Master's thesis, Universität Karlsruhe (2007)
11. Faragó, D., Schmitt, P.H.: Improving Non-Progress Cycle Checks. In: Păsăreanu, C.S. (ed.) SPIN 2009. LNCS, vol. 5578, pp. 50–67. Springer, Heidelberg (2009)
12. Holzmann, G.: The SPIN Model Checker: Primer&Ref. Man. Addison-Wesley (2011)
13. Holzmann, G.J.: Parallelizing the Spin Model Checker. In: Donaldson, A., Parker, D. (eds.) SPIN 2012. LNCS, vol. 7385, pp. 155–171. Springer, Heidelberg (2012)
14. Holzmann, G., Peled, D.: An Improvement in Formal Verification. In: Proceedings of the Formal Description Techniques, pp. 197–211. Chapman & Hall (1994)
15. Holzmann, G., Peled, D., Yannakakis, M.: On nested depth first search. In: SPIN, pp. 23–32. American Mathematical Society (1996)
16. Katz, S., Peled, D.: An Efficient Verification Method for Parallel and Distributed Programs. In: de Bakker, J.W., de Roever, W.-P., Rozenberg, G. (eds.) Linear Time, Branching Time and Partial Order in Logics and Models for Concurrency. LNCS, vol. 354, pp. 489–507. Springer, Heidelberg (1989)
17. Laarman, A., Langerak, R., van de Pol, J., Weber, M., Wijs, A.: Multi-Core nested depth-first search. In: Bultan, T., Hsiung, P.-A. (eds.) ATVA 2011. LNCS, vol. 6996, pp. 321–335. Springer, Heidelberg (2011)
18. Laarman, A., van de Pol, J., Weber, M.: Parallel Recursive State Compression for Free. In: Groce, A., Musuvathi, M. (eds.) SPIN 2011. LNCS, vol. 6823, pp. 38–56. Springer, Heidelberg (2011)
19. Laarman, A., van de Pol, J.: Variations on Multi-Core Nested Depth-First Search. In: PDMC. EPTCS, vol. 72, pp. 13–28 (2011)
20. Laarman, A., van de Pol, J., Weber, M.: Boosting Multi-Core Reachability Performance with Shared Hash Tables. In: FMCAD. IEEE Computer Society (2010)
21. Laarman, A., van de Pol, J., Weber, M.: Multi-Core LTSmin: Marrying Modularity and Scalability. In: Bobaru, M., Havelund, K., Holzmann, G.J., Joshi, R. (eds.) NFM 2011. LNCS, vol. 6617, pp. 506–511. Springer, Heidelberg (2011)
22. Moore, G.: Cramming more Components onto Integrated Circuits. Electronics 38(10), 114–117 (1965)
23. Pater, E.: Partial Order Reduction for PINS, Master's thesis. Uni. of Twente (2011)
24. Pelánek, R.: BEEM: Benchmarks for Explicit Model Checkers. In: Bošnački, D., Edelkamp, S. (eds.) SPIN 2007. LNCS, vol. 4595, pp. 263–267. Springer, Heidelberg (2007)
25. Saad, R.T., Dal Zilio, S., Berthomieu, B.: An experiment on parallel model checking of a CTL fragment. In: Chakraborty, S., Mukund, M. (eds.) ATVA 2012. LNCS, vol. 7561, pp. 284–299. Springer, Heidelberg (2012)
26. Valmari, A.: Stubborn Sets for Reduced State Space Generation. In: Rozenberg, G. (ed.) APN 1990. LNCS, vol. 483, pp. 491–515. Springer, Heidelberg (1991)
27. Vardi, M., Wolper, P.: An Automata-Theoretic Approach to Automatic Program Verification. In: LICS, pp. 332–344 (1986)

Evaluating Human-Human Communication Protocols with Miscommunication Generation and Model Checking

Matthew L. Bolton[1] and Ellen J. Bass[2]

[1] Department of Mechanical and Industrial Engineering
University of Illinois at Chicago, Chicago IL 60607
mbolton@uic.edu
[2] College of Information Science and Technology
College of Nursing and Health Professions
Drexel University, Philadelphia, PA 19104
Ellen.J.Bass@Drexel.edu

Abstract. Human-human communication is critical to safe operations in domains such as air transportation where airlines develop and train pilots on communication procedures with the goal to ensure that they check that verbal air traffic clearances are correctly heard and executed. Such communication protocols should be designed to be robust to miscommunication. However, they can fail in ways unanticipated by designers. In this work, we present a method for modeling human-human communication protocols using the Enhanced Operator Function Model with Communications (EOFMC), a task analytic modeling formalism that can be interpreted by a model checker. We describe how miscommunications can be generated from instantiated EOFMC models of human-human communication protocols. Using an air transportation example, we show how model checking can be used to evaluate if a given protocol will ensure successful communication. Avenues of future research are explored.

Keywords: Task analysis, Human-human communication, Air traffic control, Formal methods, Model checking, Human error.

1 Introduction

Human-human communication is critical to the safe operations of many complex systems. For example, until the Data Communication Integrated Services (DCIS) contract is fully implemented [25], voice communications will continue to be the primary mechanism for air traffic control clearances in the United States [1]. In many work domains, institutions develop human-human communication protocols to support safer operations. In air transportation, for example, the pilot/controller communication loop, using readbacks and other confirmation behaviors, is designed to support safety and redundancy of pilot/controller communications [32]. However miscommunications continue to impact the safety of complex systems. The Aviation Safety Reporting System (ASRS) data base, for example, identifies problems including incorrect communications, incomplete or absent communications, and correct but late communications [35].

G. Brat, N. Rungta, and A. Venet (Eds.): NFM 2013, LNCS 7871, pp. 48–62, 2013.

Further, Jones [32] has identified a number of air transportation accidents where miscommunication played a significant role.

As miscommunications continue, institutions will try to enhance human-human communication protocols. Thus having methods to verify such protocols can improve safety. There is a long tradition of formal methods being used to describe and formally verify machine communication protocols [2, 8, 19, 22, 38, 42] including the injection of communication faults or errors into the models [21, 41]. While human-human communication protocols could be modeled using these traditional formal methods approaches, human-human communication, which can include verbal statements, gestures, and related actions, is different from machine communication. Human communications are actions [3] that occur as part of the participants' larger tasks (i.e., goal directed normative behaviors to accomplish system goals [34]).

Few researchers have used formal methods to evaluate human-human communication protocols. Hörl and Aichernig [29, 30] developed a formal model of the system pilots and air traffic controllers use to communicate. However, rather than perform formal verification, they used automated test case generation to develop scenarios to guide human subject testing. Thus, Hörl and Aichernig avoided having to explicitly model and evaluate protocols with a task by having the actual tests provide that context. Others have investigated how task analytic models can be incorporated into formal models and evaluated with formal verification (see [17] for a review). Only Paternò et al. [37] and Bass et al. [4] treat human-human communication as actions [4] within a larger set of coordinated communication and task relevant activities. With the Enhanced Operator Function Model with Communications (EOFMC), Bass et al. [4] introduced an innovative means of representing goal directed behaviors requiring human-human communication and coordination as shared task structures between human operators. If a task goal is only associated with a given human operator, he or she can have separate, unshared tasks. This allows the activities associated with a given communication protocol to be contained in a separate task structure that can be analyzed on its own or with other modeled tasks. However, neither of the approaches presented in [37] and [4] have investigated how miscommunications could result in the failure of human-human communication protocols.

1.1 Objectives

Methods are needed to support formal evaluation of human-human communication protocols, including potential miscommunications. In this work, we describe a novel approach that allows an analyst to model human-human communication protocols in the context of a task analytic modeling formalism and to use formal verification with model checking to evaluate whether or not the protocol will always ensure that a correct communication will occur, even with miscommunication. In the following sections, we describe our method and its implementation. We present EOMFC, the task analytic modeling formalism we use for modeling protocols; the process that is used to translate instantiated EOFMCs into the input language of a model checker; and the modification to the translation process that allows the formal representation to be capable of generating miscommunications. We also present an air traffic control application to illustrate

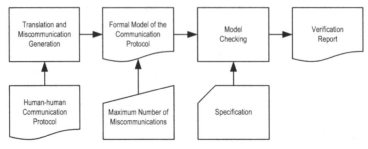

Fig. 1. Human-human communication protocol analysis method

how our method can discover problems with safety critical, human-human communication protocols. Finally, we discuss our results and outline avenues of future research.

2   Method

The method in Fig. 1 was extended from [11, 15] to allow an analyst to evaluate whether or not a human-human communication protocol will accomplish its goals for up to a specified number of miscommunications. An analyst starts by creating a human-human communication protocol in a task analytic modeling formalism. The result is run through a translation process which produces a representation of the protocol in the input language of a model checker. This version of the model includes the maximum number of miscommunications that the analyst wants in the verification process. The analyst also creates a specification which asserts desirable properties about the communication protocol in a formal specification language such as a temporal logic. Model checking performs formal verification, checking whether the formal model of the communication protocol adheres to the specification [19]. Model checking produces a verification report either confirming that the model adheres to the specification or a counterexample, illustrating how the specification was violated.

2.1   Human-Human Communication Protocol Modeling

To model human-human communication protocols, we use the Enhanced Operator Function Model with Communications [4] (an extension of the Enhanced Operator Function Model (EOFM) [9, 10, 18]). EOFMCs, with their formal semantics, are task analytic modeling formalisms capable of representing multiple human operators and human-human communication as part of a larger task model. They allow communication protocols to be modeled as shared task structures on their own or with other tasks.

EOFMC models groups of human operators engaging in shared activities as an input/output system. Inputs may come from the human-device interface, environment, and/or mission goals. Output variables are human actions. The operators' task models describe how human actions may be generated and how the values of local variables change based on input and local variables (representing perceptual or cognitive processing, task behavior, and inner group coordination and communication). All variables are defined in terms of constants, user defined types, and basic types.

Tasks in an instantiated EOFMC are represented as a hierarchy of goal directed activities and actions. Each task descends from a top level activity (there can be many tasks in a given instantiated EOFMC). Tasks can either belong to one human operator, or they can be shared between human operators. A shared task is associated with two or more associates, and a subset of associates for the general task is identified for each activity. Thus, it is explicit which human operators are participating in which activity.

Activities can have preconditions, repeat conditions, and completion conditions. These are represented by Boolean expressions written in terms of input, output, and local variables as well as constants. They specify what must be true before an activity can execute (precondition), when it can execute again (repeat condition), and what is true when it has completed execution (completion condition).

Actions occur at the bottom of the task hierarchy. They can assume several forms: (a) they can be observable, singular ways the human operator can interact with the environment; (b) they can represent a cognitive or perceptual act, where a value is assigned to a local variable; (c) they can represent human-human communications, where a communicator performs a communication action and the information conveyed (which will have a defined type) is stored in recipient local variables.

A decomposition operator specifies the temporal relationships between and the cardinality of the decomposed activities or actions (when they can execute relative to each other and how many can execute). EOFMC supports ten different decomposition operators [4]. Herein, only the following are used:

1. *and_par* – all activities or action in the decomposition must execute (in any order) and their execution can overlap;
2. *ord* – all activities or actions in the decomposition must execute in order; and
3. *com* – all of the actions in a decomposition must execute synchronously, where one human operator must perform a communication action and at least one other human operator must be the recipient of that communication.

The structure of an instantiated EOFMC can be represented visually as a tree-like graph (such as Fig. 5 on page 56) where actions are depicted by rectangular nodes and activities by rounded rectangle nodes. Conditions are connected to the activity they modify: a *precondition* is represented by a yellow, downward pointing triangle connected to the right side of the activity; a *completioncondition* is presented as a magenta, upward pointing triangle connected to the left of the activity; and a *repeatcondition* is conveyed as a recursive arrow attached to the top of the activity. These standard colors are used to distinguish condition shapes from each other and other task structures. Decompositions are arrows, labeled with the decomposition operator, extending below an activity pointing to a large rounded rectangle with the decomposed activities or actions.

By exploiting the shared activity and communication action feature of EOFMC, human-human communication protocols can be modeled as shared task activities. Human communication actions can represent human-human communication. However, other actions model the way that the human operator interacts with other elements of the work environment. Thus a human-human communication protocol can represent the human-human communication procedure and the human operator responses.

2.2   EOFMC Formal Semantics and Translation

EOFMC has formal semantics which specify how an instantiated EOFMC model executes. Each activity or action has one of three execution states: waiting to execute (*Ready*), executing (*Executing*), and done (*Done*). An activity or action transitions between states based on its current state; its start condition (*StartCondition* – when it can start executing based on the state of its immediate parent, its parent's decomposition operator, and the execution state of its siblings); its end condition (*EndCondition* – when it can stop executing based on the state of its immediate children in the hierarchy and its decomposition operators); its reset condition (*Reset* – when it can revert to *Ready* based on the execution state of its parents); and, for an activity, its strategic knowledge (the *Precondition*, *RepeatCondition*, and *CompletionCondition*). See [18] for more details.

Instantiated EOFMC task models can be translated into the language of the Symbolic Analysis Laboratory (SAL) [20] (in this case using a java program) using the EOFMC formal semantics in virtually the same manner as EOFMs [18]. The major difference between EOFMC and EOFM translation is how communications are handled – how actions in a *com* decomposition (not present in EOFM) transition out of the ready state. In the EOFMC translation, when the *StartCondition* of a human communication action is satisfied: all variables representing actions in the associated *com* decomposition are set to *Done*; the variable representing the communication value is set to the value being communicated; and the local variables human operators use to receive the communication are set to the communicated value (Fig. 2 shows the SAL notation).

The translated EOFMC can be integrated into a larger system model using a defined architecture and coordination protocol [12, 18]. Formal verifications are performed using SAL's Symbolic Model Checker (SAL-SMC). Any produced counterexamples can be visualized and evaluated using EOFMC's visual notation (extended from [13]).

```
[]StartCondition -->
    HumanComAction'        = Done;
    ComActionValue'        = ComValue;
    LocalVariableAction1'  = Done;
    LocalVariable1'        = ComActionValue';
    ...
    LocalVariableActionN'  = Done;
    LocalVariableValueN'   = ComActionValue';
```

Fig. 2. Pattern of code generated to represent a human-human communication in the SAL code (see [20]) created from translating an instantiated EOFMC. []StartCondition --> represents a nondeterministic guarded transition. An apostrophe appended to a variable indicates that the variable's value in the next state is being assigned and/or referenced. A *com* decomposition will contain a human communication action HumanComAction and N local variable actions LocalVariableAction1–LocalVariableActionN, where N is a positive integer. Each action has an associated variable containing a value. ComActionValue represents the value being communicated by the human communication action and LocalVariableValue1–LocalVariableValueN represent the values associated with local variable actions LocalVariableAction1–LocalVariableActionN respectively.

2.3   Miscommunication Generation

There are many reasons why human-human miscommunication can occur (see [24]). From an engineering and design perspective, a miscommunication can be viewed as an "action failure," where the communicator does not communicate the correct information; a "misperception," where the recipient of the communication does not correctly receive the communicated information; or both [43]. To support miscommunication generation, the translator was modified to include an additional optional transition for each original communication transition (Fig. 3).

```
[]StartCondition AND (ComErrorCount < ComErrorMax) -->
    HumanComAction'        = Done;
    ComActionValue'        IN {x: CommunicationType | TRUE};
    LocalVariableAction1'  = Done;
    LocalVariable1'        IN {x: CommunicationType | TRUE};
    ...
    LocalVariableActionN'  = Done;
    LocalVariableN'        IN {x: CommunicationType | TRUE};
    ComErrorCount'         = IF   ComActionValue' <> ComValue
                                  OR LocalVariable1' <> ComValue
                                  OR ...
                                  OR LocalVariableN' <> ComValue
                             THEN ComErrorCount + 1
                             ELSE ComErrorCount ENDIF;
```

Fig. 3. Pattern of code generated to represent a human-human miscommunication in the SAL code created from translating an instantiated EOFMC. Notation is as described in Fig. 2 with several additions. First, IN is used to indicate that the variable to the left of it can assume any value in the set to the right. Second, {x: CommunicationType | TRUE} indicates a set containing all the elements defined in type of the communication value (CommunicationType). Further, ComErrorCount represents the total number of miscommunications that have occurred and ComErrorMax represents the total number of miscommunications that are allowed to occur. Finally, the IF ... THEN ... ELSE ... ENDIF statement only allows ComErrorCount to be incremented if a miscommunication has occurred.

In these transitions, in every case where the communicated value would have normatively been assigned to a variable, the variable can assume any value that can be communicated through the associated communication action. Thus, not only can the communicator improperly communicate the information, but each of the recipients can improperly receive it. Additionally, to give analysts control over the total number of miscommunications, the method has a constant maximum (ComErrorMax) and a counter (ComErrorCount) to track the number of miscommunications. The transition ensures that a miscommunication transition can only occur if maximum has not been reached.

3   Application

To illustrate how our approach can model a safety critical human-human communication protocol, we construct an instantiated EOFMC model for an aircraft heading change in an air transportation example and we use our method to evaluate whether or not it is robust for up to one miscommunication. This example has three human operators, two pilots (a pilot flying and a pilot monitoring) and an air traffic controller. In the scenario, an air traffic controller wants to clear the aircraft to a new heading.

Both the pilots and the air traffic controller have push-to-talk switches which they press down when they want to verbally communicate information to each other over the radio. They can release this switch to end communication.

With respect to the aircraft, the Autopilot Flight Director System consists of Flight Control Computers and the Mode Control Panel (MCP). The MCP provides control of the Autopilot (A/P), Flight Director, and the Autothrottle System. When the A/P is engaged, the MCP sends commands to the aircraft pitch and roll servos to operate the aircraft flight control surfaces. Herein the MCP is used to activate heading changes. The Heading (HDG)/Tracking (TRK) window of the MCP displays the selected heading or track (Fig. 4). The 3 digit numeric display provides the current desired heading in compass degrees (between 0 and 359). Below the HDG window is the heading select knob. Changes in the heading are achieved by rotating and pulling the knob. Pulling the knob tells the autopilot to use the pilot selected value and engages the HDG mode.

The following describes a communication protocol designed to ensure that this heading is correctly communicated from the air traffic controller to the two pilots:

1. The air traffic controller contacts the pilots and gives them a new heading clearance.
2. The pilot monitoring re-contacts air traffic control and repeats the heading.
3. If the heading read back to the air traffic controller is not the heading that the air traffic controller intended, then this process needs to be repeated (starting at step 1) until the correct heading is read back.
4. Next, the pilot flying goes through the process of entering the new heading.
5. Before engaging the new heading, the pilot monitoring points at the heading window and reads off the entered heading.
6. If the heading read back by the pilot monitoring does not match the heading that the pilot monitoring hears from air traffic control, he must then repeat the process for entering and confirming the heading (going back to step 4).
7. The pilot engages the entered heading.

We next show how we can instantiate this protocol in an EOFMC and use formal verification to prove whether it will always ensure that the correct heading is engaged.

Fig. 4. Heading control and display

3.1 Modeling

This communication protocol was implemented as an instantiated EOFMC (Fig. 5). This model has three human operators: the air traffic controller (ATCo), the pilot flying (PF), and the pilot monitoring (PM). The entire process starts when the air traffic controller presses his push-to-talk switch. Then, the controller communicates the heading (*lATCoSelectedClearance*[1]) to the pilots (via the *hATCoTalk* human communication action), such as "AC1 Heading 070 for spacing." Both pilots remember this heading (stored in the local variables *lPFHeadingFromATCo* and *lPMHeadingFromATCo* for the PF and PM respectively). The ATCo releases the switch. Next, the PM presses his switch. The PM then repeats/communicates the heading that he heard (in this example, "AC1 Heading 070"), where both the ATCo and PF hear and remember the heading. The PM releases the switch. This entire process must repeat if the heading the ATCo hears from the PM does not match the heading he wanted to communicate (*lATCSelectedClearance* $\neq$ *lATCHeadingHeardFromPilots*). It completes otherwise.

Once the heading has been communicated, the pilots collaborate to set the new heading (*aSetNewHeading*). This process involves selecting and confirming the heading (*aChangeAndConfirm*) and then executing the new heading (*aExecuteTheChange*). The selection and confirmation process starts with the PF pushing and rotating the heading select knob to the heading heard from the ATCo and then pulling the knob. The PM verifies that the PF has dialed the correct heading and confirms the heading selection by pointing to the heading selection in the window and stating the entered heading. Here, two communications occur in parallel (indicated by the *and_par* decomposition operator associated with *aConfirmTheChange*): the PM points at the heading window (*aPointAtHeadingWindow*) and he speaks the heading that was entered (*aSayTheHeading*). Both are perceived by the PF. This process must repeat if the heading the PF perceived from the ATCo does not match the heading spoken by the PM (*lPFHeadingFromPM* $\neq$ *lPFHeadingFromATCo*). Once the heading is confirmed, the PF presses the heading select (hold) button to execute the heading change.

3.2 Translation

The instantiated EOFMC was translated into SAL using the automated translator. The original model contained 144 lines of XML code. The translated model contained 404 lines of SAL code. This model was composed with one representing the heading change window, where the heading can be changed when the pilot rotates the heading knob. These two model were composed together to create the full system model. The system model was then used to create two different versions: one where the maximum number of miscommunications (`ComErrorMax`) was set to zero and one where it was set to one.

---

[1] Note that in this example, all headings are modeled abstractly as either being *CorrectHeading*, if it matches the heading clearance the ATCo intended to communicate, or *IncorrectHeading*, if it does not.

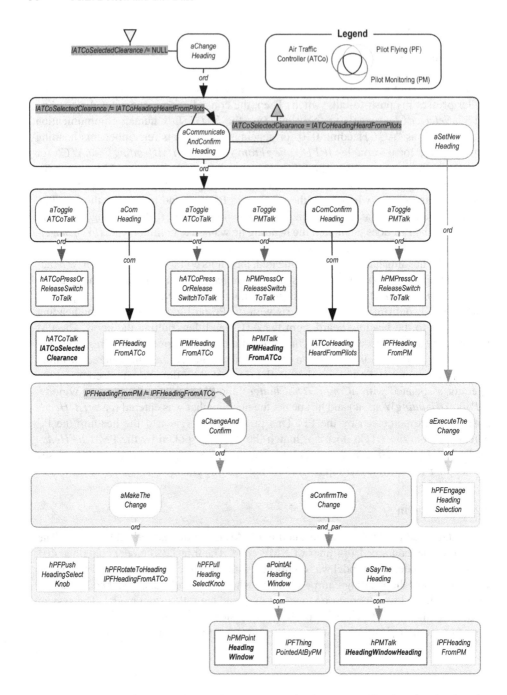

Fig. 5. Visualization of the instantiated EOFMC communication protocol for changing the aircraft heading. Activities are prefixed by "*a*", actions by "*h*", inputs by "*i*", and local variables by "*l*". Values or variables used in a communication action are bolded.

3.3 Specification and Verification

The purpose of the communication protocol is to ensure that the pilots set the aircraft heading to that intended by the air traffic controller. Thus, we can formulate this into linear temporal logic (the specification logic used by SAL) as follows:

$$\mathbf{G} \left(\begin{array}{l} (aChangeHeading = Done) \\ \rightarrow (iHeadingWindowHeading = lATCSelectedClearance) \end{array} \right) \qquad (1)$$

This specification was checked against the two versions of the formal model using SAL's symbolic model checker (sal-smc) on a workstation with 16 gigabytes of RAM, a 3.0 gigahertz dual-core Intel Xeon processor, and the Ubuntu 9.04 desktop.

The first model (ComErrorMax = 0), verified to true in 2.52 seconds (total execution time) having visited 559 states.[2]. The second model (ComErrorMax = 1) returned a counterexample after 3.2 seconds (total execution time) having visited 3726 states.

3.4 Failure Diagnosis

To help diagnose why this failure occurred, the counterexample was visualized using the technique described in [13]. This revealed the following failure sequence:

- The air traffic controller, wanting to clear the aircraft to a new heading (*Correct-Heading*), presses the switch to talk.
- The air traffic controller issues a clearance to *CorrectHeading*. However, a miscommunication occurs and the pilot flying thinks he heard *IncorrectHeading*.
- The air traffic controller releases the switch.
- The pilot monitoring presses his switch to talk.
- The pilot monitoring repeats back the heading he heard from the air traffic controller without a miscommunication occurring.
- The pilot monitoring releases the switch to talk.
- Since the correct heading was heard by the pilot monitoring, the air traffic controller allows the activity for communicating the heading (*aCommunicateAndConfirmHeading*) to complete its execution.
- The pilots begin collaborating to enter the heading from the air traffic controller.
- The pilot flying performs the activity for changing the heading: he presses the heading select knob, sets the dial to the heading he heard from the air traffic controller (*IncorrectHeading*), and pulls the heading select knob.
- The pilot monitoring then pointed at the heading display and read off the heading entered (*IncorrectHeading*) to the pilot flying.
- Because the heading just heard from the pilot monitoring (*lPFHeadingFromPM2*) matches the heading the pilot flying heard from air traffic control (*lPFHeadingFromATC*), the pilot flying engages the new heading.

Thus, although specifically designed to protect against miscommunication, the presented communication protocol does in fact allow an incorrect heading to be engaged.

---

[2] Note that an additional verification was conducted using the specification $\mathbf{F}(aChangeHeading = Done)$ to ensure that (1) was not true do to vacuity.

4   Discussion and Future Work

Human-human communication protocols can be critical to the safe operation of a system, and can fail in unexpected ways. Herein, we have introduced a method that allows human-human communication protocols to be evaluated with model checking. Because human communications during coordinated activities can include actions for communicating both verbal and non-verbal information and result in non-communication human actions, this work considers human communication as part of human task behavior. We used EOFMC to represent communication protocols as shared task behaviors that include synchronous verbal communications, gestures, activities and low level actions as well as asynchronous human behaviors associated with the communication. We described the EOFMC modeling language, its formal semantics, and the process used to translate the formal models into a model checking language. We introduced a new method for automatically generating miscommunications between human operators and showed how these could be automatically included in the translated representation of an instantiated EOFMC communication protocol. We also presented an air traffic control application to demonstrate how this method could be used to find problems in a human-human communication protocol for a safety critical system.

While the method has shown itself to be successful here, there are still a number of places for improvement and future development. These are discussed below.

4.1   Design Interventions and Additional Analyses

The failure discovered in the presented human-human communication protocol appears to occur because the protocol does not give the two pilots a means of reconciling differences between the headings they heard from air traffic control. Thus, potential solutions should support both coordinated error detection and recovery. There may be a number of ways to accomplish this. Two possible approaches are highlighted here. Firstly, if there is any disagreement between what the two pilots heard from the air traffic controller, then they could consult the air traffic controller to reconcile the disagreement. However, doing this could add additional work to the already busy air traffic controller (a potentially undesirable strategy). Alternatively, the pilots could reconcile among each other to determine what the original air traffic controller's clearance was. To determine which of these solutions is most effective, they would need to be encoded into new human-human communication protocols and evaluated with our presented method. Future work should perform these analyses.

Further, the analyses presented here only considered a maximum of one miscommunication. Ideally, a human-human communication protocol would be robust to more than just one. Thus, future work should investigate whether candidate protocols are robust for `ComErrorMax > 1`.

4.2   Scalability

The more than six times increase in state space size observed in the model checking of the model with no miscommunications (`ComErrorMax = 0`) and the one with up to one miscommunication (`ComErrorMax = 1`) suggests that there could be scalability problems with the presented method. Further, scalability assessments of formal verification analyses that have included task analytic models suggest that the state space size can increase exponentially with the size of the task model [16]. These factors could limit what types of human-human communication protocols our method could be used to evaluate and/or the maximum number of miscommunications that could be considered in a given verification. Future work should evaluate how this method scales, identify what factors most influence its scalability, and determine what types of human-human communication protocols can be evaluated using it without running into scalability problems.

4.3   Other Modeling Formalisms

SAL was used in this work because EOFM, the base task analytic modeling formalism, uses SAL. This made it easy to adapt the existing translation tools for use in EOFMC. However, it is possible that other formal tools could prove to be better suited to this particular application. For example, Communicating Sequential Processes (CSP) [26] natively models communication protocols and thus may be better suited to this work. Other formal modeling languages and tools could conceivably help address the scalability concerns discussed above. Other formal modeling infrastructures should be considered in future work.

4.4   Miscommunication Extensions

When generating miscommunications using our method, all of the ways that a miscommunication could manifest are considered to be equally probable. However, in reality, certain miscommunications will be more likely than others [24]. For example, it is much more likely that a heading clearance will be misheard as a similarly sounding heading as opposed to one that sounds nothing like the actual heading. Similarly, the target of a human's pointing communication would be more likely to be misinterpreted as something in the target's periphery rather than something further away. Thus, there could potentially be a number of miscommunications our method considers that analysts may not find probable enough to be worth including. Eliminating unlikely miscommunications could help improve the scalability of the method while improving its utility. Future work should attempt to extend the method to include this feature.

4.5   Other Erroneous Human Behavior Considerations

Miscommunication is only one type of erroneous human behavior that could impact the success of the task associated with a human-human communication protocol. For example, even when a human operator is aware of how to properly perform a task, failures of memory, attention, or human coordination can cause him or her to perform actions or activities incorrectly [7, 28, 40]. Related work has investigated how to generate erroneous human behavior in task analytic models and evaluate its impact on systems using model checking [14, 16]. Thus, it should be possible to evaluate how robust human-human communication protocols are to these other types of erroneous human behavior.

Further, the types of erroneous behaviors that have been included in task analytic models and evaluated formally have almost exclusively focused on the behavior of a single human operator [6, 14, 16, 23, 36]. Human-human communication protocols can have each of the human operators doing specific elements of a task on his or her own, but also requires coordinated behavior between the different human participants. To date, no work has focused on how to model problems with human-human coordination. Future work should investigate this subject.

4.6 Comparison to Simulation Models

A number of environments and cognitive architectures exist that allow human behavior and human-human communication to be evaluated using simulation [5, 27, 31, 33, 39]. Future work should compare our method with these, determine what the tradeoffs are between them, and investigate possible avenues of synergy.

Acknowledgement. The research was funded by NASA Ames Research Center award NNA10DE79C: NextGenAA: Integrated model checking and simulation of NextGen authority and autonomy.

References

1. Airbus: Effective pilot/controller communications. In: Human Performance. Flight Operations Briefing Notes. Airbus, Blagnac Cedex (2006)
2. Argón, P., Delzanno, G., Mukhopadhyay, S., Podelski, A.: Model checking communication protocols. In: Pacholski, L., Ružička, P. (eds.) SOFSEM 2001. LNCS, vol. 2234, pp. 160–170. Springer, Heidelberg (2001)
3. Austin, J.: How to do things with words, vol. 88. Harvard University Press (1975)
4. Bass, E.J., Bolton, M.L., Feigh, K., Griffith, D., Gunter, E., Mansky, W., Rushby, J.: Toward a multi-method approach to formalizing human-automation interaction and human-human communications. In: Proceedings of the IEEE International Conference on Systems, Man, and Cybernetics, pp. 1817–1824. IEEE, Piscataway (2011)
5. Bass, E.J., Baxter, G.D., Ritter, F.E.: Creating models to control simulations: A generic approach. AI and Simulation of Behaviour Quarterly 93, 18–25 (1995)
6. Bastide, R., Basnyat, S.: Error patterns: Systematic investigation of deviations in task models. In: Coninx, K., Luyten, K., Schneider, K.A. (eds.) TAMODIA 2006. LNCS, vol. 4385, pp. 109–121. Springer, Heidelberg (2007)
7. Baxter, G.D., Bass, E.J.: Human error revisited: Some lessons for situation awareness. In: Proceedings of the Fourth Annual Symposium on Human Interaction with Complex Systems, pp. 81–87. IEEE (1998)
8. Bochmann, G., Sunshine, C.: Formal methods in communication protocol design. IEEE Transactions on Communications 28(4), 624–631 (1980)
9. Bolton, M.L.: Automatic validation and failure diagnosis of human-device interfaces using task analytic models and model checking. Computational and Mathematical Organization Theory, 1–25 (2012), http://dx.doi.org/10.1007/s10588-012-9138-6
10. Bolton, M.L., Bass, E.J.: Enhanced operator function model: A generic human task behavior modeling language. In: Proceedings of the IEEE International Conference on Systems Man and Cybernetics, pp. 2983–2990. IEEE, Piscataway (2009)

11. Bolton, M.L., Bass, E.J.: A method for the formal verification of human interactive systems. In: Proceedings of the 53rd Annual Meeting of the Human Factors and Ergonomics Society, pp. 764–768. HFES, Santa Monica (2009)
12. Bolton, M.L., Bass, E.J.: Formally verifying human-automation interaction as part of a system model: Limitations and tradeoffs. Innovations in Systems and Software Engineering: A NASA Journal 6(3), 219–231 (2010)
13. Bolton, M.L., Bass, E.J.: Using task analytic models to visualize model checker counterexamples. In: Proceedings of the 2010 IEEE International Conference on Systems, Man, and Cybernetics, pp. 2069–2074. IEEE, Piscataway (2010)
14. Bolton, M.L., Bass, E.J.: Evaluating human-automation interaction using task analytic behavior models, strategic knowledge-based erroneous human behavior generation, and model checking. In: Proceedings of the IEEE International Conference on Systems Man and Cybernetics, pp. 1788–1794. IEEE, Piscataway (2011)
15. Bolton, M.L., Bass, E.J.: Using model checking to explore checklist-guided pilot behavior. International Journal of Aviation Psychology 22, 343–366 (2012)
16. Bolton, M.L., Bass, E.J., Siminiceanu, R.I.: Using phenotypical erroneous human behavior generation to evaluate human-automation interaction using model checking. International Journal of Human-Computer Studies 70, 888–906 (2012)
17. Bolton, M.L., Bass, E.J., Siminiceanu, R.I.: Using formal verification to evaluate human-automation interaction in safety critical systems, a review. IEEE Transactions on Systems, Man and Cybernetics: Systems (in press, expected 2013)
18. Bolton, M.L., Siminiceanu, R.I., Bass, E.J.: A systematic approach to model checking human-automation interaction using task-analytic models. IEEE Transactions on Systems, Man, and Cybernetics, Part A 41(5), 961–976 (2011)
19. Clarke, E.M., Grumberg, O., Peled, D.A.: Model checking. MIT Press, Cambridge (1999)
20. De Moura, L., Owre, S., Shankar, N.: The SAL language manual. Tech. Rep. CSL-01-01, Computer Science Laboratory, SRI International, Menlo Park (2003)
21. Dietrich, F., Hubaux, J.: Formal methods for communication services. Tech. Rep. SSC/1999/023, Institute for Computer Communications and Applications, Swiss Federal Institute of Technology (1999)
22. Edelkamp, S., Leue, S., Lluch-Lafuente, A.: Directed explicit-state model checking in the validation of communication protocols. International Journal on Software Tools for Technology Transfer 5(2), 247–267 (2004)
23. Fields, R.E.: Analysis of Erroneous Actions in the Design of Critical Systems. Ph.D. thesis, University of York, York (2001)
24. Gibson, W., Megaw, E., Young, M., Lowe, E.: A taxonomy of human communication errors and application to railway track maintenance. Cognition, Technology & Work 8(1), 57–66 (2006)
25. Harris Corporation: Harris Corporation awarded $331 million contract by FAA for data communications integrated services program (2012), http://harris.com/view_pressrelease.asp?act=lookup&pr_id=3518 (accessed December 16, 2012)
26. Hoare, C.A.R.: Communicating sequential processes. Commun. ACM 21(8), 666–677 (1978)
27. Hollan, J., Hutchins, E., Kirsh, D.: Distributed cognition: toward a new foundation for human-computer interaction research. ACM Transactions on Computer-Human Interaction 7(2), 174–196 (2000)
28. Hollnagel, E.: The phenotype of erroneous actions. International Journal of Man-Machine Studies 39(1), 1–32 (1993)
29. Hörl, J., Aichernig, B.K.: Formal specification of a voice communication system used in air traffic control, an industrial application of light-weight formal methods using VDM++. In: Wing, J.M., Woodcock, J., Davies, J. (eds.) FM 1999. LNCS, vol. 1709, pp. 1868–1868. Springer, Heidelberg (1999)

30. Hörl, J., Aichernig, B.K.: Validating voice communication requirements using lightweight formal methods. IEEE Software 17(3), 21–27 (2000)
31. John, B.E., Kieras, D.E.: The goms family of user interface analysis techniques: comparison and contrast. ACM Transactions on Computer-Human Interaction 3(4), 320–351 (1996)
32. Jones, R.K.: Miscommunication between pilots and air traffic control. Language Problems and Language Planning 27(3), 233–248 (2003)
33. Kieras, D.E., Wood, S.D., Meyer, D.E.: Predictive engineering models based on the epic architecture for a multimodal high-performance human-computer interaction task. ACM Transactions on Computer-Human Interaction 4(3), 230–275 (1997)
34. Kirwan, B., Ainsworth, L.K.: A Guide to Task Analysis. Taylor and Francis, London (1992)
35. NASA Aviation Safety Reporting System: Pilot/controller communications. Tech. rep., NASA Ames Research Center (2012)
36. Paternò, F., Santoro, C.: Preventing user errors by systematic analysis of deviations from the system task model. International Journal of Human-Computer Studies 56(2), 225–245 (2002)
37. Paternò, F., Santoro, C., Tahmassebi, S.: Formal model for cooperative tasks: Concepts and an application for en-route air traffic control. In: Proceedings of the 5th International Conference on the Design, Specification, and Verification of Interactive Systems, pp. 71–86. Springer, Vienna (1998)
38. Pek, E., Bogunovic, N.: Formal verification of communication protocols in distributed systems. In: Proceedings of MIPRO 2003, Computers in Technical Systems and Intelligent Systems, pp. 44–49. MIPRO (2003)
39. Pritchett, A.R., Feigh, K.M., Kim, S.Y., Kannan, S.: Work models that compute to support the design of multi-agent socio-technical systems (under review)
40. Reason, J.: Human Error. Cambridge University Press, New York (1990)
41. Sidhu, D.P., Leung, T.: Formal methods for protocol testing: A detailed study. IEEE Transactions on Software Engineering 15(4), 413–426 (1989)
42. Sunshine, C.A.: Formal methods for communication protocol specification and verification. Tech. rep., RAND Corporation, Santa Monica (1979)
43. Traum, D., Dillenbourg, P.: Miscommunication in multi-modal collaboration. In: AAAI Workshop on Detecting, Repairing, and Preventing Human–Machine Miscommunication, pp. 37–46. AAAI, Palo Alto (1996)

Using Model-Checking to Reveal a Vulnerability of Tamper-Evident Pairing*

Rody Kersten[1], Bernard van Gastel[2], Manu Drijvers[1],
Sjaak Smetsers[1], and Marko van Eekelen[1,2]

[1] Radboud University Nijmegen,
Institute for Computing and Information Sciences, The Netherlands
{r.kersten,s.smetsers,m.vaneekelen}@cs.ru.nl, manudrijvers@student.ru.nl
[2] Open University of the Netherlands, School of Computer Science, The Netherlands
{bernard.vangastel,marko.vaneekelen}@ou.nl

Abstract. Wi-Fi Protected Setup is an attempt to simplify configuration of security settings for Wi-Fi networks. It offers, among other methods, Push-Button Configuration (PBC) for devices with a limited user-interface. There are however some security issues in PBC. A solution to these issues was proposed in the form of Tamper-Evident Pairing (TEP).

TEP is based on the Tamper-Evident Announcement (TEA), in which a device engaging in the key agreement not only sends a payload containing its Diffie-Hellmann public key, but also sends a hash of this payload in a special, trustedly secure manner. The idea is that thanks to the special way in which the hash is sent, the receiver can tell whether or not the hash was altered by an adversary and if necessary reject it.

Several parameters needed for implementation of TEP have been left unspecified by its authors. Verification of TEA using the Spin model-checker has revealed that the value of these parameters is critical for the security of the protocol. The implementation decision can break the resistance of TEP against man-in-the-middle attacks. We give appropriate values for these parameters and show how model-checking was applied to retrieve these values.

Keywords: Security, Model-checking, Spin, Wi-Fi Protected Setup, Tamper-Evident Pairing.

1 Introduction

Security protocols aim at securing communications over networks that are publicly accessible. Depending on the application, they are supposed to ensure security properties such as authentication, integrity or confidentiality even when the network is accessible by malicious users, who may intercept and/or adapt existing, and send new messages. While the specification of such protocols is usually short and rather natural, designing a secure protocol is notoriously difficult.

---

* This work is part of the IOP GenCom GoGreen project, sponsored by the Dutch Ministry of Economic Affairs, Agriculture and Innovation.

G. Brat, N. Rungta, and A. Venet (Eds.): NFM 2013, LNCS 7871, pp. 63–77, 2013.

Flaws are often found several years later. One of the sources for the vulnerability of such protocols is that their specification is often (deliberately) incomplete. There are several reasons for the omission of certain details by the designer. For instance, a protocol may depend on properties of the hardware on which it is used. It also leaves some room for the implementer of the protocol to make implementation-dependent choices. The problem with these unspecified parameters is that it can be very hard to analyze the effects of specific choices on the correctness of the protocol itself. Mostly this is due to the fact that the protocol is specified in such a way that both designer and implementer are either convinced that the correctness is not influenced by the concrete values of these parameters, or they assume that theses values are chosen within certain (not explicitly specified) boundaries.

During the last two decades, formal methods have demonstrated their usefulness when designing and analyzing security protocols. They indeed provide rigorous frameworks and techniques that allow to discover new flaws. For example, the ProVerif tool [4] and the AVISPA platform [1] are both dedicated tools for automatically analyzing security properties. More general purpose model-checkers, such as Spin [9] and Uppaal [3], are also successfully applied to verify desired properties of protocol specifications. While this model-checking process often reveals errors, the absence of errors does in general not imply correctness of the protocol.

Secure wireless communication is a challenging problem due to the inherently shared nature of the wireless medium. For wireless home networks, the so-called Wi-Fi Protected Setup was designed to provide a standard for easy establishment of a secure connection between a wireless device with a possibly limited interface (e.g. a webcam or a printer) and a wireless access point. The wireless device, once connected to the access point, gets not only internet connectivity, but also access to shared files and content on the network. The standard provides several options for configuring security settings (referred to as *pairing* or *imprinting*). The most prominent ones are PIN and Push-Button Configuration. The PIN method has been shown to be vulnerable to brute-force attacks; see [25]. This method and its weaknesses are briefly discussed in Section 5. To establish a secure connection using the Push-Button method, the user presses a button on each device within a certain time-frame, and the devices start broadcasting their Diffie-Hellman public keys [6], which are used to agree on the encryption key to protect future communication. In [8] the authors argue that this protocol only protects against passive adversaries. Since the key exchange messages are not authenticated, the protocol is vulnerable to an active man-in-the-middle (MITM) attack. To protect key establishment against these MITM attacks, [8] presents a method called *Tamper-Evident Pairing* (TEP), that provides simple and secure Wi-Fi pairing without requiring an out-of-band communication channel (a medium, differing from the communication channel that is used for transmitting normal data). The essence of their method is that the chip-sets used in Wi-Fi devices offer the possibility not only to transmit data, but also to sense the medium to detect whether or not information is communicated. The correctness of the proposed protocol is based on the assumption that an adversary can only change or corrupt data on the medium but not completely remove the data. The TEP protocol is specified in a semi-formal way; its correctness is proven manually (i.e. on paper; not formally using e.g. a theorem prover). However, in the protocol itself some parameters are used that are not fully specified.

In this paper we investigate the TEP protocol in order to determine whether its correctness depends on the values chosen for the unspecified parameters. In other words, we analyze the protocol by varying the values of these parameters in order to find out if there exists a combination for which correctness is no longer guaranteed. Our analysis is done by using the Spin model-checker. We have modeled the essential part of the protocol (known as the Temper-Evident Announcement), and used this model to hunt for potentially dangerous combinations of parameters, which indeed appeared to exist. The next step was to explore the vulnerability boundaries, by deriving a closed predicate relating the parameters to eachother and providing a safety criterion. The derivation of this predicate, and the verification of the resulting safety criterion, was done by using the model-checker. The contribution of our work is twofold. First, it reveals a vulnerability of a protocol that was 'proven to be correct'. And secondly, it shows how model-checking can be used, not only to track down bugs, but also to establish side-conditions that are essential for the protocol to work properly.

2 Tamper-Evident Pairing

The Wi-Fi Alliance has set the Wi-Fi Protected Setup (WPS) standard in [27]. The standard provides several options for simple configuration of security settings for Wi-Fi networks (pairing). One of them is Push-Button Configuration (PBC), where two devices (enrollee and registrar) are paired by pressing a (possibly virtual) button on each of the devices within a time-out period of two minutes. Security of this method is enclosed in the fact that the user needs physical access to both devices. However, in [8], three vulnerabilities are described creating opportunity for man-in-the-middle attacks:

1. **Collision:** An attacker can create a collision with the enrollee's message and send his own message immediately after.
2. **Capture Effect:** An attacker can transmit a message at a much higher power than the enrollee. Capture effects were first described in [26].
3. **Timing Control:** an attacker can occupy the medium, prohibiting the enrollee from sending his message, and send his own message in-between.

Gollakota et al also provide an innovative solution to the PBC security problems in [8]. Their alternative pairing protocol is named Tamper-Evident Pairing (TEP). It is based on the fact that Wi-Fi devices can not only receive packets, but also simply measure the energy on the channel, as part of the 802.11 standard requirements. This provides the opportunity to encode a bit of information as a time-slot where energy is present or absent on the wireless medium. Under the assumption that an attacker does not have the ability to remove energy from the medium, this means that an attacker cannot turn an on-slot into an off-slot.

Let us start by explicating the attacker model, i.e. the assumptions about the adversary that we are securing the protocol against. The presence of an active adversary is assumed, who is trying to launch a MITM attack. She has the following capabilities:

Overwrite Data Packets. The adversary can use any of the three vulnerabilities listed above to overwrite data packets.

Introduce Energy on the Channel. The adversary can introduce energy on the channel. Energy cannot be eliminated from the wireless medium.

2.1   The Tamper-Evident Announcement

To facilitate TEP, Gollakota et al introduce the Tamper-Evident Announcement (TEA) primitive, which is sent in both directions: enrollee to registrar and vice-versa. The structure of a TEA is given in Fig. 1. It starts with the so-called *synchronization packet*. This an exceptionally long packet, filled with random data. It is detected by the receiver by measuring a burst of energy on the medium of at least its length (so in a manner similar to the on-off slots). Because this packet is exceptionally long, this uniquely identifies a TEA.

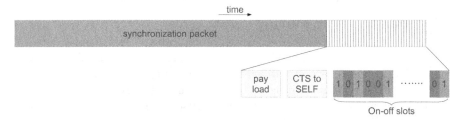

Fig. 1. The structure of a Tamper-Evident Announcement (TEA)

The synchronization packet is followed by the payload of the TEA, which contains the Diffie-Hellman public key [6] of the sender. Then, a *CTS-to-self* packet is sent. This message is part of the IEEE 802.11 specification and requests all other Wi-Fi devices not to transmit during a certain time period, here the time needed for the remainder of the TEA.

Finally, a hash of the payload is sent by either transmitting or refraining from transmitting during a series of so-called on-off *slots*. An attacker cannot change an on-slot into an off-slot, because she cannot remove energy from the medium, but she might still do the opposite. To be able to detect this as well, a specially crafted bit-balancing algorithm is applied to the 128-bit hash, prolonging it to 142 bits (71 zeros and 71 ones). Now, when an off-slot is changed into an on-slot, the balance between on and off slots is disturbed, making the tampering detectable. The 142-bit bit-balanced hash is preceded by two bits representing the direction of the TEA (enrollee to registrar or vice-versa). So, in total, 144 slots are sent.

2.2   Receiving the Slots

The sender sends out the 144 slots, which take 40 μs each, back-to-back. On the receiver-side the slots are received by measuring energy on the wireless medium. The receiver iteratively measures the energy on the medium, during so-called *sensing windows* of 20 μs. The total number of measurements m during the sensing window is stored, as well as the number of measurements e during which there was energy on the medium. If the *fractional occupancy*, given by e/m, is above a certain threshold then the medium is considered occupied during this particular sensing window.

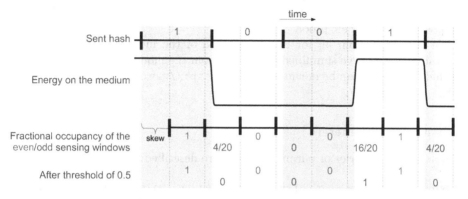

Fig. 2. Sending and receiving the slots of a 4-bit hash. The even sensing windows have the higher variance here. Therefore, those represent the received hash. Clock skew is shown in blue on the left.

The length of a sensing window is half the slot-length. The reason for this is that now either all the even sensing windows or all the odd sensing windows fall entirely within a slot, i.e. do not cross slot-boundaries, shown in Fig. 2, where the even sensing windows all fall entirely within one of the 40 μs slots. Note that the figure shows the ideal case, where measurements are exact. In reality the measurements will be less than perfect, which motivates the use of a threshold. The use of this special method of receiving the slots is motivated by the fact that there may be a slight clock-skew. This is shown in Fig. 2 on the lower-left.

After all the measurements are done and after applying the threshold, the receiver verifies that either the even or the odd sensing windows have an equal number of zeros and ones[1], and that those match a calculated hash of the payload packet. If this is not the case, then the receiver aborts the pairing process.

---

[1]   Actually, the variance of all the even sensing window measurements and that of all the odd sensing window measurements is calculated. The sensing windows with the higher variance will be the correct ones, since on and off slots are balanced. It is however not clear to us what the advantage of this approach is over simply selecting the sensing windows in which the on-off slots are balanced.

3   Modeling the Tamper-Evident Announcement in Spin

We use the same attacker model as the authors of [8], listed in Sect. 2. Given that an adversary can replace the payload packet, we will try to verify that she cannot adapt the bits of the hash that are received without being detected. Namely, if the attacker manages to send her own payload and adapt the hash such that it matches her payload and contains an equal number of zeros and ones, she can initiate a MITM attack. The payload packet itself is therefore not part of the model. We will only model the sending of the bit-balanced hash. The direction bits (i.e. the first two slots) are also not modeled. Gollakota et al. give an informal proof of the security of TEP in [8]. Effectively, we are challenging Proposition 7.2 of their proof.

We have used Spin [9] for the verification of the model. This section contains some illustrative simplified fragments from the model only. The full model (including results) can be downloaded from http://www.cs.ru.nl/R.Kersten/publications/nfm/.

3.1   Model Parameters

The model has a series of parameters that are described in this section.

Hash Length. The length of the bit-balanced hash to send. All possible hashes of this length that are bit-balanced are tried (the balancing algorithm itself is not part of the model).

Number of Measurements per Sensing Window. The number of measurements in each sensing window depends on the Wi-Fi hardware on which the protocol is implemented. The length of the window is 20 μs. During each window, the hardware logs the total number of clock-ticks, as well as the number of clock-ticks during which there was energy on the wireless medium. The number of measurements during each sensing window is thus variable. In the model though, the number of measurements is fixed and given by a parameter. The reason for this is that a variable number of measurements would highly enlarge the state-space, the number of measurements is not something that an adversary can influence and that we believe it will be fairly constant in practice. A programmer implementing the protocol could measure or calculate the average number of measurements during a sensing window and use a "safe" approximation (a little lower) in the formula. In our model, the sender puts energy on the wireless medium for the number of clock-ticks it takes to do the measurements for two sensing windows (the sensing window has half the length of an on-off slot). This means that one measurement is the unit for a clock-tick.

Sensing Window Threshold. As explained in Sect. 2.2, bits are received by measuring the *fractional occupancy* during a sensing window. It is determined whether or not the medium was occupied in a sensing window by checking if the fractional occupancy is above a certain threshold. The value of this threshold is not defined in [8], although it influences the measurements heavily. Since the number of measurements during a sensing window is constant in the model, we can omit the calculation of the fractional occupancy. This means that also the threshold should now be modeled, not as a number between 0 and 1, but as a number between 0 and the number of sensing window measurements and that its unit is clock-ticks (the medium was occupied during e ticks of the discrete clock). If the number of measurements (clock-ticks) in a sensing window where there was energy on the medium exceeds the threshold, then a one is stored for this sensing window.

Skew. The reason for the use of pairs of sensing windows for receiving the slots is that there may be an inherent clock skew. It is stated in [8] that this inherent clock skew may be up to 10 μs, i.e. half the sensing window length. By using pairs of sensing windows, either the even or the odd windows are guaranteed not to cross slot-boundaries. Furthermore, it is stated in [8] that to detect a TEA it is sufficient to detect a burst of energy "at least as long as the synchronization packet". It is not specified which is the exact synchronization point: the beginning or the end of the energy pulse. Neither is the maximum length of an energy burst that signifies a synchronization packet. The difference with the given length of 19ms introduces an extra skew. Since an adversary can introduce energy to the wireless medium, she can prolong the synchronization packet and introduce extra skew (the sign of this skew depends on the choice of synchronization point). The model variable *skew* is the total of the inherent clock skew and this *attacker skew*. Like the number of measurements and the threshold, its unit is also clock-ticks. We only consider positive skew (forward in time) in our model.

These parameters to the model are henceforth referred to as *hash_length*, *sw_measurements*, *threshold* and *skew*, respectively.

3.2   Clock Implementation

Timing is essential to modeling the TEA. However, Spin has no inherent notion of time. Luckily, in this case the exact scheduling and execution speed are not important, as the only interaction between the sender and receiver processes is sending energy to and reading the energy-level from the wireless medium. The receiver observes the value of the wireless medium once per clock cycle, the sender updates it at most once.

Due to these properties we can implement a discrete clock in Promela (the modeling language used by Spin), without the need to use specialized model-checkers with native clock support. We introduce a separate clock process, which waits until all processes using a clock are finished with a clock cycle (Listing 1, line 17), before signaling them to continue. Processes are signaled to continue by flipping the Boolean *clock* (line 23). Processes can only continue with the next clock cycle if this variable differs from their local variable *localclock* (line 10), which is also flipped after each clock-tick (line 11). Our clock implementation also supports processes which do not use a clock. A clock-tick in the model corresponds to a measurement taken by the receiver. To avoid the situation that the receiver executes before the sender, we implemented explicit turns for the processes, so the sender always executes first after a clock-tick. The process with the lowest process identifier is always executed first (line 7). We can introduce skew by letting one of the processes wait a number of clock-ticks before starting.

```
1   byte waiting = 0;
2   bool clock = false;
3   #define useClock() bool localclock = false;
4
5   inline waitTicks(procID, numberOfTicks) {
6      byte tick;
7      for (tick : 0..(numberOfTicks−1)) {
8         waiting++;
9         atomic {
10           localclock != clock;
11           localclock = clock;
12           waiting == procID;
13        }
14     }
15  }
16
17  proctype clockProc() {
18  end:
19     do
20     :: atomic {
21        waiting ==NUMBER_OF_CLOCK_PROCESSES;
22        waiting = 0;
23        clock = !clock;
24     }
25     od;
26  }
```

Listing 1. Modeling the clock. The `useClock` and `waitTicks` functions must be used in processes that use the clock.

3.3   Model Processes

The model begins with a routine that generates all possible hashes of the given length non-deterministically. It then starts four processes:

Clock. A simple clock process is used to control the other processes. The clock process is described in Sect. 3.2.

Sender. The sender process first initializes and starts the clock. It then iteratively sends a bit of the generated hash (by putting energy on the medium,
or not), waits for $2 \cdot sw\_measurements$ clock-ticks, then sends the next bit.
When finished sending, the sender must keep the clock ticking, because the
receiver process might still be running.

```
1   proctype sender() {
2     useClock();
3     waitTicks(0, 1);
4     byte i;
5     for (i : 0..(HASH_LENGTH−1)) {
6       mediumSender = get(i); //send slot
7       waitTicks(0, SW_MEASUREMENTS*2);
8     }
9     doneWithClock(0);
10  }
```

Listing 2. Sender model

Receiver. The receiver also begins with initializing and starting the clock. It
then introduces clock skew by waiting more *skew* ticks. Then, it measures
energy on the medium *sw_measurements* times (once each clock-tick) and
stores the received bit for each sensing window (one if *e* is above *threshold*).
Note that the wireless medium consists of two bits: one that is set by the
legitimate sender and one that is set by the adversary. The receiver reads
energy if either bit is set. Once measurements for all sensing windows are
done, the `checkHash()` function verifies if either the even or the odd sensing
windows have an equal number of on and off slots.

```
1   receiver() {
2     useClock();
3     waitTicks(1, SKEW+1);
4     short sw;
5     for (sw : 0..(HASH_LENGTH*2−1)) {
6       byte e = 0, ticks = 0;
7       for (ticks : 0..(SW_MEASUREMENTS−1)) {
8         e = e + (mediumSender || mediumAdversary);
9         waitTicks(1, 1);
10      }
11      store(sw, e>THRESHOLD);
12    }
13    checkHash();
14  }
```

Listing 3. Receiver model

Adversary. The adversary is modeled as a simple process that increases the
energy on the medium, then decreases it again. Because processes may be
interleaved in any possible way, this verifies all scenarios.

```
1  proctype adversary () {
2  end :
3    do
4    ::  mediumAdversary  =  1;
5        mediumAdversary  =  0;
6    od
7  }
```

Listing 4. Adversary model

4   Model-Checking Results

Verification of the model means stating the assertion that either the received hash is equal to the sent hash or it is not equal, but the tampering by the adversary is detected (because the number of ones in the hash is unequal to the number of zeros). It is thus a search for a counter-example.

The expectation was that we might be able to find such a counter-example, but that the freedom with which an adversary could modify the received hash would be limited, probably to just the first or last bit. Model-checking indeed generated a counter-example. Moreover, experimentation with different assertions turned out that the adversary actually has more freedom in modifying the hash than expected. This vulnerability is described in Sect. 4.1. After the vulnerability was discovered, we executed a large series of Spin runs to discover what the exact conditions are that enable such an attack. The results are given in Sect. 4.2.

4.1   Revealed Vulnerability in the TEA

Model-checking the TEA model using Spin generated a counter-example to the assertion that a hash that was modified by an adversary will not be accepted by the receiver. A scenario similar to the one for which this counter-example was found is shown in Fig. 3.

Figure 3 shows the case where no adversary is active. Here, the even sensing windows still have the higher variance (1001 versus 0010). Thus, those are chosen as the correct slots and the hash 1001 is received, which is equal to the sent hash.

In Fig. 4 a scenario is shown in which an adversary actively introduces energy on the wireless medium. The energy that is introduced by the attacker is shown as a dotted blue line. She manages to trick the receiver into choosing the odd sensing windows and consequently receive a modified hash: 1010. Experimentation with modified assertions has confirmed our conjecture that an adversary can use this tactic to change any 1 bit in the hash to a 0, *if and only if it is immediately followed by a 0*. Since the hash is bit-balanced, it consists of 50% zeros and 50% ones. Of the latter category, half are followed by 0 bits on average. This means that an adversary can change on average 75% of the hash.

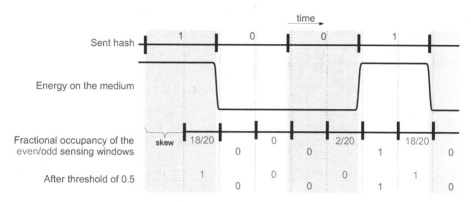

Fig. 3. Scenario in which TEP is vulnerable, for a 4-bit hash. The synchronization packet is prolonged to create a skew that is larger than the half the sensing window. The hash is still received correctly here.

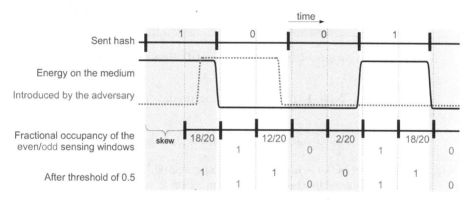

Fig. 4. The attack found by model checking, for a 4-bit hash. The adversary introduces energy to the medium to change the received hash to 1010.

4.2   Varying the Values of the Model Parameters

After discovering the vulnerability described in the previous section, we wanted to investigate what the exact circumstances are in which the vulnerability occurs. We therefore ran the Spin model-checker for many different values of the parameters *hash_length*, *sw_measurements*, *threshold* and *skew*[2]. Some of the results are shown in Table 1. As it turns out, the length of the hash has no influence on the occurrence of the vulnerability, so this is omitted from the results. Remember that the unit for all three parameters in the table is clock-ticks.

---

[2] In order to run the Spin model-checker for various values of defined parameters, we have implemented a small wrapper in the form a of C program. This wrapper can be obtained from **http://www.open.ou.nl/bvg/spinbatch/**.

Table 1. Model-checking results. Pluses indicate that the proposition is not broken. Minuses indicate the occurrence of the vulnerability.

threshold = 3 / sw_meas.	skew 0	1	2	3	4	5	6	7	8	9	10
4	+	-	-	-	-	-	-	-	-	-	-
5	+	+	-	-	-	-	-	-	-	-	-
6	+	+	+	-	-	-	-	-	-	-	-
7	+	+	+	+	-	-	-	-	-	-	-
8	+	+	+	+	+	-	-	-	-	-	-
9	+	+	+	+	+	+	-	-	-	-	-
10	+	+	+	+	+	+	+	-	-	-	-

(a) Results for *threshold* = 3

threshold = 5 / sw_meas.	skew 0	1	2	3	4	5	6	7	8	9	10
6	+	-	-	-	-	-	-	-	-	-	-
7	+	+	-	-	-	-	-	-	-	-	-
8	+	+	+	-	-	-	-	-	-	-	-
9	+	+	+	+	-	-	-	-	-	-	-
10	+	+	+	+	+	-	-	-	-	-	-

(b) Results for *threshold* = 5

threshold = 7 / sw_meas.	skew 0	1	2	3	4	5	6	7	8	9	10
8	+	-	-	-	-	-	-	-	-	-	-
9	+	+	-	-	-	-	-	-	-	-	-
10	+	+	+	-	-	-	-	-	-	-	-

(c) Results for *threshold* = 7

threshold = 9 / sw_meas.	skew 0	1	2	3	4	5	6	7	8	9	10
10	+	-	-	-	-	-	-	-	-	-	-

(d) Results for *threshold* = 9

It is obvious from Table 1 that the following predicate determines the possibility of an attack:

$$skew \geq sw\_measurements - threshold \tag{1}$$

In Fig. 4, a threshold of 0.5 is used, which is represented by a value for *threshold* of $\frac{1}{2} \cdot sw\_measurements$ in the model. If the *skew* is large enough to move a number of *threshold* measurements of the even windows over the sensing window boundary, then an adversary might change the received hash. We have model-checked the predicate for all combinations of *sw_measurements* 1–10, *threshold* 1–10 and *skew* 1–10.

5   Related Work

Before the Spin model on which this article is based was made, a simple model of the TEA and TEP in UPPAAL was made by Drijvers [7]. UPPAAL is a tool with which properties about systems modeled as networks of timed automata can be verified [3]. Because of the simple nature of this model, it did not include clock skew and therefore did not reveal the vulnerability that was later found using Spin. Apart from the TEA, Drijvers made a separate model of the overlying TEP, with which – under the assumption that the TEA is secure – no problems were identified. Since TEP was already successfully model-checked using UPPAAL and, contrary to the TEA model, not in a highly abstract form (it is much simpler), we chose not to repeat the modeling for Spin.

In [5] a method is proposed for modeling a discrete clock in Promela, without the need to alter Spin. Instead of an alternating Boolean, time is modeled as an integer which negatively impacts the state space explosion. Just as with our approach a separate clock is introduced, which waits until all the other processes are finished, before increasing the discrete clock variable. This waiting is modeled with a native feature of Promela, which only continues if no other state-transition can be made (the `timeout` keyword). Therefore, all the processes are implicitly using the modeled clock. Because of our general adversary process, this restriction is too severe for us.

Many approaches to pairing wireless devices are described in the literature. A comparison of various wireless pairing protocols is given in [24]. Often, a trusted *out-of-band* channel is used to transfer (the hash of) an encryption key, e.g. a human [10], direct electrical contact [23], Near-Field Communication [17], (ultra)sound [16], laser [18], visual/barcodes [20], et cetera. A nice overview is given in [11]. Another, slightly out-dated, overview is given in [22]. In TEP, a hash of the key is communicated in a trustedly secure manner *in-band*.

When using the PIN method that Wi-Fi Protected Setup provides, one of the devices displays an eight-digit authentication code, which the user then needs to enter on the other device. This method thus requires a screen and some sort of input device. The PIN method has been shown to be vulnerable to feasible brute-force attacks by Viehböck in [25]. The reason for this is that last digit is actually a check-sum of the first seven digits (i.e. there are only seven digits to verify) and, moreover, that the PIN is verified in two steps. The result of the verification of the first four digits is sent back to the enrollee, which may then send three more digits if this result was positive. This reduces the number of codes to try in a brute-force attack from 10^7 to $10^4 + 10^3$. A successful attack can be executed in approximately two hours on average. CERT-CC has urged users to disable the WPS feature on their wireless access points in response to this vulnerability[3]. A security and usability analysis of Wi-Fi Protected Setup, as well as Bluetooth Simple Pairing, which is similar, is given in [12].

Approaches to model-checking security protocols are described in [13] and [2]. In [14], a series of XSS and SQL injection attacks is detected using model-checking. Model-checking and theorem proving of security properties are discussed in [15]. In [19], security issues that arise from combining hosts in a network are investigated using model-checking. An entire Linux distribution is model-checked against security violations in [21].

6   Conclusions

The effects of a number of decisions to be made when implementing Tamper-Evident Pairing have been studied. In particular, the sending of a hash by using on-off slots – in which energy is present or absent on the wireless medium – was modeled. The values of several essential parameters of the protocol have not been adequately specified. Model checking proved to be very effective both in

---

[3] http://www.kb.cert.org/vuls/id/723755

uncovering a serious vulnerability for certain values of these parameters and in finding a predicate on the parameters indicating for which values the vulnerability is present. An adversary aiming to initiate a man-in-the-middle attack can thus *evidently tamper* with the received hash.

Future work could include extending the model to cover more of the TEA and investigate the feasibility of exploiting the found vulnerability. Furthermore, a full formal proof that the found vulnerability cannot occur when the predicate is not satisfied would be very valuable.

References

1. Armando, A., Basin, D., Boichut, Y., Chevalier, Y., Compagna, L., Cuellar, J., Hankes Drielsma, P., Heám, P.C., Kouchnarenko, O., Mantovani, J., Mödersheim, S., von Oheimb, D., Rusinowitch, M., Santiago, J., Turuani, M., Viganò, L., Vigneron, L.: The AVISPA tool for the automated validation of internet security protocols and applications. In: Etessami, K., Rajamani, S.K. (eds.) CAV 2005. LNCS, vol. 3576, pp. 281–285. Springer, Heidelberg (2005)
2. Armando, A., Carbone, R., Compagna, L.: LTL model checking for security protocols. Journal of Applied Non-Classical Logics 19(4), 403–429 (2009)
3. Bengtsson, J., Larsen, K., Larsson, F., Pettersson, P., Yi, W.: UPPAAL — a Tool Suite for Automatic Verification of Real–Time Systems. In: Alur, R., Sontag, E.D., Henzinger, T.A. (eds.) HS 1995. LNCS, vol. 1066, pp. 232–243. Springer, Heidelberg (1996)
4. Blanchet, B.: An Efficient Cryptographic Protocol Verifier Based on Prolog Rules. In: 14th IEEE Computer Security Foundations Workshop (CSFW-14), Cape Breton, Nova Scotia, Canada, pp. 82–96. IEEE Computer Society (June 2001)
5. Bošnacki, D., Dams, D.: Integrating real time into Spin: a prototype implementation. In: Bošnacki, D. (ed.) Enhancing State Space Reduction Techniques for Model Checking. Technische Universiteit Eindhoven (1998)
6. Diffie, W., Hellman, M.: New directions in cryptography. IEEE Transactions on Information Theory 22(6), 644–654 (1976)
7. Drijvers, M.: Model checking Tamper-Evident Pairing. Bachelor thesis, Radboud University Nijmegen (2012)
8. Gollakota, S., Ahmed, N., Zeldovich, N., Katabi, D.: Secure in-band wireless pairing. In: Proceedings of the 20th USENIX Conference on Security, SEC 2011. USENIX Association, Berkeley (2011)
9. Holzmann, G.: The model checker Spin. IEEE Transactions on Software Engineering 23(5), 279–295 (1997)
10. Kainda, R., Flechais, I., Roscoe, A.W.: Usability and security of out-of-band channels in secure device pairing protocols. In: Proceedings of the 5th Symposium on Usable Privacy and Security, pp. 11:1–11:12. ACM, New York (2009)
11. Kobsa, A., Sonawalla, R., Tsudik, G., Uzun, E., Wang, Y.: Serial hook-ups: a comparative usability study of secure device pairing methods. In: Proceedings of the 5th Symposium on Usable Privacy and Security, pp. 10:1–10:12. ACM, New York (2009)
12. Kuo, C., Walker, J., Perrig, A.: Low-cost manufacturing, usability, and security: An analysis of Bluetooth Simple Pairing and Wi-Fi Protected Setup. In: Dietrich, S., Dhamija, R. (eds.) FC 2007 and USEC 2007. LNCS, vol. 4886, pp. 325–340. Springer, Heidelberg (2007)

13. Lowe, G.: Towards a completeness result for model checking of security protocols. In: Proceedings of the 11th IEEE Computer Security Foundations Workshop, pp. 96–105 (June 1998)
14. Martin, M., Lam, M.S.: Automatic generation of XSS and SQL injection attacks with goal-directed model checking. In: Proceedings of the 17th Conference on Security Symposium, SS 2008, pp. 31–43. USENIX Association (2008)
15. Martinelli, F.: Partial model checking and theorem proving for ensuring security properties. In: Proceedings of the 11th IEEE Computer Security Foundations Workshop, pp. 44–52 (1998)
16. Mayrhofer, R., Gellersen, H.: On the security of ultrasound as out-of-band channel. In: IEEE International Parallel and Distributed Processing Symposium, IPDPS 2007, pp. 1–6 (March 2007)
17. Mayrhofer, R., Gellersen, H., Hazas, M.: Security by spatial reference: Using relative positioning to authenticate devices for spontaneous interaction. In: Krumm, J., Abowd, G.D., Seneviratne, A., Strang, T. (eds.) UbiComp 2007. LNCS, vol. 4717, pp. 199–216. Springer, Heidelberg (2007)
18. Mayrhofer, R., Welch, M.: A human-verifiable authentication protocol using visible laser light. In: The Second International Conference on Availability, Reliability and Security, ARES 2007, pp. 1143–1148 (April 2007)
19. Ritchey, R., Ammann, P.: Using model checking to analyze network vulnerabilities. In: Proceedings of the 2000 IEEE Symposium on Security and Privacy, S P 2000, pp. 156–165 (2000)
20. Saxena, N., Ekberg, J.-E., Kostiainen, K., Asokan, N.: Secure device pairing based on a visual channel. In: 2006 IEEE Symposium on Security and Privacy, pp. 306–313 (May 2006)
21. Schwarz, B., Chen, H., Wagner, D., Morrison, G., West, J., Lin, J., Tu, W.: Model checking an entire Linux distribution for security violations. In: 21st Annual Computer Security Applications Conference, pp. 10–22 (2005)
22. Smetters, D.B., Balfanz, D., Smetters, D.K., Stewart, P., Wong, H.C.: Talking to strangers: Authentication in ad-hoc wireless networks (2002)
23. Stajano, F., Anderson, R.: The resurrecting duckling: security issues for ubiquitous computing. Computer 35(4), 22–26 (2002)
24. Suomalainen, J., Valkonen, J., Asokan, N.: Security associations in personal networks: A comparative analysis. In: Stajano, F., Meadows, C., Capkun, S., Moore, T. (eds.) ESAS 2007. LNCS, vol. 4572, pp. 43–57. Springer, Heidelberg (2007)
25. Viehböck, S.: Brute forcing Wi-Fi protected setup, http://sviehb.files.wordpress.com/2011/12/viehboeck_wps.pdf
26. Ware, C., Judge, J., Chicharo, J., Dutkiewicz, E.: Unfairness and capture behaviour in 802.11 adhoc networks. In: 2000 IEEE International Conference on Communications, ICC 2000, vol. 1, pp. 159–163 (2000)
27. Wi-Fi Alliance: Wi-Fi Protected Setup Specification, version 1.0h (2006)

SMT-Based Analysis of Biological Computation

Boyan Yordanov, Christoph M. Wintersteiger,
Youssef Hamadi, and Hillel Kugler

Microsoft Research, Cambridge UK
{yordanov,cwinter,youssefh,hkugler}@microsoft.com
http://research.microsoft.com/z3-4biology

Abstract. Synthetic biology focuses on the re-engineering of living organisms for useful purposes while DNA computing targets the construction of therapeutics and computational circuits directly from DNA strands. The complexity of biological systems is a major engineering challenge and their modeling relies on a number of diverse formalisms. Moreover, many applications are "mission-critical" (e.g. as recognized by NASA's Synthetic Biology Initiative) and require robustness which is difficult to obtain. The ability to formally specify desired behavior and perform automated computational analysis of system models can help address these challenges, but today there are no unifying scalable analysis frameworks capable of dealing with this complexity.

In this work, we study pertinent problems and modeling formalisms for DNA computing and synthetic biology and describe how they can be formalized and encoded to allow analysis using Satisfiability Modulo Theories (SMT). This work highlights biological engineering as a domain that can benefit extensively from the application of formal methods. It provides a step towards the use of such methods in computational design frameworks for biology and is part of a more general effort towards the formalization of biology and the study of biological computation.

1 Introduction

Significant progress in molecular and cellular biology and breakthroughs in experimental methods have raised hopes that the engineering of biological systems can serve for technological and medical applications, with a tremendous promise ranging from the sustainable production of biofuels and other materials [31] to the development of "smart" therapeutics [4]. Among the different approaches towards such molecular programming, DNA computation (the construction of computational circuits directly from DNA strands) and synthetic biology (the re-engineering of genetic networks within organisms) have emerged as promising directions with a number of experimental studies demonstrating their feasibility [22,23]. Recently, NASA has acknowledged the importance of this domain by creating the Synthetic Biology Initiative[1] [17] designed to *"harness biology in reliable, robust, engineered systems to support NASA's exploration and science missions, to improve life on Earth, and to help shape NASA's future"*.

---

[1] http://syntheticbiology.arc.nasa.gov/

G. Brat, N. Rungta, and A. Venet (Eds.): NFM 2013, LNCS 7871, pp. 78–92, 2013.

More generally, the engineering of biological systems can lead to a better understanding of biological computation (the computational processes within living organisms) with the goal of addressing some of the following questions: *What do cells compute? How do they perform such computation?* and *In what ways can the computation be modified or engineered?* which is the focus here.

Biological complexity presents a major engineering challenge, especially since many relevant applications can be considered as "mission-critical", while robustness is hard to engineer. Computational modeling currently focuses on using simulation to help address these challenges by allowing *in silico* experiments, however simulation alone is often not sufficient to uncover design flaws. For such applications, foundational computer-aided design technologies that allow desired behavior to be specified formally and analyzed automatically are needed. However, unifying analysis frameworks capable of dealing with the biological complexity and the diverse modeling formalisms used in the field are currently missing. Inspired by the study and engineering of other computational systems such as computer hardware and software, the application of formal methods has already attracted attention in the context of biology. In this work, we take a Satisfiability Modulo Theories (SMT)-based approach, utilizing transition systems as a uniform representation for biological models, and enabling efficient analysis for important properties of DNA computing and synthetic biology. Using theories richer than Boolean logic as in SMT offers a more natural framework by allowing higher-level problem descriptions and enhanced expressive power, provided that (efficient) automatic reasoning procedures are available. Such decision procedures are being developed actively [1] and are implemented in modern solvers such as Z3 [8] where, for certain applications, SMT-based methods outperform simpler theories [28], while their model-generation capabilities are important for the problems we consider. The richness of SMT accommodates analysis procedures to address a diverse set of biological questions and leads to a framework that is expressive (can capture a variety of formalisms and specifications), scalable (can handle models of practical interest) and extensible (additional models and analysis procedures can be integrated).

The main goals of this paper are (1) to study the pertinent modeling formalisms and problems for DNA computing and synthetic biology as representative biological engineering disciplines, formalize them, and describe how they can be encoded to allow analysis using SMT-based methods; (2) to exploit domain-specific knowledge in order to identify properties of these systems to help improve the scalability of analysis methods; (3) to present results from the application of these methods on challenging examples beyond what was possible using previous analysis approaches; and (4) to explore the utility of a general framework for analyzing biological computation.

2   Preliminaries and Notation

We denote a finite set as $S = \{s_0, \ldots, s_N\}$ where $|S| = N + 1$ is the number of elements in S. We use $S = \{(s_0, n_0), \ldots, (s_N, n_N)\}$ to denote a finite multiset where each pair (s_i, n_i) denotes an element s_i and its multiplicity n_i with $n_i > 0$. Given a multiset S we use $s \in S$ when the multiplicity of s is not important and $S(s)$ to indicate the multiplicity of s when $s \in S$ and 0 otherwise. The union of multisets $(S \uplus S')$ as well as the multiplication of a multiset by a scalar (nS) are used according to their standard definitions.

3   DNA Computation

In the field of chemistry, mathematical theories such as mass-action kinetics have been developed to describe chemical reaction systems and predict their dynamical properties[12]. In molecular programming, the long term vision is to study the inverse problem where chemical and molecular systems are engineered with the goal of obtaining specific behavior of molecular events. The use of DNA as a chemical substrate has attracted attention, partially due to the availability of experimental techniques, as well as the predictability of chemical properties such as Watson-Crick pairing (the complementarity of the G-C and A-T base pairs which dictates the binding of DNA sequences). These properties have been exploited as early as in [3] where a strategy for computing a Hamiltonian path in a graph using DNA is described. DNA strand displacement (DSD) [25] is a particular DNA computation framework which, in principle, can be used to implement arbitrary computational procedures [14] and allows the use of DNA as a universal substrate for chemical reaction networks [27]. The feasibility of experimentally constructing large DNA computing circuits has been demonstrated recently [23]. Even so, the manual engineering of DNA circuits is challenging due to the parallel interactions of a large number of individual DNA species. To address these challenges, tools enabling the computational design and simulation of complex DNA circuits have been developed [16]. Here, we present an SMT-based approach for the analysis of these systems.

3.1   DNA Strand Displacement (DSD) Circuits

In a *DSD circuit*, a network of chemical reactions is constructed from *DNA species* (see Fig. 1), designed to interact according to DNA base-pairing rules. The DSD language [20] formalizes the notion of DNA species and the possible reactions between them. Briefly, a DNA species consists of a number of *strands* (individual DNA sequences)[2]. For example, in Fig. 1-A species s_0 consists of the single strand $\hat{s}_0$ while species s_3 consists of strands $\hat{s}_1$, $\hat{s}_2$, and $\hat{s}_3$ (all strands are listed in Fig. 1-D).

We are interested in studying the dynamics of a DSD circuit with single-molecule resolution by tracking how the amounts of species change as reactions take place, currently abstracting from the exact reaction kinetics (see Sec. 6 for additional discussion). A *state* of the system therefore describes the amount of molecules from each species present (Fig. 1-B). The initial state defined as part

---

[2] In the DSD language, strands are further subdivided into *domains* (*e.g.* t and x0 in strand $\hat{s}_0$ in Fig. 1-D) but for the current presentation this structure is not important.

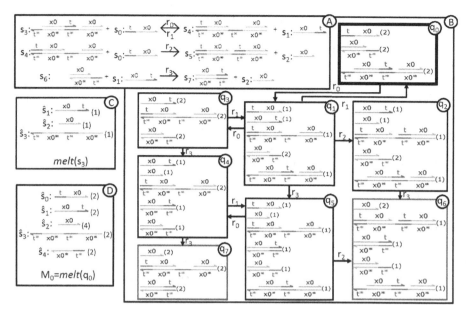

Fig. 1. A DSD circuit consisting of eight DNA species ($S = \{s_0, \dots, s_7\}$) and four reactions ($R = \{r_0, \dots, r_3\}$) represented graphically in (A). The state space of the system is shown in (B) where the multiplicity for each species is given in parenthesis and no further reactions are possible in the highlighted states (q_6 and q_7). The melting of a species and all species from a state (as discussed in Sec. 1.2) is illustrated in (C) and (D), respectively. Each strand from (D) represents a single DNA sequence.

of a DSD program (q_0 in Fig. 1-B), together with the rules of the DSD language, allows the automatic generation of possible reactions and species in the system [16]. We treat a DSD circuit as the pair $(\mathcal{S}, \mathcal{R})$ where $\mathcal{S}$ is a set of species and $\mathcal{R}$ is a set of reactions[3]. A reaction $r \in \mathcal{R}$ is a pair of multisets $r = (R_r, P_r)$ describing the reactants and products of r, where for $(s, n) \in R_r$ (resp. $(s, n) \in P_r$), $s \in \mathcal{S}$ is a species and n is the stoichiometry indicating how many molecules of s are consumed (resp. produced) through reaction r. To formalize the behavior of a DSD circuit, we construct the transition system $\mathcal{T} = (Q, q_0, T)$ where Q is the set of states, $q \in Q$ is a multiset of species ($q(s)$ indicates how many molecules of s are available in q), $q_0 \in Q$ is the initial state[4], and $T \subseteq Q \times Q$ is the transition relation. Reaction r is enabled in q, if there are enough molecules of its reactants

$$enabled(r, q) \leftrightarrow \bigwedge_{s \in \mathcal{S}} q(s) \geq R_r(s) \tag{1}$$

The transition relation T is defined as

$$T(q, q') \leftrightarrow \bigvee_{r \in \mathcal{R}} [enabled(r, q) \wedge \bigwedge_{s \in S} q'(s) = q(s) - R_r(s) + P_r(s)].$$

---

[3] Reversible reactions are treated as two non-reversible ones (*e.g.* r_0, r_1 in Fig. 1-A).
[4] We assume that the system is initialized in a single state (which is the case for DSD circuits we consider in this paper), although the methods can be generalized.

The definition of T aims to capture the firing of a single enabled reaction per transition. Still, in some special cases multiple reactions can fire in a time step (*e.g.* A → C and A + B → C + B) but this does not affect the structure of T and its subsequent analysis.

We assume that the set of species is finite and can be generated *a priory* (see discussion in Sec. 6). To enable the SMT-based analysis of DSD circuits, we represent the set of states of a transition system T using an integer encoding where $Q \subseteq \mathbb{N}^{|S|}$ and the transition relation as a function $T : \mathbb{N}^{|S|} \times \mathbb{N}^{|S|} \to \mathbb{B}$. In Sec. 3.2 we prove that for a subset of DSD models the number of molecules of each species cannot exceed some upper bound N which can be computed from the species' structures[5]- this allows a finite representation of T and can help our analysis. Finite transition systems can be encoded naturally as logical formulas [5]. As an alternative to the integer representation, we encode the amount of species $s \in S$ as a bit-vector of size $\lceil lg(N+1) \rceil$, leading to $Q \subseteq \mathbb{B}^{\hat{N}}$, $\hat{N} = |S| \lceil lg(N+1) \rceil$ where $q(s) \in \mathbb{B}^{\lceil lg(N+1) \rceil}$ amounts to a bit-vector extraction and the transition relation is encoded as a function $T : \mathbb{B}^{\hat{N}} \times \mathbb{B}^{\hat{N}} \to \mathbb{B}$. Note that, although T is finite when species bounds are available, an explicit state-space representation of Q is often unfeasible to compute for realistic DSD circuits.

3.2   Constraints Generation

Naturally occurring chemical reaction networks are often subjected to constraints such as mass-conservation. In this section, we show that the known structure of species in a DSD circuit allows us to directly compute such constraints, which we exploit in our analysis. Intuitively, the individual strands from which all species in the system are composed are preserved and their total amounts remain unchanged. In the following, we exploit this *conservation of strands* property.

Let $\hat{s}$ denote a single strand where it is possible that $\hat{s} \notin S$. Given a species $s \in S$, we use the function $melt(s)$ to compute the multiset of strands that s is composed of (Fig. 1-C). The application of $melt$ can be thought of as the "melting" of a species by increasing the temperature to dissociate all individual DNA strands. The function $melt()$ can be extended to operate on a multiset of species (Fig. 1-D), such as a state $q \in Q$

$$melt(q) \triangleq \biguplus_{s \in S} q(s)\, melt(s) \tag{2}$$

Proposition 1. *The conservation of strands allows us to restrict the set of states reachable in T to a subset $\hat{Q} \subseteq Q$, for which the strands multiset is an invariant*

$$\forall q, q' \in \hat{Q}, melt(q) = melt(q') \tag{3}$$

Corollary 1. *The invariant multiset M_0 can be computed from the initial state*

$$\forall q \in \hat{Q}, melt(q) = M_0 \text{ where } M_0 = melt(q_0) \tag{4}$$

---

[5] As an additional optimization, separate bounds for each species can be computed.

The following constraints account for the conservation of strands

$$\forall q \in \hat{Q}, \bigwedge_{\hat{s} \in \hat{S}} \left[\sum_{s \in S} q(s) M_s(\hat{s}) = M_0(\hat{s}) \right] \tag{5}$$

where $M_s = melt(s)$ denotes the multiset of strands for species s, $M_s(\hat{s})$ denotes the multiplicity of strand $\hat{s}$ in the composition of species s, and $\hat{S} = \{\hat{s} \mid \exists s \in S, \hat{s} \in melt(s)\}$ denotes the set of all individual strands in the system. In practice, Eqn. (5) is translated into constraints that might be challenging to solve. However, they can be simplified to obtain upper bounds on the multiplicities of individual species by constructing $\hat{Q}' \subseteq Q$, where in general $\hat{Q} \subseteq \hat{Q}'$ (*i.e.* $\hat{Q}'$ is an over-approximation of the states satisfying the conservation of strands invariant). Let $N_s = \min\{\lfloor M_0(\hat{s})/M_s(\hat{s}) \rfloor \mid \hat{s} \in M_s\}$ denote the maximal number of molecules of species s as restricted by its least abundant strand. Then

$$\forall q \in \hat{Q}', \bigwedge_{s \in S} q(s) \leq N_s \tag{6}$$

We encode the constraints from Eqns. (5) and (6) using functions *invariant* : $Q \rightarrow \mathbb{B}$ where, for a state $q \in Q$, *invariant*(q) iff $q \in \hat{Q}$, and *bounds* : $Q \rightarrow \mathbb{B}$ where *bounds*(q) iff $q \in \hat{Q}'$ (the exact definition of these functions depends on the encoding of Q). In the following section, we will use these functions as constraints that will allow us to study the existence of states with certain properties[6]. The upper bounds from Eqn. (6) can also serve to determine the required bit-vector size for the encoding from Sec. 3.1 (*i.e.* $N = \max\{N_s \mid s \in S\}$), while using the individual species bounds can lead to smaller encodings.

Example 1. For the DSD circuit from Fig. 1 the following constraints were generated: $s_0 + s_4 + 2s_5 = 2$, $s_2 + s_3 + s_4 + s_6 = 4$, $s_3 + s_4 + s_5 = 2$, $s_1 + s_3 + s_7 = 2$, and $s_6 + s_7 = 2$. From these, the following species bounds were obtained: $s_0 \leq 2$, $s_1 \leq 2$, $s_2 \leq 4$, $s_3 \leq 2$, $s_4 \leq 2$, $s_5 \leq 1$, $s_6 \leq 2$, and $s_7 \leq 2$.

3.3 Analysis of DNA Computation

To illustrate our method and discuss the formalization of properties relevant to DNA computation, we study a family of *transducer* circuits. Here, a transducer is a simple computational device constructed from DNA, which is intended to convert all molecules of a certain (input) species to a different (output) species through a set of chemical reactions [15]. A number of transducers can be connected *in series* (where the output of one circuit is the input for the next), which allows us to study systems of different size but with similar behavior. For these circuits, computation terminates when a state is reached where no further reactions are possible (this is also the case for the example from Fig. 1). As an additional requirement, certain reactive species denoted by $S_r \subseteq S$ must be

---

[6] For the bit-vector state encoding described in Sec. 3.1, the preclusion of overflows must be included as part of the constraints from Eqn. (5).

fully consumed throughout the computation but for some system designs this is not always the case [15]. We distinguish between "good" and "bad" termination states depending on the presence of reactive species and express the property of interest using standard temporal logic operators [21] as

$$AG(\neg bad) \wedge EF(good).$$

Formally, for a state $q \in Q$, we define

$$good(q) \leftrightarrow \bigwedge_{r \in \mathcal{R}} \neg enabled(r, q) \wedge \bigwedge_{s \in \mathcal{S}_r} s \notin q$$

$$bad(q) \leftrightarrow \bigwedge_{r \in \mathcal{R}} \neg enabled(r, q) \wedge \bigvee_{s \in \mathcal{S}_r} s \in q.$$

Using the constraints derived in Sec. 3.2, the feasibility of "good" and "bad" termination states can be analyzed. We search for a state q_g (resp. q_b) where

$$good(q_g) \wedge invariant(q_g) \tag{7}$$
$$bad(q_b) \wedge invariant(q_b) \tag{8}$$

When an unsatisfiable result is obtained for the formula from Eqn. (7) (resp. Eqn. (8)), the existence of a "good" (resp. "bad") state can be ruled out, and otherwise, a specific termination state q_g (resp. q_b) can be extracted from the model generated by the SMT solver. The constraints derived in Sec. 3.2 over-approximate the reachable states of a DSD circuit, which can only allow us to show that no reachable states with certain properties (e.g. "good" or "bad" states) exists. Identifying states q_g or q_b through this procedure, on the other hand, does not guarantee their reachability. To complete the analysis, we test the reachability of "good" and "bad" states using Bounded Model Checking (BMC) [5]. A "bad" state is reachable through K reactions or less if a trace $q_0, \ldots, q_K$ can be identified where q_0 is the initial state and

$$\bigvee_{k=0}^{K} bad(q_k) \wedge \bigwedge_{k=0}^{K-1} [T(q_k, q_{k+1}) \vee bad(q_k)] \tag{9}$$

while a similar procedure is used to search for reachable "good" states. If (9) is unsatisfiable, a "bad" ("good") state is not reachable by executing K reactions or less but increasing K might lead to the identification of such states.

Besides increasing the number of transducers, system complexity can also be controlled by including multiple copies of the circuit [15], which amounts to changing the number of molecules available in the initial state (e.g. $q_0' = mq_0$ for a system with m copies), while the set of species and reactions remain the same. This can make analysis more challenging as the length of computation traces increases. Once a reachable "bad" state q_b is identified in a system, we show that such a state is also reachable for multiple copy systems by proving that no reactions are enabled in state $q' = mq_b$. State q' can be reached in a multi-copy system if each sub-system was to independently reach state q_b.

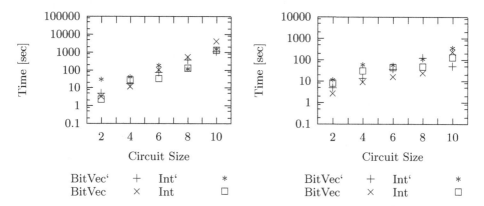

Fig. 2. Computation times for the identification of traces of lengths up to $K = 100$ in the flawed transducer circuits such that a "good" state (left panel) or a "bad" state (right panel) is reached (note the difference in scales). BitVec' and BitVec (resp. Int' and Int) indicate a bit-vector (resp. integer) encoding with or without the additional constraints from Sec. 3.2 asserted for each state $q_0, \ldots, q_{K-1}$ in (9).

We applied the procedure described in this section to DSD circuits consisting of between $n = 2, \ldots, 10$ transducers in series where all transducers were based on one of two different designs (a flawed and a corrected one). These circuits were found to include $|\mathcal{S}| = 14n + 4$ species and $|\mathcal{R}| = 8n$ reactions and, when the bit-vector encoding was used, a state was encoded as a bit-vector of size 64 (resp. 70) for the flawed (resp. corrected) circuit of size $n = 2$ and 576 (resp. 342) for $n = 10$. For the flawed system design, both "good" and "bad" states were identified using Eqns. (7) and (8) while for the corrected design only "good" termination states were possible. For each of the investigated circuits (encoded either using integers or bit-vectors) computation[7] required under 1 sec.

To confirm the reachability of states we searched for traces with depth up to $K = 100$, which was sufficient to identify computation traces leading to both "good" and "bad" states for flawed transducer circuits of different size (Fig. 2) and "good" states for the corrected one (Fig. 3-left)(the existence of "bad" states for these circuits was already ruled out). For the corrected transducers, we show that the additional constraints from Sec. 3.2 allow us to rule out the possibility of "bad" states, even for systems with many copies of the circuit (Fig. 3-right).

4   Synthetic Gene Circuits

In the field of synthetic biology, engineering principles are applied to redesign genetic networks with the goal of constructing biological systems with specific

---

[7] All computational results were obtained using the Z3 (version 4.1) theorem prover [8] on 2.5 Ghz Intel L5420 CPU machines with a 2GB memory limit per benchmark.

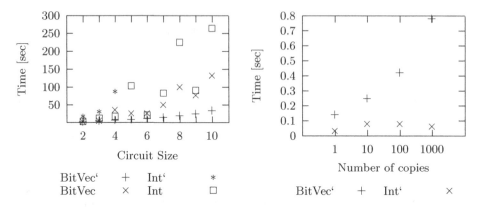

Fig. 3. Computation times for the identification of traces of lengths up to $K = 100$ in the corrected transducer circuits (left panel) and the verification of multiple copies of a circuit with ten transducers based on the corrected design (right panel). BitVec' and BitVec (resp. Int' and Int) indicate a bit-vector (resp. integer) encoding with or without the additional constraints from Sec. 3.2. For the integer encoding with the additional constraints, the memory limit was reached for circuits of size five and up during the identification of traces (left panel).

behavior (see [22] for a review). The construction of biological *devices* (relatively small gene networks which can serve as basic building-blocks) has been pursued initially and tools and programming languages to support this process have been developed (*e.g.* [19]). The construction of larger-scale systems from devices presents a challenging design problem [22], where chemical species serving as "wires" must be matched to ensure proper function and other constraints must also be satisfied (*e.g.* if the same species is an output of two separate devices in a circuit, cross-talk might occur), while in addition, specific system behavior must be obtained. The development of computational tools enabling the automated design of systems from expressive specification of the desired behavior and capable of handling the complexities of the problem can address these challenges. In the following, we formalize the constraints specific to the synthesis problem of designing a gene network with certain behavior from a library of devices and propose an SMT-based solution.

A device d is a tuple $d = (I_d, S_d, F_d)$ where I_d and S_d are finite sets of input and internally produced (output) species such that $I_d \cap S_d = \emptyset$ and $F_d = \{f_d^s \mid s \in S_d\}$ is a set of update functions (f_d^s is the update function for species s). We capture the dynamics of a device as a Boolean network - a popular formalism for modeling interaction networks [7]. In a Boolean network each species is described as available or not, thus its exact concentration (number of molecules) is abstracted (unlike the DSD formalism we described in Sec. 3). We treat a device d as a transition system $\mathcal{T}_d = (Q_d, Q_{d0}, T_d)$ where $q \in Q_d$ captures which species are available in the system (in the following, we use $q(s) \in \mathbb{B}$ as a Boolean, indicating whether species s is available in state q) and $Q_{d0} = Q_d$ (*i.e.* all states are initial). The dynamics of the system are given by the functions

Table 1. Additional constraints for constructing systems from gene network devices

Constraints	Description
$\bigwedge_{s \in S} \bigwedge_{d, d' \in D_s, d \neq d'} \neg (D(d) \wedge D(d'))$	To prevent cross-talk, two devices producing the same species are never selected at the same time.
$\bigwedge_{s \in I} \bigvee_{d \in D_s} D(d)$	All species specified as input serve as inputs to a selected device.
$\bigwedge_{s \in O} \bigvee_{d \in D^s} D(d)$	All species specified as output are produced by a selected device.
$\bigwedge_{d \in D} \left(D(d) \rightarrow \bigwedge_{s \in S_d \setminus O} \bigvee_{d' \in D_s} D(d') \right)$	To prevent the production of species that do not serve any function, all species produced by a selected device are outputs of the circuit or serve as input to another selected device.
$\bigwedge_{d \in D} \left(D(d) \rightarrow \bigwedge_{s \in I_d \setminus I} \bigvee_{d' \in D^s} D(d') \right)$	All species serving as inputs to a selected device are inputs of the circuit or are produced by another selected device in order to ensure that all device inputs are part of the system.

$f_d^s : Q_d \rightarrow \mathbb{B}$ where, for states $q, q' \in Q_d$, the *synchronous* transition relation (where all species are updated at each time step) is defined as

$$T(q, q') \leftrightarrow \left(\bigwedge_{s \in S_d} q'(s) = f_d^s(q) \right) \tag{10}$$

Note that $\mathcal{T}_d$ is finite and non-deterministic: while each species $s \in S_d$ is updated deterministically, there are no restrictions on the dynamics of species from I_d.

Given a set of devices $\mathcal{D} = \{d_0, \ldots, d_n\}$ we define the set of species $\mathcal{S} = \bigcup_{d \in \mathcal{D}} (I_d \cup S_d)$. A specification of some required system behavior is given over the dynamics of a set of input and output species denoted by $I \subseteq \mathcal{S}$ and $O \subseteq \mathcal{S}$ where $I \cap O = \emptyset$ and $I \cap (\bigcup_{d \in \mathcal{D}} S_d) = \emptyset$. Our goal is to select a subset of devices $D \subseteq \mathcal{D}$ where $D(d) \in \mathbb{B}$ indicates whether device d is used as part of the system. Let $D_s = \{d \in \mathcal{D} \mid s \in S_d\}$ denote the set of devices producing species s and $D^s = \{d \in \mathcal{D} \mid s \in I_d\}$ denote the set of devices using s as an input. We construct the transition system $\mathcal{T} = (Q, Q_0, T)$ where $q(s) \in \mathbb{B}$ indicates the availability of species $s \in \mathcal{S}$ and $Q_0 = Q$. The following constraints are asserted for all valid system states

$$\forall q \in Q, \bigwedge_{s \in S \setminus I} \left((\bigwedge_{d \in D_s} \neg D(d)) \rightarrow \neg q(s) \right) \tag{11}$$

In other words, a species s that is not produced by any device is never available in valid states of the system, unless $s \in I$. To prevent cross-talk between devices and obtain a smaller solution (*e.g.* where devices that produce unnecessary species are never included), we impose the additional constraints described in Table 1 (note that only the cross-talk constraint is required to avoid contradictions in the following definition). The transition relation of $\mathcal{T}$ is defined as

$$T(q, q') \leftrightarrow \left(\bigwedge_{s \in \mathcal{S}} q'(s) = f_d^s(q_d) \right) \qquad (12)$$

where q_d denotes the part of state q relevant for device d (i.e. describing species from $I_d \cup S_d$). With the exception of the inputs I, the system is deterministic.

For this problem, a bit-vector encoding is appropriate due to the Boolean structure of the system. For an individual device d we have $Q_d = \mathbb{B}^{|I_d|+|S_d|}$ where each $f_d^s \in F_d$ is a function $f_d^s : \mathbb{B}^{|I_d|+|S_d|} \to \mathbb{B}$. For the overall system, we have $Q = \mathbb{B}^{|\mathcal{S}|}$ where T is a function $\mathbb{B}^{|\mathcal{S}|} \times \mathbb{B}^{|\mathcal{S}|} \to \mathbb{B}$. We use a bit-vector $D \in \mathbb{B}^{|\mathcal{D}|}$ to encode the set of selected devices. Given a device d, q_d can be encoded using appropriate bit-vector extraction and concatenation to select the species from $\mathcal{S} \cap (I_d \cup S_d)$, which allows the application of functions from F_d.

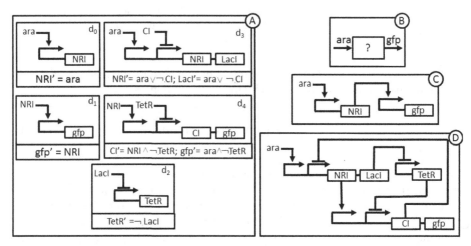

Fig. 4. A library of devices ($\mathcal{D} = \{d_0, \ldots, d_4\}$) is represented graphically in (A). Individual devices are specified by their input and output species (e.g. arabinose (ara) and the protein CI are the inputs of device d_3, while NRI and LacI are its outputs), together with a Boolean update function for each species. For example, species LacI is available in the next state (indicated by LacI') only if arabinose is available in the current state and the repressor CI is not (positive and negative regulation is represented by pointed or flat arrows). We seek a circuit with an arabinose input and green fluorescent protein (gfp) output (B) which is capable of oscillations and stabilization and satisfies the constraints discussed in Sec. 4. Our procedure identifies the solutions shown in (C, where $D = \{d_0, d_1\}$) and (D, where $D = \{d_2, d_3, d_4\}$) but only the solution from (D) has the desired dynamic behavior.

The characterization of device behavior and the construction of device libraries is currently an ongoing effort in synthetic biology. Therefore, we consider a hypothetical device library (Fig. 4-A) constructed from frequently-used components [22] to demonstrate the proposed approach. The Boolean update rules we use as an illustration abstract the detailed gene regulation behavior which has been observed and engineered experimentally. Our goal in this example is to design a circuit with the input/output characteristics shown in Fig. 4-B. In addition, we require that it is possible for the output gfp to oscillate for one value of the input ara and stabilize for the other. Two possible solutions satisfying all constraints from Table 1 were identified (Fig. 4-C,D). However, this alone does not guarantee that their dynamical properties are consistent with the required behavior. We specify two paths of the system $q_0, \ldots q_K$ and $q'_0, \ldots, q'_K$ with the properties that $\bigvee_{i=1}^{K} q_i(\mathrm{ara}) = q_0(\mathrm{ara})$, $\bigvee_{i=1}^{K} q'_i(\mathrm{ara}) = q'_0(\mathrm{ara})$ and $q_0(\mathrm{ara}) \neq q'_0(\mathrm{ara})$ (*i.e.* a different, constant input signal is applied in each case), $q_{K-1} = q_K$ (in the first case, the circuit stabilizes) and $\bigvee_{i=0}^{K-1}(q'_i = q'_K \wedge \bigvee_{j=i+1}^{K-1} q'_j(\mathrm{gfp}) \neq q'_K(\mathrm{gfp}))$ (in the second case, the circuits oscillates between multiple states where the value of gfp changes). These additional constraints eliminate the device from Fig.4-C as a possible solution, while the device from Fig.4-D is still identified as a candidate (overall, the solution was found in under 1 sec). Besides specifying behavior that the system must be capable of (*i.e.* the existence of trajectories with certain properties), specification of properties that all system trajectories must satisfy are also supported in our approach through the use of quantifiers.

5   Related Work

The application of formal methods to biology has already received attention (*e.g.* [6], among others) but here we focus specifically on biological engineering applications where formal specifications and analysis can supplement computational modeling and simulation to enable the computer-aided design of larger, more reliable systems. DNA circuits have been studied using stochastic simulation, or more recently, using probabilistic model checking [15], which also allows properties regarding the time required for computation or the probability of failure to be expressed. In synthetic biology, computational design platforms exists to target the construction of devices [29,19], while formal specifications have also been considered [30]. Here we focus on the problem of combining devices into systems, while satisfying additional design constraints, including desired system behavior. This problem is related to the synthesis of software programs from components [10] - here we formalize features of the biological design process and address this problem using SMT-based methods.

The Petri-net formalism [11] can naturally describe some properties of the DNA circuits from Sec. 3. The application of formal methods to Petri-nets has been studied extensively, and in the future, relevant analysis procedures can be adapted to the problems we consider. More specifically, the computation of invariants for Petri-nets has been studied as an analysis strategy (*e.g.* in the context of biology [26]). This problem is related to the computation we describe in Sec. 3.2 but here we derive constraints directly from the known composition of DNA species, while for Petri-nets such information is not available and invariants are computed from the network structure (*e.g.* through its incidence matrix [11]). Since the structure of species also determines the possible reactions between them combining these approaches is an interesting future direction.

6 Discussion and Future Work

Our approach is general and suitable for the analysis of biological models beyond the applications discussed in this paper. For example, with the exception of the additional species properties we exploit in Sec. 3.2, DSD circuits can be viewed as general Chemical Reaction Networks (CRNs) and therefore such systems might be analyzed using the proposed methods. Furthermore, the Boolean networks we use in Sec. 4 are a popular modeling formalisms for biological interaction networks (such as gene regulation, and signaling networks) as studied in the field of systems biology. A number of realistic models have been constructed based on this formalism, including large-scale (approaching whole-cell) regulatory and metabolic reconstructions [24] where our methods can help address challenging analysis problems. Besides providing analysis capabilities within tools such as Visual DSD [16], the discussed methods are also available as an online tool at [2].

The expressivity, scalability and extensibility of SMT, together with its model generation capabilities, which served for the identification of (counter)examples in this work but can also allow synthesis applications in the future, were the major consideration during the development of our methods. Our choice of bit-vectors as a specific theory of interest was motivated by the availability of recently developed efficient decision procedures, which allow the use of quantifiers [28]. The investigation of the integer and bit-vector representations we propose on a larger set of benchmarks is a direction of future work.

In Sec. 3 we assume that all species and reactions of a DSD circuit can be generated *a priory* (*e.g.* using Visual DSD [16]), which is often the case for circuits of practical interest with some notable exceptions [14], which might still be approached using SMT (*e.g.* through the use of recursive datatypes [18]). When a sufficient number of molecules is present in chemical and biological systems, species concentrations can be described as continuous values (*e.g.* using (non-linear) ODEs) [7], which is also a common description of the synthetic gene networks studied in Sec. 4. Such systems, as well as other infinite-state, continuous and hybrid models used in biology, can be encoded directly into SMT and analyzed using recently developed decision procedures [13]. As an alternative, (conservative) finite transition system abstractions can be constructed (*e.g.* as in [30]) to enable the SMT-based analysis of such systems.

In the modeling of biological systems, capturing individual molecules numbers (as in Sec. 3) can provide detailed and biologically accurate system descriptions, which are often difficult to analyze. Constructing (finite) transition system representations as in Sec. 3 allows us to express important properties (*e.g.* reachability) with such level of detail, which is important for applications such as DNA computing. Currently, we ignore all probabilistic aspects of these systems (which arise, for example, when reaction rates are considered) but SMT reasoning procedures for probabilistic systems (*e.g.* [9]) can help address some of the current limitations and extend our approach to other model classes (*e.g.* probabilistic Boolean networks). For challenging areas such as probabilistic SMT, it seems natural to explore biological applications for motivation and as a source of benchmarks that can help drive the development of novel methods.

7 Conclusion

As a step towards the development of an SMT-based analysis framework for studying biological computation that is scalable and supports a wide set of models and specifications, in this paper we focus on problems related to the engineering of biological systems, as part of the emerging fields of DNA computation and synthetic biology. We show that for a number of applications in these domains, transition systems capture important behavior and can be analyzed together with relevant specifications and additional constraints through SMT-based methods in an efficient manner, going beyond what was possible using other techniques. Our approach is general and is currently being applied to other biological models and formalisms. This work highlights biological engineering as a domain that can benefit extensively from the application of formal methods, while the biological complexity can also motivate the development of novel analysis methods.

References

1. Satisfiability modulo theories competition, `http://www.smtcomp.org/2012/`
2. Z34bio at `rise4fun` - software engineering tools from MSR (2012), `http://rise4fun.com/z34biology`
3. Adleman, L.: Molecular computation of solutions to combinatorial problems. Science 266(5187), 1021–1024 (1994)
4. Benenson, Y., Gil, B., Ben-Dor, U., Adar, R., Shapiro, E.: An autonomous molecular computer for logical control of gene expression. Nature 429(6990), 423–429 (2004)
5. Biere, A., Cimatti, A., Clarke, E., Zhu, Y.: Symbolic model checking without BDDs. In: Cleaveland, W.R. (ed.) TACAS 1999. LNCS, vol. 1579, pp. 193–207. Springer, Heidelberg (1999)
6. Chabrier-Rivier, N., Chiaverini, M., Danos, V., Fages, F., Schächter, V.: Modeling and querying biomolecular interaction networks. Theoretical Computer Science 325(1), 25–44 (2004)
7. de Jong, H.: Modeling and simulation of genetic regulatory systems: A literature review. Journal of Computational Biology 9(1), 67–103 (2002)
8. de Moura, L., Bjørner, N.: Z3: An efficient SMT solver. In: Ramakrishnan, C.R., Rehof, J. (eds.) TACAS 2008. LNCS, vol. 4963, pp. 337–340. Springer, Heidelberg (2008)
9. Fränzle, M., Hermanns, H., Teige, T.: Stochastic satisfiability modulo theory: A novel technique for the analysis of probabilistic hybrid systems. In: Egerstedt, M., Mishra, B. (eds.) HSCC 2008. LNCS, vol. 4981, pp. 172–186. Springer, Heidelberg (2008)
10. Gulwani, S., Jha, S., Tiwari, A., Venkatesan, R.: Synthesis of loop-free programs. SIGPLAN Not. 46, 62–73 (2011)
11. Heiner, M., Gilbert, D., Donaldson, R.: Petri Nets for Systems and Synthetic Biology. In: Bernardo, M., Degano, P., Zavattaro, G. (eds.) SFM 2008. LNCS, vol. 5016, pp. 215–264. Springer, Heidelberg (2008)
12. Horn, F., Jackson, R.: General mass action kinetics. Archive for Rational Mechanics and Analysis 47(2) (1972)

13. Jovanović, D., de Moura, L.: Solving Non-linear Arithmetic. In: Gramlich, B., Miller, D., Sattler, U. (eds.) IJCAR 2012. LNCS, vol. 7364, pp. 339–354. Springer, Heidelberg (2012)

14. Lakin, M.R., Phillips, A.: Modelling, simulating and verifying turing-powerful strand displacement systems. In: Cardelli, L., Shih, W. (eds.) DNA 17. LNCS, vol. 6937, pp. 130–144. Springer, Heidelberg (2011)

15. Lakin, M.R., Parker, D., Cardelli, L., Kwiatkowska, M., Phillips, A.: Design and analysis of DNA strand displacement devices using probabilistic model checking. Journal of the Royal Society, Interface 9(72), 1470–1485 (2012)

16. Lakin, M.R., Youssef, S., Polo, F., Emmott, S., Phillips, A.: Visual DSD: a design and analysis tool for DNA strand displacement systems. Bioinformatics 27(22), 3211–3213 (2011)

17. Langhoff, S., Rothschild, L., Cumbers, J., Paavola, C., Worden, P.: Workshop Report on What are the Potential Roles for Synthetic Biology in NASA's Mission? Technical report (2012)

18. Milicevic, A., Kugler, H.: Model checking using SMT and theory of lists. In: Bobaru, M., Havelund, K., Holzmann, G.J., Joshi, R. (eds.) NFM 2011. LNCS, vol. 6617, pp. 282–297. Springer, Heidelberg (2011)

19. Pedersen, M., Phillips, A.: Towards programming languages for genetic engineering of living cells. J. R. Soc. Interface 6(suppl. 4), S437–S450 (2009)

20. Phillips, A., Cardelli, L.: A programming language for composable DNA circuits. Journal of the Royal Society, Interface 6(suppl. 4), S419–S436 (2009)

21. Pnueli, A.: The temporal logic of programs. In: 18th Annual Symposium on Foundations of Computer Science (FOCS 1977), pp. 46–57. IEEE (1977)

22. Purnick, P.E., Weiss, R.: The second wave of synthetic biology: from modules to systems. Nature Reviews. Molecular Cell Biology 10(6) (2009)

23. Qian, L., Winfree, E.: Scaling up digital circuit computation with DNA strand displacement cascades. Science 332(6034), 1196–1201 (2011)

24. Samal, A., Jain, S.: The regulatory network of E. coli metabolism as a boolean dynamical system exhibits both homeostasis and flexibility of response. BMC Systems Biology 2(1), 21 (2008)

25. Seelig, G., Soloveichik, D., Zhang, D.Y., Winfree, E.: Enzyme-free nucleic acid logic circuits. Science 314(5805), 1585–1588 (2006)

26. Soliman, S.: Finding minimal P/T-invariants as a CSP. In: Proceedings of the fourth Workshop on Constraint Based Methods for Bioinformatics WCB, vol. 8 (2008)

27. Soloveichik, D., Seelig, G., Winfree, E.: DNA as a universal substrate for chemical kinetics. Proceedings of the National Academy of Sciences of the United States of America 107(12), 5393–5398 (2010)

28. Wintersteiger, C., Hamadi, Y., de Moura, L.: Efficiently solving quantified bit-vector formulas. In: FMCAD, pp. 239–246 (2010)

29. Yaman, F., Bhatia, S., Adler, A., Densmore, D., Beal, J.: Automated Selection of Synthetic Biology Parts for Genetic Regulatory Networks. ACS Synthetic Biology 1(8), 332–344 (2012)

30. Yordanov, B., Belta, C.: A formal verification approach to the design of synthetic gene networks. In: IEEE Conference on Decision and Control and European Control Conference, pp. 4873–4878. IEEE (2011)

31. Zhang, F., Rodriguez, S., Keasling, J.D.: Metabolic engineering of microbial pathways for advanced biofuels production. Current Opinion in Biotechnology 22(6), 775–783 (2011)

Freshness and Reactivity Analysis in Globally Asynchronous Locally Time-Triggered Systems

Frédéric Boniol[1], Michaël Lauer[2], Claire Pagetti[1], and Jérôme Ermont[3]

[1] ONERA-Toulouse, France
{frederic.boniol,claire.pagetti}@onera.fr
[2] Ecole Polytechnique de Montréal, Canada
michael.lauer@polymtl.ca
[3] IRIT-ENSEEIHT, University of Toulouse, France
jerome.ermont@enseeiht.fr

Abstract. Critical embedded systems are often designed as a set of real-time tasks, running on shared computing modules, and communicating through networks. Because of their critical nature, such systems have to meet timing properties. To help the designers to prove the correctness of their system, the real-time systems community has developed numerous approaches for analyzing the worst case times either on the processors (e.g. worst case execution time of a task) or on the networks (e.g. worst case traversal time of a message). However, there is a growing need to consider the complete system and to be able to determine end-to-end properties. Such properties apply to a functional chain which describes the behavior of a sequence of functions, not necessarily hosted on a shared module, from an input until the production of an output. This paper explores two end-to-end properties: freshness and reactivity, and presents an analysis method based on Mixed Integer Linear Programming (MILP). This work is supported by the French National Research Agency within the Satrimmap project[1].

Keywords: Real-time systems, embedded systems, end-to-end analysis.

1 Introduction

Nowadays, distributed embedded systems are widely used in domains such as nuclear power, defense or transportation. For instance in the transportation domain, a highly critical function hosted by such a system is X-by-wire, where "X" can be drive, brake or fly. Typically, such a function has to meet hard real-time requirements. In this paper, we focus on the formal verification of two kinds of requirements: (1) end-to-end freshness, i.e. the worst age of an output of the system with respect to its related input, and (2) end-to-end reactivity, i.e. the minimal duration an input must be present in order to impact an output of the system. For instance, at any time the orders given by a fly-by-wire control system to the

---

[1] Safety and time critical middleware for future modular avionics platforms:
http://www.irit.fr/satrimmap/

G. Brat, N. Rungta, and A. Venet (Eds.): NFM 2013, LNCS 7871, pp. 93–107, 2013.
© Springer-Verlag Berlin Heidelberg 2013

flight surfaces of an aircraft must be related to an aerodynamic situation not older than 200 ms. In the same way, any gust of wind longer than 100 ms must be taken into account by the system. However, because of the distributed nature of the fly-by-wire control function, and because of their increasing complexity, analyzing end-to-end properties becomes a challenge for realistic systems.

The aim of this article is to answer this challenge. More precisely, we present a scalable method for formally analyzing end-to-end worst case freshness and re-activity in distributed systems composed of time-triggered tasks communicating through an asynchronous network. Note that we use the term worst in order to designate the least favorable value. For instance, for the freshness property in the context of this paper, it refers to the oldest output, i.e. the less fresh.

1.1 Globally Asynchronous Locally Time-Triggered Systems

Critical embedded systems are often composed of tasks statically scheduled on shared computing resources and communicating through a shared network. This is the case for modern aircraft such as the Airbus A380 or the Boeing B787. These embedded systems follow the IMA standard (Integrated Modular Avionics) [ARI97]. The scheduling on each computing module is time-triggered, meaning that each task periodically executes at fixed and predetermined time intervals. However, in order to avoid the use of complex synchronization pro-tocols, modules are globally asynchronous. Such systems can be considered as Globally Asynchronous and Locally Time-Triggered (GALTT).

In the following we consider GALTT systems composed of N periodic tasks $\Gamma = \{\tau_1, \ldots, \tau_N\}$ running on a set of m modules $\mathcal{M} = \{M_1, \ldots, M_m\}$ com-municating via a shared network. We note $\Gamma(M_i)$ the set of tasks hosted by module M_i. An avionics case study of a GALTT system is given in section 3. The assumptions made for the system under analysis are:

Modules: Each module M_i is characterized by a period H_i, i.e., the hyper-period of the tasks running on the module. The hyper-period is the least common multiple of the hosted tasks periods, $H_i = lcm(\tau_j)_{\tau_j \in \Gamma_i}$.

Tasks: Each task $\tau_j \in \Gamma(M_i)$ is characterized by a set of jobs $\tau_j(k)$ for $k = 0 \ldots n_j$. $\tau_j(k)$ is the kth job of the task τ_j in the period of M_i. Each job is characterized by an interval $[b_j(k), e_j(k)]$ where $b_j(k)$ is the beginning date of the job, and $e_j(k)$ is the ending date. These dates are relative to the beginning of the period of the module M_i. A task is used to model the time required by a software task, a sensor or an actuator.

Communication: Tasks communicate in an asynchronous way. Each job $\tau_j(k)$ consumes input data arrived between $b_j(k)$ and $b_j(k-1)$. Inputs received after the beginning of the job will be consumed by the next job. Moreover, if two (or more) instances of the same input are received before the beginning of the job, only the last instance is memorized. The previous values are lost. Conversely, if no new input arrives, the task reuses the last received input. Each job produces output data at any time during its execution, meaning during interval $[b_j(k), e_j(k)]$.

Global Asynchronism: Finally, we suppose that the modules $\mathcal{M}$ are globally asynchronous, i.e., they can be shifted by an arbitrary amount of time. Nevertheless, these offsets are supposed constant.

In the paper, we do not take into account any drift between the clocks of the module. Although clock drift is a major issue in synchronized systems where a shared time reference needs to be established, in asynchronous systems, by definition, such time reference is not required. Still, the discrepancies in clock frequencies which cause the clock drift could have an impact in our analysis. Some modules could run a little faster (or slower). This may modify the actual tasks periods and executions times. However, worst case freshness or reactivity are usually measured in hundreds of ms. A high-quality quartz typically used in avionics systems is assumed to lose at most 10^8 seconds per second. Hence, clock drift could not significantly impact our results. To the best of our knowledge, it is an implicit assumption in every performance evaluation papers dealing with asynchronous systems.

1.2   The Addressed Problem: Verification of End-to-End Properties

As previously said, embedded systems must satisfy real-time properties. In general, the real-time analysis is decomposed in three steps: (1) verification of the temporal behavior of each task, which is done by proving that the worst case execution time (WCET) of each job is bounded inside its corresponding time interval, (2) evaluation of the network worst case traversal times (WCTT) for each message crossing the network, and (3) the combination of the last two analyses to verify end-to-end properties.

The first and second steps are already abundantly addressed in the literature [SAA$^+$04]. In this paper, we focus on the third step by considering two specific properties: end-to-end freshness and reactivity along a periodic functional chain. A periodic functional chain $\overset{in}{\rightarrow} \tau_n \overset{a_n}{\rightarrow} \ldots \tau_1 \overset{a_1}{\rightarrow} \tau_0 \overset{out}{\rightarrow}$ is a set of communicating tasks (including sensor and actuator tasks) such that each job of τ_n (for instance a sensor) periodically produces data a_n for τ_{n-1} from an external value in (for instance a physical parameter). τ_{n-1} then periodically produces $a_{n-1}\ldots$ upto a final task τ_0 (for instance an actuator) which delivers an output out (for instance a physical action). If the chain belongs to a critical real-time system, it has to meet a δ-freshness requirement: whenever an instance of o is observed or used by the environment, then it must be based on an instance of i acquired not earlier than δ time units before. For example, if o is the angle of a flight control surface (and τ_0 is the corresponding actuator), then it must be fresh enough with respect to the speed of the aircraft (i in that case).

The second property we are interested in is the reactivity to input changes. For instance, let us consider again the flight control system and let us imagine a gust of wind arrives in the front of the wings. In order to ensure a safe and comfortable flight, the system has to respond to any gust longer than $300ms$ by moving the ailerons. Put differently, it must be reactive to any gust of wind longer than $300ms$. More formally, if we consider again a periodic chain $\overset{in}{\rightarrow} \tau_n$

$\overset{a_n}{\rightarrow} \ldots \rightarrow \tau_0 \overset{out}{\rightarrow}$, the chain is said δ-reactive if any change on i longer than δ time units impacts o. In the previous example, if i is the measure of the external wind, then the flight control system must be $300ms$-reactive with respect to i.

The aim of this paper is to propose an efficient method for verifying δ-freshness and δ-reactivity requirements on GALTT systems.

1.3   Related Work

Latency and worst case response time analysis are already abundantly studied in the literature. The holistic approach ([TC94, Spu96]) has been introduced for analyzing worst case end-to-end response time of whole systems. The worst case scenario on each component visited by a functional chain is determined by taking into account the maximum possible jitter introduced by the component visited previously. This approach can be pessimistic as it considers worst case scenarios on every component, possibly leading to impossible scenarios. Indeed, a worst case scenario for a functional chain on a component does not generally result in a worst case scenario for this functional chain on any component visited after this component. Illustration of this pessimism is given in section 6.

The Real-Time Calculus [TCN00] (a variation of Network Calculus [LBT01]) has been proposed as an efficient method to determine worst case use of resources and latency in real-time systems. However, similarly to the holistic approach, worst case end-to-end latency is taken into account by adding the worst case delay of each component, which leads to pessimistic results.

Several methods, such as the *trajectory approach* [MM06] and the *Network Calculus* [LBT01] have been developed to deal with such over-approximations but can only be applied to the evaluation of network traversal time. A more recent work has been proposed in [BD12]. The authors suggest to extend the *Network Calculus* method in order to take into account the real-time scheduling in each computing modules connected to the network. The objective is to better characterize the communication traffic entering the network, in order to reduce the pessimism of the *Network Calculus*. However, the objective remains the evaluation of the worst case traversal time from an entry point to another one in the network. Thus these methods cannot be used on their own to compute real-time properties along functional chains. Nevertheless, as shown in section 3, they are part of the global evaluation method we propose in the following.

Upper-bounds of end-to-end properties in a networked embedded system have been proposed by [CB06]. Authors analyze the properties by modeling the functional chains and the networked architecture as a set of timed automata. In order to cope with the combinatorial explosion, they propose several abstractions. However, this work suffers from two shortcomings with respect to our objective: (1) the proposed model does not take into account the real-time behavior and scheduling of the modules, and (2) the abstractions are not efficient enough to cope with realistic systems.

Furthermore, these works are strongly focused on latency properties and do not consider more elaborate properties like freshness and reactivity.

1.4   Contribution

To the best of our knowledge, the study of freshness and reactivity properties is relatively sparse in the literature. We proposed in [LBEP11] a latency
and a freshness analysis method for a specific class of embedded systems called
Integrated Modular Avionics (IMA), composed of computing modules holding
strictly periodic tasks (i.e., composed only of one job per period). In the current
paper, we extend this work in two directions: firstly we consider more general
GALTT systems in which tasks can be composed of several jobs in the same period, and secondly we study the δ-reactivity property. As in [LBEP11], we show
that δ-freshness and δ-reactivity properties can be still modeled as a Mixed Integer Linear Program (MILP). And we show on an industrial case study that
this analysis method is scalable enough with respect to realistic systems.

2   An Avionics Case-Study

Let us consider an avionics case study depicted in Figure 1. This case study is a
part of a flight control system (FCS).

System Description. The functional chain under analysis can be summerized
as follows: the *Air sensor* periodically measures the total air pressure outside
the aircraft (TP_{ana}). This analog value is digitalized (TP_{dig}) and transmitted
through a *Remote Data Concentrator* RDC_{adr} to the *Air Data Reference function* (ADR). The ADR computes the speed of the aircraft ($speed_1$) and sends
it to the *Intertial function* (IR) which consolidates the data with data from an
inertial sensor. The consolidated speed ($speed_2$) is then returned to the ADR
for validation which sends the final speed value ($speed_3$) to the *Flight controller*
(*FlightCntrl*). It computes the angle (θ_{dig}) which must by applied to the aileron.
This last data is transmitted to the aileron actuator (*Aileron*) through RDC_{fc}.
Finally, *Aileron* transforms the digital data θ_{dig} into a physical angle (θ_{ana}).
This functional chain is formalized as $\mathcal{F} = \overset{TP_\phi}{\to} Air\_sensor \overset{TP_{dig}}{\to} RDC_{adr} \overset{TP_{dig}}{\to}$
$ADR \overset{speed_1}{\to} IR \overset{speed_2}{\to} ADR \overset{speed_3}{\to} FlightCntrl \overset{\theta_{dig}}{\to} RDC_{fc} \overset{\theta_{dig}}{\to} Aileron \overset{\theta_{ana}}{\to}$. The
architecture of the system and the real-time parameters are depicted in figure 1.

System Requirements. The chain $\mathcal{F}$ must satisfy the requirements:

– *(200ms)-freshness:* at any time, the aileron angle θ must correspond to
  a total air pressure measured at most $200ms$ before. This is illustrated in
  figure 2 and analyzed in section 4.
– *(300ms)-reactivity:* any variation of air pressure longer than $300ms$ must
  reflect on the angle applied to the aileron. This is analyzed in section 5.

3   The Analysis Approach: Overview

The analysis method is based on two steps: (1) simplification of the system by
abstracting the network with a set of timed channels, and (2) evaluation of the
worst case end-to-end freshness (WCF) or worst case end-to-end reactivity.

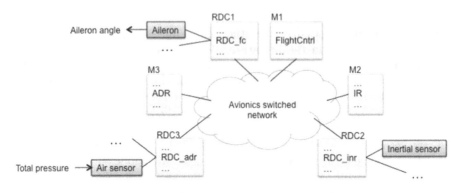

Fig. 1. Case-study: a flight control subsystem

Task	number of jobs	jobs time interval (in ms)	module & period (in ms)
ADR	2	[0,10], [25,35]	M3, 40
IR	1	[10,20]	M2, 30
$FlightCntrk$	4	[0,4], [10,14], [20,24], [30,34]	M1, 40
RDC_{adr}	1	[3,4]	RDC3, 5
RDC_{ir}	1	[5,6]	RDC2, 10
RDC_{fc}	2	[3,4], [15,16]	RDC1, 20

sensor/actuator	job time interval (in ms)	production/action period (in ms)
$Air\ sensor$	[0,1]	5
$Aileron$	[0,1]	5

First step: abstraction of the network The combinatorial complexity of the verification of real-time properties takes its root in the asynchronism of the modules,
and indeterministic congestion in the network. We showed in [LEPB10] that taking into account all these factors in the evaluation of end-to-end properties is
intractable. However, in the area of distributed embedded systems, the traversal
time of each message through the network from one module to another one must
bounded. The complexity of our analysis method can be significantly reduced
by abstracting the network with a set of timed channels. In this setting, each
communication is abstracted with a channel characterized by a time interval
$[\delta_{min}, \delta_{max}]$, where δ_{min} (resp. δ_{max}) is the lower (resp. upper) bound of the
network traversal time along the path. As said in section 1.3, these bounds can
be determined with various formal methods, depending on the nature of the
network. For instance, the *trajectory approach* has been successfully applied to
switched embedded networks in [BSF09]. The *Network Calculus* [LBT01] method
has been extended to switched networks with several priorities level [SB12]. Similarly, [HHKG09, CB10, FFF11] propose methods for evaluating lower and upper
bounds of communication delays in other classical real-time networks such as
CAN, Flexray, and SpaceWire. Generally speaking, these methods involve the
communication path parameters (route in the network, throughput of the network nodes, maximum size of the messages allocated to the path,...), and they
associate each path with its minimal and maximal traversal time. We do not

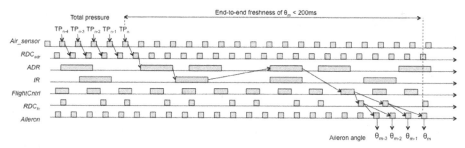

Fig. 2. A end-to-end freshness requirement in the flight control system

describe these analysis techniques in the following. Readers interested in worst case traversal times analysis are invited to consult the provided references.

By way of example, in the FCS case study we consider that each communication is abstracted by a timed channel $[1, 3]$ (in ms): each frame undergoes a delay between $1ms$ and $3ms$ to reach its destination. Note that this abstraction is an over-approximation because the bounds of the timed channels are determined with *Network Calculus*, which is an over-approximative technique. We discuss the significance of this point through experiments in section 6.

Second step: freshness and reactivity evaluation This second step constitutes the contribution of the article. It is based on an abstract model where the network and the communication paths are replaced by timed channels, and on linear programing. The idea is to characterize all the possible behaviors along a functional chain with a set of variables and constraints, and afterwards to determine the worst case scenario among all these possible behaviors with respect to the property under analysis. One of the advantage of this approach is that finding the worst case scenario can be done automatically by a solver.

4 Worst-Case End-to-End Freshness Analysis

As previously stated, we model the behavior of each element by a set of variables and constraints. The behavior of the whole system is obtained as the conjunction of all these constraints. This defines a Mixed Integer Linear Program (MILP) which can be used to determine the worst case freshness of a functional chain. In the following, all variables used for offsets and dates are reals. All variables used to designate a specific hyper-period or a job are integers. Although not mandatory, we only use integers for parameters in order to improve readability.

4.1 Modeling

Module. Let M_i be a module. The only variable which characterizes M_i is its possible offset with respect to the other modules. Modules are asynchronous, thus the time origin of their execution frame may be shifted by an offset O_i. This offset may be arbitrary. However, as we are interested in the regular behavior, and not the specific case of the initialization phase, it is not necessary to consider offsets greater than the maximal hyper-period of the system. The first constraints for M_i are then:

$$O_i \in \mathbb{R}, \quad 0 \le O_i \le \max_{k=0...m} H_k$$

Task (Including Sensor and Actuator). Tasks are the only active objects of our modeling. Let τ_j be a task running on the module M_i. Let d be a data periodically produced by τ_j. The task τ_j is characterized by a set of jobs $\tau_j(k)$ for $k = 0 \ldots n_j$. $\tau_j(k)$ is the kth job of τ_j in the hyper-period H_i. Each job is characterized by a time interval $[b_j(k), e_j(k)]$. These dates are relative to the beginning of the current hyper-period which is itself relative to the start of module M_i. Then, if n is the number of the current hyper-period, the absolute time interval corresponding to the job $\tau_j(k)$ is $[O_i + nH_i + b_j(k), O_i + nH_i + e^j(k)]$.

Let us suppose that another task reads the output data d produced by τ_j at t_{read} (t_{read} is an absolute date). To evaluate the possible freshness of d at t_{read}, one has to determine which job has produced d. This job is characterized by its index k and the index n of its hyper-period satisfying the following constraints

$$O_i + nH_i + b_j(k) \le t_{read} < O_i + nH_i + e_j(k + 1)$$

for $k < n_j$, i.e., the job is not the last job of τ_j in the nth hyper-period, as shown in the figure 3(a). And

$$O_i + nH_i + b_j(n_j) \le t_{read} < O_i + (n + 1)H_i + e_j(0)$$

for $k = n_j$, i.e., the job is the last job of τ_j in the nth hyper-period, as shown in the figure 3(b). In other terms, in the first case (left part of the figure), if d is acquired after (the relative date) $b_j(k)$ and strictly before $e_j(k + 1)$, it is possibly produced by the kth job; indeed $\tau_j(k)$ may produce d anywhere in its time interval, then possibly at $O_i + nH_i + b_j(k)$, and similarly $\tau_j(k+1)$ may take all its time interval for producing a new data, then possibly at $O_i + nH_i + e_j(k+1)$. The second case is similar.

Then, if we consider all the jobs of τ_j, determining the job and the hyper-period producing d could be done simply by considering a set of boolean variables B_k $k = 0 \ldots n_j$ (one variable per job) such that one and only one B_k is true

$$\forall k = 0 \ldots n_j, \quad B_k \in \{0, 1\}, \quad \sum_{k=0...n_j} B_k = 1$$

and such that the two following constraints are true:

$$\begin{cases} t_{read} < O_i + nH_i + \sum_{k=0...(n_j-1)} B_k \cdot e_j(k + 1) + B_{n_j}(H_i + e_j(0)) \\ O_i + nH_i + \sum_{k=0...n_j} B_k \cdot b_j(k) \le t_{read} \end{cases}$$

For a given offset of the module O_i and for a given t_{read} (acquisition date of d), these two constraints determine a set of couples (n, k), i.e., a set of jobs which can produce d. Note that the solution is note unique because of the variation of the execution time of each job.

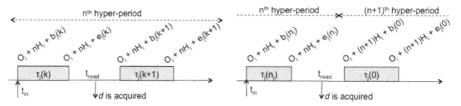

(a) first case: d is acquired between two jobs (b) second case: d is acquired between two from the same hyper-period   consecutive hyper-periods

Fig. 3. Rules determining which job has produced the data d acquired at t_{read}

Then, for any couple of hyper-period n, and job k, which respects the previous constraints, only one acquisition date (t_{in}) of the input related to the occurrence of d is acceptable. It it constrained by the beginning of the job:

$$t_{in} = O_i + nH_i + \sum_{k=0...n_j} B_k \cdot b_j(k)$$

Recall that only one of the B_k is true and denotes the job producing d; then $\sum_{k=0...n_j} B_k \cdot b_j(k)$ is the relative date at which the related input is acquired. The local freshness of d at time t_{read} is then $t_{read} - t_{in}$.

Communication through a Timed Channel. Let us now consider a timed channel characterized by a communication time in $[\delta_{min}, \delta_{max}]$ and a data d crossing that timed channel. If t_{before} and t_{after} are the input and the output dates of d from the channel, then t_{before} and t_{after} are related by

$$t_{after} - \delta_{max} \leq t_{before} \leq t_{after} - \delta_{min}$$

Communication through a Shared Memory. Tasks on a same module communicate through the local shared memory and requires no time. A shared memory is similar to a channel characterized by the interval $[0, 0]$:

$$t_{after} = t_{before}$$

4.2   Worst-Case Freshness on the Whole System

Let $\xrightarrow{in} \tau_n \xrightarrow{a_n} \dots \tau_1 \xrightarrow{a_1} \tau_0 \xrightarrow{out}$ be a functional chain. The model of this chain is simply obtained by connecting all the constraints of all the jobs and the communication involved in the chain. The set of constraints thus obtained forms a MILP. Let us note t_{out} a date at which the final output out is observed, and t_{in} the related acquisition date of the input parameter in. t_{out} and t_{in} are related by the set of the previous constraints. Then the freshness of out at t_{out} is

$$F = t_{out} - t_{in}$$

The worst case latency is obtained on a particular behavior maximizing F. This behavior can be found by using a MILP solver with the objective function:

$$maximize: F$$

4.3   Application to the Case-Study

Consider the functional chain in Figure 2. The global MILP model obtained for analyzing the worst case freshness of the chain is composed of 42 constraints and 43 variables. As an example, we only give here the beginning of the model, concerning the end of the chain, i.e., the actuator *Aileron*, and the communication task RDC_{fc} on RDC_1. The modeling language used in this listing is the one used for `lp_solve` [BEN04] input files.

```
max : t0 - t8 ;  // freshness expression to maximize

// Module offsets
OAileron <= 40; ORDC1 <= 40; OM1 <= 40; OM2 <= 40; OM3 <= 40; ORDC3 <= 40; OAir_sensor <= 40;

// Timed channels bounds
deltamin = 1; deltamax = 3;

// Aileron model where t0 is the date of the aileron angle
t0 < OAileron + 5 nAileron + 6; t0 >=  OAileron + 5 nAileron + 0;
t1 = OAileron + 5 nAileron + 0;

// From RDC_fc to Aileron
t1prime >= t1 - deltamax; t1prime <= t1 - deltamin;

// RDC_fc
t1prime < ORDC1 + 20 nRDC1 + 16 B1RDC_fc + 24 B2RDC_fc ;
t1prime >=  ORDC1 + 20 nRDC1 + 3 B1RDC_fc + 15 B2RDC_fc ;
B1RDC_fc <= 1 ; B2RDC_fc <= 1; B1RDC_fc + B2RDC_fc  = 1;
t2 = ORDC1 + 20 nRDC1 + 3 B1RDC_fc + 15 B2RDC_fc;

// From FlightCntrl to RDC_fc
t2prime >= t2 -deltamax; t2prime <= t2 - deltamin;
...
```

The MILP is solved with *lp_solve* in less than 1s on a 2.53 GHz processor. The maximal freshness returned for the case-study is 175ms. Hence, the system satisfies the (200ms)-freshness requirement.

5   Worst-Case End-to-End Reactivity Analysis

The second property we are interested in is the reactivity of a functional chain to an input signal. Let us consider again the case study figure 2. Imagine a gust of duration δms. The consequence of this gust is to suddenly increase the value of the total pressure at the input of the system. Let us suppose that for aerodynamical reasons the system has to react to any gust of duration δ is greater that 300ms; briefer gust may be ignored. Then one has to verify that it is never the case that all total pressure samples during any window greater than 300ms are lost (i.e., overwritten) somewhere in the chain, and then do not impact the aileron angle computation. For instance, in the scenario figure 2, samples TP_{n-4} to TP_{n-1} are overwritten by TP_n, and then are lost. The period of *Air_sensor* is 5ms. Then it comes directly from this scenario that the chain is not reactive to gusts of duration 20ms. The question is: can we determine the worst case end-to-end reactivity of this chain?

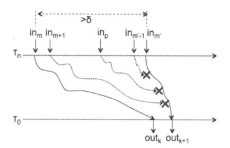

Fig. 4. a non δ-reactivity case

5.1   δ-Reactivity Modeling

Let us consider a functional chain $\overset{in}{\rightarrow} \tau_n \overset{a_n}{\rightarrow} \dots \tau_1 \overset{a_1}{\rightarrow} \tau_0 \overset{out}{\rightarrow}$. The chain is δ-reactive if and only if in any window $[t, t + \delta]$, at least one sample of in is related to a sample of out. Conversely, the chain is not δ-reactive if and only if they are two consecutive output samples out_k and out_{k+1} which depend respectively from two input samples in_m and $in_{m'}$ such that in_m and $in_{m'}$ are separated by more than δ time units. In that case, as shown in figure 4, any sample in_p acquired after in_m and before $in_{m'}$ is lost, overwritten by $in_{m'}$ somewhere in the chain.

Following this idea, a simple way to verify a chain is δ-reactive is:

1. *Consider two consecutive output samples out_k and out_{k+1}.* For the sake of simplicity, let us suppose that τ_0 is a task composed of only one job, an actuator of period T_0 for instance. As τ_0 is the last task in the chain, its processing time does not impact the reactivity. Thus, to simplify the evaluation of the reactivity of the chain, it is not necessary to consider dates of each sample out_k and out_{k+1}. It is sufficient to consider the beginning date of there respective jobs. Let t_0^k and t_0^{k+1} be these dates:

$$t_0^k = O_0 + k \cdot T_0 \text{ and } t_0^{k+1} = O_0 + (k + 1) \cdot T_0$$

   To generalize to task τ_0 composed of several jobs can be done simply by following the modeling presented in the previous section.
2. *Determine the dates t_n^m and $t_n^{m'}$,* i.e., the dates of the inputs related to o_k and o_{k+1} (i.e., in figure 4, in_m and $in_{m'}$). This analysis is done by using the constraints presented in the previous section.
3. *Determine the reactivity related to (out_k, out_{k+1})* as the difference between these two input dates: $reactivity(out_k, out_{k+1}) = t_n^{m'} - t_n^m$. The chain is then δ-reactive if

$$\forall k, \; reactivity(out_k, out_{k+1}) \leq \delta$$

As previously, the worst case reactivity is obtained on a particular behavior maximizing $reactivity(out_k, out_{k+1})$, for any k. This behavior can be found by using a MILP solver with the objective function: *maximize:* $t_n^{m'} - t_n^m$.

5.2   Application to the Case-Study

Consider the functional chain in Figure 2. The global MILP model obtained for analyzing the worst case reactivity of the chain is composed of 95 constraints and 75 variables. As an example, we only give here the beginning of the model, concerning the end of the chain, i.e., the actuator *Aileron*, and the communication task RDC_{fc} on RDC_1.

```
max : r8 - t8 ; // reactivity expression to maximize

// Offsets
OAileron <= 40; ORDC1 <= 40; OM1 <= 40; OM2 <= 40; OM3 <= 40; ORDC3 <= 40; OAir_sensor <= 40;

// Timed channels bounds
deltamin = 1; deltamax = 3;

// First sample at t0 produced by the job ntAileron
// *******************
// Aileron
t1 = OAileron + 5 ntAileron;

// From RDC_fc to Aileron
t1prime >= t1 - deltamax; t1prime <= t1 - deltamin;

// RDC_fc
t1prime <= ORDC1 + 20 ntRDC1 + 16 B1tRDC_fc + 24 B2tRDC_fc ;
t1prime >  ORDC1 + 20 ntRDC1 + 3 B1tRDC_fc + 15 B2tRDC_fc ;
B1tRDC_fc <= 1 ; B2tRDC_fc <= 1; B1tRDC_fc + B2tRDC_fc  = 1;
t2 = ORDC1 + 20 ntRDC1 + 3 B1tRDC_fc + 15 B2tRDC_fc;
...

// second sample at r0 produced by the job nrAileron
// *******************
// Aileron
nrAileron = ntAileron + 1 ;
r1 = OAileron + 5 nrAileron;

// From RDC_fc to Aileron
r1prime >= r1 - deltamax; r1prime <= r1 - deltamin;
r1prime >= t1prime ;

// RDC_fc
r1prime <= ORDC1 + 20 nrRDC1 + 16 B1rRDC_fc + 24 B2rRDC_fc ;
r1prime >  ORDC1 + 20 nrRDC1 + 3 B1rRDC_fc + 15 B2rRDC_fc ;
B1rRDC_fc <= 1 ; B2rRDC_fc <= 1; B1rRDC_fc + B2rRDC_fc  = 1;
r2 = ORDC1 + 20 nrRDC1 + 3 B1rRDC_fc + 15 B2rRDC_fc;
r2 >= t2 ;
...
```

The MILP is solved with the solver *lp_solve* in $140s$ on a 2.53 GHz processor. The maximal reactivity returned for the case-study is 130ms.

6   Discussion: Global versus Local Approach

6.1   Freshness Analysis: Local versus Global Approach

To evaluate the gain we may achieve, we benchmark our global approach against a local one. As described in section 1.3, a local approach consists in determining the local worst case freshness (LWCF) of each component visited in the functional chain with respect to the previous component only. Then the end-to-end

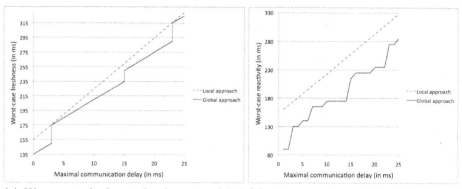

(a) Worst-case freshness: local versus global approach

(b) Worst-case reactivity: local versus global approach

Fig. 5. Local versus global approach

freshness is the sum of each LWCF. The LWCF of a timed channel is the upper bound of the communication delay: δ_{max}. In the same way, the LWCF of a task τ_i is the maximal delay between the begin and the end of two consecutive jobs (i.e., the time for a data to be refreshed). Then, in our case study, the end-to-end freshness obtained following this local reasoning is:

$$LF = 6 + 13 + 14 + 35 + 40 + 35 + 6 + 6 + 7\delta_{max} = 155 + 7\delta_{max} \text{ (in ms)} \quad (1)$$

Figure 5(a) compares the local and global approaches by varying δ_{max}. According to equation (1) the worst case freshness determined with the local approach is linear (straight dashed line). The results of the global approach form a step linear function and gives more accurate results than the local approach. The curve of the global approach varies by steps because the functional chain crosses module M_3 twice. System designers could take advantage of this more accurate evaluation technique: within certain range they could increase the network load with lower impact on the end-to-end freshness than predicted by the local approach. For instance, the curves figure 5(a) show that for a maximal traversal time through the network $\delta_{max} = 7ms$, the global WCF is equal to $195ms$ while the local one is $204ms$. Put differently, only the global method shows that the chain still meets the requirement.

6.2   Reactivity Analysis: Local versus Global Approach

We compare our global reactivity analysis with a local approach. The reactivity obtained following a local method is the difference between the maximal freshness LF and the minimal freshness plus one period of the end task of the chain τ_0. Following only a local reasoning, the minimal freshness happens when the network traversal time is minimum (δ_{min}) and when all tasks take no time and are well phased. Thus in our case study the end-to-end reactivity is:

$$LR = 155 + 7(\delta_{max} - \delta_{min}) + 5 = 160 + 7(\delta_{max} - \delta_{min}) \text{ (in ms)} \qquad (2)$$

We compare again the global approach against the local one by varying δ_{max} (δ_{min} remains equal to 1ms). The results are plotted on figure 5(b). According to equation (2) the worst case reactivity determined with the local approach is linear (straight dashed line). The results of the global approach form a more complex curve and gives more accurate results.

7   Conclusion

The article presents an analysis method for end-to-end freshness/reactivity properties on GALTT systems. This verification method is based on a MILP modeling. Worst case end-to-end properties are computed as optimal solutions of the MILP problem. An interesting feature of this approach is that one can easily compute best case end-to-end properties. It only requires to modify the objective function of the MILP form max to min. From a scalability point of view, the case study considered previously is composed of 7 tasks (including the sensor, the actuator, and the communication tasks), one of them (ADR) being crossed two times. This case study is representative from industrial systems (usually composed of 5 to 10 tasks). Our method applied to this case study does not take more than 1s for the freshness analysis and 140s for the reactivity analysis (with a non optimized solver). We think that these results are promising.

In this article, we made however a strong hypothesis about the internal behavior of the tasks. We implicitly considered that each job of each task does not induce a delay greater than its worst case response time, i.e., the length of its time interval. This implicit hypothesis is shown figure 2 where each job returns an output data before the end of its time interval. Obviously it is not always the case in realistic systems. Some tasks can implement "confirmation tests" waiting for a given amount of time (generally a multiple of its period) before producing a consolidated output. Obviously this internal latency impacts the global latency and the global reactivity of the chain. Our next work to do is to extend our global method by tasks involving internal delays.

References

[ARI97]   ARINC 653, Aeronautical Radio Inc.: Avionics Application Software Standard Interface (1997)

[BD12]   Boyer, M., Doose, D.: Combining network calculus and scheduling theory to improve delay bounds. In: RTNS 2012, pp. 51–60 (2012)

[BEN04]   Berkelaar, M., Eikland, K., Notebaert, P.: lp_solve 5.5, open source (mixed-integer) linear programming system. Software, (May 2004), http://lpsolve.sourceforge.net/5.5/

[BSF09]   Bauer, H., Scharbarg, J.-L., Fraboul, C.: Applying and optimizing tra-
            jectory approach for performance evaluation of afdx avionics network.
            In: Proceedings of the 14th IEEE International Conference on Emerging
            Technologies & Factory Automation, ETFA 2009, Piscataway, NJ, USA,
            pp. 690–697. IEEE Press (2009)

[CB06]   Carcenac, F., Boniol, F.: A formal framework for verifying distributed
            embedded systems based on abstraction methods. International Journal
            on Software Tools for Technology Transfer 8(6), 471–484 (2006)

[CB10]   Chokshi, D.B., Bhaduri, P.: Performance analysis of flexray-based sys-
            tems using real-time calculus. In: Shin, S.Y., Ossowski, S., Schumacher,
            M., Palakal, M.J., Hung, C.-C. (eds.) SAC, pp. 351–356. ACM (2010)
            (revisited)

[FFF11]   Ferrandiz, T., Frances, F., Fraboul, C.: Worst-case end-to-end delays eval-
            uation for spacewire networks. Discrete Event Dynamic Systems 21(3),
            339–357 (2011)

[HHKG09]   Herpel, T., Hielscher, K.-S.J., Klehmet, U., German, R.: Stochastic and
            deterministic performance evaluation of automotive can communication.
            Computer Networks 53(8), 1171–1185 (2009)

[LBEP11]   Lauer, M., Boniol, F., Ermont, J., Pagetti, C.: Latency and freshness anal-
            ysis on IMA systems. In: Emerging Technologies and Factory Automation
            (ETFA), Toulouse, France. IEEE (September 2011)

[LBT01]   Le Boudec, J.-Y., Thiran, P.: Network Calculus. LNCS, vol. 2050.
            Springer, Heidelberg (2001)

[LEPB10]   Lauer, M., Ermont, J., Pagetti, C., Boniol, F.: Analyzing end-to-end func-
            tional delays on an IMA platform. In: Margaria, T., Steffen, B. (eds.)
            ISoLA 2010, Part I. LNCS, vol. 6415, pp. 243–257. Springer, Heidelberg
            (2010)

[MM06]   Martin, S., Minet, P.: Worst case end-to-end response times of flows sched-
            uled with FP/FIFO. In: Proceedings of the International Conference on
            Networking, International Conference on Systems and International Con-
            ference on Mobile Communications and Learning Technologies, pp. 54–62.
            IEEE Computer Society, Washington, DC (2006)

[SAA+04]   Sha, L., Abdelzaher, T., AArzén, K.-E., Cervin, A., Baker, T., Burns, A.,
            Buttazzo, G., Caccamo, M., Lehoczky, J., Mok, A.K.: Real time schedul-
            ing theory: A historical perspective. Real-Time Syst. 28(2-3), 101–155
            (2004)

[SB12]   Mangoua Sofack, W., Boyer, M.: Non preemptive static priority with net-
            work calculus: Enhancement. In: Schmitt, J.B. (ed.) MMB & DFT 2012.
            LNCS, vol. 7201, pp. 258–272. Springer, Heidelberg (2012)

[Spu96]   Spuri, M.: Holistic Analysis for Deadline Scheduled Real-Time Distributed
            Systems. Research Report RR-2873, INRIA (1996)

[TC94]   Tindell, K., Clark, J.: Holistic schedulability analysis for distributed
            hard real-time systems. Microprocessing and Microprogramming 40(2-3),
            117–134 (1994)

[TCN00]   Thiele, L., Chakraborty, S., Naedele, M.: Real-time calculus for scheduling
            hard real-time systems. In: ISCAS, pp. 101–104 (2000)

Enclosing Temporal Evolution of Dynamical Systems Using Numerical Methods[*]

Olivier Bouissou[1], Alexandre Chapoutot[2], and Adel Djoudi[2]

[1] CEA Saclay Nano-INNOV Institut CARNOT, Gif-sur-Yvette, France
[2] ENSTA ParisTech, Palaiseau, France

Abstract. Numerical methods are necessary to understand the behaviors of complex hybrid systems used to design control-command systems. Especially, numerical integration methods are heavily used in simulation to compute approximations of the solution of differential equations, including non-linear and stiff solutions. Nevertheless, these methods only produce approximate results and they should not be used in formal verification methods as is. We propose a systematic way to make explicit Runge-Kutta integration method safe with respect to the mathematical solution. As side effect, we can hence compare different integration schemes in order to pick the right one in different situations.

1 Introduction

Verification techniques for embedded, control-command systems usually involve the modeling of the system using a hybrid automata-like formalism and then the computation of the reachable states of the system [1,2]. To compute these reachable states, one of the crucial points is the post operator for the continuous trajectories which requires to compute over-approximations of trajectories defined by ordinary differential equations (ODE in short). In the linear case (i.e. when the differential equations are linear), this can be exactly and efficiently solved using an efficient representation of convex sets as in [3]. For the non-linear case, one cannot in general compute exactly the continuous trajectories and approximation techniques such as hybridization [4,5] have been proposed. This however may result in an explosion of the number of discrete jumps and thus does not scale well to large, industrial systems.

In an industrial context, the validation of these systems (which differs to the formal verification) usually involves the modeling of the system in a Simulink-like formalism and then performing numerical simulations of the system to *test* its behavior under some input scenarios [6,7]. Numerical simulation techniques are very efficient and scale very well to large systems with many state variables. Moreover, system designers are used to tune and use these simulations to have good approximations of the system trajectories. Such simulations are however of little help for the formal verification of hybrid systems.

---

[*] This work was partially supported by the ANR project CAFEIN.

G. Brat, N. Rungta, and A. Venet (Eds.): NFM 2013, LNCS 7871, pp. 108–123, 2013.

In this article, we propose to use and adapt the numerical methods used in tools as Matlab/Simulink to define a new post operator for continuous trajectories. More formally, we define a way to transform any explicit Runge-Kutta numerical method to solve ODE into a guaranteed manner that computes over-approximations of the exact solution. We focus on explicit Runge-Kutta-like methods as they are the most widely used methods to solve differential equations. For example, in the Matlab/Simulink tool, there are 13 integration methods, 8 of which are explicit Runge-Kutta methods. It is well known that each method has its particularities and is suited for a particular kind of ODEs. So, having a collection of numerical methods allows one to choose the best one for solving its particular ODE. Our framework proposes different methods and thus allows to efficiently and precisely solve different kinds of equations.

In the rest of this article, we give in Section 2 an overview of numerical methods to solve ODEs, then in Section 3 we explain how we modified them to enclose the solution of ODEs. Then, in Section 4, we present experimentation that show the benefits of our approach compared to related work.

2   Numerical Integration

We now recall the principles of numerical integration of ordinary differential equations. An ordinary differential equation (ODE) is a relation between a function $y : \mathbb{R} \to \mathbb{R}^n$ and its derivative $\dot{y} = \frac{dy}{dt}$, written as $\dot{y} = f(t, y)$. An initial value problem (IVP) is an ODE together with an initial condition and a final time:

$$\dot{y} = f(t, y) \quad \text{with} \quad y(0) = y_0, \ y_0 \in \mathbb{R}^n \quad \text{and} \quad t \in [0, t_{\text{end}}] \ . \tag{1}$$

Example 1 (Running example). We use the following IVP as our running example:

$$\begin{cases} \dot{y} = z \\ \dot{z} = z^2 - \dfrac{3}{0.001 + y^2} \end{cases} \quad \text{with} \quad \begin{cases} y(0) = 10 \\ z(0) = 0 \end{cases}$$

and we set the final time at $t_{\text{end}} = 50$. We call this IVP the "oil-reservoir" problem, this example comes from [8]. This IVP is particularly stiff around $t = 35$, while its evolution elsewhere is slow, which makes it difficult to solve.

Solving the IVP means finding a continuous and differentiable function y_∞ such that $y_\infty(0) = y_0$ and $\forall t \in [0, t_{\text{end}}]$, $\dot{y}_\infty(t) = f(t, y_\infty(t))$. We do not address here the problem of existence of the solution and we shall always assume that $f : \mathbb{R} \times \mathbb{R}^n \to \mathbb{R}^n$ is continuous in t and globally Lipschitz in y, so Equation 1 admits a unique solution on $\mathbb{R}$ [9]. We denote the solution of (1) with initial condition y_0 at $t = 0$ as $y(t; y_0)$. Higher order differential equations can be translated into first-order ODEs by introducing additional variables for the derivatives of y.

2.1   Approximate Solution

An exact solution of Equation 1 is rarely computable so that in practice, approximation algorithms are used. The goal of an approximation algorithm is to

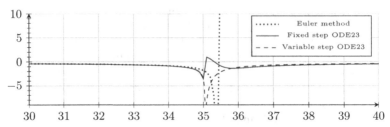

Fig. 1. Some numerical solutions of the oil-reservoir problem with different numerical methods, zooming on $t \in [30, 40]$

compute a sequence of time instants $0 = t_0 < t_1 < \cdots < t_n = t_{end}$ and a sequence of values $y_0, \ldots, y_n$ such that $\forall i \in [0, n]$, $y_i \approx y(t_i; y_0)$. In this article, we focus on single-step methods that only use y_i and approximations of $\dot{y}(t)$ to compute y_{i+1}.

The simplest method is Euler's method in which $t_{i+1} = t_i + h$ for some step-size h and $y_{i+1} = y_i + h \times f(t_i, y_i)$; so the derivative of y at time t_i, $f(t_i, y_i)$, is used as an approximation of the derivative on the whole time interval to perform a linear interpolation. This method is very simple and fast, but requires small step-sizes. More advanced methods use a few intermediate computations to improve the approximation of the derivative. For example, Bogacki-Shampine method (also named ODE23) performs three evaluations of f and then a linear interpolation from y_n using a weighted sum of the three derivative approximations (h is the chosen step-size):

$$k_1 = f(t_n, y_n) \tag{2a}$$

$$k_2 = f(t_n + (1/2)h, y_n + (1/2)hk_1) \tag{2b}$$

$$k_3 = f(t_n + (3/4)h, y_n + (3/4)hk_2) \tag{2c}$$

$$y_{n+1} = y_n + h\left((2/9)k_1 + (1/3)k_2 + (4/9)k_3\right) \tag{2d}$$

Example 2. If we consider the "oil-reservoir" problem of Example 1, Euler and Bogacki-Shampine with a fixed step-size of 0.1 produce two very different solutions, as plotted in Figure 1 in dotted and dashed lines. Note that Euler method diverges around $t = 35$, where the dynamics of the solution is very stiff.

When the derivatives of the solution exhibit high variations, for example around $t = 35$ for the "oil-reservoir" problem, it is important to adapt the step-size h to ensure that the approximate solution does not deviate too far from the exact solution. So called variable step-size methods use a second, more precise interpolation that is used as a reference of the solution. The distance between both interpolations is considered as the error made by the first interpolation. For the Bogacki-Shampine method, the second interpolation is given by:

$$k_4 = f(t_n + h, x_{n+1}) \tag{3a}$$

$$z_{n+1} = x_n + h\left((7/24)k_1 + (1/4)k_2 + (1/3)k_3 + (1/8)k_4\right) \tag{3b}$$

Then, $\| y_{n+1} - z_{n+1} \|$ is the estimated error attached to the approximation point y_{n+1} and is used to both validate the step from t_n to t_{n+1} and adapt the step-size.

$$
\begin{array}{c|ccccc}
d_2 & a_{21} \\
d_3 & a_{31} & a_{32} \\
\vdots & \vdots & & \ddots \\
d_s & a_{s1} & a_{s2} & \cdots & a_{s,s-1} \\
\hline
 & w_1 & w_2 & \cdots & & w_s \\
 & w'_1 & w'_2 & \cdots & & w'_s
\end{array}
\qquad
\begin{array}{c|cccc}
0 \\
\frac{1}{2} & \frac{1}{2} \\
\frac{3}{4} & 0 & \frac{3}{4} \\
1 & \frac{2}{9} & \frac{1}{3} & \frac{4}{9} \\
\hline
 & \frac{2}{9} & \frac{1}{3} & \frac{4}{9} & 0 \\
 & \frac{7}{24} & \frac{1}{4} & \frac{1}{3} & \frac{1}{8}
\end{array}
$$

(a) General form.   (b) Bogacki-Shampine table.

Fig. 2. Butcher table

Step-size control strategy is at the core of the performance of a numerical integration algorithms, both in terms of precision (the step-size is reduced when needed) and computation time (the step-size is increased when the solution is flat). We will present in Section 3 our method for controlling the step-size when performing guaranteed numerical integration. We refer to [9,10] for details about the step-size strategy for numerical algorithms. On Figure 1, we show the values of the approximated solution of the "oil-reservoir" problem for the Bogacki-Shampine method with a variable step-size: it greatly differs from the fixed step-size method, and it is actually very close to the actual solution (see Section 4).

In this article, we only consider methods based on Runge-Kutta methods, either fixed or variable step-size. All these methods can be described by a Butcher table (see Figure 2(a)). The d_i represent the time instants of the intermediate steps needed to compute the solution of $\dot{y} = f(t, y)$ over the interval $[t_n, t_n + h]$. The matrix made of the elements a_{ij} represents the weights used to approximate the interval solution from the previous intermediate steps. The elements w_i, w'_i (only for variable step-size methods) represent the latest weights to approximate the solution at time $t_n + h_n$ with two methods of different orders. For example, the Butcher table associated to Bogacki-Shampine is given at Figure 2(b). In consequence the elements of the Butcher table give a unified description for all the numerical integration methods members of the Rung-Kutta family. In the rest of this article, we denote by Φ a numerical method described by such a Butcher table: it relates two successive approximation points: $\forall n \in \mathbb{N}$, $(t_{n+1}, y_{n+1}) = \Phi(t_n, y_n)$.

2.2   Problems with Numerical Integration

Numerical integration only provides *approximations* of the solution of the IVP. Even when using variable step-size methods, there is no guarantee that the chosen method is close to the solution, we merely know that the smaller the step-size is, the closer the approximations are to the solution. So, if we want to use numerical methods in cases when an over-approximation of the trajectories is needed, we need to compute error bounds $y(t_n; y_0) - y_n$ for all $n \in \mathbb{N}$.

Moreover, numerical integration only concerns IVP with a single initial value, i.e. $y_0 \in \mathbb{R}^n$. In hybrid systems model verification, it is necessary to enclose all the solutions of a differential equation starting from any point in a given set. More formally, given an initial set $S_0 \subseteq \mathbb{R}^n$, we want to compute bounds on the set of trajectories $\{y(t; y_0) \mid y' = f(t, y), \; y_0 \in S_0\}$. The method we develop in the rest of the article encodes sets of values using *affine arithmetic* and compute bounds on the solutions of the differential equations by computing bounds on $y(t_n; y_0) - y_n$ whatever the initial value is within some set S_0.

Finally, implementations of numerical methods very often suffer from the use of floating-point numbers which explain why, even if theoretically a Runge-Kutta method converges towards the solution when the step-size converges towards 0, it is in practice not the case. Our method handles these errors in a safe way.

3   Guaranteed Integration

We present our solutions of the drawbacks associated to the numerical solutions of IVP. Firstly, we present our approach to manipulate sets of values for handling uncertainties. Secondly, we describe the method to bound the truncation error introduced in numerical methods to provide guaranteed numerical integration.

3.1   Computing with Sets

The simplest and most common way to represent and manipulate sets of values is interval arithmetic [11]. Nevertheless, this representation usually produces too much over-approximated results in particular because of the *dependency problem*.

Example 3. Consider the ordinary differential equation $\dot{x}(t) = -x$ solved with the Euler's method with an initial value ranging in the interval $[0, 1]$ and with a step-size of $h = 0.5$. For one step of integration, we have to compute with interval arithmetic the expression $e = x + h \times (-x)$ which produces as a result the interval $[-0.5, 1]$. Rewriting the expression e such that $e' = x(1 - h)$, we obtain the interval $[0, 0.5]$ which is the exact result. Unfortunately, we cannot in general rewrite expressions with only one occurrence of each variable.

More generally, it can be shown that for most integration schemes the width of the result can only grow if we interpret sets of values as intervals.

To avoid this problem we use an improvement over interval arithmetic named *affine arithmetic* [12] which can track linear correlation between program variables. A set of values in this domain is represented by an *affine form* $\hat{x}$ (also called a *zonotope*), i.e. a formal expression of the form $\hat{x} = \alpha_0 + \sum_{i=1}^{n} \alpha_i \varepsilon_i$ where the coefficients α_i are real numbers, α_0 being called the *center* of the affine form, and the ε_i are formal variables ranging over the interval $[-1, 1]$. Obviously, an interval $a = [a_1, a_2]$ can be seen as the affine form $\hat{x} = \alpha_0 + \alpha_1 \varepsilon$ with $\alpha_0 = (a_1 + a_2)/2$ and $\alpha_1 = (a_2 - a_1)/2$. Moreover, affine forms encode linear dependencies between variables: if $x \in [a_1, a_2]$ and y is such that $y = 2x$, then x will be represented by the affine form $\hat{x}$ above and y will be represented as $\hat{y} = 2\alpha_0 + 2\alpha_1 \varepsilon$.

Affine arithmetic extends usual operations on real numbers in the expected way. For instance, the affine combination of two affine forms $\hat{x} = \alpha_0 + \sum_{i=1}^{n} \alpha_i \varepsilon_i$ and $\hat{y} = \beta_0 + \sum_{i=1}^{n} \beta_i \varepsilon_i$ with $a, b, c \in \mathbb{R}$, is given by:

$$a\hat{x} + b\hat{y} + c \quad = \quad (a\alpha_0 + b\beta_0 + c) + \sum_{i=1}^{n} (a\alpha_i + b\beta_i)\varepsilon_i \quad . \tag{4}$$

However, unlike the addition, most operations create new noise symbols. Multiplication for example is defined by:

$$\hat{x} \times \hat{y} \quad = \quad \alpha_0 \alpha_1 + \sum_{i=1}^{n} (\alpha_i \beta_0 + \alpha_0 \beta_i)\varepsilon_i + \nu \varepsilon_{n+1} \tag{5}$$

where $\nu = (\sum_{i=1}^{n} |\alpha_i|) \times (\sum_{i=1}^{n} |\beta_i|)$ over-approximates the error between the linear approximation of multiplication and multiplication itself. Other operations, like sin, exp, are evaluated using their Taylor expansions. Note that the set-based evaluation of an expression only consists in substituting all the mathematical operators, like $+$ or sin, by their counterpart in affine arithmetic. We will denote by $\mathrm{Aff}(e)$ the evaluation of the expression e using affine arithmetic.

Example 4. Consider again $e = x + h \times (-x)$ with $h = 0.5$ and $x = [0, 1]$ which is associated to the affine form $\hat{x} = 0.5 + 0.5\varepsilon_1$. Evaluating e with affine arithmetic without rewriting the expression, we obtain $[0, 0.5]$ as a result.

One of the main difficulties when implementing affine arithmetic using floating-point numbers is to take into account the unavoidable numerical errors due to the use of finite-precision representations for values (and thus rounding on operations). We use an approach based on computations of floating-point arithmetic named *error free transformations*: the round-off error can be represented by a floating-point number and hence it is possible to exactly compute it (we refer to [13] for more details on such methods). For instance, in the case of addition, the round-off error e generated by the sum $s = a + b$ is given by ($\odot$ stands for floating-point operations): $e = (a \ominus (s \ominus (s \ominus a))) \oplus (b \ominus (s \ominus a))$.

A second comment on the implementation is that an affine form $\hat{x}$ could be represented as an array of floats encoding the coefficients α_i. However, since in practice most of those coefficients are null, it is much more efficient to adopt a sparse representation and encode it as a list of pairs (i, α_i), sorted w.r.t. the first component, containing only coefficients $\alpha_i \neq 0$. Moreover, in order to limit the growth of the number of noise symbols in affine forms, we gather during simulation all the coefficients below a given threshold into a new noise symbol.

3.2   Enclosing the Truncation Error

We recall from Section 2 that a numerical integration method computes a sequence of approximations (t_n, y_n) of the solution $y(t; y_0)$ of the IVP defined in Equation (1) such that $y_n \approx y(t_n; y_0)$. Every numerical method member of the Runge-Kutta family follows the *condition order* [9]. This condition states that a method of this family is of order p iff the $p+1$ first coefficients of the Taylor expansion of the solution and the Taylor expansion of the numerical methods are equal. Hence, at a time instant t_n the Taylor expansion of the solution with the Lagrange remainder states that $\exists \xi \in]t_n, t_{n+1}[$ such that:

$$
\begin{aligned}
y(t_{n+1}; y_0) &= y(t_n; y_0) + \sum_{i=1}^{p} \frac{h_n^i}{i!} y^{(i)}(t_n; y_0) + \frac{h_n^{p+1}}{(p+1)!} y^{(p+1)}(\xi; y_0) \\
&= y(t_n; y_0) + \sum_{i=1}^{p} \frac{h_n^i}{i!} f^{(i-1)}(t_n, y(t_n; y_0)) + \frac{h_n^{p+1}}{(p+1)!} f^{(p)}(\xi, y(\xi; y_0)) \quad .
\end{aligned}
\tag{6}
$$

In Equation (6), $g^{(n)}$ stands for the n-th derivative of function g w.r.t. time t that is $\frac{d^n g}{dt^n}$ and $h_n = t_{n+1} - t_n$ is the step-size. Moreover, the general form of an explicit s-stage Runge-Kutta formula, that is using s evaluations of f, is:

$$
y_{n+1} = y_n + h \sum_{i=1}^{s} b_i k_i \quad ,
\tag{7a}
$$

$$
k_1 = f(t_n, y_n) \quad , \qquad k_i = f\left(t_n + c_i h, y_n + h \sum_{j=1}^{i-1} a_{ij} k_j \right) \quad , \quad i = 2, 3, \ldots, s \quad .
\tag{7b}
$$

The coefficients c_i, a_{ij} and b_i are those given in a Butcher table (see Section 2). We define the function $\phi : \mathbb{R} \to \mathbb{R}^n$ by $\phi(t) = y_n + h_t \sum_{i=1}^{s} b_i k_i(t)$, $k_i(t)$ is defined as Equation (7b) where h is $h_t = t - t_n$. The Taylor expansion around t_n of the numerical solution with a Lagrange remainder states that there exists $\eta \in]t_n, t_{n+1}[$ such that:

$$
y_{n+1} = \sum_{i=0}^{p} \frac{h_n^i}{i!} \frac{d^i \phi}{dt^i}(t_n) + \frac{h_n^{p+1}}{(p+1)!} \frac{d^{p+1} \phi}{dt^{p+1}}(\eta) \quad .
$$

The truncation error measures the distance between the true solution and the numerical solution and it is defined by $y(t_n; y_0) - y_n$. If we express the truncation error with the Taylor expansions, the consequence of the condition order is that the numerical integration makes an error proportional to the Lagrange remainders. More precisely, the truncation error is defined by:

$$
y(t_n; y_0) - y_n = \frac{h_n^{p+1}}{(p+1)!} \left(f^{(p)}(\xi, y(\xi)) - \frac{d^{p+1} \phi}{dt^{p+1}}(\eta) \right) \quad \xi \in]t_k, t_{k+1}[\text{ and } \eta \in]t_n, t_{n+1}[\quad .
\tag{8}
$$

The challenge to make Runge-Kutta integration schemes safe w.r.t. the true solution of IVP is then to compute a bound of the result of Equation (8). In other words we have to bound the value of $f^{(p)}(\xi, y(\xi; y_0))$ and the value of $\frac{d^{p+1} \phi}{dt^{p+1}}(\eta)$. The latter expression is straightforward to bound because the function ϕ only depends on the value of the step-size h, and so does its $(p+1)$-th derivative. The bound is then obtain using the affine arithmetic by:

$$
\frac{d^{p+1} \phi}{dt^{p+1}}(\eta) \in \text{Aff}\left(\frac{d^{p+1} \phi}{dt^{p+1}}([t_n, t_{n+1}]) \right) \quad .
\tag{9}
$$

However, the expression $f^{(p)}(\xi, y(\xi; y_0))$ is not so easy to bound as it requires to evaluate f for a particular value of the IVP solution $y(\xi; y_0)$ at a unknown time $\xi \in]t_n, t_{n+1}[$. The solution used is the same as the one found in [14,15] and it requires to bound the solution of IVP on the interval $[t_n, t_{n+1}]$. We briefly recall the main mathematical tool used to bound the solution of IVP and we refer to [14] for a complete presentation. We consider the space of continuously differentiable functions $C^0([t_n, t_{n+1}], \mathbb{R}^n)$ and the Picard-Lindelöf operator:

$$P(f; t_n; y_n)(t) = y_n + \int_{t_n}^{t} f(s, y(s))ds \ . \tag{10}$$

Note that this operator is associated to the integral form of Equation (1). So the solution of this operator is also the solution of Equation (1).

The Picard-Lindelöf operator is used to check the contraction of the solution on a integration step in order to prove the existence and the uniqueness of the solution of Equation (1) as stated by the Banach's fixed-point theorem. Furthermore, this operator is used to compute an enclosure of the solution of IVP over a time interval $[t_n, t_{n+1}]$ using affine arithmetic. Affine arithmetic can be used to compute a bound of integral expression such that: $\int_a^b f(x)dx \in (b-a)\text{Aff}(f([a,b]))$. Using an affine version of the Picard-Lindelöf operator, we can try to prove the contraction of this operator by computing a post fixed-point over the interval $[t_n, t_{n+1}]$ that is we want to find a value z such that:

$$z \supseteq y_n + [0, h]\text{Aff}(f([t_n, t_{n+1}], z)) \ . \tag{11}$$

Note that Equation (11) is associated to an iterative process to compute z. Starting from z_0 being the interval hull of y_n and y_{n+1}, we define the sequence of affine forms z_k as $z_{k+1} = y_n + [0, h]\text{Aff}(f([t_n, t_{n+1}], z_k))$ and stop when we find k such that $z_{k+1} \subseteq z_k$. If we cannot find a post fixed-point in a given fixed number of iterations, this may be the case that the step-size is too large. Then we reject the integration step and keep going the simulation with a reduced step-size (usually $\frac{h_n}{2}$). That is Equation (11) is also used to control the integration step-size.

Furthermore, the value z is also used as an enclosure of the solution of IVP over the time interval $[t_n, t_{n+1}]$. We can hence bound the Lagrange remainder of the true solution with z such that:

$$f^{(p)}(\xi, y(\xi; y_0)) \in \text{Aff}\left(f^{(p)}([t_n, t_{n+1}], z)\right) \ . \tag{12}$$

Finally, using Equation (9) and Equation (12) we can prove Theorem 1 and thus bound the distance between the approximation points of any explicit Runge-Kutta method and any solution of the IVP.

Theorem 1. *Let $S_0 \subseteq \mathbb{R}^n$ be a set of initial states and let y_0 be an affine form such that $S_0 \subseteq y_0$. Let Φ be a numerical integration scheme and Φ_{Aff} be the evaluation of Φ using affine arithmetic. Let (t_n, y_n) be a sequence of time instants and affine forms defined by $y_{n+1} = y'_{n+1} + e_{n+1}$ where $(t_{n+1}, y'_{n+1}) = \Phi_{Aff}(t_n, y_n)$ and e_{n+1} is the truncation error as defined by Equation (8) and is evaluated using Equations (9) and (12). Then, we have that $\forall y'_0 \in S_0$: $\forall n \in \mathbb{N}$, $y(t_n; y'_0) \in y_n$.*

Example 5. We present the main steps of our method on the system $\dot{x} = x^2$ solved with Heun's method: $x_{n+1} = x_n + h/2(x_n^2 + (x_n + hx_n^2)^2)$. First, if $x(t_n) \in \hat{x}_n$, we let

$\hat{x}_{n+1} = \hat{x}_n + h/2(\hat{x}_n^2 + (\hat{x}_n + h\hat{x}_n^2)^2)$, evaluated using affine arithmetic. Next we bound the truncation error $\hat{x}_{n+1} - x(t_{n+1})$. Heun's method being of order 2 we need to bound over $[t_n, t_{n+1}]$ the third derivative of the problem and the third derivative of the method w.r.t. time, i.e. we want to bound the expressions $\dddot{x} = 6x^4$ and $\phi^{(3)}(t) = 3x_n^4$ with $\phi(t) = x_n + (t - t_n)/2(x_n^2 + (x_n + (t - t_n)x_n^2))$. For the latter, we bound it with $3\hat{x}_n^4$ using affine arithmetic. For the former, we must bound x on the whole interval $[t_n, t_{n+1}]$ into an affine form $\hat{z}$ and then we use $6\hat{z}^4$ as a bound of $\dddot{x}$. To compute $\hat{z}$, we use Equation (11) and iteratively compute a post-fixpoint of $\hat{z} = \hat{x}_n + [0, h]\hat{z}^2$. We start from the hull of $\hat{x}_n$ and $\hat{x}_{n+1}$ and evaluate the expression $\hat{x}_n + [0, h]\hat{z}^2$ using affine arithmetic until we reach a post-fixpoint.

3.3 Step-Size Strategy

Our method automatically adapts the step-size in order to validate the existence of the solution and improve the stability of the computed enclosure.

The iteration defined by Equation (11) successively computes sets z_k until $z_{k+1} = y_n + [0, h]\mathrm{Aff}(f([t_n, t_{n+1}], z_k)) \subseteq z_k$. At this point, we know that IVP (1) has a solution on $[t_n, t_{n+1}]$ and that this solution remains in z_k. As we assumed that the IVP has a solution, there exists some $h > 0$ such that Picard iteration converges. However, given some h, the iteration may diverge or take too long to converge. So we fix a maximal number of iterations K, and if we do not converge after K steps, the step is rejected and we set the step-size to $h/2$. As we start from a good approximation of the fixpoint (the hull of the enclosure at t_n and the numerical approximation at t_{n+1}), the iteration generally converges quickly.

Then, we let the user define two values, the absolute tolerance $atol$ and the relative tolerance $rtol$ that defines the acceptable error at each integration step. More formally, our method computes for each instant t_n an error e_n which is the distance between the true solution and the numerical approximation. We say that the step from t_n to t_{n+1} is accepted if e_n is such that: $\sup(e_n) \leq \mathtt{err}$ where $\mathtt{err} = \max(atol, rtol \times \max(\sup(y_{n+1}), \sup(y_n)))$. If the step is not accepted, we set the step-size to $h/2$ and restart from t_n. If the step is accepted, the next step-size is $h' = h(rtol/err)^{1/(q+1)}$, q being the order of the numerical method. So, the step-size is automatically adapted so that the error introduced at each step converges towards the user-defined tolerances. This is similar to what is done for variable step-size numerical methods, except that we now use the guaranteed error to accept and control the step-sizes. Note that we also transform fixed step-size methods such as Euler or RK4 methods into variable step-size algorithms.

Finally, our implementation also offers another algorithm to adapt the step-size: we use the PI algorithm from [15]. The main idea is the use a *proportional-integral* controller scheme to adapt h to achieve the desired error $\mathtt{err}$. This algorithm makes the step-size more stable and thus reduces the number of rejected steps due to the Picard-Lindelöf iteration and in our experiments it showed to be the best choice for controlling the step-size.

4   Experiments

In this section we present the effectiveness of our approach to make every explicit Runge-Kutta method guaranteed through different examples mainly coming from the DETEST problem set [16]. This set has been specifically defined to test numerical integration methods on various kinds of problems classified according linear/non-linear and non-stiff/stiff categories. We compare our approach against the VNODE (VNODE-LP version 0.3) software which implements the state of the art of guaranteed numerical integration methods based on interval Taylor series [14]. Despite VNODE can handle high order Taylor series we restrict our comparison to order 4 which is the highest order of the Runge-Kutta methods we consider in this article. We use the following integration methods: Euler, Heun, Runge-Kutta 4 (RK4), Bogacki-Shampine (ode23), Dormand-Prince (ode45) [10].

All the simulations were executed on a desktop (two 2.33GHz processors with 2Go of RAM) running Fedora Linux. The implementation was done in OCaml using the GiNaC library [17] to symbolically compute derivatives. In the following tables, we present: T the time (in seconds) required to simulate the problem excluding time spent to compute derivatives and TT the total time (in seconds) including time used to compute and compile derivatives[1]; $Tol = rtol = atol$ the chosen tolerance; Rej and Acc are respectively the number of rejected and accepted steps; $Evals$ is the number of function evaluations and $Prec$ is the precision, taken as the greatest width of the guaranteed enclosures calculated.

4.1   Oil-Reservoir Problem

We consider again the "oil-reservoir" problem introduced in Section 2 on which we applied different guaranteed Runge-Kutta methods. In order to give a hint on the kind of stiffness we deal with this example, in Figure 3(a) we give the temporal evolution of the variable z around $t = 35$, where the derivative varies a lot. We see that, even if the precision of the bounds decreases when the stiffness is important, our method is precise enough to make the bounds contract when the dynamics is simpler. In Figure 3(b) we give the step-size evolution of the Heun's method to emphasize the importance of the step-size control mechanism presented in Section 3.3, even for initially fixed step-size integration scheme.

Next, we present in Table 1 the results of the application of different Runge-Kutta methods on the "oil-reservoir" example. Note that VNODE is not able to solve this problem, even with an order of 50: it is not able to go beyond 2 seconds of simulation. We remark in Table 1 that the execution time increases with the chosen tolerance and the complexity of the Runge-Kutta method (number of rows in a Butcher table). Moreover, the precision varies with the chosen tolerances and methods. We recall that the precision taken in this article is the

---

[1] We distinguish both as in our implementation, we only need to compute the derivatives once, if we want to re-integrate the same problem with other parameters or from another starting point, we do not need to compute the derivatives again.

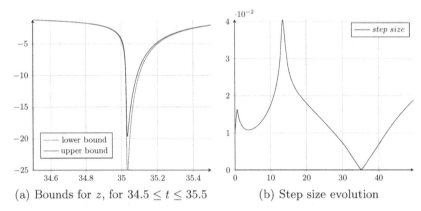

(a) Bounds for z, for $34.5 \leq t \leq 35.5$ (b) Step size evolution

Fig. 3. Oil-reservoir with guaranteed Heun's method

Table 1. Simulation results on "oil-reservoir" problem

Meth	Tol	Acc	Rej	Evals	T	TT	Prec	Prec(t_{end})
Heun	10^{-6}	2566	2561	10254	1.099	4.322	2.791	$4.541 \cdot 10^{-2}$
	10^{-9}	17626	36373	107998	8.878	12.101	$1.438 \cdot 10^{-2}$	$3.971 \cdot 10^{-3}$
	10^{-12}	220092	665081	1770346	141.848	145.071	$7.579 \cdot 10^{-5}$	$7.579 \cdot 10^{-5}$
ode23	10^{-6}	2453	2449	14706	4.833	10.713	5.412	$7.063 \cdot 10^{-2}$
	10^{-9}	8320	16633	74859	23.015	26.538	0.107	$1.891 \cdot 10^{-2}$
	10^{-12}	45495	113940	478305	132.578	136.101	$6.996 \cdot 10^{-4}$	$4.000 \cdot 10^{-4}$
RK4	10^{-6}	604	481	4340	0.909	38.646	1.413	$4.824 \cdot 10^{-2}$
	10^{-9}	1553	2031	14336	2.778	40.514	$1.368 \cdot 10^{-2}$	$3.061 \cdot 10^{-3}$
	10^{-12}	7224	14441	86660	15.409	53.145	$3.683 \cdot 10^{-5}$	$3.683 \cdot 10^{-5}$
ode45	10^{-6}	1163	1177	16380	15.791	5653.939	7.772	$1.729 \cdot 10^{-1}$
	10^{-9}	1772	2316	28616	26.046	5642.939	1.002	$6.619 \cdot 10^{-2}$
	10^{-12}	7669	15330	160993	114.609	5731.502	$2.787 \cdot 10^{-5}$	$2.787 \cdot 10^{-5}$

greatest width of the guaranteed enclosures computed during the simulation. In this example, the greatest width is computed around $t = 35$. In Table 1 the last column gives the width of the solution enclosure at the end of the simulation, which shows that we obtain precise results at $t = 50$ even if locally the error increases.

4.2   Non-stiff Problems

DETEST Problem A3. We study the behaviors of the Heun's method and the RK4 method on the following problem, for a simulation time $t \in [0, 20]$:

$$\dot{y} = y \cos(t) \quad \text{with} \quad y(0) = 1 \ . \tag{13}$$

More precisely, we emphasize the importance of the choice of the numerical methods in the trade-off of efficiency and precision even for this simple example.

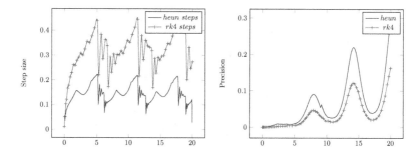

Fig. 4. Step-size (left) and precision (right) evolution for Problem A3 (Tol=10^{-3})

For this example, Heun's method and RK4 method can solve Equation (13) more efficiently than variable step-size methods as Bogacki-Shampine without loosing too much precision. Figure 4, left, shows the step-size evolution of these two methods. Note that the length of the step-size adapts to the dynamics of the problem. Furthermore, the steps chosen by RK4 method are about four times wider than those taken by the Heun's method. This is explained by the order of the method used (see Section 2). Furthermore, the precision evolution of the two methods depicted in Figure 4, right, shows that RK4 method offers more precise enclosures than Heun's method.

DETEST Problem C3. In this case study we only consider RK4 method to show the scalability of our approach. We solve for $t \in [0, 2]$ and various values of n the problem defined by:

$$\begin{pmatrix} \dot{y}_1 \\ \dot{y}_2 \\ \dot{y}_3 \\ \vdots \\ \dot{y}_n \end{pmatrix} = \begin{pmatrix} -2 & 1 & 0 & 0 & \cdots & 0 \\ 1 & -2 & 1 & 0 & \cdots & 0 \\ 0 & 1 & -2 & 1 & \cdots & 0 \\ & & & \ddots & & \\ 0 & 0 & \cdots & 0 & 1 & -2 \end{pmatrix} \begin{pmatrix} y_1 \\ y_2 \\ y_3 \\ \vdots \\ y_n \end{pmatrix} \quad \text{with} \quad y(0) = \begin{pmatrix} 1 \\ 0 \\ 0 \\ \vdots \\ 0 \end{pmatrix} . \tag{14}$$

In particular, we solved this problem with $n = \{40, 80, 120, 140\}$. Table 2 shows the time spent in simulation using RK4 method and the precision generated for each dimension and each tolerance considered. Compared to VNODE with order 4 results of the RK4 method exhibits a linear time complexity, while VNODE spends much more time to solve it. Indeed, VNODE uses standard interval arithmetic so to limit the wrapping effect during the simulation it uses a technique based on QR matrix decomposition (see [14]) which has a $O(n^3)$ complexity. Our solution to fight the wrapping effect is the use affine arithmetic which prevents the use of QR matrix decomposition then we have a better scalability without losing to much precision. Note also that with high order, e.g. 40, VNODE is able to solve this problem with only one integration step.

Table 2. Results for Problem C3

Dim	Tol	T	Prec	T VNODE	Prec VNODE
40	10^{-3}	0.378	$7.381 \cdot 10^{-4}$	0.9	$4.404 \cdot 10^{-4}$
	10^{-6}	1.064	$1.284 \cdot 10^{-5}$	7.46	$2.175 \cdot 10^{-07}$
	10^{-9}	4.628	$2.530 \cdot 10^{-8}$	72.28	$3.517 \cdot 10^{-11}$
80	10^{-3}	0.959	$1.886 \cdot 10^{-3}$	6.92	$4.404 \cdot 10^{-4}$
	10^{-6}	2.551	$1.432 \cdot 10^{-5}$	58.89	$2.175 \cdot 10^{-07}$
	10^{-9}	10.641	$2.295 \cdot 10^{-8}$	565.57	$3.517 \cdot 10^{-11}$
120	10^{-3}	1.49	$1.753 \cdot 10^{-3}$	23.21	$4.404 \cdot 10^{-4}$
	10^{-6}	4.297	$1.386 \cdot 10^{-5}$	196.56	$2.175 \cdot 10^{-07}$
	10^{-9}	17.782	$2.446 \cdot 10^{-8}$	2314.46	$3.517 \cdot 10^{-11}$
140	10^{-3}	1.846	$1.137 \cdot 10^{-3}$	37.43	$4.404 \cdot 10^{-4}$
	10^{-6}	5.285	$1.440 \cdot 10^{-5}$	334.08	$2.175 \cdot 10^{-07}$
	10^{-9}	22.286	$2.710 \cdot 10^{-8}$	3904.96	$3.517 \cdot 10^{-11}$

Table 3. Results on Problem E2

Meth	Tol	Rej	Acc	Evals	T	Prec
Heun	10^{-3}	38	11	98	0.013	$6.451 \cdot 10^{-4}$
	10^{-6}	130	129	518	0.036	$2.073 \cdot 10^{-5}$
	10^{-9}	1047	2092	6278	0.354	$8.060 \cdot 10^{-8}$
ode23	10^{-3}	36	9	135	0.046	$1.369 \cdot 10^{-3}$
	10^{-6}	99	113	636	0.156	$3.630 \cdot 10^{-5}$
	10^{-9}	653	1580	6699	1.329	$1.513 \cdot 10^{-7}$
RK4	10^{-3}	36	18	216	0.071	$5.693 \cdot 10^{-5}$
	10^{-6}	48	34	328	0.106	$7.538 \cdot 10^{-6}$
	10^{-9}	134	171	1220	0.371	$1.592 \cdot 10^{-8}$
VNODE	10^{-3}	–	–	–	0	$1.278 \cdot 10^{-4}$
	10^{-6}	–	–	–	0.02	$2.554 \cdot 10^{-07}$
	10^{-9}	–	–	–	0.18	$2.623 \cdot 10^{-10}$

4.3 Stiff Problem

We consider for a simulation time $t \in [0, 1]$ the DETEST Problem E2 defined by:

$$\begin{cases} \dot{y}_1 = y_1 \\ \dot{y}_2 = 5(1 - y_1^2)y_2 - y_1 \end{cases} \quad \text{with} \quad \begin{cases} y_1(0) = 2 \\ y_2(0) = 0 \end{cases}.$$

We look at the behaviors of different explicit Runge-Kutta methods which are known to behave not very well on such kind of problems. Table 3 gives the result on this example. For the result of VNODE, we did not succeed to access the information associated to columns Rej, Acc and Evals. Nevertheless, we note that VNODE at order 4 is more efficient and precise in this example than Runge-Kutta methods which already behave well.

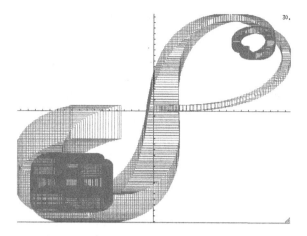

Fig. 5. Temporal evolution in (x, y)-space of the car ODE

4.4 Problem with Uncertainties

Finally, we show an example of a highly non-linear IVP, representing the movement of a car in 2D space) with some initial uncertainty:

$$\dot{x} = v \cos(\delta) \cos(\theta) \quad \dot{y} = v \cos(\delta) \sin(\theta) \quad \dot{\theta} = 0.2v \sin(0.2t) \ .$$

We integrate it up to $t = 30$ with the initial values $x(0) \in [0, 1]$, $y(0) \in [0, 1], \theta(0) = 0$ and $v \in [7, 7.1]$. Figure 5 shows the evolution of the bounds on x and y with time. This was computed using the RK4 method, with a tolerance of 10^{-8}, in $15.6s$, with $v \in [7, 7.1]$. We hence remark that our approach is efficient and robust enough to handle uncertainties.

5 Conclusion

In this article, we presented a novel method to compute guaranteed bounds on the solution of differential equations. This method is an extension of the previous work of one of the authors [15]. The main advantages of this work is that it may use various numerical methods to obtain the guaranteed bounds, so that we can treat different kinds of equations (stiff or not, linear or not). Moreover, as we use affine forms in order to enclose sets of values, we avoid the well known wrapping effect which is present in [14]. This results in a more precise and more effective method as we can make larger step-sizes. Remark that our tool computes both over-approximations at discrete time stamps t_n but also, using the Picard-Lindelöf operator, over-approximations over each intervals $[t_n, t_{n+1}]$.

To compute such over-approximations, various other tools exist. Developed for the verification of hybrid systems, SpaceEx [3] handles linear differential equations exactly using support functions and matrix exponentiation. However, when facing non-linear equations, a hybridization [5] must be performed, which can end in an explosion of the number of discrete states if the equation is stiff. Compared to tools such as VNODE [14], ValenciaIVP [18] or [19], our method relies on well-known numerical methods and can thus treat more differential equations. For example, VNODE could not integrate the "oil-reservoir" problem.

As should be clear from our experimentation, the fact that we can use various numerical methods is very interesting as each method is well adapted to a specific kind of problems. So we are confident that by adding more and more methods to our framework we will have a large enough collection to handle most kinds of problems. Three challenges arise towards this goal. First, we want to handle implicit methods in which y_{n+1} is defined via a fixpoint equation. These methods are more stable than explicit ones and thus handle better stiff systems and allow for larger step-sizes. Second, we will investigate multi-step methods that use y_n, $y_{n-1}, \ldots, y_{n-k}$ to compute y_{n+1} for some $k > 0$. Such methods are more efficient than single-step methods as they require less evaluation of f, however bounding the error is much more complicated. Finally, we will study variable order methods as in [8]. Such methods embed in one Butcher table various methods with different orders. Then, at each step, the best method is automatically chosen. This method would allow us to efficiently change the order during the integration process.

References

1. Guéguen, H., Lefebvre, M.A., Zaytoon, J., Nasri, O.: Safety verification and reachability analysis for hybrid systems. Annual Reviews in Control 33(1), 25–36 (2009)
2. Alur, R.: Formal verification of hybrid systems. In: Conference on Embedded Software, pp. 273–278. ACM (2011)
3. Frehse, G., Le Guernic, C., Donzé, A., Cotton, S., Ray, R., Lebeltel, O., Ripado, R., Girard, A., Dang, T., Maler, O.: SpaceEx: Scalable verification of hybrid systems. In: Gopalakrishnan, G., Qadeer, S. (eds.) CAV 2011. LNCS, vol. 6806, pp. 379–395. Springer, Heidelberg (2011)
4. Asarin, E., Dang, T., Girard, A.: Hybridization methods for the analysis of nonlinear systems. Acta Inf. 43(7), 451–476 (2007)
5. Dang, T., Maler, O., Testylier, R.: Accurate hybridization of nonlinear systems. In: Hybrid Systems: Computation and Control, pp. 11–20. ACM (2010)
6. Shenoy, R., McKay, B., Mosterman, P.J.: On simulation of simulink models for model-based design. Handbook of Dynamic System Modeling (2007)
7. Conrad, M., Mosterman, P.J.: Model-based design using Simulink modeling, code generation, verification, and validation. Formal Methods: Industrial Use from Model to the Code, 159–178 (2012)
8. Cash, J.R., Karp, A.H.: A variable order Runge-Kutta method for ivp with rapidly varying right-hand sides. ACM Trans. Math. Softw. 16(3), 201–222 (1990)
9. Hairer, E., Norsett, S.P., Wanner, G.: Solving Ordinary Differential Equations I: Nonstiff Problems, 2nd edn. Springer (2009)
10. Shampine, L.F., Gladwell, I., Thompson, S.: Solving ODEs with MATLAB. Cambridge Univ. Press (2003)
11. Moore, R.: Interval Analysis. Prentice Hall (1966)
12. de Figueiredo, L.H., Stolfi, J.: Self-Validated Numerical Methods and Applications. Brazilian Mathematics Colloquium monographs. IMPA/CNPq (1997)

13. Muller, J.M., Brisebarre, N., De Dinechin, F., Jeannerod, C.P., Lefèvre, V., Melquiond, G., Revol, N., Stehlé, D., Torres, S.: Handbook of Floating-Point Arithmetic. Birkhauser (2009)

14. Nedialkov, N., Jackson, K., Corliss, G.: Validated solutions of initial value problems for ordinary differential equations. Appl. Math. and Comp. 105(1), 21–68 (1999)

15. Bouissou, O., Martel, M.: GRKLib: a Guaranteed Runge Kutta Library. In: Scientific Computing, Computer Arithmetic and Validated Numerics (2006)

16. Enright, W.H., Pryce, J.D.: Two FORTRAN packages for assessing initial value methods. ACM Transations on Mathematical Software 13(1), 1–27 (1987)

17. Bauer, C., Frink, A., Kreckel, R.: Introduction to the GiNaC framework for symbolic computation within the C++ programming language. J. Symb. Comput. 33(1), 1–12 (2002)

18. Rauh, A., Brill, M., Günther, C.: A novel interval arithmetic approach for solving differential-algebraic equations with ValEncIA-IVP. Int. J. Appl. Math. Comput. Sci. 19(3), 381–397 (2009)

19. Combastel, C.: A state bounding observer for uncertain non-linear continuous-time systems based on zonotopes. In: Conference on Decision and Control. IEEE (2005)

Inferring Automata with State-Local Alphabet Abstractions*

Malte Isberner[1], Falk Howar[2], and Bernhard Steffen[1]

[1] Technical University of Dortmund, Germany
{malte.isberner,steffen}@cs.tu-dortmund.de
[2] Carnegie Mellon University, USA
howar@cmu.edu

Abstract. A major hurdle for the application of automata learning to realistic systems is the identification of an adequate alphabet: it must be small enough, in particular finite, for the learning procedure to converge in reasonable time, and it must be expressive enough to describe the system at a level where its behavior is deterministic. In this paper, we combine our automated alphabet abstraction approach, which refines the global alphabet of the system to be learned on the fly during the learning process, with the principle of state-local alphabets: rather than determining a single global alphabet, we infer the optimal alphabet abstraction individually for each state. Our experimental results show that this does not only lead to an increased comprehensibility of the learned models, but also to a better performance of the learning process: indeed, besides the drastic – yet foreseeable – reduction in terms of membership queries, we also observed interesting cases where the number of equivalence queries was reduced.

1 Introduction

The practical application of verification techniques such as model based testing [4] or model checking [6] is often hampered by the lack of adequate formal models. This is not the least a cause of the much propagated component-based software design style, as most libraries only provide very partial—if any—specifications of their components, rendering the system as a whole underspecified. As a way out of this dilemma, automata learning techniques [11] have been proposed, allowing the automated construction of behavioral models from actual runtime behavior. This has successfully been employed in applications such as Computer Telephony Integrated (CTI) systems [12,11], Web Services [20], or protocol specifications [21]. A particularly fruitful application of automata learning can be found in the EC FP7 project CONNECT [17], where behavioral models of networked systems are learned automatically, providing a basis for automated on-the-fly connector synthesis.

---

* This work was partially supported by the European Union FET Project CONNECT: Emergent Connectors for Eternal Software Intensive Networked Systems (http://connect-forever.eu/).

G. Brat, N. Rungta, and A. Venet (Eds.): NFM 2013, LNCS 7871, pp. 124–138, 2013.

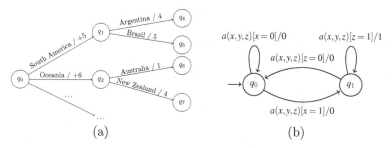

Fig. 1. (a) Fragment of the Mealy machine for generating country calling codes, (b) Mealy machine with binary action parameters

In all of the above scenarios, the learning algorithm relied on a kind of test harness, which provides an abstraction on the often infinite set of potential input actions, yielding a finite view of the system fine enough to guarantee a deterministic behavior, a precondition for most learning approaches. For real "black-box" systems, the true challenge for automata learning, these abstractions were usually determined in a laborious, manual trial and error process. The AAR algorithm presented in [16] was the first to overcome this problem: it fully automatically determines the coarsest refinement of a given abstraction that guarantees a deterministic behavior on the fly during the learning process.

In this paper we combine the AAR approach with the principle of *locality*: rather than determining one global alphabet, we fully automatically infer the optimal alphabet abstraction individually for each state. The motivation for this combination came from practical experience, in particular with learning Web applications: here, the alphabet symbols typically correspond to the actions a user can take, e.g., clicking on a link or submitting form data. An example (pattern) illustrating the need for locality is sketched in Fig. 1 (a): for an arbitrary country, it outputs the ITU country calling code (such as +1 for the US and Canada). The country is specified in a hierarchical manner, by first entering the continent and then the name of the country.

A more technical example is shown in Fig. 1 (b): here, actions are of form $a(x,y,z)$, with x,y,z ranging over the set $\{0,1\}$. The concrete input alphabet hence needs to contain every combination of values for x,y, and z, leading to $2^3 = 8$ different input symbols. The transitions are equipped with conditions checking the values of certain parameters. Obviously, the number of transitions is far lower than the size of the concrete input alphabet, as the effect of an input symbol highly depends on the current state.

A global abstraction cannot capture the specific nature of those examples; i.e., that the notion of a "valid" or "invalid" country (Fig. 1 (a)) depends on the selected continent, or that depending on the state in Fig. 1 (b), it is the value of either x or z that exposes differing behavior. A global abstraction needs to refine every single local abstraction, not only leading to an increased complexity in terms of queries, but also reducing the comprehensibility of the inferred model.

In our experimental analysis, we show that local alphabet abstraction refinement (LAAR) does not only work for systems as in Fig. 1, but also for quite differently structured third party benchmarks. In order to explore its performance, we compare the results of classical L^* learning, AAR and LAAR for the two examples displayed in Fig. 1, the first in its real-world instantiation, the latter with a growing number of parameters. Additionally, we investigated its application to a hierarchical file system navigator, and also three third-party systems. The results (cf. Table 1 in Section 4 of this paper) are quite surprising, as for some examples there was not only a decrease of membership queries, but also a decrease of equivalence queries.

However, despite the impressive performance results one should not forget the original intent of LAAR: to produce an improved and more concise abstract system model. In our experiments, the reduction factor in the number of transitions is between 4 and 10, reaching up to 500 for specific examples.

Related work. The algorithm presented in [16], which inferred alphabet abstractions at a global level, forms the basis of this paper's work. Dealing with infinite alphabets is also the aim of register automata learning [14], under the assumption that symbols are parameterized with data values from an infinite domain, and that the system behaves independently of concrete data values (i.e., permutations on the data domain do not affect the behavior).

In [10], an L^*-based approach for inferring a labeled transition system that represents an interface of a software component, classifying method execution sequences as either legal, illegal, or unknown, was introduced. The alphabet initially consists of arbitrary method invocations, and is refined subsequently to include constraints on the method's parameters. Similarly to AAR, this is done on-the-fly during the learning process. However, a fully white-box scenario is assumed, allowing to extract the precise guards from the component's source code. Unlike the approach in this paper, a homogeneous global alphabet is used.

In the context of assume-guarantee reasoning [7], active learning is employed to learn assumptions. Alphabet refinement techniques [9,3] have been used to potentially reduce the learning alphabet by starting with a smaller subset of the interface alphabet. When a seemingly spurious counterexample is found, the alphabet is extended heuristically in an additional counterexample analysis step. In contrast to [16], no abstraction is assumed on single alphabet symbols, but rather symbols not in the learning alphabet are hidden. This notion of refinement is related to predicate abstraction [5,13], and thus differs from our notion, which concerns the granularity of an abstraction. Except for the first one, all the works mentioned have in common that they do not extend the 'black box' model to the input alphabet, in contrast to our approach which describes classes of the abstraction in terms of behavioral observations.

Outline. This paper is organized as follows. Section 2 establishes the formalisms for modeling the kind of reactive systems our algorithm operates on, including a formalism for abstraction. In Section 3, we present our main contribution, an algorithm for inferring minimal abstract models of these systems. An experimental evaluation of this algorithm is presented in Section 4, and the final section concludes the paper, also giving an outlook on our intended future work.

2   Modeling Reactive Systems

Reactive systems, i.e., systems which directly respond to user interaction by producing output messages, form a large class of real-life systems, a prominent example being web services. In this paper, we will constrain ourselves to deterministic systems with finite output alphabets and state spaces, also being insensitive to real-time. For the exception of the finiteness of the input alphabet, which we do not require, these systems can be modeled by a widely known automaton model, and there exist well-studied learning algorithms for inferring such systems.

Taking into account infinite input alphabets, we will in the following subsections introduce a suitable model for this kind of systems, as well as establishing a formalism of abstraction that allows for finite representations of these models.

2.1   Mealy Machines

Mealy machines are a variant of automata which distinguish between an input alphabet and an output alphabet. Characteristic for Mealy machines is that inputs are always enabled (in other words, the transition function is totally defined for all input symbols), and that their response to an input (sequence) is uniquely determined (this property is called input determinism). Both properties fit the requirements of a large class of (reactive) systems very well.

Let Σ be a set of *input actions*. By Σ^* we denote the set of words over Σ, with the usual notation $|w|$ for the length of w. The empty word is denoted by ε. Let then $\Sigma^+ = \Sigma^* \setminus \{\varepsilon\}$ be the set of all words of nonzero length. The concatenation of two words u and v is written as $u \cdot v$ or simply uv. In the remainder of this paper we will need to distinguish between (possibly countably infinite) *concrete* input actions, referred to as Σ_C, and *abstract* (and finite) input actions, referred to as Σ_A. These indexes are applied to symbols and words in the same way.

As an extension of the well-known Mealy machine model, we now define a *countable Mealy machine (CMM)* as $M = \langle Q, q_0, \Sigma, \Omega, \delta, \lambda \rangle$, where Q is a finite nonempty set of *states*, $q_0 \in Q$ is the *initial state*, Σ is an (at most) countable set of *input actions*, Ω is a finite set of *output actions*, $\delta : Q \times \Sigma \to Q$ is the *transition function*, and $\lambda : Q \times \Sigma \to \Omega$ is the *output function*.

Intuitively, a (countable) Mealy machine evolves through states $q \in Q$, and whenever one applies an input symbol (or action) $a \in \Sigma$, the machine moves to a new state according to $\delta(q, a)$ and produces an output according to $\lambda(q, a)$.[1] The *semantics* of a Mealy machine M can sufficiently be expressed in terms of a function $[\![M]\!] : \Sigma^+ \to \Omega$ mapping each word from Σ^+ to an output symbol from Ω, defined in the following way:

$$[\![M]\!](wa) =_{def} \lambda(\delta^*(q_0, w), a).$$

---

[1] We will extend δ to words in the usual way: Let $\delta^*(q, \varepsilon) = q$ and $\delta^*(q, aw) = \delta^*(\delta(q, a), w)$ for $aw \in \Sigma^+$.

2.2   Abstractions on Countable Mealy Machines

In this section, we will describe how abstractions can serve as a way of dealing with the large (or even infinite) structure of a CMM in a more compact (finite) manner. The key idea is that the effect of each input symbol can be described in terms of the immediately produced output and the future behavior (the successor state), both of which form finite classes.

Definition 1. *For arbitrary sets Σ_C (concrete domain) and Σ_A (abstract domain), a surjective function $\alpha\colon \Sigma_C \to \Sigma_A$ is called an* abstraction. *If Σ_A is finite, α is called a* finite abstraction. *The* cardinality $|\alpha|$ *of α is defined as $|\alpha| = |\Sigma_A|$. A function $\gamma\colon \Sigma_A \to \Sigma_C$ is a* concretization *(wrt. α) if $\gamma \circ \alpha$ is the identity function on Σ_A. For $a_A \in \Sigma_A$, $\gamma(a_A)$ is called the* representative *for a_A (wrt. γ). For $a_C \in \Sigma_C$, the representative is $\rho(a_C)$ with $\rho = \alpha \circ \gamma$.* □

An abstraction α induces a partition $P_\alpha = \{\alpha^{-1}(a) \mid a \in \Sigma_A\}$ on Σ_C and therefore also an equivalence relation. Two abstractions are said to be *isomorphic* if they induce the same partition. Similarly, we adapt the concept of refinement in terms of the induced partition.

For finitely describing CMMs we identify for each state $q \in Q$ of the CMM an abstraction α_q, such that $\delta(q,\cdot)$ and $\lambda(q,\cdot)$ both are invariant under the application of ρ_q, regardless of the chosen concretization γ_q. Such an abstraction is called a *determinism-preserving abstraction (DPA)*. The following definition introduces an automaton model which captures this kind of abstraction.

Definition 2. *A (state-locally) abstract Mealy machine (AMM) $\mathcal{M}$ is defined as $\mathcal{M} = \langle Q, q_0, \Sigma_C, \Omega, A, \Delta, \Lambda \rangle$, where*

- *Q is a finite set of* states,
- *$q_0 \in Q$ is the* initial state,
- *Σ_C is a countable set of* concrete inputs,
- *Ω is a finite set of* outputs,
- *$A = \{\alpha_q\colon \Sigma_C \to \Sigma_{A,q} \mid q \in Q\}$ is a set of* local abstractions, *where $\Sigma_{A,q}$ is some (arbitrary) finite abstract domain,*
- *$\Delta = \{\delta_q\colon \Sigma_{A,q} \to Q \mid q \in Q\}$ is a set of* local transition functions *and*
- *$\Lambda = \{\lambda_q\colon \Sigma_{A,q} \to \Omega \mid q \in Q\}$ is a set of* local output functions.

An AMM evolves through states $q \in Q$ by reading input symbols $a_C \in \Sigma_C$, producing output symbols and moving to a successor state according to λ_q and δ_q respectively, beforehand transforming the input symbol a_C to an abstract symbol $a_A = \alpha_q(a_C)$. □

A CMM $M = \langle Q, q_0, \Sigma_C, \Omega, \delta, \lambda \rangle$ can be derived from an AMM $\mathcal{M} = \langle Q, q_0, \Sigma_C, \Omega, A, \Delta, \Lambda \rangle$ by defining $\delta(q, a_C) = \delta_q(\alpha_q(a_C))$ and $\lambda(q, a_C) = \lambda_q(\alpha_q(a_C))$. The semantics of an AMM can therefore also be expressed in terms of a function $[\![\mathcal{M}]\!]\colon \Sigma_C^+ \to \Omega$, and we can define a CMM M and an AMM $\mathcal{M}$ to be equivalent iff $[\![M]\!] = [\![\mathcal{M}]\!]$.

For each CMM M, there is a unique (up to isomorphism) minimal equivalent AMM $\mathcal{M}$. Here, minimal refers to both the number of states as well as the cardinality of each local abstraction $|\alpha_q|$. Considering the possibility to derive a CMM from $\mathcal{M}$, it is obvious that the same number of states as the minimal CMM is both necessary and sufficient. For each state $q \in Q$ in the minimal CMM $M = \langle Q, q_0, \Sigma_C, \delta, \lambda \rangle$, we define the equivalence relation $\simeq_q \subseteq \Sigma_C \times \Sigma_C$ by

$$a_C \simeq_q a'_C :\Leftrightarrow \delta(q, a_C) = \delta(q, a'_C) \wedge \lambda(q, a_C) = \lambda(q, a'_C).$$

The abstraction α_q^* corresponding to $\simeq_q$ obviously is determinism-preserving. Furthermore, if an abstraction α_q does not refine α_q^*, there exist $a_C, a'_C \in \Sigma_C$ such that $\alpha_q(a_C) = \alpha_q(a'_C)$ but $\alpha_q^*(a_C) \neq \alpha_q^*(a'_C)$ and therefore $a_C \not\simeq_q a'_C$. By the definition of $\simeq_q$, α_q cannot be determinism preserving.

The minimal AMM $\mathcal{M}$ of some system modeled by a CMM is the *most concise* representation of this system: it only contains a single transition for each *distinguishable* transition (wrt. either source or target state, or output symbol) in the CMM. This qualifies the minimal AMM as the desired model in terms of comprehensibility.

3   The Learning Algorithm

In this section we will present our main contribution: an active learning algorithm that produces an abstract model of a system under learning (*SUL*) at the level of an optimal local abstraction. Before describing the concepts of our algorithm, we will briefly revisit the algorithm L_M^* [25,23], an adaptation of the classical L^* algorithm [2] for Mealy machines.

3.1 L_M^* Revisited

Active automata learning algorithms infer models of unknown regular systems under learning (SUL) for which initially only an input alphabet is known, using two kinds of queries.

- *Membership queries* (MQ) test the reaction of the *SUL* to a specific input (e.g., a word over the input alphabet).
- *Equivalence queries* (EQ) test whether an intermediate hypothesis correctly models the *SUL*, and returns a counterexample in case it does not.

In principle, learning starts with a one state hypothesis automaton that treats all words over the considered alphabet (of elementary observations) alike and refines this automaton on the basis of query results iterating two steps: *hypothesis construction* and *hypothesis verification*.

During hypothesis construction the dual way of how states of the unknown SUL are characterized is central:

- by an incrementally growing prefix-closed set of words reaching each state of the *SUL* exactly once. This set defines a spanning tree of the intermediate hypothesis automata.

- by their future behavior wrt. a dynamically growing set of 'distinguishing' suffixes from Σ_C^+. This characterization is too coarse throughout the learning process and will be refined continuously following the pattern of the well-known Nerode congruence [19] (or [24] for Mealy machines).

This evolving characterization is established using membership queries. From certain well-defined sets of prefixes and suffixes, hypothesis automata can be constructed, which are then subjected to an equivalence query. In case the hypothesis is not equivalent to the target system, a counterexample highlighting some difference is returned and will be exploited to further refine the hypothesis. If, on the other hand, *ok* is returned, learning can terminate.

At this point it should be mentioned that, in general, equivalence queries for black box systems are undecidable. Realizing them for a concrete application is very much dependent on the application scenario itself. As this is a matter of research independent from the approach presented in this paper, we will not discuss it here. For the most generic way of approximating equivalence queries in black-box scenarios by means of membership queries, a quite efficient way is discussed in [15].

The central data structure of the L_M^* algorithm is an *observation table*. An observation table is a tuple $\langle Sp, Lp, \mathcal{D}, T \rangle$, where

- Sp is a prefix-closed set of *access sequences* identifying states in the hypothesis ('short prefixes'),
- Lp is a set of *one-step futures* identifying the transitions in the hypothesis ('long prefixes'); in the classical scenario Lp is usually chosen as $Lp = Sp \cdot \Sigma \setminus Sp$,
- $\mathcal{D}$ is a set of *distinguishing suffixes* used for distinguishing states, resp. for matching the states reached by the words in Lp against those identified by words in Sp (usually initialized with Σ for Mealy machines),
- $T \colon (Sp \cup Lp) \to (\mathcal{D} \to \Omega)$ is a mapping assigning to each word in $Sp \cup Lp$ the observable future behavior (wrt. $\mathcal{D}$) of the corresponding (possibly unknown) state in the *SUL*, i.e., $T(u)(v) = [\![SUL]\!](uv)$.

An observation table is used to maintain the dual characterization of states discussed above. It is *closed* iff for every word $u \in Lp$, there exists a corresponding word $u' \in Sp$ such that $T(u) = T(u')$. Intuitively, this guarantees that in a hypothesis automaton all transitions have well-defined destinations. A table can be closed by subsequently moving words $u \in Lp$ violating this condition to Sp and adjusting Lp accordingly (e.g., by adding all words $u \cdot \Sigma$). An example of a slightly extended observation table can be found in Fig. 2 (c): The rows in the upper part correspond to words in Sp, while those in the lower part correspond to one-step futures from Lp. The columns are labeled by suffixes in $\mathcal{D}$, such that each cell corresponds to a $T(u)(v)$ for $u \in Sp \cup Lp, v \in \mathcal{D}$.

From a closed observation table, a hypothesis automaton $\mathcal{H}$ can be constructed to which an equivalence query may yield a counterexample exposing a behavioral difference between the *SUL* and $\mathcal{H}$. More precisely, a counterexample exposes a state in the hypothesis whose future behavior wrt. some suffix

$v \notin \mathcal{D}$ differs from every state in the hypothesis (i.e., prefix in $\mathcal{S}p$). This suffix is added to the set $\mathcal{D}$, resulting in an unclosed table and thus the creation of additional states in a subsequent hypothesis. Both hypothesis construction and counterexample handling are described in detail for our new algorithm in Sections 3.3 and 3.4.

3.2   Alphabet Abstraction Refinement

In [16], an extension to L_M^* was presented, which combines active automata learning with inferring a globally coarsest determinism-preserving abstraction on the input alphabet. As in this paper, a pure black-box scenario was assumed: abstraction classes were defined in terms of query outcomes, and the refinement was triggered by counterexamples exposing non-determinism due to the current abstraction.

The key technical idea was to introduce a *middle congruence* relation on concrete alphabet symbols: two symbols $a_C, a_C' \in \Sigma_C$ could be shown to be inequivalent by a prefix $p \in \Sigma_C^*$ and a suffix $d \in \Sigma_C^*$ such that $[\![SUL]\!](pa_Cd) \neq [\![SUL]\!](pa_C'd)$. In the context of the learning algorithm, the pair (p,d) could be used to classify arbitrary concrete symbols a_C by looking at the result of a membership query $MQ(pa_Cd)$. This resembles the general idea of active automata learning to approximate the *Nerode* congruence [19] for separating words $u, u' \in \mathcal{S}p$ using suffixes $v \in \mathcal{D}$ such that $[\![SUL]\!](uv) \neq [\![SUL]\!](u'v)$.

In principle, the global AAR approach can be thought of as the combination of two relatively independent components: (i) a classical active learning algorithm, supporting a dynamically growing input alphabet, and (ii) an alphabet abstraction refinement module, which is triggered by otherwise inexplicable counterexamples; i.e., words $w = w_1 \ldots w_n \in \Sigma_C^*$, which cease to be counterexamples when pointwisely transforming each w_i to the corresponding representative symbol.

Naturally, a global determinism-preserving abstraction is also determinism-preserving when applied to each state locally. However, it was already sketched in the introductory examples in Fig. 1 that this global perspective is not always adequate. While it would be possible to coarsen each abstraction locally for each state until reaching the respective coarsest DPA, our approach is to perform the abstraction refinement locally from the starting point on. This is a considerably more involved task: first, there no longer exists a homogeneous, global input alphabet. When introducing new representative symbols, it is crucial to pinpoint the exact state of which to extend the alphabet. Second, the approach of transforming a counterexample into a representative word is bound to fail, as the abstraction to choose depends on the corresponding state – an information which can be erroneous as well. In combination, this calls for a much stronger integration of the alphabet abstraction refinement part with the existing learning and counterexample handling algorithm.

Before laying our focus on the treatment of counterexamples in Sec. 3.4, we will first introduce the data structure for managing abstractions, and show how these are connected to the usual observation table.

Definition 3. *An abstraction tree $\mathcal{T}$ for a prefix $u \in \Sigma_C^*$ is a tuple $\mathcal{T} = \langle u, r \rangle$, where r is the root node of a binary tree consisting of two kinds of nodes: (i) inner nodes are labeled with a classifier $\langle d, o \rangle \in \Sigma_C^* \times \Omega$ and have two child nodes, an equals-child, and an other-child; (ii) leaves are labeled with a pair of concrete and abstract inputs $(a_C, a_A) \in \Sigma_C \times \Sigma_A$.*

An abstraction tree $\mathcal{T}$ is a special kind of a decision tree, realizing both an abstraction function $\alpha_{\mathcal{T}}$ as well as the representative function $\rho_{\mathcal{T}}(a_C)$ as following, for a concrete symbol $a_C \in \Sigma_C$: starting at the root of the tree, we choose at each inner node labeled with $\langle d, o \rangle$ the *equals*-child if $MQ(ua_Cd) = o$, and the *other*-child otherwise. This step directly reflects the middle congruence on alphabet symbols from [16], as mentioned above. The step is repeated until a leaf (a_R, a_A) is reached. Then, $a_A = \alpha_{\mathcal{T}}(a_C)$ is the corresponding abstract symbol and $a_R = \gamma_{\mathcal{T}}(a_A) = \rho_{\mathcal{T}}(a_C)$ its representative.

The corresponding abstraction can be *refined* by splitting leaves: We call a tuple $\langle a_C, d, o \rangle$ a *witness* (for the insufficiency of the abstraction) if $[\![SUL]\!](ua_Rd) \neq [\![SUL]\!](ua_Cd) = o$, i.e., it demonstrates a deviating behavior when concretizing a_A by a_C instead of a_R. Let (a_R, a_A) be the leaf found by the lookup operation for a_C, and let a_A' be a new abstract symbol that does not yet appear anywhere else. We replace the leaf by an inner node $\langle d, o \rangle$, which has the leaf (a_C, a_A') as its *equals*-child and the leaf (a_R, a_A) as its *other*-child.

For an abstraction tree $\mathcal{T}$, we denote by $\Sigma_C(\mathcal{T})$ the set of representatives, i.e., the set of all concrete symbols appearing at leaves, and by $\Sigma_A(\mathcal{T})$ the corresponding abstract domain. The cardinality $|\mathcal{T}|$ is the total number of leaves in the tree, it holds that $|\alpha_{\mathcal{T}}| = |\mathcal{T}|$.

Abstraction trees can always be initialized with a leaf $(a_C, a_A) \in \Sigma_C \times \Sigma_A$ as its rood node, where a_C, a_A are arbitrary concrete respectively abstract actions. Of course, if prior knowledge about the semantics of the alphabet exists, a more fine-grained initial abstraction can be used.

3.3   Modifications for Observation Tables

As in [16], the learning algorithm operates on a concrete level: the sets Sp, Lp and $\mathcal{D}$ all form subsets of Σ_C^*. For constructing the set Lp, we need to know the local (representative) alphabet for each state corresponding to a prefix $u \in Sp$. We hence associate with each $u \in Sp$ a corresponding state-local abstraction (tree) $\mathcal{T}_u = \langle u, r_u \rangle$. The set Lp can then be defined as $Lp = \{ua_C \mid u \in Sp, a_C \in \Sigma_C(\mathcal{T}_u)\} \setminus Sp$.

For obvious reasons, the set $\mathcal{D}$ is not initialized with the full learning alphabet, but rather with a finite arbitrary nonempty subset of Σ_C^+. For determining transition outputs in the hypothesis, L_M^* assumes that for each prefix $u \in Sp$ and input $a \in \Sigma$ there exists a table cell $T(u)(a)$ containing the corresponding output. As we cannot rely on this (as $\mathcal{D}$ is not guaranteed to contain all $a_C \in \Sigma_C(\mathcal{T}_u)$ for every $u \in Sp$), the output of each transition is stored separately by means of an *output table* $O : (Sp \cup Lp) \setminus \{\varepsilon\} \to \Omega$. The additional $|Sp \cup Lp| - 1$ MQs will obviously neither change asymptotic query complexity nor will hamper practical applicability. In Fig. 2 (c), the output is shown next to the respective row label.

Closing tables. Since closing a previously unclosed observation table augments the set Sp, this also requires the introduction of a new local abstraction. Similar to beginning with a one-state hypothesis for the automaton, as a new abstraction we will initially use a maximally coarse one that treats all symbols from Σ_C alike (i.e., $\mathcal{T}_u = \langle u, (a_C, a_A) \rangle$, where a_C is an arbitrary concrete representative).

Hypothesis construction. The generation of an abstract Mealy machine (cf. Def. 2) hypothesis $\mathcal{H}$ from a closed observation table $\langle Sp, Lp, \mathcal{D}, T \rangle$, abstraction trees $\mathcal{T}_u$ for every $u \in Sp$ and an output table O mostly resembles the method for ordinary Mealy machines [24]: States are identified with words $u \in Sp$, where ε corresponds to the initial state. Since the observation table is closed, it follows that for each $a_C \in \Sigma_C(\mathcal{T}_u)$ there is $ua_C \in Sp \cup Lp$, and thus a word $u' \in Sp$ such that $T(ua_C) = T(u')$. Transitions are then constructed by applying the local abstraction α_u on a_C, thus $\delta_u(\alpha_u(a_C)) = u'$. Outputs are handled accordingly.

3.4 Handling Counterexamples

Once we have generated a hypothesis automaton $\mathcal{H}$, an equivalence query will either signal success or return a counterexample, i.e., a word $c \in \Sigma_C^+$ such that $[\![\mathcal{H}]\!](c) \neq [\![SUL]\!](c)$. In the classical scenario, a counterexample gives rise to at least one new state by exposing future behavior that differs from all states currently present in the hypothesis. This *splitting* of states is done implicitly by augmenting the set $\mathcal{D}$ of distinguishing suffixes and consequently closing the table. As a starting point for handling counterexamples, we use the approach described in [22] and detailed in [24], not the original way proposed by Angluin [2].

When also inferring alphabet abstractions, the situation is different: the cause of deviating behavior can also be an abstraction that is too coarse and thus imposes non-determinism. Accordingly, the treatment of counterexamples becomes a much more complicated task. The following paragraphs will explain in detail how a counterexample is processed.

Consider a counterexample $c = c_1 \ldots c_m \in \Sigma_C^+$. We decompose c into $c = ua_C v$, where $u, v \in \Sigma_C^*$ and $a_C = c_i \in \Sigma_C$. Values for i range from 1 to m and are considered in ascending order. The idea now is to transform the prefix u to the word leading to the same state in $\mathcal{H}$. This word is referred to as the *access sequence* of u and denoted by $\lfloor u \rfloor$. For each decomposition $c = ua_C v$, we determine the local representative $a_R = \rho_{\lfloor u \rfloor}(a_C)$ and perform the following checks:

1. $[\![SUL]\!](\lfloor u \rfloor a_R v) \neq [\![SUL]\!](\lfloor u \rfloor a_C v)$: In the state reached via $\lfloor u \rfloor$ in the SUL, a_C and a_R may not be treated equivalently. Let $o = [\![SUL]\!](\lfloor u \rfloor a_C v)$, then $\langle a_C, v, o \rangle$ is a witness for splitting the leaf labeled with the concrete symbol a_R in the abstraction tree $\mathcal{T}_{\lfloor u \rfloor}$. The word $\lfloor u \rfloor a_C$ is added to the set Lp, introducing a new transition in the hypothesis.

2. $[\![SUL]\!](\lfloor u \rfloor a_R v) \neq [\![SUL]\!](\lfloor ua_R \rfloor v)$: The future behavior wrt. v of the state reached by $\lfloor u \rfloor a_R$ and $\lfloor ua_R \rfloor$ differs (this is the classical case). In the hypothesis, these two words must lead to different states. The suffix v is added to the set $\mathcal{D}$, resulting in an unclosed table caused by $T(\lfloor ua_R \rfloor)(v) \neq T(\lfloor u \rfloor a_R)(v)$ and thus the creation of a new state in the hypothesis.

If none of the above cases applies, i is incremented and the steps described above are repeated. Obviously, for $i = 1$ the initial counterexample c is considered, whereas after the last step c has been transformed into a word ua_R fully supported by the hypothesis. As c is a counterexample, both words lead to different outputs, guaranteeing that one of the above cases will eventually apply. As a single counterexample may expose both an insufficient number of states as well as an alphabet abstraction being too coarse, it usually is a good idea to re-evaluate a counterexample after having updated the hypothesis.

3.5   Correctness and Complexity

The following theorem states that our algorithm is guaranteed to terminate after a certain number of queries, and that it does so with an optimal result.

Theorem 1. *If $\mathcal{M}$ is an optimal abstraction of SUL, the algorithm infers $\mathcal{M}$ using $O(t(n + am)) = O(mk^2 n^3)$ membership queries and at most $n + t = O(t) = O(n^2 k)$ equivalence queries, where $n = |Q|$, $k = |\Omega|$, $t = \sum_{q \in Q} |\alpha_q|$, $a = \max_{q \in Q} |\alpha_q|$ and m is the maximum length of a counterexample returned by an equivalence query.*

We will omit the proof of the complexity at this point, and only sketch the idea for proving optimality. For this, we can resort to the optimality argument from [2]: New states are introduced only when differing future behavior is explicitly discovered. This can be applied to the refinement level of the alphabet as well: local alphabets are augmented only when necessary, hence the refinement level of the minimal CMM is never exceeded. As long as the refinement level is too coarse, however, counterexamples can be found.

3.6   An Example Run of the Algorithm

In order to give a better impression of how exactly the algorithm works, we present an execution fragment of applying it to the system depicted in Fig. 1 (b). In all contexts, we will use $a(0,0,0)$ as the default concrete representative, hence we initialize the data structure with $Sp = \{\varepsilon\}$, $Lp = \mathcal{D} = \{a(0,0,0)\}$ and the only abstraction tree $\mathcal{T}_\varepsilon = \langle \varepsilon, (a(0,0,0), a_1) \rangle$. This leads to a trivial initial hypothesis, consisting only of a single state and transition, outputting 0 on each input symbol.

When conducting an equivalence query, a possible counterexample is $c = a(0,0,1)a(1,0,1)a(1,1,1)$, whose output 1 contradicts the hypothesis. We now stepwise transform this counterexample according to the process described in Sec. 3.4. Substituting the representative $a(0,0,0)$ for the first symbol does not change the output, neither does replacing $a(0,0,0)$ by its access sequence $\lfloor a(0,0,0) \rfloor = \varepsilon$. After the first iteration of the loop, we transformed the counterexample to $a(1,0,1)a(1,1,1)/1$. However, replacing $a(1,0,1)$ with the standard representative $a(0,0,0)$ changes the observed output behavior to 0. We refine the abstraction tree $\mathcal{T}_\varepsilon$ using the witness $\langle a(1,0,1), a(1,1,1), 1 \rangle$. The resulting abstraction tree is shown in Fig. 2 (a), and $a(1,0,1)$ is added to the local alphabet of the state represented by ε and thus to Lp.

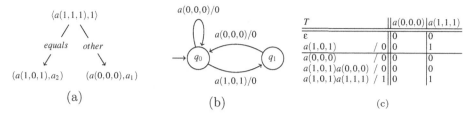

Fig. 2. (a) Abstraction tree for ε after first refinement, (b) intermediate hypothesis after two counterexample evaluations, (c) final observation table

Reevaluation shows that the counterexample still conflicts with our hypothesis. Since the abstraction of ε has changed, we have to start transforming from the beginning. $a(0,0,1)a(1,1,1)$ produces 0 as last output, so the first symbol is still replaced by $a(0,0,0)$ and subsequently by ε. The remaining word $a(1,0,1)a(1,1,1)$ already starts with a representative symbol, but when substituting $a(1,0,1)$ with $\lfloor a(1,0,1)\rfloor = ε$, the output changes to 0. $a(1,1,1)$ is added to $\mathcal{D}$, leading to a new state with access sequence $a(1,0,1)$ being added to the hypothesis. The corresponding abstraction tree is again initialized with the maximally coarse abstraction, using $a(0,0,0)$ as a representative symbol. The intermediate hypothesis is shown in Fig. 2 (b), the observation table at this point is the one shown in Fig. 2 (c) without the last line.

A final reevaluation again exposes that we still have a counterexample. A change in output from 1 to 0 is observed during the transformation $a(1,0,1)a(1,1,1) \rightarrow a(1,0,1)a(0,0,0)$, leading to the abstraction $\mathcal{T}_{a(1,0,1)}$ being refined using as a witness $\langle a(1,1,1), ε, 1 \rangle$, and we end up with a representative version of the final model. The corresponding observation table is shown in Fig. 2 (c).

4   Experimental Results

We have implemented the algorithm outlined in the previous sections as part of LearnLib[2] [21] and conducted several experiments, the results of which are depicted in Table 1. We compared our new algorithm with both the classical L_M^* and the global AAR algorithm presented in [16]. In the case of infinite alphabets, we restricted the domain to those symbols which have non-error semantics in at least one state, as otherwise it would not have been possible to use L_M^*.

Besides taking into account the number of membership and equivalence queries, we also considered the sizes of the abstractions: $|\Sigma_A|$ for global, $|\alpha| = \max_{q \in Q} |\alpha_q|$ for local AAR. A cache for avoiding multiple membership queries for the same word was used in all experimental setups. Finally, we also recorded the wallclock times (on a 2.5GHz Intel Core i5-2520M with 8GB RAM).

We considered the following example systems for our experiments: The country calling code (CCC) example, as displayed in Fig. 1, and a similar problem,

---

[2] http://www.learnlib.de/

Table 1. Results of the experimental evaluation. Lowest values are marked bold (comparison only between global and local AAR for EQ).

Example	Size		L^*_M			Global AAR				Local AAR			
	$|Q|$	$|\Sigma_C|$	# MQ	# EQ	Time	# MQ	# EQ	Time	$|\Sigma_A|$	# MQ	# EQ	Time	$|\alpha|$
CCC	204	200	320,200	1	51s	10,953	201	5m55s	196	**2,600**	204	22s	55
FHN1	95	88	190,122	3	28s	39,456	93	39s	36	**3,798**	99	4s	15
FHN2	310	262	7,391,946	9	58m0s	1,766,688	354	6h50m16s	258	**50,371**	417	7m30s	39
BV7	71	128	1,269,564	14	4m27s	175,458	146	2m00s	128	**10,926**	91	26s	2
BV8	84	256	5,994,280	24	25m51s	677,176	287	16m49s	256	**25,168**	116	1m43s	2
BV9	72	512	19,370,515	15	2h00m09s	890,475	535	53m48s	512	**39,507**	99	2m54s	2
BV10	75	1024	80,473,959	26	13h19m02s	2,795,183	1060	8h57m32s	1024	**80,455**	111	10m13s	2
Bio.Pass.	5	264	348,744	1	1m34s	**2,052**	14	4s	10	2,966	24	6s	6
Pots2	664	32	1,504,181	39	14m03s	1,483,594	96	16m28s	32	**234,289**	2,840	58m58s	7
Peterson3	1,328	57	8,775,306	43	3h21m48s	> 8,000,000[3]	—	> 4h30m	—	**590,786**	3,986	5h45m36s	4

a file system hierarchy navigator (FHNi), modeling the navigation through a directory structure, a model of the biometric passport (cf. [1]) and two rather large models (Pots2 and Peterson3), distributed with the CADP tool set [8] and the Concurrency Workbench [18]. Finally, we considered a series of automatically generated automata (BVk) of the type sketched in Fig. 1 (b), with k binary parameters.

The results underline the improvement in terms of efficiency: In all cases, the number of membership queries could vastly be reduced, depending on the concrete example by several orders of magnitude. For the systems with hierarchical structure, namely CCC and FHNi, there are major improvements regarding the number of membership queries, the size of the abstraction as well as the execution times, compared to both global AAR and L^*_M, while the number of equivalence queries is only moderately increased in comparison to global AAR. The biggest improvement could be observed for the BVk examples, where an increase in two to three orders of magnitude in MQs, execution times as well as conciseness of the model could be seen. While we expected local AAR to outperform the other two algorithms in terms of membership queries, we found it surprising that, compared to global AAR, also the number of equivalence queries was reduced significantly.

When looking at the remaining examples, which were not chosen with local abstraction (Bio.Pass.) or even abstraction in general (Pots2 and Peterson3) in mind, the results are still promising. Of all the considered examples, Pots2 is the only one were LAAR falls behind. While there is a reduction in terms of membership queries by an order of magnitude, due to the computational overhead, the execution time is much higher than for global AAR as well as L^*_M. One should keep in mind, however, that we performed MQs by simulation, which is extremely quick. The more time a single membership query takes, the more does local AAR profit.

Particularly striking is the conciseness of the Peterson3 model inferred using local abstractions: L^*_M produces a model with 57 outgoing transitions in each state, where LAAR automatically infers a model where no state has more than four outgoing transitions. Global AAR failed to learn this system, as it repeatedly ran into out-of-memory-conditions.

---

[3] Execution aborted due to out-of-memory-condition.

5 Conclusions

We have presented an automata learning algorithm that infers a model of a system at an abstract level, while in parallel inferring a set of state-local alphabet abstractions just fine enough to preserve determinism. This allows us to handle input alphabets of infinite cardinality for which no further information is known, that is, they are – just like the system itself – treated in a 'black box' fashion.

By an experimental evaluation, we show that this not only leads to more concise and thus more comprehensible models, but also is in the majority of cases a significant improvement in terms of performance compared to our previous algorithm, treating abstraction at a global level only. Moreover, in the case of finite but large input alphabets, it compares very well to the classical L_M^* algorithm, provided that a state-local perspective on alphabet abstraction is by any means adequate considering the system's behavior.

Currently, we are investigating the impact of LAAR by inferring models for a variety of real-life web applications, and the generality of the local alphabet abstraction for enhancing learning of richer automaton models, in particular register automata [14].

References

1. Aarts, F., Schmaltz, J., Vaandrager, F.: Inference and Abstraction of the Biometric Passport. In: Margaria, T., Steffen, B. (eds.) ISoLA 2010, Part I. LNCS, vol. 6415, pp. 673–686. Springer, Heidelberg (2010)
2. Angluin, D.: Learning Regular Sets from Queries and Counterexamples. Information and Computation 2(75), 87–106 (1987)
3. Gheorghiu Bobaru, M., Păsăreanu, C.S., Giannakopoulou, D.: Automated Assume-Guarantee Reasoning by Abstraction Refinement. In: Gupta, A., Malik, S. (eds.) CAV 2008. LNCS, vol. 5123, pp. 135–148. Springer, Heidelberg (2008)
4. Broy, M., Jonsson, B., Katoen, J.-P., Leucker, M., Pretschner, A. (eds.): Model-Based Testing of Reactive Systems. LNCS, vol. 3472. Springer, Heidelberg (2005)
5. Clarke, E., Grumberg, O., Jha, S., Lu, Y., Veith, H.: Counterexample-guided Abstraction Refinement for Symbolic Model Checking. J. ACM 50(5), 752–794 (2003)
6. Clarke, E.M., Grumberg, O., Peled, D.A.: Model Checking. Springer (1999)
7. Cobleigh, J.M., Giannakopoulou, D., Păsăreanu, C.S.: Learning Assumptions for Compositional Verification. In: Garavel, H., Hatcliff, J. (eds.) TACAS 2003. LNCS, vol. 2619, pp. 331–346. Springer, Heidelberg (2003)
8. Garavel, H., Lang, F., Mateescu, R., Serwe, W.: CADP 2010: A Toolbox for the Construction and Analysis of Distributed Processes. In: Abdulla, P.A., Leino, K.R.M. (eds.) TACAS 2011. LNCS, vol. 6605, pp. 372–387. Springer, Heidelberg (2011)
9. Gheorghiu, M., Giannakopoulou, D., Păsăreanu, C.S.: Refining Interface Alphabets for Compositional Verification. In: Grumberg, O., Huth, M. (eds.) TACAS 2007. LNCS, vol. 4424, pp. 292–307. Springer, Heidelberg (2007)
10. Giannakopoulou, D., Rakamarić, Z., Raman, V.: Symbolic Learning of Component Interfaces. In: Miné, A., Schmidt, D. (eds.) SAS 2012. LNCS, vol. 7460, pp. 248–264. Springer, Heidelberg (2012)

11. Hagerer, A., Hungar, H., Niese, O., Steffen, B.: Model Generation by Moderated Regular Extrapolation. In: Kutsche, R.-D., Weber, H. (eds.) FASE 2002. LNCS, vol. 2306, pp. 80–95. Springer, Heidelberg (2002)

12. Hagerer, A., Margaria, T., Niese, O., Steffen, B., Brune, G., Ide, H.-D.: Efficient Regression Testing of CTI-systems: Testing a Complex Call-center Solution. Annual Review of Comm., Int. Engineering Consortium (IEC) 55, 1033–1040 (2001)

13. Henzinger, T.A., Jhala, R., Majumdar, R., Sutre, G.: Lazy abstraction. In: POPL 2002, pp. 58–70. ACM, New York (2002)

14. Howar, F., Steffen, B., Jonsson, B., Cassel, S.: Inferring Canonical Register Automata. In: Kuncak, V., Rybalchenko, A. (eds.) VMCAI 2012. LNCS, vol. 7148, pp. 251–266. Springer, Heidelberg (2012)

15. Howar, F., Steffen, B., Merten, M.: From ZULU to RERS: Lessons learned in the ZULU challenge. In: Margaria, T., Steffen, B. (eds.) ISoLA 2010, Part I. LNCS, vol. 6415, pp. 687–704. Springer, Heidelberg (2010)

16. Howar, F., Steffen, B., Merten, M.: Automata Learning with Automated Alphabet Abstraction Refinement. In: Jhala, R., Schmidt, D. (eds.) VMCAI 2011. LNCS, vol. 6538, pp. 263–277. Springer, Heidelberg (2011)

17. Issarny, V., Steffen, B., Jonsson, B., Blair, G.S., Grace, P., Kwiatkowska, M.Z., Calinescu, R., Inverardi, P., Tivoli, M., Bertolino, A., Sabetta, A.: CONNECT Challenges: Towards Emergent Connectors for Eternal Networked Systems. In: ICECCS, pp. 154–161 (2009)

18. Moller, F., Stevens, P.: Edinburgh Concurrency Workbench User Manual (Version 7.1), http://homepages.inf.ed.ac.uk/perdita/cwb/

19. Nerode, A.: Linear Automaton Transformations. Proceedings of the American Mathematical Society 9(4), 541–544 (1958)

20. Raffelt, H., Margaria, T., Steffen, B., Merten, M.: Hybrid Test of Web Applications with Webtest. In: TAV-WEB 2008, pp. 1–7. ACM, New York (2008)

21. Raffelt, H., Steffen, B., Berg, T., Margaria, T.: LearnLib: A Framework for Extrapolating Behavioral Models. International Journal on Software Tools for Technology Transfer (STTT) 11(5), 393–407 (2009)

22. Rivest, R.L., Schapire, R.E.: Inference of Finite Automata Using Homing Sequences. Inf. Comput. 103(2), 299–347 (1993)

23. Shahbaz, M., Groz, R.: Inferring Mealy Machines. In: Cavalcanti, A., Dams, D. (eds.) FM 2009. LNCS, vol. 5850, pp. 207–222. Springer, Heidelberg (2009)

24. Steffen, B., Howar, F., Merten, M.: Introduction to Active Automata Learning from a Practical Perspective. In: Bernardo, M., Issarny, V. (eds.) SFM 2011. LNCS, vol. 6659, pp. 256–296. Springer, Heidelberg (2011)

25. Steffen, B., Margaria, T., Raffelt, H., Niese, O.: Efficient test-based model generation of legacy systems. In: HLDVT 2004, Sonoma (CA), USA, pp. 95–100. IEEE Computer Society Press (November 2004)

Incremental Invariant Generation Using Logic-Based Automatic Abstract Transformers*

Pierre-Loïc Garoche[1,2], Temesghen Kahsai[2], and Cesare Tinelli[2]

[1] Onera, the French Aerospace Lab, France
[2] The University of Iowa

Abstract. Formal analysis tools for system models often require or benefit from the availability of auxiliary system invariants. Abstract interpretation is currently one of the best approaches for discovering useful invariants, in particular numerical ones. However, its application is limited by two orthogonal issues: (*i*) developing an abstract interpretation is often non-trivial; each transfer function of the system has to be represented at the abstract level, depending on the abstract domain used; (*ii*) with precise but costly abstract domains, the information computed by the abstract interpreter can be used only once a post fix point has been reached; this may take a long time for large systems or when widening is delayed to improve precision. We propose a new, completely automatic, method to build abstract interpreters which, in addition, can provide sound invariants of the system under analysis before reaching the end of the post fix point computation. In effect, such interpreters act as on-the-fly invariant generators and can be used by other tools such as logic-based model checkers. We present some experimental results that provide initial evidence of the practical usefulness of our method.

1 Introduction and Motivation

Abstract interpretation and symbolic model checking have led independently over the years to the creation of analysis tools that are starting to have a substantial impact on the development of real world software, in particular for safety- or mission-critical systems. Interestingly, the two exhibit complementary strengths and weaknesses [13]. Model checking techniques so far have proved stronger on software that is mostly control-driven and not heavily data-dependent. To be effective with data-dependent programs, these techniques may require programs to be judiciously annotated with data invariants. Also, model checking has been traditionally limited to finite-state systems although new approaches, such as those based on solvers for Satisfiability Modulo Theories (SMT), can lift that restriction in some cases.

Dually, abstract interpretation techniques are quite effective with data-dependent programs, in particular numerical ones, requiring in principle no program annotations. On the other hand, they have more difficulties in dealing with control aspects [13]. Also, although abstract interpretation is a very general framework, most of its applications focus on the analysis of source code. Even tools, such as Nbac [16], that target software artifacts at a higher level of abstraction (e.g., software models expressed in dataflow

---

* Work supported by AFOSR grant #AF9550-09-1-0517, FNRAE Cavale project and ANR INS Project CAFEIN, with the support of the Aerospace Space cluster.

G. Brat, N. Rungta, and A. Venet (Eds.): NFM 2013, LNCS 7871, pp. 139–154, 2013.

specification languages) do not analyze those artifacts directly and work instead with their compilation into an intermediate imperative representation such as LLVM or byte code. This is possibly a consequence of the fact that developing an abstract interpreter for a complete language can be time consuming: even if a large set of abstract domains, such as those provided by the APRON library [17], is readily available, defining sound abstract transformers for every construct of the target language requires substantial work. Another limitation of current abstract interpretation techniques is that they typically depend on Kleene-style fix point algorithms to construct an abstract semantics of the program under analysis. The properties of such semantics, characterized by the concretization of a post fix point of an abstract transformer, can be obtained only once the post fix point has been (completely) computed. Depending on the widening strategies used or, in general, the complexity of the abstractions and the semantics considered, one may have to wait a long time before getting any interesting information from the analysis of the program.

Contribution and Significance. In this work we try to address some of the issues above by combining techniques from abstract interpretation and logic-based model checking. Specifically, we propose a general method for the automatic definition of abstract interpreters that compute numerical invariants of transition systems. We rely on the possibility of encoding the transition system in a decidable logic to compute transformers for an abstract interpreter *completely automatically*. Our method has the significant added benefit that the abstract interpreter can be instrumented to generate system invariants on the fly, during its iterative computation of a post fix point. A prototype implementation of the method provides initial evidence of the feasibility of our approach.

While motivated by practical issues (namely, the generation of auxiliary invariants for a k-induction model checker) the current work is more general and can be adapted to a wide variety of contexts. It only requires that the transition system semantics be expressible in a decidable logic with an efficient solver, such as SAT or SMT solvers, and that the elements of the chosen abstract domain be effectively representable in that logic, as discussed later in more detail. Such requirements are satisfied by a large number of abstract domains used in current practice. As a consequence, we believe that our approach could help considerably in expanding the reach of abstract interpretation techniques to a variety of target languages, as well as facilitate their integration with complementary techniques from model checking.

Related Work. With the current efficiency of SMT solvers on the one hand and the ability of abstract interpretation to compute numerical invariants on the other, the issue of combining SMT and Abstract Interpretation is receiving increasing attention. In [7], Cousot *et al,* draw a parallel between SMT-based reasoning and abstract interpretation. They identify the Nelson-Oppen procedure as a reduced product over different interpretations. While this work is more general, it allows one to understand ours as follows: the concrete domain is an abstract logical domain, our concrete transformer—computed with the aid of an SMT solver—can be seen as an over-approximation of the concrete transition relation in this abstract logical domain. The abstraction we build amounts to computing a reduction between a logical and an algebraic domain, as suggested in [7, §6]. Comparable work in [30], gives an overview of techniques embedding logical predicates as elements of *logical lattices*. Some SMT theories are then formalized within this abstract interpretation view of the analysis: uninterpreted function symbols, linear arithmetic, and their combination.

Another, more practical approach by Monniaux and Gonnord [23] uses bounded reachability with an SMT solver to compute a chaotic iteration strategy. The solver identifies the equation that needs propagating in order to achieve a better widening. However, unlike ours, this solution does not use the actual models found by the SMT solver. In [10], an SMT solver is used to choose among different strategies in an iteration-based policy analysis. The solver identifies the next strategy that will improve the current abstract property. While both works rely on SMT solvers to aid the fix point computation, they do not encode, as we do, the concrete transition relation as a SMT formula in order to compute the abstract property. Also related is Monniaux's automatic modular abstraction for linear constraints [22]. A predicate transformer is defined using quantifier elimination over the semantics of C statements, as in an axiomatic semantics (weakest precondition or strongest postcondition). The transformer is exact for the linear template abstractions considered. It is unclear, however, how this approach can scale to a complete program analysis, since the use of quantifier elimination on a complete transition system is not usually feasible (the blocks analyzed in [22] are small functions used in a symbol library for Lustre/Scade). King and Sondergaard [21] follow a similar approach but rely on reasoning in a concrete logic, as we do, and then abstract the result. As in [22], they aim at computing a very precise transformer but restrict themselves to a specific setting with finite domains, whereas we do not.

A line of work by Reps and various collaborators [24,31,28,29] shares similar foundations with our approach: relying on a decidable logic to construct abstract transformers. The work in [24] over-approximates least fix points but is restricted to domains admitting only finite height chains, while that in [31] adopts the dual approach—to avoid the convergence issue in infinite height domains—by over-approximating greatest fix points from above. Both works are based on manually defined abstract transformers. Very recent work [28,29], concurrent with ours, extends those approaches by synthesizing automatically the abstract transformer via a logic encoding, in a way similar to ours. The first paper combines a least and a greatest fix point computation, while the second only relies on a greatest fix point over-approximation. In case of infinite height domains (e.g., intervals or polyhedra), the least fix point approximation will never converge and only the greatest fix point may be used. In contrast, we target the over-approximation of the least fix point, using widening to ensure convergence. Regarding the ability to produce safe abstract values before the end of the fix point computation, it is not clear how a greatest fix point approach would compare in practice to our incremental invariant generation mechanism (cf. Section 4). A comparative experimental evaluation would require a substantial effort that is outside the scope of this paper.

Finally, the static analysis tools to which we compare ours experimentally in Section 5 are based on sophisticated techniques to improve the precision of the fix point computation, such as lookahead widening [12], or to accelerate convergence [11,26]. These techniques, as well as others such as delayed widening could be integrated in principle in our approach since they mainly focus on the iteration strategy for the fix point computation rather than a specific abstract transformer.

2   Formal Preliminaries

We use basic notions and results from abstract interpretation (e.g. [4,5]). We introduce below those that are most relevant to this work, to have a more self-contained presentation. Similarly, we also introduce relevant notions from symbolic logic and automated reasoning. As customary, we model computational systems as transition systems. A *transition system* S is a triple $(\mathbf{Q}, \mathbf{I}, \leadsto)$ where $\mathbf{Q}$ is a set of *states*, the *state space*; $\mathbf{I} \subseteq \mathbf{Q}$ is the set of S's *initial states*; and $\leadsto \subseteq \mathbf{Q} \times \mathbf{Q}$ is S's *transition relation*. A state $q' \in \mathbf{Q}$ is *reachable* if $q' \in \mathbf{I}$ or $q \leadsto q'$ for some reachable state q.

Abstract Interpretation. Abstract interpretation allows one to analyze a transition system $S = (\mathbf{Q}, \mathbf{I}, \leadsto)$ by first defining a *concrete domain* for S, a partially ordered set $\langle D, \subseteq \rangle$, and a *concrete transformer*, a monotonic function $f : D \to D$. In this paper we will focus on the *collecting semantics*

$$\mathbb{S} \overset{\text{def}}{=} \mathrm{lfp}_{\mathbf{I}}^{\subseteq}(f)$$

of S where $D = \wp(\mathbf{Q})$, the power set of $\mathbf{Q}$; $\subseteq$ is set inclusion; $f(X) = X \cup \{x' \mid x \in X, \; x \leadsto x'\}$; and $\mathrm{lfp}_{\mathbf{I}}^{\subseteq}(f)$ is the least-fix point of f greater than $\mathbf{I}$, obtained as the stationary limit of the ascending sequence $X_0 \subseteq X_1 \subseteq \ldots$ with $X_0 = \mathbf{I}$ and $X_n = f(X_{n-1})$ for all $n > 0$.

An abstract representation of the concrete domain is provided by another partial order $\langle D^{\#}, \sqsubseteq^{\#} \rangle$ the *abstract domain*. The two are related by an *abstraction function* $\alpha : D \mapsto D^{\#}$ and a *concretization function* $\gamma : D^{\#} \mapsto D$. An *abstract transformer* is any monotonic function $g : D^{\#} \to D^{\#}$. We will consider domains $\langle D, \subseteq \rangle$ and $\langle D^{\#}, \sqsubseteq \rangle$ that are lattices, and abstraction and concretization functions that form a *Galois connection* (which we denote by $\alpha : \langle D, \subseteq \rangle \leftrightarrows \langle D^{\#}, \sqsubseteq \rangle : \gamma$). In a Galois connection, both α and γ are monotonic; $\alpha(\gamma(y)) \sqsubseteq y$ for all $y \in D^{\#}$; and $x \subseteq \gamma(\alpha(x))$ for all $x \in D$.

First-Order Logic. Our method works with several logics (including propositional and quantified Boolean logic) that can be more or less directly embedded in many-sorted first-order logic with equality (e.g. [8]). For generality then, we present our work in terms of the latter. We fix a set $\mathbf{S}$ of *sort symbols* and let $\mathbf{X} = \bigcup_{\sigma \in \mathbf{S}} \mathbf{X}_\sigma$ where each $\mathbf{X}_\sigma$ is an infinite set of *variables (of sort σ)*. Given a many-sorted signature Σ of function and predicate symbols, well-sorted terms and formulas (resp. Σ-*terms* and Σ-*formulas*) are defined as usual. If F is a Σ-formula, and $\mathbf{x} = (x_1, \ldots, x_n)$ a tuple of variables with no repetitions, we write $F[\mathbf{x}]$ to denote that F's free variables are from $\mathbf{x}$; furthermore, if $\mathbf{t} = (t_1, \ldots, t_n)$ is a term tuple, we write $F[\mathbf{t}]$ to denote the formula obtained from F by simultaneously replacing each occurrence of x_i in F by t_i for $i = 1, \ldots, n$.

We adopt a standard notion of Σ-*interpretation* $\mathcal{M}$ for each signature Σ. A satisfiability relation $\models$ between such interpretations and Σ-formulas with variables in $\mathbf{X}$ is defined inductively as usual. A Σ-interpretation $\mathcal{M}$ *satisfies* a Σ-formula F if $\mathcal{M} \models F$. We are normally interested in specific classes of Σ-formulas and Σ-interpretations. We collect these restrictions in the notion of a *(sub)logic* (of many-sorted logic): a triple $\mathcal{L} = (\Sigma, \mathbf{F}, \mathbf{M})$ where Σ is a signature; $\mathbf{F}$, the *language* of $\mathcal{L}$, is a set of Σ-formulas; and $\mathbf{M}$ is a class of Σ-interpretations, the *models* of $\mathcal{L}$, that is closed under variable reassignment, (i.e., every Σ-interpretation that differs from one in $\mathbf{M}$ only for how it interprets the variables is also in $\mathbf{M}$). A formula $F[\mathbf{x}]$ of $\mathcal{L}$ is *satisfiable (resp., unsatisfiable) in* $\mathcal{L}$

if it is satisfied by some (resp., no) interpretation in **M**. A set Γ of formulas *entails in* $\mathcal{L}$ a Σ-formula F, written $\Gamma \models_{\mathcal{L}} F$, if $\Gamma \cup \{F\} \in \mathbf{F}$ and every interpretation in **M** that satisfies all formulas in Γ satisfies F as well. The set Γ is *satisfiable in* $\mathcal{L}$ if $\Gamma \not\models_{\mathcal{L}}$ false.

3   Computable Abstract Transformer via Logic Encodings

For the rest of the paper we fix a transition system $S = (\mathbf{Q}, \mathbf{I}, \rightsquigarrow)$ and its collecting semantics $\mathbb{S} = \mathrm{lfp}_{\mathbf{I}}^{\subseteq}(f)$ introduced earlier, which coincides with the set of reachable states of S. Our main concern will be how to define a sound abstract counterpart $f_{\mathbf{A}}$ of f in a suitable abstract domain $\langle \mathbf{A}, \sqsubseteq_{\mathbf{A}} \rangle$ with abstraction function $\alpha : \wp(\mathbf{Q}) \to \mathbf{A}$ and concretization function $\gamma : \mathbf{A} \to \wp(\mathbf{Q})$ so that we can define S's abstract semantics as

$$\mathbb{S}^{\#} \stackrel{\mathrm{def}}{=} \mathrm{lfp}_{\mathbf{I}_{\mathbf{A}}}^{\sqsubseteq_{\mathbf{A}}}(f_{\mathbf{A}})$$

where $\mathbf{I}_{\mathbf{A}}$ is in turn a suitable abstraction of $\mathbf{I}$. By well-known results [4,5], the fix point $\mathbb{S}^{\#}$ above can be computed or over-approximated so that its concretization by γ is a sound approximation (i.e., an over-approximation) of the concrete fix point $\mathbb{S}$.

A major issue when using abstract interpretation in general is how to define $f_{\mathbf{A}}$. In practice, when the transition system is induced by a program, as is often the case, the concrete transformer f is defined constructively in terms of the programming language's idioms (e.g., assignment, loop and conditional statements for imperative languages) and memory model (e.g., heap, stack, etc.). The corresponding abstract transformer must then handle all those constructs as well, and reflect their respective actions in the abstract domain $D_{\mathbf{A}}$. When the abstraction function α is defined from γ by the unique adjoint property of Galois connections the definition of $f_{\mathbf{A}}$ is usually a manual, laborious chore. One has to design the transformer in detail and then prove it sound, by showing that $f(X) \in \gamma(f_{\mathbf{A}}(a))$ for all $a \in \mathbf{A}$ and $X \in \gamma(a)$.

We present a method that can instead compute a sound abstraction of f completely automatically. The method is applicable when the transition system and the concrete and abstract domains can be encoded as we explain below in a logic $\mathcal{L}$ satisfying the requirements listed in the next subsection. For generality, we will describe our method in terms of an arbitrary logic $\mathcal{L}$ satisfying those requirements. To have an intuition, however, depending on the concrete domain, possible examples of $\mathcal{L}$ would be propositional logic or several of the many logics used in SMT: linear real arithmetic, linear integer arithmetic with arrays, and so on.

The basic idea of our method for computing the abstract transformer is fairly simple. It depends on the availability of a $\mathcal{L}$-formula T encoding S's transition relation and a computable function $\gamma_{\mathbf{F}}$ mapping each abstract element a to a formula $\gamma_{\mathbf{F}}(a)$ satisfied by the states abstracted by a. Given an $a \in \mathbf{A}$, the transformer uses $T, \gamma_{\mathbf{F}}(a)$ and a solver for $\mathcal{L}$ to look for a state $\mathbf{v}'$ that is not abstracted by a but is the successor of a state abstracted by a. If such a state does not exist then a is a fix point and is returned. Otherwise, the transformer computes an abstraction a' of state $\mathbf{v}'$ and returns the join of a and a'.

The main appeal of this approach is that logic solvers enumerating satisfying assignments are readily available, and abstracting single states is straightforward for most abstract domains used in practice. In principle, a better approach would be to compute not a single state like $\mathbf{v}'$ above but a formula G denoting a whole set of them. The resulting abstract transformer would then require a smaller number of iterations to reach a fix point. This would both accelerate convergence and, since we use widening, improve precision by possibly needing fewer widening steps. However, computing the formula G and mapping it to a corresponding abstract element is considerably more challenging and expensive, if possible at all for a chosen logic and abstract domain. So we leave the investigation of this approach to further work. The rest of this section formalizes our current approach and describes it in more detail.

Logic Requirements. We assume a logic $\mathcal{L} = (\Sigma, \mathbf{F}, \mathbf{M})$ with a decidable entailment relation $\models_{\mathcal{L}}$ and a language $\mathbf{F}$ closed under all the Boolean operators.[1] For each sort σ in $\mathcal{L}$, we distinguish a set V_{σ} of variable-free terms, which we call *values*, such that $\models_{\mathcal{L}} \neg(v_1 = v_2)$ for each distinct $v_1, v_2 \in V_{\sigma}$. Examples of values would be Boolean, integer or rational constants. We assume that the satisfiable formulas of $\mathcal{L}$ are *satisfied by values*, that is, for every formula $F[\mathbf{y}]$ (with free variables from $\mathbf{y}$) satisfied by a model $\mathcal{M}$ of $\mathcal{L}$ there is a value tuple $\mathbf{v}$ such that $F[\mathbf{v}]$ is satisfied by $\mathcal{M}$.

We assume a total surjective encoding of S's state space $\mathbf{Q}$ to n-tuples of values, for some fixed n, where each n-tuple encodes a state. Depending on $\mathcal{L}$, states may be encoded, for instance, as tuples of Boolean constants, or integer constants, or mixed tuples of Boolean, integer and rational constants, and so on. From now on then *we will identify states with tuples of values*. Note that, thanks to our various assumptions, each formula $F[\mathbf{y}_1, \ldots, \mathbf{y}_k]$ in $k \cdot n$ variables denotes a subset of $\mathbf{Q}^k$, namely the set of all k-tuples of states that satisfy F. We call that set the *extension* of F and define it formally as follows: $\llbracket F \rrbracket \overset{\text{def}}{=} \{(\mathbf{v}_1, \ldots, \mathbf{v}_k) \in \mathbf{Q}^k \mid F[\mathbf{v}_1, \ldots, \mathbf{v}_k] \text{ is satisfiable in } \mathcal{L}\}$. We refer to formulas like F above as *state formulas* and say they are *satisfied* by the state tuples in $\llbracket F \rrbracket$. For each state $\mathbf{v} = (v_1, \ldots, v_n) \in \mathbf{Q}$ and distinct variables $\mathbf{x} = (x_1, \ldots, x_n)$ of corresponding sort, we denote by $A_{\mathbf{v}}$ the *assignment formula* $x_1 = v_1 \wedge \cdots \wedge x_n = v_n$, which is satisfied exactly by $\mathbf{v}$. Finally, we assume the existence of an *encoding of S in $\mathcal{L}$*, i.e., a pair $(I[\mathbf{x}], T[\mathbf{x}, \mathbf{x}'])$ of formulas of $\mathcal{L}$ with $\mathbf{x}$ and $\mathbf{x}'$ both of size n, where $I[\mathbf{x}]$ is a formula satisfied exactly by the initial states of S, and $T[\mathbf{x}, \mathbf{x}']$ is a formula satisfied by two reachable states $\mathbf{v}, \mathbf{v}'$ iff $\mathbf{v} \rightsquigarrow \mathbf{v}'$.

First Abstraction—From Sets of States to Formulas. For theoretical convenience, we start with an intermediate abstraction that maps sets of states to possibly infinitary formulas representing those states precisely. To do that, we extend the language of $\mathcal{L}$ by closing it under a disjunction operator $\bigvee$ that applies to (possibly infinite) sets of formulas of $\mathcal{L}$. We then extend the notions of satisfiability, entailment and equivalence in $\mathcal{L}$ to the new language as expected—e.g., for every set Γ of formulas of $\mathcal{L}$, $\bigvee \Gamma$ is satisfied by an interpretation $\mathcal{M}$ if some $F \in \Gamma$ is satisfied by $\mathcal{M}$, and so on.[2]

Let $\mathbf{F}_{\mathbf{x}}$ be the set of all formulas in the extended language above whose free variables are from the same n-tuple $\mathbf{x}$. One can show that mutual entailment between two formulas in $\mathbf{F}_{\mathbf{x}}$ is an equivalence relation. Let $[F]$ denote the equivalence class of a formula F with respect to this relation, and let $\mathbf{E}$ denote the set of all those equivalence classes. Let $\llbracket [F] \rrbracket \overset{\text{def}}{=} \llbracket F \rrbracket$ for each $[F] \in \mathbf{E}$. The poset $\langle \mathbf{E}, \sqsubseteq_{\mathbf{E}} \rangle$ where

---

[1] The latter is to simplify the exposition. Weaker assumptions are possible.

[2] In practice, our method will never need to work with formulas $\bigvee \Gamma$ where Γ is infinite.

$$[F] \sqsubseteq_{\mathbf{E}} [G] \quad \text{iff} \quad F \models_{\mathcal{L}} G$$

has a lattice structure with the following join and meet operators: $[F] \sqcup_{\mathbf{E}} [G] \stackrel{\text{def}}{=} [F \vee G]$ and $[F] \sqcap_{\mathbf{E}} [G] \stackrel{\text{def}}{=} [F \wedge G]$. It can be shown that the two functions[3]

$$\alpha_{\mathbf{E}} : \wp(\mathbf{Q}) \to \mathbf{E} \stackrel{\text{def}}{=} \lambda V. [\bigvee\{A_{\mathbf{v}} \mid \mathbf{v} \in V\}] \qquad \text{and} \qquad \gamma_{\mathbf{E}} : \mathbf{E} \to \wp(\mathbf{Q}) \stackrel{\text{def}}{=} \lambda E. [\![E]\!]$$

form a Galois connection. By standard results [5], the best sound abstract transformer of f with respect to this connection is

$$f_{\mathbf{E}} : \mathbf{E} \to \mathbf{E} \stackrel{\text{def}}{=} \alpha_{\mathbf{E}} \circ f \circ \gamma_{\mathbf{E}} = \lambda E. [\bigvee\{A_{\mathbf{v}} \mid \mathbf{v} \in [\![E]\!] \cup \{\mathbf{u}' \mid \mathbf{u} \in [\![E]\!], \mathbf{u} \rightsquigarrow \mathbf{u}'\}\}]$$

By our logic requirements, the most precise abstraction of the set $\mathbf{I}$ of S's initial states is $\alpha_{\mathbf{E}}(\mathbf{I}) = [I]$ where, recall, I is the formula denoting $\mathbf{I}$ in $\mathcal{L}$. It follows that in the abstract domain $\langle \mathbf{E}, \sqsubseteq_{\mathbf{E}} \rangle$ we can define the following semantics for S: $\mathbb{S}^{\mathbf{E}} \stackrel{\text{def}}{=} \text{lfp}_{[I]}^{\sqsubseteq_{\mathbf{E}}}(f_{\mathbf{E}})$.

Second Abstraction—Changing Fix Point Computation. For our later needs, we would like to have a fix point computation that actually enumerates the additional states discovered by the collecting semantics. The abstraction $\alpha_{\mathbf{E}}$ above, over-approximating sets of states by disjunctions of assignment formulas, is not well suited for that because these disjunctions can be infinitary. Hence, we introduce another abstract transformer, on the same lattice $\langle \mathbf{E}, \sqsubseteq_{\mathbf{E}} \rangle$:

$$g_{\mathbf{E}} : \mathbf{E} \to \mathbf{E} \stackrel{\text{def}}{=} \lambda E. E \sqcup_{\mathbf{E}} \text{choose}(\{[A_{\mathbf{v}'}] \mid T[\mathbf{v}, \mathbf{v}'] \text{ is sat. in } \mathcal{L}, \mathbf{v} \in [\![E]\!], \mathbf{v}' \notin [\![E]\!]\})$$

where choose is some choice function over subsets of $\mathbf{E}$, returning one element of its input set if the set is non-empty, and [false] otherwise. This function maps each equivalence class E to a class E' such that $[\![E']\!] \setminus [\![E]\!]$ contains just one state, chosen among the successors of the states in $[\![E]\!]$ according to the transition formula T. We can use $g_{\mathbf{E}}$ instead of $f_{\mathbf{E}}$ in the fix point computation thanks to the following result.[4]

Proposition 1 (Soundness). *The transformers $f_{\mathbf{E}}$ and $g_{\mathbf{E}}$ have the same least fix point above $[I]$, i.e., $\text{lfp}_{[I]}^{\sqsubseteq_{\mathbf{E}}}(f_{\mathbf{E}}) = \text{lfp}_{[I]}^{\sqsubseteq_{\mathbf{E}}}(g_{\mathbf{E}})$ where $\text{lfp}^{\sqsubseteq_{\mathbf{E}}}$ is defined using transfinite iterations.*

Main Abstraction—Abstracting Formulas in $\mathbf{F_x}$. We now introduce our last abstraction, mapping formulas in $\mathbf{F_x}$ to elements of an abstract domain $\langle \mathbf{A}, \sqsubseteq_{\mathbf{A}} \rangle$ like those typically used in abstract interpretation tools (intervals, polyhedra, and so on). We assume that $\mathbf{A}$ is fitted with a lattice structure with meet $\sqcap_{\mathbf{A}}$ and join $\sqcup_{\mathbf{A}}$. We also assume the existence of a *computable* monotonic function $\gamma_F : \mathbf{A} \to \mathbf{F_x}$ that associates a formula of $\mathbf{F_x}$ to each element of $\mathbf{A}$. Intuitively, we are requiring that each element of $\mathbf{A}$ be effectively representable as a formula denoting a set of states. This requirement is easily satisfied for many numerical abstract domains and the sort of logics used in SMT. For instance, intervals can be mapped to conjunctions of inequalities between variables

---

[3] We borrow λ-calculus' notation to denote mathematical functions.
[4] All proofs of our results can be found in a companion technical report available at
http://www.cs.uiowa.edu/~tinelli/html/publications.html.

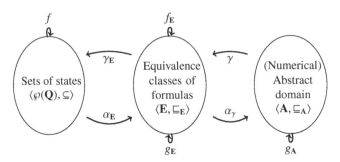

Fig. 1. Global framework: combination of abstractions

Input: $a \in \mathbf{A}$
$F[\mathbf{x}, \mathbf{x}'] := \gamma_{\mathbf{F}}(a)[\mathbf{x}] \wedge T[\mathbf{x}, \mathbf{x}'] \wedge \neg\gamma_{\mathbf{F}}(a)[\mathbf{x}']$
if F is satisfiable in $\mathcal{L}$ **then**
    let $\mathbf{v}, \mathbf{v}'$ be two states that satisfy $F[\mathbf{x}, \mathbf{x}']$
    return $a \sqcup_{\mathbf{A}} \alpha_{\mathbf{Q}}(\mathbf{v}')$
return a

Fig. 2. Basic version of the automatic abstract transformer $g_{\mathbf{A}}$

and values; similarly, any linear-based abstraction can be mapped to a conjunction of linear arithmetic constraints. As concretization function we use the monotonic function $\gamma : \mathbf{A} \mapsto \mathbf{E} \overset{\text{def}}{=} (\lambda F.[F]) \circ \gamma_{\mathbf{F}}$ which maps each abstract element to an equivalence class in $\mathbf{E}$. Since $\mathbf{E}$ and $\mathbf{A}$ are lattices, γ induces a Galois connection $\alpha_\gamma : \langle \mathbf{E}, \sqsubseteq_{\mathbf{E}} \rangle \leftrightarrows \langle \mathbf{A}, \sqsubseteq_{\mathbf{A}} \rangle : \gamma$ where α_γ is uniquely determined by γ.

In summary, we obtain the combination of abstractions illustrated in Figure 1. However, *we do not use α_γ at all* by assuming instead the existence of a *state abstraction* function $\alpha_{\mathbf{Q}} : \mathbf{Q} \mapsto \mathbf{A}$ which directly associates states to their abstract counterparts in $\mathbf{A}$. For our approach to be sound, it is enough for $\alpha_{\mathbf{Q}}$ to be such that $a \sqsubseteq_{\mathbf{A}} \alpha_{\mathbf{Q}}(\mathbf{v})$ for each $\mathbf{v} \in \mathbf{Q}$ and $a \in \mathbf{A}$ where a is $\mathbf{v}$'s best abstraction—i.e., the smallest element of $\mathbf{A}$ with $[A_{\mathbf{v}}] \sqsubseteq_{\mathbf{E}} \gamma(a)$. In the actual domains we have considered in our implementation, the definition of $\alpha_{\mathbf{Q}}$ is straightforward and such that $a = \alpha_{\mathbf{Q}}(\mathbf{v})$. For instance, let $\mathbf{v} = (4, -2, 5)$ Then $\alpha_{\mathbf{Q}}(\mathbf{v})$ is $([4; 4], [-2; -2], [5; 5])$ if $\mathbf{A}$ is the integer interval domain, and is the abstract element described by the system $\{4 \leq x_1 \leq 4, \ -2 \leq x_2 \leq -2, \ 5 \leq x_3 \leq 5\}$ if $\mathbf{A}$ is a relational domain such as octagons or polyhedra.

The Abstract Transformer. Recall that our main goal was to generate a computable sound abstract transformer $g_{\mathbf{A}}$ for $g_{\mathbf{E}}$ *automatically*. We can do that by relying solely on (*i*) the function $\gamma_{\mathbf{F}}$, (*ii*) the state abstraction $\alpha_{\mathbf{Q}}$, and (*iii*) a sound, complete and terminating satisfiability solver for the logic $\mathcal{L}$ that is also able to return for each satisfiable state formula $F[\mathbf{x}_1, \ldots, \mathbf{x}_k]$ a tuple $\mathbf{v}_1, \ldots, \mathbf{v}_k$ of states that satisfies it.

A basic procedure for computing $g_{\mathbf{A}}$ is given in Figure 2. The satisfiability tests and the choice of the states $\mathbf{v}$ and $\mathbf{v}'$ in the figure are performed by the solver for $\mathcal{L}$, which effectively plays for $g_{\mathbf{A}}$ the role of the choice function in the definition of $g_{\mathbf{E}}$. We note that, while fix points are traditionally computed in the abstract domain, with our approach it is not necessary to transfer back the element $g_{\mathbf{A}}(a)$ to detect that a is a fix point: it is enough to detect that the formula F in Figure 2 is unsatisfiable.

Theorem 1 (Soundess). *The transformer g_A is a sound approximation of g_E: for all* $a \in A$, $(g_E \circ \gamma)(a) \sqsubseteq (\gamma \circ g_A)(a)$.

Our eventual goal is to over-approximate the fix point $\mathrm{lfp}_{I_A}^{\sqsubseteq_A}(g_A)$ where I_A is a sound approximation of the initial state formula I; more precisely, where $[I] \sqsubseteq_E \gamma(I_A)$. When I is satisfied by a single state $\mathbf{v}$, the abstract element I_A is just $\alpha_Q(\mathbf{v})$. In general, we can use the logic solver again to compute an I_A iteratively. A basic procedure for that (also used in [24]) is the following, starting with I_A equal to the bottom element of A:

> **while** (there is a state $\mathbf{v}$ satisfying $I[\mathbf{x}] \wedge \neg \gamma_F(I_A)[\mathbf{x}]$) **do**
> $\quad I_A := I_A \sqcup_A \alpha_Q(\mathbf{v})$

Proposition 2 (Soundness). *When the loop above terminates, the computed element I_A is a sound approximation of $[I]$.*

In practice, we are mostly interested in abstract domains that do not satisfy the ascending chain condition [4]. In those cases, a widening operator ∇ is needed in addition to the join $\sqcup_A$, in the computation of I_A and of $\mathrm{lfp}_{I_A}^{\sqsubseteq_A}(g_A)$ to ensure convergence. Although any of the widening operators and strategies developed in the field could be used for that, we have been able to obtain pretty good experimental results already with rather unsophisticated widening strategies, as we discuss in Section 5.

4 On-the-Fly Invariant Generation

A one-state formula $F[\mathbf{x}]$ is an *invariant for S* if $[\![F]\!]$ includes the set R_S of all reachable states of S. Invariants have many useful applications in static analysis, logic-based model checking, and deductive verification in general. In our abstract domain E from the previous section, any formula F such that $\mathrm{lfp}_{[I]}^{\sqsubseteq_E}(f_E) \sqsubseteq_E [F]$ is an invariant, since $R_S = [\![\mathrm{lfp}_{[I]}^{\sqsubseteq_E}(f_E)]\!] \subseteq [\![F]\!].$[5] By the construction of our abstraction in the domain A, any fix point computation for the transformer $g_A : A \to A$ starting with the element I_A from Proposition 2 produces a value a such that $\gamma_F(a)$ is an invariant for S.

A distinguishing feature of our approach is that, in practice, we can modify the fix point computation for g_A to generate *intermediate* invariants as it goes and *before* reaching the fix point. We capitalize on the fact that $\gamma_F(a)$ is typically a conjunction of formulas, or *state properties*, $P_1[\mathbf{x}], \ldots, P_m[\mathbf{x}]$. For any intermediate value $a \in A$ constructed during the fix point computation for g_A, if $\gamma_F(a) = P_1 \wedge \cdots \wedge P_m$ we can check whether any of the P_i's is already invariant.

Since the fix point computation using g_A starts with an over-approximation of the initial states, we know that the whole $\gamma_F(a)$ is inductive, and hence invariant, if the satisfiability test on the formula F in Figure 2 fails. However, it is possible to do better by turning that test into one that checks the *k-inductiveness* [27] of the individual P_i's simultaneously. We discuss an efficient mechanism for doing that in previous work [18]. We refer the reader to that work for more details, but the important point here is that,

---

[5] Of course, obtaining a formula from the equivalence class $\mathrm{lfp}_{[I]}^{\sqsubseteq_E}(f_E)$ would be enough for all analysis purposes since that class consists of the strongest invariant for S. However, in general, such formulas may be infinitary or impractical to compute.

given a bound on k, we can identify fairly quickly, for each $i = 0, \ldots, k$, which subsets of $\{P_1, \ldots, P_m\}$ are conjunctively i-inductive.[6] If the whole $\{P_1, \ldots, P_m\}$ is proven k-inductive, which is equivalent to proving that the formula

$$G[\mathbf{x}_0, \ldots, \mathbf{x}_{k+1}] \overset{\text{def}}{=} \gamma_{\mathbf{F}}(a)[\mathbf{x}_0] \wedge T[\mathbf{x}_0, \mathbf{x}_1] \wedge \cdots \wedge \gamma_{\mathbf{F}}(a)[\mathbf{x}_k] \wedge T[\mathbf{x}_k, \mathbf{x}_{k+1}] \wedge \neg\gamma_{\mathbf{F}}(a)[\mathbf{x}_{k+1}]$$

is unsatisfiable, then $g_{\mathbf{A}}$ can return a because in that case it is a fix point. Otherwise, the state $\mathbf{v}_{k+1}$ from a state tuple $(\mathbf{v}_0, \ldots, \mathbf{v}_{k+1})$ that satisfies G can be used to generalize a as done with $\mathbf{v}'$ in Figure 2. In either case, any subset of $\{P_1, \ldots, P_n\}$ that has been proven k-inductive can be output as a set of (intermediate) invariants.

This in effect turns an abstract interpreter for $\mathbf{A}$ using $g_{\mathbf{A}}$ into an on-the-fly invariant generator. The invariants generated in the earlier iterations of the interpreter are usually, but not necessarily, the simplest ones (e.g., interval bounds on a variable, equalities between variables, and so on) and become increasingly more elaborate as the computation proceeds. The main point is that one does not need to wait until the end of a possibly complex fix point computation using a wide set of costly abstractions to obtain potentially useful invariants. Our experimental results confirm this conjecture.

An additional, if secondary, benefit of identifying intermediate invariants is that they can be used to improve the preciseness of later iterations of the very fix point computation that generated them. This can be done by maintaining at all times a conjunction $J[\mathbf{x}]$ of all the intermediate invariants generated until then, and using at each call of $g_{\mathbf{A}}$ the formula $T_J[\mathbf{x}, \mathbf{x}'] \overset{\text{def}}{=} T[\mathbf{x}, \mathbf{x}'] \wedge J[\mathbf{x}]$ in place of the original transition relation formula T. Using the strengthened transition formula T_J helps counterbalance the loss of precision caused by widening while maintaining the soundness of $g_{\mathbf{A}}$—since the strengthening discards only states that are definitely unreachable for not satisfying the invariant $J[\mathbf{x}]$.

Application: Invariant Generation for Lustre Programs

This work was originally motivated by the problem of proving invariant properties of Lustre programs. Lustre [15] is a synchronous data-flow specification/programming language with infinite streams of values of three basic types: Booleans, integers, and reals. It is used to model control software in embedded devices. Properties to be proven are typically introduced within Lustre programs as observer Boolean streams so that checking that a property is invariant amounts to checking that its corresponding stream is constantly true. In previous work, we developed a k-induction-based parallel model checker for Lustre programs, called Kind [20], which uses SMT solvers as its main reasoning engine. Kind benefits from the use of auxiliary invariant generators to strengthen its basic k-induction procedure [19]. We implemented the fix point computation method described here as an additional on-line invariant generator for Kind.

Kind works with an idealized version of Lustre with infinite-precision numerical types. Idealized Lustre programs can be readily recast as transition systems in a three-sorted concrete domain with Booleans and (mathematical) integers and reals. Such systems can be almost directly encoded and reasoned about in a quantifier-free logic of

---

[6] For the reader unfamiliar with k-induction, it is enough to know that every k-inductive formula is invariant, and is k'-inductive for every $k' > k$. Also, 0-inductive formulas are inductive in the traditional sense.

```
1 node p_count (a,b,c:bool) returns (x,y:int; obs:bool);
2  var n₁, n₂:int;
3  let
4    n₁ = 10000;  n₂ = 5000;
5    x = 0 -> if b or c then 0 else if a and (pre x) < n₁ then (pre x) + 1 else pre x;
6    y = 0 -> if c then 0 else if a and (pre y) < n₂ then (pre y) + 1 else pre y;
7    obs = (x != n₁) or (y = n₂);
8 tel
```

Fig. 3. Double counter example in Lustre

mixed integer and real arithmetic with uninterpreted function symbols. The linear fragment of that logic, which we could call QF_UFLIRA in the nomenclature of SMT-LIB [3], can be efficiently decided by the SMT solvers used by Kind. This means that Lustre programs limited to linear arithmetic are amenable to analysis with our method.

We have built an abstract interpreter, called Kind-AI, for such Lustre programs that computes the abstract transformer automatically as explained earlier, and generates a stream of invariants (for Kind's benefit) during its fix point computation.[7] As abstract domain we use one defined, as usual, as a reduced product of a variety of abstract domains, including relational and non-relational ones. Our implementation of the function γ_F converts abstract elements into formulas of QF_UFLIRA as one would expect: an interval $[a; b]$ for a variable x is converted into the formula $a \le x \wedge x \le b$; a linear constraint $\Sigma_i \, a_i \cdot x_i \ge c$ is mapped directly to the corresponding formula of QF_UFLIRA. The translation is extended homomorphically to more complex elements. For instance, elements that are the meet of other ones (such as polyhedra, etc.) are converted to the conjunction of the translation of the components.

Kind-AI is written in OCaml and relies on the APRON abstract domain library [17]. It shares with Kind, also written in OCaml, modules to encode Lustre programs as transition systems in the QF_UFLIRA logic, and to interact with an SMT solver. A basic partitioning mechanism allows Kind-AI to express certain conditional properties. Specifically, it is possible to specify any Boolean term or finite range term t from the Lustre program as a *partitioning variable*. Then the premises of the conditional properties are conjunctions of predicates of the form $t = v$, where v is one of the possible values of t. We illustrate the use of Kind-AI here with a typical example: counters, which are used widely within safety mechanisms for critical systems.

Example 1. In the Lustre program shown in Figure 3, two counters x and y are incremented up to their respective maximum value whenever the input value a is **true**; both are reset to 0 when the input c is **true**. The counter x is reset also when the input b is **true**. Suppose we would like to prove that whenever x reaches its maximum value, so does y. This property is expressed by the synchronous observer *obs*. It is enough to show then that the Boolean stream *obs* is equal to the constant stream **true**.

With a partitioning using the Boolean terms $x < n_1$ and $y < n_2$, chosen for being if-then-else guards in the program that involve stateful variables, Kind-AI behaves as follows with respect to the state variable tuple (x, y). Its fix point algorithm finds and

---

[7] Kind-AI and the input problems used in the experiments described in the next section can be found at http://clc.cs.uiowa.edu/Kind/NFM13.

injects, in order, into the abstract domain the states $(0, 0)$, $(0, 1)$, $(1, 1)$ and $(2, 2)$. After the injection of $(1, 1)$, the computed abstract element contains the sub-properties $0 \leq x$, $x \leq 1$, $0 \leq y$, $y \leq 1$ and $x \leq y$. After the injection of $(2, 2)$, Kind-AI identifies three sub-properties as invariants: $0 \leq x$, $0 \leq y$ and $y < n_2 \Rightarrow x \leq y$.[8] Using the same widening heuristics described in the next section, a fix point that also includes the invariants $x \leq 10000$ and $y \leq 5000$ is reached in 3.95 seconds after 31 iterations.

With this program, using k-induction alone Kind is not able to prove in reasonable time the property expressed by *obs*. However, when run concurrently with Kind-AI, Kind is able to prove the target property as soon as it receives the intermediate invariants $0 \leq x$, $x \leq 10000$, $0 \leq y$, $y \leq 5000$ and $y < n_2 \Rightarrow x \leq y$.   □

5   Experimental Evaluation

Our approach relies heavily on widening in practice to ensure convergence. As a consequence, one might wonder about the logical strength of the invariants produced by our invariant generator. To evaluate that we did an initial experimental comparison with a couple of other static analysis tools, ASPIC and SMT-AI, that can generate linear numerical invariants for (finite and) infinite-state systems. The first is a tool combining linear relation analysis with widening and acceleration techniques [11]. The second tool is an abstract interpreter that targets specifically Lustre programs and employs a number of AI techniques to produce program invariants [25].[9]

We looked at the set of infinite-state transition systems collected by Gonnord on the ASPIC website [1]. These are mostly toy numerical systems, specified in the FAST language [9], which however admit interesting conditional and unconditional numerical invariants. FAST expresses transition systems essentially as unbounded counter automata, with a finite control structure and transitions that have linear integer arithmetic guards, and effects described by affine functions. We translated each automaton to a Lustre program by encoding the automaton's states by means of a *mode variable*, a finite range variable with each value representing one of the states.

We ran four different configurations of ASPIC on the FAST systems. We also ran Kind-AI and SMT-AI on the corresponding Lustre programs, with partitioning over the mode variable above and with the *full packs* option, which builds a relational abstraction (using polyhedra and octagons in Kind-AI, and just polyhedra in SMT-AI) on all the stateful variables of the program. In Kind-AI, we used a very simple widening heuristics, which applies widening every two join operations and uses as widening thresholds the numerical constants in the input program. We set an upper bound of 4 for the k-induction loop used in the computation of the abstract transformer g_A described in Section 4. All tests were executed with a 60 second timeout on a Linux machine with a quad-core 2.80 GHz Xeon processor with 12 GB of RAM.

Finally, we compared for each problem the invariants generated by ASPIC and SMT-AI at the end of their analysis with the conjunction of the intermediate invariants progressively generated by Kind-AI. Figure 4 summarizes the results of this comparison.

---

[8] Note that fast pre-analyses used in abstract interpretation tools, such as constant propagation, will not produce implications like the one above.

[9] The "SMT" in the name is just because it works with formulas in the SMT-LIB format [3].

Benchmarks	ASPIC				SMT-AI	Kind-AI	SMT-AI
	Ch79	Ch79V2	Lookahead	Native		runtime	runtime
apache1	= 004	= 004	= 004	= 004	+ 004	005	005
car7	‖	−	‖	−	‖	12,120	083
dummy1	= 003	= 003	−	−	+ 003	005	003
dummy4	+ 014	= 014	= 014	= 014	+ 006	014	005
dummy6	+ 004	+ 028	+ 028	−	+ 002	028	timeout
gb	+ 783	+ 783	= 783	‖	+ 009	7,830	026
goubault1b	+ 011	= 011	= 011	= 011	+ 011	026	025
goubault2b	+ 057	+ 072	+ 072	+ 072	+ 057	102	018
hal79a	‖	−	−	−	+ 047	1,430	024
hal79b	+ 101	+ 101	−	−	+ 101	1,020	021
simplecar	+ 066	−	= 066	−	+ 005	066	006
sp	‖	−	‖	‖	+ 035	12,300	timeout
subway	‖	−	‖	‖	‖	19,130	05,330
swap	‖	−	−	−	+ 022	022	006
t4x0	+ 014	+ 014	+ 014	+ 014	+ 014	067	027
train1	‖	−	‖	‖	‖	19,040	05,330
wcet1	‖	‖	‖	−	‖	5,530	027
wcet2	‖	‖	‖	‖	‖	38,870	2,270

Fig. 4. Comparison of final invariants computed by Kind-AI vs. those computed by the other tools. The symbol + means Kind-AI's invariant is stronger; − weaker; = equivalent; and ‖ incomparable. All runtimes are in milliseconds.

The various configuration of ASPIC are explained in [1]. The first three implement earlier methods developed by others [14,2,12]; the last one corresponds to ASPIC's own method. The last two columns in the figure show the time SMT-AI and Kind-AI respectively took to compute their fix point. The corresponding runtimes for ASPIC are not reported because they were 3ms in almost all cases, with a maximum of 7ms. The numbers in the ASPIC and SMT-AI columns indicate at what time during Kind-AI's computation the conjunction of its intermediate invariants became equivalent or stronger than the final invariant generated by the other tools.

We stress that Kind-AI was designed to quickly compute auxiliary invariants for Kind, not to produce comprehensive analyses. So it incorporates none of the sophisticated techniques used by ASPIC to increase the precision of its analysis [11]. In spite of that, in many cases it computed stronger or equivalent invariants. This suggests that the sound abstract transformers generated automatically with our method can produce fairly accurate analyses out of the box. The results also confirm that while convergence to a fix point may take considerably longer in Kind-AI than in the other tools, good invariants (i.e., stronger or equivalent to those from the other tools) are produced a lot sooner.

6   Conclusion and Further Work

The framework we presented offers two main contributions: (*i*) a systematic and automatic generation of abstract transformers based on a combination of logic solvers and abstract domain libraries; (*ii*) the gradual generation of invariants during the computation of post fix points. Our approach is truly automatic whenever the target system can be encoded in a suitable decidable logic and abstract domain elements are representable in that logic. Such conditions are often easy to satisfy for systems already analyzable with SMT solvers, and for numerous abstract domains. Thanks to continuous advances in SMT, we expect that more and more domains, such as those for finite precision integers and floating point numbers, will be supported by SMT solvers. Our approach will then immediately provide for free abstract interpreters/invariant generators for them. Although our current implementation works with Lustre programs, our general method is language independent. Also, it imposes no restrictions on the abstract domains that can be used as long as, in essence, the domains admit a concretization in a decidable logic with an available solver. Furthermore, our framework facilitates the expression of big-step semantics (on the logical side) and therefore avoids the loss of precision obtained when applying abstract transfer functions at a small-step semantics level.

About the second contribution, to our knowledge, our initial implementation of the framework is the only available tool based on abstract interpretation and Kleene-style fix point computation that provides invariants *before* the post fix point is reached. Even if reduced domains share knowledge about their current state, this information is not a guaranteed fix point and cannot be soundly communicated to other tools. In a multi-analyzer setting, the ability to share invariants before the end of the computation can drastically increase performance. But that sort of intermediate but guaranteed information can be extremely valuable even in standalone use. For example, when statically analyzing a 200k-loc critical embedded software for the absence of run time errors [6], one could start looking at sections of the code that are already proven to be error free while the automatic analysis continues. This contrasts with the current general practice for least-fix point approximations where one gets at most alarms during the computation and has to wait, possibly for hours, for that computation to end before interpreting the results, and realizing perhaps that certain parameters need further tuning.

We have implemented our method and verified the general quality of its generated invariants with a comparative evaluation on some benchmarks admitting interesting numerical invariants. Further work will involve a more extensive experimental evaluation of the method to assess the effects of its generated invariants on the performance of our Kind model checker, which already relies on auxiliary invariants generated by other means. One source of imprecision in our method, leading to weaker invariants, is the generalization of the current abstract value to include successor states that may in fact be unreachable. Additional work will focus on developing enhancements for mitigating this problem.

References

1. Aspic website, http://laure.gonnord.org/pro/aspic/benchmarks.html
2. Bagnara, R., Hill, P.M., Ricci, E., Zaffanella, E.: Precise widening operators for convex polyhedra. In: Cousot, R. (ed.) SAS 2003. LNCS, vol. 2694, pp. 337–354. Springer, Heidelberg (2003)
3. Barrett, C., Stump, A., Tinelli, C.: The SMT-LIB Standard: Version 2.0. In: SMT (2010)
4. Cousot, P., Cousot, R.: Abstract interpretation: A unified lattice model for static analysis of programs by construction or approximation of fixpoints. In: POPL, pp. 238–252 (1977)
5. Cousot, P., Cousot, R.: Systematic design of program analysis frameworks. In: POPL, pp. 269–282 (1979)

6. Cousot, P., Cousot, R., Feret, J., Mauborgne, L., Miné, A., Monniaux, D., Rival, X.: The ASTREÉ Analyzer. In: Sagiv, M. (ed.) ESOP 2005. LNCS, vol. 3444, pp. 21–30. Springer, Heidelberg (2005)
7. Cousot, P., Cousot, R., Mauborgne, L.: The reduced product of abstract domains and the combination of decision procedures. In: Hofmann, M. (ed.) FOSSACS 2011. LNCS, vol. 6604, pp. 456–472. Springer, Heidelberg (2011)
8. Enderton, H.B.: A Mathematical Introduction to Logic, 2nd edn. Academic Press (2001)
9. Fast website, http://www.lsv.ens-cachan.fr/fast/
10. Gawlitza, T.M., Monniaux, D.: Improving strategies via SMT solving. In: Barthe, G. (ed.) ESOP 2011. LNCS, vol. 6602, pp. 236–255. Springer, Heidelberg (2011)
11. Gonnord, L., Halbwachs, N.: Combining widening and acceleration in linear relation analysis. In: Yi, K. (ed.) SAS 2006. LNCS, vol. 4134, pp. 144–160. Springer, Heidelberg (2006)
12. Gopan, D., Reps, T.: Lookahead widening. In: Ball, T., Jones, R.B. (eds.) CAV 2006. LNCS, vol. 4144, pp. 452–466. Springer, Heidelberg (2006)
13. Gurfinkel, A., Chaki, S.: Combining predicate and numeric abstraction for software model checking. STTT 12(6), 409–427 (2010)
14. Halbwachs, N.: Détermination automatique de relations linéaires vérifiées par les variables d'un programme. PhD thesis, University of Grenoble (1979)
15. Halbwachs, N., Caspi, P., Raymond, P., Pilaud, D.: The synchronous data-flow programming language LUSTRE. Proceedings of the IEEE 79(9), 1305–1320 (1991)
16. Jeannet, B., Halbwachs, N., Raymond, P.: Dynamic partitioning in analyses of numerical properties. In: Cortesi, A., Filé, G. (eds.) SAS 1999. LNCS, vol. 1694, pp. 39–50. Springer, Heidelberg (1999)
17. Jeannet, B., Miné, A.: Apron: A library of numerical abstract domains for static analysis. In: Bouajjani, A., Maler, O. (eds.) CAV 2009. LNCS, vol. 5643, pp. 661–667. Springer, Heidelberg (2009)
18. Kahsai, T., Garoche, P.-L., Tinelli, C., Whalen, M.: Incremental verification with mode variable invariants in state machines. In: Goodloe, A.E., Person, S. (eds.) NFM 2012. LNCS, vol. 7226, pp. 388–402. Springer, Heidelberg (2012)
19. Kahsai, T., Ge, Y., Tinelli, C.: Instantiation-based invariant discovery. In: Bobaru, M., Havelund, K., Holzmann, G.J., Joshi, R. (eds.) NFM 2011. LNCS, vol. 6617, pp. 192–206. Springer, Heidelberg (2011)
20. Kahsai, T., Tinelli, C.: PKIND: a parallel k-induction based model checker. In: PDMC. EPTCS, vol. 72, pp. 55–62 (2011)
21. King, A., Søndergaard, H.: Automatic abstraction for congruences. In: Barthe, G., Hermenegildo, M. (eds.) VMCAI 2010. LNCS, vol. 5944, pp. 197–213. Springer, Heidelberg (2010)
22. Monniaux, D.: Automatic modular abstractions for linear constraints. In: POPL, pp. 140–151. ACM (2009)
23. Monniaux, D., Gonnord, L.: Using bounded model checking to focus fixpoint iterations. In: Yahav, E. (ed.) SAS 2011. LNCS, vol. 6887, pp. 369–385. Springer, Heidelberg (2011)
24. Reps, T., Sagiv, M., Yorsh, G.: Symbolic implementation of the best transformer. In: Steffen, B., Levi, G. (eds.) VMCAI 2004. LNCS, vol. 2937, pp. 252–266. Springer, Heidelberg (2004)
25. Roux, P., Delmas, R., Garoche, P.-L.: SMT-AI: an abstract interpreter as oracle for k-induction. Electr. Notes Theor. Comput. Sci. 267(2), 55–68 (2010)
26. Schrammel, P., Jeannet, B.: Extending abstract acceleration methods to data-flow programs with numerical inputs. Electr. Notes Theor. Comput. Sci. 267(1), 101–114 (2010)
27. Sheeran, M., Singh, S., Stålmarck, G.: Checking safety properties using induction and a SAT-solver. In: Johnson, S.D., Hunt Jr., W.A. (eds.) FMCAD 2000. LNCS, vol. 1954, pp. 108–125. Springer, Heidelberg (2000)

28. Thakur, A., Elder, M., Reps, T.: Bilateral algorithms for symbolic abstraction. In: Miné, A., Schmidt, D. (eds.) SAS 2012. LNCS, vol. 7460, pp. 111–128. Springer, Heidelberg (2012)
29. Thakur, A., Reps, T.: A method for symbolic computation of abstract operations. In: Madhusudan, P., Seshia, S.A. (eds.) CAV 2012. LNCS, vol. 7358, pp. 174–192. Springer, Heidelberg (2012)
30. Tiwari, A., Gulwani, S.: Logical interpretation: Static program analysis using theorem proving. In: Pfenning, F. (ed.) CADE 2007. LNCS (LNAI), vol. 4603, pp. 147–166. Springer, Heidelberg (2007)
31. Yorsh, G., Reps, T., Sagiv, M.: Symbolically computing most-precise abstract operations for shape analysis. In: Jensen, K., Podelski, A. (eds.) TACAS 2004. LNCS, vol. 2988, pp. 530–545. Springer, Heidelberg (2004)

Numerical Abstract Domain Using Support Functions

Yassamine Seladji and Olivier Bouissou

CEA Saclay Nano-INNOV Institut CARNOT
91 191 Gif sur Yvette CEDEX, France
{yassamine.seladji,olivier.bouissou}@cea.fr

Abstract. An abstract interpretation based static analyzer depends on the choice of both an abstract domain and a methodology to compute fixpoints of monotonic functions. Abstract domains are almost always representations of convex sets that must provide efficient algorithms to perform both numerical and order-theoretic computations. In this paper, we present a new abstract domain that uses support functions to represent convex sets. We define the order-theoretic operations and, using a predefined set of directions, we define an efficient method to compute the fixpoint of linear and non-linear programs. Experiments show the efficiency and precision of our methods.

1 Introduction

Almost all static analysers rely on a method to efficiently compute numerical invariants. This is particularly true for highly numerical programs like digital filters for which we are interested in computing a possibly tight over-approximation of the range of values the variables can take. The theory of abstract interpretation defines such invariants as the least fixpoint of a system of semantics equations operating on elements of some abstract domain. The quality of the invariant then depends on both the algorithm to compute the least fixpoint and the choice of the abstract domain to encode sets of values.

For this second point, most domains over-approximate the sets of variables values by convex sets, very often using a (sub) polyhedral representation [6,14,9,15]. More recently, new domains were proposed that allow to encode non-convex (even non-connected) sets [3,1] but these are convex sets in another space. So it is clear that the static analyser efficiency relies on a precise and efficient representation of convex sets, that allows for both numeric and order-theoretic transformations. In this paper, we define a new abstract domain based on the support function representation of a convex set and show that this domain allows to efficiently and precisely compute numerical invariants.

Support function is a popular representation of convex sets for numerical analysis [11]: a set S is represented as a function mapping each direction d with the distance between the origin and the supporting hyperplane of S in the direction d. Support functions offer a very compact and precise representation of

G. Brat, N. Rungta, and A. Venet (Eds.): NFM 2013, LNCS 7871, pp. 155–169, 2013.

convex sets and allow for an exact computation of affine transformation of sets (see Section 2). Support functions with finite supports were successfully used in the hybrid systems analysis [10] to represent value sets or in our previous work to speed up the convergence of the Kleene algorithm on general polyhedra [16].

In this article, we present a new abstract domain which is based on a sub-polyhedral representation of convex sets using support functions with finite supports. It allows for a compact representation of sets and we define efficient algorithms to compute the fixpoint of affine and non-linear loops. This domain is similar to the template domain [15] in that it depends on a fixed direction set $\Delta \subseteq \mathbb{R}^n$ (n: the space dimension) and bounds the convex sets in each Δ direction. However, as it benefits from the algorithms on support functions, linear operations are very efficient and do not depend on linear programming solvers.

This article is organized as follows. Section 2 gives some basic definitions and results on support functions. Section 3 formally defines our abstract domain, in particular the order-theoretic operations. Sections 4 and 5 show how to adapt Kleene algorithm to our domain for linear and non-linear loops, respectively. For the non-linear case, the notion of interval based support function is introduced which allows to compute both an over- and under-approximation of the least fixpoint. Section 6 concludes the article with some experimentation.

Notations. We put $\mathbb{R}_\infty = \mathbb{R} \cup \{-\infty, +\infty\}$ and $\mathbb{I}_\mathbb{R} = \{[a,b] | a \leq b : a, b \in \mathbb{R}_\infty\}$. Given two vectors $v, w \in \mathbb{R}^n$, let $\langle v, w \rangle \in \mathbb{R}$ be the scalar product of u and w. Let $\mathbb{B}^n$ be the unit sphere in $\mathbb{R}^n$.

2   Support Function

In this section, we give the definition of the support function of a convex set and give some usefull properties that show how a support function is modified by set transformations. Given a convex set $S \subseteq \mathbb{R}^n$, the support function of S, denoted δ_S, is a functional representation of S, as stated by Definition 1 and Property 1.

Definition 1 ([11, Def. C.2.1.1]). *Let* $S \subseteq \mathbb{R}^n$ *be a convex set. The support function* δ_S *is defined by:*

$$\delta_S : \begin{cases} \mathbb{B}^n \to \mathbb{R}_\infty \\ d \mapsto \sup\{\langle x, d \rangle : x \in S\} \end{cases}$$

Property 1 ([11, Corollary. C.3.1.2]). *Let* $S \subseteq \mathbb{R}^n$ *be a convex set and let* δ_S *be its support function. Then,* $S = \bigcap_{d \in \mathbb{B}^n} \{x \in \mathbb{R}^n \mid \langle x, d \rangle \leq \delta_S(d)\}$.

Property 1 states that a convex set is uniquely determined by its support function. Stated differently, any positively homogeneous function $\delta : \mathbb{B}^n \to \mathbb{R}_\infty$ determines exactly one convex set defined as the intersection of all hyperplanes $\{x \in \mathbb{R}^n \mid \langle x, d \rangle \leq \delta(d)\}$ for all $d \in \mathbb{B}^n$. We recall that δ is positively homogeneous (of degree 1) if $\forall d \in \mathbb{B}^n, k \in \mathbb{R}, \delta(kd) \leq k\delta(d)$.

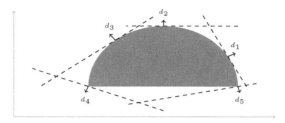

Fig. 1. Graphical representation of the support function of a convex set (in gray). The dashed lines are the lines $\langle x, d \rangle = \delta_S(d)$ for various directions d.

Figure 1 shows a convex set (in gray) and the value of its support function for some directions $d \in \mathbb{B}^n$. It should be clear from Property 1 and Figure 1 that it holds that, for a given direction set $\Delta \subseteq \mathbb{B}^n$, $S \subseteq \bigcap_{d \in \Delta} \{x \in \mathbb{R}^n | \langle x, d \rangle \leq \delta_S(d)\}$. Note that if Δ is a finite set, then $S_\Delta = \bigcap_{d \in \Delta} \{x \in \mathbb{R}^n | \langle x, d \rangle \leq \delta_S(d)\}$ is a convex polyhedron [11, Def. A.4.2.5]. So, the restriction of a support function of a set S over a finite domain Δ defines a convex polyhedron that over-approximates S. The faces of this polyhedron have a pre-defined shape: they are orthogonal to the chosen directions $d \in \Delta$. This is the basic idea behind our abstract domain based on support functions, see Section 3.

Support function computation. In the rest of this section, we show how the support function of a convex set can be computed efficiently in some cases. Obviously Definition 1 shows that the value of $\delta_S(d)$ for each $d \in \mathbb{B}^n$ can be obtained using a convex optimization problem [2], if an appropriate description of S is known. Property 2 below shows that we can compute efficiently the support function of a transformation of S. In this property, we denote by:

- MS for a given matrix $M \in \mathbb{R}^{n \times m}$ the set $MS = \{Mx | x \in S\}$,
- $S \oplus S'$ given two convex sets S and S' the Minkowski sum of S and S' defined by $S \oplus S' = \{x + x' \mid x \in S, \ x' \in S'\}$,
- λS for $\lambda \in \mathbb{R}$ the set $\lambda S = \{\lambda x \mid x \in S\}$.
- $S \cup S'$ the convex hull of convex sets S and S' and $S \cap S'$ their intersection.

Property 2 ([10, Prop. 3]). *Let S, S' be two convex sets. We have:*

1. $\forall M \in \mathbb{R}^{n \times m}$, $\delta_{MS}(d) = \delta_S(M^T d)$.
2. $\forall \lambda \geq 0$, $\delta_{\lambda S}(d) = \lambda \delta_S(d)$.
3. $\delta_{S \cup S'}(d) = \max(\delta_S(d), \delta_{S'}(d))$.
4. $\delta_{S \cap S'}(d) \leq \min(\delta_S(d), \delta_{S'}(d))$.
5. $\delta_{S \oplus S'}(d) = \delta_S(d) + \delta_{S'}(d)$.

Note that all relations are exact, except for the computation of the support function of the intersection for which we only have an over-approximation.

Another important case for which we can efficiently compute the support function of a convex set S is when S is a convex polyhedron. Then, the convex optimization problem of Definition 1 becomes a linear programming problem

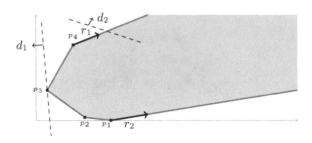

Fig. 2. Support function of a convex polyhedron. In direction d_1 the supremum is realized by a generator, in direction d_2 it is unbounded.

for which we have efficient algorithms (although linear programming may be exponential in the worst case). Moreover, Property 3 below shows that a more efficient method exists if the polyhedron is described by its generators.

Property 3 ([11, Ex. C.3.4.3]). *Let* $\mathsf{P} \subseteq \mathbb{R}^n$ *be a convex polyhedra generated by the set of generators* $v_1, \ldots, v_k$ *and rays* $r_1, \ldots, r_l$. *The support function* δ_P *is defined by:*

$$\forall d \in \mathbb{B}^n, \ \delta_\mathsf{P}(d) = \begin{cases} \max_{i \in [1,k]} \langle v_i, d \rangle & \textit{if } \forall j \in [1,l], \ \langle r_j, d \rangle \leq 0 \\ +\infty & \textit{otherwise} \end{cases}.$$

Property 3 shows that for a convex polyhedron P represented by its generator, the support function δ_P in a direction d can be computed in linear time. The condition $\forall j \in [1,l], \langle r_j, d \rangle \leq 0$ in Property 3 allows us to efficiently detect when the polyhedron supremum $\sup_{x \in \mathsf{P}} \langle x, d \rangle$ is finite or not, as illustrated on Figure 2.

3   Abstract Domain

In this section, we formally define our abstract domain based on support functions: we define both the order theoretic operations and the effect of an affine and non-linear affectation. Our domain is an abstraction of convex polyhedra over $\mathbb{R}^n$, where n is the number of variables of the program being analyzed. We denote by $\mathbb{P}$ the abstract domain of convex polyhedra over $\mathbb{R}^n$.

3.1   Lattice Structure

Let $\Delta = \{d_1, \ldots, d_l\}$ be a finite set of directions, i.e. $\Delta \subseteq \mathbb{B}^n$. Our abstract domain $\mathbb{P}^\sharp_\Delta$ is parametrized by this set Δ and is defined in Definition 2.

Definition 2. *Let* $\Delta \subseteq \mathbb{B}^n$ *be the set of directions. We define* $\mathbb{P}^\sharp_\Delta$ *as the set of all functions from* Δ *to* $\mathbb{R}_\infty$, *i.e.* $\mathbb{P}^\sharp_\Delta = \Delta \to \mathbb{R}_\infty$. *We denote* $\perp_\Delta$ *(resp.* $\top_\Delta$*) the function such that* $\forall d \in \Delta, \ \perp_\Delta(d) = -\infty$ *(resp.* $\top_\Delta(d) = +\infty$*).*

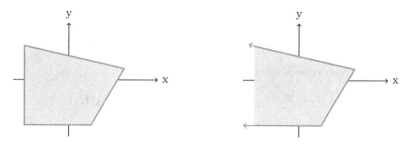

Fig. 3. The geometrical representation of $\gamma_\Delta(\Omega_1)$ (left) and $\gamma_\Delta(\Omega_2)$ (right)

For each $\Omega \in \mathbb{P}^\sharp_\Delta$, we write $\Omega(d)$ the value of Ω in direction $d \in \Delta$. Intuitively, Ω is a support function with finite domain.

The abstraction and concretization functions of $\mathbb{P}^\sharp_\Delta$ are given in Definition 3.

Definition 3. *Let $\Delta \subseteq \mathbb{R}^n$ be the set of directions. We define the concretizatiion function $\gamma_\Delta : \mathbb{P}^\sharp_\Delta \to \mathbb{P}$ by:*

$$\forall \Omega \in \mathbb{P}^\sharp_\Delta, \ \gamma_\Delta(\Omega) = \bigcap_{d \in \Delta} \{x \in \mathbb{R}^n \mid \langle x, d \rangle \leq \Omega(d)\} \ .$$

The abstraction function $\alpha_\Delta : \mathbb{P} \to \mathbb{P}^\sharp_\Delta$ is defined by:

$$\forall P \in \mathbb{P}, \alpha_\Delta(P) = \begin{cases} \bot & \text{if } P = \emptyset \\ \top & \text{if } P = \mathbb{R}^n \\ \lambda d. \ \delta_P(d) & \text{otherwise} \end{cases} \ .$$

Example 1. *Let $\Delta \subseteq \mathbb{R}^2$ with $\Delta = \{(-3,5),(1,3),(-1,0),(0,-1)\}$. For the abstract element $\Omega_1 = \{3,4,3,2\}$[1]. The result of $\gamma_\Delta(\Omega_1)$ is given in Figure 3(left). The right of the Figure 3 is the result of $\gamma_\Delta(\Omega_2)$, with $\Omega_2 = \{3,3,+\infty,2\}$. In this case, for $d_3 = (-1,0)$, $\Omega_2(d_3) = +\infty$, which means that the resulting polyhedron is unbounded in the direction d_3.*

Definition 3 shows that the concretization of an abstract element of $\mathbb{P}^\sharp_\Delta$ is a polyhedron defined by the intersection of half-spaces, where each one is characterized by its normal vector $d \in \Delta$ and the coefficient $\Omega(d)$. The abstraction function on the other side is the restriction of the support function of the polyhedra on the set of directions Δ. We next define the order, join and meet of $\mathbb{P}^\sharp_\Delta$ and then show that $(\alpha_\Delta, \gamma_\Delta)$ is a Gallois connection.

Definition 4 (Order structure of $\mathbb{P}^\sharp_\Delta$). *We define the inclusion operation $\sqsubseteq_\Delta$ as $\forall \Omega_1, \Omega_2 \in \mathbb{P}^\sharp_\Delta, \Omega_1 \sqsubseteq_\Delta \Omega_2 \iff \gamma_\Delta(\Omega_1) \sqsubseteq \gamma_\Delta(\Omega_2)$, where $\sqsubseteq$ is the inclusion on $\mathbb{P}$. The join $\sqcup_\Delta$ and meet $\sqcap_\Delta$ are defined by:*

- *$\forall \Omega_1, \Omega_2 \in \mathbb{P}^\sharp_\Delta, \ \Omega_1 \sqcup_\Delta \Omega_2 = \lambda d. \ \max(\Omega_1(d), \Omega_2(d))$;*
- *$\forall \Omega_1, \Omega_2 \in \mathbb{P}^\sharp_\Delta, \ \Omega_1 \sqcap_\Delta \Omega_2 = \lambda d. \ \min(\Omega_1(d), \Omega_2(d))$.*

---

[1] We identify $\mathbb{P}^\sharp_\Delta = \Delta \to \mathbb{R}_\infty$ with $\mathbb{R}_\infty^{|\Delta|}$, so that $\Omega_1 = \{3,4,3,2\}$ is the function mapping the first direction to 3, the second to 4,..

Note that the join operation is exact:

$$\forall \Omega_1, \ \Omega_2 \in \mathbb{P}^{\sharp}_{\Delta}, \ \gamma_{\Delta}(\Omega_1 \sqcup_{\Delta} \Omega_2) = \gamma_{\Delta}(\Omega_1) \sqcup \gamma_{\Delta}(\Omega_2)$$

while the meet operation is over-approximated:

$$\forall \Omega_1, \ \Omega_2 \in \mathbb{P}^{\sharp}_{\Delta}, \ \gamma_{\Delta}(\Omega_1 \sqcap_{\Delta} \Omega_2) \supseteq \gamma_{\Delta}(\Omega_1) \sqcap \gamma_{\Delta}(\Omega_2) \ .$$

Property 4. *The function pair* $(\alpha_{\Delta}, \gamma_{\Delta})$ *form a Galois connection [5] between* $\mathbb{P}$ *and* $\mathbb{P}^{\sharp}_{\Delta}$.

PROOF. See our extended version [17]. □

Note that $\forall \Omega \in \mathbb{P}^{\sharp}_{\Delta}$, if $\Omega = \alpha_{\Delta}(\mathsf{P})$, then $\mathsf{P} \subseteq \gamma_{\Delta}(\Omega)$, and the vertices of the polyhedron P touch the faces of $\gamma_{\Delta}(\Omega)$. This is stated in Proposition 5.

Property 5 ([10, Prop. 3]). *Let* P *be a polyhedron and* $\Omega \in \mathbb{P}^{\sharp}_{\Delta}$ *such that* $\Omega = \alpha_{\Delta}(\mathsf{P})$. *We have that,* $\mathsf{P} \subseteq \gamma_{\Delta}(\Omega)$. *This over approximation is tight as the vertices of* P *touch the faces of* $\gamma_{\Delta}(\Omega)$.

3.2   Affine Transformations

We now explain how an element $\Omega \in \mathbb{P}^{\sharp}_{\Delta}$ is modified by an affine transformation of the form $X = AX + b$ where X is the variable set of the program, $A \in \mathbb{R}^{n \times n}$ is a square matrix and $b \in \mathbb{R}^n$ is a vector. Let thus P_0 be a polyhedron and $\Omega_0 = \alpha_{\Delta}(\mathsf{P}_0)$ be the initial abstract state. Let also $\mathsf{P}_1 = [\![X = AX + b]\!](\mathsf{P}_0)$ be the polyhedron obtained after applying the affine transformation. Our goal is to compute the best possible abstraction Ω_1 of P_1, without computing P_1. Note that, using the operation set defined in Section 2, we have that $\mathsf{P}_1 = A\mathsf{P}_0 \oplus b$. Thus, using Property 2 we have: $\forall d \in \Delta, \delta_{\mathsf{P}_1}(d) = \delta_{A\mathsf{P}_0 \oplus b}(d) = \delta_{A\mathsf{P}_0}(d) + \delta_b(d) = \delta_{\mathsf{P}_0}(A^T d) + \langle b, d \rangle$. So we define Ω_1 as:

$$\forall d \in \Delta, \ \Omega_1(d) = \delta_{\mathsf{P}_0}(A^T d) + \langle b, d \rangle. \tag{1}$$

Note that $\Omega_1 = \alpha_{\Delta}(\mathsf{P}_1)$, while $\mathsf{P}_1 \subseteq \gamma_{\Delta}(\Omega_1)$. However, we do not need compute P_1, we only need to evaluate δ_{P_0} on directions $A^T d$, which can be done efficiently if P_0 is described using generators, as stated by Proposition 3. Moreover, Proposition 5 ensures that P_1 vertices touch $\gamma_{\Delta}(\Omega_1)$ faces. The precision of $\gamma_{\Delta}(\Omega_1)$ depends strongly on the chosen Δ: more directions we have more precise Ω_1 is.

3.3   Non-linear Transformations

We now deal with non-linear transformation, i.e. we want to apply the transformation $X = f(X)$, where $f : \mathbb{R}^n \to \mathbb{R}^n$ is non-linear. We use the notion of *linearisation* presented in [13] to abstract the transformation into an interval linear form. Interval linear forms are given by $i + \sum_{k=1}^{n} i_k X_k$, where $\forall k \in [1, n]$, X_k is a program variable and $i, \ i_k \in \mathbb{I}_{\mathbb{R}}$. For example, the expression $X_1 \times X_2$ can be transformed into $i_1 \times X_2$ where i_1 is the interval concretization of X_1. After the linearisation process, the transformation $X = f(X)$ can be abstracted by $X = AX + b$, where $A \in \mathbb{I}_{\mathbb{R}}^{n \times n}$ and $b \in \mathbb{I}_{\mathbb{R}}^n$.

As for Section 3.2, we want to compute $\Omega \in \mathbb{P}_{\Delta}^{\sharp}$, which is an abstraction of $P_1 = [\![X = AX + b]\!](P_0)$ (the semantics of interval linear forms is given in [13]). We cannot use Equation 1 directly because $\forall d \in \Delta$, $A^T d$ is an interval vector and δ_{P_0} is only defined on $\mathbb{R}^n$. To deal with that, we introduce the notion of *interval based support function*. In the rest of this article, $\forall i \in \mathbb{I}_{\mathbb{R}}$, $\overline{i}$ represents the upper bound of i and $\underline{i}$ its lower bound.

Let P be a polyhedron represented by its generators $v_1, \ldots, v_k$ and rays $r_1, \ldots, r_l$. We define the function σ_{P} by:

$$\sigma_{\mathsf{P}} : \begin{cases} \mathbb{I}_{\mathbb{R}}^n \to \mathbb{R} \\ d \mapsto \begin{cases} \max\limits_{i \in [1,k]} \overline{\langle v_i, d \rangle} & \text{if } \forall j \in [1,l], \langle r_j, d \rangle \cap]0, +\infty[= \emptyset \\ +\infty & \text{otherwise} \end{cases} \end{cases}.$$

In the same way, we define ι_{P} by:

$$\iota_{\mathsf{P}} : \begin{cases} \mathbb{I}_{\mathbb{R}}^n \to \mathbb{R} \\ d \mapsto \max_{i \in [1,k]} \underline{\langle v_i, d \rangle} \end{cases}.$$

Property 6 shows that δ_{P}, the support function of P, can be approximated using ι_{P} and σ_{P}. We call this approximation *interval based support function*.

Property 6 (Interval based support function). *Let P be a polyhedron and δ_{P} be its support function. Let $d \in \mathbb{I}_{\mathbb{R}}^n$ be an interval vector, representing a set of possible directions. We have that:*

$$\forall d \in d, \iota_{\mathsf{P}}(d) \leq \delta_{\mathsf{P}}(d) \leq \sigma_{\mathsf{P}}(d)$$

PROOF. On the one hand, we have that $\exists v \in \mathsf{P}$ s.t. $\iota_{\mathsf{P}}(d) = \underline{\langle v, d \rangle} = b$. So,

$$(\forall d \in d), \delta_{\mathsf{P}}(d) \geq \langle v, d \rangle \geq b. \tag{2}$$

On the other hand, we have that $\exists v \in \mathsf{P}$ s.t. $\sigma_{\mathsf{P}}(d) = \overline{\langle v, d \rangle} = b'$. So,

$$\forall d \in d, \exists v_i \in \mathsf{P} \text{ s.t. } \delta_{\mathsf{P}}(d) = \langle v_i, d \rangle \leq \overline{\langle v_i, d \rangle} \leq b'. \tag{3}$$

Thus from Equations 2 and 3, we have that: $b \leq \delta_{\mathsf{P}}(d) \leq b'$. $\square$

Let us now define Ω, abstraction of P_1. We know that, for all $d \in \Delta$ and for all $d' \in A^T d$, $\delta_{P_0}(d') \leq \sigma_{P_0}(A^T d)$. We have, $\forall d \in \Delta, \delta_{P_1}(d) = \delta_{AP_0 \oplus b}(d)$, so $\delta_{P_1}(d) \leq \sigma_{AP_0}(d) + \langle b, d \rangle$. So we define Ω as

$$\forall d \in \Delta, \ \Omega(d) = \sigma_{P_0}(A^T d) + \overline{\langle b, d \rangle}. \tag{4}$$

Note that in this case, Ω is an over-approximation of δ_{P_1}, i.e. $\alpha_{\Delta}(P_1) \sqsubseteq_{\Delta} \Omega$. In the same way, we can use ι_{P} to under approximate δ_{P_1}, i.e. we have that:

$$\forall d \in \Delta, \ \delta_{\mathsf{P}}(d) \geq \iota_{P_0}(A^T d) + \underline{\langle b, d \rangle}.$$

This under-approximation can be combined with the over-approximation to evaluate the precision of Ω.

4   Fixpoint Computation for Affine Loops

In this section, we present a specialization of Kleene algorithm to compute the fixpoint of an affine loop using our domain $\mathbb{P}_\Delta^\sharp$. We consider loops of the form:

```
while(C)
  X=AX+b;
```

We suppose that A is a real matrix, b may be a set of values, given as a polyhedra P_b, and C is a guard. Such loops include for example linear filters in which P_b represents the possible values of the new input at each loop iteration. We assume that the program variables lie initially in the polyhedra P_0.

4.1   Loops without Guards

We first consider the case where the loop is not conditioned by a guard, i.e. C is $\texttt{true}$. We want to compute an over-approximation in $\mathbb{P}_\Delta^\sharp$ of P_∞, the loop invariant defined as the least fixpoint of the equation $P = P_0 \sqcup (AP + P_b)$. Usually, P_∞ is defined as the limit of the Kleene iterates given by $P_i = P_{i-1} \sqcup (AP_{i-1} + P_b)$.

Property 7 defines the abstract element Ω_i at each iteration and shows that for all $d \in \Delta, \Omega_i(d) = \delta_{P_i}(d)$. Thus, we have that $\Omega_i = \alpha_\Delta(P_i)$, which means that Ω_i is the best abstraction of P_i in $\mathbb{P}_\Delta^\sharp$.

Property 7. *Let P_i be the polyhedron obtained in the ith iteration using polyhedra abstract domain, then*

$$\delta_{P_i}(d) = \Omega_i(d) = \max\left(\delta_{P_0}(d), \max_{j \in [1,i]}\left(\delta_{P_0}(A^{Tj}d) + \sum_{k=1}^{j}\delta_{P_b}(A^{T(k-1)}d)\right)\right) \quad (5)$$

PROOF. The proof runs by induction on i. We begin by $i = 1$. $\forall d \in \Delta$, we have, using Property 2, that $\delta_{P_1}(d) = \delta_{P_0 \cup AP_0 + P_b}(d) = \max\left(\delta_{P_0}(d), \delta_{P_0}(A^T d) + \delta_{P_b}(d)\right)$. Let now $i \geq 1$ such that Equation (5) is true.
Then, we have, $\forall d \in \Delta$: $\delta_{P_{i+1}} = \delta_{P_i \sqcup (AP_i + P_b)}(d) = \max\left(\delta_{P_i}(d), \delta_{P_i}(A^T d) + \delta_{P_b}(d)\right)$.
Now, we have that:

$$\delta_{P_i}(A^T d) = \max\left(\delta_{P_0}(A^T d), \max_{j \in [1,i]}\left(\delta_{P_0}(A^{Tj}A^T d) + \sum_{k=1}^{j}\delta_{P_b}(A^{T(k-1)}A^T d)\right)\right)$$

$$= \max\left(\delta_{P_0}(A^T d), \max_{j \in [1,i]}\left(\delta_{P_0}(A^{T(j+1)}d) + \sum_{k=1}^{j}\delta_{P_b}(A^{Tk}d)\right)\right)$$

$$= \max\left(\delta_{P_0}(A^T d), \max_{j \in [2,i+1]}\left(\delta_{P_0}(A^{T(j)}d) + \sum_{k=2}^{j}\delta_{P_b}(A^{T(k-1)}d)\right)\right)$$

We can deduce with a case analysis that:

$$\delta_{P_i}(A^T d) + \delta_{P_b}(d) = \max_{j \in [1,i+1]}\left(\delta_{P_0}(A^{Tj}d) + \sum_{k=1}^{j}\delta_{P_b}(A^{T(k-1)}d)\right)$$

From that we deduce Equation 5 for $i + 1$.   □

Algorithm 1. Kleene Algorithm using support function

Input: $\Delta \subset \mathbb{R}^n$, set of l directions
Input: P_0, The initial polyhedron
Input: $A \in \mathbb{R}^{n \times n}, b \in \mathbb{R}^n$
1: $D = \Delta$
2: $\Omega = \delta_{\mathsf{P}_0}(\Delta)$
3: **repeat**
4:     $\Omega' = \Omega$
5:     **for all** $i = 0, \ldots, (l-1)$ **do**
6:         $\Theta[i] = \Theta[i] + \delta_{\mathsf{P}_b}(D[i])$
7:         $D[i] = A^T D[i]$
8:         $\Upsilon[i] = \delta_{\mathsf{P}_0}(D[i]) + \Theta[i]$
9:         $\Omega[i] = \max(\Omega[i], \Upsilon[i])$
10:    **end for**
11: **until** $\Omega \sqsubseteq_\Delta \Omega'$

Property 7 defines a normal form of Ω_i *i.e.* $\Omega_i = \alpha_\Delta(\gamma_\Delta(\Omega_i))$. From that, we have that $\sqsubseteq_\Delta$ can be performed in linear time, such that:

$$\forall \Omega_1, \Omega_2 \in \mathbb{P}_\Delta^\sharp, \Omega_1 \sqsubseteq_\Delta \Omega_2 \iff \forall d \in \Delta, \Omega_1(d) \leq \Omega_2(d).$$

In Algorithm 1, the computation of the abstract element Ω depends on the computation of δ_{P_0}, Θ and D. We know that P_0 represents the polyhedron of the initial condition of the analysed program, so its representation, in general, is quite simple. In particular, the number of its generators is usually small. This means that the computation of δ_{P_0} does not require LP solvers. So, what changes in each iteration is the direction set in which δ_{P_0} is computed. Thus, Algorithm 1 has a polynomial complexity in the number of iteration and linear in the number of directions in Δ. In addition, its result is as accurate as possible: at each iterate, we have that $\Omega_i = \alpha_\Delta(\mathsf{P}_i)$. So $\Omega_\infty = \alpha_\Delta(\mathsf{P}_\infty)$, with Ω_∞ is the fixpoint obtained in our analysis and P_∞ is the one obtained using polyhedra domain. Note that, $\gamma_\Delta(\Omega_\infty)$ can have redundant constraints *i.e.* $\exists d \in \Delta$ *s.t.* $\gamma_{\Delta \setminus \{d\}}(\Omega_\infty) = \gamma_\Delta(\Omega_\infty)$. However, $\gamma_\Delta(\Omega_\infty)$ can be used for another analysis, so a redundancy removal method is needed. The one defined on polyhedra domain is time consuming, so we want to develop an efficient redundancy removal method based on our domain, which is the subject of our ongoing work.

Remark 1. *1) Like in the standard Kleene algorithm, Algorithm 1 does not guarantee the termination of the analysis. To handle this problem, we can use a widening operator on support functions which is very easy to define: if the support function in a given direction increases, we set it to $+\infty$. Of course using threshold [12] can help to limit this over-approximation. Another solution to speed-up the convergence is the use of the acceleration method presented in our previous work [16]. For that, we construct for each $d \in \Delta$ the numerical sequence $S_d = (\Omega_i(d))_{i \in \mathbb{N}}$, and then use acceleration methods to compute its limit.*

2) Our results are more precise than those obtained using template domain [4] with the chosen direction set Δ as a TCM [16, Sect. 5.1]. The difference is *that, in $\mathbb{P}^{\sharp}_{\Delta}$ the analysis is done with the precision of the polyhedra domain and the over-approximation is done only, at the end, in the concretization function. When with template domain, all the analysis is done in a less expressive domain.*

4.2   Loops with Linear Guard

We now consider the case when the loop has a guard of the form $\langle X, c \rangle \leq l$, with $c \in \mathbb{R}^n$ and $l \in \mathbb{R}$. Let H be the half space $H = \{x \in \mathbb{R}^n | \langle x, c \rangle \leq l\}$. In this case, the polyhedra P_i is defined as: $\mathsf{P}_{i+1} = \mathsf{P}_i \cup ((A_i \mathsf{P}_i \oplus \mathsf{P}_b) \cap H)$. $\forall d \in \Delta$, we have $\delta_{\mathsf{P}_{i+1}}(d) = \delta_{\mathsf{P}_i \cup ((A_{i+1}\mathsf{P}_i \oplus \mathsf{P}_b) \cap H)}(d)$ so:

$$\delta_{\mathsf{P}_{i+1}}(d) \leq \max(\delta_{\mathsf{P}_i}(d), \min(\delta_{\mathsf{P}_i}(A^T d) + \delta_{\mathsf{P}_b}(d), \delta_H(d)))$$

Note that $\delta_H(d) = l$ if $d = \lambda c$ for some $\lambda \geq 0$ and $\delta_H(d) = +\infty$ otherwise. We thus distinguish two cases: $d = \lambda c$ with $(\lambda \geq 0)$ or $\not\exists \lambda \geq 0$, $d = \lambda c$. Let us thus put $\Delta_1 = \{d \in \Delta | d = \lambda c, \lambda \geq 0\}$, and $\Delta_2 = \Delta \setminus \Delta_1$, if Δ_1 is empty we put $\Delta_1 = \{c\}$. Note that Δ is defined such that its elements are not two per two parallel i.e. $\forall d \in \Delta, \not\exists d' \in \Delta \setminus \{d\} : d = \lambda.d' (\lambda \geq 0)$. So, the cardinality of Δ_1 is 1. For the fixpoint computation, we separate the two cases. If $d \in \Delta_2$, as $\delta_H(d) = +\infty$, we have the same relation between $\delta_{\mathsf{P}_{i+1}}$ and δ_{P_i} as for the case of loops without guards, so $\Omega_i(d)$ defined as in Property 7.

Now, for $d \in \Delta_1$, we put $\Omega_i(d) = \max(\delta_{\gamma_\Delta(\Omega_{i-1})}(d), \min(\delta_{\gamma_\Delta(\Omega_{i-1})}(A^T d) + \delta_{\mathsf{P}_b}(d), l))$ which is an over approximation of $\delta_{\mathsf{P}_i}(d)$:

$$\begin{aligned}
\delta_{\mathsf{P}_i}(d) &= \delta_{\mathsf{P}_{i-1} \cup ((A\mathsf{P}_{i-1} \oplus \mathsf{P}_b) \cap H)}(d) \\
&\leq \max(\delta_{\mathsf{P}_{i-1}}(d), \min(\delta_{\mathsf{P}_{i-1}}(A^T d) + \delta_{\mathsf{P}_b}(d), \delta_H(d))) \\
&\leq \max(\delta_{\gamma_\Delta(\Omega_{i-1})}(d), \min(\delta_{\gamma_\Delta(\Omega_{i-1})}(A^T d) + \delta_{\mathsf{P}_b}(d), l)) \\
&\leq \Omega_i(d)
\end{aligned}$$

To compute $\Omega_i(d)$, we use $\delta_{\gamma_\Delta(\Omega_{i-1})}(d)$ and $\delta_{\gamma_\Delta(\Omega_{i-1})}(A^T d)$, which are obtained using linear programming. This does not affect a lot our method efficiency, because it is applied at most for one direction in Δ. So, in the case of affine loops with linear guard $\langle X, c \rangle \leq l$, we use Algorithm 1 but distinguish when $d \in \Delta_1$ from $d \in \Delta_2$. Then, we have that $\alpha_\Delta(\mathsf{P}_i) \sqsubseteq_\Delta \Omega_i$ such that the P_i vertices touch $\gamma_\Delta(\Omega_i)$ faces, except for the face of $\gamma_\Delta(\Omega_i)$ whose normal vector belongs to Δ_1.

5   Fixpoint Computation for Non-linear Loops

Let us now handle the case of non-linear loop, i.e. we consider a loop whose body is $X = f(X)$, f being a (possibly) non-linear function of the program variables. We again compute over-approximations of P_i, the Kleene algorithm iterates over the polyhedra domain. Basically, we apply, at each iteration, a linearisation of the function f and then use the interval based support function to compute Ω_i.

Let us denote $\boldsymbol{A}_i X + \boldsymbol{b} = L(f, \Omega_i)$ the interval linear form produced by linearisation of f when the value of variables X are in $\gamma_\Delta(\Omega_i)$. Note that this means that the matrix A of Algorithm 1 is now an interval matrix which may change from one iteration to the other. We compute A_i using techniques from [13], which requires that we have bounds on variables $X_k \in X$. Such bounds are very easy to get in our case: we assume that in Δ we added each direction $\pm X_k$, for every variable X_k. Then, the bounds on X_k are given by $\Omega_i(X_k)$ and $\Omega_i(-X_k)^2$.

To compute Ω_{i+1} from Ω_i, we will thus: first compute A_i using the linearisation process, and then apply the interval linear transformation $A_i X + b$ to Ω_i. Using functions σ and ι defined in Section 3.3, we can have bounds for Ω_{i+1}. In the polyhedra abstract domain, let P_i be the polyhedron obtained in the ith Kleene iteration. Property 8 below shows that we can compute bounds on δ_{P_i}.

Property 8. *Let $d \in \Delta$. For all $i \in \mathbb{N}$, we define $d_i^\star = \prod_{k=1}^{i} A_k^T d$ and :*

$$\overline{\Psi_i} = \sum_{k=1}^{i-1} \sigma_{P_b}\left(\prod_{q=k+1}^{i} A_q^T d \right) + \delta_{P_b}(d), \quad \underline{\Psi_i} = \sum_{k=1}^{i-1} \iota_{P_b}\left(\prod_{q=k+1}^{i} A_q^T d \right) + \delta_{P_b}(d) .$$

We have that:

$$\begin{cases} \delta_{P_i}(d) \geq \max\left(\delta_{P_0}(d), \max_{j \in [1,i]}\left(\iota_{P_0}(d_j^\star) + \underline{\Psi_j} \right) \right) \\ \delta_{P_i}(d) \leq \max\left(\delta_{P_0}(d), \max_{j \in [1,i]}\left(\sigma_{P_0}(d_j^\star) + \overline{\Psi_j} \right) \right) \end{cases}$$

PROOF. We do not give the whole proof as it is technical and long, but rather show how it runs for $i = 1, 2$. The general case is then a generalization of this.

Case $i = 1$. We know that $P_1 = P_0 \sqcup A_1 P_0 + P_b$. This means that

$$P_1 = P_0 \sqcup \left(\bigsqcup_{A_1 \in A_1} A_1 P_0 + P_b \right) .$$

The property of σ proves that $\forall A_1 \in A_1$, we have $\delta_{A_1 P_1}(d) \leq \sigma_{P_0}(A_1^T d)$, and equivalently for ι. This proves the property for $i = 1$.

Case $i = 2$. We notice that $P_2 = P_0 \sqcup (A_1 P_0 + P_b) \sqcup (A_2 A_1 P_0 + A_2 P_b + P_b)$. And then, for all $d \in \Delta$:

$$\forall A_1 \in A_1, \ A_2 \in A_2, \ \delta_{A_2 A_1 P_0 + A_2 P_b}(d) = \delta_{P_0}(A_1^T A_2^T d) + \delta_{P_b}(A_2^T d)$$
$$\leq \sigma_{P_0}(A_1^T A_2^T d) + \sigma_{P_b}(A_2^T d)$$

We equivalently get the lower bound using the ι function, and using the fact that $\delta_{S \cup S'}(d) = \max(\delta_S(d), \delta_{S'}(d))$, we get the result for $i = 2$. □

Let $\Delta \subseteq \mathbb{R}^n$ be a set of directions. Property 8 allows us to define the abstract element $\Omega_i \in P_\Delta^\sharp$ as given in Definition 5.

Definition 5. *Let $d_i^\star$ and Ψ_i be defined as in Property 8. The abstract element $\Omega_i \in P_\Delta^\sharp$ obtained in the ith Kleene iteration is given by:*

$$\forall d \in \Delta, \ \Omega_i(d) = \max\left(\delta_{P_0}(d), \max_{j \in [1,i]}\left(\sigma_{P_0}(d_j^\star) + \overline{\Psi_j} \right) \right)$$

---

[2] We let X_k denote the vector of $\mathbb{B}^n$ with a 1 in the dimension corresponding to X_k.

We have that $P_i \subseteq \gamma_\Delta(\Omega_i)$, so Ω_i of Definition 5 is sound. Note that we are no-longer guaranteed to have the best abstraction, i.e. we only have $\alpha_\Delta(P_i) \sqsubseteq_\Delta \Omega_i$ (compared to the linear case in which we had an equality). We can also compute an under-approximation of the fixpoint using the lower bound of Property 8.

We can modify Algorithm 1 for non-linear loops. Due to lack of place, we can not present this new algorithm (see the extended version [17]). We here explain the main differences with Algorithm 1 and why the complexity is increased. The main difference is that we now need to keep track of the list of all matrices $\prod_{k=1}^{i} A_k$ and $\prod_{q=k+1}^{i} A_q$. This list, called θ in the algorithm, is used as follows:

1. we extend it at the beginning of each iteration by computing the linearisation matrix A_{i+1} and multiplying each term of the list by A_{i+1}.
2. we iterate on it to compute $\overline{\Psi}$ and thus the upper bound of $\Omega(d)$.

The θ list length at iteration i is i, so we must make i call to σ_{P_0} or σ_{P_b} at iteration i, which makes the complexity of this algorithm quadratic in the number of generators of P_0 and P_b, while the algorithm for the linear case is linear.

Now let us extend this method to loops with non-linear guard. Again, we linearize at each iteration the guard and thus get a guard of the form $\langle X, C_i \rangle \leq L$, where $C_i \in \mathbb{I}_\mathbb{R}^n$ and $L \in \mathbb{I}_\mathbb{R}$. In this case, C_i changes in each iteration. To compute $\Omega_i \in P_\Delta^\sharp$, we distinguish two cases, $\forall d \in \Delta$:

- If $d \notin C_i$ then Property 8 is used to compute $\Omega_i(d)$.
- If $d \in C_i$, $\Omega_i(d) = \max(\delta_{\gamma_\Delta(\Omega_{i-1})}(d), \min(\boldsymbol{\sigma}_{\gamma_\Delta(\Omega_{i-1})}(A_i^T d) + \overline{\langle b, d \rangle}, \overline{L}))$.

Here more than one direction in each iteration may belong to C_i, so we may need to perform many calls to a linear programming solver to compute Ω_i.

Remark 2. *To analyse programs with floating point numbers, we can use the same technique as in the octagon domain with floating point [13]. The idea is to use the interval analysis and so we can use the interval based support function.*

6   Experimentation

To show the efficiency of our abstract domain, we use it to analyze different numerical programs. The implementation is done using the PPL[3]. The experi-mentation was done on a computer with 4 $2.0GHz$ processors and $8Gb$ of RAM. The linear programs that we analyze are digital filters [4] of order 2 to 10, to show the impact of the number of variables on the efficiency of the analysis. These filters are taken from the tests of Filter Verification Framework [7]. Note that Kleene iteration using the polyhedra abstract domain without widening fails to analyze these programs, i.e. the analysis does not terminate. So to compare our results, we use polyhedra abstract domain with widening with delay (15 iterations). The table of Figure 4 shows that our domain, using the octagonal

---

[3] Parma Polyhedra Library : `http://bugseng.com/products/ppl/`
[4] Programs are at `http://www.lix.polytechnique.fr/~bouissou/filters/`

Program				$\mathbb{P}^{\sharp}_{\triangle}$		
Name	$|V|$	t(s)	Bounded	t(s)	Iteration	$|y_n|$
`lp_iir_9600_2`	6	0.12	No	0.023	47	19.16
`lp_iir_9600_4`	10	TO	-	0.186	100	2.96
`lp_iir_9600_4_elliptic`	10	TO	-	0.471	276	3.74
`lp_iir_9600_6_elliptic`	14	TO	-	3.636	702	4.89
`bs_iir_9600_12000_10_chebyshev`	22	TO	-	53.986	2391	7.93
`non_linear_ODE`	3	TO	-	0.059	13	8.047

Fig. 4. Results of analysis obtained using different methods

```
begin
  while (0<=10) do
    xn = 0.5 *x - y - 2.5;
    yn = 0.9 *y + 10;
    x = xn; y = yn;
  done;
end
```

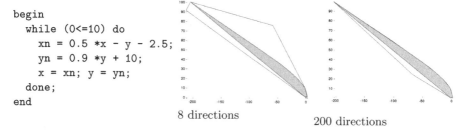

8 directions   200 directions

Fig. 5. A simple program (left) and the obtained post-fixpoints (right)

direction set and without widening, allows us to obtain a good fixpoint quickly, when the analysis using polyhedra abstract domain returns $\top$ in the best cases. The column $|y_n|$ is the width of the bounding box for the output of the filter, it is computed as $|y_n| = |\Omega(y_n) - \Omega(-y_n)|$, where Ω is the obtained post-fixpoint. $|V|$ is the number of variables, columns labeled t are the execution time (in seconds), the value TO meaning that the execution took more than 10 minutes, the column "Bounded" tells whether the polyhedra analysis could compute a bounded post-fixpoint. For most programs the analysis with widening did not terminate before the time-out. Note that increasing the delay did not help in getting a bounded fixpoint for the polyhedra domain. Note also that we did not use thresholds for the widening because our programs contain infinite loops, which means without guard, so it is hard to define relevant thresholds statically. This table thus shows the efficiency of our algorithm for linear loops. Remember that the computed post-fixpoint is also precise: it is the abstraction, in $\mathbb{P}^{\sharp}_{\triangle}$, of the least fixpoint obtained with polyhedra domain.

For the experimentation, we took also a non-linear program, which represents the Euler scheme to solve a non-linear ODE given by the formulas:

$$x_1 = x_1 + dt \times (-(1 + \gamma \times x_2^2) \times x_1)$$
$$x_2 = x_2 + dt \times (-0.5 \times x_2 \times (1 - \gamma \times x_1^2) + 2 \times x_3)$$
$$x_3 = x_3 + dt \times (-(1 - \gamma \times x_1) \times 2x_2 - 0.5 \times x_3)$$

where $dt = 0.01, \gamma = 0.1$ and the initial variables values are in $[-2, 2]$. Its analysis using polyhedra[5] could not give a result in a reasonable time.

---

[5] Using INTERPROC analyser
http://pop-art.inrialpes.fr/interproc/interprocwebf.cgi

We know that the precision of our analysis result depends strongly on the chosen direction set. To show that, we analyse the program given in the left of Figure 5 using $\mathbb{P}^{\sharp}_{\Delta_1}$ and $\mathbb{P}^{\sharp}_{\Delta_2}$, s.t. Δ_1 and Δ_2 represent, respectively, set of 8 and 200 random directions. We display on Figure 5 (right) our analysis result (in white) and the polyhedron obtained using Kleene iteration on the polyhedra domain (filled in gray). Note that, the polyhedron is obtained after 200 iterations and is not the least fixpoint in the polyhedra domain, which is contained in the white polyhedron obtained with our method. Execution time using Δ_1 is $0.046s$ and $3.15s$ using Δ_2, which shows our method scalability in the directions number.

Finally, as mentionned in Section 4, our algorithm combines easily with widening: we just set $\Omega_i(d) = +\infty$ if $\Omega_i(d) > \Omega_{i-1}(d)$. Using this widening, we can compute post-fixpoints of unbounded programs. For example, the simple translation $x = x + 1 \wedge y = y + 1$ starting from $x \in [0,1]$ and $y \in [0,1]$, we could compute the fixpoint $x \geq 0 \wedge y \geq 0 \wedge -y \geq x - 1 \wedge y \leq x + 1$ in 3 iterations.

7   Conclusion

In this article, we showed a new abstract domain that uses support functions to represent convex sets. Depending on the chosen set of directions, our domain $\mathsf{P}^{\sharp}_{\Delta}$ holds an over-approximation of the support functions of the set in each direction. Clearly, both the definition and the order defined in our domain are the same as for the template abstract domain. However, the linear assignments are very different as we can always rely on the support function of the initial polyhedron which is easily computed. Using this technique, we showed that our domain is very precise: for a loop, the ith iterate is the best abstraction in $\mathsf{P}^{\sharp}_{\Delta}$ of the ith iterate one would have computed using the polyhedra domain.

As already stated, the precision of our domain depends on the relevancy of the used direction set. Our analysis, in most cases, is not time consuming, so we can get a precise post-fixpoint using a large number N of random directions. The problem is that the resulting polyhedron contains a lot of constraints, and is thus hard to be, eventually, re-used as an entry of another analysis. We plan to develop a minimization method, that allows us to keep only $K \leq N$ relevant directions. For that, we are looking to apply pruning methods developed in [8], which allow to keep K linear functions from a set of N templates in order to best approximate the value function of an optimal control problem. We believe that the use of support functions to represent a polyhedron will allow us to use efficient methods to compute the importance of one constraint of the polyhedron, which is an apriori to the algorithm of [8]. Clearly, the choice of random directions is not optimal, so we are also interested in adapting the techniques of parametrized templates used in [4] to define the set of directions we use. In this way, we believe we could change it during the analysis and thus gain in precision. These ideas are the subject of our ongoing works.

Acknowledgement. We want to thank A. Adjé, E. Goubault and the anonymous reviewers for their helpful comments, and precious advices.

References

1. Allamigeon, X., Gaubert, S., Goubault, É.: Inferring Min and Max Invariants Using Max-plus Polyhedra. In: Alpuente, M., Vidal, G. (eds.) SAS 2008. LNCS, vol. 5079, pp. 189–204. Springer, Heidelberg (2008)
2. Bertsekas, D.P., Nedić, A., Ozdaglar, A.E.: Convex Analysis and Optimization. Athena Scientific Series in Optimization and Neural Computation. Athena Scientific (2003)
3. Chen, L., Miné, A., Wang, J., Cousot, P.: Interval polyhedra: An abstract domain to infer interval linear relationships. In: Palsberg, J., Su, Z. (eds.) SAS 2009. LNCS, vol. 5673, pp. 309–325. Springer, Heidelberg (2009)
4. Colón, M.A., Sankaranarayanan, S.: Generalizing the template polyhedral domain. In: Barthe, G. (ed.) ESOP 2011. LNCS, vol. 6602, pp. 176–195. Springer, Heidelberg (2011)
5. Cousot, P., Cousot, R.: Abstract interpretation: a unified lattice model for static analysis of programs by construction or approximation of fixpoints. In: Conference Record of the Fourth ACM Symposium on Principles of Programming Languages (POPL 1977), pp. 238–252. ACM Press (1977)
6. Cousot, P., Halbwachs, N.: Automatic discovery of linear restraints among variables of a program. In: Conference Record of the Fifth ACM Symposium on Principles of Programming Languages (POPL 1978), pp. 84–97. ACM Press (1978)
7. Cox, A., Sankaranarayanan, S., Chang, B.-Y.E.: A bit too precise? Bounded verification of quantized digital filters. In: Flanagan, C., König, B. (eds.) TACAS 2012. LNCS, vol. 7214, pp. 33–47. Springer, Heidelberg (2012)
8. Gaubert, S., McEneaney, W.M., Qu, Z.: Curse of dimensionality reduction in max-plus based approximation methods: Theoretical estimates and improved pruning algorithms. In: CDC-ECE (2011)
9. Goubault, E., Putot, S.: Perturbed affine arithmetic for invariant computation in numerical program analysis. CoRR, abs/0807.2961 (2008)
10. Le Guernic, C., Girard, A.: Reachability analysis of hybrid systems using support functions. In: Bouajjani, A., Maler, O. (eds.) CAV 2009. LNCS, vol. 5643, pp. 540–554. Springer, Heidelberg (2009)
11. Hiriart-Urrut, J.-B., Lemaréchal, C.: Fundamentals of Convex Analysis. Springer (2004)
12. Lakhdar-Chaouch, L., Jeannet, B., Girault, A.: Widening with thresholds for programs with complex control graphs. In: Bultan, T., Hsiung, P.-A. (eds.) ATVA 2011. LNCS, vol. 6996, pp. 492–502. Springer, Heidelberg (2011)
13. Miné, A.: Weakly relational numerical abstract domains. PhD thesis, École Polytechnique (2004), http://www.di.ens.fr/~mine/these/these-color.pdf
14. Miné, A.: The octagon abstract domain. Higher-Order and Symbolic Computation 19 (2006)
15. Sankaranarayanan, S., Sipma, H.B., Manna, Z.: Scalable analysis of linear systems using mathematical programming. In: Cousot, R. (ed.) VMCAI 2005. LNCS, vol. 3385, pp. 25–41. Springer, Heidelberg (2005)
16. Seladji, Y., Bouissou, O.: Fixpoint computation in the polyhedra abstract domain using convex and numerical analysis tools. In: Giacobbazzi, R., Berdine, J., Mastroeni, I. (eds.) VMCAI 2013. LNCS, vol. 7737, pp. 149–168. Springer, Heidelberg (2013)
17. Seladji, Y., Bouissou, O.: Numerical abstract domain using support functions (extended version) (2013), http://www.lix.polytechnique.fr/~bouissou/pdf/publications/NFM13_extended.pdf

Widening as Abstract Domain

Bogdan Mihaila, Alexander Sepp, and Axel Simon

Technical University of Munich, Garching b. München, Germany
firstname.lastname@in.tum.de

Abstract. Verification using static analysis often hinges on precise numeric invariants. Numeric domains of infinite height can infer these invariants, but require widening/narrowing which complicates the fixpoint computation and is often too imprecise. As a consequence, several strategies have been proposed to prevent a precision loss during widening or to narrow in a smarter way. Most of these strategies are difficult to retrofit into an existing analysis as they either require a pre-analysis, an on-the-fly modification of the CFG, or modifications to the fixpoint algorithm. We propose to encode widening and its various refinements from the literature as cofibered abstract domains that wrap standard numeric domains, thereby providing a *modular* way to add numeric analysis to any static analysis, that is, without modifying the fixpoint engine. Since these domains cannot make any assumptions about the structure of the program, our approach is suitable to the analysis of executables, where the (potentially irreducible) CFG is re-constructed on-the-fly. Moreover, our domain-based approach not only mirrors the precision of more intrusive approaches in the literature but also requires fewer iterations to find a fixpoint of loops than many heuristics that merely aim for precision.

Adding numeric domains of infinite height to a static analysis requires that widening and/or narrowing is applied within each loop of the program to ensure termination [7]. Commonly, this is implemented by modifying the fixpoint algorithm to perform upward and downward iterations while a pre-analysis determines necessary widening points. Firstly, downward iterations can be problematic since a widened state can induce a precision loss in other domains that cannot be reverted with the narrowed numeric state [17]. Secondly, determining a minimal set of widening points requires non-trivial algorithms for irreducible control flow graphs (CFGs) [6]. Worse, these algorithms cannot be applied in the context of analyzing machine code, as the CFG is re-constructed on-the-fly while computing the fixpoint [3]. Moreover, narrowing alone is often not enough to obtain precise fixpoints which has been illustrated in many papers that present improved widenings/narrowings [10,11,12,15,17]. All of these approaches require disruptive changes to the fixpoint engine, for instance, tracking several abstract states [10,12], temporarily disabling parts of the CFG [11], performing a pre-analysis with different semantics [13,15], collecting "landmarks" [17] or referring to user-supplied thresholds [5]. This paper shows that widening and its various refinements can be implemented without modifying an existing fixpoint engine, thereby making numeric domains available to analyses that are oblivious to the

G. Brat, N. Rungta, and A. Venet (Eds.): NFM 2013, LNCS 7871, pp. 170–184, 2013.

```
1  int x = 0;
2  int y = 0;
3  while (x < 100) {
4      x = x + 1;
5      y = y + 1;
6  }
7
```

step	line		intervals		affine	thresholds
			x	y		
1	2		$[0,0]$		$x=0$	
2	3		$[0,0]$	$[0,0]$	$x=0,y=0$	
3	4		$[0,0]$	$[0,0]$	$x=0,y=0$	$x\leq 99$
4	5		$[1,1]$	$[0,0]$	$x=1,y=0$	$x\leq 100$
5	6		$[1,1]$	$[1,1]$	$x=1,y=1$	$x\leq 100$
6	3	$\sqcup$	$[0,1]$	$[0,1]$	$x=y$	$x\leq 100$
6'	3'	$\triangledown$	$[0,100]$	$[0,100]$	$x=y$	
7	4		$[0,99]$	$[0,99]$	$x=y$	
8	5		$[1,100]$	$[0,99]$	$x=y+1$	
9	6		$[1,100]$	$[1,100]$	$x=y$	
10	3	$\sqsubseteq$	$[0,100]$	$[0,100]$	$x=y$	
11	7		$[100,100]$	$[100,100]$		

Fig. 1. Rapid convergence during widening

challenges of widening [1]. Specifically, we propose to implement the inference of widening points and the various widening heuristics as abstract domains that can be plugged into an analysis in a modular way. This modular approach not only reduces the overall complexity of an analysis, it also facilitates the comparison and combination of various heuristics.

The key idea of our approach is to implement abstract domains as cofibered domains [18], an approach sometimes called "functor domains" [5]. Here, each domain $\mathcal{D}$ has a child $\mathcal{C}$ that it controls. The combined domain is written $\mathcal{D} \triangleright \mathcal{C}$. Only the leaf, namely the interval domain $\mathcal{I}$, has no child. The benefit is that a transfer function of domain $\mathcal{D}$ on a state $s \in \mathcal{D} \triangleright \mathcal{C}$ may execute any number of transfer functions on its child $\mathcal{C}$ before returning a new state s'. We illustrate this idea using a cofibered threshold domain $\mathcal{T}$ and a cofibered affine domain $\mathcal{A}$ to build the domain stack $\mathcal{T} \triangleright (\mathcal{A} \triangleright \mathcal{I})$. A state is written as a tuple $\langle t, \langle a, i \rangle \rangle \in \mathcal{T} \triangleright (\mathcal{A} \triangleright \mathcal{I})$ containing the individual domain states $t \in \mathcal{T}$, $a \in \mathcal{A}$ and $i \in \mathcal{I}$.

Figure 1 presents the analysis of a simple loop over $\mathcal{T} \triangleright (\mathcal{A} \triangleright \mathcal{I})$ where the state of each domain is written in a separate column. The states of the interval and affine domain for steps 1 to 6 are straightforward. The threshold domain tracks all conditions in tests that are redundant, here x<100, i.e. $x \leq 99$ in step 3. These so-called predicates are changed by assignments, here yielding $x \leq 100$ after x=x+1;. In step 6, the state after one loop iteration is joined with the previous state at line 3, yielding the intervals $[0,1]$ for both, x and y together with the affine relation $x = y$ and the threshold $x \leq 100$ since it is still redundant in the joined state. The interim step 6' shows how the state obtained at step 2 is widened with respect to the state at step 6: the threshold domain applies widening on its child, yielding $x, y \in [0, \infty]$ for the interval domain while the affine domain returns the join $x = y$ since its lattice is of finite height. The threshold domain then refines this state by applying the test $x \leq 100$. The affine domain passes this test to its child, the interval domain, but also applies the tests $\sigma(x \leq 100)$ for any substitution $\sigma = [x/y]$ that can be derived from equalities over x. This refines the interval domain to $x, y \in [0, 100]$ as shown as step 6'. Steps 7 to 10 ascertain that this state is indeed a fixpoint of the loop, yielding the post-condition shown as step 11.

The example illustrates two consequences of this cofibered arrangement of domains: firstly, it is a modular way of combining several domains, thus keeping each domain simple; secondly, information can be propagated between domains by applying several operations on a child C for each operation on the parent $\mathcal{D}$.

One might argue that the modular design itself creates the need for propagation which is unnecessary when using a monolithic domain such as an off-the-shelf polyhedra package [2]. However, combining several simple domains allows for a more flexible trade-off between efficiency and precision by adjusting the interaction between domains [16]. For instance, in all polyhedra packages we tested, the widening operation is reduced to a join when the affine relations are not stable, thereby requiring a third fixpoint iteration for this simple example. In our modular setup, the information in the affine domain is not intermingled with information on variable bounds, thereby allowing the affine domain (which has finite height) to compute a join while the interval domain performs widening. This alternative design yields the same precision while requiring fewer iterations.

The implementation of the various widening strategies builds on the ability to separate various concerns into individual domains. These domains are as follows:

Widening Point Domain: Rather than enhancing a fixpoint engine to identify widening points in loops, we propose a domain that turns a join operation into a widening when it observes that the state is propagated along a back-edge of the CFG. This simple technique for irreducible CFGs [6] and CFGs that are constructed on-the-fly [3] works surprisingly well in practice.

Threshold Domain: We implement widening with thresholds [5,13] but infer the thresholds automatically. We present the basic domain that infers thresholds from tests. Unlike previous work [15] that extracts thresholds from a preanalysis using the domain of polyhedra [9], only relevant tests are tracked.

Delay Domain: A domain which postpones widening is presented that ensures precise results for loops containing assignments of constants.

Phased Domain: We provide an automatic way to separate the state space of loops into several phases, where phase boundaries are automatically inferred from tests within the loop, similar to guided static analysis [11]. This domain can be seen as an instance of a decision tree domain combinator [8].

Besides these specific domains, our paper makes the following contributions:

- Even though cofibered abstract domains only allow to selectively delay widening or to restrict the result of widening by applying tests, they suffice to implement even the most complex widening heuristic in the literature [11].
- Our domains can be added to existing analyses without modification to the fixpoint engine. Our modular approach allows for combining several heuristics and even to retrofit an existing analysis that has no notion of widening.
- We give experimental evidence of the precision of our widening domains.

The remainder of the paper is organized as follows. The next section introduces notation and defines a domain that determines when to widen. Sections 2 to 4 introduce the threshold, delay, and phased domain to improve precision. Section 5 evaluates our domains before Sect. 6 presents related work and concludes.

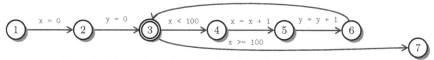

Fig. 2. The control flow graph of the introductory example

1 Preliminaries

This section details the program analysis problem we address. The CFG is represented by a set of vertices labeled $l_1, l_2, \ldots \in Lab$ and directed edges for assignments $l_i \xrightarrow{x=e} l_j$ and tests $l_i \xrightarrow{e \leq 0} l_j$. Given the lattice $\langle \mathcal{D}, \sqsubseteq_{\mathcal{D}}, \sqcup_{\mathcal{D}}, \sqcap_{\mathcal{D}}, \top_{\mathcal{D}}, \bot_{\mathcal{D}} \rangle$ of an abstract domain $\mathcal{D}$, we associate each vertex at l_i with a state $d_i \in \mathcal{D}$ which initially are $d_0 = \top_{\mathcal{D}}$ and $d_i = \bot_{\mathcal{D}}$ for $i \neq 0$. The semantics of an assignment edge $l_i \xrightarrow{x=e} l_j$ in $\mathcal{D}$ is given by $F_i^j = [\![l_i : x = e]\!]^{\mathcal{D}} : \mathcal{D} \to \mathcal{D}$; likewise for test edges. As an example, Fig. 2 shows the CFG of the introductory example of Fig. 1. Here, nodes l_i are labeled with i and an empty edge $l_6 \longrightarrow l_3$ was added so that labels match line numbers. The solution of analysing a program is characterized by a set of equations $s_j \sqsupseteq_{\mathcal{D}} F_i^j(s_i)$, each corresponding to an edge from l_i to l_j. It can be inferred using chaotic iteration [1,6] which picks a location l_i that is not stable and, for all edges $s_i \longrightarrow s_j$ updates s_j to $s_j := s_j \sqcup_{\mathcal{D}} F_i^j(s_i)$.

Inferring numeric information about program variables usually requires the use of abstract domains that have infinite increasing chains such as intervals where $[0,1] \sqsubseteq [0,2] \sqsubseteq [0,3] \ldots$ or convex polyhedra [9]. In these cases, termination of the fixpoint computation is not guaranteed unless at least one widening operator is inserted into each cycle of the graph. The idea of a widening operator is to extrapolate the change in the abstract state between consecutive iterations at a node in the graph. It must obey the following definition [9]:

Definition 1. *Given a domain $\mathcal{D}$, define $\nabla_{\mathcal{D}}^l : \mathcal{D} \times \mathcal{D} \to \mathcal{D}$ such that:*

$$\forall x, y \in \mathcal{D} : x \sqsubseteq_{\mathcal{D}} x \nabla_{\mathcal{D}}^l y$$
$$\forall x, y \in \mathcal{D} : y \sqsubseteq_{\mathcal{D}} x \nabla_{\mathcal{D}}^l y$$

and for all increasing chains $x_0 \sqsubseteq_{\mathcal{D}} x_1 \sqsubseteq_{\mathcal{D}} \ldots$ the increasing chain $y_0 = x_0$, $\ldots y_{i+1} = y_i \nabla_{\mathcal{D}}^l x_{i+1}$ is not strictly increasing.

Consider inserting a widening operator into the equation of the no-op edge from l_6 to l_3, yielding $s_3 := s_3 \nabla_{\mathcal{D}}^l (s_3 \sqcup_{\mathcal{D}} F_6^3(s_6)) = s_3 \nabla_{\mathcal{D}}^l (s_3 \sqcup_{\mathcal{D}} s_6)$. Although termination is now guaranteed, the result of, say, an interval analysis is imprecise: $\{x \in [0,0], y \in [0,0]\} \nabla_{\mathcal{D}}^l \{x \in [0,1], y \in [0,1]\} = \{x \in [0,\infty], y \in [0,\infty]\}$. This stable state can, in principle, be made more precise by replacing the widening with a narrowing operator and re-running the fixpoint computation just for the loop body. However, this requires meddling with the fixpoint engine in order to identify the loop and its in- and outgoing edges and changing the way states are handled: for example our updates $s_j := s_j \sqcup_{\mathcal{D}} F_i^j(s_i)$ are *expansive* ($s_i \sqsubseteq_{\mathcal{D}} s_j \sqcup_{\mathcal{D}} F_i^j(s_i)$) so that the states cannot shrink by evaluating the updates [15]. We therefore avoid narrowing altogether to avoid changing the way states are stored. Instead, Sect. 2

$$\begin{aligned}
[\![l : x = e]\!]^{\mathcal{W}} \langle \langle l^w, f^w \rangle, c \rangle &= \langle \langle l, f^w \vee (l < l^w) \rangle, [\![l : x = e]\!]^{\mathcal{C}} c \rangle \rangle \\
[\![l : e \leq 0]\!]^{\mathcal{W}} \langle \langle l^w, f^w \rangle, c \rangle &= \langle \langle l, f^w \vee (l < l^w) \rangle, [\![l : e \leq 0]\!]^{\mathcal{C}} c \rangle \rangle \\
\langle w_1, c_1 \rangle \sqsubseteq_{\mathcal{W}} \langle w_2, c_2 \rangle &= c_1 \sqsubseteq_{\mathcal{C}} c_2 \\
\langle \langle l_1^w, f_1^w \rangle, c_1 \rangle \sqcup_{\mathcal{W}} \langle \langle l_2^w, f_2^w \rangle, c_2 \rangle &= \begin{cases} \langle \langle l, false \rangle, c_1 \nabla_{\mathcal{C}}^l c_2 \rangle & \text{if } f_1^w \vee f_2^w \\ \langle \langle l, false \rangle, c_1 \sqcup_{\mathcal{C}} c_2 \rangle & \text{otherwise} \end{cases} \\
& \text{where } l = \max(l_1^w, l_2^w)
\end{aligned}$$

Fig. 3. Lattice and transfer functions for the widening point domain

and 3 present domains that implement more precise widenings. Before detailing these, we address the task of identifying widening points.

1.1   Inferring Widening Points

For programs made up of well-nested loops, widening is only required at each loop head in the program [5], which renders fixpoint computations relatively straightforward. For programs with irreducible CFGs, it is generally necessary to place more than one widening point in each cycle [6] and, hence, a widening heuristic must not lose precision when widening is applied several times within a loop. This, in turn, implies that a conservative heuristic, that places rather many widening points, suffices. We now present such a heuristic that is appropriate for machine code, implemented as abstract domain $\mathcal{W}$. The domain observes back-edges, that is, information flowing from larger to smaller addresses. Once observed, the next join on $\mathcal{W} \triangleright \mathcal{C}$ translates to a widening on the child $\mathcal{C}$.

For the sake of finding back-edges, we assume that statement labels $l \in Lab$ represent the code address of a statement or test. The widening point domain is given by the lattice $\langle \mathcal{W} \triangleright \mathcal{C}, \sqsubseteq_{\mathcal{W}}, \sqcup_{\mathcal{W}}, \sqcap_{\mathcal{W}}, \top_{\mathcal{W}}, \bot_{\mathcal{W}} \rangle$ where $\mathcal{W} : Lab \times \{true, false\}$ is a tuple of the last program point and a flag indicating if a backward edge has been observed. If set, widening is applied at the next junction node at which point the loop is usually completely traversed. Figure 3 defines the domain operations. The transfer functions for assignment and the lattice functions for subset and join are shown. Each function operates on tuples $\langle w, c \rangle \in \mathcal{W} \triangleright \mathcal{C}$ where $w \equiv \langle l^w, f^w \rangle \in \mathcal{W}$. The transfer functions $[\![\cdot]\!]^{\mathcal{W}}$ on $\mathcal{W}$ apply the corresponding operation $[\![\cdot]\!]^{\mathcal{C}}$ on the child $c \in \mathcal{C}$ while tracking the current label l and whether a backward edge $l^w \to l$ with $l < l^w$ has been observed. The subset test $\sqsubseteq_{\mathcal{W}}$ translates to a subset test on the child, indicating that the $\mathcal{W}$ domain does not actually infer any information about the state of the program and is therefore, per definition, stable. The only effect of the domain is that the $\sqcup_{\mathcal{W}}$ translates to a widening operation on the child if one of the flags is true. Note that this domain may be more precise than a standard algorithm for determining widening points [6] since widening is applied only after a back-edge. For instance, in Fig. 2, widening is only applied when updating node l_3 with a state from l_6 but no widening is applied when propagating the state from l_2 to l_3, as this path is not a back-edge.

The ability to add widening to an analysis without changing the fixpoint can also be carried over to various widening heuristics, as detailed next.

$$[\![l : x = e]\!]^{\mathcal{T}}\langle t, c\rangle \quad = \langle [p \mapsto \langle \bar{l}_o, \bar{l}_w\rangle \in t \mid x \notin vars(p)] \cup [\sigma^{-1}(p) \mapsto \langle \bar{l}_o, \bar{l}_w\rangle \mid p \mapsto \langle \bar{l}_o, \bar{l}_w\rangle \in t$$
$$\wedge \sigma = [x/e], \sigma^{-1}(p) \text{ exists}], [\![l : x = e]\!]^{\mathcal{C}} c\rangle$$

$$[\![l : e \leq 0]\!]^{\mathcal{T}}\langle t, c\rangle \quad = \langle filter(t'[e \leq 0 \mapsto \langle \{l\}, \emptyset\rangle \mid \exists p. t(p) = \langle \bar{l}_o, \emptyset\rangle \wedge l \in \bar{l}_o], c), [\![l : e \leq 0]\!]^{\mathcal{C}} c\rangle|$$

$$\langle t_1, c_1\rangle \sqsubseteq_{\mathcal{T}} \langle t_2, c_2\rangle = c_1 \sqsubseteq_{\mathcal{C}} c_2 \qquad\qquad \text{where } t' = [p \mapsto \langle \bar{l}_o, \bar{l}_w\rangle \in t \mid l \notin \bar{l}_o \vee \bar{l}_w \neq \emptyset]|$$

$$\langle t_1, c_1\rangle \sqcup_{\mathcal{T}} \langle t_2, c_2\rangle = \langle filter(t, c), c\rangle \text{ where } t = join(t_1, t_2) \text{ and } c = c_1 \sqcup_{\mathcal{C}} c_2$$

$$\langle t_1, c_1\rangle \nabla^l_{\mathcal{T}} \langle t_2, c_2\rangle = \langle filter(t[p_i \mapsto \langle \bar{l}_o, \bar{l}_w \cup \{l\}\rangle \mid \langle \bar{l}_o, \bar{l}_w\rangle \in t \wedge \bar{l}_o \cap \bar{l}_{upd} \neq \emptyset], c), c\rangle \text{ where}$$
$$t = join(filter(t_1, c_2), filter(t_2, c_2)) \wedge c = [\![l : p_1]\!]^{\mathcal{C}} \dots [\![l : p_n]\!]^{\mathcal{C}} (c_1 \nabla^l_{\mathcal{C}} c_2)$$
$$p_i \in \{e_1 \leq 0, \dots, e_n \leq 0\} = \{p \in dom(t) \mid t(p) = \langle \bar{l}_o, \bar{l}_w\rangle \wedge l \notin \bar{l}_w\} \text{ and}$$
$$\bar{l}_{upd} = \bigcup_{i=1}^n \{\bar{l}_o \mid t(p_i) = \langle \bar{l}_o, \bar{l}_w\rangle \wedge \max(e_i, c) = \min_{i=1}^n(\max(e_i, c))\}$$

Fig. 4. Transfer and lattice functions for the threshold domain

2   Widening with Thresholds as Abstract Domain

Widening is necessary to ensure termination when a fixpoint is computed over a domain of infinite height. One problem of widening is that the obtained fixpoint is almost always a post-fixpoint, that is, it is larger than the least fixpoint. This section shows how predicates occurring in tests can be used as *thresholds* to restrict the widened state, thereby often giving better results than a narrowing can provide. Let *Pred* be a set of predicates that are used as conditions in tests. We only require that the negation $\neg p$ of $p \in Pred$ exists and that $\neg p \in Pred$ where $\neg(\neg p) \equiv p$. In practice, we gather all tests convertible to linear inequalities and assume integer arithmetic: $\neg(a_1 x_1 + \dots + a_n x_n \leq c) \equiv a_1 x_1 + \dots + a_n x_n \geq c + 1$.

The threshold domain is given by the lattice $\langle \mathcal{T} \triangleright \mathcal{C}, \sqsubseteq_{\mathcal{T}}, \sqcup_{\mathcal{T}}, \sqcap_{\mathcal{T}}\rangle$ where the universe $\mathcal{T} : Pred \dashrightarrow \wp(Lab) \times \wp(Lab)$ is a partial map from redundant tests $p \in Pred$ to two sets of program points. The first set $\bar{l}_o$ contains the program points of the test where p originated. The second set $\bar{l}_w$ denotes the widening points at which p has been used as thresholds. We update $t \in \mathcal{T}$ to $t' = t[p \mapsto l] \in \mathcal{T}$ with $t'(p) = l$ and $t'(q) = t(q)$ for $q \neq p$. In abuse of notation we use $[p \mapsto \dots]$ to construct a new mapping and $\emptyset$ for the empty map. We enforce the invariant that all tests $p \in Pred$ are redundant in the child domain by applying $filter : \mathcal{T} \times \mathcal{C} \to \mathcal{T}$ which is defined as $filter(t, c) = [p \mapsto t(p) \mid p \in dom(t) \wedge [\![\neg p]\!]^{\mathcal{C}} c = \bot_{\mathcal{C}}]$ where $[\![\neg p]\!]^{\mathcal{C}} c \in \mathcal{C}$ computes a state of the child domain in which the test $\neg p$ has been applied. Note that instead of $[\![p]\!]^{\mathcal{C}} c = c$ we use the cheaper test $[\![\neg p]\!]^{\mathcal{C}} c = \bot_{\mathcal{C}}$.

Figure 4 presents the transfer functions and lattice operations of the threshold domain. An assignment $x = e$ at program point $l \in Lab$ is forwarded to the child. All thresholds that are not affected by the write to x are kept as is (first line) while predicates p that mention x are kept if an inverted substitution σ^{-1} exists where $\sigma = [x/e]$. For instance, consider the assignment x=x+1; in Fig. 1 where $t = [x \leq 99 \mapsto \langle \{3\}, \emptyset\rangle] \in \mathcal{T}$ and intervals $\mathcal{C} = \mathcal{I}$ with $x \in [0, 1]$. With $\sigma = [x/x + 1]$, we obtain $\sigma^{-1} = [x/x - 1]$ and $\sigma^{-1}(x \leq 99) = x \leq 100$. Thus, the state after the assignment is $\langle [x \leq 100 \mapsto \langle \{3\}, \emptyset\rangle], x \in [1, 2]\rangle$. Note that the resulting threshold is again 98 units away from the current state space. Indeed, applying a linear substitution ensures that each threshold remains redundant. If $x \notin vars(e)$ or if e is not linear, σ^{-1} does not exist and the threshold is removed.

```
1   int n = 0;
2   while (true) {
3       if (!read_sec())
4           continue;
5       if (n<60) {
6           n = n+1;
7       } else {
8           n = 0;
9       }
10  }
```

Fig. 5. A loop whose fixpoint cannot be obtained by narrowing

The transfer function for tests replaces tests that originate here ($l \in \bar{l}_o$) and which have not been applied yet ($\bar{l}_w = \emptyset$) with a fresh threshold $e \leq 0$. Here, t' contains the remaining mappings. Tests that happen to actually restrict the incoming state space c are removed by *filter*.

With respect to the lattice operation, the entailment test $\langle t_1, c_1 \rangle \sqsubseteq_{\mathcal{T}} \langle t_2, c_2 \rangle$ reduces to an entailment test on the child. The join $\langle t_1, c_1 \rangle \sqcup_{\mathcal{T}} \langle t_2, c_2 \rangle$ uses a function *join* that merges the program points where tests originate and where they are applied point-wise as follows:

$$join(t_1, t_2) = \left[p \mapsto \langle \bar{l}_1^o \cup \bar{l}_2^o, \bar{l}_1^w \cup \bar{l}_2^w \rangle \mid \langle \bar{l}_i^o, \bar{l}_i^w \rangle = \begin{cases} t_i(p) & \text{if } p \in dom(t_i) \\ \langle \emptyset, \emptyset \rangle & \text{otherwise} \end{cases} \right]_{\substack{p \in dom(t_1) \\ \cup dom(t_2)}}$$

Again, applying *filter* removes thresholds that are not redundant in $c_1 \sqcup_{\mathcal{C}} c_2$. Given the collected thresholds, the widening $\langle t_1, c_1 \rangle \nabla_{\mathcal{T}}^l \langle t_2, c_2 \rangle$ is now able to refine the widened child state $c_1 \nabla_{\mathcal{C}}^l c_2$ by applying those predicates $e_1 \leq 0$, $\dots e_n \leq 0$ as tests that have not yet been used at this widening point, that is, for which $l \notin \bar{l}_w$ holds. For each such predicate, we check if $e_i \leq 0$ has actually contributed to restricting $c_1 \nabla_{\mathcal{C}}^l c_2$ by checking if the distance $max(e_i, c)$ to the state c is the smallest of all predicates. The set $\bar{l}_{upd}$ is defined to contain the locations of all contributing tests. The idea is that, from two tests $l_1 : x \leq 10, l_2 : x \leq 50$, only l_1 is marked as being applied, thereby allowing the test $x \leq 50$ to serve as a threshold in future widenings. The merged domain state t is then updated so that all tests at locations $l \in \bar{l}_{upd}$ are marked as applied at l. Overall, widening is delayed at most $|\bar{l}_o|$ times at each of the $|\bar{l}_w|$ widening points. Since there are only a finite number of program locations, termination follows.

Widening with thresholds can find least fixpoints where narrowing cannot [12]. Consider the program in Fig. 5 that tracks the seconds within a minute. The loop repeatedly waits for a seconds signal that causes `read_sec` to return 1. The simplified CFG of the program contains three loops. After propagating $n = 0$ to node 2, the loops through node 3 and 4 are stable. The loop via node 5 yields $n \in [0, 1]$ in node 2 which is widened to $n \in [0, \infty]$. The threshold $n \leq 59$ is transformed by `n=n+1` to $n \leq 60$ and is applied after widening, yielding $n \in [0, 60]$. Narrowing cannot deduce this fixpoint due the cycle via node 4 [12].

$$[\![l : x = e]\!]^{\mathcal{D}}\langle d, c\rangle = \langle d \cup \bar{l}, [\![l : x = e]\!]^{C} c\rangle \text{ where } \bar{l} = \begin{cases} \{l\} & \text{if } e \in \mathbb{Z} \\ \emptyset & \text{otherwise} \end{cases}$$

$$\langle d_1, c_1\rangle \sqsubseteq_{\mathcal{D}} \langle d_2, c_2\rangle = c_1 \sqsubseteq_C c_2$$

$$\langle d_1, c_1\rangle \sqcup_{\mathcal{D}} \langle d_2, c_2\rangle = \langle d_1 \cup d_2, c_1 \sqcup_C c_2\rangle$$

$$\langle d_1, c_1\rangle \nabla_{\mathcal{D}}^l \langle d_2, c_2\rangle = \langle d_1 \cup d_2, c\rangle \text{ where } c = \begin{cases} c_1 \nabla_C^l c_2 & \text{if } d_2 \backslash d_1 = \emptyset \\ c_1 \sqcup_C c_2 & \text{otherwise} \end{cases}$$

Fig. 6. Lattice and transfer functions for the delaying domain

```
1  int x = 0;
2  int y = 0;
3  while (x < 100) {
4    if (read()) y = 1;
5    x = x + 4;
6  }
7
```

step	line		intervals		congruences	$\mathcal{T}$		$\mathcal{D}$
			x	y				
1	2		$[0,0]$					$\{1\}$
2	3		$[0,0]$	$[0,0]$				$\{1,2\}$
3	4		$[0,0]$	$[0,0]$		$x \le 99$		$\{1,2\}$
4	5		$[0,0]$	$[1,1]$		$x \le 99$		$\{1,2,4\}$
5	6		$[4,4]$	$[1,1]$		$x \le 103$		$\{1,2,4\}$
6	3	$\sqcup$	$[0,4]$	$[0,1]$	$x \equiv 4$	$x \le 103$		$\{1,2,4\}$
6'	3'	∇	$[0,100]$	$[0,\infty]$	$x \equiv 4$			$\{1,2,4\}$
7	4		$[0,96]$	$[0,\infty]$	$x \equiv 4$			$\{1,2,4\}$
8	5		$[0,96]$	$[0,\infty]$	$x \equiv 4$			$\{1,2,4\}$
9	6		$[4,100]$	$[0,\infty]$	$x \equiv 4$			$\{1,2,4\}$
10	3	$\sqsubseteq$	$[0,100]$	$[0,\infty]$	$x \equiv 4$			$\{1,2,4\}$
11	7		$[100,100]$	$[0,\infty]$				$\{1,2,4\}$

Fig. 7. Widening after one iteration loses the bound on y

3 Restricting Widening after Constant Assignments

It is widely acknowledged that computing a few iterations of a loop without widening can improve the precision of the computed fixpoint [2]. For instance, the program in Fig. 7 may set the variable y to 1 depending on some external event where read() may return the value of some sensor in a control software [5,8]. Given the threshold domain $\mathcal{T}$ as-is, the table in Fig. 7 shows how widening the state at step 6' with respect to that at step 2 yields $x \in [0,0] \nabla_{\mathcal{I}}^l [0,4] = [0,\infty]$ and $y \in [0,0] \nabla_{\mathcal{I}}^l [0,1] = [0,\infty]$ where the former interval can be refined by the threshold $x \le 103$ to $[0,100]$ since $x \equiv 4$, i.e. x is a multiple of four. The loop test x<100 then yields the precise value for x in step 7. However, the upper bound for y is lost. The common approach to improve the precision is to delay widening [13], that is, to compute another iteration of the loop using the state at step 6. After the second iteration, $y \in [0,1] \nabla_{\mathcal{I}}^l [0,1] = [0,1]$ is as desired.

Rather than fixing the number of times widening should be delayed, we track if widening would alter variables that were set to a constant. To this end, we define a delaying domain given by the lattice $\langle \mathcal{D} \rhd \mathcal{C}, \sqsubseteq_{\mathcal{D}}, \sqcup_{\mathcal{D}}, \sqcap_{\mathcal{D}}\rangle$ where $\mathcal{D} : \wp(Lab)$ is a set of program points with constant assignments. The transfer functions in Fig. 6 simply collect those program points that assign a constant to a variable. Performing widening on $\mathcal{D}$ will check if this set has increased and, if so, perform a join instead of a widening. For example, in step 6' of Fig. 7, location 4 is new relative to the state at step 2, thereby performing another iteration based on the state at step 6. Note that the delaying domain also delays widening if a new if-branch becomes enabled that contains a constant assignment. Note further that i=i+1 is never considered constant so as not to delay widening unnecessarily.

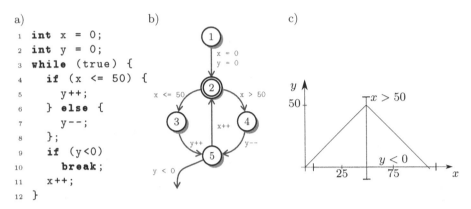

Fig. 8. A loop containing phase transitions

4   Guided Static Analysis as Abstract Domain

Numeric domains are usually convex approximations of the possible set of numeric values. One drawback of convexity is that joining two states can incur a precision loss that cannot later be recovered from. For example, the join of two intervals $[0,5] \sqcup_\mathcal{I} [15,20] = [0,20]$ adds the spurious values $6, \ldots 14$ and applying $x \leq 10$ to this state is less precise than applying it to the individual intervals. The idea of guided static analysis [11] is to avoid this kind of precision loss by identifying different phases of a loop and to track a separate state for each phase. The original proposal is formulated in terms of operations that restrict the CFG to increasingly larger sub-graphs and to perform widening/narrowing on these sub-graphs. In this section, we show that the same effect can be obtained by adding a cofibered *phase domain* into the domain hierarchy, thereby avoiding any modification to the fixpoint engine or to the handling of states.

Consider the loop in Fig. 8a) that increments x, starting from zero. For the first fifty iterations, y is incremented while in the next fifty iterations y is decremented. The loop exits in the 102th iteration when y becomes negative. The state space is depicted in Fig 8c) where the two hyperplanes annotated with the predicates $p_x \equiv x > 50$ and $p_y \equiv y < 0$ mark the different phase transitions. In particular, observe that the three phases can be characterized by the predicates that hold: for the first phase $\neg p_x \wedge \neg p_y$ holds, for the second phase $p_x \wedge \neg p_y$ and for the third phase $p_x \wedge p_y$. Thus, rather than characterizing the loop phases by enabled sub-graphs of the CFG, we construct an abstract domain that tracks a different child domain for each feasible valuation of the predicates. In a child c that is tracked for the predicates $p_1, \ldots p_n$, we assume that each predicate p_i holds and, lest the domain is imprecise, $[\![\neg p_i]\!]^\mathcal{C} c = \bot_\mathcal{C}$ for all $i \in [1,n]$. Thus, in the example, the predicates $\neg p_x \wedge \neg p_y$ hold in the state of the first phase c_1 and propagating c_1 over the edge from CFG node 2 to 4 in Fig. 8b) yields an empty state, thereby simulating the fact that this sub-path of the CFG is disabled. Analogous, a state c_2 in which $p_x \wedge \neg p_y$ holds has the path $2 \rightarrow 3 \rightarrow 5$ disabled since it is guarded by $p_x \equiv x > 50$.

step	line		intervals x	y	affine	phased $c; p_1 : t_1; \ldots p_n : t_n; \bar{p}$	threshold
1	2		$[0,0]$		$x=0$	$c_1; \emptyset$	
2	3		$[0,0]$	$[0,0]$	$x=0, y=0$	$c_1; \emptyset$	
3	5		$[0,0]$	$[0,0]$	$x=0, y=0$	$c_1; \{x>50\}$	$x \leq 50$
4	6		$[0,0]$	$[1,1]$	$x=0, y=1$	$c_1; \{x>50\}$	$x \leq 50$
5	11		$[0,0]$	$[1,1]$	$x=0, y=1$	$c_1; \{x>50, y<0\}$	$x \leq 50$
6	12		$[1,1]$	$[1,1]$	$x=1, y=1$	$c_1; \{x>50, y<0\}$	$x \leq 51, y \geq 0$
7	3	$\sqcup$	$[0,1]$	$[0,1]$	$x=y$	$c_1; \{x>50, y<0\}$	$x \leq 51, y \geq 0$
8	3'	∇	$[0,50]$	$[0,50]$	$x=y$	$c_1; x>50 : t_2; \{y<0\}$	$y \geq 0$
	3'		$[51,51]$	$[51,51]$	$x=51, y=51$	$c_2; \{y<0\}$	
9	5		$[0,50]$	$[0,50]$	$x=y$	$c_1; x>50 : t_2; \{y<0\}$	$y \geq 0$
	5					$\perp_{A \rhd I}; \{y<0\}$	
10	6		$[0,50]$	$[1,51]$	$x=y-1$	$c_1; x>50 : t_2; \{y<0\}$	$y \geq 1$
	6					$\perp_{A \rhd I}; \{y<0\}$	
11	7					$\perp_{A \rhd I}; x>50 : t_2; \{y<0\}$	$y \geq 0$
	7		$[51,51]$	$[51,51]$	$x=51, y=51$	$c_2; \{y<0\}$	
12	8					$\perp_{A \rhd I}; x>50 : t_2; \{y<0\}$	$y \geq -1$
	8		$[51,51]$	$[50,50]$	$x=51, y=50$	$c_2; \{y<0\}$	
13	9		$[0,50]$	$[1,51]$	$x=y-1$	$c_1; x>50 : t_2; \{y<0\}$	$y \geq -1, y \geq 1$
	9		$[51,51]$	$[50,50]$	$x=51, y=50$	$c_2; \{y<0\}$	
14	12		$[1,50]$	$[1,50]$	$x=y$	$c_1; x>50 : t_2; \{y<0\}$	$y \geq 0$
	12		$[51,52]$	$[50,51]$	$x+y=102$	$c_2; \{y<0\}$	
15	3'	$\sqsubseteq$	$[1,50]$	$[1,50]$	$x=y$	$c_1; x>50 : t_2; \{y<0\}$	
	3'	∇	$[51,102]$	$[0,51]$	$x+y=102$	$c_2; \{y<0\}$	
16	5	$\sqsubseteq$	$[0,50]$	$[0,50]$	$x=y$	$c_1; x>50 : t_2; \{y<0\}$	
	5					$\perp_{A \rhd I}; \{y<0\}$	
17	6	$\sqsubseteq$	$[0,50]$	$[1,51]$	$x=y-1$	$c_1; x>50 : t_2; \{y<0\}$	
	6					$\perp_{A \rhd I}; \{y<0\}$	
18	7					$\perp_{A \rhd I}; x>50 : t_2; \{y<0\}$	
	7		$[51,102]$	$[0,51]$	$x+y=102$	$c_2; \{y<0\}$	
19	8					$\perp_{A \rhd I}; x>50 : t_2; \{y<0\}$	
	8		$[51,101]$	$[0,50]$	$x+y=101$	$c_2; y<0 : t_3; \emptyset$	
	8		$[102,102]$	$[-1,-1]$	$x=102, y=-1$	$c_3; \emptyset$	
20	9		$[0,50]$	$[1,51]$	$x=y-1$	$c_1; x>50 : t_2; \{y<0\}$	
	9		$[51,100]$	$[0,50]$	$x+y=101$	$c_2; y<0 : t_3; \emptyset$	
	9		$[102,102]$	$[-1,-1]$	$x=102, y=-1$	$c_3; \emptyset$	
21	10		$[102,102]$	$[-1,-1]$	$x=102, y=-1$	$c_3; \emptyset$	
22	12		$[1,50]$	$[1,50]$	$x=y$	$c_1; x>50 : t_2; \{y<0\}$	
	12		$[51,102]$	$[0,51]$	$x+y=102$	$c_2; y<0 : \perp_{A \rhd I}; \emptyset$	
23	3	$\sqsubseteq$	$[1,50]$	$[1,50]$	$x=y$	$c_1; x>50 : t_2; \{y<0\}$	
	3	$\sqsubseteq$	$[51,102]$	$[0,51]$	$x+y=102$	$c_2; y<0 : \perp_{A \rhd I}; \emptyset$	

Fig. 9. Computing the fixpoint for the example in Fig. 8

We implement the ideas of tracking several children depending on which predicates hold in the cofibered *phase domain* that is given by the lattice $\langle \mathcal{P} \rhd \mathcal{C}, \sqsubseteq_{\mathcal{P}}, \sqcup_{\mathcal{P}}, \sqcap_{\mathcal{P}}, \top_{\mathcal{P}}, \perp_{\mathcal{P}} \rangle$ where $\mathcal{P} : \mathcal{C} \times (Pred \times \mathcal{P})^* \times \wp(Pred)$ is a recursive type, representing a multi-way decision tree. A node in this tree $\langle c; p_1 : t_1; \ldots p_n : t_n; \bar{p} \rangle \in \mathcal{P}$ contains a child domain c in which predicates $p_1, \ldots, p_n \in Pred$ do not hold. The node has n sub-trees $t_1, \ldots t_n \in \mathcal{P}$ where p_i holds in t_i. The set $\bar{p} \subseteq Pred$ is a set of predicates that are unsatisfiable and represent phases that have not (yet) been entered. Before we detail the transfer and lattice functions, we consider the fixpoint computation in Fig. 9 using a domain stack $\mathcal{T} \rhd \mathcal{P} \rhd \mathcal{A} \rhd \mathcal{I}$, that is, thresholds wrapping the phase domain, that wraps affine and intervals.

Initially, the phase domain contains a single child domain c_1 and no sub-trees as shown in step 1 of Fig. 9. The idea of the phased domain is to gather all unsatisfiable tests as possible phase predicates, adding them to the set $\bar{p}$. Thus, step 3 adds the predicate $x > 50$ and step 5 adds $y < 0$. Note that, unlike the threshold predicates, the phase predicates are not transformed. Once widening is applied

$[\![l : x = e]\!]^{\mathcal{T}} \langle c; p_1 : t_1; \dots p_n : t_n; \bar{p} \rangle =$
$\quad$ let $c_e = [\![l : x = e]\!]^{\mathcal{C}} c$ and $c' = [\![l : \neg p_i]\!]^{\mathcal{C}} \cdots [\![l : \neg p_n]\!]^{\mathcal{C}} c_e$ and $c_i = [\![l : p_i]\!]^{\mathcal{C}} c_e$
$\quad$ and $\langle \tilde{c}_e^i; part^i \rangle = [\![l : x = e]\!]^{\mathcal{T}} t_i$
$\quad$ and $\tilde{c}_{res}^i = c_i \sqcup_{\mathcal{C}} [\![l : p_i]\!]^{\mathcal{C}} \tilde{c}_i$ and $c'' = c' \sqcup_{\mathcal{C}} [\![l : \neg p_1]\!]^{\mathcal{C}} \tilde{c}_e^1 \sqcup_{\mathcal{C}} \cdots \sqcup_{\mathcal{C}} [\![l : \neg p_n]\!]^{\mathcal{C}} \tilde{c}_e^n$
$\quad$ and $\bar{p}^{red} = \{ p \in \bar{p} \mid [\![l : \neg p]\!]^{\mathcal{C}} c'' = \bot_{\mathcal{C}} \}$ and $\langle p_{n+1}, \dots p_{n+k} \rangle = \bar{p} \setminus \bar{p}^{red}$
$\quad$ and $c_{res} = [\![l : \neg p_{n+1}]\!]^{\mathcal{C}} \cdots [\![l : \neg p_{n+k}]\!]^{\mathcal{C}} c''$ and $c_{new}^{n+j} = [\![l : p_{n+j}]\!]^{\mathcal{C}} c''$ for $j = 1 \dots k$
$\quad$ in $\langle c_{res}; p_1 : \langle \tilde{c}_{res}^1; part^1 \rangle; \dots p_n : \langle \tilde{c}_{res}^n; part^n \rangle; p_{n+1} : \langle c_{new}^{n+1} \rangle; \dots p_{n+k} : \langle c_{new}^{n+k} \rangle; \bar{p}^{red} \rangle$

$[\![l : e \le 0]\!]^{\mathcal{T}} \langle c; p_1 : t_1; \dots p_n : t_n; \bar{p} \rangle =$
$\quad$ let $\langle \tilde{c}_e^i : part^i \rangle = [\![l : e \le 0]\!]^{\mathcal{T}} t_i$ and $c_e = [\![l : e \le 0]\!]^{\mathcal{C}} c$
$\quad$ in if $\bigwedge_{i=1}^n \tilde{c}_e^i = \bot_{\mathcal{T}} \wedge c_e = \bot_{\mathcal{C}}$ then $\bot_{\mathcal{T}}$ else
$\quad$ $\langle c_e; p_1 : \langle \tilde{c}_e^1; part^1 \rangle; \dots p_n : \langle \tilde{c}_e^n; part^n \rangle; \text{if } [\![l : e > 0]\!]^{\mathcal{C}} c = \bot_{\mathcal{C}} \text{ then } \bar{p} \cup \{ e \le 0 \} \text{ else } \bar{p} \rangle$

$\langle c_1; part_1 \rangle \sqsubseteq_{\mathcal{T}} \langle c_2; part_2 \rangle =$
$\quad$ let $\langle \langle p_1^1 : t_1^1; \dots p_n^1 : t_n^1; \bar{p}^1 \rangle, \langle p_1^2 : t_1^2; \dots p_n^2 : t_n^2; \bar{p}^2 \rangle \rangle = compatible(part_1, part_2)$
$\quad$ in $c_1 \sqsubseteq_{\mathcal{C}} c_2 \wedge \bigwedge_{i=1}^n t_i^1 \sqsubseteq_{\mathcal{T}} t_i^2$

$\langle c_1; part_1 \rangle \sqcup_{\mathcal{T}} \langle c_2; part_2 \rangle =$
$\quad$ let $\langle \langle p_1^1 : t_1^1; \dots p_n^1 : t_n^1; \bar{p}^1 \rangle, \langle p_1^2 : t_1^2; \dots p_n^2 : t_n^2; \bar{p}^2 \rangle \rangle = compatible(part_1, part_2)$
$\quad$ in $\langle c_1 \sqcup_{\mathcal{C}} c_2; p_1^1 : t_1^1 \sqcup_{\mathcal{T}} t_1^2; \dots p_n^1 : t_n^1 \sqcup_{\mathcal{T}} t_n^2; \bar{p}^1 \rangle$

$\langle c_1; part_1 \rangle \nabla_{\mathcal{T}}^l \langle c_2; part_2 \rangle =$
$\quad$ let $\langle \langle p_1^1 : t_1^1; \dots p_n^1 : t_n^1; \bar{p}^1 \rangle, \langle p_1^2 : t_1^2; \dots p_n^2 : t_n^2; \bar{p}^2 \rangle \rangle = compatible(part_1, part_2)$
$\quad$ and $c_e = [\![l : \neg p_1^1]\!]^{\mathcal{C}} \cdots [\![l : \neg p_n^1]\!]^{\mathcal{C}} c_1 \nabla_{\mathcal{T}}^l c_2$ and $\langle \tilde{c}_e^i; part^i \rangle = \langle [\![l : p_i^1]\!]^{\mathcal{T}} (t_i^1 \nabla_{\mathcal{T}}^l t_i^2);$
$\quad$ and $\bar{p}^{red} = \{ p \in \bar{p} \mid [\![l : \neg p]\!]^{\mathcal{C}} c'' = \bot_{\mathcal{C}} \}$ and $\langle p_{n+1}, \dots p_{n+k} \rangle = \bar{p} \setminus \bar{p}^{red}$
$\quad$ and $c_{res} = [\![l : \neg p_{n+1}]\!]^{\mathcal{C}} \cdots [\![l : \neg p_{n+k}]\!]^{\mathcal{C}} c_e$ and $c_{new}^{n+j} = [\![l : p_{n+j}]\!]^{\mathcal{C}} c_e$ for $j = 1 \dots k$
$\quad$ in $\langle c_{res}; p_1^1 : \langle \tilde{c}_e^1; part^1 \rangle \dots p_n^1 : \langle \tilde{c}_e^n; part^n \rangle; p_{n+1} : \langle c_{new}^{n+1} \rangle; \dots p_{n+k} : \langle c_{new}^{n+k} \rangle; \bar{p}^{red} \rangle$

Fig. 10. Transfer and lattice functions for the phase domain

in step 8, the subtree $t_2 = c_2; \{ y < 0 \}$ is added. This new subtree is immediately disabled in step 9 and 10 due to the test `x <= 50`. Analogously, only the subtree t_2 is enabled in steps 11 and 12. Both states are joined in step 13. Incrementing `x` to obtain step 14 poses the challenge that x in c_1 straddles the phase bound $x > 50$. Thus, the state $c_e = [\![\text{x++}]\!]^{A \triangleright \mathcal{I}} c_1$ is split into $c_1' = [\![x \le 50]\!]^{A \triangleright \mathcal{I}} c_e$ and $\tilde{c} = [\![x > 50]\!]^{A \triangleright \mathcal{I}} c_e = \langle x = 51, y = 51 \rangle$. The latter is joined with the updated state of the subtree $[\![\text{x++}]\!]^{A \triangleright \mathcal{I}} c_2 = \langle x = 52, y = 50 \rangle$ yielding the downward slope $x + y = 102$ in the second line of step 14. Widening is applied again, thereby consuming the last threshold $y \ge 0$. The same state is propagated in steps 16 and 17 whereas the **else**-branch sees a larger state. Indeed, decrementing `y` in c_2 surpasses the phase threshold $y < 0$, thereby creating a third subtree $t_3 = c_3; \emptyset$ in step 19. Step 20 computes the joined state from which the state at loop exit is split off (step 21). Step 22 increments `x` which again propagates the point $\langle x = 51, y = 51 \rangle$ from c_1 to c_2 as for step 14. A fixpoint is observed in step 23.

$\quad$ The domain operations are formally defined in Fig. 10. We allow for several subtrees per node to cater for sequences of **if**-statements. The assignment $l : x = e$ first computes the effect on the state in the current node c, yielding c_e, and its subtrees t_i, yielding $\tilde{c}_e^i$. The state space that spills over the phase predicates $p_1, \dots p_n$ is cut off and merged into the respective parent or subtree. Any previously unsatisfiable phase predicates are checked against the new node state c'' and new subtrees $p_{n+1} : \langle c_{new}^{n+1} \rangle; \dots p_{n+k} : \langle c_{new}^{n+k} \rangle;$ are added.

	our analysis						interproc		conc.
example	time	insns.	#wp	steps	iter.	exact	iter.	exact	exact
simple loop Fig. 1	7	14	1	23	2	✓	3+1	✓	✓
nested loops random	7	20	2	42	3	✓	5+2	✓	✓
nested loops random (mod)	7	20	2	43	3	✓	5+2		✓
nested loops medium	4	18	2	39	3	✓	4+2		✓
nested loops hard	4	19	2	40	3	✓	4+2		✓
nested loops hard (mod 1)	5	19	2	48	4	✓	4+2		✓
nested loops hard (mod 2)	10	19	2	96	8		4+3		✓
Halbwachs Fig. 1a [12]	2	9	1	15	2	✓	3+2	✓	✓
Halbwachs Fig. 1b	5	17	2	51	4	✓	4+2		✓
Halbwachs Fig. 1b (mod)	4	17	2	49	4	✓	5+2		✓
Halbwachs Fig. 2a	2	10	1	23	3	✓	3+2	✓	✓
Halbwachs Fig. 2b	3	12	1	28	3	✓	4+1		✓
Halbwachs Fig. 2b (mod)	4	14	1	46	4	✓	3+2	✓	✓
Halbwachs Fig. 4	18	18	2	84	9		4+2		✓
⋆Gopan Fig. 1a [10]	15	14	1	36	4	✓	5+2		
⋆Gopan Fig. 1a (mod)	13	14	1	33	4	✓	5+1		
Chaouch Fig. 2 [15]	2	12	1	19	2	✓	3+2		✓
Chaouch Fig. 3	7	23	1	83	6	✓	4+2		✓
Chaouch Fig. 3 (mod)	4	25	3	66	3	✓	4+1		
Chaouch Fig. 4	2	10	1	22	3	✓	4+1		✓
Chaouch Fig. 5	2	17	2	51	4	✓	4+2		✓
⋆Chaouch Fig. 6	13	14	1	36	4	✓	5+2		

Fig. 11. Widening examples

Much simpler is the test $l : x \leq e$ which is applied recursively and is also added as phase predicate to $\bar{p}$ if it is unsatisfiable. The domain operations all rely on a function *compatible* that recursively adds missing phases by adding a subtree $p_i : \bot_{\mathcal{C}}; \ldots \bar{p}$ whenever $p_i : c_i; \ldots; \bar{p}$ only exists in the respective other domain. The lattice operations $t_1 \sqsubseteq_{\mathcal{P}} t_2$ and $t_1 \sqcup_{\mathcal{P}} t_2$ then reduce to a point-wise lifting of the respective operations on the child domain. Widening is defined similarly to join, however, the phase boundaries are enforced after widening in order to ensure that the various states remain separated by the phase predicates. If widening makes unsatisfiable phase predicates satisfiable, new subtrees are added.

5   Experimental Results

We evaluated the presented domains in our analyzer for machine code [16], using a domain stack $\mathcal{W} \rhd \mathcal{D} \rhd \mathcal{T} \rhd \mathcal{A} \rhd \mathcal{C} \rhd \mathcal{I}$ where $\mathcal{C}$ tracks congruences, except for examples marked with ⋆ that use $\mathcal{W} \rhd \mathcal{D} \rhd \mathcal{T} \rhd \mathcal{P} \rhd \mathcal{A} \rhd \mathcal{C} \rhd \mathcal{I}$. The benchmarks in Fig. 11 represent challenging loops that were mostly put forth in the literature [10,12,15]. Our own "nested loops" increase two variables, with various bounds and resets. Examples marked with "(mod)" are modifications of the same problem. These include changing the loop exit conditions in nested loops or adding loop exit points (**break**, **continue**), adding further variables or loop counter increments on separate paths through the loop. We also modified examples, where applicable, to contain non-deterministic paths and multiple widening points inside the loops, both features that can be found in irreducible graphs. The measurements are as follows: *insns.* gives the number of instructions in the program; *#wp* is the number of widening back-edges; *steps* the number of instructions the analyzer evaluated to reach the fixpoint; *iter.* is the maximum number of fixpoint iterations at any program point; *exact* denotes if the best interval bounds were found; *time* shows the analysis time in milliseconds. The time shown is the median of 2000 runs on a 2.4 GHz Core i5 machine running Linux.

We compared our results with those of the Interproc and ConcurInterproc analyzers [15]. For both we used polyhedra with congruences which is the domain that is closest to our domain stack. Interproc can count iteration steps but only uses narrowing to refine the post-fixpoint. The table shows that the number of iterations in our analysis is usually smaller than that of Interproc, even without the narrowing iterations (which are indicated by $+n$). In all benchmarks, we used no explicit delay. Since most examples are engineered not to work with narrowing, the least fixpoint is rarely obtained. ConcurInterproc uses a pre-analysis to infer thresholds but does not perform an iteration count. Assuming that these thresholds are applied to the states after widening, ConcurInterproc must require at least as many iterations as the number of upward iterations of Interproc. Our precision and that of the threshold widening in ConcurInterproc match. Entries where our analysis is less precise than ConcurInterproc require a polyhedral invariant that our domains cannot express. For the examples requiring disjunctive invariants ConcurInterproc is imprecise in that it infers, for example, $x \in [51, 102]$ for line 10 in Fig. 8. Our benchmarks used for Interproc are available on-line at http://tinyurl.com/cwdg5qr.

6   Related Work

Many authors address the task of improving widening, be it for specific domains such as polyhedra [2,14], or by altering the way fixpoints are inferred. With respect to the latter, Halbwachs pioneered the idea of using thresholds to refine widening and to delay widening [13]. Thresholds over variables are created from a set of constants, an idea later successfully used in the large [4]. Chaouch et al. [15] recently proposed a pre-analysis to infer thresholds automatically. This pre-analysis uses the polyhedron abstract domain [9] and requires a way to extract individual inequalities from it. Rather than extracting thresholds, widening with landmarks [17] measures the distance of the current state space to the loop condition and extrapolates the state space accordingly. Both approaches require special domain functions, e.g. for widening, and are thus not easily portable between different numeric domains. Our threshold domain is easier to use as it is agnostic to the underlying domain and infers the possible thresholds by itself.

Bagnara et al. generalizes the idea of delaying widening by using a finite number of tokens: a widening may use any non-terminating strategy if there are still tokens to consume [2]. Rather than requiring the user to fix the set of tokens, our delay domain in Sect. 3 uses program points instead of tokens, thereby ensuring termination without depending on user input.

One challenge of using convex numeric domains is the problem of spillage of state into branches of the program or behaviors of the transfer function that cannot be recovered from by narrowing. In this context, Halbwachs et al. propose to re-start the analysis at a different pre-fixpoint from which widening and narrowing infer a new post-fixpoint. The intersection of the previous and the new post-fixpoint is still sound and may be more precise [12]. Rather than removing the spillage, Gopan et al. propose to avoid spillage into currently unreachable branches immediately after widening [10]. They require one state to determine which branches of the loops are enabled and a second state to compute widening and narrowing on the enabled part of the loop. Instead of duplicating the analysis cost by tracking a second abstract state, the authors later propose to directly track which parts of the CFG are enabled [11]. They generalize their idea to track different states for each phase, that is, for each set of enabled branches in a loop. While none of the three approaches require changes to the transfer functions of the domains as was the case for widening with thresholds, each approach requires intrusive changes to the fixpoint engine and the handling of states. Our threshold domain in Sect. 2 has the same functionality as the Guided Static Analysis approach [11] but requires no changes to the way states are handled. Interestingly, the transfer functions of our threshold domain are similar to those of the decision tree domain of Astrée [8]. However, the latter tracks Boolean flags as predicates and requires a user-supplied limit to avoid an exponential explosion. Since our domain creates a tree that mirrors the finite branching inside the loop body, its size is always limited by the program.

6.1   Conclusion

Implementing widening strategies as abstract domains is beneficial due to its modularity and independence of the fixpoint engine. This approach provides equal or better precision combined with fewer iterations required to obtain stability.

References

1. Apinis, K., Seidl, H., Vojdani, V.: Side-Effecting Constraint Systems: A Swiss Army Knife for Program Analysis. In: Jhala, R., Igarashi, A. (eds.) APLAS 2012. LNCS, vol. 7705, pp. 157–172. Springer, Heidelberg (2012)
2. Bagnara, R., Hill, P.M., Ricci, E., Zaffanella, E.: Precise Widening Operators for Convex Polyhedra. Science of Computer Programming 58(1-2), 28–56 (2005)
3. Balakrishnan, G., Gruian, R., Reps, T., Teitelbaum, T.: CodeSurfer/x86 – A Platform for Analyzing x86 Executables. In: Bodik, R. (ed.) CC 2005. LNCS, vol. 3443, pp. 250–254. Springer, Heidelberg (2005)
4. Blanchet, B., Cousot, P., Cousot, R., Feret, J., Mauborgne, L., Miné, A., Monniaux, D., Rival, X.: Design and Implementation of a Special-Purpose Static Program Analyzer for Safety-Critical Real-Time Embedded Software. In: Mogensen, T.Æ., Schmidt, D.A., Sudborough, I.H. (eds.) The Essence of Computation. LNCS, vol. 2566, pp. 85–108. Springer, Heidelberg (2002)

5. Blanchet, B., Cousot, P., Cousot, R., Feret, J., Mauborgne, L., Miné, A., Monniaux, D., Rival, X.: A Static Analyzer for Large Safety-Critical Software. In: Programming Language Design and Implementation, San Diego, California, USA. ACM (June 2003)

6. Bourdoncle, F.: Efficient Chaotic Iteration Strategies with Widenings. In: Bjørner, D., Broy, M., Pottosin, I.V. (eds.) FMP&TA 1993. LNCS, vol. 735, pp. 128–141. Springer, Heidelberg (1993)

7. Cousot, P., Cousot, R.: Abstract Interpretation and Application to Logic Programs. Journal of Logic Programming 13(2-3), 103–179 (1992)

8. Cousot, P., Cousot, R., Feret, J., Mauborgne, L., Miné, A., Monniaux, D., Rival, X.: Combination of Abstractions in the ASTRÉE Static Analyzer. In: Okada, M., Satoh, I. (eds.) ASIAN 2006. LNCS, vol. 4435, pp. 272–300. Springer, Heidelberg (2008)

9. Cousot, P., Halbwachs, N.: Automatic Discovery of Linear Constraints among Variables of a Program. In: Principles of Programming Languages, Tucson, Arizona, USA, pp. 84–97. ACM (January 1978)

10. Gopan, D., Reps, T.: Lookahead Widening. In: Ball, T., Jones, R.B. (eds.) CAV 2006. LNCS, vol. 4144, pp. 452–466. Springer, Heidelberg (2006)

11. Gopan, D., Reps, T.: Guided Static Analysis. In: Riis Nielson, H., Filé, G. (eds.) SAS 2007. LNCS, vol. 4634, pp. 349–365. Springer, Heidelberg (2007)

12. Halbwachs, N., Henry, J.: When the Decreasing Sequence Fails. In: Miné, A., Schmidt, D. (eds.) SAS 2012. LNCS, vol. 7460, pp. 198–213. Springer, Heidelberg (2012)

13. Halbwachs, N., Proy, Y.-E., Roumanoff, P.: Verification of Real-Time Systems using Linear Relation Analysis. Formal Methods in System Design 11(2), 157–185 (1997)

14. Jeannet, B., Miné, A.: Apron: A Library of Numerical Abstract Domains for Static Analysis. In: Bouajjani, A., Maler, O. (eds.) CAV 2009. LNCS, vol. 5643, pp. 661–667. Springer, Heidelberg (2009)

15. Lakhdar-Chaouch, L., Jeannet, B., Girault, A.: Widening with Thresholds for Programs with Complex Control Graphs. In: Bultan, T., Hsiung, P.-A. (eds.) ATVA 2011. LNCS, vol. 6996, pp. 492–502. Springer, Heidelberg (2011)

16. Sepp, A., Mihaila, B., Simon, A.: Precise Static Analysis of Binaries by Extracting Relational Information. In: Pinzger, M., Poshyvanyk, D. (eds.) Working Conference on Reverse Engineering, Limerick, Ireland. IEEE Computer Society (October 2011)

17. Simon, A., King, A.: Widening Polyhedra with Landmarks. In: Kobayashi, N. (ed.) APLAS 2006. LNCS, vol. 4279, pp. 166–182. Springer, Heidelberg (2006)

18. Venet, A.: Abstract Cofibered Domains: Application to the Alias Analysis of Untyped Programs. In: Cousot, R., Schmidt, D.A. (eds.) SAS 1996. LNCS, vol. 1145, pp. 366–382. Springer, Heidelberg (1996)

LiquidPi: Inferrable Dependent Session Types

Dennis Griffith and Elsa L. Gunter

University of Illinois at Urbana-Champaign

Abstract. The Pi Calculus is a popular formalism for modeling distributed computation. Session Types extend the Pi Calculus with a static, inferable type system. Dependent Types allow for a more precise characterization of the behavior of programs, but in their full generality are not inferable. In this paper, we present LiquidPi an approach that combines the dependent type inferencing of Liquid Types with Honda's Session Types to give a more precise automatically derived description of the behavior of distributed programs. These types can be used to describe/enforce safety properties of distributed systems. We present a type system parametric over an underlying functional language with Pi Calculus connectives and give an inference algorithm for it by means of efficient external solvers and a set of dependent qualifier templates.

1 Introduction

In a world of multiproccessors, embedded systems, and cloud computing, parallel, concurrent, and distributed programs have become ubiquitous. With their growth comes an increased need for tools and theory to design, implement and verify these programs. One of the most successful verification efforts have been type systems [12]. By providing a static characterization of program behavior type systems allow for programmers to prove that certain dangerous behaviors are impossible. Particularly useful have been automatically inferable types since they can allow access to the guarantees of type systems at a low overhead for users. Dependent types [9] focus on increasing the expressivity of type systems by allowing for types to depend on, i.e., be constructed from, the value of terms instead of only on other types. In general, this gives up on inferability, but Rondon *et al.* [13] describe an approach, liquid typing, that can allow for inferencing of certain dependent type systems.

One standard tool for the design of parallel systems is the Pi Calculus [10]. When discussing types for the Pi Calculus the notion of input and output of a process is mostly closely associated with the input and output of its channels. Thus instead of finding the type of variables and expressions like we might in a functional language, we instead look at providing types for channels. As a first pass we might say that each channel has a type like `int` to denote that it can only transmit integers. This notion of channel typing (and similar homogeneous typings [6]) gives almost no ability to characterize the temporal behavior of channels. An improvement on this approach are session types [7] which allow for a rich characterization of the temporal behavior of the channels involved in a

G. Brat, N. Rungta, and A. Venet (Eds.): NFM 2013, LNCS 7871, pp. 185–197, 2013.

system. LiquidPi is an application of the liquid typing approach to session types. The contributions of this paper are the following:

- A dependent session type system for LiquidPi (Section 3)
- An inference algorithm for the LiquidPi type system (Section 4)

2   Basic Syntax and Session Types

The Pi Calculus [10] is a process algebra for modeling distributed computation. It uses synchronous channels to pass data (including channel names) between processes that execute in parallel. The Pi Calculus can be viewed as a wrapper providing these distributed communication constructs around some underlying language of data and computation. For the purposes of this paper we will assume that the underlying language is a simple functional language. We will impose a few other requirements on this underlying language in later sections. The syntax of the Pi Calculus, along with some informal meaning, is presented in the following grammar, where x ranges over a set of data variables, e ranges over expressions in the underlying functional language, k ranges over a distinct set of channel names, τ is a type from the underlying functional language, P_i is a τ-indexed family of processes, and X ranges over a distinct set of definition variables.

$$P ::= 0 \mid P\|P \mid \text{accept } X(k).P \mid \text{request } X(k).P \mid k!(e).P \mid k!(k).P \mid k?(x).P$$
$$\mid k?(k).P \mid \text{if } e \text{ then } P \text{ else } P \mid (\nu k)P \mid k \triangleleft e.P_i \mid \text{case}_\tau\ k \Rightarrow P_i$$
$$\mid \text{def } X(\boldsymbol{x}; \boldsymbol{k}) = P \text{ in } P \mid X(\boldsymbol{e}, \boldsymbol{k})$$

Informally, 0 is the terminated process. The process $P_1\|P_2$ is the processes P_1 and P_2 executing in parallel. The process accept $X(k).P$ initiates the session X along k and proceeds as P. The process request $X(k).P$ is the counterpart to accept that requests the initiation of session X along k and proceeds as P. The process $k!(e).P$ sends the result of e along k and then continues as P. The process $k_1!(k_2).P$ sends the channel k_2 over k_1 and then continues as P. The process $k?(x).P$ binds the next data value sent on k to x and then continues as P. The process $k_1?(k_2).P$ receives the next channel sent on k_1 and then continues as P. The process if e then P_1 else P_2 evaluates e and proceeds as P_1 or P_2 as appropriate. The process $(\nu k)P$ generates a fresh channel and binds it to k. The process $k \triangleleft e.P$ evaluates e and sends it along k then proceeds as P. This will be distinguished from $k!(e).P$ in the type system by allowing the receiving process to offer differently typed behaviors based on the value of e. The process case$_\tau$ $k \Rightarrow P_i$ receives a value of type τ along k then proceeds as the corresponding P_i. The declaration def $X(\boldsymbol{x}; \boldsymbol{k}) = P_1$ in P_2 defines X as process P_1 that can use the variables in scope along with those supplied by $\boldsymbol{x}$ and $\boldsymbol{k}$, binds the definition to X, and proceeds as P_2. The process $X(\boldsymbol{e}, \boldsymbol{k})$ calls the process defined by X and supplies it as arguments the evaluated $\boldsymbol{e}$ and $\boldsymbol{k}$.

Pi Calculus semantics are traditionally given in terms of a transition semantics that assumes a structural congruence that brings together compatible send/receive instructions so that communication can occur. For more details on semantics see Yoshida's survey [16].

Session Types [7,16] were introduced to provide a static characterization of the temporal behavior of the Pi Calculus. They rule out some dangers present in the Pi Calculus like the nondeterminism possible with channels held by more than two processes and sending and receiving processes disagreeing over the type of data being communicated. The type system disallows these while still allowing for a high degree of expressiveness such as communicating channel names and heterogeneous channel usage. The syntax of session types, S, is given by the following grammar where t ranges over a set of type variable names, τ is a type from the underlying functional language, and S_i is a τ-indexed family of session types.

$$S ::= 0 \mid t \mid \mu t.S \mid !\tau.S \mid ?\tau.S \mid ![S].S \mid ?[S].S \mid \&_\tau S_i \mid \oplus_\tau S_i$$

The informal meaning of these are as follows. 0 is the type of channels that will have no further communication. The types $\mu t.S$ and t allow us to construct (possibly infinite) recursive types. We treat types equirecursively (i.e., we identify a recursive type with its unfolding $\mu t.S = S\{\mu t.S/t\}$). The type $!\tau.S$ is that of a channel that sends a data value of type τ and then proceeds as S. The type $?\tau.S$ is that of a channel that receives a data value of type τ and then proceeds as S. The type $![S_1].S_2$ is that of a channel that sends a channel with type S_1 and then proceeds as S_2. The type $?[S_1].S_2$ is that of a channel that receives a channel with type S_1 and then proceeds as S_2. The type $\&_\tau S_i$ is that of a channel that sends a piece of data of type τ and then proceeds as the appropriate τ-index S_i. The type $\oplus_\tau S_i$ is that of a channel that receives a piece of data of type τ and then proceeds as the appropriate τ-index S_i. As with processes, our types have a notion of send/receive pairs. We define the notion of a dual type to encode this correspondence. The dual of a session type S is denoted $\overline{S}$ and defined below.

$$\overline{0} = 0 \qquad \overline{!\tau.S} = ?\tau.\overline{S} \qquad \overline{?\tau.S} = !\tau.\overline{S}$$

$$\overline{![S_1].S_2} = ?[S_1].\overline{S_2} \quad \overline{?[S_1].S_2} = ![S_1].\overline{S_2} \quad \overline{\&_\tau S_i} = \oplus_\tau \overline{S_i} \quad \overline{\oplus_\tau S_i} = \&_\tau \overline{S_i}$$

The session type system will use duality to match up compatible channel users. A channel typing is a mapping from channel variables to session types. The last notation needed is for marking polarity. Polarity markings are superscripts on channel names that will allow us to distinguish the two conceptual "ends" of a channel so that we can rule out send/receive confusion and more than two processes using a channel at once. We use k^+ to denote the positive end of channel k, k^- to denote the negative "end", and $k^{\overline{p}}$ to denote swapping the polarity of k^p.

Using the notions above we can give the rules for session types. We use Θ to denote a mapping from process variables to tuples of their argument types, Γ to denote typings for our functional variables, and Δ to denote channel typings. We use $\Delta_1 \cdot \Delta_2$ to denote the merger of two channel typings that share no

$$\frac{\Theta; \Gamma \vdash_S P : \Delta \cdot (k : S) \qquad \Gamma \vdash e : \tau}{\Theta; \Gamma \vdash_S k!(e).P : \Delta \cdot (k :! \tau.S)} \text{ T.SEND} \qquad \frac{\Theta; \Gamma \cdot x : \tau \vdash_S P : \Delta \cdot (k : S)}{\Theta; \Gamma \vdash_S k?(x).P : \Delta \cdot (k :? \tau.S)} \text{ T.REC}$$

$$\frac{\text{for } (k, S) \in \Delta : S=0}{\Theta; \Gamma \vdash_S 0 : \Delta} \text{ T.END} \qquad \frac{\Theta; \Gamma \vdash_S P : \Delta \cdot k_1 : S_1}{\Theta; \Gamma \vdash_S k_1!(k_2).P : \Delta \cdot (k_1 :![S_2].S_1) \cdot (k_2 : S_2)} \text{ T.THR}$$

$$\frac{\Theta; \Gamma \vdash_S P : \Delta \cdot (k^p : S) \cdot (k^{\overline{p}} : \overline{S})}{\Theta; \Gamma \vdash_S (\nu\, k)P : \Delta} \text{ T.NU} \qquad \frac{\Theta; \Gamma \vdash_S P : \Delta \cdot (k_1 : S_1) \cdot (k_2 : S_2)}{\Theta; \Gamma \vdash_S k_1?(k_2).P : \Delta \cdot (k_1 :?[S_2].S_1)} \text{ T.CAT}$$

$$\frac{\Theta; \Gamma \vdash_S P : \Delta \cdot (k^+ : G(X))}{\Theta; \Gamma \vdash_S \text{accept } X(k).P : \Delta} \text{ T.ACC} \qquad \frac{\Theta; \Gamma \vdash_S P : \Delta \cdot (k^- : \overline{G(X)})}{\Theta; \Gamma \vdash_S \text{request } X(k).P : \Delta} \text{ T.REQ}$$

$$\frac{\Theta; \Gamma \vdash_S P : \Delta_1 \qquad \Theta; \Gamma \vdash_S P : \Delta_2}{\Theta; \Gamma \vdash_S P \| Q : \Delta_1 \cdot \Delta_2} \text{ T.PAR}$$

$$\frac{\Gamma \vdash e : \mathsf{Bool} \qquad \Theta; \Gamma \vdash_S P : \Delta \qquad \Theta; \Gamma \vdash_S Q : \Delta}{\Theta; \Gamma \vdash_S \text{if } e \text{ then } P \text{ else } Q : \Delta} \text{ T.IF}$$

$$\frac{\Gamma \vdash e : \tau : \text{ENUM} \qquad \text{for } i \in \tau : \Theta; \Gamma \vdash_S P_i : \Delta \cdot (k : S_i)}{\Theta; \Gamma \vdash_S k \lhd e.P_i : \Delta \cdot k : \&_\tau S_i} \text{ T.INT}$$

$$\frac{\tau : \text{ENUM} \qquad \text{for } i \in \tau : \Theta; \Gamma \vdash_S P_i : \Delta \cdot (k : S_i)}{\Theta; \Gamma \vdash_S \text{case}_\tau\, k \Rightarrow P_i : \Delta \cdot k : \oplus_\tau S_i} \text{ T.EXT}$$

$$\frac{\text{for } i \in \text{dom}(\Delta) : \Delta(i) = 0 \qquad \text{for } i : \Gamma \vdash e_i : \tau_i \qquad \text{for } (k, S) \in \Delta : S=0}{\Theta \cdot X : (\boldsymbol{\tau}, \boldsymbol{S}); \Gamma \vdash_S X(\boldsymbol{e}, \boldsymbol{k}) : \Delta \cdot \boldsymbol{k} : \boldsymbol{S}} \text{ T.CALL}$$

$$\frac{\Theta \cdot X : (\boldsymbol{\tau}, \boldsymbol{S}); \Gamma \cdot \boldsymbol{x} : \boldsymbol{\tau} \vdash_S P : (\boldsymbol{k} : \boldsymbol{S}) \qquad \Theta \cdot X : (\boldsymbol{\tau}, \boldsymbol{S}); \Gamma \vdash_S Q : \Delta}{\Theta; \Gamma \vdash_S \text{def } X(\boldsymbol{x}; \boldsymbol{k}) = P \text{ in } Q : \Delta} \text{ T.DEF}$$

Fig. 1. Typing Rules for Simple Session Types

common bindings. We use the hypothesis $\tau : \text{ENUM}$ to denote that the type τ is a finite enumeration. Depending on the details underlying functional language this may have different interpretations. These enumerations could be smoothly generalized to algebraic datatypes, but we present only the simplified view to avoid unneeded clutter. The judgment $\Theta; \Gamma \vdash_S P : \Delta$ denotes that, assuming the definitions of Θ and the functional types in Γ, the free channel variables of process P have the session types in Δ. We use $\Gamma \vdash e : \tau$ to denote that the type system for the underlying functional language proves that e has type τ from the assumptions in Γ. We assume that sessions have some globally visible type and so assume a mapping, G, from session names to session types. Figure 1 contains a listing of the typing rules for simple session types. To see how the rules eliminate dangerous behavior consider the rule T.NU. This rule ensures two things:

the fresh channel has two and only two "ends"; the users of each end agree both in the direction of communication at every step and the type of value or channel being communicated.

3   Refinement Type System

Dependent Types [9] are types that allow the meaning of types to depend on data values. As an example, when trying to describe the type of division we might be interested in allowing only non-zero `int`s instead of all `int`s as divisors. What we mostly will be interested in are a restricted class of dependent types called refinement types. A refinement type is a basic type (i.e., a non-compound type–`int` but not `int->float`) with a predicate attached to it; e.g., the positive integers are given by $\{v : \text{int}|0 \leq v\}$. Simple types can naturally be viewed as refinement types by using the trivial always-true predicate. From this follows a natural notion of subtyping (with the normal contravariance for functions). In addition to allowing predicates to incorporate constants, we will want them to allow for dependency on previously bound terms, e.g., $\{v : \text{int}|v \leq x\}$ for some previously bound x. For compound functional types we assume that refinements are available on the "leaf" types [13]. Refined session types, Υ, are generated by the following grammar, where ρ denotes a refined simple type and Υ_i denotes a τ-indexed family of refined session types.

$$\Upsilon ::= 0 \mid t \mid \mu t.\Upsilon \mid !\rho.\Upsilon \mid ?x \in \rho.\Upsilon \mid ![\Upsilon].\Upsilon \mid ?[\Upsilon].\Upsilon \mid \&_\tau \Upsilon_i \mid \oplus_\tau \Upsilon_i$$

These types are nearly the same as their simple counterparts but utilizing refined functional types instead of simple functional types. A construct that does change is $?x \in \rho.\Upsilon$. This construct allows refined session types to bind the data value that was sent across the channel and refer to this in later refined types. In particular, this allows for session types like $?x \in \{v : \text{int}|\text{TRUE}\}.!\{v : \text{int}|v \geq x\}.0$, which would be a refined session type for describing a process that receives an integer and then returns the absolute value of that integer. Why not provide more binders? For the sending of data there is no new value introduced, e could always be reconstructed in our refinement as needed, so there is nothing to bind. An additional practical consideration is that it is not obvious what variable to use to bind the result of e. For sending and receiving channels, we assume that the logic that Section 4 uses cannot analyze channels and so have no need to refer to a received channel in our predicates. For the two choice constructs, there is no need to provide an explicit binding for the enumeration value chosen, the τ-indexed family of types can already implicitly use this knowledge.

We will need a few more definitions before introducing the typing rules for refined session types. First, $\rho\downarrow$ is a refined type with all the refinement information striped out (e.g., $\{v : \text{int}|0 \leq v\}\downarrow = \text{int}$). This has a natural generalization to environments and typings. The notion of the dual of a session type is essentially unchanged except for the need to handle bindings during the reception of data, so we say that for any x, $\overline{!\rho.\Upsilon} =?x \in \rho.\overline{\Upsilon}$ and $\overline{?x \in \rho.\Upsilon} =!\rho.\overline{\Upsilon}$. Additionally, refinements introduce a notion of subtyping. We use $\Gamma \vdash \rho_1 \sqsubseteq \rho_2$ to denote that

$$\frac{\Theta; \Gamma \vdash_{SL} P : \Delta \cdot k : \Upsilon \qquad \Gamma \vdash_L e : \rho \qquad \Gamma \vdash \rho \sqsubseteq \rho'}{\Theta; \Gamma \vdash_{SL} k!(e).P : \Delta \cdot (k : !\rho'.\Upsilon)} \text{ R.Send}$$

$$\frac{\Theta; \Gamma \cdot x : \rho \vdash_{SL} P : \Delta \cdot (k : \Upsilon) \qquad \Gamma \vdash \rho' \sqsubseteq \rho}{\Theta; \Gamma \vdash_{SL} k?(x).P : \Delta \cdot (k : ?x \in \rho'.\Upsilon)} \text{ R.Rec}$$

$$\frac{\Theta; \Gamma \vdash_{SL} P : \Delta \cdot k_1 : \Upsilon_1}{\Theta; \Gamma \vdash_{SL} k_1!(k_2).P : \Delta \cdot (k_1 : ![\Upsilon_2].\Upsilon_1) \cdot (k_2 : \Upsilon_2)} \text{ R.Thr}$$

$$\frac{\Theta; \Gamma \vdash_{SL} P : \Delta \cdot (k_1 : \Upsilon_1) \cdot (k_2 : \Upsilon_2)}{\Theta; \Gamma \vdash_{SL} k_1?(k_2).P : \Delta \cdot (k_1 : ?[\Upsilon_2].\Upsilon_1)} \text{ R.Cat} \qquad \frac{\Theta; \Gamma \vdash_{SL} P : \Delta \cdot (k^p : \Upsilon) \cdot (k^{\overline{p}} : \overline{\Upsilon})}{\Theta; \Gamma \vdash_{SL} (\nu\, k)P : \Delta} \text{ R.Nu}$$

$$\frac{\Theta; \Gamma \vdash_{SL} P : \Delta_1 \qquad \Theta; \Gamma \vdash_{SL} P : \Delta_2}{\Theta; \Gamma \vdash_{SL} P \| Q : \Delta_1 \cdot \Delta_2} \text{ R.Par} \qquad \frac{\text{for } (k, \Upsilon) \in \Delta : \Upsilon = 0}{\Theta; \Gamma \vdash_{SL} 0 : \Delta} \text{ R.End}$$

$$\frac{\Theta; \Gamma \vdash_{SL} P : \Delta \cdot (k^+ : G_L(X))}{\Theta; \Gamma \vdash_{SL} \text{accept } X(k).P :} \text{ R.Acc} \qquad \frac{\Theta; \Gamma \vdash_{SL} P : \Delta \cdot (k^- : \overline{G_L(X)})}{\Theta; \Gamma \vdash_{SL} \text{request } X(k).P :} \text{ R.Req}$$

$$\frac{\Gamma \vdash_L e : \rho \qquad \rho\downarrow = \text{Bool}}{\Theta; \Gamma \cdot e \vdash_{SL} P : \Delta_1 \qquad \Theta; \Gamma \cdot \neg e \vdash_{SL} Q : \Delta_2 \qquad \Gamma \cdot e \vdash \Delta_1 \sqsubseteq \Delta \qquad \Gamma \cdot \neg e \vdash \Delta_2 \sqsubseteq \Delta}{\Theta; \Gamma \vdash_{SL} \text{if } e \text{ then } P \text{ else } Q : \Delta} \text{ R.If}$$

$$\frac{\Gamma \vdash_L e : \rho \qquad \rho\downarrow : \text{Enum} \qquad \text{for } i \in \rho\downarrow : \Theta; \Gamma \vdash_{SL} P_i : \Delta \cdot (k : S_i)}{\Theta; \Gamma \vdash_{SL} k \lhd e.P_i : \Delta \cdot k : \&_\tau S_i} \text{ R.Int}$$

$$\frac{\tau : \text{Enum} \qquad \text{for } i \in \tau : \Theta; \Gamma \vdash_{SL} P_i : \Delta \cdot (k : S_i)}{\Theta; \Gamma \vdash_{SL} \text{case}_\tau\, k \Rightarrow P_i : \Delta \cdot k : \oplus_\tau S_i} \text{ R.Ext}$$

$$\frac{\text{for i: } \Gamma \vdash_L e_i : \rho_i' \qquad \text{for i: } \Gamma \vdash \rho_i' \sqsubseteq \rho_i \qquad \text{for } (k, \Upsilon) \in \Delta : \Upsilon = 0}{\Theta \cdot X : (\rho, \Upsilon); \Gamma \vdash_{SL} X(e, k) : \Delta \cdot k : \Upsilon} \text{ R.Call}$$

$$\frac{\Theta \cdot X : (\rho, \Upsilon); \Gamma \cdot x : \rho \vdash_{SL} P : (k : \Upsilon) \qquad \Theta \cdot X : (\rho, \Upsilon); \Gamma \vdash_{SL} Q : \Delta}{\Theta; \Gamma \vdash_{SL} \text{def } X(x; k) = P \text{ in } Q : \Delta} \text{ R.Def}$$

Fig. 2. Type Rules for Refined Session Types

ρ_1 is a subtype of ρ_2 under the assumptions in Γ (defined by Rondon [13]) and $\Gamma \vdash \Upsilon_1 \sqsubseteq \Upsilon_2$ for subtyping of refined session types, defined below.

$$\frac{}{\Gamma \vdash 0 \sqsubseteq 0} \qquad \frac{\Gamma \vdash \rho_1 \sqsubseteq \rho_2 \qquad \Gamma \vdash \Upsilon_1 \sqsubseteq \Upsilon_2}{\Gamma \vdash !\rho_1.\Upsilon_1 \sqsubseteq !\rho_2.\Upsilon_2}$$

$$\frac{\Gamma \vdash \rho_1 \sqsubseteq \rho_2 \qquad \Gamma \vdash \Upsilon_1 \sqsubseteq \Upsilon_2}{\Gamma \vdash ?x \in \rho_1.\Upsilon_1 \sqsubseteq ?x \in \rho_2.\Upsilon_2} \qquad \frac{\Gamma \vdash \Upsilon_1 \sqsubseteq \Upsilon_2}{\Gamma \vdash ![\Upsilon].\Upsilon_1 \sqsubseteq ![\Upsilon].\Upsilon_2}$$

$$\frac{\Gamma \vdash \Upsilon_1 \sqsubseteq \Upsilon_2}{\Gamma \vdash ?[\Upsilon].\Upsilon_1 \sqsubseteq ?[\Upsilon].\Upsilon_2} \qquad \frac{\Gamma \vdash \Upsilon_1 \sqsubseteq \Upsilon_2}{\Gamma \vdash ?[\Upsilon].\Upsilon_1 \sqsubseteq ?[\Upsilon].\Upsilon_2}$$

$$\frac{\Gamma \vdash \text{for } i: \Upsilon_i \sqsubseteq \Upsilon_i'}{\Gamma \vdash \&_\tau \Upsilon_i \sqsubseteq \&_\tau \Upsilon_i'} \qquad \frac{\text{for all } i: \Gamma \vdash \Upsilon_i \sqsubseteq \Upsilon_i'}{\Gamma \vdash \oplus_\tau \Upsilon_i \sqsubseteq \oplus_\tau \Upsilon_i'}$$

Figure 2 introduces the typing rules for Refined Session Types. $\Theta; \Gamma \vdash_{SL} P : \Delta$ denotes that, using the definitions of Θ and assumptions of Γ (many of which are just functional typing assignments), the free process channels of process P have the refined session types in Δ. $\Gamma \vdash_L e : \rho$ denotes that, under the assumptions of Γ, e has refined type ρ, the details of which depend on the underlying functional language. The rules are similar to the rules presented for unrefined session types but with the addition of subtyping information where appropriate. R.SEND uses the idea that a process may transmit a subtype of its declared type and still maintain correct behavior. Conversely, R.REC encodes that a process may use a looser approximation of its received data than required while still maintaining correctness. R.NU remains "unchanged" for two reasons. First, the notion of duality has changed a bit, so an implicit change to handle refinements occurs. Second, while this would be a reasonable place to include subtyping information but the rules R.SEND and R.REC already account for this. Similarly R.CALL and not R.DEF encapsulates the idea that definitions usage can accepted more tightly constrained types for a particular instance than they accept in general. Perhaps the most interesting rule is R.IF. This rule makes refined session types path sensitive [1] by allowing for both branches to have different types and slightly different assumptions (e vs. $\neg e$) and then combining to have one unified typing for the whole process.

The type system for refined session types has a close connection with the simple session types as exhibited by the following lemma.

Lemma 1 (Judgement Correspondence). *For refined definition environment Θ, refined functional assumptions Γ, process P and refined channel environment Δ, $\Theta; \Gamma \vdash_{SL} P : \Delta$ implies $\Theta \downarrow; \Gamma \downarrow \vdash_S P : \Delta \downarrow$. For simple definition environment Θ_1, simple functional environment Γ_1, and simple channel typing Δ_1, $\Theta_1; \Gamma_1 \vdash_S P : \Delta_1$ implies there exists Θ_2, Γ_2, and Δ_2 s.t. $\Theta_2; \Gamma_2 \vdash_{SL} P : \Delta_2$ and $\Theta_2 \downarrow = \Theta_1$, $\Gamma_2 \downarrow = \Gamma$, and $\Delta_2 \downarrow = \Delta_1$.*

Proof (Sketch). Both proofs proceed by induction on the size of proof trees. For the first result, notice that by dropping all the refinement information (and subtyping) each of the refined session type rules becomes a simple session typing rule. For the second result, use the trivial always-true predicate to (not) constrain the types.

4   Inferencing

Inferring arbitrary refinement predicates is undecidable in general (consider trying to infer the type of a function that generates random primes) so we will restrict our attention significantly. In particular, we will fix some set of basic predicates and then infer predicates that are finite conjunctions drawn from this set. For example, if wishing to infer simple interval properties we might have a set of predicates like $\{v \leq 5, v \leq x, y \leq v, \dots\}$. Following [13], we will assume that this set is generated by a finite set of templates instantiated by program variables. We then look for conjunctions of ground substitutions for these templates that are suitable solutions to our constraints.

Inferring refined session types proceeds in three major steps:

1. Infer simple types and record some information from doing so
2. Add predicate variables to types and gather constraints on them
3. Solve these constraints

4.1 Simple Types

Inferring simple types is done by utilizing prior work [7,1,3]. In particular, we assume that for our functional language we can infer simple types. During this inferencing we will need to record a bit of extra information. Specifically, we will assume that the simple session type inferencing algorithm annotates channel generation with the channel's session type. Because of polarity considerations there is not a single type for a channel but two dual types, one for each end. For presentational compactness, we will assume that $(\nu k)P$ is annotated to become $(\nu\ k : S)P$ were S was the type of k^+ found during inferencing. Additionally, we will assume that parallel compositions are annotated with how to split the combined channel typing environment for the process into one typing for each of the two subprocesses. We will denote this split by converting $P_1 \| P_2$ into $P_{1\,K_1} \| _{K_2} P_2$ with the names of K_i being those for P_i. Last, we assume that definitions are annotated with their argument types. That is def $X(\boldsymbol{x}; \boldsymbol{k}) = P_1$ in P_2 becomes def $X(\boldsymbol{x}; \boldsymbol{k}) : (\boldsymbol{\tau}; \boldsymbol{S}) = P_1$ in P_2. With these annotations we will be able to calculate at any point the simple channel typing of a subprocess of the process that we are trying to infer types. A more complicated implementation might be able to cache information closer to its use location, but we think these annotations provide a good trade-off between clarity and completeness.

4.2 Constraints

We utilize constraints of the following forms during constraint generation. $\varGamma \vdash_{\mathrm{wf}} \varUpsilon$ indicates that $\varUpsilon$ is well-formed w.r.t. $\varGamma$, i.e., that the free variables in $\varUpsilon$ are bound in $\varGamma$, $(\mathrm{FN}(\varUpsilon) \subseteq \mathrm{dom}(\varGamma))$. Additionally, we use subtyping requirements of the form $\varGamma \vdash \varUpsilon_1 \sqsubseteq \varUpsilon_2$ and $\varGamma \vdash \rho_1 \sqsubseteq \rho_2$. The constraint $\varUpsilon_1 = \overline{\varUpsilon_2}$ is used to enforce duality. We also lift our constraints to work on (equal length) vectors of types pointwise (e.g., $\varGamma \vdash_{\mathrm{wf}} \boldsymbol{\rho}$ is equivalent to $\bigcup\{\varGamma \vdash_{\mathrm{wf}} \rho_i\}$).

We assume that we have some constraint generation algorithm that will produce correct constraints for our underlying functional language [13]. Armed with this we can read our typing rules as generating constraints by inserting subtyping constraints as appropriate (and in the case of T.Nu a duality constraint). Throughout the process of constraint gathering we will occasionally need to generate new refined session types with predicate variables, we denote this by $\tau\!\uparrow$ for basic types and $S\!\uparrow$ for session types. Whenever we perform this generation we will provide some well-formedness constraint in addition to any subtyping constraints generated by the typing rules.

As an example consider the rule R.Send. Suppose that we know $\varTheta\!\downarrow; \varGamma\!\downarrow\vdash_{SL}$ $k!(e).P : \varDelta \cdot (k :!\tau.S)$ from our simple inference step. When we generate constraints for this we will make one call to our functional constraint generation algorithm $(\varGamma \vdash_L e : \rho)$, one recursive call to our session type constraint generation algorithm $(\varTheta; \varGamma \vdash_{SL} P : \varDelta \cdot k : \varUpsilon)$, generate one refined type $\tau\!\uparrow$, and add the constraints $\varGamma \vdash \rho \sqsubseteq \tau\!\uparrow$ and $\varGamma \vdash_{\mathrm{wf}} \tau\!\uparrow$, which corresponds to the constraints imposed by the typing rule.

Figure 3 provides a listing of the constraint generation algorithm for refined session types. $\mathrm{CONSTR}_{SL}(\varTheta, \varGamma, P, \varDelta_S)$ returns $(\varDelta, C)$ a pair of refined channel

$\text{CONSTR}_{SL}(\Theta, \Gamma, 0, \Delta_S) = (\Delta_S, \emptyset)$
$\text{CONSTR}_{SL}(\Theta, \Gamma, \text{accept } X(k).P, \Delta_S) =$
  $\quad (\Delta \cdot (k^+ : \Upsilon), C) \leftarrow \text{CONSTR}_{SL}(\Theta, \Gamma, P, \Delta \cdot (k^+ : G(X)))$
  $\quad \text{Return } (\Delta, C \cup \{\Gamma \vdash \Upsilon \sqsubseteq G_L(X)\})$
$\text{CONSTR}_{SL}(\Theta, \Gamma, \text{request } X(k).P, \Delta_S) =$
  $\quad (\Delta \cdot (k^- : \Upsilon), C) \leftarrow \text{CONSTR}_{SL}(\Theta, \Gamma, P, \Delta \cdot (k^- : \overline{G(X)}))$
  $\quad \text{Return } (\Delta, C \cup \{\Gamma \vdash \Upsilon \sqsubseteq \overline{G_L(X)}\})$
$\text{CONSTR}_{SL}(\Theta, \Gamma, k!(e).P, \Delta_S \cdot (k :!\tau.S)) =$
  $\quad (\Delta \cdot k : \Upsilon, C) \leftarrow \text{CONSTR}_{SL}(\Theta, \Gamma, P, \Delta_S \cdot (k : S))$
  $\quad (\rho, C') \leftarrow \text{CONSTR}_L(\Gamma, e)$
  $\quad \rho' \leftarrow \tau \uparrow$
  $\quad \text{Return } (\Delta \cdot k :!\rho'.\Upsilon, C \cup C' \cup \{\Gamma \vdash_{wf} \rho'; \Gamma \vdash \rho \sqsubseteq \rho'\})$
$\text{CONSTR}_{SL}(\Theta, \Gamma, k?(x).P, \Delta_S \cdot (k :?\tau.S)) =$
  $\quad \rho \leftarrow \tau \uparrow$
  $\quad \rho' \leftarrow \tau \uparrow$
  $\quad (\Delta \cdot k : \Upsilon, C) \leftarrow \text{CONSTR}_{SL}(\Theta, \Gamma \cdot x : \rho, P, \Delta_S \cdot (k : S))$
  $\quad \text{Return } (\Delta \cdot k :?x \in \rho'.\Upsilon, C \cup \{\Gamma \vdash_{wf} \rho; \Gamma \vdash_{wf} \rho'; \Gamma \vdash \rho \sqsubseteq \rho'\})$
$\text{CONSTR}_{SL}(\Theta, \Gamma, k_1!(k_2).P, \Delta_S \cdot (k_1 :![S_2].S_1) \cdot (k_2 : S_2)) =$
  $\quad (\Delta \cdot k_1 : \Upsilon_1, C) \leftarrow \text{CONSTR}_{SL}(\Theta, \Gamma, P, \Delta_S \cdot (k_1 : S_1))$
  $\quad \Upsilon_2 \leftarrow S_2 \uparrow$
  $\quad \text{Return } (\Delta \cdot k_1 :![\Upsilon_2].\Upsilon_1, C \cup \{\Gamma \vdash_{wf} \Upsilon_2\})$
$\text{CONSTR}_{SL}(\Theta, \Gamma, k_1?(k_2).P, \Delta_S \cdot (k_1 :?[S_2].S_1)) =$
  $\quad (\Delta \cdot (k_1 : \Upsilon_1) \cdot (k_2 : \Upsilon_2), C) \leftarrow \text{CONSTR}_{SL}(\Theta, \Gamma, P, \Delta_S \cdot (k_1 : S_1) \cdot (k_2 : S_2))$
  $\quad \text{Return } (\Delta \cdot (k_1 :?[\Upsilon_2].\Upsilon_1), C)$
$\text{CONSTR}_{SL}(\Theta, \Gamma, P_1{}_{K_1} \| _{K_2} P_2, \Delta_S) =$
  $\quad (\Delta_1, C_1) \leftarrow \text{CONSTR}_{SL}(\Theta, \Gamma, P_1, \Delta_S \upharpoonright_{K_1})$
  $\quad (\Delta_2, C_2) \leftarrow \text{CONSTR}_{SL}(\Theta, \Gamma, P_2, \Delta_S \upharpoonright_{K_2})$
  $\quad \text{Return } (\Delta_1 \cdot \Delta_2, C_1 \cup C_2)$
$\text{CONSTR}_{SL}(\Theta, \Gamma, k \lhd e.P_i, \Delta_S \cdot (k : \&_\tau S_i)) =$
  $\quad \text{for } i: (\Delta \cdot (k : \Upsilon_i), C_i) \leftarrow \text{CONSTR}_{SL}(\Theta, \Gamma \cdot (e = i), P_i, \Delta_S \cdot (k : S_i))$
  $\quad \text{Return } (\Delta \cdot (k : \&_\tau \Upsilon_i), \bigcup C_i)$
$\text{CONSTR}_{SL}(\Theta, \Gamma, \text{case}_k\ e \Rightarrow P_i, \Delta_S \cdot (k : \oplus_\tau S_i)) =$
  $\quad \text{for } i: (\Delta \cdot (k : \Upsilon_i), C_i) \leftarrow \text{CONSTR}_{SL}(\Theta, \Gamma \cdot (e = i), P_i, \Delta_S \cdot (k : S_i))$
  $\quad \text{Return } (\Delta \cdot (k : \&_\tau \Upsilon_i), \bigcup C_i)$
$\text{CONSTR}_{SL}(\Theta, \Gamma, \text{if } e \text{ then } P_1 \text{ else } P_2, \Delta_S) =$
  $\quad (\Delta_1, C_1) \leftarrow \text{CONSTR}_{SL}(\Theta, \Gamma \cdot e, P_1, \Delta_S)$
  $\quad (\Delta_2, C_2) \leftarrow \text{CONSTR}_{SL}(\Theta, \Gamma \cdot (\neg e), P_2, \Delta_S)$
  $\quad \text{for } k \in \text{dom}(\Delta_S): \Upsilon_k \leftarrow \Delta_S(k) \uparrow$
  $$\text{Return } \left(\mathbf{k} : \mathbf{\Upsilon}, C_1 \cup C_2 \cup \bigcup_{k \in \text{dom}(\Delta)} \left\{ \begin{array}{l} \Gamma \vdash_{wf} \Upsilon_k; \\ \Gamma \cdot e \vdash \Delta_1(k) \sqsubseteq \Upsilon_k; \\ \Gamma \cdot (\neg e) \vdash \Delta_2(k) \sqsubseteq \Upsilon_k \end{array} \right\} \right)$$
$\text{CONSTR}_{SL}(\Theta, \Gamma, (\nu\ k : S)P, \Delta_S) =$
  $\quad (\Delta \cdot (k^+ : \Upsilon_1) \cdot (k^- : \Upsilon_2), C) \leftarrow \text{CONSTR}_{SL}(\Theta, \Gamma, P, \Delta \cdot (k^+ : S) \cdot (k^- : \overline{S}))$
  $\quad \text{Return } (\Delta, C \cup \{\Upsilon_1 = \overline{\Upsilon_2}\})$
$\text{CONSTR}_{SL}(\Theta \cdot (X : (\boldsymbol{\rho}, \boldsymbol{\Upsilon})), \Gamma, X(e, k), \Delta_S \cdot (\mathbf{k} : \mathbf{S})) =$
  $\quad \text{for } i: (\rho'_i, C_i) \leftarrow \text{CONSTR}_L(\Gamma, e_i)$
  $\quad \text{Return } (\Delta_S \cdot (\mathbf{k} : \boldsymbol{\Upsilon}), \bigcup C_i \cup \{\Gamma \vdash \rho' \sqsubseteq \rho\})$
$\text{CONSTR}_{SL}(\Theta, \Gamma, \text{def } X(\boldsymbol{x}; \mathbf{k}) : (\boldsymbol{\tau}; \mathbf{S}) = P_1 \text{ in } P_2, \Delta_S \cdot (\mathbf{k} : \mathbf{S})) =$
  $\quad (\boldsymbol{\rho}; \boldsymbol{\Upsilon}) \leftarrow (\boldsymbol{\tau} \uparrow; \mathbf{S} \uparrow)$
  $\quad (\Delta_1 \cdot (\mathbf{k} : \boldsymbol{\Upsilon'}), C_1) \leftarrow \text{CONSTR}_{SL}(\Theta \cdot (X : (\boldsymbol{\rho}; \boldsymbol{\Upsilon})), \Gamma \cdot (\boldsymbol{x} : \boldsymbol{\rho}), P_1, (\mathbf{k} : \mathbf{S}))$
  $\quad (\Delta_2, C_2) \leftarrow \text{CONSTR}_{SL}(\Theta \cdot (X : (\boldsymbol{\rho}; \boldsymbol{\Upsilon'})), \Gamma, P_2, \Delta_S)$
  $\quad \text{Return } (\Delta_2, C_1 \cup C_2 \cup \{\Gamma \vdash_{wf} \boldsymbol{\rho}; \Gamma \vdash_{wf} \boldsymbol{\Upsilon}; \Gamma \vdash \boldsymbol{\Upsilon'} \sqsubseteq \boldsymbol{\Upsilon}\})$

Fig. 3. Constraint Generation Algorithm

typing (with predicate variables) and a set of constraints. We use $\text{CONSTR}_L(\Gamma, e)$ to denote the assumed constraint gatherer of our underlying functional language. The algorithm assumes that, for functional assumptions Γ, $\text{CONSTR}_L(\Gamma, e)$ returns (ρ, C) a pair of a refined functional type and a set of constraints (both well-formedness and subtyping). A small abuse of notation occurs in the case for terminated processes and in process variable definition. Specifically, we use Δ_S as both a simple session typing and as a refined one. From our typing rules we know in both cases it must be entirely composed of mappings of the form $(k : 0)$

and so can be reasonably used in both contexts. While most of the cases used to define CONSTR$_{SL}$ are relatively straightforward we highlight a few rules here.

Consider the case for conditional branching, perhaps the most complicated case. First we make recursive calls with the altered assumptions, allowing for sensitivity to the value of e. From R.IF we know that both of the typings returned by these must be subtypes of our overall typing. Since we do not have a preexisting typing use for this subtyping we have to generate one ($\Delta_S(k) \uparrow$). We then return this typing along with our recursively generated constraints and three new constraints for each channel in our typing. The first new constraint ensures that our freshly generated types are well-formed. The other encodes the subtyping present in the rule. One might worry that if both k^p and $k^{\overline{p}}$ appear in our typing that this might cause them to become delinked. Since we will only use our constraint generation on closed processes after simple session type inferencing we know that these paired channel ends will eventually be generated by some $((\nu\ k)P)$ and thus duality will be ensured there.

The following lemma gives us the correctness of our constraint generation algorithm.

Lemma 2 (Constraint Correctness). *For a closed annotated process P, empty definition and functional environments and simple typing, CONSTR$_{SL}(\emptyset, \emptyset, P, \emptyset)$ returns (Δ, C), s.t. $\emptyset; \emptyset \vdash_{SL} P : \Delta$ if and only if C has a solution.*

Proof (Sketch). Induction on the proof trees of $\Theta; \Gamma \vdash_{SL} P : \Delta$ for a generalization of the lemma to non-empty environments.

4.3   Solving

Once all constraints have been generated, we will have many predicate variables left. A solution to a system of constraints is a ground substitution for predicate variables such that all constraints are satisfied. Assuming that our constraints allow all legal solutions (Lemma 2), we know that there is at least one possible solution, the trivial always-true solution. The important question is then that of finding a maximally specific solution. We search for a maximal solution using the normal implication ordering lifted to maps (i.e., $\sigma_1 \geq \sigma_2 \iff \forall x.\sigma_1(x) \implies \sigma_2(x)$).

A first pass removes all duality constraints by performing the substitutions implied by the equations. Since all Γ in our constraints are finite and every predicate variable has at least one well-formedness constraint, we know that for any given predicate variable, there can be at most a finite number of ground substitutions admissible by its well-formedness constraints. This together with the observation that only the predicate variables mentioned in our constraints matter for a substitution's admissibility, we have only a finite number of "interesting" substitutions that might be solutions. Assuming that we can decide admissibility and solution ordering (e.g., via an SMT solver) then we can just try all solutions and select a maximal one. This requirement for being able to decide ordering is perhaps the biggest constraint on what we can choose as our templates, since we need to stay away from choosing those that are incompatible with our choice of SMT solver.

This proposed solution process is unsatifyingly slow, so we instead suggest using Iterative Weakening [13]. Iterative Weakening is a technique that starts from the strongest admissible ground substitution (for each predicate variable a conjunction of all predicates admissible by its well-formedness constraints) and iteratively removes an offending conjunct. Since we deal with conjunctions of instantiated templates we know that removing a conjunct can at most preserve a substitution's strength and the always-true substitution is a solution, we know that iterative weakening will find a maximally specific solution. From the above arguments we have the following lemma.

Lemma 3 (Solver Correctness). *For a given set of constraints, s.t. every predicate variable has at least one (finite) well-formedness constraint, iterative weakening produces a maximally specific solution.*

Proof (Sketch). Outlined above, this is proven by a generalization of Rondon [13]. ▢

5   Related Work

The most direct related work are the series of papers by Rondon *et al.* [13,8,14] applying their liquid typing approach to infer refinement types for various languages. Our work can be seen as a continuance of this line of work by applying it to the Pi Calculus.

Gay and Hole [5] present a Pi Calculus with session types and subtyping on the choice operators, allowing flexibility on the number of branches for the type of an internal choice and its corresponding external choice. Additionally, read-write permission using Pi Calculus type systems tend to have subtyping for their permissions [6]. Here subtyping is utilized to track permissions with having only read or write permissions being viewed as a subtype of having both. Both of these notions of subtyping are orthogonal to the subtyping used in this paper.

Perhaps closest to our dependent session types are those found in Caires *et al.* [2]. They allow for full dependent types and envision writing proof carrying code, at the functional level, by transmitting proofs across channels. They do not (as expected) address inferring types for their programs. Additionally they use linear logic as a basis for their typing system which gives a fairly different feeling, since we do not need to worry about differentiating between linear and replicateable resources.

While we use some of the simplest session types as a basis for LiquidPi a number of extensions to them have been made [15,4,11]. In particular, these recent works have studied global types, providing a holistic description of system communication, instead of per channel types using asynchronous communication. These too also involve a notion of subtyping, but it is used for dealing with asynchrony and not at the functional level. We expect that the liquid typing approach would likely apply in these cases, though with extra complexity arising from their more complicated type systems.

6   Conclusion and Future Work

We have presented LiquidPi an approach that combines the dependent type inferencing of Liquid Types with Hondas Session Types to give a more precise automatically derived description of the behavior of distributed programs. These types can be used to describe/enforce safety properties of distributed systems. We presented a type system parametric over an underlying functional language with Pi Calculus connectives and give an inference algorithm for it by means of efficient external solvers and a set of dependent qualifier templates. By doing this we demonstrate that inferring dependent types for communication is achievable, gaining a fair amount of expressivity compared to previous techniques.

As described in Section 5, there are many variations of type systems for distributed systems that have been presented, it would be interesting to integrate inferable dependent types into them as well to yield greater expressivity. Another natural thing to do with this work is to create an efficient implementation. With the ease of use of modern SMT solvers a simple prototype shouldn't be infeasible, but heuristics for the weakening step of iterative weakening might need more investigation.

Acknowledgments. This material is based upon work supported by the Army Research Office under Award No. W911NF-09-1-0273 and by NASA Contract No. NNA10DE79C . Any opinions, findings, and conclusions or recommendations expressed in this publication are those of the author(s) and do not necessarily reflect the views of the Army Research Office or NASA.

References

1. Aho, A.V., Sethi, R., Ullman, J.D.: Compilers: Principles, Techniques and Tools. Addison-Wesley (1988)
2. Caires, L., Pfenning, F., Toninho, B.: Towards concurrent type theory. In: Pierce, B.C. (ed.) TLDI, pp. 1–12. ACM (2012)
3. Damas, L., Milner, R.: Principal type-schemes for functional programs. In: DeMillo, R.A. (ed.) POPL, pp. 207–212. ACM Press (1982)
4. Demangeon, R., Honda, K.: Nested protocols in session types. In: Koutny, M., Ulidowski, I. (eds.) CONCUR 2012. LNCS, vol. 7454, pp. 272–286. Springer, Heidelberg (2012)
5. Gay, S.J., Hole, M.: Subtyping for session types in the pi calculus. Acta Inf. 42(2-3), 191–225 (2005)
6. Hennessy, M.: A Distributed Pi-Calculus. Cambridge University Press (2007)
7. Honda, K., Vasconcelos, V.T., Kubo, M.: Language primitives and type discipline for structured communication-based programming. In: Hankin, C. (ed.) ESOP 1998. LNCS, vol. 1381, pp. 122–138. Springer, Heidelberg (1998)
8. Kawaguchi, M., Rondon, P.M., Jhala, R.: Type-based data structure verification. In: Hind, M., Diwan, A. (eds.) PLDI, pp. 304–315. ACM (2009)
9. Martin-Löf, P.: Intuitionistic type theory (1984)
10. Milner, R., Parrow, J., Walker, D.: A calculus of mobile processes, i. Inf. Comput. 100(1), 1–40 (1992)

11. Mostrous, D., Yoshida, N., Honda, K.: Global principal typing in partially commutative asynchronous sessions. In: Castagna, G. (ed.) ESOP 2009. LNCS, vol. 5502, pp. 316–332. Springer, Heidelberg (2009)
12. Pierce, B.C.: Types and programming languages. MIT Press, Cambridge (2002)
13. Rondon, P.M., Kawaguchi, M., Jhala, R.: Liquid types. In: Gupta, R., Amarasinghe, S.P. (eds.) PLDI, pp. 159–169. ACM (2008)
14. Rondon, P.M., Kawaguchi, M., Jhala, R.: Low-level liquid types. In: Hermenegildo, M.V., Palsberg, J. (eds.) POPL, pp. 131–144. ACM (2010)
15. Toninho, B., Caires, L., Pfenning, F.: Functions as session-typed processes. In: Birkedal, L. (ed.) FOSSACS 2012. LNCS, vol. 7213, pp. 346–360. Springer, Heidelberg (2012)
16. Yoshida, N., Vasconcelos, V.T.: Language primitives and type discipline for structured communication-based programming revisited: Two systems for higher-order session communication. Electr. Notes Theor. Comput. Sci. 171(4), 73–93 (2007)

Automated Verification of Chapel Programs Using Model Checking and Symbolic Execution

Timothy K. Zirkel, Stephen F. Siegel, and Timothy McClory*

Verified Software Laboratory, Department of Computer and Information Sciences
University of Delaware, Newark DE 19716, USA
{zirkeltk, siegel, tmcclory}@udel.edu

Abstract. Chapel is a new programming language targeting high performance computing. Chapel makes it easier to write parallel code, but is still subject to concurrency problems such as deadlocks, race conditions, and nondeterministic results. In theory, model checking and symbolic execution tools can help with these problems, but certain Chapel primitives are difficult to represent in the models used by existing tools. For example, some primitives dynamically create arbitrarily nested scopes with threads executing within those scopes. We present (1) a new formal model that naturally represents these dynamic concepts and (2) a new prototype model checking/symbolic execution tool for Chapel programs that uses this model as its intermediate representation. We describe how the tool translates Chapel into this IR and the results of applying the tool to several synthetic Chapel programs.

1 Introduction

Currently, most high performance scientific programs are written in C, C++, or Fortran, in combination with one or more concurrency extensions, such as the Message Passing Interface library [13] or OpenMP [14]. These approaches, based on old programming languages and concurrency models, pose well-known challenges to programmer productivity and to writing correct, efficient code. Much research effort has focused on ameliorating these problems with better debugging and analysis tools, but there have also been a number of recent initiatives introducing entirely new programming languages for HPC (e.g., [1,3,5,18]).

These new languages include Chapel [5], a programming language designed for high productivity parallel programming. It incorporates high level constructs for expressing common parallel programming patterns. While these constructs simplify programs, they also make it easier to introduce unintended forms of nondeterminism. Such nondeterminism can lead to deadlock or unexpected results. We present a prototype verification tool for programs written in the subset of

---

* Supported by the U.S. National Science Foundation grant CCF-0953210 and the U.S. Department of Defense.

G. Brat, N. Rungta, and A. Venet (Eds.): NFM 2013, LNCS 7871, pp. 198–212, 2013.

```
prog ::= decl+
decl ::= (config | extern)? (const | var | param) v : type (= expr)? ;
       | (iter | proc) f ( ( v : type (, v : type)* )? ) (: type)? block
block ::= { (decl | stmt) * }
type ::= sync? (real | int | void | bool | string | [ expr ] type)
stmt ::= block | call | expr = expr ; | return expr? ; | yield expr ;
       | while ( expr ) block | if ( expr ) then stmt (else stmt)?
       | cobegin block
       | (for | forall | coforall) v in (expr .. expr | call) block
expr ::= x | int_literal | float_literal | string_literal | true | false
       | call | expr [ expr ] | ( expr ) | (+ | - | !) expr
       | expr (|| | && | == | != | < | > | >= | <= | + | - | * | / | %) expr
call ::= f ( (expr (, expr)*)? )
```

Fig. 1. Abstract syntax of Chapel subset

Chapel shown in Figure 1. The tool can automatically detect such defects or show that none exist within specified parameters.

The Chapel programming runtime spawns *tasks* (threads) that interact via shared memory. The cobegin statement creates a new task for each statement in a block. The coforall statement creates a new task for each iteration of a loop. The forall statement spawns one or more tasks and partitions the iterations of the loop among those tasks. The number of tasks created depends on the runtime configuration. Execution is halted after cobegin, coforall, and forall statements until all created tasks have completed. An example of a forall statement is included in Figure 2.

The iteration domain of a loop is specified by a special type of function called an *iterator*. Ordinary functions that yield one return value are called *procedures*. Iterators are defined using the same syntax as a procedure except return statements are replaced with yield statements. An iterator definition is preceded by the keyword iter and a procedure definition is preceded by the keyword proc. Iterators are used to generate a sequence of values.

Constant variable declarations begin with the keyword const and must contain an initialization expression. Regular variables are declared with keyword var. Each variable is permitted to have one of two modifiers: config or extern. Config variables must be in the global scope. These variables may be initialized at compile time through some platform-dependent means. Extern variables are assumed to be defined outside of the program. No memory is allocated for extern variables and they are not initialized.

Tasks can be coordinated with sync variables. A sync variable is declared using the sync keyword. Each sync variable has a boolean flag associated with it, which indicates whether the variable is *empty* or *full*. A sync variable can only be read when full and can only be written to when empty. A write to a sync variable makes it full and a read from the variable makes it empty. A task that attempts to read or write a sync variable must wait until it is in the correct state. The flag is initially set to be empty.

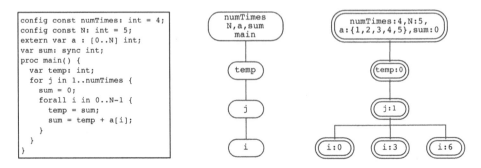

Fig. 2. adderPar.chpl. Left: This program computes the sum of the elements in a and stores the result in sum. This process is repeated numTimes times. If sum is not declared to be a sync variable then the program is incorrect; center: static scope tree for this program; right: the dynamic scope tree in a state.

The program in Figure 2 demonstrates some of the challenges for Chapel verification. The dynamic state illustrates how the tasks share certain memory regions. The tasks created have their own scopes for the variables that are declared in the body of the forall loop. However, they share all the variables above that point in the static scope tree. Hence the dynamic scope tree shown on the right. The ability to declare and instantiate procedures in arbitrary scopes is fundamental to our modeling approach, but is absent from standard model checking languages such as Promela [10].

State space explosion is always an issue with model checking, but the dynamic nature of Chapel concurrency exacerbates the problems. For example, to execute a nested pair of coforall statements, each with an iteration space of size N, N^2 concurrent processes are instantiated.

Our Chapel Verification Tool (CVT) uses model checking with symbolic execution [4, 11, 12] to verify correctness properties of Chapel programs. It can also verify the functional equivalence of two programs, using comparative symbolic execution [16]. We constructed CVT by re-using certain components of the Toolkit for Accurate Scientific Software (TASS) [17]. TASS supports a subset of MPI, but not dynamic process creation, and the only scope shared by TASS processes is the one global ("shared") scope. Verifying Chapel programs requires a substantially different state representation.

2   CIR: The Chapel Intermediate Representation

In this section we describe the Chapel Intermediate Representation (CIR). CIR is a "guarded command" style representation [7] that provides simple primitives for dynamic process creation, procedure calls, nondeterminism, and message-passing. It also adds to the usual model a notion of scopes, which have both a static and a dynamic aspect.

SPIN [10] uses a model which allows dynamic process creation and (as of version 6) allows nested local scopes within a process definition. The dSPIN [6] extension to SPIN allowed additional dynamic constructs, such as heap-allocated data and procedures with local scope nests. In both SPIN and dSPIN, however, a process or procedure can be declared only in the outermost (global) scope. CIR goes further by allowing procedure definitions in any scope. The "forking" of such procedures leads to states like the one depicted in Figure 2(right). In that state, there are three processes, each with its own copy of i, but sharing j and variables in the scopes above. This general model of concurrency and scopes is similar to the threading model in some functional languages, such as Racket [8].

2.1   CIR Models

A *CIR model* consists of the following components. First, there is a set Σ of (static) *scopes*, which has the structure of a rooted tree with root σ_0. These correspond to the lexical scopes in the source code, plus scopes that may be added to translate complex statements (see §3). The root scope represents the outermost scope encompassing the entire program. If τ is a child of σ, the lexical scope represented by τ is immediately contained in that represented by σ.

The model associates to each $\sigma \in \Sigma$ a set of typed variables and a set of procedure symbols. We say these variables and procedure symbols are *declared in* σ. All of these sets are pairwise disjoint; in particular, the variables declared in σ do not include those declared in any child of σ. We say a variable or procedure symbol is *visible in* σ if it is declared in σ or an ancestor of σ.

Types include *boolean*, *real*, *int*, *string*, arrays of any element type, and a type *process* for process IDs. For simplicity, in this paper, the *real* and *int* types represent the mathematical real numbers and integers, though no fundamental changes are required in the model to incorporate finite-precision or other types.

For each procedure symbol f declared in the model, there is a *procedure scope*, which is a child of the scope in which f is declared. A scope can be the procedure scope of at most one procedure. The *root procedure* has σ_0 as its procedure scope, and is the only procedure that does not have a declaration scope.

Every scope σ "belongs to" a unique procedure: if σ is the procedure scope for some f then σ belongs to f, else σ belongs to the procedure to which the parent of σ belongs.

The model associates to each procedure symbol f a *procedure signature*, which consists of a return type (possibly "void") and a sequence of parameter types. Finally, there is a *guarded transition system* associated to f. This system includes a set of locations, including a start location. Each location l has an associated scope $\mathsf{lscope}(l)$ which must belong to f; there is no other restriction on $\mathsf{lscope}(l)$. The location also has some number (possibly 0) of outgoing transitions. Each transition comprises (1) a *guard*, a boolean-valued expression specifying when the transition is enabled, (2) a destination location, and (3) an *atomic CIR statement*.

The kinds of atomic statements are listed below. In the list, v, w and b denote left-hand side (LHS) expressions, $e, \mathsf{dest}, \mathsf{src}, \mathsf{tag}, e_1, \ldots$ denote expressions, f is a procedure symbol, and x is a variable. In all cases, the variables and procedure symbols must be visible in lscope(l). An asterisk indicates an optional element. The semantics of these statements is given in Section 2.2.

1. $v = e$
2. return e^*
3. $v^* = f(e_1, \ldots, e_n)$
4. $v^* = $ fork $f(e_1, \ldots, e_n)$, where v has *process* type
5. join(e), where e has *process* type
6. $v = $ choose(e), where v and e have integer type
7. send(dest, e, tag), where dest has *process* type, tag has integer type
8. receive(src, v, tag) (like above, but src and tag may have form any(w))
9. write(e)
10. noop
11. sync-read(b, v, x), where b has boolean type
12. sync-write(b, x, e), where b has boolean type.

2.2   CIR Semantics

We assume given a set of (typed) *values*. The values of type *process* are integers. Given this, the *state* of a CIR model comprises

1. a set Δ of *dyscopes* (dynamic scopes) which has the structure of a rooted tree with with root δ_0;
2. a function static: $\Delta \to \Sigma$ which respects tree structure, i.e., if $\delta_1, \delta_2 \in \Delta$ and δ_1 is a child of δ_2 then static(δ_1) is a child of static(δ_2). We say δ *is an instance of* static(δ);
3. for each $\delta \in \Delta$, a function which assigns a value (of the correct type) to each variable declared in static(δ);
4. a set of integers P (the *process IDs* used in the state);
5. a function which assigns to each $p \in P$ a *call stack*, which is a sequence of frames, each frame consisting of a location l in some procedure and a dyscope δ such that static(δ) = lscope(l);
6. a function which assigns to each ordered pair of processes a finite sequence of *messages*, where a message consists of a value for the message data and an integer tag.

Figure 3(right) shows a state of the model to its left. This state has two dyscopes which are instances of scope 1, no instance of scope 6, and 1 instance of each of the remaining scopes. There are 3 processes, whose call stacks are illustrated. (The locations are not shown.)

The semantics of a CIR model are specified in a small-step operational style using an interleaving view of concurrency. For a transition to be enabled, its guard must evaluate to *true*. In addition, certain statements have an *implicit guard* which must also hold; these are discussed below. For the most part, all of this is standard, so we limit the discussion to aspects of the semantics that may be particular to CIR.

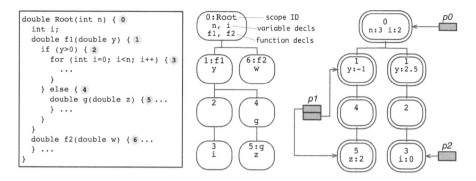

Fig. 3. CIR scopes. left: pseudocode representation of a CIR model with lexical scopes numbered; center: the static scope tree; right: a state consisting of 3 processes and 7 dynamic scopes.

To execute $v = \mathsf{choose}(e)$, e is evaluated to yield an integer n. An integer in the range $[0, n-1]$ is chosen nondeterministically and assigned to v.

A send statement specifies the destination process, the data to be sent, and an integer tag. Tags are used by the receiver to select messages for reception. The data may have any type, including an array type. The execution of the send creates a message and appends it to the message sequence for (p, q), where p is the process ID of the sender and q that of the receiver. The receive has an implicit guard which holds when a message matching the tag is available in an appropriate queue and pulls out the oldest message matching the tag. The "any" variant used as the source argument means the receive will nondeterministically choose one of the incoming queues which has a matching message, and then pull out the oldest matching message from that queue; the process ID of the sender will be stored in v. The use of "any" as the tag argument simply means the oldest message will be removed from the queue, regardless of its tag; the tag of that message will be stored in tag.

The sync-read and sync-write are used to model accesses to a sync variable x. The sync-read has implicit guard b and when executed it performs the assignment of x to v and sets b to *false* in one atomic step. A sync-write behaves dually.

When control moves from one location to another within a procedure's transition system, the scope may change. When this happens, new dyscopes are created and added to the state. This is carried out in such a way that the correspondence between dynamic and static scopes is preserved. The protocol requires computing the "join" in the static scope tree of the old and new scopes, considering the path from the old scope to the join to the new scope, and then creating a corresponding structure in the dynamic tree; see Figure 4(a–c).

A dyscope is *unreachable* if it does not occur in any frame and is not an ancestor of a dyscope occurring in a frame. Such a dyscope may be removed from the state; see Figure 4(d).

If a call or fork is executed in dyscope δ then since f is visible, it must be the case that f is declared in $\mathsf{static}(\delta')$ where δ' is δ or an ancestor of δ. A new

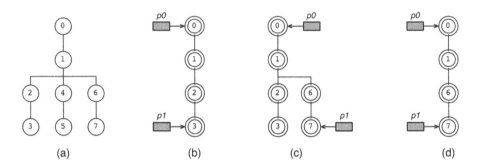

Fig. 4. Jump protocol. (a) a static scope tree; (b) a dyscope tree; p_1 is about to move from a location in scope 3 to a location in scope 7; (c) new dyscopes are added corresponding to the path from scope 1 (the join of 3 and 7) to 7; (d) dyscopes 2 and 3 became unreachable so were removed.

dyscope is created whose parent is δ' and whose scope is the procedure scope of f. A new frame is created referring to the new dyscope. For a call, the frame is pushed onto the existing stack; for a fork, a new process is created whose stack consists of the single frame.

If a process has terminated and there are no references to that process in the state, it can be removed from the state. At any point, process IDs can also be re-assigned throughout the state, for example, to remove gaps or put the state into a canonical form.

Symbolic semantics. We have described the "concrete" semantics of a CIR model. Minimal changes are required to apply symbolic execution to CIR. These techniques are now well-known: values associated to variables become (typed) symbolic expressions, a path condition variable is added to the state, any time a guard *may* be *true* a transition is enabled in the symbolic space, and so on. Currently, our symbolic representation uses concrete representations of the dynamic scope tree, call stacks, and message queues (but the data in a message is symbolic), although it is conceivable that these structures could also be represented symbolically, thereby enabling reasoning for unbounded numbers of processes, dyscopes, and so on.

3   Translating from Chapel to CIR

In this section we present the translation of several Chapel structures into CIR. The translations are provided in a pseudocode for CIR. For readability, the pseudocode utilizes common sequential constructs (e.g., `for`, `if`) that do not exist in CIR, but are translated to the transition system in standard ways. There is no proof of soundness of the translation because there is no formal semantics of Chapel, just a natural language description in the manual. In fact, translation to CIR could be a way to give a formal semantics to the language.

3.1   Built-In Constants

CVT uses four built-in constants. These do not appear in the Chapel code being verified, but are used in the translation of several constructs. Three of these constants are used as message tags:

1. _CVT_NEXT_TAG indicates the next value yielded by an iterator.
2. _CVT_TERM_TAG indicates that an iterator has run out of values or that a process should terminate.
3. _CVT_FORALL_TAG indicates that the message data is the next value for a worker to use when running the body of a forall loop.

The fourth constant is _CVT_MAX_WORKERS, an upper bound on the number of tasks used when executing a forall loop. Each forall loop may be assigned any number of workers from 1 to _CVT_MAX_WORKERS, and CVT will explore executions of the code with each possible number. While this bounds the number of workers used in any particular forall loop, the use of nested loops, cobegin statements, iterators, etc. yields programs with a high degree of concurrency.

3.2   Iterators

In the CIR model, an iterator is represented as a procedure. The procedure takes the same arguments as the original iterator plus an argument of process type to indicate the calling process. Yield statements are replaced by statements to send the yielded value to the calling process. Before the procedure returns, it sends a termination message to the caller.

```
iter foo(arg0, ..., argN) : T {...; yield e; ...}
```

is translated as

```
void foo(process caller, arg0, ..., argN) {
  ...;
  send(caller, e, _CVT_NEXT_TAG);
  ...;
  send(caller, NULL, _CVT_TERM_TAG);
}
```

When a range literal a..b is used as an iterator, CVT replaces this with a call to a built-in implementation of the range literal as an iterator.

```
iter _CVT_range_iterator(lower : int, upper : int) {
  var current : int;
  current = lower;
  while (current <= upper) {
    yield current;  current = current + 1;
  }
}
```

During model construction, the range literal iterator is then translated like any other user-defined iterator.

3.3   Loops

While loops are straightforward to translate into CIR. The various flavors of for loops have more complicated translations due to their use of iterators and implicit parallelism.

For Loops. Recall that iterators are modeled as procedures that use send statements to yield values to the calling process. When translating a for loop, CVT forks a new process running the iterator, then executes the loop body on each value received from the iterator.

The expression self has type process and returns the ID of the process in which the expression is evaluated.

```
for x in f(...) S
```

is translated as

```
{ T x;  process p;  int tag;
  p = fork f(self, ...);
  while (true) {
    receive(p, x, any(tag));
    if (tag == _CVT_TERM_TAG) break;
    S
  }
}
```

Parallel Loops. Forall loops exhibit the greatest degree of nondeterminism of the for loop varieties. CVT models forall loops as a manager-worker pattern:

```
forall x in f(...) S
```

is translated as

```
{ int numWorkers = 1 + choose(_CVT_MAX_WORKERS);
  int i;  process workers[numWorkers];
  void _CVT_tmp_1(process manager) {
    T x;  int tag;
    while (true) {
      receive(manager, x, any(tag));
      if (tag == _CVT_TERM_TAG) break;
      S
    }
  }
  for (i = 0..numWorkers-1) workers[i] = fork _CVT_tmp1(self);
  { T x;  process iterator;  int tag, dest;
    iterator = fork f(self, ...);
    while (true) {
```

```
    receive(iterator, x, any(tag));
    if (tag == _CVT_TERM_TAG) break;
    dest = choose(numWorkers);
    send(workers[dest], x, _CVT_FORALL_TAG);
  }
  for (i = 0..numWorkers-1)
    send(workers[i], NULL, _CVT_TERM_TAG);
  for(i = 0..numWorkers-1) join workers[i];
  }
}
```

The manager receives values from the iterator and assigns them to workers. All possible numbers of workers between one and _CVT_MAX_WORKERS, inclusive, are explored.

Coforall loops are translated similarly to forall loops, but there is always exactly one worker process for each iteration of the loop.

3.4 Cobegin

For each statement in the body of a cobegin, a new temporary procedure is created. Each temporary procedure takes no arguments and its body contains just the statement from the cobegin. The cobegin statement is then translated into a series of fork statements followed by a series of join statements.

cobegin{S1; ...; SN}

is translated as

```
{ process _CVT_tmp_procs[N];
  void _CVT_tmp_1() {S1} ... void _CVT_tmp_N() {SN}
  _CVT_tmp_procs[0] = fork _CVT_tmp_1();
  ...;
  _CVT_tmp_procs[N-1] = fork _CVT_tmp_N();
  join _CVT_tmp_procs[0]; ...; join _CVT_tmp_procs[N];
}
```

3.5 Sync Variables

A sync variable has additional state information indicating whether it is full or empty. CVT tracks this information by introducing a new boolean-valued control variable (initially *false*) for each sync variable. For a sync variable foo$ (the symbol $ is by convention used in sync variable identifiers, but otherwise has no special meaning), the associated control variable is _CVT_sync_foo$. foo$ = x; is translated as sync-write(_CVT_sync_foo$, foo$, x); and x = foo$; is translated as sync-read(_CVT_sync_foo$, x, foo$);. We introduce additional temporary variables as needed to conform to this syntax.

3.6 Composite Models

To compare two programs, CVT creates a composite CIR model. It does this by creating models for each individual program. Each of these will have a procedure *system* which begins execution and has the outermost scope for that program. CVT then creates a new system procedure. The new system procedure's only task is to fork and join the individual models' system procedures. Variables in the outermost scope of the individual models are moved to the new outermost scope. Any variables with the `extern` modifier are considered to be inputs. Any other variables which are not `const` in the outermost scope are considered to be outputs. When this new model is executed and reaches a terminal state, it checks that all output variables with the same name have the same value.

4   Evaluation

4.1   Tool Characteristics

CVT supports two modes. It can be applied to a single Chapel program to verify (or find counterexamples to) certain safety properties, including absence of deadlocks, out-of-bounds array indexing, division by 0, and uses of uninitialized variables. It may also be used to compare two Chapel programs for functional equivalence. This comparison mode can also detect data races and other inappropriate nondeterminism, as such defects can cause two programs to produce different outputs on the same input. Like TASS, CVT uses symbolic execution to verify properties for all possible input values. When CVT compares two programs, it uses the same symbolic values for corresponding input variables. Thus the values of output variables can be compared at termination to check that they hold equivalent symbolic expressions.

CVT is conservative in its analysis. If it says that a program is correct or that two models are equivalent, then those properties must hold within the bounds specified by the program and `_CVT_MAX_WORKERS`. However, CVT is not necessarily precise: it may produce spurious counterexamples.

4.2   Tool Structure and Implementation

CVT is comprised of several components. These components, and the way data flows between them, are illustrated in Figure 5.

Front End. CVT contains a new front end for the currently supported subset of Chapel. A Java parser generated by the ANTLR parser generator [15] parses the source and builds a Chapel AST. The AST is processed (e.g., adding the range literal iterator implementation) to prepare for conversion to a CIR model.

CVT Model Builder. CVT converts the Chapel AST into a CIR model using the translations discussed in Sec. 3.

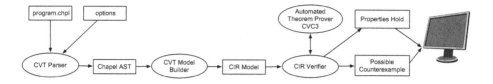

Fig. 5. Dataflow through CVT tool chain

CIR Verifier. The TASS components used by CVT provide a general framework for symbolic execution and utilize an external theorem prover (currently CVC3 [2]). [17] describes several nontrivial numerical programs whose computations are handled by CVC3. CVT defines the state of a CIR model as described above, and also guarded transitions between states. A *simple transition* represents a deterministic move from one state to another. The state is modified based on the statement wrapped by the transition, and there is exactly one resulting state. A *choose transition* provides a nondeterministic choice between a number of values. These are used when a CIR statement utilizes the expression choose(N). In a choose transition, CVT will explore the states resulting from each possible value of the choose expression.

4.3   Partial Order Reduction

The state space explosion problem is a major issue for formal verification of parallel programs. While any parallel code allows statement executions to interleave in many ways, a language such as Chapel provides the added challenge of dynamically creating an unknown number of processes when executing certain statements. Partial order reduction (POR) [9] is a technique to mitigate the state space explosion problem.

There is a well-known POR result for concurrent systems with a simple "local/global" scope hierarchy: suppose that in the search of the state space, some process p is at a local location, i.e., all transitions emanating from that location refer only to variables local to p. Then it is safe to restrict the search to the set of transitions enabled at p.

CVT uses a generalization of this technique. Suppose p is at location l and in dyscope δ. Recall that the set of dyscopes is structured as a tree rooted at δ_0. The outgoing transitions of l may contain expressions which refer to variables in δ or in any dyscope along the path from δ to δ_0. Let δ' be the highest dyscope referred to by the outgoing transitions of l. Suppose no other process can reach (following parent edges from the dyscopes referenced in its call stack) δ'. Then it is safe to restrict the search to transitions enabled in p. For verification of *adderSpec* with $N = 10$, *numTimes* $= 5$, and _CVT_MAX_WORKERS $= 2$ (see §4.4), this POR technique reduced runtime from 15.3s to 0.7s and the number of states encountered from 55331 to 505.

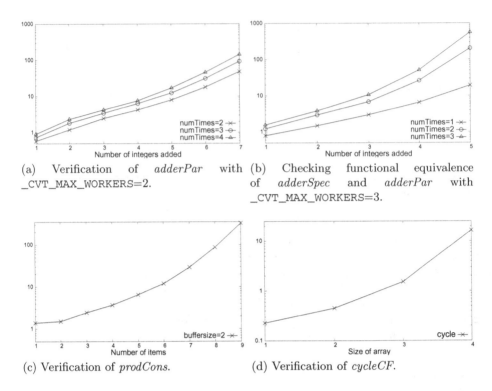

(a) Verification of *adderPar* with (b) Checking functional equivalence
_CVT_MAX_WORKERS=2.   of *adderSpec* and *adderPar* with
                                     _CVT_MAX_WORKERS=3.

(c) Verification of *prodCons*.   (d) Verification of *cycleCF*.

Fig. 6. Results of experiments in which properties were verified to hold. In all graphs, y-axis is total time in seconds.

4.4   Scaling Experiments

We designed several synthetic Chapel programs to test CVT. Each program has several variants. Some variants are believed to be correct, while others contain known defects. While simple, the programs illustrate a number of realistic errors in Chapel codes. Figure 6 summarizes the results of scaling experiments which verified that all checked properties hold. While these results use the POR technique discussed in §4.3, we believe that there are many additional improvements and optimizations that will further improve scaling in the future. Figure 7 provides some statistics for experiments which were able to detect violations. We next describe the sample programs. The code and experimental results are available at http://vsl.cis.udel.edu/cvt.

Adder. This program adds numbers in an array multiple times. The simplest version of the code, *adderSpec*, uses nested for loops. The inner loop sums the numbers, while the outer loop controls the number of times the addition is performed. Another correct version, *adderPar*, uses a forall statement for the inner loop to distribute the addition among multiple tasks. A sync variable is used to store the sum in order to prevent data races. An erroneous version,

Experiment	max workers	states	transitions	max procs	time (s)
adderPar vs *adderNoSync*	20	14495	14496	10	6.260
adderSpec vs *adderND*	2	7675	7819	12	5.027
locks	N/A	5562	5742	5	2.712
cycle	20	1067	1066	4	1.224
prodCons vs *prodConsNoSync*	N/A	3011	3010	6	2.779

Fig. 7. Results of experiments which detect violations, indicating time to produce the first counterexample. Column "max workers" gives the values of _CVT_MAX_WORKERS for that run. The "max procs" column gives the maximum number of active processes at one time during the experiment.

adderNoSync, neglects to make the sum a sync variable. Another erroneous version, *adderND*, replaces the outer for loop with a forall loop; the output then becomes nondeterministic even though synchronization is used correctly.

locks. The *locks* program is a classic deadlock example. A cobegin spawns two processes. Each process runs a loop that tries to acquire and release two locks, but the processes acquire the locks in different orders.

cycle. The *cycle* program in Figure 8 performs reads and writes on a circular array of sync variables. Depending on how the loop iterations are partitioned among tasks, it may deadlock. In particular, *cycle* will deadlock if it is executed using one task. The version *cycleCF* avoids this problem by using a coforall in place of the forall.

```
config const N : int = 100;
var a: [0..N-1] sync int;
proc main() {
  forall i in 0..N-1 {
    var t : int;
    a[(i+1)%N] = i;
    writeln("Wrote ",i);
    t = a[i];
    writeln("Read ",t);
  }
}
```

Fig. 8. The *cycle* program

prodCons. The *prodCons* program implements a producer-consumer pattern. The producer adds items from an input array to a circular buffer of sync variables. The consumer reads items from the buffer. The erroneous version, *prodConsNoSync*, neglects to use sync variables in the buffer.

5   Conclusion and Future Work

We have described a new model for verification of Chapel programs. The parallel constructs and spawning of threads in arbitrary scopes in Chapel map naturally to this model. Using model checking with symbolic execution, we have demonstrated the feasibility of automatic verification and defect-detection for non-trivial Chapel programs.

CVT is a prototype tool which works only on a small subset of the full Chapel language. We would like to extend CVT to cover a larger portion of Chapel. In particular, more complex datatypes and arbitrary domains are interesting directions for future work. We would also like to improve scalability, possibly by developing improved partial order reduction techniques.

References

1. Allen, E., Chase, D., Hallett, J., Luchangco, V., Maessen, J.W., Ryu, S., Steele Jr., G.L., Tobin-Hochstadt, S.: The Fortress language specification, version 1.0 (March 2008), http://labs.oracle.com/projects/plrg/Publications/fortress.1.0.pdf
2. Barrett, C., Tinelli, C.: CVC3. In: Damm, W., Hermanns, H. (eds.) CAV 2007. LNCS, vol. 4590, pp. 298–302. Springer, Heidelberg (2007)
3. Charles, P., Grothoff, C., Saraswat, V., Donawa, C., Kielstra, A., Ebcioglu, K., von Praun, C., Sarkar, V.: X10: an object-oriented approach to non-uniform cluster computing. In: Proceedings of the 20th Annual ACM SIGPLAN Conference on Object-Oriented Programming, Systems, Languages, and Applications, OOPSLA 2005, pp. 519–538. ACM, New York (2005)
4. Clarke, L.A.: A system to generate test data and symbolically execute programs. IEEE Trans. Softw. Eng. 2, 215–222 (1976)
5. Cray, Inc.: The Chapel parallel programming language (2012), http://chapel.cray.com/
6. Demartini, C., Iosif, R., Sisto, R.: dSPIN: A dynamic extension of SPIN. In: Dams, D.R., Gerth, R., Leue, S., Massink, M. (eds.) SPIN 1999. LNCS, vol. 1680, pp. 261–276. Springer, Heidelberg (1999)
7. Dijkstra, E.W.: Guarded commands, nondeterminacy and formal derivation of programs. Commun. ACM 18(8), 453–457 (1975)
8. Flatt, M., PLT: The Racket reference, version 5.3.1, http://docs.racket-lang.org/reference/ (retrieved November 19, 2012)
9. Godefroid, P.: Partial-Order Methods for the Verification of Concurrent Systems. LNCS, vol. 1032. Springer, Heidelberg (1996)
10. Holzmann, G.J.: The SPIN Model Checker. Addison-Wesley, Boston (2004)
11. Khurshid, S., Păsăreanu, C.S., Visser, W.: Generalized symbolic execution for model checking and testing. In: Garavel, H., Hatcliff, J. (eds.) TACAS 2003. LNCS, vol. 2619, pp. 553–568. Springer, Heidelberg (2003)
12. King, J.C.: Symbolic execution and program testing. Communications of the ACM 19(7), 385–394 (1976)
13. Message Passing Interface Forum: MPI: A message-passing interface standard, version 3.0 (September 2012), http://www.mpi-forum.org/docs/docs.html
14. OpenMP Architecture Review Board: OpenMP application program interface, version 3.1 (July 2011), http://www.openmp.org/mp-documents/OpenMP3.1.pdf
15. Parr, T.: ANTLR Parser Generator, http://www.antlr.org
16. Siegel, S.F., Mironova, A., Avrunin, G.S., Clarke, L.A.: Combining symbolic execution with model checking to verify parallel numerical programs. ACM TOSEM 17(2), Article 10, 1–34 (2008)
17. Siegel, S.F., Zirkel, T.K.: TASS: The Toolkit for Accurate Scientific Software. Mathematics in Computer Science 5(4), 395–426 (2011)
18. Yelick, K.A., Semenzato, L., Pike, G., Miyamoto, C., Liblit, B., Krishnamurthy, A., Hilfinger, P.N., Graham, S.L., Gay, D., Colella, P., Aiken, A.: Titanium: A high-performance Java dialect. Concurrency - Practice and Experience 10(11-13), 825–836 (1998)

Formal Analysis of GPU Programs with Atomics via Conflict-Directed Delay-Bounding*

Wei-Fan Chiang[1], Ganesh Gopalakrishnan[1], Guodong Li[2], and Zvonimir Rakamarić[1]

[1] School of Computing, University of Utah, USA
{wfchiang,ganesh,zvonimir}@cs.utah.edu
[2] Fujitsu Labs of America, USA
gli@us.fujitsu.com

Abstract. GPU based computing has made significant strides in recent years. Unfortunately, GPU program optimizations can introduce subtle concurrency errors, and so incisive formal bug-hunting methods are essential. This paper presents a new formal bug-hunting method for GPU programs that combine *barriers* and *atomics*. We present an algorithm called _conflict-directed delay-bounded scheduling algorithm_ (CD) that exploits the occurrence of conflicts among atomic synchronization commands to trigger the generation of alternate schedules; these alternate schedules are executed in a *delay-bounded* manner. We formally describe CD, and present two correctness checking methods, one based on final state comparison, and the other on user assertions. We evaluate our implementation on realistic GPU benchmarks, with encouraging results.

1 Introduction

General purpose Graphics Processing Units ("GPU") are being widely deployed in both low-end (mobile) and high-end (supercomputing) systems in order to accelerate computation [12]. Unfortunately, GPU program optimizations can introduce subtle concurrency errors such as data races and deadlocks. While many tools for formally debugging GPU programs have been proposed [3,14,15, 17,29], none of these tools cater to programs that combine *barriers* and *atomics*—features found in popular GPU programming languages such as CUDA [23] and OpenCL [24]. In this paper, we present an extension of our tool GKLEE [17] to address this program class. The extension is based on a new scheduling algorithm called _conflict-directed delay-bounded scheduling algorithm_ (CD). The subject of this paper is a formal description as well as a thorough evaluation of the CD algorithm on programs that employ CUDA atomics in subtle ways.

While programs employing *barriers* (*e.g.*, `__syncthreads()` in CUDA) and *atomic operations* (*e.g.*, *atomic add, atomic min, compare-and-swap* [11] in CUDA) are not numerous, there are many important programs, including the GPU Gem [22] called *N*-body simulation [19, 21] that use them. In this paper, we

---

* Supported by NSF CCF 1255776, OCI 1148127, and the Microsoft SEIF Award.

G. Brat, N. Rungta, and A. Venet (Eds.): NFM 2013, LNCS 7871, pp. 213–228, 2013.
© Springer-Verlag Berlin Heidelberg 2013

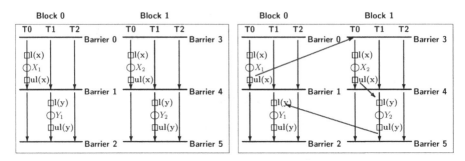

Fig. 1. Basics of CUDA, Thread Blocks, Races, and Conflicts

formally describe CD, and present two correctness checking methods, one based on final state comparison across two schedules, and the other on user assertions. We evaluate our implementation on realistic GPU benchmarks, with encouraging results; we also publicly release our benchmark suite [2].

1.1 Background

Consider a contrived GPU "kernel" program `ArraySum` that employs threads to update each location `a[i]` of an array to the value `a[(N+i-1)%N]+b`:

```
void __global__ ArraySum (int *a, int b) {
  __shared__ int temp[N];
  __syncthreads(); // Barrier 0; also Barrier 3 for threads in [512-1023]
  int idx = blockIdx.x * blockDim.x + threadIdx.x;
  if (idx < N) temp[idx] = a[(N+idx-1)%N] + b;
  __syncthreads(); // Barrier 1; also Barrier 4 for threads in [512-1023]
  if (idx < N) a[idx] = temp[idx];
  __syncthreads(); // Barrier 2; also Barrier 5 for threads in [512-1023]
}
```

CUDA[1] presents three memory spaces: the *Global* space visible to all threads, the *Shared* space visible to threads within a *thread block* (typically 512 contiguous threads, abstractly referred to as `BLOCK_SIZE`), and the *Local* space visible to specific threads.[2] Assume that arrays `a` and `temp` are allocated in the *Shared* memory space. An invocation of kernel `ArraySum` with `N = BLOCK_SIZE` creates `BLOCK_SIZE` threads in block Block 0. Fig. 1 (left) provides a high level illustration of this situation.[3] The use of `__syncthreads()` in this example enforces the fact that threads before the barrier are executed before those after the barrier.

---

[1] Other GPU languages also have similar notions.

[2] CUDA threads are scheduled in batches called *warps*. While the typical warp-size is 32, it is not guaranteed to be so in all situations. In this paper, we take the conservative approach of taking the warp-size to be 1.

[3] Please momentarily ignore `l(x)`, `l(y)`, `ul(x)`, and `ul(y)` of this figure. Also, for simplicity, we highlight only three threads, namely T0, T1, and T2.

For uniformity, we also assume the presence of `__syncthreads()` statements at entry/exit (if not already present). For example, Barrier 0 and Barrier 2 in Fig. 1 (left) illustrate this convention.

Continuing our explanation of kernel `ArraySum`, as per CUDA conventions, all its threads execute the same code; however, each thread computes it own specific location `idx` to act upon. Each thread reads location `(N+idx-1)%N`, adds `b` to the value read, and assigns it to location `idx` of array `temp`. Now, if one were to remove Barrier 1, data races would be introduced; for example, `temp[2] = a[1]` and `a[1] = temp[1]` would be executed in parallel.

Now imagine the *same* kernel being executed concurrently by *twice* as many (*i.e.*, 1,024) threads. The threads are now split between Block 0 and Block 1 (see Fig. 1(left)), and observe that inter-block synchronization through barriers no longer works. For example, even with Barrier 1 and Barrier 4 present, accesses X_1 and X_2 can *conflict* (*i.e.*, involve the same memory location with one of them being a write). Similarly, potential conflicts are also (X_1,Y_2), (Y_1,X_2), and (Y_1,Y_2). Next, imagine that the user has realized "lock" (`l`) and "unlock" (`ul`) instructions using CUDA atomics. (Also, you may now stop ignoring the `l()` and `ul()` instructions in the figure.) Now, if we protect the pair (X_1,X_2) using the same lock variable `x`, we will avoid one data race. Likewise, assuming that (X_1,Y_2) and (Y_1,X_2) involve different addresses, we can protect (Y_1,Y_2) using another lock variable `y`. This will prevent data races among all pairs of accesses.

Following standard terminology (*e.g.*, [10, 27]), we distinguish between *ordinary* and *synchronizing* memory accesses. Two conflicting *synchronization* instructions are *not* involved in a race; however, two conflicting ordinary instructions are involved in a race. For example, lock instructions in Fig. 1 are conflicting, but are not involved in a data race. In general, property checking requires that non-commuting actions [5], such as atomic regions protected by locks, be explored under all interleavings. For illustration, suppose Fig. 1(left) executes the program in the order the barriers are numbered 0 through 5 (thus performing the Y_1 action before the Y_2 action). Then, Fig. 1(right) illustrates a *conflict-directed* alternative schedule in which the order is $Y_2; Y_1$.

Let us now turn to Fig. 2 to understand the basics of scheduling. As it turns out, data races can be detected by running a *single* schedule. In particular, as described in our previous work [17], we can execute a specific sequential schedule [1] shown by the zig-zag lines, running T0, T1,.... We call this schedule the *canonical* schedule. During a canonical schedule, suppose we record every access (read/write), and the (symbolic) path conditions under which the access occurs. Then, at the end of the canonical schedule, we can check for a race as follows. For each access pair containing at least one write, such as (P,Q), we check whether the conjunction of the path conditions can be satisfied, and also whether the address expressions become equal; if so, we report a race. If all access pairs visited along the single (canonical) schedule avoid a conflict, then no other schedule needs to be considered for race checking. Essentially, all schedules are equivalent for finding a *"first race"* [16]. Clearly, the canonical schedule can detect races across thread blocks (such as between (A,B) in the figure) as well.

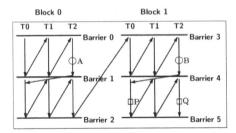 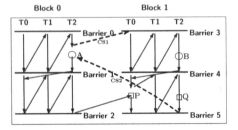

Fig. 2. Illustration of Canonical (left) and CD (right) Scheduling

Historically, it was the canonical scheduling approach that allowed us to extend the KLEE [4] *sequential* program concolic analyzer to handle GPU *concurrency*.

As illustrated previously with respect to Y_1 and Y_2, property checking in the presence of synchronization instructions requires generating alternative schedules of non-commuting actions. Unfortunately, the conflict-directed approach can require us to explore *all possible* orderings of the atomic regions (*e.g.*, similar to dynamic partial order reduction or DPOR [9]). In this context, the CD algorithm can be understood to be a suitable search bounding method inspired by previous work [8], but tailored to handle atomics in the context of canonical scheduling. Assume that we have executed a canonical schedule, and in this schedule we observe a conflict between A and P, with A encountered before P (see Fig. 2 (right)). As per the DPOR algorithm, we will be required to execute another schedule where P is executed before A. However, before we can execute P, we must execute *all* the threads in the barrier interval [3-4] (including instruction B), cross **Barrier 4**, and only then be able to execute P. The CD algorithm has been designed to smoothly handle such details, and also apply bounding.

In summary, the CD algorithm can be seen as a light-weight design that (1) is conflict-directed in its approach to delay-bounding (original paper [8] was not so), (2) is a light-weight approximation to DPOR while also incorporating the barrier semantics and happens-before predecessors, and (3) is built on the backbone of canonical scheduling, allowing us to incorporate other interesting heuristics related to canonical scheduling to improve performance and scalability. In particular, one such technique that enables scalability to a large number of threads is described in our recent work [18].

2 CD Algorithm for Schedule Generation

We now provide a rough sketch of the CD algorithm. Consider Fig. 2, where instructions {A,B,P,Q} are synchronization instructions (e.g., `atomicCAS`, `lock`, `atomicMin`) guarding specific regions of the user code. We first execute the CUDA program along a canonical schedule while checking for data races (among ordinary accesses) as well as recording conflicts among synchronization instructions. These conflicts are inserted into a delay list D,[4] and used to delay threads

---

[4] Later, we will show that D is in fact a list of lists, but for now a simple list suffices.

when the program is re-executed to generate alternate schedules. We now walk through an illustrative CD execution with the help of Fig. 2(left and right).[5] Initially, let list $D = []$ and delay-bound $K = 2$. Anytime $|D| > K$, skip over this D list (details in §4). We present step-by-step several executions of the algorithm.

• First, while executing the initial canonical schedule shown in Fig. 2(left), collect the conflicting pairs, which are (A,B) and (P,Q) in our example. Based on the collected conflict pairs, obtain a list L of *delay points*. The delay points are the first instructions of each conflict pair, where the notion of first is defined by the delaying canonical scheduling order. In our example, we will obtain $L = [A, P]$.

• For each member l of L, append l at the end of D, thus obtaining an augmented D list. In our example, given that we started with $D = []$, the initial augmented D lists are $[A]$ and $[P]$. Now re-execute with D set to $[A]$ and $[P]$ in turn.

• Consider the execution with $D = [A]$. This delays A, switching (via the CS1 arrow) to T0 of Block 1. After we remove A from D, we have $D = []$. Continue the canonical execution of Block 1 entirely (Barrier 3 through Barrier 5). By this time, we would have observed instruction B in Block 1's barrier interval [3-4], and the conflict (P,Q) again. At the end of the execution of T2 at Barrier 5, the execution resumes with A, and then finishes the code between Barrier 1 and Barrier 2. The conflicts observed are (B,A) and (P,Q), and we augment the initial $D = [A]$ with B and P to obtain $D = [A, B]$ and $D = [A, P]$, respectively.

• Re-execute with $D = [A, B]$, which generates the following execution: (1) delay A; (2) go to Block 1 and there delay B; (3) resume by executing A, and then resume with B. This traverses the conflicting instructions in the order A, B, P, Q. *Notice that because of the barrier semantics, we must necessarily cycle over A and B again before we reach into P and Q.*

• Re-execute with $D = [A, P]$. (It is helpful to point out that Fig. 2(right) depicts how CD executes with $D = [A, P]$.) This generates the following execution: (1) execute till A, then delay A; (2) execute through Block 1's Barrier 4; (3) descent into the barrier interval [4-5] of Block 1; (4) delay P since it is now at the head of D; (5) switch via transition CS2 to resume A and finish the barrier interval [1-2] of Block 0; (6) finally, resume at P and finish up Block 1 entirely.

• Since we assumed delay-bound $K = 2$, after exploring the delay list $[A, P]$, we do not augment it any further. (Such augmentations generate 3-instruction delay lists which are skipped.) Instead, we backtrack and re-execute with $D = [P]$. *Implementation note: we process all smaller D sets before going to larger sets.*

The above CD execution achieves several interesting schedules, and in the end we get the following orders of dependent actions in global traces:

− ...; A ;...; B ;...; P ;...; Q ;... (in the run with $D = []$),
− ...; B ;...; P ;...; Q ;...; A ;... (in the run with $D = [A]$),
− ...; A ;...; B ;...; Q ;...; P ;... (in the run with $D = [P]$),
− ...; B ;...; Q ;...; A ;...; P ;... (in the run with $D = [A, P]$).

---

[5] For simplicity, assume here that the same instructions A, B, P, Q will be encountered each time we replay. In general, the control flow will change due to global state differences caused by delaying, and different instructions are likely to be encountered.

```
1  leafid := tree[target] ;
2  if leafid ≠ LOCK then
3  |    leafid := tree[target] ;
4  |    if leafid = atomicCAS(&tree[target], leafid, LOCK) then
5  |    |    assert(leafid ≠ LOCK) ;
6  |    |    tree[target] := func() ;
```

Fig. 3. Code Excerpt from a GPU Implementation of the N-Body Algorithm

A precise formal specification of CD is in §4. Next, we present a case study and assess how well CD performs on it.

3   Motivating Example

In this section, we motivate the need for CD with a realistic example: an aggressively optimized GPU-based implementation of the well-known Barnes-Hut algorithm for performing an N-body simulation [21]. The pseudocode shown in Fig. 3 is a variant of the original code excerpt containing a bug planted by us. In the example, each thread tries to insert a node into a tree structure (encoded by *tree* array) where *target* is

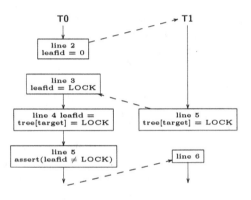

Fig. 4. Schedule Revealing N-Body Bug

the index of the intended insertion. It is possible for multiple threads to have the same *target*. Variable *leafid* contains the value pointed by *target* in *tree*; if this value is $LOCK$, then the target location is currently unavailable for modification. Note that line 3 is the extraneous line—a bug—not present in the original code. It presents a redundant read from *tree[target]* that had already been done on line 1. The value read is used by the consequent *atomicCAS*.

The central operation of our interest is *atomicCAS(addr, expected, new)* which atomically: (1) checks whether *addr* holds the *expected* value; (2) if so, it replaces it with *new*, else it leaves the value in *addr* unaffected; (3) it always returns the original value in *addr*. In the example, *atomicCAS* instruction on line 4 tries to put $LOCK$ in *tree[target]* and returns the original value in *tree[target]*. Once a thread succeeds on condition in line 4 and proceeds to line 5, it exclusively owns *tree[target]* until it releases the ownership by assigning to it on line 6. Therefore, the old value of *tree[target]* should not be $LOCK$ on line 5; if it were, it would mean that the location is already owned by another thread. We consider this to be our safety property of interest, and we encoded it as an assertion on line 5.

Fig. 4 shows why the code in Fig. 3 is erroneous. Suppose that threads T0 and T1 are accessing the same target, whose value was initialized to 0. Thread T0 first executes lines 1-2, then is delayed, and preempted by T1. Thread T1 executes lines 1-5, then is delayed, and preempted by T0. Thread T0 on line 3 reads *leafid* from *tree[target]*; since its value is *LOCK*, after T0 executes line 3, *leafid* is *LOCK*. (If buggy line 3 was not introduced, *leafid* would still be a non-*LOCK* value thanks to the conditional on line 2.) Then, T0 proceeds to line 4 and *atomicCAS* succeeds even though it has also succeeded for T1. On line 5, T0 triggers a failure of our safety property of interest. Note that this error takes at least two delays to be discovered. As our experimental results will show, our implementation of CD was successful in detecting such bugs within a reasonable number of overall delays and with acceptable runtimes.

4   Formal Description of CD

Let $\mathbb{N} = \{0, 1, 2, \ldots\}$ where numbers can also be viewed as sets, *e.g.*, $3 = \{0, 1, 2\}$. Consider a CUDA program *pgm* meant for execution within $BID \in \mathbb{N}$ thread blocks. Let $barid \in \mathbb{N}$ number the barriers within each block, with $lastbar(bid) \in \mathbb{N}$ being the number assigned to the last barrier within block $bid \in BID$.[6] A barrier interval (BI) is the interval (block of code) enclosed by two successive barriers. There are $TID \in \mathbb{N}$ threads per block with identifiers $tid \in TID$. For each thread, let $pc \in \mathbb{N}$ be its program counter.

We employ the tuple $cs = \langle bid, barid, tid, pc \rangle$ to specify the control state of execution. The way in which cs advances is depicted in Fig. 2. A canonical schedule begins at $InitCS = \langle 0, 0, 0, 0 \rangle$. (Here, $barid = 0$ models being in barrier interval [0-1].) Predicate $DoneBar(bid, barid, tid)$ tells whether thread tid has executed barrier $barid$ within block bid. This predicate is initialized to $InitDoneBar$ where $InitDoneBar(0, 0, 0)$ is true.

The entire state of the execution of *pgm* is captured by cs and S, where S is the data state (CUDA shared, global, and local variables). We do not elaborate on S, nor the CUDA instructions that update S. We maintain $S0$, a shadow copy of the initial data state used during program re-execution. Given the current instruction $ins = cur(S, cs, pgm)$, the state update of S caused by ins is modeled using $nxt(S, pgm, cs, ins)$.

Consider a CUDA program *pgm*, and let ins be Bar (barrier) for all S and cs. Informally speaking, a canonical schedule that begins in this state moves each thread until its pc is at the next barrier; then another thread is picked, and so on until all threads are at their next barrier. Whenever a thread is at the next barrier, the $DoneBar$ predicate associated with that thread and barrier is set to true. When all the threads are at their next barrier, execution must switch over to the "next" barrier interval, determined as $nxtBI(S, pgm, cs)$. Any reasonable implementation of these abstract functions is permissible. For instance, $nxtBI$ could mean either (1) *stay within the same thread block and execute the next sequential barrier interval*; or (2) *switch over to the next thread block and execute the earliest unexecuted barrier interval*.

---

[6] CUDA programs are assumed to be terminating. We also assume the usual *textually aligned* barriers. For example, CUDA programs are expected not to branch on thread IDs, with only half the threads encountering a barrier.

Delay List: Let $[a, b, c]$ be a list. Then $hd([a, b, c])$ is a and $tl([a, b, c])$ is $[b, c]$. We maintain the delay list D as a list of lists.[7] For example, $D = [[], [a, b, c], [p, q, r]]$, where a, b, c and p, q, r are instructions, is a delay list.

We describe the operational semantics of CD in terms of the rules in Fig. 5. The rules are of the form $\frac{pre}{\Sigma \to \Sigma'}$, where if $pre(\Sigma)$ holds then Σ can evolve to Σ'; Σ is maintained as $\langle S0, S, cs, DoneBar, D0, D, RW, Confl \rangle$, where $cs = \langle bid, barid, tid, pc \rangle$. The CD algorithm starts with $D = [[]]$. If no conflicts are encountered, D remains $[[]]$ until the entire program execution is finished, at which point D becomes $[]$. The only inference rule provided for the case $D = []$ is to stop the entire execution of CD (Rule TERMINATION). We keep a shadow-copy of the starting delay list in $D0$. Suppose $D0 = D = [[]]$ at the beginning, and say it grows to $D = [[a, b], [p, q]]$ at the end of execution as per the CD schedule. We then re-initialize $D0$ and D according to $D0 = D = [[a, b], [p, q]]$ and re-execute the whole program. Here are the details of such a re-execution:

- When instruction a is encountered, it will be delayed, and D will be updated to $[[b], [p, q]]$, meaning that a (already delayed) need not be delayed any more. (Rules NXTTIDCSDEL and NXTBIDCS cover these cases.)
- Thereafter when b is encountered, it is delayed, and D is updated to $[[], [p, q]]$. Then (and only then) we start recording conflicts (Rule NXTPCBI$_{rec}$; notice that it checks for $hd(D) = []$). This is because the conflicts recorded must be as a consequence of delaying a, b (and further conflicts discovered in the process will later augment D). At the end of the entire *pgm* execution, let us say we have encountered conflicts in the order (i, j) and (k, l). Then we update D to $[[p, q], [a, b, i], [a, b, k]]$ (Rule RETRIG).
- Now if the delay bound K is 2, we will execute again with $[p, q]$, but skip over $[a, b, i]$ and $[a, b, k]$ (Rule BOUND).

Read-Write Set: We maintain a read-write set RW that records all reads and writes encountered; function $rwOf(ins)$ obtains the reads and writes of instruction ins. These will be used for race checking and also for forming conflicts. (We do not detail race checking here.) Entries will be added to RW as/when memory accesses (reads/writes) are encountered (Rule NXTPCBI).

Conflict List: We maintain a conflict list *Confl* as a list of pairs of the kind shown above, *e.g.*, $Confl = [(i, j), (k, l)]$. *Confl* is updated via function *rec* only when $hd(D) = []$ (Rule NXTPCBI$_{rec}$). At the end of *pgm*, we will change $D0$ from $[[a, b], [p, q]]$ to $[[p, q], [a, b, i], [a, b, k]]$.

Delay Bounding, Termination, Retriggering: Whenever $length(hd(D0)) > K$, we update D to $tl(D)$, which achieves delay bounding (Rule BOUND). The algorithm terminates when $D = D0 = []$ (Rule TERMINATION). On the other hand, if $D \neq []$, $length(hd(D0)) \leq K$, and $DoneBar(bid, lastbar(bid), tid)$ for all bid, tid, we retrigger the execution with the augmented (function *aug*) D and

---

[7] In our implementation, we maintain D sorted ascending in size. This allows all shorter delay sequences to be executed before executing any longer delay sequence. This is purely a heuristic, and has no bearing on the overall correctness of CD.

- TERMINATION:

$$\frac{D = []}{\langle S0, S, cs, DoneBar, D0, D, RW, Confl \rangle \rightarrow STOP}$$

- BOUND:

$$\frac{D \neq [] \ \wedge \ length(hd(D0)) > K}{\langle S0, S, cs, DoneBar, D0, D, RW, Confl \rangle \rightarrow \langle S0, S, cs, DoneBar, tl(D0), tl(D), RW, Confl \rangle}$$

Assume $D \neq [] \ \wedge \ length(hd(D0)) \leq K$ is a part of the precondition of the rules below.

- RETRIG:

$$\frac{\forall b \in BID : \ \forall t \in TID : \ DoneBar(b, lastbar(b), t) \ \wedge \ D1 = aug(D0, Confl)}{\langle S0, S, cs, DoneBar, D0, D, RW, Confl \rangle \rightarrow \langle S0, S0, InitCS, InitDoneBar, D1, D1, \emptyset, [] \rangle}$$

- NXTBI:

$$\frac{cur(S, cs, pgm) = \mathsf{Bar} \ \wedge \ \forall t \in TID \setminus \{tid\} : \ DoneBar(bid, barid + 1, t)}{\wedge \ Db = DoneBar[\langle bid, barid + 1, tid \rangle \leftarrow true]}{\langle S0, S, cs, DoneBar, D0, D, RW, Confl \rangle \rightarrow \langle S0, S, nxtBI(S, pgm, cs), Db, D0, D, RW, Confl \rangle}$$

- NXTTIDCS:

$$\frac{cur(S, cs, pgm) = \mathsf{Bar} \ \wedge \ \exists t \neq tid \in TID : \ \neg DoneBar(bid, barid + 1, t)}{\wedge \ Db = DoneBar[\langle bid, barid + 1, tid \rangle \leftarrow true] \ \wedge \ cs1 = nxtTidCS(S, pgm, cs)}{\langle S0, S, cs, DoneBar, D0, D, RW, Confl \rangle \rightarrow \langle S0, S, cs1, Db, D0, D, RW, Confl \rangle}$$

- NXTPCBI:

$$\frac{hd(D) \neq [] \ \wedge \ ins = cur(S, cs, pgm) \ \wedge \ ins \neq \mathsf{Bar}}{\wedge \ ins \neq hd(hd(D)) \ \wedge \ cs1 = nxtPCBI(S, pgm, cs) \ \wedge \ RW1 = add(RW, rwOf(ins))}{\langle S0, S, cs, DoneBar, D0, D, RW, Confl \rangle \rightarrow \langle S0, S, cs1, DoneBar, D0, D, RW1, Confl \rangle}$$

- NXTTIDCSDEL:

$$\frac{hd(D) \neq [] \ \wedge \ cur(S, cs, pgm) = hd(hd(D)) \ \wedge \ cs1 = nxtTidCS(S, pgm, cs)}{\wedge \ \exists t \neq tid \in TID : \ \neg DoneBar(bid, barid, t) \ \wedge \ D1 = D[hd(D) \leftarrow tl(hd(D))]}{\langle S0, S, cs, DoneBar, D0, D, RW, Confl \rangle \rightarrow \langle S0, S, cs1, DoneBar, D0, D1, RW, Confl \rangle}$$

- NXTBIDCS:

$$\frac{hd(D) \neq [] \ \wedge \ cur(S, cs, pgm) = hd(hd(D)) \ \wedge \ cs1 = nxtBidCS(S, pgm, cs)}{\wedge \ \forall t \in TID \setminus \{tid\} : \ DoneBar(bid, barid, t) \ \wedge \ D1 = D[hd(D) \leftarrow tl(hd(D))]}{\langle S0, S, cs, DoneBar, D0, D, RW, Confl \rangle \rightarrow \langle S0, S, cs1, DoneBar, D0, D1, RW, Confl \rangle}$$

- NXTPCBI$_{rec}$:

$$\frac{hd(D) = [] \ \wedge \ ins = cur(S, cs, pgm) \ \wedge \ ins \neq \mathsf{Bar}}{\wedge \ cs1 = nxtPCBI(S, pgm, cs) \ \wedge \ Confl1 = rec(Confl, RW, rwOf(ins))}{\langle S0, S, cs, DoneBar, D0, D, RW, Confl \rangle \rightarrow \langle S0, S, cs1, DoneBar, D0, D1, RW, Confl1 \rangle}$$

Fig. 5. Operational Semantics of the CD Algorithm

$D0$, with cs reset to $InitCS$, S to $S0$, $DoneBar$ to $InitDoneBar$, RW to $\emptyset$, and $Confl$ to $[]$ (Rule RETRIG).

Setting $DoneBar$: When $cur(S, cs, pgm)$ equals Bar, we update $DoneBar$ to true for $\langle bid, barid + 1, tid \rangle$, and cs to $nxtBI(S, pgm, cs)$ (Rules NXTBI, NXTTIDCS).

Staying within a BI upon Delay: If $cur(S, cs, pgm) = hd(hd(D))$, we set D to $D[hd(D) \leftarrow tl(hd(D))]$, *i.e.*, $hd(D)$ is replaced with $tl(hd(D))$ in D. Now, if there is a *tid* for which $DoneBar(bid, barid, tid)$ is false, we stay in the same BI and use function $nxtTidCS(S, pgm, cs)$ to update cs (Rule NXTIDCSDEL).

Moving over to Another BI upon Delay: When $DoneBar$ is true of all the threads except a thread *tid*, and this thread is delayed, we move over to the next block in the scheduling order. Such a block must exist because (1) we are replaying a schedule already traversed before, but with an instruction to delay, (2) we recorded the *first* part of a conflict pair, (3) which means there is another instruction (conflict partner in the pair) that is "yet to be seen", and (4) we will hit that instruction. Our selection policy in this case is to context-switch to the next *bid* (in a modulo fashion) and the lowest *barid* such that for that *bid*, *barid*, there is a lowest ranked *tid* for which $DoneBar$ is false. We will use function $nxtBidCS(S, pgm, cs)$ to return this control state (Rule NXTBIDCS).

5 Experimental Results

We have implemented CD in an extension of our tool GKLEE called $GKLEE_{atm}$. $GKLEE_{atm}$ was evaluated using the following CUDA benchmarks [2]: **nbody:** the classical Barnes-Hut N-body algorithm [21], [260 LOC]; **tsp:** traveling salesman algorithm [28], [130 LOC]; **aMin:** implements atomicMin for double-precision floating point, [20 LOC]; **aMinUpdate:** use of atomicMin to set a shared location to min, [35 LOC]; **bintree:** tree insertion designed similar to wait-free ray tracing cache [7], [75 LOC]. The N-body (nbody) and traveling salesman (tsp) benchmarks are real-life CUDA programs; others are synthetic benchmarks we modeled after real programs. We created both bug-free and buggy versions for each benchmark. Each buggy benchmark contains a non-trivial realistic bug related to a potential algorithm implementation error. We also inserted assertions for checking correctness, which is a commonly used approach by programmers. The first four benchmarks (nbody, tsp, aMin, aMinUpdate) contain *lost-atomicity* bugs similar to the bug shown in §3. Such bugs are commonly created by programmers when they are trying to prevent side-effects of preemptions using atomics, but fail at their attempt. Our last benchmark, bintree, contains a *missing-atomicity* bug caused by unprotected shared memory accesses. In the experiments, we test two versions of $GKLEE_{atm}$ with different conflict selection policies: (1) unoptimized picks any detected conflict to trigger the generation of a new schedule; (2) optimized picks conflicts containing at least one read/write belonging to a "conditional atomic operation" such as atomicCAS.

For all of our benchmarks a delay bound of $K = 2$ was sufficient. We performed two sets of experiments with two different CUDA configurations: (1) 2 thread-blocks with each of them containing one thread, and (2) 3 thread-blocks with

benchmark	buggy						bug-free					
	unoptimized			optimized			unoptimized			optimized		
	#sch.	t.	rlt.	#sch.	t.	rlt.	#sch.	t.	rlt.	#sch.	t.	rlt.
nbody(pa)	221	910	TP	64	182	TP	356	1134	TN	106	271	TN
nbody(fc)	44	278	TP	17	52	TP	356	1231	TN	106	295	TN
tsp(pa)	4	40	TP	4	40	TP	39	432	TN	27	293	TN
tps(fc)	4	41	TP	4	40	TP	39	426	TN	27	297	TN
aMin(pa)	25	28	TP	25	28	TP	53	57	TN	53	57	TN
aMin(fc)	4	5	TP	4	7	TP	53	56	TN	53	57	TN
aMinUpdate(pa)	18	32	TP	10	11	TP	51	81	TN	27	33	TN
aMinUpdate(fc)	18	32	TP	10	11	TP	51	88	TN	27	34	TN
bintree(pa)	83	90	FN	53	56	FN	83	90	TN	66	66	TN
bintree(fc)	2	3	FP	2	3	FP	2	3	FP	2	3	FP

(a) Experimental Results for 2 Thread-Blocks with 1 Thread Each

benchmark	buggy						bug-free					
	unoptimized			optimized			unoptimized			optimized		
	#sch.	t.	rlt.	#sch.	t.	rlt.	#sch.	t.	rlt.	#sch.	t.	rlt.
nbody(pa)	448	2414	TP	126	429	TP	1195	4900	TN	336	1019	TN
nbody(fc)	83	606	TP	28	126	TP	1195	5366	TN	336	1137	TN
tsp(pa)	4	53	TP	4	56	TP	114	1738	TN	60	1019	TN
tps(fc)	4	55	TP	4	55	TP	114	2331	TN	60	1091	TN
aMin(pa)	107	117	TP	107	117	TP	431	463	TN	431	463	TN
aMin(fc)	6	7	TP	6	7	TP	431	464	TN	431	465	TN
aMinUpdate(pa)	6	8	TP	5	5	TP	653	912	TN	294	361	TN
aMinUpdate(fc)	6	7	TP	4	5	TP	653	882	TN	294	350	TN
bintree(pa)	14	17	TP	191	202	FN	835	902	TN	405	431	TN
bintree(fc)	2	3	FP	2	3	FP	2	3	FP	2	3	FP

(b) Experimental Results for 3 Thread-Blocks with 1 Thread Each

Fig. 6. Experimental Results. *pa* tags benchmarks with manually inserted assertions for correctness checking; *fc* tags benchmarks where final state comparison is performed for correctness checking; *#sch.* gives number of schedules explored; *t.* gives runtimes in seconds; *rlt.* gives analysis results.

each of them containing one thread. Other configurations were not necessary due to the high symmetry of CUDA programs.

5.1 Results and Discussion

Our experimental results are shown in Fig. 6. The result (*rlt.*) column shows the outcome of the analysis:

- true-positive (TP): a true bug was reported (successful detection);
- true-negative (TN): no bug reported, none exists (no false alarm or omission);
- false-positive (FP): a bug was reported, but no error exists (false alarm);
- false-negative (FN): no bug was reported, but a real bug exists (omission).

Note that none of these bugs can be detected using previous tools due to the lack of support for atomic operations.

Comparison between Different Thread Configurations. Benchmarks in Fig. 6a use fewer blocks/threads than those of Fig. 6b. Using fewer blocks generates fewer conflicts and therefore also fewer schedules to explore. However, using the two-block configuration for the bintree benchmark results in GKLEE$_{atm}$ missing a bug, since bintree requires at least three threads to trigger the bug scenario.

```
 1  while true do
 2      if T[curr] ≠ null then
 3          if T[curr] ≤ val then  child := curr+2 ;
 4          else child := curr+1 ;
 5          if T[child] = null then
 6              new := atomicAdd(&TSize, 3) ;
 7              T[new] := val ;
 8              T[child] := new; break ;
 9          else curr := T[child] ;
10      else
            if null = atomicCAS(&T[curr], null, val) then break ;
11  assert(the tree is valid and connected) ;
```

Fig. 7. Pseudocode Showing a Bug in our bintree Benchmark

Next we further elaborate why our bintree benchmark bug requires at least three threads to be discovered.

Fig. 7 gives an abstraction of our bintree kernel. The tree is encoded as usual into an array T, where three consecutive elements in T denote a node. The first of these elements is the value of the node (hence the index of this element is also the index of the node). The value of the second element is the index of the left subtree (node), which contains all values less than the value of the current node. The value of the third element is the index of the right subtree (node), which contains all values greater than or equal to the value of the current node. In the pseudocode, $curr$ denotes the index of the current traversed node, $child$ denotes the index of the subtree to visit, and new denotes the index of a newly created node. Lines 2-9 perform tree traversal and the insertion of new nodes, lines 3-4 decide which subtree to traverse, and lines 5-8 insert a new node into an empty subtree. Line 9 sets the current traversed index to continue the tree traversal. The introduced bug is on line 8 where the user should have used an *atomicCAS* operation to update $T[child]$ and continue the tree traversal upon failure. The buggy code instead directly updates the tree, resulting in dangling nodes.

Fig. 8 illustrates a buggy scenario where T0 builds the root node (line 10), and T1 and T2 are concurrently attempting to insert a value (val) into the tree. Suppose that T0 has value 1 to insert, T1 has value 2, and T2 has value 3. First, T0 runs through the code and generates the root node. Then, T1 traverses the tree and decides to insert value 2 in the right subtree of the root node. However, it is

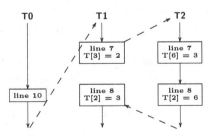

Fig. 8. Schedule Revealing bintree Bug

preempted just before line 8. Thread T2 then traverses the tree and inserts value 3 in the right subtree of the root node. When T1 resumes, it overwrites the right subtree with value 2. The final tree is (1, 3, null, 2, null, null, 3, null, null). The node (3, null, null) is a dangling node and the tree is not connected. Note that while this scenario has 3 context-switches, it requires just one delay (of T1) to be discovered.

Comparison between Different Conflict Selection Policies. We observe that using the optimized strategy explores fewer schedules and produces the same results as the unoptimized strategy, except for bintree under the three-block configuration. The most remarkable savings are obtained for the nbody kernel: our conflict selection optimization reduces the number of schedules to explore by nearly a third (221 versus 64 in Fig. 6a), while producing the same test outcomes. However, in general, this optimization might prune a certain "critical conflict" necessary to trigger a schedule leading to a bug. For example, in Fig. 6b, the bug in bintree can only be detected without conflict selection optimization. The "lost atomicity" bug in this example pertains to two instances of line 8 in Fig. 7. In a sense, since the programmer "forgot" to guard $T[child] = new$ on line 8 with an atomic construct, these lines are in a real data race.

Comparison between Different Correctness Checking Strategies. Our two correctness checking strategies, fc and pa, produce different outcomes on 3 of our benchmarks: bintree, aMin, and nbody. In particular, fc produces a false positive outcome for bintree in all experiments. This is because the bintree benchmark inherently produces two distinct states (*i.e.*, bit-level state layouts) even for two logically equivalent trees. Therefore, checking correctness by simply comparing final states will end up generating a false alarm for GPU programs that generate nondeterministic bit-state outcomes (which are nevertheless logically equivalent). In contrast, for aMin and nbody, the fc strategy shows distinct advantages, often exploring only a fifth of the number of schedules (*e.g.*, 448 versus 83 for nbody) before finding a bug. Our results suggest that the final state comparison strategy is better overall in terms of the number of schedules that get explored before a bug is reached.

6   Discussion, Related Work, and Conclusions

GKLEE$_{atm}$ is the first tool we know that employs the combination of conflict-directed and delay-bounded testing. Its CD algorithm extends the canonical scheduling method which has already proven successful [17]. Since the intended semantics of most CUDA programs is sequential, race/conflict freedom is the norm. In these cases, we avoid generating interleavings. GKLEE$_{atm}$ also inherits additional features of GKLEE (*e.g.*, test-case generation, test-case reduction, bank conflict and memory coalescing estimation) that are now available for examples that employ CUDA atomics.

CD is not formally complete. For example, the initial canonical schedule in §2 gave us the delay points $[A, P]$. Suppose we had executed the sequential schedule that began with thread T2 of Block 1, we would initially encounter $[B, Q]$. At that point, the control flows may change, and instead of seeing $[P, A]$ later, we may see some other conflicting operations (or perhaps no conflicts at all). Our future work may combine static analysis with CD to determine which other sequential schedules to consider. The manner in which CD is realized using the abstract functions $nxtTidCS$, $nxtBidCS$, $nxtBI$, and $nxtPCBI$ gives us the intriguing possibility of choosing these functions based on static analysis or randomizing them for separate runs. In the paper, we have explored prioritizing atomics involving conditional comparisons, such as atomicMin (see §5).

Race-Directed Testing. Race-directed testing for traditional multithreaded programs was proposed previously [25, 26]. It detects races in a schedule and takes them as "hints" for introducing context-switches, which in turn generate more schedules for detecting property violations. $GKLEE_{atm}$ extends race-directed testing with delay-bounding, and selects a subset of races suitable for testing CUDA programs with atomic operations.

Bounded Testing. Bounded testing is a well-known technique for analysis of traditional multithreaded programs (e.g., [8, 13, 20]). It was empirically shown that most of concurrency bugs can be detected by introducing only a limited amount of nondeterminism (e.g., context-switches, delays). $GKLEE_{atm}$ takes this approach to efficiently detect bugs in CUDA programs, and mixes it with our conflict-directed feedback for obtaining new delay locations. Traditional bounded testing typically does not employ such feedback and blindly introduces delays at all potential conflict locations.

GPU Program Testing Tools. Recently, several GPU program testing tools were proposed [3, 6, 14]. Test amplification [14] starts with dynamic testing of GPU programs, but employs a test amplification technique to generalize the results of the dynamic analysis over a large space of inputs. The amplification relies on a static information flow analysis to prune inputs not affecting the property to be verified. GPUVerify [3] performs symbolic analysis of GPU programs similar to PUG [15], but provides a precise CUDA operational semantics for predicated executions. KLEE-CL [6] employ symbolic analysis to perform equivalence checking for C programs and their accelerated OpenCL implementations. KLEE-CL can also check data race for OpenCL programs. However, none of these tools support atomic instructions.

Conclusions. We propose the first conflict-directed delay-bounding approach to schedule multithreaded programs. We formally describe our CD algorithm that implements this approach as a new tool $GKLEE_{atm}$, and apply it for testing aggressively optimized GPU programs that employ atomic instructions and barriers. Furthermore, we evaluate several scheduling policies and property checking approaches. In addition to detecting subtle concurrency bugs, CD proves to be a light-weight and tailorable approximation to more complete (but also more expensive) algorithms such as DPOR. Our future work will include exploiting thread symmetry [18] and informing concolic verification through static analysis.

References

1. Attiya, H., Guerraoui, R., Hendler, D., Kuznetsov, P., Michael, M.M., Vechev, M.: Laws of order: expensive synchronization in concurrent algorithms cannot be eliminated. In: POPL, pp. 487–498 (2011)
2. http://www.cs.utah.edu/fv/CdDb
3. Betts, A., Chong, N., Donaldson, A.F., Qadeer, S., Thomson, P.: GPUVerify: a verifier for GPU kernels. In: OOPSLA, pp. 113–132 (2012)
4. Cadar, C., Dunbar, D., Engler, D.R.: KLEE: Unassisted and automatic generation of high-coverage tests for complex systems programs. In: OSDI (2008)
5. Clarke, E.M., Grumberg, O., Peled, D.A.: Model Cheking. MIT Press (1999)
6. Collingbourne, P., Cadar, C., Kelly, P.H.J.: Symbolic testing of openCL code. In: Eder, K., Lourenço, J., Shehory, O. (eds.) HVC 2011. LNCS, vol. 7261, pp. 203–218. Springer, Heidelberg (2012)
7. Debattista, K., Dubla, P., dos Santos, L.P.P., Chalmers, A.: Wait-free shared-memory irradiance caching. Comp. Graphics and Applications 31(5), 66–78 (2011)
8. Emmi, M., Qadeer, S., Rakamarić, Z.: Delay-bounded scheduling. In: POPL, pp. 411–422 (2011)
9. Flanagan, C., Godefroid, P.: Dynamic partial-order reduction for model checking software. In: POPL, pp. 110–121 (2005)
10. Goetz, B., Bloch, J., Bowbeer, J., Lea, D., Holmes, D., Peierls, T.: Java Concurrency in Practice. Addison-Wesley Longman, Amsterdam (2006)
11. Herlihy, M., Shavit, N.: The Art of Multiprocessor Programming (2008)
12. Hwu, W.-M.W.: GPU Computing Gems Emerald Edition (2011)
13. Lal, A., Reps, T.: Reducing concurrent analysis under a context bound to sequential analysis. Form. Methods Syst. Des. 35(1), 73–97 (2009)
14. Leung, A., Gupta, M., Agarwal, Y., Gupta, R., Jhala, R., Lerner, S.: Verifying GPU kernels by test amplification. In: PLDI, pp. 383–394 (2012)
15. Li, G., Gopalakrishnan, G.: Scalable SMT-based verification of GPU kernel functions. In: FSE, pp. 187–196 (2010)
16. Li, G., Li, P., Sawaya, G., Gopalakrishnan, G., Ghosh, I., Rajan, S.: GKLEE technical report, http://www.cs.utah.edu/fv/GKLEE/gklee_tr.pdf
17. Li, G., Li, P., Sawaya, G., Gopalakrishnan, G., Ghosh, I., Rajan, S.P.: GKLEE: concolic verification and test generation for GPUs. In: PPOPP (2012)
18. Li, P., Li, G., Gopalakrishnan, G.: Parametric flows: Automated behavior equivalencing for symbolic analysis of races in CUDA programs. In: SC (2012)
19. Méndez-Lojo, M., Burtscher, M., Pingali, K.: A GPU implementation of inclusion-based points-to analysis. In: PPOPP, pp. 107–116 (2012)
20. Musuvathi, M., Qadeer, S.: Iterative context bounding for systematic testing of multithreaded programs. In: PLDI, pp. 446–455 (2007)
21. CUDA implementation of the tree-based Barnes-Hut N-body algorithm, http://www.gpucomputing.net/?q=node/1314
22. Nguyen, H.: GPU Gems 3, 1st edn. Addison-Wesley Professional (2007)
23. Nvidia. CUDA parallel computing platform, http://www.nvidia.com/object/cuda_home_new.html
24. OpenCL. OpenCL - the open standard for parallel programming of heterogeneous systems, http://www.khronos.org/opencl

25. Sen, K.: Race directed random testing of concurrent programs. In: PLDI (2008)
26. Sen, K., Agha, G.: A race-detection and flipping algorithm for automated testing of multi-threaded programs. In: Bin, E., Ziv, A., Ur, S. (eds.) HVC 2006. LNCS, vol. 4383, pp. 166–182. Springer, Heidelberg (2007)
27. Sorin, D.J., Hill, M.D., Wood, D.A.: A Primer on Memory Consistency and Cache Coherence (2011)
28. http://www.cs.txstate.edu/~burtscher/research/TSP_GPU/
29. Zheng, M., Ravi, V.T., Qin, F., Agrawal, G.: GRace: a low-overhead mechanism for detecting data races in GPU programs. In: PPOPP, pp. 135–146 (2011)

Bounded Lazy Initialization

Jaco Geldenhuys[1], Nazareno Aguirre[2,4],
Marcelo F. Frias[3,4], and Willem Visser[1]

[1] Computer Science Division, Department of Mathematical Sciences,
Stellenbosch University, Private Bag X1, 7602 Matieland, South Africa
{jaco,wvisser}@cs.sun.ac.za
[2] Department of Computer Science, FCEFQyN, Universidad Nacional de
Río Cuarto (UNRC), Argentina
naguirre@dc.exa.unrc.edu.ar
[3] Department of Computer Engineering, Instituto Tecnológico de
Buenos Aires (ITBA)
mfrias@itba.edu.ar
[4] National Scientific and Technical Research Council (CONICET), Argentina

Abstract. Tight field bounds have been successfully used in the context of bounded-exhaustive bug finding. They allow one to check the correctness of, or find bugs in, code manipulating data structures whose size made this kind of analyses previously infeasible. In this article we address the question of whether tight field bounds can also contribute to a significant speed-up for symbolic execution when using a system such as Symbolic Pathfinder. Specifically, we propose to change Symbolic Pathfinder's lazy initialization mechanism to take advantage of tight field bounds. While a straightforward approach that takes into account tight field bounds works well for small scopes, the lack of symmetry-breaking significantly affects its performance. We then introduce a new technique that generates only non-isomorphic structures and consequently is able to consider fewer structures and to execute faster than lazy initialization.

1 Introduction

Many techniques have been devised in order to determine to what extent a software artifact is correct. Testing [1], for instance, is one of these techniques. Two main reasons justify the place testing occupies in most software development projects: it is lightweight, and it is scalable. The downside, as is well-known, is that testing only allows one to detect errors that occur when code is executed on the tested inputs. In order to achieve greater guarantees of software correctness, more conclusive program analysis techniques have to be considered. For instance, bounded verification [7] and model checking [2] guarantee that no errors can be exhibited on significantly larger input sets (i.e., on that part of the input state space that was successfully explored by the corresponding technique), compared to testing. This is achieved, of course, at the expense of scalability. Therefore, improving the scalability of the latter analysis techniques is a *must*.

G. Brat, N. Rungta, and A. Venet (Eds.): NFM 2013, LNCS 7871, pp. 229–243, 2013.

Bounded exhaustive verification automatically checks code correctness, but subject to a *scope*, consisting of a maximum number of iterations and object instances for the classes involved [7,4,5]. Therefore, if the technique is successful in verifying code, it does not guarantee absolute correctness, but correctness within the established scope (i.e., no errors exist that require at most the established maximum number of iterations, and involve at most the established number of object instances). As shown in [5], by appropriately bounding the values that class fields can take, bounded exhaustive verification based on SAT-solving can be significantly improved. In particular, field bounds allowed bounded exhaustive verification to significantly increase data domains scopes for analysis, and to detect bugs that other tools based on bounded verification, model checking, or SMT-solving failed to detect [5]. Here, we explore whether by using field bounds one can also improve the scalability of symbolic execution of structures, as performed by Symbolic PathFinder (SPF) [10], an extension of Java PathFinder (JPF).

The field bounds considered in this work are the *tight bounds* computed by the approach in [5], which uses the structural invariants of the classes under analysis (the so-called repOK). Intuitively, by changing SPF's lazy initialization approach [8], where all possible aliasing possibilities are explored, to only take into account those included in pre-computed field bounds, considerably fewer structures should be considered. Interestingly, as the results for binary search trees in Section 5 show, this intuition holds for structures up to 6 nodes, but then lazy initialization starts to perform better. As it will be discussed later on, it turns out that the benefit of considering fewer options for each reference to be lazily initialized is outweighed by the fact that the bounded approach considers isomorphic structures whereas lazy initialization does not. That is, although lazy initialization constructs many structurally invalid structures, they are quickly pruned by repOK, whereas in the bounded case duplicate (isomorphic) valid structures are considered throughout the analysis and are never pruned.

The above problem is overcome by a new algorithm, introduced in this paper, that not only bounds lazy initialization, but also produces only non-isomorphic structures. This algorithm can be shown to strictly consider fewer structures than lazy initialization, since it behaves similarly except that some aliasing options are not considered. This algorithm constitutes the main contribution of the paper.

Contributions. In this paper we make the following contributions:

1. We study of the usefulness of field bounds in the context of symbolic execution of structures.
2. We show that symmetry-breaking, as a mechanism to prevent considering isomorphic structures, is important for efficiency.
3. We propose an algorithm that incorporates field bounds with symmetry breaking into symbolic execution, and implement it within SPF.
4. We assess the above on three classic data structures: linked lists, binary trees and red-black trees.

Structure of the article. In Sections 2 and 3, we introduce and discuss field bounds and lazy initialization, respectively. In Section 4 we present the notion of *Bounded Lazy Initialization*, and introduce both a straightforward algorithm for it, and a more efficient one that performs symmetry-breaking. In Section 5, we present experimental results showing that, on a relevant data structures benchmark, bounded lazy initialization with symmetry breaking scales better than standard lazy initialization. In Section 6 we discuss related work, and in Section 7 we present our conclusions and proposals for future work.

2   Tight Field Bounds and Program Analysis

Bounded program verification was introduced in [7] as a technique for bug detection. In [4,5] it is implemented by translating Java code annotated with contracts to a propositional formula, which is solved using a SAT-solver. This approach requires the engineer to provide a *scope*, consisting of a maximum number of iterations and object instances for the classes involved [7,4,5]. The existence of a satisfying valuation for the formula can then be traced back to an execution exhibiting an erroneous behavior (unhandled exception or contract violation) within the provided scope. If no valuation is found, we know that the method is *correct within the prescribed scope*.

The encoding of bounded program correctness as a satisfiability problem involves interpreting programs in terms of relations. Given a class C, a class field f of type C' defined in C can be semantically interpreted, in a given program state, as a total function f mapping object references from C (the semantic domain associated with class C), to C' (the domain associated with class C'). That is, in a given program state, f can be seen as a binary relation contained in $C \times C'$. Notice that properties of the state may make some tuples of $C \times C'$ infeasible as part of the interpretation of a field f. In particular, if the state is assumed to satisfy certain representation invariant (e.g., the states prior to the execution of the code under analysis are assumed to satisfy a precondition, which would include the wellformedness of the inputs), all tuples corresponding to ill-formed structures will necessarily be out of the semantic interpretation of f in that state. For instance, in linked lists, if the representation invariant indicates that lists must be acyclic, then tuples of the form $\langle N, N \rangle$, with $N \in Node$ (the semantic domain associated with the Node class) cannot belong to *next* (the semantic interpretation of next), if the corresponding state is assumed to satisfy the invariant.

The above observation about infeasible tuples in fields' semantic domains can be enhanced if one is able to prevent isomorphic structures via symmetry-breaking. Symmetry breaking enforces a canonical ordering on the way references are stored in the model of the memory heap used during analysis. In [5], a mechanism for automatically defining symmetry-breaking predicates, for any Java class, is introduced. These predicates force assigning node references to structures following a breadth-first ordering. Figure 1 shows examples of the ordering for singly linked lists and binary trees. The ordering imposed by symmetry-breaking predicates prevents some references from being connected. For instance, in a list, a node reference N_i can only point (through field next) to N_{i+1} or the

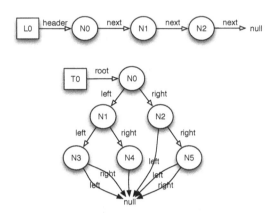

Fig. 1. Node ordering for list-like and tree-like data structures

value null, if symmetry-breaking is imposed. Similarly, reference N_0 can only point through field left to N_1 or the value null (any other candidate would violate the breadth-first ordering). If we instead consider field right, N_0 can point to N_1 (only in case N_0.left = null), N_2, or null.

Also in [5], the notion of *tight field bound* is introduced. Tight field bounds allow us to remove from fields' semantic domains the tuples that are infeasible due to representation invariants and symmetry-breaking, and lead to exponential speed-ups in analysis. Let us describe this notion. Let us consider a class C and a field f in C, of type C' (i.e., declared as C' f). A *scope* determines sets C and C' of object instances of classes C and C', respectively (e.g., if the scope for class Node is 3, then $Node = \{N_0, N_1, N_2\}$). Notice that the scope does not determine the set of objects live at a specific runtime configuration, but rather the runtime objects in any configuration. A sample scope would be, for instance, 7 Node (e.g., for performing a bounded verification on all linked lists, or binary search trees, composed of up to 7 nodes). Consider the lattice of binary relations $\langle \mathcal{P}(C \times (C' \cup \{\texttt{null}\})), \subseteq \rangle$ (disregard null if C' is a basic type). A *tight bound* for field f is a member U_f of $\mathcal{P}(C \times (C' \cup \{\texttt{null}\}))$ in which all pairs must belong to some semantic interpretation for field f. Since the semantic interpretations might be constrained by certain state properties (e.g., representation invariants or symmetry breaking predicates), some tuples might necessarily be out of tight field bounds.

As an example, consider scope 4 Node for acyclic linked lists with symmetry-breaking. Then, relation

$$\{(N_0, N_1), (N_0, \texttt{null}), (N_1, N_2), (N_1, \texttt{null}), (N_2, N_3), (N_2, \texttt{null}), (N_3, \texttt{null})\}$$

is a tight bound for field next. Similarly, relation

$$\{(N_0, N_1), (N_0, \texttt{null}), (N_1, N_2), (N_1, N_3), (N_1, \texttt{null}), (N_2, N_3), (N_2, \texttt{null}), (N_3, \texttt{null})\}$$

is a tight bound for field `left` of binary search trees, under scope 4 `Node`. We invite the reader to refer to Figure 1 to verify that pair (N_0, N_2), for instance, cannot belong to the tight bounds for fields `next` (resp., `left`) of linked lists (resp., binary search trees) under symmetry breaking.

To take advantage of tight field bounds, these must be computed prior to actual program analysis. In [5], an effective distributed algorithm for computing tight field bounds is presented. The implementation, that is designed using a master/slave architecture, allows for the removal, from the field's semantic domain, of those pairs that cannot belong to any valid instance that satisfies the symmetry breaking-induced ordering and other constraints such as a representation invariant. Precomputing field bounds contributes to the scalability of analysis, since bounds only depend on the class, its invariant and the scope, but are independent from the code of the method under analysis. Also, once the bounds are computed, they are stored in a bounds database, and often reused. For instance, the same bound can be used for the analysis of all the methods in a class, and for different kinds of analysis (verification, test input generation, etc.). Therefore, the cost of computing bounds is amortized by their frequent use.

3   Lazy Initialization

Lazy initialization [8] is a technique for symbolic execution especially tailored for handling complex, possibly unbounded data structures. Symbolic execution begins with uninitialized field values and, along symbolic execution of a method m, class fields are initialized only when they are accessed. Whenever a (previously uninitialized) field f for an existing object o is accessed, the lazy initialization for o.f takes place. When o.f is a reference to an instance of object type, the following possibilities are, non-deterministically, considered:

- o.f may take the value `null`,
- o.f may refer to an already existing object,
- o.f refers to a new object.

This is formalized in the algorithm presented in Figure 2, extracted from [8]. In order to make the contribution of this paper more clear we separate the above choices into a function called *options()* which will be adapted in the following sections.

3.1   A Running Example

Let us consider the algorithm in Figure 3. This algorithm searches for an integer value stored in a `TreeSet`. It returns the node that stores the valuer, if the value is stored in the `TreeSet`, or it returns `null` otherwise. Figure 4 portrays 13 out of the 57 structures generated by the Lazy Initialization mechanism along the symbolic execution of method `Contains` (we present those structures where only fields `root` or `left` are being initialized). In Section 4, where we introduce *Bounded Lazy Initialization*, we will come back to this example in order to compare the number of generated structures.

```
if (f is uninitialized) {
    if (f is a reference field of type T) {
        nondeterministically initialize f to each element of options()
        if (method precondition is violated) {
            backtrack()
        }
    }
    if (f is primitive (or string) field) {
        initialize f to a new symbolic value of appropriate type
    }
}
```

function options()
    return the set consisting of
      1. `null`
      2. a new object of class T (with uninitialized field values)
      3. every object created during a prior initialization of a field of type T

Fig. 2. Lazy Initialization Algorithm

4   Bounded Lazy Initialization

Bounded Lazy Initialization profits from the existence of pre-computed tight field bounds in order to prune the state space exploration performed by lazy initialization even further. Let us consider an object o and a field f such that $o.f$ is next to be lazily initialized. For the sake of intuition, consider the partially initialized `TreeSet` from Figure 5, with $o = N_1$ and $f = $ `left`. According to Figure 2, the following possibilities arise during lazy initialization:

- $o.f = $ `null`,
- $o.f = N_2$, with N_2 a new uninitialized node, or
- $o.f$ may refer to N_0 or N_1.

The tight bound for `TreeSet` field `left` with up to 3 nodes is

$$\{(N_0, \mathtt{null}), (N_0, N_1), (N_1, \mathtt{null}), (N_2, \mathtt{null})\} \ .$$

Out of the 4 alternatives that would be explored using lazy initialization, only one is feasible according to the bound, namely, initializing $o.f = $ `null`. The remaining options introduce tuples to field `left` that were already deemed infeasible by the bound pre-computation. Certainly, initializing $o.f = N_0$ or $o.f = N_1$ leads to a cyclic structure, and therefore these initializations are correctly prevented by the bounds. Even more interesting, $o.f = N_2$ is also prevented since the resulting structure would become unbalanced, with no nodes remaining to regain the balance. It is worth noticing that tight field bounds capture these subtleties that elude lazy initialization.

```
public TreeSetNode Contains(int key) {
        TreeSetNode p = root;
        while (p != null) {
            if (key == p.key) {
                    return p;
            }
            else if (key < p.key) {
                    p = p.left;
            }
            else {
                    p = p.right;
            }
        }
        return null;
}
```

Fig. 3. Method `Contains` from class `TreeSet`

Unlike lazy initialization, bounded lazy initialization bounds the size of the generated structures. Lazy initialization produces partially initialized structures that eventually have to be made concrete. The concretization process may require generating a structure that, because of its size, exceeds the capabilities of the concretization technique. Therefore, whenever possible, keeping the size of the structures under control is beneficial for analysis.

Bounded Lazy Initialization modifies the lazy initialization algorithm by filtering those initializations that are incompatible with the tight field bounds. In Section 4.1 we present a first approach to Bounded Lazy Initialization that is particularly useful for explaining the concept, as well as for exposing a limitation that is later on addressed, in Section 4.2.

4.1 First Approach: Initializing from Bounds

The first algorithm for Bounded Lazy Initialization is given in Figure 6. When a field f has to be initialized, the algorithm allows one to consider all the options provided by the tight bound for field f. In Figure 7, we show all the structures produced by Bounded Lazy Initialization during the symbolic execution of method `Contains` (cf. Figure 3). There are clear differences with the outcome of lazy initialization (cf. Figure 4). The reduction on the number of generated structures (57 for lazy initialization versus 13 for its bounded version) is obviously significant. Besides, as argued above, this "pruning" is sound, since the structures that are no longer produced by the bounded lazy initialization procedure stand no chance of satisfying the class invariant.

An important property of lazy initialization is that no isomorphic partially initialized structures are ever generated. Therefore, no obviously redundant structures are being produced. When we move to bounded lazy initialization, this

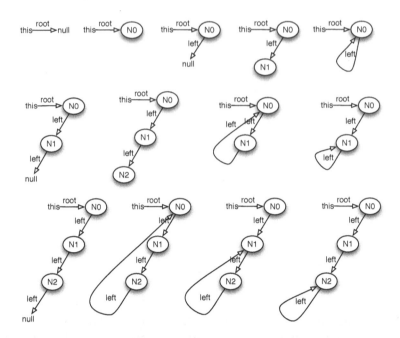

Fig. 4. Some of the structures generated by lazy initialization along the symbolic execution of method `Contains`

property is lost. Notice in particular that in Figure 7, the 6th and the 7th partially initialized structures (also shown on the left side of Figure 8) are indeed isomorphic (also the 10th and 12th as well as 11th and 13th). Unfortunately, the number of isomorphic structures grows to a point where the advantage of using the bounds is seriously reduced. In Section 4.2 we present an alternative approach that follows the same intuition, yet avoids producing isomorphic partially initialized structures.

4.2   Second Approach: Regaining Full Symmetry Breaking

Let us analyze the 6th and 7th structures from Figure 7 (see left part of Figure 8). The reason for having these two isomorphic initialization alternatives for N_0.`right` is that by making use of the information provided by the tight bound for field `right`, the options for this field, for node N_0, are `null`, N_1, or N_2. However, it is not necessary to consider two different "non-null" initializations. In order to avoid these isomorphic structures, we will use sets of references as labels for nodes in the partially initialized structure. Figure 8 illustrates how the structures get merged into a common structure under this new approach. The intuition is the following: *each node is labeled with a set of references that can be reached by traversing the fields, and are compatible with the tight field bounds.* The new algorithm for bounded lazy initialization is presented in Figure 9.

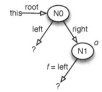

Fig. 5. A partially initialized `TreeSet` instance

Input: Receiver object this, and field **f**
Input: Tight bound U_f for field **f**
  function options()
     return $\{t : \text{T such that (this}, t) \in U_f\}$

Fig. 6. The Bounded Lazy Initialization algorithm (version 1)

Let us consider a node n in the partially initialized structure whose label set is N. Let **f** be the field that has to be initialized, and let U_f be its tight bound. Since U_f is a binary relation, we can compute $N' = N; U_f$ (N' is then the set of all images of elements in N, with respect to relation U_f). As it was the case for lazy initialization, the new algorithm also considers three cases, whose discussion follows:

- If $\text{null} \in N'$, there must be a reference $r \in N$ such that $\langle r, \text{null} \rangle \in U_f$. Therefore, there may be a concrete structure instance in which $n.\text{f} = \text{null}$. Thus, **null** is a candidate definition that has to considered. Equally important, if $\text{null} \notin N'$ there cannot be any node pointing to **null**. Therefore, **null** does not need to be considered. Notice that the lazy initialization algorithm *always* evaluates the possibility of using **null**.
- If N' contains some reference, then we consider adding a new node to the structure. Notice that if $N' = \{\text{null}\}$, we do not add a new node. This decision, consistent with the tight bound information, prunes options that are unnecessarily considered by the lazy initialization algorithm.
- In lazy initialization, the third case initializes **f** as pointing to previously introduced nodes. But, if N' does not intersect the label set for a previously introduced node m, it is not possible (due to the bound induced constraints), that $this.\text{f} = m$. This prunes initialization options that are currently considered by lazy initialization.

Notice that no isomorphic partially initialized structures can ever be generated. This immediately follows from the fact that we are generating structures in the same order lazy initialization does, yet we are skipping (probably many) initializations. If we use the algorithm from Figure 9, out of the 13 partially initialized structures considered in Figure 7 only 10 remain.

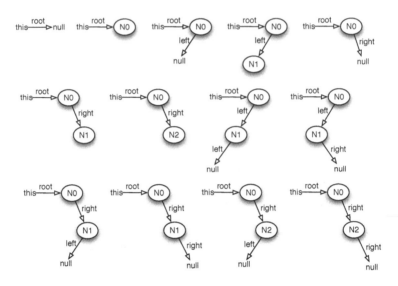

Fig. 7. The 13 structures generated by Bounded Lazy Initialization along the symbolic execution of method `Contains`

5   Evaluation

The bounded lazy initialization algorithms described in the previous section were implemented in Symbolic PathFinder [10], and compared to the already-implemented lazy initialization algorithm. Three data structures are used to illustrate the performance of the new approach:

- **LList:** An implementation of sequences based on singly linked lists;
- **BSTree:** A binary search tree implementation from [14]; and
- **TreeSet:** An implementation based on red-black trees as found in `java.util`.

They cover linear and tree-like structures. Since the number of partially initialized structures generated during bounded lazy initialization strongly depends on the cardinality of the tight bounds, it is relevant to analyze the impact of the technique on heavily constrained structures (such as `TreeSet`, where tight bounds are smaller) and on less constrained structures (such as `BSTree`).

5.1   Experimental Setting

Tight field bounds were not computed as part of our experiments. Instead, precomputed databases for the data structures were reused. Computing tight field bounds, as put forward in [5], requires checking, via SAT solving, the feasibility of each tuple in the corresponding field's semantic domain. Thus, a high number of SAT queries, which depends on the scope, must be performed. However, these checks are all independent from one another, and therefore are subject to

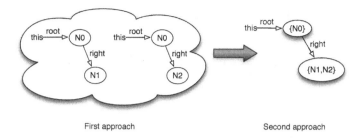

First approach   Second approach

Fig. 8. From isomorphic partially initialized structures to a single partially initialized structure

Input: Receiver object this, with node set N as label
Input: Tight bound U_f for field f
  function options()
    Let N' be the node set $N; U_f$. **return** the set
      1. null, if null belongs to N'
      2. a new object of class T (with uninitialized field values), if $N' \setminus \{\texttt{null}\} \neq \emptyset$
      3. every object created during a prior initialization of a field of
         object type T whose label node set intersects with N'

Fig. 9. The Bounded Lazy Initialization algorithm (version 2)

parallelization. Indeed, in [5] the approach to compute tight field bounds uses a cluster. As a sample, the time required to compute tight bounds for lists, binary search trees and red black trees using the approach in [5] is 68:53, 00:38 and 02:51 (in minutes and seconds, mm:ss), for scopes 100, 12 and 12, respectively, and using a cluster of 16 quad-core PCs. These scopes exceed those used in this paper, and therefore the corresponding tight bound computation times serve as upper bounds of the actual times for the experiments in the paper. Each PC in the cluster had two Intel Dual Core Xeon 2.67 GHz processors, a 2 MB L2 cache, and 2 GB of RAM. The cluster used Debian GNU/Linux (kernel 2.6.18-6) and the Argonne National Laboratory's MPICH2 for message-passing.

The results reported in the rest of this section were computed on an Apple MacBook Pro with a 2.3 GHz Intel i5 processor with 4 Gb of memory, running the Mac OS X 10.8.2 operating system and the Darwin 12.2.0 kernel.

5.2   Experimental Results

Each experiment explores the execution of repOK(t) on a symbolic data structure t with n nodes. The value of n is a parameter for the experiments. The repOK routine checks that t satisfies the constraints on the wellformedness of the corresponding data structure; for example, in the implementation of TreeSet, repOK makes sure that t is a valid binary search tree, that node parent pointers are

Table 1. Experimental results for `LList`

		LI		BLI1			BLI2	
n	unique	explored	time	explored	duplicates	time	explored	time
1	1	2	<00:01	1	0	<00:01	1	<00:01
10	10	74	<00:01	19	0	<00:01	19	<00:01
100	100	5 249	00:02	199	0	<00:01	199	<00:01

Table 2. Experimental results for `BSTree`

		LI		BLI1			BLI2	
n	unique	explored	time	explored	duplicates	time	explored	time
1	1	4	<00:01	2	0	<00:01	2	<00:01
2	3	21	<00:01	10	0	<00:01	11	<00:01
3	8	82	<00:01	36	1	<00:01	44	<00:01
4	22	306	<00:01	145	9	<00:01	164	<00:01
5	64	1 140	00:01	668	61	00:01	639	00:01
6	196	4 275	00:02	3 554	393	00:02	2 464	00:01
7	625	16 144	00:04	21 165	2 523	00:05	9 604	00:03
8	2 055	61 332	00:09	140 996	16 927	00:17	35 695	00:06
9	6 917	234 154	00:29	1 030 989	119 747	01:43	136 260	00:16
10	23 713	897 596	01:44	8 259 479	908 563	13:47	516 376	00:53
11	82 499	3 452 526	06:34	–	–	–	1 972 260	03:12

correct, and that the red-black color constraints are satisfied, resulting in a balanced tree. As `repOK` traverses the data structure, the fields are initialized using the lazy, bounded lazy, and the symmetry-breaking bounded lazy techniques.

Tables 1, 2, and 3 (for `LList`, `BSTree`, and `TreeSet`, respectively) show the number of structures explored, and the execution times (in minutes and seconds, mm:ss). The last two tables show only those experiments that completed in less than 30 minutes. The results for `LList` in Table 1 do not convey much information. The first two columns show the value of n (the number of nodes) and the number of unique data structures of this size. As expected, these values are identical in the case of `LList`. The next three major columns show the results for the LI (lazy initialization), BLI1 (the first bounded lazy initialization), and BLI2 (the second bounded lazy initialization) techniques. The times, shown in columns 4, 7, and 9, are negligible. The values in columns 3, 5, and 8 are the number of choices made during the exploration according to the algorithms in Figures 2, 6, and 9, respectively. Because the last two values are bounded, not many such choices are explored; LI is entirely unconstrained and make all possible choices. Nevertheless, the times remain small.

The results for `BinTree` show a different case, since the number of choices is much larger, and the `repOK` implementation is more involved. Up to $n = 6$, LI makes more choices because it is not constrained by bounds. However, at $n = 7$ it is overtaken by BLI1 in this regard, because of the number of duplicates the latter explores. The number of duplicates explored (over and above the unique

Table 3. Experimental results for `TreeSet`

n	unique	LI explored	LI time	BLI1 explored	BLI1 duplicates	BLI1 time	BLI2 explored	BLI2 time
1	2	4	00:01	2	0	<00:01	2	<00:01
2	4	27	<00:01	20	2	<00:01	15	<00:01
3	7	110	00:01	22	1	<00:01	21	<00:01
4	15	409	00:01	90	1	00:01	101	00:01
5	29	1 509	00:04	239	14	00:02	158	00:01
6	49	5 610	00:08	1 231	58	00:05	883	00:04
7	84	21 043	00:27	7 636	178	00:23	4 715	00:13
8	148	79 530	02:14	51 291	576	03:13	16 146	00:53
9	270	302 402	11:51	267 750	1 775	27:11	39 583	02:59
10	518	–	–	–	–	–	149 133	17:11

structures) is given in the middle column of the table. This extra work is also reflected in the execution times. The BLI2 technique explores fewer choices than either LI and BLI1, meaning that it can analyze significantly more structures in the same amount of time. This same trend is also clear in the case of `TreeSet`.

6   Related Work

Constraint based bounded verification has its origins in [7], where a translation from annotated code to SAT is proposed, and off-the-shelf SAT-solvers are used in order to determine the existence of bugs in the code under analysis. Several articles suggest improvements over [7]. For instance, [12] uses properties of functional relations to improve Java code analysis, and provides improvements for integer and array analyses. Bounded verification can be performed modularly, as shown in [4]. In [5], the use of tight field bounds allowed us to improve bounded verification significantly.

Symbolic execution [9] is a technique for program analysis that executes a path in the program control flow graph using symbolic values. During the symbolic execution, conditions from branching statements are conjoined into a *path condition*. The satisfaction of the path condition allows one to create inputs that exercise the symbolically executed path. Lazy initialization [8] is an optimization of symbolic execution where dynamically allocated data structures are partially initialized on demand, deferring the initialization process as much as possible. Dynamic symbolic execution [6] (also called *concolic* execution), uses concrete executions to guide the symbolic execution phase.

Symbolic execution and bounded verification were combined in [11]. Symbolic execution was used to build path conditions that were later on solved using bounded verification. Bounds have also been used in the context of symbolic execution; tools like Kiasan [3] and Symbolic Pathfinder [10] bound the length of reference chains. In [13] symbolic execution was used to generate tests for containers similar to those used here. Various different approaches were used for test generation, including symbolic execution of repOK(), but no bounds were considered. All the techniques that resort to symbolic execution may profit from using a mechanism such as, bounded lazy initialization, as defined in this paper.

7 Conclusions and Future Work

Tight field bounds have been successfully used in the context of bounded-exhaustive bug finding, in order to increase this analysis' scalability. In this paper, we studied whether field bounds can also contribute to improve the efficiency of symbolic execution. We showed not only that field bounds can be employed to improve the symbolic execution of structures, but also that symmetry breaking, as a mechanism to prevent considering isomorphic structures, is important for efficiency. We proposed two algorithms that incoporate field bounds into Symbolic Pathfinder's lazy initialization, resulting in what we call *bounded lazy initialization*. The first is a straightforward extension of lazy initialization to take into account field bounds, whereas the second prevents the generation of isomorphic structures. We carried out experiments with classic data structure implementations, that show the usefulness of our approach, and the importance of avoiding generating isomorphic structures.

The presented approach requires pre-computing tight bounds for the fields of the program under analysis. Computing tight field bounds, as put forward in [5], requires a high number of satisfiability queries, which are independent and therefore are subject to parallelization. So, a cluster is used to compute these bounds. We are working on alternative, more efficient, ways of computing tight bounds. In particular, we are currently developing tight bound computation mechanisms that can be run on a single workstation, with an efficiency comparable to the approach in [5], but which may lead to less precise bounds.

We used symbolic execution on the repOK() method, to analyze the effectiveness of using field bounds. This can be used, e.g., to generate all valid structures (within a provided scope), to be employed later on for testing. Moreover, since the repOK() method typically uses all fields of a structure, it does not have any bias towards particular visits of the analyzed structures. A different approach, that we plan to explore, would be to symbolically execute the code under analysis, and then to check which valid structures are required. This would produce structures without necessarily having to instantiate all their parts. The contribution of tight field bounds in such contexts might be different from what we obtained in this work, so we plan to evaluate our approach in such scenarios.

Acknowledgements. The authors would like to thank the anonymous referees for their helpful comments. This work was partially supported by the Argentinian Ministry of Science and Technology and the South-African Department of Science and Technology, through grant MINCyT-DST SA1108; by the Argentinian Agency for Scientific and Technological Promotion (ANPCyT), through grants PICT PAE 2007 No. 2772 and PICT 2010 No. 1690; and by the MEALS project (EU FP7 programme, grant agreement No. 295261).

References

1. Ammann, P., Offutt, J.: Introduction to Software Testing. Cambridge University Press (2008)
2. Clarke Jr., E.M., Grumberg, O., Peled, D.A.: Model Checking. MIT Press, Cambridge (1999)
3. Deng, X., Lee, J., Robby: Bogor/Kiasan: A k-bounded symbolic execution for checking strong heap properties of open systems. In: Proceedings of the 21st IEEE/ACM International Conference on Automated Software Engineering, ASE 2006, pp. 157–166. IEEE Computer Society, Washington, DC (2006)
4. Dennis, G., Yessenov, K., Jackson, D.: Bounded verification of voting software. In: Shankar, N., Woodcock, J. (eds.) VSTTE 2008. LNCS, vol. 5295, pp. 130–145. Springer, Heidelberg (2008)
5. Galeotti, J.P., Rosner, N., Pombo, C.L., Frias, M.F.: Analysis of invariants for efficient bounded verification. In: Proceedings of the 19th International Symposium on Software Testing and Analysis, pp. 25–36 (July 2010)
6. Godefroid, P., Klarlund, N., Sen, K.: DART: directed automated random testing. In: Proceedings of the 2005 ACM SIGPLAN Conference on Programming Language Design and Implementation, PLDI 2005, pp. 213–223. ACM, New York (2005)
7. Jackson, D., Vaziri, M.: Finding bugs with a constraint solver. In: Proceedings of the 2000 ACM SIGSOFT International Symposium on Software Testing and Analysis, ISSTA 2000, pp. 14–25. ACM, New York (2000)
8. Khurshid, S., Păsăreanu, C.S., Visser, W.: Generalized symbolic execution for model checking and testing. In: Garavel, H., Hatcliff, J. (eds.) TACAS 2003. LNCS, vol. 2619, pp. 553–568. Springer, Heidelberg (2003)
9. King, J.C.: Symbolic execution and program testing. Commun. ACM 19(7), 385–394 (1976)
10. Păsăreanu, C.S., Rungta, N.: Symbolic PathFinder: symbolic execution of Java bytecode. In: Proceedings of the IEEE/ACM International Conference on Automated Software Engineering, ASE 2010, pp. 179–180. ACM, New York (2010)
11. Shao, D., Khurshid, S., Perry, D.E.: Whispec: white-box testing of libraries using declarative specifications. In: Proceedings of the 2007 Symposium on Library-Centric Software Design, LCSD 2007, pp. 11–20. ACM, New York (2007)
12. Vaziri, M., Jackson, D.: Checking properties of heap-manipulating procedures with a constraint solver. In: Garavel, H., Hatcliff, J. (eds.) TACAS 2003. LNCS, vol. 2619, pp. 505–520. Springer, Heidelberg (2003)
13. Visser, W., Pasareanu, C.S., Khurshid, S.: Test input generation with Java PathFinder. In: Avrunin, G.S., Rothermel, G. (eds.) ISSTA, pp. 97–107. ACM (2004)
14. Visser, W., Păsăreanu, C.S., Pelánek, R.: Test input generation for Java containers using state matching. In: Pollock, L.L., Pezzè, M. (eds.) Proceedings of the ACM/SIGSOFT International Symposium on Software Testing and Analysis, pp. 37–48. ACM (July 2006)

From UML to Process Algebra and Back: An Automated Approach to Model-Checking Software Design Artifacts of Concurrent Systems

Daniela Remenska[1,3], Jeff Templon[3], Tim A.C. Willemse[2], Philip Homburg[1],
Kees Verstoep[1], Adria Casajus[4], and Henri Bal[1]

[1] Dept. of Computer Science, VU University Amsterdam, The Netherlands
[2] Dept. of Computer Science, TU Eindhoven, The Netherlands
[3] NIKHEF, Amsterdam, The Netherlands
[4] Universitat de Barcelona, Spain

Abstract. One of the challenges in concurrent software development is early discovery of design errors which could lead to deadlocks or race-conditions. For safety-critical and complex distributed applications, traditional testing does not always expose such problems. Performing more rigorous formal analysis typically requires a model, which is an abstraction of the system. For object-oriented software, UML is the industry-adopted modeling language. UML offers a number of views to present the system from different perspectives. Behavioral views are necessary for the purpose of model checking, as they capture the dynamics of the system. Among them are sequence diagrams, in which the interaction between components is modeled by means of message exchanges. UML 2.x includes rich features that enable modeling code-like structures, such as loops, conditions and referring to existing interactions. We present an automatic procedure for translating UML into mCRL2 process algebra models. Our prototype is able to produce a formal model, and feed model-checking traces back into any UML modeling tool, without the user having to leave the UML domain. We argue why previous approaches of which we are aware have limitations that we overcome. We further apply our methodology on the Grid framework used to support production activities of one of the LHC experiments at CERN.

Keywords: formal methods, software engineering, UML.

1 Introduction

As modern software systems become more complex and distributed, a major challenge is faced in maintaining their quality and functional correctness. Early discovery of design errors which could lead to deadlocks, race-conditions and other flaws, before they can surface, is of a paramount importance. The Unified Modeling Language (UML) [1] has become the lingua franca of software engineering, in particular for the domain of object-oriented systems. Over time, several mature CASE tools have already adopted UML as the industry-standard visual modeling language for describing software systems. However, use of these tools alone does not assure the correctness of the design, nor does it provide direct means to test the software under design. For safety-critical

G. Brat, N. Rungta, and A. Venet (Eds.): NFM 2013, LNCS 7871, pp. 244–260, 2013.
© Springer-Verlag Berlin Heidelberg 2013

and complex distributed applications, traditional testing does not always expose such problems. Performing more rigorous formal analysis typically requires a model, which is an abstraction of the system. In the last decades, more rigorous methods and tools for modeling and analysis have been proposed. Despite the research effort, these methods are still not widely accepted in industry. One problem is the lack of expertise and the necessary time investment in the OO development cycle, for becoming proficient in them. A more substantial problem is the lack of a systematic connection between actual implementation and the semantics of the existing formal languages.

To bridge the gap between industry-adopted methodologies based on UML software designs, and the sophisticated analysis, verification and optimization tools, several approaches have been proposed for automated extraction of the necessary analysis models from the UML artifacts. For instance, Petri Nets [2, 3], Layered Queuing Networks [4] and stochastic process algebras [5, 6] are used for performance analysis. Model checking for certain properties of the system is often done via translation into process algebra [7, 8]. Automatic synthesis of functional test cases from UML models is possible as well [9, 10]. Model-to-model transformations can also be done within the UML domain itself, for the purpose of model optimization or refactoring [11]. In each of these cases, the translation is mediated by defining graph-transformation rules between the meta models of UML and the target language.

A UML model of a system is typically a combination of multiple views. Devising an automated transformation methodology requires that behavioral views of the system be available. The static views of a system (such as Class and Deployment UML diagrams) are rarely sufficient to extract the necessary information for constructing a target model for meaningful analysis. Activity, Sequence, and State Machines are among the most commonly used behavioral diagrams for this purpose. State Machines (SM) represent the reaction of individual objects on different stimuli; they are suitable for describing specific parts of systems, such as a critical control component, but are very rarely used [8] as the sole paradigm for developing large distributed object-oriented systems. Developers almost never create a fully-formed object a-priori and in isolation, with all the behavior that the object will ever need. Activity Diagrams (AD) describe the system at a higher level of abstraction, where objects and message exchanges are not captured. They represent workflows of activities, with support for choice and concurrency, and are commonly used for business process modeling. Sequence Diagrams (SD) provide the most fine-grained runtime view of the system. They model a set of interacting objects by means of message-exchanges over time. These diagrams contain information about the control flow during the interaction, capturing conditions and iterations. With the introduction of UML 2.x set of rich features such as combined fragments, SDs have become popular for expressing scenarios because of their clear and intuitive visual layout and close correspondence with actual code-like structures. However, most of the proposed transformation approaches up to date target only one particular type of behavioral diagram, mostly AD or SM diagrams [5, 8, 12, 13]. When it comes to interactions (SDs) or targeting multiple diagram types, the existing approaches either deal with UML 1.x semantics [6, 14–17], largely limiting the expressiveness by not taking into account all elements which allow designers to describe complex traces in compact manner, or their semantical models suffer from flaws [6, 17], as we will show. Furthermore, rarely [18] does an approach give feedback to the software developer on the results of the formal analysis, back into the UML domain.

Our interest in this paper is obtaining a formal model in the process algebra mCRL2 [19], taking a UML model as starting point. We chose mCRL2 because it is able to deal with abstract data types as well as user-defined functions for data transformation. Familiarity with the toolset's simulation, debugging, visualization and model-checking capabilities has influenced our decision, but mCRL2 has many commonalities with other process algebraic formalisms, so in principle the methodology can be easily adapted. Due to the true-concurrency nature (multi-actions) of mCRL2, we can faithfully express the partial-order semantics of SDs, rather than the limited interleaving semantics that many approaches adopt. This is important in distributed systems where the representation of parallelism by non-determinism ignores real asynchronous behaviors that may exist. The proposed approach in this paper is based on UML 2.x semantics, and makes use of both sequence and activity diagrams to automatically derive the target formal model. We rely on the XMI representation to devise the model transformation procedure. XMI [1] is an XML-based vendor-independent format for metadata exchange between compliant UML tools. Based on the approach, we have developed a prototype tool that can take a UML model in XMI representation as input, and construct the mCRL2 model. Our methodology allows traces from the model checking tool to be conveniently displayed back in any UML tool. We have further applied the tool to the DIRAC [20] Grid framework used to support production activities for one of the LHC experiments.

The paper is structured as follows: Section 2 gives a brief overview of the syntax and semantics of the UML and mCRL2 language notation necessary for understanding the Transformation Methodology (Section 3). In Section 4 we apply it on a case study from the Grid domain, and we conclude in Section 5.

2   Preliminaries

The UML abstract syntax and semantics is described in terms of its *UML metamodel*, which defines the relationships between model elements. To translate a system composed of different diagrams, we chose Sequence Diagrams as a driving behavior description type, and we take the necessary additional information about concurrency from Activity Diagrams. Our choice is motivated by the fact that SDs provide the richest set of constructs for low-level behavior expression, and as such have a close correspondence with actual code. Additional information from ADs is necessary for deriving the actual (OS level) processes, relevant for concurrent and distributed systems.

2.1   Sequence Diagrams

Sequence diagrams model the interaction among a set of participants, with emphasis on the sequence of messages exchanged over time. The participants are class instances (objects) shown as rectangular boxes, with the vertical lines falling from them known as *Lifelines* (See Fig. 1, left). Each *Message* sent between the lifelines defines a specific act of communication, synchronous or asynchronous. The start and end of the directed

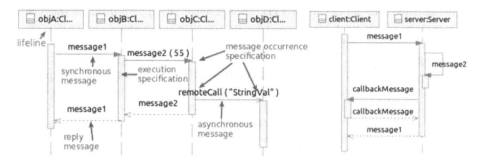

Fig. 1. Sequence Diagrams notation

edge representing a message are called *MessageEnds*, and are marked with a so called *MessageOccurrenceSpecification* element of the UML metamodel.Synchronous messages are drawn with filled arrow-head, while asynchronous ones have an open arrow-head. Reply messages are drawn as dashed lines. All message types can carry arguments.

Messages are sent between objects with the aim of invoking specific behavior, known as *ExecutionSpecification*, and visualized as a thin rectangle on the receiver's lifeline. Thus, execution specifications specify when a particular object is busy executing the invoked method. Execution specifications can be nested/overlapping, as a result of a callback message, or an object invoking its own method, an example of both shown in Fig. 1 (right). In this example, the *client* object sends a request for *message1* execution on the *server* side, after which it is blocked until it receives a reply from that method call. However, this does not stop other potential objects from invoking any method of the *client* interface. This possibility of overlapping method executions on the lifeline on a single object thus plays an important role in our transformation methodology choices.

Combined Fragments. Combined Fragments were introduced to add more expressiveness to SDs by means of constructs capturing complex control flows, thus overcoming

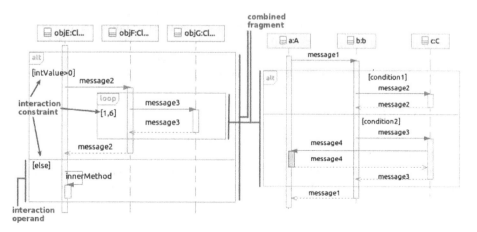

Fig. 2. Combined Fragments examples

many limitations present in UML 1.x [1]. The specification supports different fragment types, such as *alt, opt, loop, break, par*. They are visualized as rectangles with a keyword indicating the type. Combined Fragments consist of one or more *InteractionOperands*. Depending on the type of the fragment, *InteractionConstraints* can guard each of the interaction operands. Combined fragments can be nested with an arbitrary nesting depth, to capture complex workflows. Figure 2 shows how some of them can be used. The guards play a crucial role in deciding which fragment's operand(s) will be executed at runtime. All fragment types above have equivalent constructs in most object oriented languages. Another useful enhancement is the *InteractionUse* fragment. Thus, for expressing complex scenarios, one can include a reference to another SD, which is semantically equivalent to including the behavior of the called diagram in the current one. This promotes reuse of already defined sequence diagrams.

Runtime Semantics. Unlike the syntax, the SD semantics is scattered through the UML specification, and defined by the means of natural language. The most important points can be summarized as follows: an object sends a message as a result of earlier behavior invocations on its interface, and is the object's reaction to these receptions. In that sense, an object does not control the reception of a message. Message and execution completion are considered local concepts. For a message m sent from object $o1$ to object $o2$, the sender's view of that message completion is the sending, the receiver's view of the message completion is its reception, while other objects have no knowledge of m. Thus, the only synchronization points between the objects are the message exchanges. *This semantics does not impose a total ordering of the messages in a given SD.*

2.2   Activity Diagrams

As already stated, we use ADs to extract concurrency information necessary for deriving OS-level processes in a distributed system setup. Although the notion of concurrency is present in some form in SDs, the *par* fragment only indicates that the implementation can execute any interleaving of the operands' behaviors, without mandating that the implementation be concurrent or distributed. In a concurrent or distributed setup, each of the SDs could be parts of multiple processes that must be initialized by the system environment at some point, and this is where elements of ADs help. We defer the explanation of the limited subset of used elements to the section where we explain the transformation methodology, illustrating it on an example.

2.3   The mCRL2 Language

mCRL2 is a process algebra language for specification and analysis of concurrent systems. Our choice of mCRL2 as a formal language is motivated by its rich set of abstract data types as first-class citizens, as well as its powerful toolset for analysis, simulation, and visualization of specifications. The syntax of mCRL2 is given by the following BNF grammar:

$$p ::= a(d_1, \ldots, d_n) \mid \tau \mid \delta \mid p + p \mid p.p \mid p \| p \mid \sum_{d:D} p \mid c \to p \diamond p$$

A basic action a of a process may have a number of data arguments $d_1, ..., d_n$. The action τ denotes an internal step, which cannot be observed from the external world. Non-deterministic choice between two processes is denoted by the $+$ operator. Processes can be composed sequentially and in parallel by means of "." and "$||$". The sum operator $\sum_{d:D} p$ denotes (possibly infinite) choice among processes parameterized by d. $c \rightarrow p \diamond p$ is a conditional process, and depending on the value of the boolean expression c, the first or second operand is selected.

To enforce synchronization, the allow operator $\nabla_H(p)$ specifies the set of actions H that are allowed to occur. To show possible communications in a system and the resulting actions, the communication operator $\Gamma_C(p)$ is used. The elements of set C are so-called multi-actions of the form $a_1 \mid a_2 \mid ... \mid a_n \rightarrow c$, which intuitively means that action c is the result of the multi-party synchronization of actions $a_1, a_2, ...$ and a_n. There are a number of built-in data types in mCRL2, such as (unbounded) integers, (uncountable) reals, booleans, lists, and sets. Furthermore, by a **sort** definition one can define a new data type. A new process is declared by **proc**.

The semantics associated with the mCRL2 syntax is a Labeled Transition System system that has multi-action labeled transitions. A more elaborate description of mCRL2 and its features can be found in [19].

3 Transformation Methodology

3.1 The Rationale

Before describing the transformation methodology, we outline the rationale behind the choices we made, and why they differ from previous approaches that deal with SDs as behavioral description diagrams of a system. The approaches of which we are aware, and which use a process algebra formalism for a target model, translate each lifeline (hence, each object) into a sequential process[1]. However, this implies that an object behaves intrinsically sequentially, which is not the case. The object's individual processing capabilities are exposed via its methods. In a concurrent setting, multiple threads of a process (or even multiple processes sharing an object, if the implementation language permits this) could be invoking methods of the same object, thus, that object could be executing multiple behaviors at the same time. Consider the simple SD in Fig. 2 (right). Even if we assume that the scenario is executed by a single OS process, treating each object as a sequential process is problematic. In the example, after invocation of *message1*, object a needs to know the choice that object b has made (modeled with the *alt* fragment), while this choice is based on local conditions that only b is aware of. Therefore, a cannot know whether its method *message4* will be invoked by object c, before a return from *message1* is received on the same lifeline. Consequently, a single process representation of the lifeline a should not control the reception of *message4* and execution of the associated behavior. Some approaches attempt to deal with this by making all involved processes aware of each others' local decisions, but this quickly becomes cumbersome and prone to errors, given how complex UML 2.x SDs can be made by nesting combined fragments.

---

[1] The only exception made to this rule is when dealing with the *par* fragment.

We wish to preserve the OO paradigm in the transformation to a formal model. In this paradigm, unless an object is active, it does not control the invocation of its methods; it only responds by executing the associated behavior. An OS process is then essentially a chain of method invocations on objects. To achieve this, we associate an mCRL2 process *description* with each class method. A description (be it actual program code or a UML model) of a class method should not differ across objects that are instances of that class. Of course, at runtime objects execute only one of the multiple possible traces captured by that description, based on variable values. In our methodology, each such mCRL2 process *instance* carries data parameters that encode the class, object, and OS process instance to which the exhibited method behavior belongs at runtime. As an important consequence of this choice, *we preserve information on objects, classes and method calls in the mCRL2 model*, which makes it easy to reverse model-checking traces back into the UML domain.

3.2   The Approach

Figure 3 gives an overview of our approach and implemented toolset. Both the source (UML) and the target (mCRL2) models adhere to their respective metamodels. Although any UML modeling tool with XMI export/import capabilities can be used, we chose IBM's Rational environment because of the excellent support for SDs and consistency preservation across multiple views of the same model. For parsing and manipulation of the XMI representations we use Eclipse's MDT-UML2 plugin, which implements the UML 2.x metamodel. The transformation rules define how to generate a model that conforms to a particular metamodel, from a model that conforms to another metamodel.

To achieve the basic idea of mapping each method along a lifeline into an mCRL2 process description, we process the ordered events along every lifeline individually, thus decomposing the lifeline into individual *ExecutionSpecifications*. We take into account both synchronous and asynchronous messages, so there are essentially 6 different

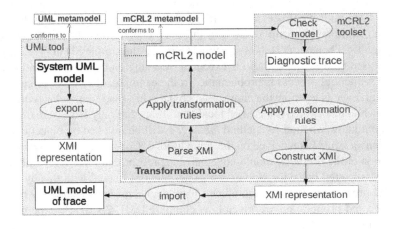

Fig. 3. Automated verification of UML models

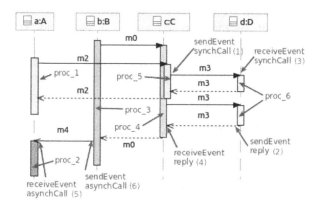

Fig. 4. Identifying event types along lifelines

types of message events (shown in Fig. 4) that we consider: (1) *SendEvent_synchCall*; (2) *SendEvent_reply*; (3) *ReceiveEvent_synchCall*; (4) *ReceiveEvent_reply*; (5) *ReceiveEvent_asynchCall*; and (6) *SendEvent_asynchCall*. In UML metamodel terms, each of these events correspond to *MessageOccurrenceSpecifications*, and refer to the ends of each *Message*. Readers familiar with class diagrams are referred to the UML superstructure[1] for the Interactions metamodel, though the transformation process in the sequel can be understood without it. An *Interaction* (a Sequence Diagram) essentially encloses *Messages*, *Lifelines* and an ordered list of *InteractionFragments*. Each *Message* is accompanied by a pair of *MessageOccurrenceSpecifications*, and has a reference to the lifelines at which the message is sent and and received. Both *MessageOccurrenceSpecifications* and *CombinedFragments* are specializations of *InteractionFragment*. We exploit these relationships in our algorithm for matching and transforming into an mCRL2 model.

All fragments of an *Interaction* are processed sequentially, and depending on their type, different mapping rules are applied. In case of *MessageOccurrenceSpecifications*, each event type is treated separately. In case of a *CombinedFragment*, each *InteractionOperand*'s nested fragments are treated by applying the same procedure recursively.

1: **procedure** PROCESSFRAGMENTS($fragments \leftarrow interaction.getFragments()$)
2:   **for each** $fragment$ in $fragments$ **do**
3:    **if** $fragment.type = MessageOccurrenceSpecification$ **then**
4:      $message \leftarrow fragment.getMessage()$
5:      $arguments \leftarrow message.getArguments()$
6:      $event \leftarrow fragment.getEvent()$
7:      $objName, className \leftarrow fragment.getCovered.getObjectAndClass()$
8:      $theReadyStack \leftarrow readyProcessesPerLifeline.get(objName)$
9:      $theBusyStack \leftarrow busyProcessesPerLifeline.get(objName)$

Two in-memory stacks are kept for the currently "ready" and the "busy" methods on each lifeline, for cases of overlapping invocations. Busy methods are waiting (blocked)

for a reply from another method execution that they have invoked, while ready processes
are active, but not blocked. The message, arguments, class, and object corresponding to
the handling event are retrieved.

```
10:    switch event do
11:      case SendEvent_synchCall :                                          ▷ Case (1)
12:        mcrl2Process ← theReadyStack.pop()
13:        if insideInteractionOperand & firstEvent then
14:          operator ← getCombinedFragmentOperand()
15:          guard ← getCombinedFragmentOperandGuard()
16:          if operator = "alt" then
17:            mcrl2Process.addAltFragment(guard)
18:            [...]
19:          else if operator = "par" then
20:            mcrl2Process.addParFragment(guard)
21:          else if operator = "loop" then
22:            loopProcess ← newLoopProcess()
23:            mcrl2Process.addCallToLoopProcess(loopProcess)
24:            theReadyStack.push(mcrl2Process)
25:            loopProcess.addCondition(guard)
26:          end if
27:        end if
28:        mcrl2Process.addInvocation(
29:          "synch_call_send(id, className, objName, message, arguments)")
30:        theBusyStack.push(theProcess)
```

The above pseudocode handles the case of *SendEvent_synchCall* observed on a lifeline.
For invocation to be possible, the object representing that lifeline must already be active in some method, at the same time **not** being blocked and awaiting for a return from
a method call. We obtain that "ready" method (or mCRL2 *process*) from a stack, on
line 12. In addition, this is the only valid UML case where it is possible for a *SendE-
vent_synchCall* to be the first event inside a *CombinedFragment*. The different fragment
types are handled by associating a corresponding mCRL2 structure in the mCRL2 process (lines 14-27). The details of how each type of fragment is mapped to an mCRL2
structure will be explained after the algorithm walk-through, where also invocations
(line 28) added to each process will be discussed.

```
31:    case SendEvent_reply :                                               ▷ Case (2)
32:      mcrl2Process ← theReadyStack.pop()
33:      mcrl2Process.setProcessed()
34:      mcrl2Process.addInvocation("
35:        synch_reply_send(id, className, objName, message, arguments)")
```

Once a method sends a reply (*SendEvent_reply*), that mCRL2 process description is
finished. The process is removed from the appropriate "ready" stack, as it no longer
exhibits behavior after this point.

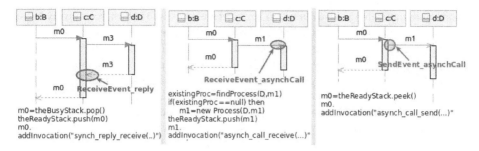

Fig. 5. Handling Case 4(left), Case 5(middle) and Case 6(right)

36:	**case** $ReceiveEvent\_synchCall$: ▷ Case (3)
37:	$findProcess \leftarrow findProcess(className, message)$
38:	**if** $findProcess = null$ **then**
39:	$findProcess \leftarrow newProcess(className, message)$
40:	**end if**
41:	**if** $\neg findProcess.isProcessed$ **then**
42:	$theReadyStack.push(findProcess)$
43:	$findProcess.addInvocation($
44:	$"synch\_call\_receive(id, className, objName, message, arguments)")$
45:	**end if**

Reception of a synchronous call on a lifeline indicates method invocation. Unless the mCRL2 process corresponding to this method has already been fully constructed, a new one is created, and pushed to the "ready" stack.

To get an intuition on how the algorithm proceeds, we treat Cases 4, 5, and 6 along with a graphical notation (Fig. 5), rather than an algorithmic exposition. Upon reception of a reply from a method (Case (4)), the one initiating it is no longer blocked, so the corresponding mCRL2 process is removed from the "busy" stack and added to the "ready" one. Handling of Case (5) is analogous to Case (3), except that a different kind of invocation is added to the mCRL2 process. Finally, handling Case (6) is also analogous to Case (1), with the important difference being that the active method invoking this asynchronous call on another object will not be blocked after the call. This is why the process is not removed from the "ready" stack nor pushed to the busy one.

46:	**else if** $fragment.type = CombinedFragment$ **then**
47:	**getOperandsForCombinedFragment**($fragment$)
48:	**end if**
49:	**end for**
50:	**end procedure**

1:	**procedure** GETOPERANDSFORCOMBINEDFRAGMENT($fragment$)
2:	$operands \leftarrow fragment.getOperands()$
3:	**for each** $operand$ in $operands$ **do**
4:	$processFragments(operand.getFragments())$ ▷ handle recursively
5:	**end for**
6:	**end procedure**

All operands that belong to a *CombinedFragment* are processed in turn, recursively handling all fragments (possibly also nested *CombinedFragments*) contained in them, by calling *processFragments* again. This concludes the basic algorithm for transformation of SDs of arbitrary complexity into mCRL2 process descriptions. When the algorithm is applied to the example in Fig. 4 it results in 6 different process definitions. The data that messages convey, and which takes part in decisions, are owned by the objects representing the lifelines. This data is maintained by introducing a recursive "memory" process for each object within the mCRL2 specification, which carries all data values as parameters [21]. Most of the primitive data types used have a direct mapping into mCRL2 types. Strings are handled using mCRL2's abstract data type capabilities. Due to space limitations we will not explain the transformation rules for activity diagrams, although they are rather simple. We will demonstrate them on an example instead.

The different invocation types added to the mCRL2 processes in the course of the transformation are mCRL2 actions. They carry all parameters necessary for exchange of data between processes, and are used for synchronizing the processes on the corresponding send/receive events. The actions *synch_call_send* and *synch_call_receive* represent two ends of a synchronous message exchanged between two processes. Similarly, *synch_reply_send* and *synch_reply_receive* correspond to a reply message, while *asynch_call_send* and *asynch_call_receive* represent an asynchronous call. By applying the mCRL2 communication (Γ) and allow (∇) operator in the following manner:

$$\nabla_{\{synch\_call,\ synch\_reply,\ asynch\_call\}}$$
$$\Gamma_{\{synch\_call\_send|synch\_call\_receive\ \rightarrow synch\_call,}$$
$$synch\_reply\_send|synch\_reply\_receive\ \rightarrow synch\_reply,$$
$$asynch\_call\_send|asynch\_call\_receive\ \rightarrow asynch\_call\}$$

,communication is enforced between processes as a result of the multi-action synchronization at the corresponding events.

Figure 6 demonstrates the transformation rules on a simple example. Classes, objects, method names and string values are represented by enumerated data types (**struct**). Replies are distinguished from their respective method calls, as they may also carry parameters. The mCRL2 summation (**sum**) operator is used for binding parameter identifiers to actual values when two processes communicate. This example illustrates how the *alt* fragment is translated into the mCRL2 conditional operator. To avoid deadlocks, and permit the process to continue in case none of the guards evaluates to true, the **internal** (τ) step is added as a last "artificial" choice. Note that the introduction of this internal step is deliberate, in order to match the mCRL2 *if-then-else* operator with UML's *alt* fragment semantics, and as such, should not mask proper deadlocks. The translation of the *opt* and *break* fragments uses the conditional operator in a very similar manner. In a *par* fragment, all communication inside each operand is set to run in parallel with the "∥" mCRL2 operator. The *loop* fragment has a special treatment. It is translated into a recursive process referenced by the mCRL2 process representing the method active at the moment of entering the loop. There are several less-known combined fragments (like *ignore, consider, neg*) which are not presented here. While they can be included in the transformation, we have not encountered implementation-language counterparts in object-oriented distributed software, so they are not tackled here.

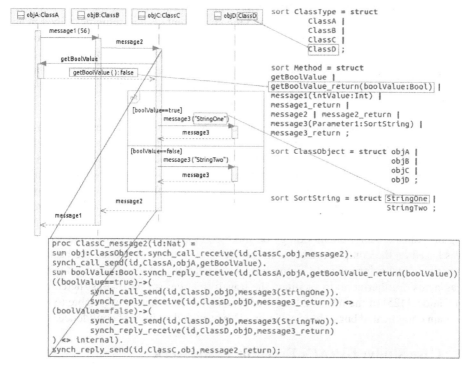

Fig. 6. Application of the SD transformation rules

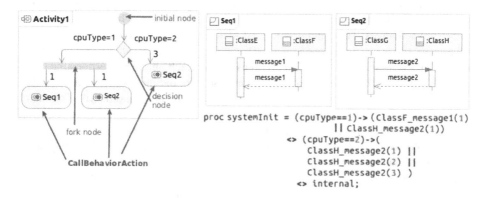

Fig. 7. Application of AD transformation rules for system-level concurrency setup

Finally, Fig. 7 shows how a simple system-level concurrency can be expressed in an AD, and how it is translated into an mCRL2 specification. ADs consist of *Actions* and *Control Nodes* connected by *Activity Edges*, with each diagram having one *Initial Node*. The control nodes have their intuitive meaning as in traditional flow charts, namely to depict concurrent flows (*Fork*), and decision points (*Decision*). While there are various action types, we are primarily interested in the *CallBehaviorAction*, which invokes a referenced behavior directly. Since SDs are classified as behavior, we use this action type to provide the link between SDs and the concurrent system setup described in an AD. In the given example, depending on the condition, three concurrent OS process instances are started with the *Seq2* SD, or alternatively one instance of *Seq1* and *Seq2* in parallel. The *id:Nat* parameter that each mCRL2 process carries is used to bind it to an OS process in the system setup. It is also possible to add *Activity Final Node* for systems where execution terminates, by design.

Validating the Transformation. The current UML specification uses a combination of semi-formal diagrams, a constraints language, and natural language descriptions. While there has been a substantial effort [22–24] on formalization, there is still no official mathematically-formalized semantics definition. In this context, formal correctness proofs to support the validity of the transformation approach are not possible. To assess the correctness of our proposed semantics, we used the simulation and visualization mCRL2 tools on simple diagrams in isolation, in order to get confidence before applying the transformation methodology on more complex ones. This informal validation was based on the compositional nature of UML; we closely examined the basic UML constructs' behavior reflected in the formal model, with a special focus on combined fragments. Furthermore, to facilitate the transformation, we have constructed a UML metamodel [25] of the mCRL2 language syntax. The fact that we were able to reliably explain complicated bugs observed in practice provided additional confidence.

4   Case Study: DIRACs Executor Framework

DIRAC [20] is the grid framework used to support production activities of the LHCb experiment at CERN. Jobs submitted via its interface undergo several processing steps between the moment they are submitted to the grid, to the point when their execution on the grid actualizes. The crucial Workload Management components responsible for orchestrating this process are the *ExecutorDispatcher* and the *Executors*. Executors process any task sent to them by the ExecutorDispatcher, each one being responsible for a different step in the handling of tasks (such as resolving the input data for a job). The ExecutorDispatcher takes care of persisting the state of the tasks and distributing them amongst all the Executors, based on the requirements of each task. It maintains a queue of tasks waiting to be processed, and other internal data structures to keep track of the distribution of tasks among the Executors. During testing, certain problems have manifested: occasionally, tasks submitted in the system would not get dispatched, despite the fact that their responsible Executors were idle at the moment. The root cause of this problem could not be identified by testing with different workload scenarios, nor by analysis of the generated logs.

We used our toolset to generate an mCRL2 model, based on the reverse-engineered SDs of the Executor Framework implementation. To reason about the correctness of the generated model behavior, mCRL2 relies on the modal μ-calculus language [19], extended with regular expressions and data. Regular expressions are constructed using the boolean constants *true* and *false* and the modalities "[]" (*necessity*) and "<>" (*possibly*). The behaviors inside the modalities are specified using *action formulas*. The constants *true* and *false* have their usual meaning: *true* holds in every state, while

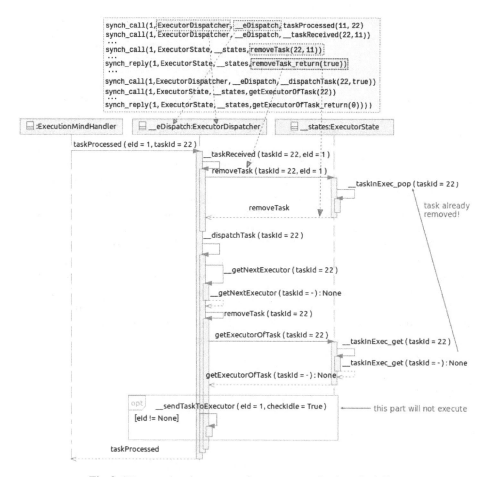

Fig. 8. SD trace showing a case of no-progress of tasks scheduling

false does not hold in any state of the model. Together with operators like "∗", used for expressing cardinality (actions can occur any number of times), ".", which allows for concatenating behaviors, and "!" for the set complement, or negation, powerful expressions can be formulated. The *action-based* formulas are a good match for our transformation methodology: actions correspond to message exchanges, which already contain the information on the sender/receiver class and object of a particular message. As will be discussed in the next section, we plan to utilize this for expressing modal μ-calculus formulas as sequence diagrams. The above-mentioned Executors problem can be formulated as the following safety property:

```
[ true * .
synch_call (1 , ExecutorQueues ,__queues , pushTask ( JobPath , taskId , false )) .
true *.
!( synch_call (1 , ExecutorQueues ,__queues , popTask ([ JobPath ]))) *.
synch_reply (1 , ExecutorDispatcher ,__eDispatch ,__sendTaskToExecutor_return (OK, 0))] false
```

, meaning that a task pushed in the queue must be processed, i.e., removed from the queue before the ExecutorDispatcher declares that there are no more tasks for processing.

Explicit model checking was not feasible in this case due to the model size (50 concurrent processes), so we resorted to using a standard monitoring process which is set to run in parallel with the original model and observe the relevant actions that the system itself takes. This technique, combined with a depth-first traversal choice in the tool, effectively discovered a trace violating the property within minutes. The counter-example (Fig. 8) is a rather long trace (available at [25]), and traverses a large fraction of the SDs (27 in total), but the bug was localized in a single SD, covering the behavior of the ExecutorDispatcher component. We only present the most important part for understanding the cause. Whenever a task has been processed by some of the Executors, the ExecutorDispatcher is notified (*taskProcessed(eId,taskId)*), and this removes it from its internal list of processing tasks. To further dispatch the task to another Executor, this task is removed from the ExecutorDispatcher's memory of processing tasks, followed by retrieval of the next responsible Executor. In case it was actually processed by the last Executor in the chain, the dispatcher attempts to retrieve its last Executor (*getExecutorOfTask(taskId)*), so that more tasks can be dispatched by this (now free) Executor. However, this information is already removed, as can be seen from the figure. As a result, the *opt* fragment (shown only for clarity, not generated by the toolset) will not be executed, and no further tasks waiting for this Executor will be dispatched. The bug was reported and fixed. The figure also demonstrates how the trace is translated back in the UML domain, to facilitate debugging the actual problem. The process is relatively simple, since each action of the trace already contains the information necessary to build the message exchange sequence in the SD.

5   Conclusions and Future Work

We have presented an automated transformation methodology for verification of UML models, based on sequence and activity diagrams, preserving the object-oriented view of the system in the transformation. Although the mCRL2 toolset automatically discovers deadlocks, model checking for application-specific properties requires the use of temporal logic. Part of the future work is expressing modal μ-calculus formulas as sequence diagrams of accept/reject scenarios: behaviors that the designer wants to either confirm or avoid in the model. This can be easily achieved, given that μ-calculus formulas are action-based, and actions correspond to message exchanges in our transformation methodology. Furthermore, we plan to explore the limitations of this approach, given that process proliferation is likely to happen in larger systems. In our case study, we have as many as 50 processes, and already generating the entire state space can be problematic at this scale, given that the generated model is over 2k lines of model code.

Besides discovering behavioral problems, automating performance analysis is on our road-map as well. UML provides extension mechanisms called *Profiles* which allow annotating models with quantitative information, such as expected execution time, resource usage, number of requests, etc. These quantities permit assessing the system's efficiency and reliability. Our approach can be easily extended in this direction, by taking into account not only message occurrences, but also annotated execution specifications within SDs. We can use the same target formalism for enhancing the models with such quantitative information. The CADP toolset [26] for analysis of stochastic models is well integrated with mCRL2 for this purpose.

References

1. OMG: UML Specifications, `http://www.omg.org/spec`
2. Distefano, S., Scarpa, M., Puliafito, A.: From UML to Petri Nets: The PCM-Based Methodology. IEEE Trans. Software Eng. 37(1), 65–79 (2011)
3. Bernardi, S., Donatelli, S., Merseguer, J.: From UML Sequence Diagrams and Statecharts to Analysable Petri Net Models. In: Proc. WOSP 2002, pp. 35–45 (2002)
4. Petriu, D.C., Shen, H.: Applying the UML Performance Profile: Graph Grammar-Based Derivation of LQN Models from UML Specifications. In: Field, T., Harrison, P.G., Bradley, J., Harder, U. (eds.) TOOLS 2002. LNCS, vol. 2324, pp. 159–177. Springer, Heidelberg (2002)
5. Tribastone, M., Gilmore, S.: Automatic Extraction of PEPA Performance Models from UML Activity Diagrams Annotated with the MARTE Profile. In: Proc. WOSP 2008 (2008)
6. Tribastone, M., Gilmore, S.: Automatic Translation of UML Sequence Diagrams into PEPA Models. In: Proc. QEST 2008, pp. 205–214 (2008)
7. Guelfi, N., Mammar, A.: A Formal Semantics of Timed Activity Diagrams and its PROMELA Translation. In: Proc. APSEC 2005, pp. 283–290 (2005)
8. Jussila, T., et al.: Model Checking Dynamic and Hierarchical UML State Machines. In: Proc. MoDeVa 2006 (2006)
9. Bandyopadhyay, A., Ghosh, S.: Test Input Generation Using UML Sequence and State Machines Models. In: Proc. ICST 2009. IEEE Computer Society (2009)
10. Pickin, S., Jard, C., Le Traon, Y., Jéron, T., Jézéquel, J.-M., Le Guennec, A.: System Test Synthesis from UML Models of Distributed Software. In: Peled, D.A., Vardi, M.Y. (eds.) FORTE 2002. LNCS, vol. 2529, pp. 97–113. Springer, Heidelberg (2002)
11. Whittle, J.: Transformations and Software Modeling Languages: Automating Transformations in UML. In: Jézéquel, J.-M., Hussmann, H., Cook, S. (eds.) UML 2002. LNCS, vol. 2460, pp. 227–242. Springer, Heidelberg (2002)
12. Cao, H., Ying, S., Du, D.: Towards Model-based Verification of BPEL with Model Checking. In: Proc. CIT 2006. IEEE Computer Society (2006)
13. Siveroni, I., Zisman, A., Spanoudakis, G.: Property Specification and Static Verification of UML Models. In: Proc. ARES 2008. IEEE Computer Society (2008)
14. Sarma, M., Kundu, D., Mall, R.: Automatic Test Case Generation from UML Sequence Diagram. In: Proc. ADCOM 2007 (2007)
15. Rasch, H., Wehrheim, H.: Checking the Validity of Scenarios in UML Models. In: Steffen, M., Zavattaro, G. (eds.) FMOODS 2005. LNCS, vol. 3535, pp. 67–82. Springer, Heidelberg (2005)
16. María, Merino, P., Pimentel, E.: Debugging UML Designs with Model Checking. Journal of Object Technology 1(2), 101–117 (2002)
17. Korenblat, K.P., Priami, C.: Toward Extracting pi-calculus from UML Sequence and State Diagrams. Electronic Notes in Theoretical Computer Science 101 (2004)
18. Hvid Hansen, H., Ketema, J., Luttik, B., Mousavi, M., van de Pol, J., dos Santos, O.M.: Automated Verification of Executable UML Models. In: Aichernig, B.K., de Boer, F.S., Bonsangue, M.M. (eds.) FMCO 2010. LNCS, vol. 6957, pp. 225–250. Springer, Heidelberg (2011)
19. Cranen, S., Groote, J.F., Keiren, J.J.A., Stappers, F.P.M., de Vink, E.P., Wesselink, W., Willemse, T.A.C.: An Overview of the mCRL2 Toolset and Its Recent Advances. In: Piterman, N., Smolka, S.A. (eds.) TACAS 2013. LNCS, vol. 7795, pp. 199–213. Springer, Heidelberg (2013)
20. Tsaregorodtsev, A., et al.: DIRAC: A Community Grid Solution. In: Proc. CHEP 2007 (2007)

21. Remenska, D., et al.: Using Model Checking to Analyze the System Behavior of the LHC Production Grid. In: Proc. CCGRID 2012, pp. 335–343 (2012)
22. Broy, M., Crane, M.L., Dingel, J., Hartman, A., Rumpe, B., Selic, B.: 2nd UML 2 Semantics Symposium: Formal Semantics for UML. In: Kühne, T. (ed.) MoDELS 2006. LNCS, vol. 4364, pp. 318–323. Springer, Heidelberg (2007)
23. Lazăr, C., Lazăr, I., Pârv, B., Motogna, S., Czibula, I.: Tool Support for fUML Models. Int. J. of Computers, Communications & Control 5(5) (2010)
24. Diskin, Z., Dingel, J.: Mappings, maps and tables: Towards formal semantics for associations in UML2. In: Wang, J., Whittle, J., Harel, D., Reggio, G. (eds.) MoDELS 2006. LNCS, vol. 4199, pp. 230–244. Springer, Heidelberg (2006)
25. Remenska, D., Homburg, P.: The mCRL2⇔UML transformation toolset, https://github.com/remenska/NFM
26. Garavel, H., Lang, F., Mateescu, R., Serwe, W.: CADP 2010: A Toolbox for the Construction and Analysis of Distributed Processes. In: Abdulla, P.A., Leino, K.R.M. (eds.) TACAS 2011. LNCS, vol. 6605, pp. 372–387. Springer, Heidelberg (2011)

Automatically Detecting Inconsistencies in Program Specifications

Aditi Tagore and Bruce W. Weide

Dept. of Computer Science and Engineering
The Ohio State University
Columbus, Ohio 43210, USA
{tagore.2,weide.1}@osu.edu

Abstract. A verification system relies on a programmer writing mathematically precise descriptions of code. A specification that describes the behavior of an operation and a loop invariant for iterative code are examples of such mathematical formalizations. Due to human errors, logical defects may be introduced into these mathematical constructs. Techniques to detect certain logical errors in program specifications, loop invariants, and loop variants are described. Additionally, to make program specifications more concise and to make it easier to create them, RESOLVE has parameter modes: each formal parameter is annotated with a mode that is related to the intended roles of the incoming and outgoing values of that parameter. Methods to check whether the programmer has chosen a plausibly correct mode for each parameter are also explained. The techniques described are lightweight and are applied at an early stage in the verification process.

1 Introduction

The primary value of a formal verification system is to verify a program implementation against its specification and to report an implementation error if there is one. The robustness of such a system depends as much on the programmer supplying a correct specification for her program as it does on the theorem prover's ability to prove the verification conditions (VCs) generated from a proposed implementation of that specification. However, inconsistencies in the specification may be introduced during the software development process due to human errors. In such scenarios, either an implementation may be declared as correct for an incorrect specification, or it may not be possible to write a valid implementation at all. In a similar way, defects may occur when a programmer annotates a loop with an invariant and a variant.

The idea described in this paper is used to detect certain errors at an early stage in the formal verification process. Typically, errors are only detected in a verification system when a VC cannot be proved by the theorem prover and subsequently the VC is traced back to its origin in the program to identify the error. We describe a lightweight method that checks consistency of certain programming constructs before VCs are generated. Since the cost of detecting

G. Brat, N. Rungta, and A. Venet (Eds.): NFM 2013, LNCS 7871, pp. 261–275, 2013.

and fixing errors increases as software development reaches the later stages of its life-cycle, eliminating errors early is widely regarded as a best practice in software engineering.

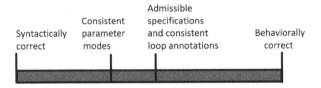

Fig. 1. Types of correctness checks

Formal verification ensures that a program is behaviorally correct, i.e., it matches its specification. It is far stonger than syntactic correctness of a program, which is checked by an ordinary compiler. The techniques outlined here lie between these two extremes. The consistency of program specifications and loop annotations is accomplished with the help of a theorem prover (also used for formal verification), but instead of proving an entire program to be correct, we perform local checks on mathematical statements that do not depend on the entire body of code. Additionally, we also illustrate methods to accomplish consistency checks on the modes of operation parameters. These are syntactic checks, but of a slightly different order than those that are normally carried out by a compiler. This classification is shown in Figure 1.

Our specifications and their implementations are written in RESOLVE [1]. To detect logical inconsistencies in program specifications and their implementations, we use an SMT solver, Z3 [2], as a back-end prover. The example programs are chosen from the RSRG software components library, some of which have been suggested as software verification benchmarks [3]. Students in computer science classes have been observed to make the kinds of errors that are mentioned in this paper, as have the authors and other more experienced specifiers.

The contributions in this paper are three-fold:

- The conditions for admissibility of program specifications are formulated.
- Techniques to establish logical consistency of loop annotations (invariants and variants) are developed.
- Methods for ascertaining that a programmer has supplied the correct modes for the parameters of an operation are described.

A reader's familiarity with formal specifications, pre- and post-conditions, and loop invariants and variants is assumed. However, no prior knowledge of RESOLVE or of the intricate mechanisms of Z3 is necessary. The ideas apply to specifications and formal verification / theorem-proving technology in general.

Section 2 provides an overview of the types of defects considered. Sections 3,4 and 5 expound on the techniques for detecting such defects with examples. Discussion and related work are presented in Section 6, with conclusions in Section 7.

2   Types of Specification Defects Detected

2.1   Defective Contracts

An operation (or method) specification promises certain properties that
the implementer can assume at the
time of a call via the requires
clause (pre-condition) and, in turn,
demands that certain properties
hold upon return via the ensures
clause (post-condition). We first divide specifications into two distinct
groups: those that are implementable
and those that are not. Unimplementable specifications are, for our
(practical) purposes, considered inadmissible. A specification with an
unsatisfiable post-condition is unim-

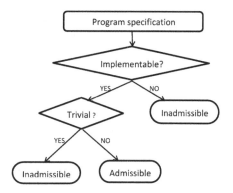

Fig. 2. Program Specifications

plementable and hence inadmissible. On the other hand, not all specifications
that are implementable are admissible[1]. Some of them may be trivially correct
and hence are inadmissible. This happens if the pre-condition is unsatisfiable.
This characterization is shown in Figure 2. In short, an inadmissible specification is one that, for practical purposes, must have resulted from a specification
error. In Section 3 we discuss various techniques to detect these different types
of problems in specifications.

2.2   Defective Loop Annotations

Loop invariants and variants are important constructs needed to formally verify a program. Loop invariants are needed to reason about the loop, without
considering the loop iterations individually. Correspondingly, to prove the total correctness of programs, variants (called progress metrics in RESOLVE) are
used. A variant is usually a natural number that has a positive value before each
time the loop body is executed, and must be reduced in each iteration. Invariants
and variants are together used to prove total correctness of loops.

As mentioned earlier, there is a benefit to detecting defects in loop annotations at an early stage, even before VCs are generated. In Section 4 we discuss
techniques to ensure admissibility of its constituent parts.

2.3   Inconsistent Parameter Modes

Each parameter of a RESOLVE operation is annotated with a *mode* in the
header of that operation. A programmer may fail to select parameter modes that

---

[1] "Admissible" refers to a specification that does not contain any checkable defects,
not to one that "correctly formalizes the requirements".

are consistent with how the parameter values are utilized and changed in the operation. In other words, the modes may not be consistent with the `requires` and the `ensures` clause.

For example, the `replaces` mode indicates that the outgoing parameter value is determined by the operation and that the incoming value is inconsequential. Thus the operation should not refer to the incoming value of the parameter. Hence if the programmer uses a `replaces` mode when the incoming value of the parameter appears in the pre- or post-condition, then she is alerted of this anomaly.

A detailed explanation of the modes is presented in Section 5 where we also discuss the methods we employ to detect modes that are inconsistent with the specification of the operation.

3   Inconsistent Specifications

3.1   Methodology

A specification may be inadmissible for various reasons, as discussed in Section 2.1. We perform a series of checks to identify those that are not admissible. The following lists a taxonomy of defects that may occur in the specifications.

Contradiction in the Pre-condition: An implementation may be declared as trivially correct if the pre-condition (say *pre*) is *false*. Logical contradictions appearing in *pre* make it *false* and hence the post-condition (say *post*) is irrelevant. To avoid such *default* correctness, the `requires` clause is tested for satisfiability.

Contradiction in the Post-condition: On the other hand, a specification is unimplementable if *post* is *false*. A contradiction in *post* implies that it is impossible to create an implementation that meets the specification. In this case too, the `ensures` clause is tested for satisfiability.

Appropriateness of *pre* **and** *post* **Together**: Even when the `requires` and `ensures` clauses are individually contradiction-free, they may still preclude an implementation that satisfies the program specification.

```
procedure DecrementBy3 (updates x: Integer)
 requires
   x >= 3
 ensures
   x = #x - 3 and x > 0
```

Fig. 3. Proposed specification of `DecrementBy3`

As an example, consider the specification of a procedure `DecrementBy3` shown in Figure 3. The parameter mode `updates` for the parameter x indicates the value of this parameter may be changed by the operation. The # symbol in the ensures clause refers to the parameter at the time of the call; no # symbol is used in the requires clause as it always refers to the incoming value. The pre-condition of the procedure DecrementBy3 says that the incoming value of x should be greater than or equal to 3. The post-condition of the procedure says that the outgoing value of x is equal to 3 less than its incoming value (denoted by #x) *and* that the outgoing value is positive.

The requires and ensures clauses are individually satisfiable: both are *true* for #x = 4 and x = 1. Even so, a valid implementation (that is correct for all the input values that satisfy the pre-condition) is still not possible, because the input value #x = 3 satisfies the requires clause, but the outgoing value of x must be 0 and that makes the second conjunct $(x > 0)$ *false*, and hence invalidates the ensures clause.

To detect logical inconsistencies in program specifications (e.g., the one in Figure 3), we need to ascertain that for *all* possible values that can satisfy *pre*, there *exist* values of the variables that satisfy *post*. So we check the validity of

$$\forall x_1, \ldots, x_n(pre \implies \exists y_1, \ldots, y_m(post)) \tag{1}$$

where $(x_1, \ldots, x_n)$ are the incoming values of the variables appearing in *pre* and $(y_1, \ldots, y_m)$ are the outgoing values of the variables in *post*.

Thus the specification in Figure 3 is tested with the help of the formula

$$\forall \#x(\#x >= 3 \implies \exists x(x = \#x - 3 \land x > 0)) \tag{2}$$

3.2   Example: A Divide Operation for Unbounded Integers

In RESOLVE, a contract contains the client-view of a software component that describes a model of that component's behavior. A realization module contains operation bodies that implement the operations specified in the contract. Consider the contract Divide for *unbounded* integers, i.e, integer values without an upper or lower bound.

```
contract Divide enhances UnboundedIntegerFacility

  procedure Divide (updates i: Integer, restores j: Integer,
                                        replaces r: Integer)
      ensures
          #i = i * j + r  and  0 < r  and  r < |j|

end Divide
```

Fig. 4. Proposed specification of Divide

In the Divide operation (shown in Figure 4), the incoming value of i (denoted by #i) is the dividend and the quotient is the outgoing value of i. Since the value of the divisor j remains unchanged, its parameter mode is restores.

The remainder from the division is returned in r. Since, the incoming value of r is inconsequential, its parameter mode is replaces.

An important observation needs to be made about the variable j. The parameter mode of j is restores, which means the incoming and the outgoing values are the same; it is equivalent to having j = #j as part of the ensures clause. For simplicity, a programmer can leave such a clause out of the post-condition. But while constructing the formula to check for validity, this additional conjunct needs to be appended to the ensures clause. First, we check whether the precondition (there isn't one and hence by default is it considered to be *true*) and post-condition are individually satisfiable; they are. Then, we construct formula (3) to check for the admissibility of the specification.

$$\forall \#i, \#j(true \implies \exists i, j, r((\#i = i * j + r) \wedge (0 < r) \wedge (r < |j|) \wedge (j = \#j)))$$
(3)

To test whether the specification is admissible, formula (3) is automatically translated into Z3's SMT2 input format and Z3 is invoked to prove it. Z3 determines that it is invalid. This gives a flag to the programmer that the specification contains an error. When a formula is determined to be invalid, Z3 produces a counter-example, i.e., values for which the formula does not hold. Here, it suggests a value 0 for #j. As we know that j = #j, the last two conjuncts of the ensures clause in Figure 4 are reduced to $0 < r$ and $r < 0$. Since a conflict arises, the programmer (we hope) sees that a value of 0 cannot be allowed for the divisor j. Hence, this should be prevented by the requires clause.

```
requires
  j /= 0
ensures
  #i = i * j + r  and  0 < r  and  r < |j|
```

Fig. 5. New proposed pre- and post-condition of Divide

The specification in Figure 4 is now corrected as shown in Figure 5, and it is checked again:

$$\forall \#i, \#j((\#j \neq 0) \implies \exists i, j, r((\#i = i*j+r) \wedge (0 < r) \wedge (r < |j|) \wedge (j = \#j)))$$
(4)

Z3 declares this formula invalid as well and produces a counter-example where $\#j = 1$. On substituting this value, the last two conjuncts of the ensures clause are $0 < r$ and $r < 1$. The variable r cannot satisfy both these conjuncts at the same time, since r is an integer. Hence, the programmer should realize at this point, that the remainder from the Divide operation may be equal to 0.

```
requires
  j /= 0
ensures
  #i = i * j + r  and  0 <= r  and  r < |j|
```

Fig. 6. Correct Pre- and post-condition of `Divide`

Hence, the specification for `Divide` is updated one last time to the admissible one in Figure 6.

3.3   Example: An Increment Operation for Bounded Integers

We next consider a contract for *bounded* integers, where two constants MIN and MAX represent the minimum and the maximum bounds respectively. The bounds are used with the restriction that MIN <= 0 and 0 < MAX. Figure 7 shows (some of) a proposed contract for the `BoundedIntegerFacility`.

```
contract
  BoundedIntegerFacility                  type Integer is modeled
                                            by INTEGERMODEL
  definition MIN: integer                 exemplar i
  satisfies restriction                   initialization ensures
    MIN <= 0                                i = 0

  definition MAX: integer                 procedure Increment
  satisfies restriction                   (updates i: Integer)
    0 < MAX                               requires
                                            i <= MAX
  math subtype INTEGERMODEL               ensures
  is integer                                i = #i + 1
  exemplar i                              ...
  constraint                              end BoundedIntegerFacility
    MIN <= i  and  i <= MAX
```

Fig. 7. A proposed `BoundedIntegerFacility` contract

The specification of each operation that appears in this contract can be tested for correctness using the method described in Section 3.1. However, a bounded integer (say i) in this contract must satisfy MIN <= i < MAX that is introduced by the `constraint` clause. Thus, to check the validity of each of the operation specifications in this contract, formula (1) needs to be updated such that the `constraint` clause (say *constr*) on the program variables (an abstract invariant) is not violated. The `constraint` clause must hold for both the incoming and the outgoing parameter values and thus needs to be appended to both the `requires` and the `ensures` clauses. In addition, the `restriction` clause (say *restr*) on the boundary values (i.e., `MAX` and `MIN`) must also be accounted for in the formula in the same way as the `constraint`. The resultant formula is shown in (5).

$$\forall x_1, \ldots, x_n((pre \land constr \land restr) \implies \exists y_1, \ldots, y_m(post \land constr \land restr)) \tag{5}$$

where $(x_1, \ldots, x_n)$ are the incoming values of the parameters appearing in *pre*, *constr* and *restr* and $(y_1, \ldots, y_m)$ are the outgoing values of the parameters in *post*, *constr* and *restr* .

The specification of the operation `Increment`, like all others, needs to be tested for validity using the formula from (5). Substituting values, the formula evaluates to

$$\forall \#i, MAX, MIN(((\#i <= MAX) \land (\#i <= MAX) \land (MIN <= \#i)$$
$$\land (0 < MAX) \land (MIN <= 0)) \implies \exists i((i = \#i + 1) \land (i <= MAX)$$
$$\land (MIN <= i) \land (0 < MAX) \land (MIN <= 0))) \tag{6}$$

Z3 concludes that the formula in (6) is invalid, and produces a counter-example with a value 1 for each of the variables `#i` and `MAX`. Substituting these values in the formula (6), the programmer notices that the `ensures` clause no longer holds true, as the value of `i` becomes greater than `MAX`. This gives the programmer a clue that to keep the value of `i` within bounds, the value of `#i` should have been less than `MAX`.

On correcting the `requires` clause of the specification, the resulting specification of `Increment` is tested for validity and Z3 determines it to be valid.

3.4 Example: A Halve Operation

Like many other languages for writing specifications, RESOLVE supports user-defined mathematical functions and predicates. The procedure `Halve` in Figure 9 contains a user-defined predicate `IS_ODD`, that is presented in Figure 8. The ability to make up new definitions helps the specifier: instead of writing out the expression for *odd* each time, she can condense it with the help of the predicate. This also can help the prover [4].

To test the admissibility of the `Halve` specification, the formula to be checked for validity is in (7).

$$\forall \#i(true \implies \exists i((IS\_ODD(\#i) \implies \#i = i + i)$$
$$\land (\neg IS\_ODD(\#i) \implies \#i = i + i + 1))) \tag{7}$$

Z3 declares this as invalid and produces a value 0 for each of the variables `#i` and `i`. Since 0 does not satisfy the `IS_ODD` predicate, substituting the values gives rise to the expression $0 = 0 + 0 + 1$, which is impossible. At this point the programmer realizes that the conditions are simply flipped and she updates the specification to the correct one. The new check of the specification indicates that it is admissible.

```
definition IS_ODD(i: Integer)
          : boolean
  is
      i mod 2 /= 0
```

Fig. 8. The predicate *IS_ODD*

```
procedure Halve(
    updates i: Integer)
  ensures
    if IS_ODD(#i) then
      #i = i + i
    else
      #i = i + i + 1
```

Fig. 9. Proposed specification
for Halve

4   Consistency of Loop Annotations

In RESOLVE, a loop invariant for a while loop is introduced via a maintains clause. This clause formalizes the relation between the variable values just before the loop (prefixed with a #) and the variable values at any time the while loop condition is checked (unadorned). Additionally, the progress metric (variant) of a loop is stated in a decreases clause.

```
procedure Add (updates n: Natural, restores m: Natural)
  variable k, z: Natural
  loop
    maintains n + m = #n + #m  and   k + m = #k + #m  and  z = 0
    decreases m
  while not AreEqual (m, z) do
    Increment (n)
    Increment (k)
    Decrement (m)
  end loop
  m :=: k
end Add
```

Fig. 10. Procedure Add for UnboundedNaturalFacility

Figure 10 shows the code for operation Add for natural numbers. This procedure adds two natural numbers n and m and stores the result in n. The body of this procedure makes calls to two other operations: Increment and Decrement, which have been defined in the UnboundedNaturalFacility contract. The primary data-movement operator in RESOLVE, :=:, swaps (exchanges) the values of its two operands, which must be simple variables. We perform the following checks to ensure that the constituent parts of a loop are admissible.

4.1   The Invariant and the Boolean Condition Are Contradiction-Free

If two or more conjuncts in the loop invariant (say *inv*) contradict each other, then the invariant evaluates to *false* and the loop will never execute. For a

similar reason, the boolean loop condition (say B) should not contain any contradictions. Thus we first check to see that inv and B are individually satisfiable.

4.2   The Variant Is Positive Every Time the Loop Executes

In order for a loop to execute, the loop variant (say var) must (a) be positive
every time the loop body executes, and (b) decrease during every iteration of the
loop (we restrict attention to loop variants that are non-negative integers). We
perform consistency checks to see that case (a) holds. Since to prove the validity
of (b), the loop body needs to be involved, this is generated as a VC later in the
tool chain.

To ensure that case (a) holds, we check the validity of the following formula.

$$\forall x_1, \ldots, x_n(B \wedge inv \implies var > 0) \tag{8}$$

where $(x_1, \ldots, x_n)$ are the variables that occur in the boolean condition, the
invariant and the variant. Applying this formula to check the validity of the
variant in Figure 10, the formula to be tested for validity is

$$\forall m, \#m, n, \#n, k, \#k, z(m \neq z \wedge n + m = \#n + \#m \wedge \\ k + m = \#k + \#m \wedge z = 0 \implies m > 0) \tag{9}$$

Here, since m and z are natural numbers, their values have to be at least 0 and
thus, the above formula is valid.

4.3   The Loop Invariant Is Valid Before the Loop Executes for the First Time

Some fundamental properties of a loop invariant are that it holds (a) the first
time before entering the loop, and (b) at the end of each iteration of the loop. As
in the case of variants, to prove case (b), the loop body needs to be examined,
and thus a VC is generated later for this purpose. Here for case (a), we perform
a simple check of the logical consistency of the loop invariant before entering the
loop. We need to ensure that there *exist* some values of variables in the invariant
such that it is potentially true. Thus we check the validity of (10).

$$\exists x_1, \ldots, x_n(inv_{init}) \tag{10}$$

where inv_{init} is the invariant with $\#$ symbols removed and $(x_1, \ldots, x_n)$ are
the variables in the invariant. By definition of $\#$, before the loop executes for
the first time, each unadorned variable in the invariant has the same value as
the adorned version.

Application of this procedure to the invariant in Figure 10 results in

$$\exists k, z, n, m(n + m = n + m \wedge k + m = k + m \wedge z = 0) \tag{11}$$

The validity of formula (11) confirms that the loop invariant *might* be valid
at the beginning of the loop. A VC is generated later in the tool-chain to see
whether it is *always* valid at this point.

5   Detecting Incorrect Parameter Modes

RESOLVE has multiple parameter modes: `restores`, `updates`, `replaces` and `clears`. Although some of them have been mentioned in previous sections, their meanings are consolidated in Table 1.

Table 1. Parameter modes

Parameter Mode	Description
restores	The incoming and the outgoing values of the parameter are the same
updates	The incoming and outgoing values of the parameter are potentially different
replaces	The operation's behavior does not depend on the incoming value (a special case of updates)
clears	The outgoing value of the parameter is an initial value of its type (a special case of updates)

The programmer supplies a mode for each parameter, as discussed in Section 2.3. In our technique, syntactic checks are employed to give suggestions to the programmer about the appropriate mode in case the way in which the parameter values in an operation are utilized are not consistent with the parameter mode. In our method, we allow that there might be an error either in the pre- or post-condition or in the parameter mode. In other words, we do not assume the parameter mode or the body of the specification to be absolutely correct; instead we make suggestions to assist the programmer write a correct specification when these are not consistent with each other.

5.1   A Variable with **Replaces** Mode Appears in the **Requires** Clause

If a variable occurs in the `requires` clause, the incoming value of the variable is relevant to the operation's behavior. But this cannot occur if the mode is `replaces`. Thus if the incoming value of a variable annotated with the `replaces` parameter mode is used in the `requires` or `ensures` clause, the programmer is issued a warning message.

```
procedure Divide (updates i: Integer, replaces j: Integer,
                                       replaces r: Integer)
   requires
        j /= 0
...
```

Fig. 11. Incorrect header of Divide

As an example, consider the `Divide` procedure from Section 3.2. The value of the divisor j remains unchanged, and thus the parameter mode should correctly be `restores`. Suppose instead, as shown in Figure 11, if the programmer incorrectly uses the `replaces` mode, an error is detected, since the incoming value of j is used in the `requires` clause to state that division by 0 is not allowed.

5.2   Incoming Value of a Variable in the Post-condition

The incoming value of a variable (say x) may occur in the `ensures` clause *if and only if* the parameter mode is `updates` or `clears`. For the `restores` mode, since the incoming and outgoing values of the variables are the same, $\#x$ should not appear in the `ensures` clause (because x should be used). Although the value of the variable is changed with `replaces` mode, the `ensures` clause cannot refer to the incoming value of the variable, since the incoming value is supposed to be immaterial.

Thus, a warning is given to the programmer in the following two cases:

- She used the parameter mode `updates` or `clears` and yet did not use $\#x$ in the post-condition. This could mean that either she wanted the mode to be either `restores` or `replaces` or that she missed out an additional conjunct in the `ensures` clause that refers to the incoming value of the variable.
- She designated the mode to be `restores` or `replaces` and $\#x$ appeared in the `ensures` clause.

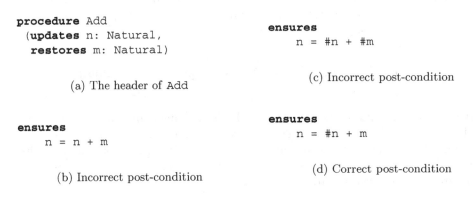

```
procedure Add
  (updates n: Natural,
   restores m: Natural)
```
(a) The header of Add

```
ensures
    n = n + m
```
(b) Incorrect post-condition

```
ensures
    n = #n + #m
```
(c) Incorrect post-condition

```
ensures
    n = #n + m
```
(d) Correct post-condition

Fig. 12. The Add operation

Figure 12 shows the contract for `Add` for natural numbers. The body of `Add` operation was illustrated in Figure 10. The header for this procedure is shown in (a). If the programmer writes the post-condition as shown in (b), an error is detected since the parameter mode for n is declared as `updates`, yet the incoming value #n does not appear in the post-condition. On the other hand, if the programmer writes the post-condition as in (c), an error is detected again since the mode for m is `restores`, and yet the incoming value #m appears. The correct post-condition is shown in (d).

5.3   Other Warnings

In addition to the errors listed above, warnings are given to the programmer when the following anomalies are noticed:

- **The `clears` parameter mode**: When the parameter mode is `clears`, typically the outgoing parameter value is not referenced in the post-condition since the parameter value is reset to an initial value of its type.

  For example, suppose a programmer declares the parameter mode of i to be `clears`, and then adds a conjunct to the post-condition which says i = 0. This conjunct is unecessary, since the RESOLVE compiler automatically adds the conjunct i = 0 to the post-condition when the parameter mode of i is `clears`.

- **The outgoing parameter equals a constant value in the post-condition**: If the mode of the variable is `restores`, then a conjunct i = `constant` should not appear in the post-condition. Since the parameter value is not changed by the operation, it is not meaningful to add a conjunct stating that the outgoing value should be equal to a particular value. (It is okay, of course, to say that some other variable is equal to this parameter.)

6   Discussion and Related Work

The examples of inconsistent specifications that are presented in Section 3 concern integers. The method presented here to detect such inconsistencies can also be applied for other datatypes such as arrays, stacks, queues, etc. However, Z3 is frequently unable to determine a formula as valid / invalid if it contains recursive definitions of datatypes. In addition, our primary admissibility-check formula contains an alternation of quantifiers that automated solvers have trouble with. It is expected that if provers become more adept at handling such datatypes and quantifiers, a larger range of specifications can be automatically checked for admissibility.

Validating program specifications has been previously described as generating test-cases [5] and as symbolic execution [6, 7]. Both of these methods rely on making the specifications executable. However, formal specifications are non-executable mathematical statements, and to conform with this characteristic, our technique uses a theorem prover to establish their validity. Heitmeyer, *et.al* [8] describe a toolset to carry out syntactic and critical property checks like safety, timing, etc., on specifications. In contrast, the analyses in this paper are more general in that they do not depend only on certain properties of particular types of specifications, but check for logical consistency of *every* program specification. They are also more involved than mere syntactic checks (as depicted in Figure 1).

Some program verifiers such as Dafny [9] are capable of detecting a subset of inconsistent specifications that are described in this paper. Dafny is capable of detecting a "division by zero" error in the `ensures` clause that states the return value as `i/j`, i.e., it explicitly uses the divide operator, when a `requires` clause stating that $j \neq 0$ is missing. But, it does not detect a more involved division by zero error such as the one present in the `Divide` specification shown in Figure 4.

Ponsini *et.al* [10] describe a way of determining the correctness of loop invariants using constraint solvers. Their correctness proof closely follows Hoare logic [11]. The admissibility checks presented in this paper are of a different nature and are more comprehensive in that consistency of loop variants is also considered.

7   Conclusions

In this paper, we developed methods to detect logical inconsistencies in program specifications and errors in loop invariants and variants. Methods to help the programmer annotate each parameter in operation headers with the correct mode are also presented.

Most inconsistencies that are identified by our techniques are logical ones: those that if present might cause an error during verification. By detecting them early, we prevent the programmer from making more mistakes further along. However, some of the inconsistencies (mentioned in Section 5.3) are warnings and not errors, in that they do not cause the verification process to fail and yet are better eliminated so that a better program specification is achieved.

In the future, we will contine to enhance our technique to detect logical inconsistencies in other specification constructs. We hope that others also implement and extend this idea to create useful lightweight tools that help programmers by leveraging formal specifications.

Acknowledgment. The authors are grateful for the suggestions of the members of RSRG. This material is based upon work supported by the National Science Foundation under Grants No. CCF-0811737, ECCS-0931669, and CCF-1162331. Any opinions, findings, conclusions, or recommendations expressed here are those of the authors and do not necessarily reflect the views of the National Science Foundation.

References

1. Sitaraman, M., Weide, B.: Component-based software using RESOLVE. SIGSOFT Softw. Eng. Notes 19, 21–63 (1994),
   http://doi.acm.org/10.1145/190679.199221
2. de Moura, L., Bjørner, N.: Z3: An efficient SMT solver. In: Ramakrishnan, C.R., Rehof, J. (eds.) TACAS 2008. LNCS, vol. 4963, pp. 337–340. Springer, Heidelberg (2008)

3. Weide, B.W., et al.: Incremental benchmarks for software verification tools and techniques. In: Shankar, N., Woodcock, J. (eds.) VSTTE 2008. LNCS, vol. 5295, pp. 84–98. Springer, Heidelberg (2008)

4. Tagore, A., Zaccai, D., Weide, B.W.: Automatically proving thousands of verification conditions using an SMT solver: An empirical study. In: Goodloe, A.E., Person, S. (eds.) NFM 2012. LNCS, vol. 7226, pp. 195–209. Springer, Heidelberg (2012)

5. Kemmerer, R.: Testing formal specifications to detect design errors. IEEE Transactions Software Engineering, 32–43 (1985)

6. Kneuper, R.: Symbolic execution as a tool for validation of specifications. PhD thesis, University of Manchester (1989)

7. Bouquet, F., Dadeau, F., Legeard, B., Utting, M.: Symbolic animation of JML specifications. In: Fitzgerald, J.S., Hayes, I.J., Tarlecki, A. (eds.) FM 2005. LNCS, vol. 3582, pp. 75–90. Springer, Heidelberg (2005)

8. Heitmeyer, C., Kirby, J., Labaw, B., Bharadwaj, R.: SCR: A toolset for specifying and analyzing software requirements. In: Vardi, M.Y. (ed.) CAV 1998. LNCS, vol. 1427, pp. 526–531. Springer, Heidelberg (1998)

9. Leino, K.R.M.: Dafny: An automatic program verifier for functional correctness. In: Clarke, E.M., Voronkov, A. (eds.) LPAR-16. LNCS, vol. 6355, pp. 348–370. Springer, Heidelberg (2010)

10. Ponsini, O., Collavizza, H., Fedele, C., Michel, C., Rueher, M.: Automatic verification of loop invariants. In: Proceedings of the 2010 IEEE International Conference on Software Maintenance, ICSM 2010, pp. 1–5. IEEE Computer Society, Washington, DC (2010)

11. Hoare, C.A.R.: An axiomatic basis for computer programming. Commun. ACM 12(10), 576–580 (1969)

BLESS: Formal Specification and Verification of Behaviors for Embedded Systems with Software*

Brian R. Larson, Patrice Chalin, and John Hatcliff

Kansas State University, Kansas, USA
{brl,chalin,hatcliff}@ksu.edu

Abstract. Recent experience in the avionics sector has demonstrated the benefits of using rigorous system architectural models, such as those supported by the standard Architectural and Analysis Definition Language (AADL), to ensure that multi-organization composition and integration tasks are successful. Despite its ability to capture interface signatures and system properties, such as scheduling periods and communication latencies as model attributes, AADL lacks a formal interface specification language, a formal semantics for component behavioral descriptions, and tools for reasoning about the compliance of behaviors to interface contracts. In this paper we introduce the Behavioral Language for Embedded Systems with Software (BLESS)—a behavioral interface specification language and proof environment for AADL. BLESS enables engineers to specify contracts on AADL components that capture both functional and timing properties. BLESS provides a formal semantics for AADL behavioral descriptions and automatic generation of verification conditions that, when proven by the BLESS proof tool, establish that behavioral descriptions conform to AADL contracts. We report on the application of BLESS to a collection of embedded system examples, including definition of multiple modes of a pacemaker.

1 Introduction

Recent experiences in the avionics sector have demonstrated the benefits of using rigorous system architectural models, such as those supported by the SAE standard Architectural and Analysis Definition Language (AADL) [19], to ensure that multi-organization integration tasks are successful. For example, on the System Architecture Virtual Integration (SAVI) effort, members of the Avionics Vehicle Systems Institute, including Boeing, AirBus, Honeywell, and Rockwell Collins, conducted pilot studies in the use of AADL to define precise system architectures [23]. Using an "integrate then build" design approach, important interactions are specified, interfaces are designed, and compatibility of modules and crucial system properties are verified before the internals of components are built. Subsequently, stakeholders provide implementations that are compliant with the architecture [9]. This development approach focuses on defining

* Work supported in part by the US National Science Foundation (NSF) (#0932289, #1239543), the NSF US Food and Drug Administration Scholar-in-Residence Program (#1065887, #1238431) the National Institutes of Health / NIBIB Quantum Program, and the US Air Force Office of Scientific Research (AFOSR) (#FA9550-09-1-0138). The authors with to thank engineers from the US Food and Drug Administration for feedback on this work.

G. Brat, N. Rungta, and A. Venet (Eds.): NFM 2013, LNCS 7871, pp. 276–290, 2013.
© Springer-Verlag Berlin Heidelberg 2013

precise interface descriptions and exposing in architectural models important properties needed to perform component-wise and system-wide analysis of real-time scheduling and error propagation properties.

Despite its ability to capture interface signatures and system properties—such as scheduling periods and communication latencies—as model attributes, AADL lacks (i) a formal behavioral interface specification language, (ii) a formal semantics for component behavioral descriptions, and (iii) tools for reasoning about the compliance of behaviors to interface specifications. Obviously, such capabilities are needed to fully support the "integrate then build" vision of SAVI, as well as the full potential of AADL in other contexts.

Previous work on Behavioral Interface Specification Languages (BISLs) [11] has produced a number of specification and verification technologies for programming languages used in system development, and has demonstrated that these techniques can support the type of formal compositional reasoning that would greatly benefit the safety-critical architecture-centric development supported by AADL and illustrated by, *e.g.*, the SAVI project. While several technical concepts and lessons learned from previous work on BISLs can be carried over and applied to the design of a BISL for AADL, there are a number of interesting differences that give rise to significant challenges not considered in BISLs such as JML [8] and Spec# [5]. For instance, while conventional programming languages focus on interactions via method calls and shared variable concurrency, AADL emphasizes component-based designs with synchronous and asynchronous communication via ports. Thus, a different approach is needed for positioning contracts in source artifacts and for generating verification conditions to support compositional reasoning in the presence of buffered and unbuffered port behavior. A behavioral specification framework for AADL must be carefully designed to align with the real-time operating system (RTOS) concepts defined in the standardized AADL runtime environment, which supports systems targeted for deployment on real-time platforms like the ARINC 653, a platform for modular avionics [12]. A behavioral specification framework for AADL must also provide a means of specifying and reasoning about crucial timing properties phrased in terms of the RTOS concepts of scheduling periods exposed as architecture attributes . Finally, since AADL is used in domains that require certification, it is desirable for tools that reason about envisioned AADL specifications produce auditable artifacts that can be assessed as part of the certification process.

In this paper, we introduce the *Behavioral Language for Embedded Systems with Software* (BLESS)—a BISL and an associated proof environment for AADL [13]. The AADL standard provides the notion of an "AADL Annex" to support extensions to the modeling language, and BLESS uses this mechanism to introduce notations for (a) specifying behaviors on component interfaces, (b) defining AADL-runtime aware transition systems that capture the internal behavior of AADL components, and (c) writing assertions to capture important state and event properties within the transition system notation. BLESS annex subclauses can be inserted into AADL components transparently to other uses of the system architecture. Successful definition and tool engineering for formal reasoning frameworks like BLESS require a precisely defined formal semantics, and we have invested considerable effort in defining a such a semantics for

BLESS[1]. Finally, BLESS includes a verification-condition (VC) generation framework and an accompanying proof tool that enables engineers to prove VCs via proof scripts build from system axioms and rules from a user-customizable rule library.

BLESS and AADL are rich, expressive languages. Due to space constraints, this paper gives a cursory introduction to AADL (Section 2), and then focuses on the *core features* of the BLESS language (Sections 3 & 4) and its associated specification and verification methodology which is assisted by the BLESS tool (Section 5). Material is presented using a running example from the medical device domain: a pacemaker [21].

The BLESS tool framework [24] is implemented as a publicly available open source plug-in to the Eclipse-based OSATE environment for AADL [18], and includes and editor for BLESS specifications and an environment operating the BLESS proof engine.

2   Background and Motivation

Avionics & origins of AADL: To manage the ever increasing complexity of electronic control systems, engineers devised ways to recursively partition complex systems into collections of simpler sub-systems. As a result, several *architectural* domain specific languages (DSLs) were invented[2] to capture system structure and, more importantly, the specification of interfaces—which are crucial to successful system composition.

In a movement to standardize an architectural description language for avionics and aerospace systems, SAE International sponsored standard subcommittee AS-2C; it is from this effort that SAE AS5506 *Architecture Analysis & Design Language* (AADL) was created, and revised upon use, now AS5506C. Both commercial and open source tools for creating and analyzing AADL models are available [18].

AADL Core and Annex Sublanguages: AADL was designed with extensibility in mind. It has a core language defined in its own standards document. The core language allows one to express architectural structure—using components, interfaces, connections, containment—but not behavior. The core language is extensible with *annex sublanguages*, some of which have been standardized by an annex standard document approved by AS-2C. The AADL (core) grammar allows insertion, into the text representing components, an annex subclause of the form: `annex AnnexName {** ... **}`. Key standardized annexes include [20]:

- Behavior Annex (BA) extends AADL with the ability of defining component behavior via state machines having: states, state variables and (guarded) state transitions with associated actions written in a simple imperative language.
- Data Modeling Annex (DM) supports the definition of data components.
- ARINC653 Annex defines properties relevant to the elaboration of ARINC653 compliant embedded systems.

BLESS, inspired from BA, improves and extends the state-transition formalism and, more importantly, introduces the notion of *Assertion* as a basic building block for contractual specifications. BLESS also adds contracts to AADL subprograms, though this feature is not covered here.

---

[1] Due to space constraints, the semantics cannot be presented here. We refer interested readers to [13] for the formal semantics and details of the VC generation process.

[2] The section on related work describes some of these DSL.

Upon reviewing an early draft of the proposed standard annex document, a committee member pondered whether a tool made to transform proof outlines of highly-concurrent programs could be adapted for a suitably-annotated state-transition system. Motivated by this possibility, the first author created BLESS: an AADL annex sublanguage that can be used to annotate BA behavior with Assertions[3].

3 BLESS by Example: A Simple Pacemaker

3.1 Cardiac Pacing

Cardiac pacing is used for a compact illustration of BLESS, because it is a simple safety-critical cyber-physical systems having crucial timing properties. Figure 1 depicts a pacemaker (Pulse Generator) connected by pacing leads to the inside of a heart's right atrium and ventricle.

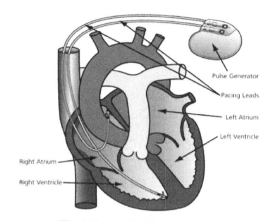

Fig. 1. Pacemaker Environment

The first pacemakers emitted a short (<1 ms), low voltage (1V to 10V) "pace" at a rate fixed (60-80 bpm) in the factory through a single lead to the right ventricle. A pace causes a cascade of cell contractions in both right and left ventricles, expelling blood to lungs and body, respectively. The earliest electrophysiologists selected the pacing rate and voltage when ordering a device. When everything worked, people whose bradycardia[4] made simple walking activities tiresome, felt "normal" after the implant, instead of incessantly-increasing fatigue until succumbing to their heart disease.

However, constant-rate electrical-pacing interfered intrinsic pacing of a patient's heart. Fortunately, the same leads implanted to deliver electrical paces, can also sense intrinsic electrical activity of the heart (approx. 1mV). These signals, sensed within the heart, are called *electrograms*.

Analog design wizards devised ways to amplify and filter millivolt electrograms, and then to compare the signal with a programmable threshold to determine whether an intrinsic contraction occurred (Figure 2). This allowed the pacemaker to monitor the patient and inhibit electrical-pacing when intrinsic pacing voltage exceeds a lower limit. This inhibitory behavior became known as "VVI", short for: Ventricle (chamber(s) paced), Ventricle (chamber(s) sensed), Inhibit [5].

Complicating matters, real hearts are electrically noisy during and after contraction, so the pacemaker must ignore any sensed voltage for a period of time after either pacing or sensing heart contraction. By adjusting this *ventricular refractory period* (VRP) and sensing threshold, an electrophysiologist can tune a pacemaker for a specific patient, and by choosing a *lower rate limit* (LRL), ensure minimum heart rate.

---

[3] Capital 'A' as the proper-noun for assertions defined by BLESS.

[4] Bradycardia is the class of cardiac diseases in which the heart beats too slowly.

[5] Constant-rate pacing is referred to as VOO, for "pace ventricle, no sensing, constant rate".

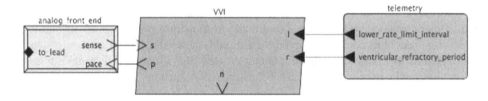

Fig. 2. Pacemaker System Diagram in AADL Graphical Notation

```
thread VVI
  features
    s: in event port;      -- sense of a ventricular contraction
    p: out event port;     -- pace ventricle
    n: out event port;     -- non-refractory ventricular sense
    lrl: in data port BLESS_Types::Time;   -- lower rate limit interval
    vrp: in data port BLESS_Types::Time;   -- ventricular refractory period
  properties
    Dispatch_Protocol => Aperiodic;
end VVI;
```

Fig. 3. AADL VVI Thread Component Type

The first author worked for five years at a leading pacemaker company, and was responsible for the release of a requirements document for a previous generation pacemaker that since been used in over 25 research papers within the formal methods community [21]. The pacing examples that we discuss in this paper adhere to those requirements.

3.2 AADL VVI Component

Presented using the standardized graphical view of AADL models, Figure 2 shows the top-level architecture of a pacing system where the structure has been simplified to focus tightly on the elements needed to present a description of the VVI pacing mode. Figure 3 shows the AADL component type that describes the interface of a thread that performs the VVI control function. The interface has three asynchronous *event* ports s, p and n. Events arrive at port s (ventricular-sense) whenever the analog front end detects electrograms exceeding the prescribed threshold. Events sent out on port p (ventricular-pace) cause the front end to administer a pace of prescribed voltage. An event sent out on port n (non-refractory ventricular-sense) indicates that a ventricular-sense was detected after expiration of the ventricular refractory period (VRP). Data ports support the automatic propagation of state values from one component to another, without triggering a thread dispatch within the receiving component. Data ports lrl and vrp communicate the lower rate limit interval and ventricular refractory period programmed by the physician through the telemetry subsystem.

3.3 Behavior for VVI

Figure 4 shows a BLESS state machine (without BLESS Assertions) that captures the behavior of the VVI component. Without Assertions, BLESS annex language subclauses deliberately appear similar to BA subclauses . BLESS annex subclauses have sections for `variables`, `states`, and `transitions`.

Variable values persist from thread suspension to next dispatch . States must be one of `initial`, `complete`, `final`, or *execute* if none of these. Behavior begins in the `initial` state, terminates in a `final`, suspends upon entry to `complete` states until next dispatch. State transitions (in BA and BLESS) are of the form:

transition_name: *source_state(s)* -[*condition*]-> *destination_state* {*action*};

Transitions are named (*e.g.*, `T2`[6]), and each transition includes one or more source states (*e.g.*, the `pace` and `sense` states of `T2`), a single target state (*e.g.*, the `off` state of `T2`), guard expression (*e.g.*, the `on dispatch s` of `T4` which holds when an event arrives on the `s` event port), and a (possibly empty) set of actions to execute (*e.g.*, `p! & last_beat := now` of `T3`). Transitions must be written to guarantee that only a finite number of execute states are passed through before entering a complete or final state. Transitions leaving `complete` states have dispatch conditions evaluated by the run time system . The special dispatch condition `on dispatch` **stop** holds when an event is received on a **stop** (which is predeclared for every AADL component to cause normal termination). Transitions leaving execute states may have a boolean expression as transition condition, so long as there is at least one enabled transition and a complete state will eventually be reached. Sending an event out on a port `p` is written `p!`. The current time is written as `now`. Action sets separated by "`&`" may be executed in any order, or concurrently; action sequences separated by "`;`" must be executed in order; assignment uses "`:=`". A `timeout` with a port list and a duration is reset by event arrival or departure at a listed port, and expires when the most recent event on a listed port occurred the duration previously.

The transition system captures the behavior of VVI as follows. The time of the most recent cardiac event is retained in the persistent variable `last_beat`. After causing a ventricular pace to begin operation [T1], VVI waits for either a ventricular sense [T4] (which it then checks for VRP [T5,T6]) or a timeout of the patient's lower-rate-limit interval since the most-recent cardiac event [T3]. If the time since the most recent cardiac event to the current ventricular sense is within the VRP, then return to the `pace` state and wait some more [T5]. Otherwise, reset `last_beat` to "now", and send an event out on `n` to reset the timeout [T6]. When no cardiac events have occurred in the previous lower-rate-limit interval (timeout), send an event out on `p` to cause an electrical-pace, and reset the timeout [T7]. The behavior from the `sense` state is similar [T8,T9,T10].

3.4   Adding BLESS Assertions to VVI

BLESS introduces Assertions to AADL as a basic block to forming rich behavioral specifications. Syntactically, Assertions are always enclosed in double angle brackets, `<< >>`. Semantically, an Assertion is a temporal logic formula extending a first-order predicate calculus with simple temporal operators for continuous `p@t` and discrete time `p^k`, where `t` is the time at which `p` occurs, and `k` is the number of dispatch periods from now. As indicated by operators such as `p^k`, BLESS Assertions are able to reason

---

[6] We will sometimes abbreviate transition names, using only the "T#" prefix.

```
annex BLESS {**
variables
  last_beat: BLESS_Types::Time;
states
  power_on : initial state;
  pace : complete state;
  sense : complete state;
  check_pace_vrp : state;
  check_sense_vrp : state;
  off : final state;
transitions
  T1_POWER_ON:
    power_on -[ ]-> pace  {p! & last_beat := now};
  T2_STOP:
    pace,sense -[on dispatch stop]-> off {};
  T3_PACE_LRL_AFTER_VP:
    pace -[on dispatch timeout (p n) lrl ms]-> pace
      {p! & last_beat := now};
  T4_VS_AFTER_VP:
    pace -[on dispatch s]-> check_pace_vrp {};
  T5_VS_AFTER_VP_IN_VRP:
    check_pace_vrp -[(now-last_beat) < vrp]-> pace {};
  T6_VS_AFTER_VP_IS_NR:
    check_pace_vrp -[(now-last_beat) >= vrp]-> sense
      {n! & last_beat := now};
  T7_PACE_LRL_AFTER_VS:
    sense -[on dispatch timeout (p n) lrl ms]-> pace
      {p! & last_beat := now};
  T8_VS_AFTER_VS:
    sense -[on dispatch s]-> check_sense_vrp {};
  T9_VS_AFTER_VS_IN_VRP:
    check_sense_vrp -[(now-last_beat) < vrp]-> sense {};
  T10_VS_AFTER_VS_IS_NR:
    check_sense_vrp -[(now-last_beat) >= vrp]-> sense
      {n! & last_beat := now};
**};
```

Fig. 4. VVI Thread Behavior (without BLESS assertions)

directly in terms of the logical scheduling periods captured in the AADL run-time environment – which forms an abstraction of common threading and scheduling services, *etc.*, found in widely-used real-time operating systems. Thus, in contrast to other modeling languages and model checking frameworks that assume arbitrary interleaving of concurrent transitions, BLESS assumes an interleaving semantics corresponding to the scheduling abstractions in the standardized AADL run-time environment.

BLESS supports the following kinds of Assertion:

- *Port Assertion* expresses what is true when an event is sent or received on a port.
- *State Assertion* expresses what is true while the machine is in that state.
- *Action Step Assertion* expresses what is true during the execution of a transition's action steps, at that point where the Assertion is inserted.
- *Thread Invariant* expresses a predicate that must be true of every state.

As will be illustrated next, VVI relevant examples of each kind of Assertion are given in Figure 5.

Before doing so we will review BLESS's support for "predicate abstraction" allowing (parameterized) predicates to be named and subsequently used in Assertions. As an example, refer to the LRL predicate defined on line 14 in Figure 5. It captures the property that the patient had an intrinsic or electrically-paced heartbeat in the previous lower-rate-limit interval (cf. lrl defined in Figure 3). The identifier x is a formal parameter representing a particular time. The predicate can be read as follows: there exists a time t in the closed interval $[x - lrl, x]$ such that an event was issued on port n or port p at time t.

```
   thread VVI
2    features
       s: in event port;        -- ventricular contraction has been sensed
4      p: out event port        -- pace ventricle
         {BLESS::Assertion=>"<<VP()>>";};
6      n: out event port        -- non-refractory ventricular sense
         {BLESS::Assertion=>"<<VS()>>";};
8      lrl: in data port T;     -- lower rate limit interval
       vrp: in data port T;     -- ventricular refractory period
10   properties
       Dispatch_Protocol => Aperiodic;
12   annex BLESS {**
   assert
14   <<LRL:x: exists t:T in x-lrl..x that (n@t or p@t)>>  -- Lower Rate Limit
     <<VS: : s@now and notVRP()>> -- ventricular sense detected, not in VRP
16   <<VP: :  -- ventricular pace
       (n or p)@(now-lrl)  --last beat occurred LRL interval ago,
18     and  -- not since then ("," means open interval)
         not (exists t:T in now-lrl,,now that (n or p)@t) >>
20   ... -- Not shown are notVRP(), PACE(t), SENSE(t), etc.
   invariant
22   <<LRL(now)>>  -- LRL is "always" true
   variables
24   last_beat : T
       <<LAST: : (n or p)@last_beat>>;  -- time of last pace or NR sense
26   states
     power_on : initial state <<VS()>>;  --start with "sense"
28   pace : complete state
       -- ventricular pace occurred in previous LRL interval
30     <<PACE(now)>>;
     sense : complete state
32     -- ventricular sense occurred in previous LRL interval
       <<SENSE(now)>>;
34   check_pace_vrp : state
       -- execute state to check if s is in vrp after pace
36     <<s@now and PACE(now)>>;
     check_sense_vrp : state
38     -- execute state to check if s is in vrp after sense
       <<s@now and SENSE(now)>>;
40   off : final state;
   transitions
42   T1_POWER_ON:  power_on -[ ]-> sense
       {<<VS()>> n! <<n@now>> & last_beat := now <<last_beat=now>>};
44   ...
     T6_VS_AFTER_VP_IS_NR: check_pace_vrp -[(now-last_beat)>=r]-> sense
46   -- s after VRP, go to "sense" state, send n!, reset timeouts
       {<<VS()>> n! <<n@now>> & last_beat := now <<last_beat=now>>};
48 ... **}; ...
```

Fig. 5. BLESS-annotated VVI Thread Component Type

Figure 5 also illustrates how a `BLESS::Assertion` can be attached to a port (cf. lines 5 and 7). By attaching such Assertions one is specifying that the given predicate will be true whenever an event is issued over the port. The VVI thread invariant (`LRL(now)`) is given on line 22; it is effectively stating that: from when the thread leaves its initial state until it enters a final state, the patient has a heart beat in the previous lower rate limit interval. Finally, an example of a state Assertion is given on line 30 for the `pace` state; and inlined action step Assertions are given on, *e.g.*, line 43.

The complete BLESS source for the VVI example is available in [14]. (As a convenience of reviewers, we have included the complete BLESS source for VVI.aadl in an appendix.)

4 Thread Verification Obligations

For a subprogram annotated with a contract, its correctness argument (which we will call a proof obligation) takes the form of: under the assumption that the precondition holds, if the body is executed (and terminates), then the postcondition must hold.

A thread has a proof obligation for each complete or execute state, and each transition. In the subsections that follow, we illustrate each of these kinds of proof obligation. As we shall see, all proof obligations have the form $<<P>>S<<Q>>$ where P and Q are Assertions, and S is an action (possibly Skip, the empty action).

Complete State Assertions Imply Invariant: Entering a complete state suspends the thread until next dispatch. Therefore each complete state's Assertion must imply the thread's invariant. Thus, *e.g.*, the complete state pace has Assertion <<PACE(now)>>. Its proof obligation, as generated by the BLESS proof tool, is:[7]

```
P [64] <<PACE(now)>>
S [51]->
Q [51] <<LRL(now)>>
   What for: <<M(pace)>> -> <<I>> from invariant I when complete
   state pace has Assertion <<M(pace)>> in its definition.
```

The "What for" part explains why the proof tool generated the proof obligation; M(...) represents a meaning function. Thus, the "meaning" of the pace state is the pace state Assertion.

Execute States Have Enabled Outgoing Transition: Execute states are transitory and so they must always have an enabled, outgoing transition. If more than one transition is enabled, the choice is nondeterministic. Each execute state's Assertion must imply the disjunction of outgoing transition conditions[8]. Proof obligation for execute states check_pace_vrp is:

```
P [71] <<s@now and PACE(now)>>
S [71]->
Q [71] <<((now-last_beat) < vrp) or ((now-last_beat) >= vrp)>>
   What for: Serban's Theorem:  disjunction of execute conditions
   leaving execution state check_pace_vrp,
   <<M(check_pace_vrp)>> ->  <<e1 or e2 or . . . en>>
```

Execute Transitions without Actions: For transitions without actions, the conjunction of the Assertion of the source state and the transition condition must imply the Assertion of the destination state. Execute transitions have Boolean-valued expressions for transition conditions. Proof obligation for execute transition T5 is:

```
P [71] <<s@now and PACE(now) and ((now-last_beat) < vrp)>>
S [97]->
Q [64] <<PACE(now)>>
   What for:  <<M(check_pace_vrp) and x>> -> <<M(pace)>> for
   T5_VS_AFTER_VP_IN_VRP:check_pace_vrp-[x]->pace{};
```

The transition condition T5 occurs when a sense was in VRP, thus ignored. As was mentioned earlier, M(check_pace_vrp) stands for the meaning of check_pace_vrp, which is its Assertion: <<s@now and PACE(now)>>. Since the T5 transition condition is (now-last_beat) < vrp, their conjunction is the predicate given as P in the proof obligation. The Assertion for state pace, <<M(pace)>>, is <<PACE(now)>>, shown as Q.

Execute Transitions with Actions: For execute transitions with actions, the conjunction of the Assertion of the source state and the transition condition becomes the

---

[7] Numbers in square brackets correspond to line #s in the full VVI source given in [14].

[8] Named for Serban Georghe.

precondition; and the Assertion of the destination state is the postcondition. The proof obligation for execute transition with actions T6 is:

```
 P [71] <<s@now and PACE(now) and ((now-last_beat) >= r)>>
 S [104]<<VS()>>n!<<n@now>> & last_beat := now<<last_beat=now>>
 Q [68] <<SENSE(now)>>
    What for:   <<M(check_pace_vrp) and x>> A <<M(sense)>> for
    T6_VS_AFTER_VP_IS_NR:check_pace_vrp-[x]->sense{A};
```

Note that it is similar for T10. For both T6 and T10, the sense was after expiration of the ventricular refractory period, with the same action A: an event sent out port n, and last_beat set to the current time.

Initial and Stop Transitions: Transitions leaving initial states have proof obligations like execute transitions, with or without actions.

Every AADL component has an implicit **stop** port meant to signal orderly termination and transition to a final state. Because final states don't do anything, stop transitions without actions like T2 generate trivial proof obligations logically equivalent to *true*.

Dispatch Transitions with Timeout: Transitions leaving complete states must have dispatch conditions evaluated by the runtime system . BLESS follows BA in requiring that dispatch conditions be disjunctions of conjunctions of dispatch triggers. Relative to BA, BLESS extends the definition of the timeout dispatch trigger to include port lists. Without a port list, BLESS, like BA, defines the timeout starting at the *time-of-previous-suspension* (**tops**). With a port list, BLESS timeouts are reset by any event, sent or received, on a listed port.

Dispatch trigger from timeout occurs when

- an event was sent or received on a listed port (one timeout period in the past),
- no other event has been sent or received by any listed port since then, and
- none of the other dispatch conditions leaving the same source state has occurred since the time-of-previous-suspension (tops).

For transition T3 events leaving either port p or port n, reset the timeout.

```
  T3_PACE_LRL_AFTER_VP:  --pace when LRL times out
  pace -[on dispatch timeout (p n) lrl ms]-> pace
    {<<VP()>> p! <<p@now>> & last_beat := now< <last_beat=now>>};
```

The proof obligation for T3 in Figure 6 has a complex precondition:

- Assertion of the pace source state invariant: PACE(now).
- Port event LRL occurred previously: (p **or** n)@(now-lrl).
- No port events to reset timeout:
  not (exists t:T **in** now-lrl,,now that (p **or** n)@t).
- No stop since time-of-previous-suspension (tops) [T2]:
  not (exists u:T **in** tops,,now that **stop**).
- No sense since tops [T4]:**not** (exists u:T **in** tops,,now that s@u).
- No timeout since tops: **not** (exists u:T **in** tops,,now that
  ((p **or** n)@(u-lrl) **and**
  not (exists t:T **in** u-lrl,,u that (p **or** n)@t)))

The full listing of initial proof obligations from which these examples are excerpted, can be found in [14].

```
P [88] <<PACE(now) and (p or n)@(now-lrl)
   and not (exists t:T in now-lrl,,now that (p or n)@t)
   and not (exists u:T in tops,,now  that stop)
   and not (exists u:T in tops,,now that s@u)
   and not (exists u:T in tops,,now that ((p or n)@(u-lrl) and
            not (exists t:T in u-lrl,,u that (p or n)@t)))>>
S [91]<<VP()>>p!<<p@now>> & last_beat := now<<last_beat = now>>
Q [64] <<PACE(now)>>
  What for:  <<M(pace) and x>> A <<M(pace)>> for
  T3_PACE_LRL_AFTER_VP:pace-[x]->pace{A};
```

Fig. 6. Verification Obligation for Transition With Timeout

5 Using the BLESS Proof Tool

5.1 Discharing Proof Oblications

The BLESS proof tool both: (i) generates proof obligations from AADL models having
BLESS annex subclauses defining behavior adorned with Assertions, and (ii) transforms proof obligations into simpler ones, with human guidance, successively by applying inference rules.When all proof obligations have been solved, the BLESS proof
tool produces a formal proof as a list of theorems, each of which is axiomatic, or derived from earlier theorems in the sequence by a stated inference rule. The last theorem
in the sequence asserts that all proof obligations have been discharged.

The BLESS proof tool works as a plug-in to the Open-Source AADL Tool Environment version 2 (OSATE 2) for editing and analyzing AADL models [18], together with
a growing family of architectural analysis plug-ins. Typically, after loading a model in
BLESS, all of the proof obligations are generated together, but solved one-at-a-time, by
applying (groups of) proof rules.

The first proof obligation for VVI is:

```
P [64]  <<PACE(now)>>
S [51]->
Q [51]  <<LRL(now)>>
```

It shows that the Assertion of complete state pace, <<PACE(now)>>, needs to imply
the thread invariant, <<LRL(now)>>. By expanding the named predicates we obtain:

```
P [64] <<p@last_beat and
         (exists t:BLESS_Types::Time in now-lrl..now that p@t )>>
S [51]->
Q [51] <<exists t:BLESS_Types::Time in now-lrl..now
         that (n@t or p@t)>>
```

By splitting existential quantification we get:

```
P [64] <<p@last_beat and
         (exists t:BLESS_Types::Time in now-lrl..now that p@t)>>
S [51]->
Q [51] <<(exists t:BLESS_Types::Time in now-lrl..now that n@t)
     or (exists t:BLESS_Types::Time in now-lrl..now that p@t)>>
```

After some normalization of the predicates we get:

```
P [64] <<(exists t:BLESS_Types::Time in now-lrl..now  that p@t)
    and p@last_beat>>
S [51]->
Q [51] <<(exists t:BLESS_Types::Time in now-lrl..now that n@t )
    or (exists t:BLESS_Types::Time in now-lrl..now that p@t)>>
```

which is then recognized as an axiom of the form $(P \wedge Q) \rightarrow (P \vee Q)$.

```
Theorem (1)                          [serial 1020]
P [64] <<(exists t:BLESS_Types::Time in now-lrl..now that p@t )
       and p@last_beat>>
S [51] ->
Q [51] <<(exists t:BLESS_Types::Time in now-lrl..now that n@t )
       or (exists t:BLESS_Types::Time in now-lrl..now that p@t )>>
by And-Elimination/Or-Introduction Schema:
   (P and Q)->(P or R)
Theorem (2)                          [serial 1019]
P [64] <<(p@last_beat and (exists t:BLESS_Types::Time
       in now-lrl..now that p@t ))>>
S [51] ->
Q [51] <<((exists t:BLESS_Types::Time in now-lrl..now that n@t )
       or (exists t:BLESS_Types::Time in now-lrl..now that p@t ))>>
by Normalization:
      Reflexivity of Conjunction: (m and k) = (k and m)
      Add Unnecessary Parentheses For No Good Reason: a = (a)
and Theorem (1) [serial 1020]

...

Theorem (4)                          [serial 1003]
P [64] <<PACE(now)>>
S [51] ->
Q [51] <<LRL(now)>>
by Substitution of Assertion Labels
and Theorem (3) [serial 1018]
Theorem (119)                        [serial 1002]
P     <<VVI proof obligations>>
S [51] ->
Q     <<VVI proof obligations>>
by Initial Thread Obligations
and theorems 4 8 11 14 28 29 30 50 52 53 74 94 96 97 118:

...

Theorem (97) [serial 1016] used for:
   <<M(check_sense_vrp) and x>> -> <<M(sense)>> for
   T9_VS_AFTER_VS_IN_VRP:check_sense_vrp-[x]->sense{};
Theorem (118) [serial 1017] used for:
   <<M(check_sense_vrp) and x>> A <<M(sense)>> for
   T10_VS_AFTER_VS_IS_NR:check_sense_vrp-[x]->sense{A};
```

Fig. 7. Selected Theorems from the Complete VVI Proof

Then the next proof obligation is placed in the set of currently unsolved proof obligations. The BLESS proof tool accepts script files, and writes actions to a script file that can be edited, and invoked, to make re-play of proof strategies easy. When all of the proof obligations have been solved, theorem numbers are assigned depth first, and the complete proof is emitted.

While the current proof process is manual, we plan to capitalize on the growth in power and usability of theorem provers (*e.g.*, SMT solvers) to help automate as much of the proof process as possible.

5.2 Complete Formal Proof for VVI

In all, the complete proof for VVI requires 119 theorems, some of which are illustrated in Figure 7. Sample theorems include: Theorem (4), which discharges the first proof obligation considered in Section 5.1; the last theorem (119) states that all the proof obligations have been discharged.

6 Evaluation

As can be seen from Table 1, we have been writing BLESS architectural specifications on progressively large case studies and attempting to complete verification proofs. The table gives the AADL/BLESS Model name, the number of AADL components in the

Table 1. BLESS Models

AADL Model	Number of Component	SLOC	Number of Theorems	Number of Proof script steps
VVI pacemaker	1	100	119	101
DDD pacemaker	1	302	1274	582
PulseOx Smart Alarm App	5	949	1003	460
Isolette	15	628	verif. in progress	288
PCA Pump	43	1389	verif. not started	-

model and the number of Source Lines Of Code (SLOC). In addition to the VVI pacing mode described here, the examples include DDD pacing mode (a more complex pacing mode in which both atrium and ventricle are paced and sensed instead of just the ventricle as in VVI), an application that implements "smart alarms" for pulse oximetry monitoring, the control logic for an infant incubator (Isolette), and a detailed architectural specification (43 software and hardware components) for a Patient-Controlled Analgesia Pump developed in collaboration with engineers from the US Food and Drug Administration. The verification proofs for the two pacemaker case studies have been completed, as indicated by the availability of the number of theorems required to complete the proof. The last three examples have arisen as part of our work on a Medical Application Platform (MAP) for coordinating collections of networked devices [10]. While these case studies are larger, their verification proofs are still in progress. This is due, in part, to the fact that the models are still evolving. Each case study has allowed us to identify the need to enhance the BLESS tool's set of rules for use in discharging proofs. It has also made evident, especially in the context of evolving models, of the need for further proof automation.

7 Related Work

Much work has been done on formal methods for reasoning about behavioral descriptions in high-level modeling languages such as UML. While model checking applied to notations such as Statecharts and other state machine notations has been well-studied (*e.g.*, [16]), such approaches primarily focus on verifying temporal properties or simple assertions, instead of the strong functional properties expressible in BLESS, or properties that relate directly to timing and scheduling periods in the run-time environment. Relatively little has been done on proof tools for behavioral descriptions in architecture definition languages. In one example, Thums and Balser [22] provide an interactive verification framework for Statecharts based on Dynamic Logic.

The B Method [1] and successor Event-B [2] are nice examples of mature frameworks with tool support that emphasize proof for high-level designs of realistic systems. The Atelier B tool generates proof obligations from behavioral models and provides a manually oriented proof environment. Recent work, *e.g.*, [15], provides tools that translate Atelier B proof obligations into Why3 so as to leverage SMT solvers. Rodin [3] provides proof support for Event B by generating proof obligations. Both B and Event-B focus much more heavily on refinement of high-level semantic descriptions rather than on behaviors in the context of architectural descriptions.

For previous work on verification of the behavioral aspects of AADL models, a translation of a subset of AADL BA into an extension of Petri nets is given by [7], while Ölveczky *et al.* translate AADL BA into Real-Time Maude [17]. These strategies employ model checking and term rewriting, respectively, to verify simple assertions and temporal properties. Thus, they achieve a much higher degree of automation, but treat less expressive specification languages.

Also mentioned in the introduction was the important class of specification language named Behavioral Interface Specification Languages. Notable members of this class include the Java Modeling Language and Spec# (a BISL for C#). Most BISLs are enriched contract-based languages intended for the specification and verification of single-threaded software systems. The KeY Project supports the addition of specifications to software models expressed in UML using languages such as JML and OCL [4, 6].

8   Conclusion

The primary result of this paper—the BLESS framework for behavioral interface specification and verification—represents a significant advance in AADL capabilities that relates directly to AADL's core objectives of supporting rigorous system integration in critical systems. The key technical contributions include designing specifications that capture both functional and timing properties in a manner that aligns with AADL's inter-component communication primitives, scheduling framework, and run-time environment.

Working from the specification notations, formal semantics, and tool support developed here, multiple automated verification methods, including model checking and symbolic execution, can be developed to support verification of AADL component behaviors and interface descriptions. In this first stage of our work, our goal has been to provide tool support that exercises the entirety of the BLESS language, provides strong verification, and provides a formal framework on which more automated, lighter-weight analyses can be built.

In addition to directly supporting interface specification and verification, BLESS annotations can support other facets of critical system development. For example, BLESS is being used in US Army-funded work at the Software Engineering Institute (SEI) on AADL's Error Model Annex to capture system conditions under which faults/errors may arise and propagate. BLESS is also being used in the AADL Requirements Definition and Analysis Language (RDAL) Annex to formally define requirements.

References

1. Abrial, J.-R.: The B-book: assigning programs to meanings. Cambridge University Press, New York (1996)
2. Abrial, J.-R.: Modeling in Event-B: System and Software Engineering. Cambridge University Press, New York (2010)
3. Abrial, J.-R., Butler, M., Hallerstede, S., Hoang, T.S., Mehta, F., Voisin, L.: Rodin: an open toolset for modelling and reasoning in Event-B. Int. J. Softw. Tools Technol. Transf. 12(6), 447–466 (2010)

4. Ahrendt, W., Baar, T., Beckert, B., Bubel, R., Giese, M., Hähnle, R., Menzel, W., Mostowski, W., Roth, A., Schlager, S., Schmitt, P.H.: The KeY tool. Software and Systems Modeling 4, 32–54 (2005)
5. Barnett, M., Leino, K.R.M., Schulte, W.: The spec# programming system: An overview. In: Barthe, G., Burdy, L., Huisman, M., Lanet, J.-L., Muntean, T. (eds.) CASSIS 2004. LNCS, vol. 3362, pp. 49–69. Springer, Heidelberg (2005)
6. Beckert, B., Hähnle, R., Schmitt, P.H. (eds.): Verification of Object-Oriented Software. LNCS (LNAI), vol. 4334. Springer, Heidelberg (2007)
7. Berthomieu, B., Bodeveix, J.-P., Chaudet, C., Dal Zilio, S., Filali, M., Vernadat, F.: Formal verification of AADL specifications in the topcased environment. In: Kordon, F., Kermarrec, Y. (eds.) Ada-Europe 2009. LNCS, vol. 5570, pp. 207–221. Springer, Heidelberg (2009)
8. Burdy, L., Cheon, Y., Cok, D.R., Ernst, M.D., Kiniry, J.R., Leavens, G.T., Leino, K.R.M., Poll, E.: An overview of JML tools and applications. Journal on Software Tools for Technology Transfer (STTT) 7(3), 212–232 (2005)
9. Feiler, P.H., Hansson, J., de Niz, D., Wrage, L.: System architecture virtual integration: An industrial case study. Technical Report CMU/SEI-2009-TR-017 (2009)
10. Hatcliff, J., King, A., Lee, I., Fernandez, A., Goldman, J., McDonald, A., Robkin, M., Vasserman, E., Weininger, S.: Rationale and architecture principles for medical application platforms. In: Proceedings of the 2012 International Conference on Cyberphysical Systems (2012)
11. Hatcliff, J., Leavens, G.T., Leino, K.R.M., Müller, P., Parkinson, M.: Behavioral interface specification languages. ACM Comput. Surv. 44(3), 16:1–16:58 (2012)
12. Januzaj, V., Mauersberger, R., Biechele, F.: Performance modelling for avionics systems. In: Moreno-Díaz, R., Pichler, F., Quesada-Arencibia, A. (eds.) EUROCAST 2009. LNCS, vol. 5717, pp. 833–840. Springer, Heidelberg (2009)
13. Larson, B.R.: Behavior Language for Embedded Systems with Software Annex Sublanguage for AADL (2012), Available at [24]
14. Larson, B.R., Chalin, P., Hatcliff, J.: BLESS: Formal specification and verification of behaviors for embedded systems with software. Technical Report SAnToS 2012-12-01, Kansas State University, Computing and Information Sc. Dept. (2012), Available at [24]
15. Mentré, D., Marché, C., Filliâtre, J.-C., Asuka, M.: Discharging proof obligations from Atelier B using multiple automated provers. In: Derrick, J., Fitzgerald, J., Gnesi, S., Khurshid, S., Leuschel, M., Reeves, S., Riccobene, E. (eds.) ABZ 2012. LNCS, vol. 7316, pp. 238–251. Springer, Heidelberg (2012)
16. Mikk, E., Lakhnech, Y., Siegel, M., Holzmann, G.J.: Implementing Statecharts in PROMELA/SPIN. In: Proceedings of the Workshop on Industrial Strength Formal Specification Techniques (WIFT). IEEE Computer Society, Washington, DC (1998)
17. Ölveczky, P.C., Boronat, A., Meseguer, J.: Formal semantics and analysis of behavioral AADL models in Real-Time Maude. In: Hatcliff, J., Zucca, E. (eds.) FMOODS/FORTE 2010. LNCS, vol. 6117, pp. 47–62. Springer, Heidelberg (2010)
18. Osate 2 web site (2012), `wiki.sei.cmu.edu/aadl/index.php/Osate_2`
19. SAE International. SAE AS5506A. Architecture Analysis & Design Language (AADL) (2009)
20. SAE International. SAE AS5506/2. Architecture Analysis & Design Language (AADL) Annex, vol. 2 (2011)
21. Boston Scientific. Pacemaker system specification (2007), `sqrl.mcmaster.ca/pacemaker.html`
22. Thums, A., Balser, M.: Interactive verification of statecharts. Integration of Software Spec. Tech. (INT) (2002)
23. System Architecture Virtual Integration (SAVI) Initiative (2012), `wiki.sei.cmu.edu/aadl/index.php/Projects_and_Initiatives`
24. SAnToS TR 2012-12-01 web site, `info.santoslab.org/research/aadl/bless`

Towards Complete Specifications with an Error Calculus

Quang Loc Le[1], Asankhaya Sharma[1], Florin Craciun[2], and Wei-Ngan Chin[1]

[1] Department of Computer Science, National University of Singapore
[2] Faculty of Mathematics and Computer Science, Babes-Bolyai University, Romania

Abstract. We present an error calculus to support a novel specification mechanism for sound and/or complete safety properties that are to be given by users. With such specifications, our calculus can form a foundation for both proving program safety and/or discovering real bugs. The basis of our calculus is an algebra with *a lattice domain* of four abstract statuses (namely *unreachability*, *validity*, *must-error* and *may-error*) on possible program states and *four operators* for this domain to calculate suitable program status. We show how *proof search* and *error localization* can be supported by our calculus. Our calculus can also be extended to *separation logic* with support for user-defined predicates and lemmas. We have implemented our calculus in an automated verification tool for pointer-based programs. Initial experiments have confirmed that it can achieve the dual objectives, namely of safety proving and bug finding, with modest overheads.

1 Introduction

Traditionally, program specifications are given primarily for safety scenarios and are used to describe the states under which program execution would occur safely. When successfully verified, such specifications are said to be *sound* for their specified input scenarios. That is, a specification is said to be *sound* if it has identified input scenarios (or preconditions) that are guaranteed to lead to safe program execution. However, we are also interested in *complete* specifications that will additionally verify the remaining input scenarios (that lead to execution failure) as invalid ones. Informally, a specification is said to be *complete* if it has unambiguously identified both input scenarios that lead to safe code execution, and input scenarios that lead to code execution failure.

Such complete specifications for programs are helpful for two reasons. Firstly, they can be used to specify precisely (through weakest precondition[1]) when inputs can be handled correctly by programs. Conversely, we are also able to precisely identify when programs would fail to work correctly (or safely). Secondly, the specifications on erroneous inputs can be used to help pinpoint actual software *bugs* in programs as they could be used to precisely indicate where each given error occurs.

Though useful, the task of capturing complete specifications is very challenging, and may not always be possible since the input scenarios under which failures could

---

[1] While it may be desirable to have weakest precondition that guarantee safety or correctness, we also allow flexibility for users to specify a wider range of specifications that include those with either stronger preconditions and/or weaker postconditions. Though weaker specifications give fewer guarantees, they are more easily verified and may be enough to ensure reliability.

G. Brat, N. Rungta, and A. Venet (Eds.): NFM 2013, LNCS 7871, pp. 291–306, 2013.
© Springer-Verlag Berlin Heidelberg 2013

occur may not be unambiguously specified and verified. In this paper, we shall provide the basic mechanisms that can help specify complete specifications, where possible. To achieve this goal, we propose *a lattice domain* of four abstract statuses (namely *unreachability*, *validity*, *must-error* and *may-error*) and make use of the validity (must-error) status for specifying safe (unsafe, resp.) execution scenarios. Furthermore, when the complete requirements are hard (or impossible) to specify, we have also provided approximation mechanisms that can help us specify *near-complete* specifications through the use of *may-error* as opposed to *must-error* classification in weakened postcondition.

Our motivation for developing complete specifications for programs was further heightened by the recent VSTTE competition [1] that was held in November 2011. Out of five problems that the participants were asked to verify for safety and correctness, there were two problems (problem 4 and problem 5) where more complex specifications that satisfy *completeness* were requested. As complete specifications must additionally address erroneous scenarios, we have recently developed a comprehensive verification framework that could just as easily deal with input scenarios that invoke errors, as it would with input scenarios that led to safe program execution

At the heart of our proposal is a calculus that can uniformly specify both safe and unsafe execution scenarios. Our calculus uses *an algebra* with the lattice domain of four-point program statuses and four binary operations over these program statuses. The program statuses can be used for each program state, and also to decorate more precisely the post-conditions of program specification. To support modular verification, we provide our calculus with *two entailment procedures* (one for pre-condition checks at method calls, and another for post-condition checks) and a set of *sound structural rules*. Furthermore, this extension also helps to classify (into must or may) as well as to localize errors when the verification fails. This enables our verifier to work both as a safety and correctness proving tool and as a bug finding tool.

The paper makes the following main contributions

- a lattice domain with four distinct statuses on possible program states.
- a specification mechanism to support both sound and complete properties.
- a calculus (for the lattice) to reason about safety and must/may errors (Sec. 3)

  - support for separation logic with user-defined predicates and lemmas (Sec. 4).
  - support for error calculus within a modular verification framework (Sec. 5).

- an extension to support error localization (Sec. 4.3).

We also demonstrate the calculus capability of proving safety and detecting bugs with modest overheads through an implementation and two experiments in Sec. 6. Next section presents the algebra and new specification mechanism. It also illustrates the use of calculus through examples on modular verification and error localization.

2   Motivation and Overview

2.1   An Algebra on Status of Program States

The basis of our proposal is the identification of an algebra $(\mathcal{E}, \mathcal{F})$ in which $\mathcal{E}$ is a lattice domain with four points used to capture the status of each program state, while

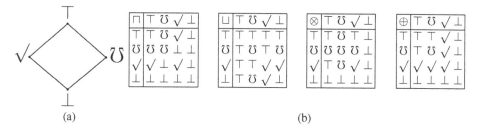

Fig. 1. An Algebra on Status of Program States

$\mathcal{F}$ is a set of four binary operators (meet ($\sqcap$), join ($\sqcup$), compose ($\otimes$) and search ($\oplus$)) to combine the statuses of program states. The four points that are used for program status are as follows:

- $\bot$: denotes an unreachable state.
- $\sqrt{}$: denotes a valid program state from normal program execution.
- $\mho$: denotes a state that corresponds to a must (or definite) error scenario.
- $\top$: denotes a state that corresponds to a may error or an unknown scenario. That is, it could either be $\bot$, or $\sqrt{}$ or $\mho$.

Note that the must error status ($\mho$) subsumes the unreachable $\bot$ status. The may error status ($\top$) comes from imprecision or from dependency on some unknown input. In our system, potential sources of imprecision include imprecise specifications, imprecise invariants of complex data structures and incomplete domains. Although we could separately identify those kinds of imprecision, for simplicity we uniformly specify them with the $\top$ status value. In the implementation, we distinguish them through different messages with status (see Sec. 4.3).

Let $\preceq$ be a partial ordering relation on status whereby $\tau_1 \preceq \tau_2$ means status τ_1 is more precise than status τ_2. The $\sqcup$ and $\sqcap$ operators denote the least upper bound and the greatest lower bound, respectively, over the lattice domain. The domain $\mathcal{E}$ and two operations $\sqcap$, $\sqcup$ form a complete lattice $\mathcal{D} = \langle \mathcal{E}, \preceq, \sqcup, \sqcap, \bot, \top \rangle$ organized as shown in Fig. 1a. This lattice forms a core part of the underlying abstract semantics for our system. Furthermore, $\bot$ is *zero* element of $\otimes$ and $\oplus$ operations; it means $x \oplus \bot = \bot$ and $\bot \otimes x = \bot$ for any values x. The remaining calculations of $\otimes$ and $\oplus$ are illustrated in Fig. 1b. The $\otimes$ operator is meant to support conjunctive proving, and searches for *failures* from $\mho$ and $\top$ status. The $\oplus$ operator is meant to support *proof search*, and searches for $\sqrt{}$ status to succeed in proving. Thus the priority order of the $\otimes$ operator is $\mho$, $\top$ and lastly $\sqrt{}$, and the priority order of the $\oplus$ operator is $\sqrt{}$, $\top$ and lastly $\mho$. Contrast this with the $\sqcup$ operator which doesn't have any priority between $\sqrt{}$ and $\mho$. So it would simply yield $\top$ when the two statuses are combined together.

2.2 Mechanism for Sound and Complete Specifications

To illustrate our new specification mechanism, we consider a method that returns the data which its input points to, as shown below

```
int get_data(node x)
  case{ x≠null → requires x↦node⟨d, p⟩ ensures (res=d) √;
        x=null → ensures (true) ℧; }
```

where `res` is a reserved identifier denoting the method's result and the data structure `node` is declared as: `data node { int val; node next }`.

In our system, each method is specified by pre- and post-conditions (through separation logic formulas), denoted by `requires` and `ensures` keyword, respectively. In the specification above, we also use structured specifications [9] where disjoint conditions are expressed using case construct for expressing both sound (with x≠null condition) and complete (with x=null condition) requirements, as can be seen for the above specification of `get_data` (with the √ and ℧ statuses in postconditions, resp.). In comparison, if we are only interested in sound specification, we could just use the following instead:

```
int get_data(node x)
  requires x↦node⟨d, p⟩ ensures (res=d) √;
```

Occasionally, it may be possible to automatically generate complete specification by negating the input conditions of sound specification. However, this may not always be feasible. Firstly, negation computation may be hard to implement in complex domains. For example, it is unclear how to compute negation in separation logic (which our system relies on). Secondly, not all methods have clearly delineated boundary between sound and complete conditions, as an example consider the interactive schedule (ischedule) method in Fig. 2. With prio=0 condition, this method's status depends on the user input which is unknown at verification time. Therefore, there exists a gap between soundness and completeness that cannot be derived simply through the negation operation. For this example, we can instead provide a *near-complete* specification, as shown in the bottom right of Fig. 2. Informally, a specification is said to be *near-complete* if it captures all possible input conditions but contains either ⊤ program status or an ambiguous disjunction, comprising of both √ and ℧ statuses, in one or more of its postconditions.

```
1. int ischedule(int prio){                       Sound Specification:
2.   if (prio>0)/*run it */return 0;               l₁. int ischedule(int prio)
3.   else if (prio<0) abort();                      l₂. requires prio>0 ensures (res=0)√;
4.   else{                                          Near-Complete Specification:
5.     printf("Allow this task to run? y or n");    l₃. int ischedule(int prio)
6.     char c=getc();                               l₄. case { prio>0 → ensures (res=0)√;
7.     if (c =' y')/*run it */return 0;             l₅.        prio<0 → ensures (true)℧;
8.     else abort(); } }                            l₆.        prio=0 → ensures (true)⊤; }
```

Fig. 2. Code and Specification of *ischedule* Method

We note that our approach for proving the completeness of program is based on the assumption that the user-supplied specification is complete; namely that it covers all values of the input domain and that each error program state denotes an input scenario where no valid output state is possible. Checking (or even inferring) the completeness of specifications is a challenging research direction that could be investigated in future.

2.3   Essence of Error Calculus

To highlight how our calculus can be used to verify programs, consider the method foo in Fig. 3. Furthermore, to illustrate the possibility of incompleteness, we assume a method, complexTest, whose specification cannot be handled by current automated provers. We shall verify the code of foo in a forward manner, and would compute a program state for each of its program point. Each program state, Φ, is a formula on the state of variables and heap. Each program state can be combined with a status and is represented by (Φ, τ) where τ denotes a status value from our lattice.

```
1 int foo(int x, int y)
2 requires x≥0
3 ensures (res>0)√; {
4  if (x<0) return −1; /*L1*/
5  else{
6    if (y>1) return 1; /*L2*/
7    else if (y<0) return −1; /*L3*/
8    else return y; /*L4*/
9 }}
```

Fig. 3. Code of *foo* Method

As part of compositional verification, the precondition of each callee is checked against the current calling context and the postcondition is checked at the exit of the method's body. In the example, we can identify four program states of interests that correspond to four exits (L1, L2, L3 and L4) of the method. The following illustrates how the statuses are decided at exits through proof obligations discharged for postcondition checking with the help of the entailment procedure $\vdash_C$ that conforms to our error calculus. Given a program state π_a and a *post-condition* π_c, we can determine the status s for such checking with the help of the following judgment: $\pi_a \vdash_C \pi_c \rightsquigarrow s$. The resulting statuses generated by the entailment procedure are as follows:

$$L1 : x\geq0 \wedge x<0 \wedge \text{res}=-1 \qquad\qquad \vdash_C \text{res}>0 \rightsquigarrow \bot$$
$$L2 : x\geq0 \wedge \neg(x<0) \wedge y>1 \wedge \text{res}=1 \qquad \vdash_C \text{res}>0 \rightsquigarrow \sqrt{}$$
$$L3 : x\geq0 \wedge \neg(x<0) \wedge \neg(y>1) \wedge y<0 \wedge \text{res}=-1 \quad \vdash_C \text{res}>0 \rightsquigarrow \mho$$
$$L4 : x\geq0 \wedge \neg(x<0) \wedge \neg(y>1) \wedge \neg(y<0) \wedge \text{res}=y \vdash_C \text{res}>0 \rightsquigarrow \top$$

Each of the above proofs yields a status based on the outcome of its entailment. This status can be added to program state for each of these program points. At L1, the antecedent is unsatisfiable which corresponds to an unreachable scenario (either infinite loop[2] or dead code) that can be captured by (false, $\bot$) with false denoting contradiction at that program point. At L2, the consequent can be directly proven using the antecedent. This yields a valid program state that can be represented by $(x\geq0\wedge\neg(x<0)\wedge y>1\wedge\text{res}=1, \sqrt{})$. This program state indicates that the method will exit safely at this location with res=1. At L3, the negation of the consequent can be proven from its antecedent. The program state at L3 can be computed to be a must error as $x\geq0\wedge\neg(x<0)\wedge y<0, \mho)$. The sub-formula on result res=−1 is dropped since we have a must error outcome where the output state is unimportant. At L4, the antecedent can neither prove the consequent nor its negation. Hence, we would need to classify this program point as a may error whose state is $(x\geq0\wedge\neg(x<0) \wedge \neg(y>1) \wedge \neg(y<0) \wedge \text{res}=y, \top)$. A formula on result res=y is still captured since the $\top$ status includes possibly safe output.

---

[2] Although we provide a mechanism to specify infinite loop, proving termination is beyond the scope of this paper.

When an entailment checking fails, an error messages is generated with relevant information to help debugging process. For example, the error message at L_3 is:

> Verify method foo. Proving postcondition fails:
> Failure (must):
> $(x{\geq}0, 2) \wedge (\neg(x{<}0), 5) \wedge (\neg(y{>}1), 6) \wedge (y{<}0, 7) \wedge (\text{res}{=}{-}1, 7) \vdash_C (\text{res}{>}0, 3)$

where irrelevant formulas are sliced away and failures are localized by pairs of the relevant failing formulas and their corresponding statement code or specification line numbers.

3 Assertion Language

In this section, we introduce the concepts and terminology that are used to describe our calculus throughout the paper. Our formalism includes inductive predicates in separation logic which are written in an assertion language. We extend this language with program status (τ) to support error calculus with different program states.

$$
\begin{array}{llll}
pred & ::= p(v^*) \equiv \Phi\ [\texttt{inv}\ \pi] & \alpha & ::= v_1{=}v_2\ |v{=}\texttt{null}\ |a{\leq}0\ |a{=}0\ |\cdots \\
\Psi & ::= \{(\Phi_1, \tau_1); ...; (\Phi_i, \tau_i)\} & a & ::= k\ |\ k{\times}v\ |\ a_1 + a_2 \\
\Phi & ::= \bigvee\ (\exists w^* {\cdot} \kappa {\wedge} \pi)^* & L & ::= lemma\ [\texttt{l}]\ p(v^*){\wedge}\pi \bowtie \exists w^* {\cdot} (\kappa{\wedge}\pi)[\tau] \\
\kappa & ::= \texttt{emp}\ |\ v{\mapsto}c(v^*)\ |\ p(v^*)\ |\ \kappa_1 * \kappa_2 & \bowtie & ::= \rightarrow\ |\ \leftarrow\ |\ \leftrightarrow \\
\pi & ::= \alpha\ |\ \neg\alpha\ |\ \pi_1{\wedge}\pi_2 & \tau & ::= \bot\ |\ \circlearrowleft\ |\ \sqrt{}\ |\ \top
\end{array}
$$

$$\text{where } p/l \text{ is a predicate/lemma name; } v, w \text{ are variable names;}$$
$$c \text{ is a data type name; } k \text{ is an integer or a float constant;}$$

Fig. 4. The Assertion Language

Separation logic can provide concise and precise notations for specifying pointer-based programs and their data structures. We enhance the separation logic fragment presented in [2,19]. Figure 4 describes our assertion language. Each data structure and its properties can be defined by an inductive predicate *pred*, that consists of a name p, a main separation formula Φ and an optional pure invariant formula π that must hold for every predicate instance. The separation logic formula Φ is a disjunction of symbolic heap. Each symbolic heap is a conjunction of a heap formula κ and a pure formula π. The pure part captures a rich constraint from the domains of Presburger arithmetic, monadic set or polynomial real arithmetic. The heap part includes points-to predicate $\mapsto$, spatial conjunction predicate $*$ for combining two disjoint heap memory, and user-defined predicates $p\langle v_1, .., v_n \rangle$ to capture more complex data structures with selected properties. For examples, with the simple data structure *node* declared in Sec. 2.2, we define variants of list segment, as follows:

$$
\begin{array}{l}
\texttt{pred lseg}\langle \texttt{root}, \texttt{n}, \texttt{p}\rangle \equiv (\texttt{root}{=}\texttt{p} \wedge \texttt{n}{=}0) \\
\qquad \vee\ \exists \texttt{d}, \texttt{q} \cdot (\texttt{root}{\mapsto}\texttt{node}\langle \texttt{d}, \texttt{q}\rangle * \texttt{lseg}\langle \texttt{q}, \texttt{n}{-}1, \texttt{p}\rangle)\ \texttt{inv n}{\geq}0 \\
\texttt{pred plseg}\langle \texttt{root}, \texttt{n}, \texttt{p}\rangle \equiv \exists \texttt{d} \cdot (\texttt{root}{\mapsto}\texttt{node}\langle \texttt{d}, \texttt{p}\rangle \wedge \texttt{n}{=}1 \wedge \texttt{d}{\geq}0) \\
\qquad \vee\ \exists \texttt{d}, \texttt{q} \cdot (\texttt{root}{\mapsto}\texttt{node}\langle \texttt{d}, \texttt{q}\rangle * \texttt{plseg}\langle \texttt{q}, \texttt{n}{-}1, \texttt{p}\rangle \wedge \texttt{d}{\geq}0)\ \texttt{inv n}{\geq}1
\end{array}
$$

The predicate lseg describes a list segment of nodes whose length is captured by the parameter n. Similarly, the predicate plseg describes a list segment with only non-negative integers.

Lemmas are used to relate data structures beyond their original predicate definitions [18]. A lemma specification consists of a head $p(v^*)$, a guard π, a body Φ and a direction to apply (left $\rightarrow$, right $\leftarrow$ or both $\leftrightarrow$) that denotes a weakening, strengthening or equivalence, respectively. For example, to illustrate that $\text{plseg}\langle\text{root}, \text{n}, \text{p}\rangle$ is an instance of $\text{lseg}\langle\text{root}, \text{n}, \text{p}\rangle$, we can use the following left (or weakening) coercion lemma:

$$\text{lemma } w_1 \; \text{plseg}\langle\text{root}, \text{n}, \text{p}\rangle \wedge \text{n} > 0 \; \rightarrow \text{lseg}\langle\text{root}, \text{n}, \text{p}\rangle$$

4 A Calculus on Errors

In this section, we initially formalize the calculus with pure (without heap) formulas π. The extension of the calculus to heap formulas will be presented in the next section.

4.1 The Entailment Procedures

In this subsection, we introduce two entailment procedures for discharging the proof obligations with support for the four-points status.

Entailment Procedure for Postconditions Checking. The basic machinery for the judgment $\pi_a \vdash_C \pi_c \rightsquigarrow s$ is captured by the following four rules. We use underlying theorem solvers for answering sastifiability. Note that $\text{UNSAT}(\pi)$ denotes that π is definitely unsatisfiable and $\text{PSAT}(\pi)$ denotes that π is possibly satisfiable (as a complement of unsatisfiability checking and due to its incompleteness).

$$\frac{\text{UNSAT}(\pi_1)}{\pi_1 \vdash_C \pi_2 \rightsquigarrow \bot} \; [\text{EC}-[\textbf{BOTTOM}]] \qquad \frac{\text{PSAT}(\pi_1) \quad \text{UNSAT}(\pi_1 \wedge \neg\pi_2)}{\pi_1 \vdash_C \pi_2 \rightsquigarrow \sqrt{}} \; [\text{EC}-[\textbf{OK}]]$$

$$\frac{\text{PSAT}(\pi_1) \quad \text{UNSAT}(\pi_1 \wedge \pi_2)}{\pi_1 \vdash_C \pi_2 \rightsquigarrow \mho} \; [\text{EC}-[\textbf{MUST-ERROR}]] \qquad \frac{\text{PSAT}(\pi_1 \wedge \neg\pi_2) \quad \text{PSAT}(\pi_1 \wedge \pi_2)}{\pi_1 \vdash_C \pi_2 \rightsquigarrow \top} \; [\text{EC}-[\textbf{MAY-ERROR}]]$$

Two rules at the first line check the success of the entailment and classify it as unreachable ($\bot$) or valid ($\sqrt{}$) as usual (checking $\text{UNSAT}(\pi_1 \wedge \neg\pi_2)$ is equivalent to checking $\pi_1 \implies \pi_2$). Next two rules at the second line check and classify the must/may error scenarios; in the first rule, a must error is identified when $\pi_a \implies \neg\pi_c$ is provable: lastly, due to the imprecision, entailments which has not been proven so far are marked with unknown status through the second rule. (In the last rule, the condition $\text{PSAT}(\pi_1)$ is discarded because it can be implied from two present conditions.)

To illustrate this entailment procedure, let us consider a postcondition check, $x \geq 0$, under four different program states, as shown below.

$$x \leq -1 \wedge x = 0 \vdash_C x \geq 0 \rightsquigarrow \bot \qquad x \leq -1 \vdash_C x \geq 0 \rightsquigarrow \mho$$
$$x > 0 \qquad\qquad \vdash_C x \geq 0 \rightsquigarrow \sqrt{} \qquad \text{true} \; \vdash_C x \geq 0 \rightsquigarrow \top$$

Entailment Procedure for Preconditions Checking. Furthermore, to support the checking of preconditions from specifications with soundness and/or completeness, we introduce another entailment judgment of the form: $\pi_a \vdash_E \pi_c \rightsquigarrow s$.

$$
\frac{\text{UNSAT}(\pi_1)}{\pi_1 \vdash_E \pi_2 \rightsquigarrow \bot} \; [\text{EE-}[\text{BOTTOM}]]
\qquad
\frac{\text{PSAT}(\pi_1) \;\; \text{UNSAT}(\pi_1 \wedge \neg\pi_2)}{\pi_1 \vdash_E \pi_2 \rightsquigarrow \surd} \; [\text{EE-}[\text{OK}]]
\qquad
\frac{\text{PSAT}(\pi_1 \wedge \neg\pi_2)}{\pi_1 \vdash_E \pi_2 \rightsquigarrow \top} \; [\text{EE-}[\text{MAY}]]
$$

The status for this entailment is now limited to only three possible values, namely $\bot$, $\surd$ and $\top$, without the $\mho$ status, as illustrated below:

$$
\begin{array}{ll}
x{\le}{-}1{\wedge}x{=}0 \vdash_E x{\ge}0 \rightsquigarrow \bot & x{\le}{-}1 \vdash_E x{\ge}0 \rightsquigarrow \top \\
x{>}0 \quad\quad\;\; \vdash_E x{\ge}0 \rightsquigarrow \surd & \text{true} \;\; \vdash_E x{\ge}0 \rightsquigarrow \top
\end{array}
$$

Unlike the earlier entailment procedure, this new entailment has introduced a $\top$ status value where $\mho$ was derived previously, since the precondition may be under-approximated. We can recover from this lack of information by leveraging on the status from postconditions, where applicable. We defer formalization of the recovery to Sec. 6, we now illustrate it through the check of the calling context, `prio<0`, against the near-complete specification of the `ischedule` procedure (presented in Fig. 2) as follows:

$$
\begin{aligned}
\texttt{prio<0} \vdash \texttt{case \{ prio>0} &\rightarrow \texttt{ensures (res=0)}\surd; \\
\texttt{prio<0} &\rightarrow \texttt{ensures (true)}\mho; \\
\texttt{prio=0} &\rightarrow \texttt{ensures (true)}\top; \} \\
\rightsquigarrow (\bot{\otimes}\surd) \sqcup (\surd{\otimes}\mho) &\sqcup (\bot{\otimes}\top) \rightsquigarrow \bot \sqcup \mho \sqcup \bot \\
\rightsquigarrow \mho
\end{aligned}
$$

This compositional check is performed through two steps. Firstly, for each scenario (1) the calling context is combined with the condition of current scenario; (2) unsatisfiability check is performed by the $\vdash_E$ procedure; and (3) the status from postcondition is combined (by $\otimes$). Secondly, those scenarios are joined (by $\sqcup$).

4.2 Structural Rules

We provide sound structural rules that would carry out the entailment proving process in smaller entailments. These rules support error localization, separation entailment procedure and modular verification.

$$
\frac{\pi_1 \vdash \pi \rightsquigarrow \tau_1 \quad \pi_2 \vdash \pi \rightsquigarrow \tau_2}{\pi_1 \vee \pi_2 \vdash \pi \rightsquigarrow \tau_1 \sqcup \tau_2} \; [\text{SE-}[\sqcup \text{ JOIN}]]
\qquad
\frac{\pi \vdash \pi_1 \rightsquigarrow \tau_1 \quad \pi \vdash \pi_2 \rightsquigarrow \tau_2}{\pi \vdash \pi_1 \wedge \pi_2 \rightsquigarrow \tau_1 \otimes \tau_2} \; [\text{SE-}[\otimes \text{ COMPOSE}]]
\qquad
\frac{\pi \vdash \pi_1 \rightsquigarrow \tau_1 \quad \pi \vdash \pi_2 \rightsquigarrow \tau_2}{\pi \vdash \pi_1 \vee \pi_2 \rightsquigarrow \tau_1 \oplus \tau_2} \; [\text{SE-}[\oplus \text{ SEARCH}]]
$$

These rules use the algebraic operations presented in Sec. 2.1 to combine the results. Note that, $\vdash$ is generic, and can be $\vdash_C$ or $\vdash_E$. The first rule decomposes disjunction on the antecedent, while the second rule decomposes conjunction on the consequent. Both these rules can be implemented without any loss of information. The third rule performs a search over a disjunction in the consequent. This search returns a set of possible proofs for the entailment. According to the $\oplus$ operator, if at least one $\surd$ status is found in this solution set, the entailment will succeed.

Theorem 1 (Soundness of the Structural Rules). *Given an entailment* $\pi_1 \vdash \pi_2$. *($\vdash$ is either* $\vdash_C$ *or* $\vdash_E$). *If the application of the structural rules* [SE-[...]] *on the given antecedent* π_1 *and consequent* π_2 *returns the result* τ, *then the application of the* [EC-[...]] *([EE-[...]]) rules on the given antecedent* π_1 *and consequent* π_2 *returns the same result* τ, *namely* $\pi_1 \vdash_C \pi_2 \rightsquigarrow \tau$ *($\pi_1 \vdash_E \pi_2 \rightsquigarrow \tau$, respectively).*

The proof is by an induction on the structural rules [SE-[...]] and a case analysis on the returned result τ. We present full proof of the theorem in the technical report [16].

4.3   Error Localization Extension to Calculus

To provide support for error localization, we must extend the four-point lattice with messages that capture the reason for each success or failure (see the left of Fig. 5).

Status $\perp$ does not carry any message which is denoted by $\emptyset$. When faced with a message with error from $m_1 \sqcup m_2$ and $m_1 \otimes m_2$, both of the two smaller messages (with possible errors), denoted by m_1 and m_2, must be resolved, before the main message is said to be resolved. When faced with a message with error of the form $m_1 \oplus m_2$, only one of the messages with errors from either m_1 or m_2 needs to be resolved, before the main message $m_1 \oplus m_2$ is resolved. We may now modify the three operators $\sqcup$, $\otimes$ and $\oplus$, to propagate messages capturing the localizations for successes and failures. Let us denote this using a generic name $\diamond$ for three operators. We propagate every message, where possible, as shown at the right of Fig. 5. In case empty message $\emptyset$ is generated, we remove it from the main message as shown in the second and third rules. In case the resulting status from $\tau_1 \diamond \tau_2$ is $\perp$, we remove its messages, as shown in the last rule.

$$
\begin{array}{ll}
\tau[m] ::= \perp[\emptyset] \mid \mho[m] \mid \surd[m] \mid \top[m] & \tau_1[m_1] \diamond \tau_2[m_2] \Rightarrow (\tau_1 \diamond \tau_2)[m_1 \diamond m_2] \\
m \quad ::= bm \mid m_1 \sqcup m_2 \mid m_1 \otimes m_2 \mid m_1 \oplus m_2 & m \quad \diamond \quad \emptyset \quad \Rightarrow m \\
bm \quad ::= \pi_1 \Longrightarrow \pi_2 \ (\texttt{valid}) & \emptyset \quad \diamond \quad m \quad \Rightarrow m \\
\qquad \mid \pi_1 \Longrightarrow \overline{\pi_2} \ (\texttt{must error}) & \perp[m] \quad \Rightarrow \perp[\emptyset] \\
\qquad \mid \pi_1 \Longrightarrow \underline{\pi_2} \ (\texttt{may error}) &
\end{array}
$$

Fig. 5. Program State: Status and Message

5   Error Calculus for Separation Logic

In this section, we show how our calculus can be used to support the reasoning of pointer-based programs via the fragment of separation logic presented in Sec.3. As separation logic is a sub-structural logic, we have to account for heap memory as a resource. Thus, entailment in separation logic is typically supported with a frame inference capability [2,19], similar to the following format:

$$ \Phi_1 \vdash \Phi_2 * \Phi_3 $$

whereby antecedent Φ_1 entails Φ_2 with a residue frame captured by Φ_3. Logically, the above entailment is equivalent to $\Phi_1 \Longrightarrow \Phi_2 * \Phi_3$ where Φ_3 may contain existential variables that have been instantiated and pure formula that were already established in Φ_1.

We enhance the entailment procedure for separation logic in two steps. First, we extend the entailment procedure above to support the error calculus by the following judgment:

$$\Phi_1 \vdash \Phi_2 \rightsquigarrow (\Phi_3, \tau)$$

If the antecedent semantically entails the consequent, the entailment succeeds and we expect status τ to be set to $\sqrt{}$. Otherwise, the entailment fails and we expect τ to be set to either $\mho$ or $\top$. Second, this procedure is extended to support proof search with disjunctive formulas and lemma as elaborated in Sec. 5.1.

To illustrate the first step, let us examine four simple examples to better understand how status outcome is being determined by the entailment procedure of separation logic.

Entailment 1

$x{\mapsto}\texttt{node}(\_, q) * q{\mapsto}\texttt{node}(\_, \texttt{null})$
$\vdash_C x{\mapsto}\texttt{node}(\_, p)$
$\rightsquigarrow (q{\mapsto}\texttt{node}(\_, \texttt{null}) \wedge p{=}q \wedge x{\neq}\texttt{null}, \sqrt{})$

Entailment 2

$x{\mapsto}\texttt{node}(\_, q) * q{\mapsto}\texttt{node}(\_, \texttt{null})$
$\vdash_C x{\mapsto}\texttt{node}(\_, \texttt{null})$
$\rightsquigarrow (q{\mapsto}\texttt{node}(\_, \texttt{null}), \mho)$

The entailment 1 yields a residue $q{\mapsto}\texttt{node}(\_, \texttt{null})$ and an instantiation $p{=}q$ from (implicit) existential variable p. It also carries a pure formula $x{\neq}\texttt{null}$ from the antecedent. The entailment 2 yields a must failure, denoted by $\mho$. The consequent expects $q{=}\texttt{null}$, but the antecedent had $q{\mapsto}\texttt{node}(\_, \texttt{null})$. This contradiction has caused a $\mho$ failure to be raised. The residue captures the state when failure was detected.

Entailment 3

$$x{\mapsto}\texttt{node}(\_, q) * q{\mapsto}\texttt{node}(\_, \texttt{null}) \vdash_C x{\mapsto}\texttt{node}(3, p)$$
$$\rightsquigarrow (q{\mapsto}\texttt{node}(\_, \texttt{null}) \wedge p{=}q \wedge x{\neq}\texttt{null}, \top)$$

The entailment 3 yields a may failure, denoted by $\top$. The consequent expects value 3 to be proven as the data field of x. However, the antecedent has no information on that field position. Hence, a $\top$ failure was raised.

5.1 Separation Entailment with Proof Search

To support proof search the entailment procedure for separation logic shall now be presented as a judgment of the following (full) form:

$$\Phi_1 \vdash \Phi_2 \rightsquigarrow (\Psi, \tau)$$

whereby Ψ captures a set of residual program states with status information. We use a set of program states (Ψ) since our entailment procedure may have to conduct a proof search with the help of lemmas. Furthermore, we must extend our entailment procedure in the following ways. First, rules are added to support proof search that adds to our set of outcomes with the help of lemmas. Proof search is performed in the order as follows:

- Status values of the proof search with lemmas are combined by the union ($\oplus$) operator (where $\sqrt{}$ or $\top$ take priority over $\mho$). Hence, if a proof search attempt fails, we return a $\top$ (unknown) status, rather than a $\mho$ status since the latter prevents a $\sqrt{}$ success from being reported, even if they can be confirmed in a different proof search.

– If a complete set of lemmas have already been explored, then a must error status is returned.

Second, when our entailment procedure becomes stuck with a non-empty consequent, comprising some heap predicates, we shall firstly determine a pure approximation of the consequent for both heap and pure data through XPure procedure [2]. For examples:

$$\text{XPure}(x \mapsto \text{node}\langle \_, \_ \rangle) \implies x \neq \text{null}$$
$$\text{XPure}(\text{lseg}\langle \text{root}, n, p \rangle) \implies \text{root}=p \wedge n = 0 \vee \text{root} \neq \text{null} \wedge n > 0$$

where $\implies$ denotes our over-approximation, and lseg is a predicate defined in Sec 3. We may then determine if there is any contradiction with the antecedent to decide whether must or may failure is going to be reported.

6 Modular Verification with Error Calculus

Code verification is typically formalised using Hoare triples of the form $\{pre\}c\{post\}$, where pre, $post$ are the initial and final states of program code c. To incorporate status into our program state, we shall use disjunctive program state of form $\bigvee(\Phi, \tau)$, giving us a new Hoare triple of the form $\{\bigvee(\Phi_1, \tau_1)\} c \{\bigvee(\Phi_1, \tau_1)\}$. To simplify our presentation, we shall use (Φ, τ) instead of the more general disjunctive program state $\bigvee(\Phi, \tau)$ that was implemented. To provide sound and complete requirements, we shall also use structured specification from [9] of the form below:

$$Y ::= \text{requires } \Phi \, Y \mid \text{case}\{\pi_1 \Rightarrow Y_1; \ldots; \pi_n \Rightarrow Y_n\} \mid \text{ensures } (\Phi)\tau$$

This extends the pre/post specifications to support case analysis and staged verification. The verification requirement for methods can be affected by progressively collecting the precondition in the structured specification, prior to the verification of its method body. As this process is straightforward, we omit the details here.

The abstract semantics of each method call is captured by its specifications. We encode its verification with the rule $[\text{FV}-[\text{CALL}]]$. Note that $(t \, v)^*$ and $(\text{ref } t \, u)^*$ denote *pass-by-value* and *pass-by-reference* parameters, respectively. Each method call $mn(v^*, u^*)$ in our core language has only variables as arguments. To avoid the need for argument substitutions, we assume that each method declaration from Program has been suitably renamed so that actual arguments are identical to the formal arguments.

$$\frac{[\text{FV}-[\text{CALL}]]}{\begin{array}{c} t_0 \, mn \, ((t \, v)^*, (\mathit{ref} \, t \, u)^*) \, Y \, \{c\} \in \text{Program} \\ \Phi_1 \vdash Y \rightsquigarrow (\Phi_2, \tau_2) \\ \Phi_R = \text{if } \tau_1 = \sqrt{} \text{ then } (\exists v'^* \cdot \Phi_2) \text{ else } \Phi_1 \\ \hline \{(\Phi_1, \tau_1)\} \, mn \, ((t \, v)^*, (\mathit{ref} \, t \, u)^*)\{(\Phi_R, \tau_1 \otimes \tau_2)\} \end{array}}$$

The proof obligations are generated and verified at the second line, provided that the incoming status τ_1 is $\sqrt{}$. Furthermore, output states from proving entailment are composed with status from pre-state at the third line. By default, if the caller context contains errors, such errors are simply propagated to the next instruction in a similar manner as exceptions. However, unlike exceptions, error states are never caught. To generate proof obligations for the extended specification, we propose to extend the entailment procedure to handle specification with separation formulas. The revised judgment has the form $\Phi_1 \vdash Y \rightsquigarrow (\Phi_2, \tau_2)$, where Φ_1 is the current state, Y is the specification and (Φ_2, τ_2) is the residual state and its status. Three syntax-directed rules are extended. They are used to prove each precondition and assume its respective postcondition for the callee, as shown below:

$$\frac{\Phi_1 \vdash_E \Phi \rightsquigarrow (\Phi_2, \tau_2) \qquad (\Phi_2) \vdash Y \rightsquigarrow (\Phi_3, \tau_3)}{\Phi_1 \vdash \text{requires } \Phi\, Y \rightsquigarrow (\Phi_3, \tau_2 \otimes \tau_3)} \text{[FV-[C-REQUIRES]]}$$

$$\frac{\Phi \wedge \pi_i \vdash Y_i \rightsquigarrow (\Phi_i, \tau_i)\ i = 1 \ldots n}{\Phi \vdash \text{case}\{\pi_i \Rightarrow Y_i\}^* \rightsquigarrow (\bigvee \Phi_i, \sqcup \tau_i)} \text{[FV-[C-CASE]]} \qquad \frac{\Phi_1 \vdash_C \text{true} \rightsquigarrow (\Phi, \tau_1)}{\Phi_1 \vdash \text{ensures } (\Phi_2)\tau_2 \rightsquigarrow (\Phi_1 * \Phi_2, \tau_1 \otimes \tau_2)} \text{[FV-[C-ENSURES]]}$$

7   Implementation and Experiments

We have implemented our error calculus inside a program verification system for separation logic, called HIPEE. We use HIPEE to verify C-based programs against user-given specifications. The verification is performed compositionally for each method, and loops are transformed to recursive methods. HIPEE eventually translates separation logic proof obligations to pure formulae that can be discharged by different theorem provers. Our system uses Omega [21], MONA [15], Redlog [7] and Z3 [4] as underlying theorem provers for answering the satisfiability and simplification queries. When program code is not successfully verified against safety properties, HIPEE not only further classifies the failures into the must or may errors but also localizes program statements and specifications relevant to the errors.

7.1   Calculus Performance for Heap-Based Programs

To evaluate the overheads of error calculus, we executed our system HIPEE twice, once *with* error calculus and a second time *without*, on a suite of bug-free pointer-based programs. We stress that although the sizes of these programs are fairly small, they deal with fairly complex heap-based data structures, such as linked lists, doubly-linked lists and AVL-trees. Therefore, these programs can be used to *fully* evaluate the performance of our calculus which has been embedded inside a separation logic prover. The results are summarized in Table 1. The first column contains the list of the verified programs and their proven properties while the second, third and fourth columns describe number of lines of code (LOC), number of lines of specification (LOS) and number of procedures in each program. On average, LOS is around 12% of LOC and specifications are complicated enough to demonstrate the performance of our calculus. The fifth and sixth columns show the total verification time (in seconds) for the system HIPEE without and with error calculus, respectively. The last two columns capture the number of satisfiability and simplification queries sent to the provers for each experiment.

Table 1. Verification Performance with (w) and without (wo) Error Calculus

Programs (specified props)	Size		Proc	Time(sec.)		Invo.(#)	
	LOC	LOS	#	wo	w	wo	w
Linked list (size,interval)	327	50	26	0.44	0.46	2738	3202
Linked list (size,sets)	157	27	13	0.58	0.6	1520	1724
Sorted llist (size,sness,sets)	98	11	6	0.46	0.49	955	1060
Doubly llist (size,interval)	186	23	13	0.34	0.34	1864	2083
Doubly llist (size,sets)	91	13	5	0.5	0.5	1309	1429
CompleteT (size,minheight)	106	12	5	0.87	0.94	2149	2533
Heap trees (size,maxelem)	179	13	5	1.9	1.91	4540	4954
AVL (height, size)	313	27	12	3.44	3.59	7863	8585
AVL2 (height,size,bal)	152	37	7	2.83	3	6959	7876
BST (size,height)	177	18	9	0.35	0.37	1883	2192
BST (size,height,interval)	153	12	6	0.3	0.31	1581	1836
RBT (size,blackheight)	508	48	19	3.32	3.38	13069	16687
Bubble sort (size)	75	9	4	0.21	0.21	1092	1254
Quick sort (size, sets)	82	10	4	0.27	0.28	778	832
Merge sort (size,sets)	109	11	6	0.47	0.5	1035	1074
Quick sort - queue (size)	127	4	2	4.25	5.27	13218	21139
Total	2840	325	142	20.53	22.15	62553	78460

In Table 1, the results show that the total overhead introduced by our error calculus is around 1.62 seconds (8%). This overhead is proportional to the number of extra satisfiability and simplification queries shown in the last two columns. These experimental results have shown that must/may error calculus with messages can be supported with modest overhead.

7.2   Calculus Usability

In order to show the usability of our error calculus on bugs finding and localizing, we evaluated our system on the Siemens test suite [12] of programs. The test suite contains programs with complex data structures (e.g. linked lists, queues), arrays and loops. Each program in the suite has one non-faulty version, v_0, and a number of seeded faulty versions (#Ver. column in Table 2) from v_1 to v_n. Each of these faulty versions has one or more (seeded) faults. Total number of faults is captured in #Fault column. These faulty versions are suitable for checking the ability of tools in finding bugs and localizing errors (as used in [14]).We provide specifications for each program such that HIPEE (1) successfully verifies safety (sound or complete requirements) in the non-faulty versions, and (2) captures potential must-bug errors that are complementary to the safety scenarios. We emphasize that these specifications were designed primarily to verify safety scenarios *without* considering the faulty versions of each program. Nevertheless, HIPEE is able to utilize the same specification to find and explain the presence of bugs in the faulty versions, as elaborated below.

Table 2 shows the result of running our system on six programs from the suite. The properties our tool proved include: (i) memory safety (all), (ii) size of data structures (`schedule1a`, `schedule1b` and `schedule2` program), (iii) array-related properties

Table 2. Bugs finding and localizing with small programs in the Siemens Test Suite

Programs	LOC	LOS	#Proc.	#Ver.	#Fault	$\mho$	$\top^1$	$\top^2$	LOE	time(s)
tcas	173	48	9	41	48	31	14	3	3.48	3.06
schedule2	374	108	16	10	10	5	0	3	3	8.25
schedule1a	412	50	18	10	16	15	0	1	4.38	18.13
schedule1b	413	50	18	9	8	7	0	1	4.25	32.29
replace	564	73	21	24	24	18	0	6	4.21	17.89
print_tokens2	570	64	19	10	10	7	0	1	4.88	20.42
print_tokens	726	87	18	7	9	8	0	1	3.67	6.73
Total/(Average)	3232	480	119	111	125	91	14	16	(3.98)	(15.25)

(`tcas`, `print_token`, `print_token2` and `replace` program), (iv) functional arithmetic constraints between input and output (all). We are interested in finding out all the errors in the programs and classifying them as must ($\mho$), disjunctive may ($\top^1$) or may ($\top^2$) errors. For instance, from 48 faults of program `tcas`, HiPEE was able to detect all the errors in the program, and classified 31 of them as must ($\mho$) errors, 14 as disjunctive may ($\top^1$) errors and 3 as may ($\top^2$) errors. In summary, HiPEE detected 97% of real bugs including 73%, 11% and 13% of $\mho$, $\top^1$ and $\top^2$ errors, respectively.

However, a few errors were not detected by our system, e.g. v_4, v_9 of `schedule2` and v_1, v_2 of `print_tokens2` were verified successfully by HiPEE. Upon careful examination, we found that the substituted statement in v_9 is semantically equivalent with the non-faulty one in v_0. Hence, we consider it as a bug in constructing the benchmark rather than a real program bug. For v_1, v_2 and v_4, there were omitted statements that are related to the I/O systems. For instance, the following statement is omitted in v_1:

if(ch == EOF) fprintf(stdout, "It can not get character");

This was not picked up by our system since the specification of I/O operations were not being modelled. It would be interesting to see I/O operations being modelled in future.

Our calculus further supports debugging in localizing the errors. The LOE column shows the average number of lines of program code and specification relevant to the errors for each program. We are able to provide concise (between 3-5 lines) error locations for all the bugs in the suite. Such short but accurate localizations make it easier for users to comprehend the discovered errors. The last column shows the average time which HiPEE took for verifying a faulty version of each program.

Purely from the system point of view and on the assumption that specifications have already been provided, HiPEE took on average 16 seconds for safety proving, bug finding and error localization on one faulty version of each program.

8   Related Work and Conclusion

The most relevant idea to our new specification mechanism is exception safety in Spec# language [17]. While Spec# uses *otherwise* keyword to explicate scenarios which definitely lead to exceptions, our proposal uses must error values $\mho$ to model erroneous scenarios. Hence, it is possible to integrate our mechanism into exception handling.

Moreover, our specification mechanism with the error calculus has well supported our verifier not only in proving safety/functional correctness and validating input parameter (like Spec#) but also in finding and classifying bugs.

Static analysis based bug finding is not new and already exists [6,8,11,13]. Recent work in first order relational logic [6,13] also addresses the problem of finding bugs in programs with pointers and linked data structures. The method is based on under approximation for loops and heap, thus it only finds the must bugs ($\mho$) in the code. Similarly, Exorcise [11] is only capable of detecting must errors ($\mho$) based on evaluating *weakest liberal precondition*. Since both consider only postcondition violation as a must error, they do not report on the more common bugs that are due to preconditions. Our calculus is more expressive (with uncovering not only must error but may error and with proving safety) through the help of new specification mechanism on sound and/or complete properties. Moreover, to handle pointer-based programs, while the underlying assumption in [13] is that most bugs can be found in the programs with small scope (loop unrolling) and small heap size, we have also shown how our error calculus can handle data structures with aliasing through a simple integration with separation logic.

As static analysis suffers from precision problem, there have been attempts to use dynamic or hybrid analysis for safety proving and bugs finding. An approach based on dynamic analysis to infer likely invariants from code is implemented in [3]. Invariants discovered can be used as method annotations or assumptions, which can aid static checkers in detecting bugs. This hybrid analysis uses a combination of under approximation and over approximation in different phases of analysis. Similarly, SMASH [10] integrates safety with bug finding via a synergy between static analysis and testing. In our approach we do not rely on dynamic analysis as our complete lattice can symbolically capture a richer set of possible program states. Our method integrates both bug-finding and safety proving within a single calculus, without prejudice to working with dynamic-based analyses for unknown scenarios. Other attempts are based on dual static analysis. An over-approximation for safety and another over-approximation for bugs finding was presented in [20] but it has only been applied to numerical imperative programs. Another related approach using over- and under-approximation was presented in [5]. In [5], the may and must queries correspond to safety and liveness properties. Their conditions are computed with respect to a finite abstraction for each particular property. In comparison, the conditions for our must/may error are captured in terms of symbolic (infinite) domain that relies *only* on over-approximation mechanisms.

Conclusion. In this paper, we described a novel specification mechanism for both sound and complete requirements via the calculus for must/may errors. The calculus also enables bug finding (with safety checking) during modular verification. We can provide fairly precise and concise failure localization from our calculus. Using separation logic, we can support sound and complete safety verification, in the presence of data structures with sophisticated invariants, via user-defined predicates and lemmas. We have extended an automated tool for verifying complex data structures to use our error calculus. Initial sets of experiments have shown that bug finding and safety checking via the modular verification can be supported with modest overheads.

Acknowledgement. This work is being supported by MoE research grant 2009-T2-1-063. Florin Craciun is supported by the project POSDRU 89/1.5/S/60189 "Postdoctoral Programs for Sustainable Development in a Knowledge Based Society".

References

1. VSTTE 2012 Software Verification Competition (2012),
   https://sites.google.com/site/vstte2012/compet
   (accessed July 27, 2012)
2. Chin, W.N., David, C., Nguyen, H.H., Qin, S.: Automated verification of shape, size and bag properties via user-defined predicates in separation logic. Sci. Comput. Program. 77(9), 1006–1036 (2012)
3. Csallner, C., Smaragdakis, Y., Xie, T.: DSD-Crasher: A hybrid analysis tool for bug finding. ACM Trans. Softw. Eng. Methodol. 17(2) (2008)
4. de Moura, L., Bjørner, N.: Z3: An Efficient SMT Solver. In: Ramakrishnan, C.R., Rehof, J. (eds.) TACAS 2008. LNCS, vol. 4963, pp. 337–340. Springer, Heidelberg (2008)
5. Dillig, I., Dillig, T., Aiken, A.: Reasoning about the unknown in static analysis. Commun. ACM 53(8), 115–123 (2010)
6. Dolby, J., Vaziri, M., Tip, F.: Finding bugs efficiently with a SAT solver. In: ESEC/SIGSOFT FSE, pp. 195–204 (2007)
7. Dolzmann, A., Sturm, T.: Redlog: computer algebra meets computer logic. SIGSAM Bull. 31, 2–9 (1997)
8. Flanagan, C., Leino, K.R.M., Lillibridge, M., Nelson, G., Saxe, J.B., Stata, R.: Extended static checking for Java. In: PLDI, pp. 234–245 (2002)
9. Gherghina, C., David, C., Qin, S., Chin, W.-N.: Structured specifications for better verification of heap-manipulating programs. In: Butler, M., Schulte, W. (eds.) FM 2011. LNCS, vol. 6664, pp. 386–401. Springer, Heidelberg (2011)
10. Godefroid, P., Nori, A.V., Rajamani, S.K., Tetali, S.D.: Compositional may-must program analysis: unleashing the power of alternation. In: POPL 2010, pp. 43–56. ACM (2010)
11. Hoenicke, J., Leino, K.R.M., Podelski, A., Schäf, M., Wies, T.: It's doomed; we can prove it. In: Cavalcanti, A., Dams, D.R. (eds.) FM 2009. LNCS, vol. 5850, pp. 338–353. Springer, Heidelberg (2009)
12. Hyunsook, D., Sebastian, E., Gregg, R.: Supporting controlled experimentation with testing techniques: An infrastructure and its potential impact. Empirical Softw. Engg. 10, 405–435 (2005)
13. Jackson, D., Vaziri, M.: Finding bugs with a constraint solver. In: ISSTA 2000, pp. 14–25 (2000)
14. Jose, M., Majumdar, R.: Cause clue clauses: error localization using maximum satisfiability. In: PLDI, pp. 437–446. ACM, New York (2011)
15. Klarlund, N., Moller, A.: MONA Version 1.4 - User Manual. BRICS Notes Series (2001)
16. Le, Q.L., Sharma, A., Craciun, F., Chin, W.-N.: Towards complete specifications with error calculus. Technical report, SoC, National Univ. of Singapore (July 2012),
    http://www.comp.nus.edu.sg/~locle/papers/mme.pdf
17. Leino, K.R.M., Schulte, W.: Exception safety for c#. In: SEFM, pp. 218–227 (2004)
18. Nguyen, H.H., Chin, W.-N.: Enhancing program verification with lemmas. In: Gupta, A., Malik, S. (eds.) CAV 2008. LNCS, vol. 5123, pp. 355–369. Springer, Heidelberg (2008)
19. O'Hearn, P.W.: Tutorial on separation logic (Invited tutorial). In: Gupta, A., Malik, S. (eds.) CAV 2008. LNCS, vol. 5123, pp. 19–21. Springer, Heidelberg (2008)
20. Popeea, C., Chin, W.N.: Dual analysis for proving safety and finding bugs. In: SAC (2010)
21. Pugh, W.: The Omega Test: A fast practical integer programming algorithm for dependence analysis. Communications of the ACM 8, 102–114 (1992)

A Probabilistic Quantitative Analysis
of Probabilistic-Write/Copy-Select*

Christel Baier, Benjamin Engel, Sascha Klüppelholz, Steffen Märcker,
Hendrik Tews, and Marcus Völp

Institute for Theoretical Computer Science and Institute for Systems Architecture
Technische Universität Dresden, Germany
{baier,klueppel,maercker}@tcs.inf.tu-dresden.de,
{engel,tews,voelp}@os.inf.tu-dresden.de

Abstract. Probabilistic-Write/Copy-Select (PWCS) is a novel synchronization scheme suggested by Nicholas Mc Guire which avoids expensive
atomic operations for synchronizing access to shared objects. Instead,
PWCS makes inconsistencies detectable and recoverable. It builds on the
assumption that, for typical workloads, the probability for data races is
very small. Mc Guire describes PWCS for multiple readers but only one
writer of a shared data structure. In this paper, we report on the formal
analysis of the PWCS protocol using a continuous-time Markov chain
model and probabilistic model checking techniques. Besides the original PWCS protocol, we also considered a variant with multiple writers.
The results were obtained by the model checker PRISM and served to
identify scenarios in which the use of the PWCS protocol is justified
by guarantees on the probability of data races. Moreover, the analysis
showed several other quantitative properties of the PWCS protocol.

1 Introduction

Control mechanisms for shared data is a central task for the design of parallel
systems. Various protocols to ensure exclusive access to shared data have been
developed by the operating system community. Most prominent are sophisticated
locking schemes. These, however, became more and more complex. Moreover,
scalability turns out to be problematic because atomic operations and cache
synchronization between an ever growing number of cores became more and
more expensive [MCS91].

At a recent Real-Time Linux Workshop, Nicholas Mc Guire proposed
a promising idea to exploit the increasing complexity of modern manycore systems for synchronizing shared objects [Gui11]. Rather than avoiding inconsistencies at all cost by locking objects or updating their state with increasingly

---

* This work was in part funded through the DFG project QuaOS, the CRC 912 Highly-
Adaptive Energy-Efficient Computing (HAEC), the EU under FP-7 grant 295261
(MEALS), the DFG/NWO-project ROCKS, the cluster of excellence cfAED (center
for Advancing Electronics Dresden) and by the EU and the state Saxony through
the ESF young researcher group IMData 100098198.

G. Brat, N. Rungta, and A. Venet (Eds.): NFM 2013, LNCS 7871, pp. 307–321, 2013.
© Springer-Verlag Berlin Heidelberg 2013

more expensive atomic operations, Mc Guire proposed to not synchronize readers and writers at all. Instead, he proposed to explicitly allow data races on the shared object but to make inconsistencies from ongoing writes detectable. As such, Mc Guire's protocol is an instance of a new class of algorithms that make use of the randomness that is inherent in complex modern computer architectures. This randomness is caused by differences in the content of the core-local caches and by arbitration at the hardware level, which together induce small, but almost unpredictable differences in the execution time. In the approach of Mc Guire, writers are viewed as fault injectors that access the shared data items probabilistically. Instead of single data items that are protected by some locking scheme, Mc Guire's approach deals with a fixed number of replicas of the shared objects (called "copies" in [Gui11]) that are written and read in reversed order. The idea is that, thanks to the inherent randomness of the writers, the probability for a reader to find at least one consistent replica is sufficiently high. For this reason, Mc Guire used the notion *Probabilistic-Write/Copy-Select*, PWCS for short, for his approach. Mc Guire reports in [Gui11] on measure-based experiments illustrating that PWCS is indeed a promising approach that outperforms most locking schemes in high-end cache coherent systems. Moreover, PWCS makes no special assumptions on the memory consistency model except that modifications will eventually propagate to prospective readers.

In this paper, we report on a formal analysis of Mc Guire's protocol using probabilistic model checking techniques. We designed a continuous-time Markov chain (CTMC) to model the PWCS protocol, using exponential distributions as a formalization of the inherent randomness of complex systems observed by Mc Guire. While [Gui11] only addresses the case of a single writer and multiple readers, we analyzed the protocol for multiple writers. This requires the consideration that the replica of shared data items can be in three modes: consistent, currently modified (by precisely one writer) or damaged (concurrently modified by two or more writers). We identified a series of quantitative measures that serve to evaluate the adequacy of the PWCS protocol and that address different aspects. From the readers perspective, guarantees on the success rate and the required time to find at least one consistent replica are most relevant. The average repairing time provides a formal criterion for the usefulness of the implicit repairing mechanism of damaged replica, given by the possibility that eventually some writer modifies the damaged replica without being interfered by other writers. These and other quantitative measures have been formalized as quantitative queries using continuous stochastic logic (CSL) [ASSB00,BHHK03] and its extension for reasoning about rewards (CSRL) [BHHK00] and analyzed using the model checker PRISM [KNP04,KNP09]. The model checking results indeed confirm Mc Guire's observations.

At its current stage, it is too early to give affirmative answers to the applicability of PWCS. But both, Mc Guire's measure-based evaluation and our quantitative analysis, give evidence in the potential of PWCS-like protocols that make use of the inherent probabilism in complex systems to avoid the drawbacks of standard locking schemes or other coordination mechanisms relying on a deterministic protocol or explicit probabilistic algorithms (e.g., using random number generators).

Related Work. Probabilistic model checking was already used in various application areas, ranging from distributed randomized algorithms over energy management, communication, gossiping and cryptographic protocols to network on chip design and system biology. See e.g. the homepages of the model checkers PRISM [KNP04,KNP05,KNP09], MRMC [KZH+11] or the CADP tool set [CGH+10]. Most related to our approach are case studies that address the quantitative analysis of non-randomized mutual exclusion protocols where stochastic distributions were used to model the delay or duration of actions. Examples are the case studies performed by Mateescu and Serwe with the CADP toolbox [MS10] and a series of classical mutual exclusion algorithms and our recent work on a simple spinlock protocol using PRISM and MRMC [BDE+12b,BDE+12a]. The timing behavior of standard mutual exclusion protocols using mathematical reasoning with stochastic distributions was also investigated by the algorithm community, see e.g. [GM99].

2 Probabilistic-Write/Copy-Select

In [Gui11], Mc Guire presented two alternative implementations of PWCS [Gui11] projected objects, which differ in the type of token they use for making object inconsistencies detectable: tag-based consistency tokens complement the object with a pair of version numbers that have to match for the data to be read consistent; hash-based consistency tokens on the other hand store a hash of the data, which up to collision uniquely identifies the consistent states of the object.

Writes proceed by first marking the object inconsistent, either by incrementing the version of the end tag or, in case of hashes, by simply modifying some part of the object to cause a mismatch between the stored hash and data. After the modification completes, the begin tag is incremented to mark the data consistent again. In case of hashes, consistency is established automatically once the stored hash and all modifications become visible.

Readers match this operation by taking a copy of the object and its consistency token. More precisely, they first copy the begin tag and then the data into a private buffer. After that, they match the buffered begin tag with the end tag stored in the object to determine whether they have read a consistent version. If not they retry or follow some other back-off strategy. Replicas of the object are used to further reduce the chance of a reader finding an inconsistent object.

To enforce the order in which end tag, data and begin tag become visible, fences have to be used on modern processor architectures possibly in combination with some delay loop or packet ordering scheme to ensure that the respective updates become visible in the desired order. Hashes further relax these hardware dependencies because no matter in which order the data and tags are read or written, once all data plus the corresponding hash arrives at a reader, it will find its copy to be consistent.

Mc Guire does permits only one writer process. Here, we extend PWCS and consider multiple writers that may modify all replicas of the object concurrently. It may therefore happen that some replicas get damaged because different writers succeed in storing parts of their data. In this case, the stored data and the hash do not match, which allows a reader to recognize an inconsistency. Note that tags would not allow for a reliable damage detection. In contrast to our model, a reader cannot distinguish between a damaged replica and a temporarily inconsistent one that is currently updated by a single writer. We assume that a damaged replica becomes consistent again, and is thus implicitly repaired, when a single writer can modify it without others interfering.

3 Stochastic Model of PWCS

To model the PWCS protocol we use exponential distributions for representing the inherent randomness in an explicit way. This leads to a continuous-time Markov chain (CTMC), which then serves as basis for the formal analysis using the CTMC engine of the PRISM model checker. The CTMC is obtained in a compositional way, using CTMCs with action labels for each writer and each reader. The replica are represented by a non-stochastic transition system that synchronize with the writers to change their states.

3.1 Preliminaries

We briefly summarize the relevant principles of continuous-time Markov chains. Further details can be found in textbooks on Markov chains, see e.g. [Kul95,KS60].

If S is a finite set then a distribution on S is a function $\nu : S \to [0, 1]$ with $\sum_{s \in S} \nu(s) = 1$. For $U \subseteq S$, $\nu(U)$ is a shortform notation for $\sum_{s \in U} \nu(s)$.

The CTMCs we use here are tuples $\mathcal{M} = (S, Act, R, \mu)$ where S is a finite state space, Act a finite set of action names and R a function of the type $R : S \times Act \times S \to \mathbb{R}_{\geq 0}$, called the rate matrix of $\mathcal{M}$. The last component μ is a distribution on S specifying the probabilities for the starting states. If ν is a distribution on S then we write $\mathcal{M}_\nu$ for the CTMC (S, Act, R, ν) that results from $\mathcal{M}$ by replacing the initial distribution μ with ν.

We write $s \xrightarrow{\lambda:\alpha} s'$ if $R(s, \alpha, s') = \lambda > 0$ with the intuitive meaning that $\mathcal{M}$ has a transition from state s to state s' with action label α and rate λ. The value λ specifies the rate of an exponential distribution. That is, the probability for the transition $s \xrightarrow{\lambda:\alpha} s'$ to be ready for firing some time in the interval $[0, t]$ is $1 - e^{-\lambda t}$. Thus, the average delay of this transition is $1/\lambda$. If $R(s, \alpha, s') = 0$ then $\mathcal{M}$ cannot move from s to s' via action α. The choice between several enabled transitions in state s relies on the race condition. Thus, the time-abstract probability to fire a particular transition $s \xrightarrow{\lambda:\alpha} s'$ in state s is $P(s, \alpha, s') = \lambda/E(s)$ where $E(s)$ denotes the exit rate of state s, i.e., the sum of the rates of all outgoing transitions of state s. The probability that $s \xrightarrow{\lambda:\alpha} s'$ will fire within t time units is then $P(s, \alpha, s') \cdot (1 - e^{-E(s) \cdot t})$.

Paths in a CTMC are sequences of consecutive transitions augmented by the time points when they are taken. The quantitative analysis using the logics CSL [ASSB00,BHHK03] relies on the standard σ-algebra on infinite paths and probability measure (see e.g. [Kul95,KS60]). To specify measurable sets of infinite paths, we will use LTL-like notations, such as $\Diamond T$ ("eventually T") where $T \subseteq S$ denotes the set of all infinite paths that contain at least one T-state. Similarly, $\mathcal{U}$ denotes the until-operator and $\mathcal{U}^{\leq t}$ the time-bounded until with time bound t. To formalize measurable sets of paths in a state-based logical framework, we will also use state predicates and propositional formulas built upon them as a symbolic formalism for sets of states. The state predicates and their meanings will be obvious from the names of the states in our model.

For our analysis, we are chiefly interested in the long-run behavior, i.e., the system behavior when time tends to infinity and when the system is in equilibrium. For this purpose, we deal with the *steady-state distribution* $\theta : S \to [0,1]$ where $\theta(s)$ represents the average fraction of time to be in state s on the long-run. Formally, $\theta(s)$ is defined by

$$\theta(s) \;\;=\;\; \lim_{t \to \infty} \theta(s,t)$$

where $\theta(s,t)$ denotes the probability for $\mathcal{M}$ being in state s at time instant t. For finite CTMCs, function θ is well-defined and it is indeed a distribution on S. Long-run probabilities refer to the probability measure obtained for the CTMC $\mathcal{M}_\theta$ where the original initial distribution μ of $\mathcal{M}$ is replaced with the steady-state distribution θ.

Suppose now that U is a set of states such that $\theta(U) > 0$. Conditional long-run probabilities under condition U refer to the long-run behavior of $\mathcal{M}$ when starting in one of the U-states. These are obtained by using the probability measure of the CTMC $\mathcal{M}_\theta^U = \mathcal{M}_\nu$ where ν is the distribution on S given by $\nu(s) = 0$ if $s \in S \setminus U$ and $\nu(s) = \theta(s)/\theta(U)$ if $s \in U$. If Π is a measurable set of infinite paths, then the *conditional long-run probability* for Π under condition U is the probability measure of Π in the CTMC $\mathcal{M}_\theta^U$ and denoted by $\Pr(\Pi \mid U)$.

We will also study reward-based properties formalized using the logic CSRL [BHHK00]. These require an extension of $\mathcal{M}$ by a reward function $rew : S \to \mathbb{R}_{\geq 0}$ where $rew(s)$ specifies the reward to be earned per time unit when staying in state s. For finite paths one can then reason about the accumulated reward. Suppose π is a finite path where the underlying state sequence is $s_0 s_1 \ldots s_n$ and let $t_0 = 0$ and t_i the time point where π takes the i-th transition. The accumulated reward of π is:

$$Rew(\pi) \;\;=\;\; \sum_{i=0}^{n-1} (t_{i+1} - t_i) \cdot rew(s_i)$$

Suppose U is a set of states with $\theta(U) > 0$ and $\Pr(\Diamond T \mid U) = 1$. The *conditional long-run accumulated reward* for eventually reaching T under condition U is defined as the expected value of the random variable that assigns to each infinite path in $\Diamond T$ the accumulated reward of the shortest prefix that ends in a T-state under the probability measure in the CTMC $\mathcal{M}_\theta^U$. It is denoted by

AccRew($\lozenge T \mid U$). In the analysis of the PWCS-protocol, we will deal with the reward function that assigns value 1 to all states. In this case, AccRew($\lozenge T \mid U$) can be interpreted as the average amount of time to reach T from U on the long-run.

For the quantitative analysis of the PWCS-protocol, we will consider several instances of $\text{Pr}(\Pi \mid U)$ and AccRew($\lozenge T \mid U$), including those where U is given a set of actions rather than a set of states. In those cases, U is identified with the set of states that can be entered via taking some transition with an action label in U.

3.2 Modeling the PWCS-Protocol

The CTMC for the PWCS-protocol will be obtained by composing CTMCs for the writers and readers and ordinary (non-stochastic) transition systems for the replica. For the synchronization of the writers with the replica, we use CSP-like notations for actions: $!a$ for the sending of a signal by some writer and $?a$ for the matching receive action by the replica. Since all state changes of the replica are triggered by the writers, the action alphabet of the replica consists of actions of the form $?a$ where the corresponding send action $!a$ is in the action alphabet of some writer. The other actions of the writers and all actions of the readers are executed in an interleaved way. Since only the sending actions are augmented with rates, the rate for the synchronization of $?a$ and $!a$ in the composite CTMC is the rate of the sending action $!a$ in the CTMC of the writer. This corresponds to the following SOS-rules to combine the CTMCs for the writers and the readers with the transition system for the replica to obtain a CTMC for the PWCS-protocol:

$$\frac{s \xrightarrow{\lambda:\alpha} s'}{\langle s, \overline{x} \rangle \xrightarrow{\lambda:\alpha} \langle s', \overline{x} \rangle} \qquad \frac{w \xrightarrow{\lambda:!a} w', \ r \xrightarrow{?a} r'}{\langle w, r, \overline{y} \rangle \xrightarrow{\lambda:a} \langle w', r', \overline{y} \rangle}$$

In the first rule, $s \xrightarrow{\lambda:\alpha} s'$ stands for a transition of some writer or reader, while $\overline{x}$ stands for the tuple consisting of the local states of all other components.

In the second rule, $w \xrightarrow{\lambda:!a} w'$ and $r \xrightarrow{?a} r'$ stand for a transition of some writer and replica, respectively. Here, $\overline{y}$ stands for the tuple consisting of the local states of all readers and all other writers and replica.

Replicas. The replicas themselves are interpreted as shared data objects among the readers and writers and behave according to the control-flow diagram shown in Fig. 1. We abstract away from the concrete values stored in the object, and only represent the three possible modes of a replica: it can be either consistent, currently modified, or damaged. Therefore, the model for the kth replica consists of the three locations $consistent_k$, $currently\_modified_k$, or $damaged_k$. An integer variable w_k keeps track of the number of writers that are currently writing the kth replica. The edges in the control-flow diagram partly refer to the counter variable w_k by means of a guard or an assignment. The usual unwinding of the control-flow diagram yields a transition system where each state consists of a

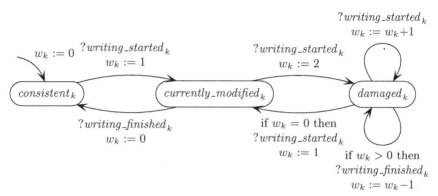

Fig. 1. Control-flow diagram for the kth replica

location and a value for the counter variable w_k and where the transitions are labeled by some receive action $?a$ (without any reference to the counter variable).

Each replica is assumed to be initially consistent and no writer is currently actively writing. In Fig. 1, the transitions $writing\_started_k$ and $writing\_finished_k$ stand for sets of transitions $writing\_started_k^i$ and $writing\_finished_k^i$, $1 \leq i \leq I$ which synchronize with the respective actions triggered by any of the writers. That is, whenever some writer starts operating on the kth replica, which is indicated by the synchronous action $writing\_started_k^i$, the replica changes its location, where it is now considered to be under modification and the counter variable w_k is increased accordingly. Similarly, the synchronous action $writing\_finished_k$ indicates the end of a write operation on the kth replica. A replica is said to be damaged if more than one writer is operating on the replica at the same time. A replica can only become consistent if one writer can successfully write its data without interference from another writer. We mark a damaged replica as currently modified once a single writer starts modifying the replica exclusively. If it succeeds writing the replica without interference from another writer, we consider the replica to be repaired and hence consistent. We say a writer interferes with another reader or writer if it writes a replica that is concurrently read or written by this other process.

Readers. Fig. 2 shows the CTMC formalizing the operational behavior of the jth reader. For each transition we assign a rate of an exponential distribution. The jth reader is initially in the state $idle^j$ before it starts reading the replica in the order of decreasing indices. The delay of the transition from the idle state to the state $reading_K^j$ is exponentially distributed with rate κ. Intuitively, κ defines the "read rate" of an individual reader, which can be understood as the average number of reading requests per time unit in state $idle^j$. The transition from state $reading_k^j$ to state $check_k^j$ with action $reading\_finished_k^j$ fires with rate δ. In states $check_k^j$ the reader checks whether or not the read of the kth replica was successful. The read operation is successful if the replica was found consistent at the beginning of the read and there was no interference from a concurrent write operation of some

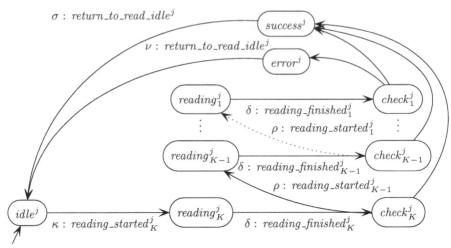

Fig. 2. CTMC for the jth reader

writer. For the latter, the jth reader has access to the shared boolean variables $corrupted_k^j$. The variables $corrupted_k^j$ are set to *false* whenever a transition with action $reading\_started_k^j$ is fired and set to *true* by the writers as specified in the next paragraph of this section. In case that the replica was found consistent and no writer was writing the replica concurrently, the jth reader changes its state to $success^j$, from where it returns to state $idle^j$ with rate σ. Otherwise it proceeds reading the next replica with rate $\rho \in \mathbb{R}_{>0}$. If the reader could not find a consistent replica without interference from a writer, the reader moves to the state $error^j$. The transition from $error^j$ to $idle^j$ can be understood as a high-level representation of some error handling which is modeled here stochastically using an exponential distribution with rate ν. (Also the original PWCS protocol proposed by Mc Guire does not consider any concrete policy for the error handling.) In the following, we say a reader is in a read cycle if it is in some state other than $idle^j$ and define the term write cycle accordingly.

Writers. The writers are modeled by the CTMC shown in Fig. 3. The ith writer starts in its initial state $idle^i$ and changes its state to $writing_1^i$ with rate $\gamma \in \mathbb{R}$, while firing the send action $!writing\_started_1^i$ synchronously with the matching receive action $?writing\_started_1^i$ by the first replica. Hence, the writer starts writing the first replica when it enters the location $writing_1^i$. Once the writer has started, it will write all replica in the order of increasing indices (i.e., in reversed order of the readers). When the write operation of the kth replica ($k \in \mathbb{N}$) is finished, the writer changes its state to $ready_k^i$ with the synchronous action $writing\_finished_k^i$ and rate λ before continuing with the next replica. The time to access the next replica is exponentially distributed with rate $\mu \in \mathbb{R}$. After the writer has finished writing the last replica it changes back to state $idle^i$ via action $return\_to\_write\_idle^i$ with rate η. We assume that the effect of firing $writing\_started_k^i$ will be that the shared variables $corrupted_k^j$ are set to *true* for all readers (i.e., $1 \leq j \leq J$). This is to "inform" the readers which are currently reading the kth replica about the

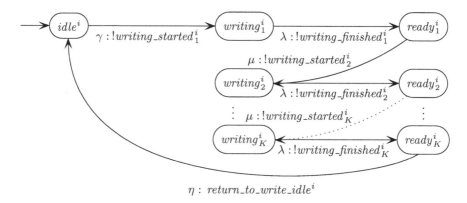

$$\eta : \; return\_to\_write\_idle^i$$

Fig. 3. CTMC for the ith writer

interfering write operation. We have introduced this signaling mechanism because the interfering write may corrupt the data the reader retrieves from the replica. Concurrent reads may retrieve corrupt data even though the replica may be consistent before and after the write.

To obtain the PRISM model, we did some technical modifications on the CTMC models presented above. Action labels have been encoded as variables. This enables references to actions in the state-labeled logics CSL and CSRL. Furthermore, we identify the last ready-state $ready^i_K$ with the idle-state $idle^i$.

4   Quantitative Analysis

We now proceed to the quantitative analysis of PWCS. There are several interesting questions to ask about PWCS when one seeks to use it in a specific scenario. For example, what is the likelihood to read a consistent object, how many replicas have to be read for that and how long does it take on average. The following queries, which we have model checked, give answers to these questions and insights into the balance between repair and damage that we found to be crucial for the performance of PWCS in the presence of multiple concurrent writers.

Queries. To obtain deeper insight in PWCS and have analyzed the following six queries. The writer index $1 \le i \le I$ and reader index $1 \le j \le J$ are arbitrarily chosen but fixed.

Q1: *"Probability to successfully read a replica (on the long run)"*: The jth reader successfully reads a replica, when it finds one consistent replica during its read cycle without interference. That is, the reader starts its read cycle when performing the first read action $reading\_started^j_K$ and reaches location $idle^j$ via $success^j$ (rather than via $error^j$). Formally, the task is to compute:

$$\Pr\big(\neg error^j \; \mathcal{U} \; idle^j \; \big| \; reading\_started^j_K\big)$$

Q2: *"The $p \in [0,1]$ time-quantile for a successful read (on the long run) within time bound t":*

$$\min\{t \; : \; p \le \Pr(\neg error^j \; \mathcal{U}^{\le t} \; idle^j \mid reading\_started^j_K)\}$$

In this query we are interested in the minimum time bound t such that the probability to successfully read a replica on the long run (cf. Query Q1) is above a certain threshold p.

Q3: *"Fraction of time in which all K replica are damaged"*: While all replicas stay damaged, readers have no chance to successfully read a single replica.

$$\theta(damaged_1 \wedge \ldots \wedge damaged_K)$$

For this query we will investigate the effect on the model checking outcome when increasing the number of replicas K present in the model, as this should raise the probability of finding a consistent replica for the readers.

Q4: *"Average time (on the long run) for repairing a damaged replica"*: In this query we are interested in the average repair time once a replica becomes damaged. For the computation we annotate all states of the model with reward 1 and compute the following conditional long-run accumulated reward:

$$\mathrm{AccRew}(\Diamond \; consistent_k \mid just\_damaged_k)$$

Here, $just\_damaged_k$ is a shorthand notation for the transition in which a second writer starts operating on the kth replica, i.e., the transition from location $currently\_modified_k$ to location $damaged_k$ with an action $writing\_started^i_k$ (cf. Fig. 1).

Q5: *"The $p \in [0,1]$ time-quantile for repairing a damaged replica (on the long run) within time bound t"*: In this query we are interested in the minimum time bound t such that the probability to successfully repair a damaged replica on the long run (cf. Query Q4) is above a certain threshold p.

$$\min\{t \; : \; p \le \Pr(\Diamond^{\le t} \; consistent_k \mid just\_damaged_k)\}$$

Q6: *"The probability to write at least c consistent replica within one write cycle where $c \le K$."*: We say that the ith writer successfully writes at least c replicas in one write cycle if on the path through the cycle there are at least c indices $\ell = \ell_1, \ldots, \ell_c$, where $w_\ell = 0$, $writing\_started^i_\ell$ is executed and followed by $writing\_finished^j_\ell$ without interfering writes on the ℓth replica by any of the other writers.

$$\Pr(\Pi_c \mid writing\_started^i_1)$$

Here, the set Π_c consists of all infinite paths that have a finite prefix that meets the constraints imposed above.

5   Evaluation

We have evaluated PWCS for the three different scenarios depicted in Table 1: Scenario 1 (*frequent reads and writes*) is a worst-case setup for PWCS where readers and writers access the shared object as fast as they can. Scenario 2

Table 1. Parameters for the three evaluated scenarios

	Scenario 1		Scenario 2		Scenario 3	
	time	rate	time	rate	time	rate
idle time (writer)	1	$\gamma = 1$	20	$\gamma = 0.05$	200	$\gamma = 0.005$
idle time (reader)	1	$\kappa = 1$	2	$\kappa = 0.5$	20	$\kappa = 0.05$

parameters common to all scenarios

	time	rate
write duration	2	$\lambda = 0.5$
read duration	1	$\delta = 1$
other	0.01	$\mu = \rho = \sigma = \nu = 100$

(*frequent reads/moderate writes*) characterizes a read-most data structure where writers access the object only every 10th read access in average. Scenario 3 (*moderate reads/occasional writes*) is a setup where both readers and writers access different parts of fine-granular synchronized objects or where the times to access objects are significantly smaller than the computation phases between subsequent accesses. Due to the cache-agnostic nature of our CTMC model and because we are primarily interested in the synchronization behavior of one selected reader, we will instantiate our model with one reader (i.e., $J = 1$) and vary the number of writers I between 1 and 5. For the queries Q1, Q3 and Q5, we vary the number of replicas K between 1 and 5. For the remaining queries we fix K to 5. All times are average durations relative to the average read duration.

The computations were carried out on an Intel Core i7 2640M @ 2.8 GHz. For our parameter sets, the model sizes ranged from 13 states ($I = K = 1$) up to approximately 50 million states ($I = K = 5$). By applying PRISM's built-in symmetry reduction, we were able to reduce the state space significantly to about 0.65 million states. Using PRISM's sparse engine, we observed model checking times between a fraction of a second and 6 minutes (Q1, $I = K = 5$). To obtain the long-run probabilities and accumulated rewards, we applied our PRISM extension [BDE+12b] that calculates the weighted sums using the steady-state distribution θ. For Q2 we approximated the time-quantile by sampling with a period of 0.25 time units. In order to compute property Q6 efficiently, we translated it into a nested PCTL query that yields a compact Rabin automaton for the converse property: "The probability to write at most c damaged replicas where $c \leq K$".

Reader Performance (Queries Q1 – Q2). Figs. 4(a), 4(c) and 4(e) show the probability to read a consistent replica in the three analyzed scenarios. For Scenario 2 and 3, we clearly see that as few as four respectively two replicas suffice to reach success rates over 95 % even if replicas are damaged by interfering writers. In the worst case Scenario 1, reads are still successful in over 45 % of all cases once the number of replicas exceeds the number of writers.

Query Q2 projects the Q1 results into the time domain. Figs. 4(b), 4(d) and 4(f) show the probability of reading the shared object successfully within

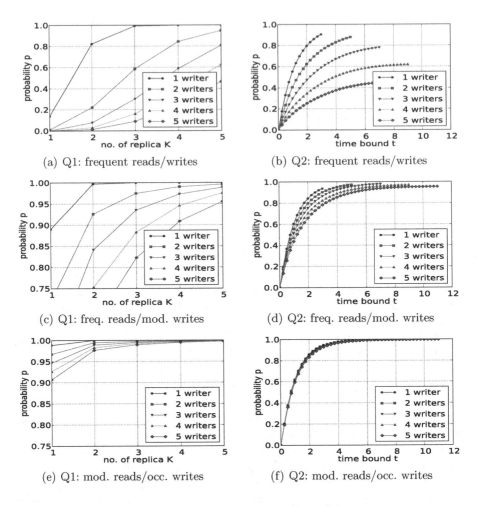

Fig. 4. Results for the Queries Q1 and Q2

the time bound t. Recall, the average time to read a replica is one time unit. As expected, additional writers cause more replica to be inconsistent. The time to find a consistent replica increases with the number of writers. There are two important points to notice. First, if we take the average write duration multiplied by the number of writers plus the average time to read a replica (i.e., 3, 5, 7, 9 and 11 time units for $1, \ldots, 5$ writers, respectively) the probability to have read the object successfully is well over 90 % for Scenario 2 and well over 99 % for Scenario 3 and 2 or more writers. Another point to notice is the gap between the curves and probability 1. In particular for Scenario 1, the 4-writer curve approaches 62 % but never reaches 1. Part of this gap can be explained by writers currently modifying the replica, which renders the replica temporarily inconsistent. To better grasp the influence of damage on this gap, we have analyzed queries Q3 to Q6.

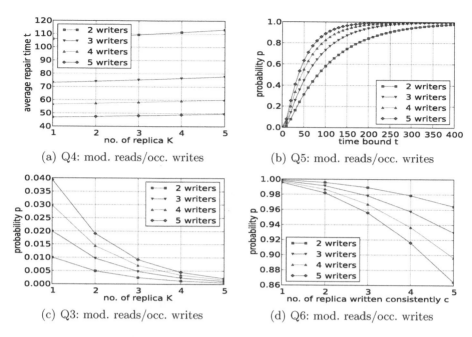

(a) Q4: mod. reads/occ. writes

(b) Q5: mod. reads/occ. writes

(c) Q3: mod. reads/occ. writes

(d) Q6: mod. reads/occ. writes

Fig. 5. Results for the Queries Q3 – Q6

Replica Damage (Queries Q3 – Q6). Fig. 5 shows the results for queries Q3 to Q6. Due to the limited space, we present only the results for Scenario 3. However, we confirmed that the results for Scenario 2 follow the same trend. Q3 shows that in a system with only a single replica, the likelihood that it is damaged is below 4 %. The probability that all replicas are damaged further decreases when the number of replicas is increased. Queries Q4 (Fig. 5(a)) and Q5 (Fig. 5(b)) address the time a replica stays damaged. In both figures, we see a superposition of two effects: more writers damage a replica with higher probability but the higher write rate reduces the time before a replica gets repaired. Q6 confirms these observations by answering the question how likely it is to write c consistent replicas out of 5 replicas. Over 99 % of all writes manage to produce at least one replica, which explains the high success rate of readers.

From these observations, we can conclude: (1) PWCS preserves a high chance of finding the shared object consistent as long as the number of replica exceeds the number of writers. (2) Special precautions to avoid damage or to make damage distinguishable from temporary inconsistencies are not justified.

Experimental Confirmation. To confirm our findings about damaged replicas, we have implemented an element-wise PWCS-protected array. We vary the size of the array to adjust read and write rates. Fig. 6 shows the results for queries Q1 and Q6. All measurements were taken on an Intel Xeon X5650 @ 2.67 GHz (hyperthreading disabled). The array remains in the shared L3 cache throughout our benchmark. The measurements confirm the analytical results except in the one replica case in Q1. We attribute this deviation to interference from the cache

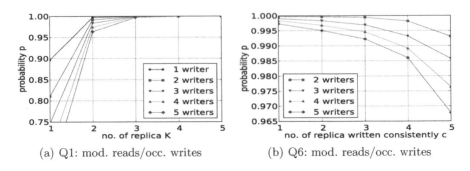

(a) Q1: mod. reads/occ. writes   (b) Q6: mod. reads/occ. writes

Fig. 6. Measurement results for the Queries Q1 and Q6

coherence protocol, which prior to writing invalidates copies of the replica of all other readers and writers. Our model does not take cache effects into account.

Notice that we do not give graphs for Q4 and Q5 because both queries are very hard to measure, since they require global knowledge and very tight synchronized clocks. Moreover, the operations to gather and distribute this information from the damaging writers to the repairing writer would influence the measurement code such that they conceal the actual effect we would like to measure.

6   Conclusions

This work presented a quantitative analysis of Probabilistic-Write/Copy-Select (PWCS) using continuous-time Markov chains and probabilistic model-checking techniques implemented in the model checker PRISM. PWCS is a new synchronization protocol based on the implicit-randomness induced by the complexity of todays many-core systems. In our analysis, we were able to confirm Mc Guire's measure-based experiments: few replicas suffice to maintain a high probability ($> 95\,\%$) of finding a consistent replica. We established these results for the common situations where reads dominate the shared object accesses. In addition, we also confirmed these findings for more exceptional scenarios with frequent writes.

We extended PWCS and considered multiple, parallel writers without additional synchronization. Our analysis revealed a high probability of repairing damaged replicas within reasonable time bounds. This high repair rate translates into a low probability ($< 4\,\%$) to actually damage the object by damaging all its replicas.

A particularly interesting point of our formal analysis is that it revealed insights in the behavior of PWCS that evade measurement-based investigations. We consider this as a general advantage of probabilistic-model checking and plan to investigate further low-level algorithms that exhibit very short runtimes and where the instrumentation-induced interfere conceals the quantities to measure. In addition, we plan to look into further variants of PWCS and, more generally, into implicit-randomness based stochastic algorithms.

References

ASSB00.   Aziz, A., Sanwal, K., Singhal, V., Brayton, R.K.: Model checking continuous-time Markov chains. ACM Transactions on Computational Logic 1(1), 162–170 (2000)

BDE$^+$12a. Baier, C., Daum, M., Engel, B., Härtig, H., Klein, J., Klüppelholz, S., Märcker, S., Tews, H., Völp, M.: Chiefly symmetric: Results on the scalability of probabilistic model checking for operating-system code. In: SSV 2012. EPTCS, vol. 102, pp. 156–166 (2012)

BDE$^+$12b. Baier, C., Daum, M., Engel, B., Härtig, H., Klein, J., Klüppelholz, S., Märcker, S., Tews, H., Völp, M.: Waiting for locks: How long does it usually take? In: Stoelinga, M., Pinger, R. (eds.) FMICS 2012. LNCS, vol. 7437, pp. 47–62. Springer, Heidelberg (2012)

BHHK00.   Baier, C., Haverkort, B.R., Hermanns, H., Katoen, J.-P.: On the logical characterisation of performability properties. In: Welzl, E., Montanari, U., Rolim, J.D.P. (eds.) ICALP 2000. LNCS, vol. 1853, pp. 780–792. Springer, Heidelberg (2000)

BHHK03.   Baier, C., Haverkort, B.R., Hermanns, H., Katoen, J.-P.: Model checking algorithms for continuous-time Markov chains. IEEE Transactions on Software Engineering 29(6), 524–541 (2003)

CGH$^+$10.   Coste, N., Garavel, H., Hermanns, H., Lang, F., Mateescu, R., Serwe, W.: Ten years of performance evaluation for concurrent systems using CADP. In: Margaria, T., Steffen, B. (eds.) ISoLA 2010, Part II. LNCS, vol. 6416, pp. 128–142. Springer, Heidelberg (2010)

GM99.   Gafni, E., Mitzenmacher, M.: Analysis of timing-based mutual exclusion with random times. In: 18th Annual ACM Symposium on Principles of Distributed Computing (PODC), pp. 13–21. ACM (1999)

Gui11.   Mc Guire, N.: Probabilistic write copy select. In: 13th Real-Time Linux Workshop, pp. 195–206 (October 2011)

KNP04.   Kwiatkowska, M.Z., Norman, G., Parker, D.: Probabilistic symbolic model checking with PRISM: a hybrid approach. STTT 6(2), 128–142 (2004)

KNP05.   Kwiatkowska, M.Z., Norman, G., Parker, D.: Probabilistic model checking in practice: case studies with prism. SIGMETRICS Performance Evaluation Review 32(4), 16–21 (2005)

KNP09.   Kwiatkowska, M.Z., Norman, G., Parker, D.: PRISM: probabilistic model checking for performance and reliability analysis. SIGMETRICS Performance Evaluation Review 36(4), 40–45 (2009)

KS60.   Kemeny, J., Snell, J.: Finite Markov Chains. D. Van Nostrand (1960)

Kul95.   Kulkarni, V.: Modeling and Analysis of Stochastic Systems. Chapman & Hall (1995)

KZH$^+$11.   Katoen, J.-P., Zapreev, I.S., Moritz Hahn, E., Hermanns, H., Jansen, D.N.: The ins and outs of the probabilistic model checker MRMC. Performance Evaluation 68(2), 90–104 (2011)

MCS91.   Mellor-Crummey, J., Scott, M.: Scalable reader-writer synchronization for shared-memory multiprocessors. In: PPOPP 1991, pp. 106–113. ACM (April 1991)

MS10.   Mateescu, R., Serwe, W.: A study of shared-memory mutual exclusion protocols using CADP. In: Kowalewski, S., Roveri, M. (eds.) FMICS 2010. LNCS, vol. 6371, pp. 180–197. Springer, Heidelberg (2010)

Statistical Model Checking of Wireless Mesh Routing Protocols

Peter Höfner[1,3] and Annabelle McIver[2,1]

[1] NICTA
[2] Department of Computing, Macquarie University
[3] Computer Science and Engineering, University of New South Wales

Abstract. Several case studies indicate that model checking is limited in the analysis of mesh networks: state space explosion restricts applicability to at most 10 node networks, and quantitative reasoning, often sufficient for network evaluation, is not possible. Both deficiencies can be overcome to some extent by the use of statistical model checkers, such as SMC-Uppaal. In this paper we illustrate this by a quantitative analysis of two well-known routing protocols for wireless mesh networks, namely AODV and DYMO. Moreover, we push the limits and show that this technology is capable of analysing networks of up to 100 nodes.

1 Introduction

Wireless Mesh Networks (WMNs) are self-organising ad-hoc networks that support broadband communication without relying on a wired backhaul infrastructure. They have gained popularity through their flexibility which allows them to be used in a diverse range of applications, from emergency response to transportation systems. Automatic route-discovery, maintenance and repair play a fundamental role in reliability and performance of such networks where typical scenarios include dynamic topologies. The engineering challenge is to design protocols which facilitate good service in spite of these harsh operating conditions.

Traditional approaches to the analysis of WMN protocols are simulation and test-bed experiments. While these are important evaluation methods they are typically used for testing implementations rather than design specifications. Moreover, the analysis is restricted to global properties such as overall throughput or message delay. Formal analysis of specifications is one way to systematically screen protocols for flaws and to present counterexamples to diagnose them. It has been used in locating problems in automatic route-finding protocols [2,9].

Unfortunately, current state-of-the art model checkers are unable to handle protocols of the complexity needed for WMN routing in realistic settings. In previous work [8] we used the model checker Uppaal to analyse basic qualitative properties of the Ad hoc On-Demand Distance Vector (AODV) routing protocol, one of four protocols currently standardised by the IETF MANET working group. We were able to analyse systematically *all* network topologies of up to five nodes. Although this provides a partial analysis, as does simulation, the

G. Brat, N. Rungta, and A. Venet (Eds.): NFM 2013, LNCS 7871, pp. 322–336, 2013.

network sizes are far from realistic and quantitative information such as probabilities were not included. In this paper we investigate whether *statistical model checking* can combine the systematic methodology of "classical" model checking with the ability to analyse quantitative properties and realistic scenarios.

Statistical Model Checking (SMC) [20,19] combines ideas of model checking and simulation with the aim of supporting quantitative analysis as well as addressing the size barrier that currently prevents useful analysis of large models. SMC trades certainty for approximation, using Monte Carlo style sampling, and hypothesis testing to interpret the results. We are interested in timed systems and so we use SMC-Uppaal, the Statistical extension of Uppaal (release 4.1.11) [4], which supports the composition of timed and/or probabilistic automata. The sampling is carried out according to the probability distribution defined by the probabilistic automata. Parameters setting thresholds on the probability of false negatives (α) and on probabilistic uncertainty (ε) can be used to specify the statistical confidence on the result. SMC-Uppaal computes the number of simulation runs needed by using the theoretical Chernoff-Hoeffding bounds ($O(\frac{1}{\varepsilon^2}\ln\frac{2}{\alpha})$), which crucially is independent of the size of the model. SMC-Uppaal generates an interval $[p-\varepsilon, p+\varepsilon]$ for estimating p, the probability of CTL-property ψ holding w.r.t. the underlying probability distribution.

In this paper we model two routing protocols for WMNs: AODV and DYMO (Dynamic MANET On-demand).[1] One aim is to understand the role of the different design choices via a number of performance and correctness measures. We analyse the performance, both over a complete set of topologies for small networks as well as for medium-to-large network sizes. Since the complexity and size of these protocols go far beyond what can be analysed with standard model checking, these case studies provide excellent test bases for demonstrating the power and capacity of the new statistical tools. We illustrate here the range and depth of the analysis which is achievable with statistical analysis, which we believe is currently not possible using traditional simulation alone.

In Sect. 2, we give an informal summary of routing, followed by a description of our Uppaal models, concentrating particularly on timing aspects. Four categories of experiments are discussed in Sect. 3. The first presents a timing analysis of AODV; the second and third provide a thorough comparison of AODV against DYMO both w.r.t. overall performance and quality of the routes discovered, where we find some surprising trends. Finally we demonstrate that this analysis is scalable, illustrated by redoing a selection of experiments for networks consisting of up to 100 nodes. In Sect. 4 we review related work and in Sect. 5 we reflect on the challenges ahead for SMC.

2   Routing Protocols and Their Architecture

On demand routing protocols such as AODV and DYMO are designed to establish routes only when needed, typically when a new data packet is injected by a user (application layer). Each node maintains its own routing table thereby

---

[1] Since March 2012, DYMO is sometimes referred to as AODVv2.

enabling it to act as its own router. Routing tables can be updated whenever new messages are handled, since incoming messages carry a wealth of information concerning network connectivity simply because they have just successfully travelled from somewhere. Nodes mine that information in different ways, which, as our analysis shows, yields different behavioural profiles.

The collective information in the nodes' routing tables is at best a partial representation of network connectivity as it was sometime in the past; in the most general scenarios mobility continually modifies that representation. Nodes following either AODV or DYMO store information about a route towards a possible destination d (if a route has been discovered) as follows. The total number of hops in the route (**hops**), the identity of the very next hop in the route (**nhop**), a "destination sequence number" (**dsn**) (a measure of the freshness of the entry), and a "validity flag" (**flag**),[2] which is unset whenever information arrives indicating that one of the downstream links in the route is broken. Whilst currently our analysis only looks at static topologies we nevertheless find that these protocols do not always perform as we would expect.

2.1 Basic Architecture for Ad Hoc Routing

AODV and DYMO follow the same basic architecture. Each node maintains a message queue to store incoming messages and a processor for handling messages. Whilst the queue is always enabled to receive messages, message handling can take time and so communication between queue and handler occurs only when the handler has successfully processed a message. The workflow of the handler is as follows: first, the next (oldest) message is loaded from its message queue. Depending on the type of message (see below) the routing table is updated and, if necessary, a new message is created, and either broadcast or unicast.

The AODV Architecture. Each node maintains its own destination sequence number, routing table and keeps a record of the messages it has already received (or initiated). It also manages a queue to store data packets waiting to be delivered. Messages are handled appropriately according to their type:

PKT   Messages containing data packets play no part in route-finding. In the case that a node has a valid route for the PKT's destination, the packet is forwarded to **nhop**, the next hop on the route. In the case that the data packet is injected by the application layer and no (valid) route is known, the packet is placed on the node's packet queue, and a route discovery process is initiated by broadcasting an appropriate RREQ message.

RREQ Route requests are messages, broadcast to every node within transmission range. They contain information about the originator of the route discovery process, the neighbour that most recently sent it, and the number of nodes through which the request travelled. All of this information is available for updating routing tables. The same request can be received via different routes and so nodes maintain a record of those that have already

---

[2] AODV calls it *Valid Destination Sequence Number flag*; DYMO *Route.Broken*.

been handled so that duplicates can be discarded. For new requests, the following actions are taken. (a) If the node is either the destination or has a valid route to the destination stored in its routing table, a route reply (RREP) message is generated, which is unicast back to most recent sender. (b) If the node is neither the destination nor has any information about the destination, it increments the hop count and broadcasts it on.

RREP Replies are "logically" matched up with the corresponding request that gave rise to it so that a route for the requested destination can be established. The routing table is updated for that destination, by recording nhop as the neighbour from which the RREP was received and similarly taking hops and dsn from the RREP. Only if the routing table was changed during the update, the hop count of the RREP is increased and then (in the case that the node was not the original initiator) forwarded to the neighbour from which the corresponding request was received.

RERR Error messages are generated whenever link breaks are detected by some nodes. Often this occurs when a message (RREP or PKT) fails to be sent. In these cases an error message is sent to all neighbours. If an RERR message is received the routing tables are updated—in particular routes are marked as *invalid*, and the error message is forwarded to all neighbours.

This informal introduction to AODV should be sufficient to understand the experiments described below. A detailed description can be found in [14].

The DYMO Architecture. DYMO [15] follows the same basic workflow as AODV. In this section we only highlight the major design differences.[3]

(a) DYMO's mechanism for managing duplicate requests is no longer based on a queue of handled RREQ messages. Instead DYMO uses sequence numbers to judge whether information contained in a message should be forwarded. While this modification saves some memory, it has been shown that the change can lead to loss of route requests [6].

(b) On the other hand AODV can lose route replies since RREP messages are only forwarded if the routing table of an intermediate node is updated (changed).[4] To avoid this, a node generating a route reply increments the sequence number for the destination, thereby guaranting that the routing table of nodes receiving the RREP message will be updated, and the RREP forwarded.

(c) DYMO establishes *bidirectional* routes between originator and destination. When an intermediate node initiates a route reply, it unicasts a message back to the originator of the request (as AODV does), but at the same time it forwards a route reply to the intended destination of the route request.

(d) DYMO uses the concept of *path accumulation*: whenever a control message (RREQ, RREP, RERR) travels via more than one node, information about *all* intermediate nodes is stored in the message. In this way, a node receiving a message establishes routes to *all other intermediate nodes*. In AODV nodes only establish routes to a the initiator and to the sender of a message.

---

[3] Our model is based on DYMO's internet draft version 22.

[4] http://www.ietf.org/mail-archive/web/manet/current/msg05702.html

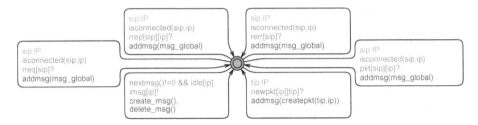

Fig. 1. Automaton modelling the `Queue`

These changes imply (as intended) quite different behaviour: for example (c) and (d) might mean that DYMO establishes many more routes in the network as a whole than does AODV. On the other hand (a) could imply that some routes might not be discovered at all. We investigate some of these differences below.

2.2   AODV and DYMO in Uppaal

In previous work [8], an untimed Uppaal model of AODV was developed and used to analyse some basic qualitative properties. In this paper we extend that analysis to quantitative properties combining time and probability. As a consequence the models needed a significant redesign to include timing constraints on sending messages between nodes, as well as redesigning communication between nodes so that the unicast behaviour of DYMO and AODV was correctly rendered using SMC-Uppaal's (only) broadcast mechanism.

We model AODV and DYMO as a parallel composition between node processes, where each process is a parallel composition of two timed automata, the `Handler` and the `Queue`. Communication between nodes i and j is only feasible if they are in transmission range of each other. This is modelled by predicates of the form `isconnected[i][j]`, which is true if and only if i and j can communicate. Communication between different nodes i, j are on channels named according to the type of message being delivered (`rerr`, `rrep`, `rreq`).

The `Queue` of a node `ip` is depicted in Fig. 1. Messages (arriving from other nodes) are stored in a queue, by using the function `addmsg`. Our model guarantees that messages sent by nodes within transmission range are received.

The `Handler`, modelling the message-handling protocol, is far more complicated and has around 20 locations. It is busy while sending messages, and can only accept a new message from the `Queue` once it has completely finished handling a message. Whenever it is not processing a message and there are messages stored in the `Queue`, the `Queue` and the `Handler` synchronise via channel `imsg[ip]`, transferring the relevant message data from the `Queue` to the `Handler`. The `Handler` then follows the workflow sketched in Sect. 2.1. Due to lack of space, we cannot present the full timed automaton modelling the `Handler`, but it is available in full online[5]. Here, we concentrate on our treatment of time.

According to the specification of AODV [14], the most time consuming activity is the communication between nodes, which takes on average 40 milliseconds.

---

[5] http://www.hoefner-online.de/nfm2013/

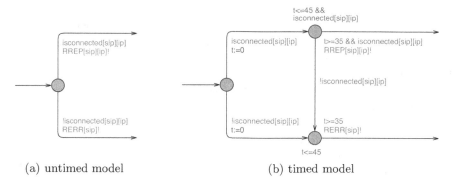

(a) untimed model   (b) timed model

Fig. 2. Part of `Handler`—unicast a message

In Fig. 2 we compare the extract of a model without time (as used in [8]) with the corresponding extract including time. For the untimed model we simply guard the communication with `isconnected` so that the message (here a `rrep`) is sent whenever the nodes are connected, and an error message is generated otherwise. In the timed model, we use a clock variable `t`, set to 0 before transmission, and then we use an intermediate location which has the effect of selecting a delay of at least 35 milliseconds and no more than 45 milliseconds uniformly at random. In the case that the nodes are still connected at the time of sending then the `rrep` message is successfully transmitted, and otherwise an error is reported.[6]

3 Experiments

The experiments split into four categories: a timing analysis of AODV (Sect. 3.1); a comparison between AODV and DYMO (Sect. 3.2); a quantitative analysis of the two protocols (Sect. 3.3); and a feasibility study of networks of realistic size (Sect. 3.4). The experiments of the first three categories use the following setup: 3.1 GHz Intel Pentium 5 CPU, with 16 GB memory, running the Mac OS X 10.7 operating system. The final category needs 128 GB memory (3.3 GHz). For all experiments we use SMC-Uppaal 4.1.11 (June 2012). In the first three categories, the parameters of false negatives (α) and probabilistic uncertainty (ε) are both set to 0.01—yielding a confidence level of 99% and SMC-Uppaal checks 26492 runs (cf. Chernoff-Hoeffding bound). The last category uses, due to its calculational complexity, only 738 runs and a confidence level of 95% ($\alpha = \varepsilon = 0.05$).

3.1 A Timing Analysis of AODV

The first category extends experiments performed for the untimed model for AODV [8], exploring in more depth the surprising result that AODV might fail to discover an existing route in 47% of all network topologies with up to 5 nodes.

---

[6] This complexity needs to be inserted because a change in connectivity could result in nodes being connected at the start of transmission, but become disconnected before the transmission is completed.

For the experiments we generate all topologies of up to 5 nodes, where for each topology we consider three distinct nodes A, B and C; each with particular originator/destination roles as per scenario described below. Up to symmetry this yields 444 topologies. For each scenario we analyse three properties; in total this requires approximately 4000 experiments for this category.

Initially, for each scenario no routes are known. Then, with a time gap of 35–45 milliseconds, two of the distinct nodes receive a data packet and have to find routes to the packets' destinations. The scenarios assign roles as follows:

(i) A is the only originator sending a packet first to B and afterwards to C;
(ii) B and C are originators both sending to A;
(iii) A is sending to B first and then B is also an originator sending to C;
(iv) B is an originator sending to C followed by A sending to B.

For each scenario we analyse two properties and their combination. The first property examines the time taken for the protocol to complete, i.e., until all messages have been handled, which encoded in Uppaal's syntax as

$$\texttt{Pr[<=10000](<> (tester.final \&\& emptybuffers()))} \tag{1}$$

This query asks for the probability estimate (`Pr`) satisfying the CTL-path expression `<>(tester.final && emptybuffers())` within 10000 time units (milliseconds); we choose this bound as a conservative upper bound to ensure that the analyser explores paths to a depth where the protocol is guaranteed to have terminated. `tester` refers to a process which injects the data packets to the originators (`tester.final` means that all data packets have been injected), and the function `emptybuffers()` checks whether the nodes' message queues are empty.

The second property examines the time for requested routes to be established. This differs from (1) since routes are usually found before all buffers are emptied.

$$\texttt{Pr[<=10000](<> (OIP1.rt[DIP1].nhop!=0 \&\& OIP2.rt[DIP2].nhop!=0))} \tag{2}$$

Here, `o.rt[d].nhop` is the next hop in `o`'s routing table entry for destination `d`. As soon as this value is set (is different to 0), a route to `d` has been established.

The third property combines the first two and analyses the time which is needed to finish the protocol and to establish the routes; this estimates the proportion of runs which end without ever finding a route.

$$\texttt{Pr[<=10000](<> (tester.final \&\& emptybuffers() \&\&}$$
$$\texttt{OIP1.rt[DIP1].nhop!=0 \&\& OIP2.rt[DIP2].nhop!=0))} \tag{3}$$

For every scenario, SMC-Uppaal evaluates the property under consideration for 26492 runs and returns a probability interval $[p-0.01, p+0.01]$, where p is the averaged probability over all runs. Probability theory implies that with a likelihood of 99% the "real" value is inside this interval.

Fig. 3 displays the results for all 5-node networks.[7] The x-axis represents the time (in milliseconds) for the property to be satisfied; the y-axis represents the average number of simulation runs per topology for the property to be satisfied.

---

[7] The graphs for network sizes 3 and 4 look similar and can be found at
   `http://www.hoefner-online.de/nfm2013/`

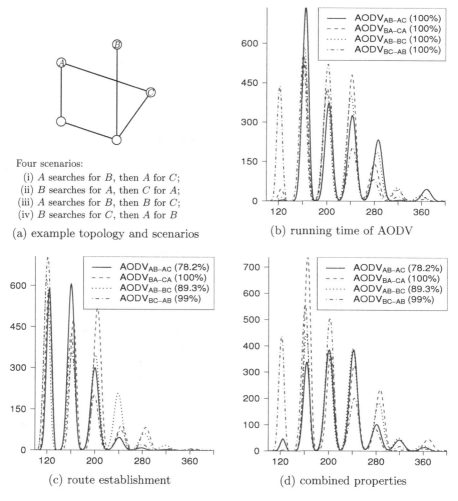

Four scenarios:
  (i) A searches for B, then A for C;
  (ii) B searches for A, then C for A;
  (iii) A searches for B, then B for C;
  (iv) B searches for C, then A for B

(a) example topology and scenarios

(b) running time of AODV

(c) route establishment

(d) combined properties

Fig. 3. A timed analysis of AODV (5-node topologies).[8]

For example the highest peak in (b) shows that 720 simulation runs (out of 26492) need 164 ms to finish the protocol. Figs. (b–d) refer to Properties (1), (2) and (3). Each graph depicts the results for each scenario. For example the solid graph corresponds to the the first scenario (A is the originator and B and C are the destinations). The overall probability that the property is satisfied is indicated by the percentage given in the legend.[9]

Analysis of the Results. All of the experiments yield a periodic behaviour of roughly 40 milliseconds corresponding to the average time for sending a message. Surprising is that the performance of AODV is fairly stable across scenarios.

---

[8] Figures 3, 4 and 7 have been produced using the tool R [16].
[9] More precisely, the probability shown is the average of all medians of the probability intervals returned by Uppaal.

Fig. 3(b) shows that AODV always terminates and presents the running times for termination. Fig. 3(c) shows that in general route establishment occurs much earlier; the results also show that AODV cannot always establish routes: in the case of 3-node topologies routes are not established in 11.7% of all cases; for networks with 4 nodes in 10.85% of all cases; and in case of 5 nodes in approximately 10% of all cases.

Fig. 3(d) confirms that the quantitative analysis gives significantly more insight than an untimed analysis such as reported in [8]. There, we considered a similar property and found that in 47.3% of all 5-node topologies there is the possibility of route-discovery failure—a quantitative analysis was not possible. Our quantitative analysis shows that failure to find a route can now be estimated at around 10%. There are two reasons for this dramatic difference. First, the inclusion of time ruled out some scenarios where route failure was due to messages overtaking each other. Second, and more significant, the new analysis determines the number of runs (not the number of topologies), where route discovery fails and indicates that discovery failures are rare: whereas in half of the topologies route failure is possible [8], in only ∼10% of all runs failure actually happens.

3.2   AODV versus DYMO

In Sect. 2 we have outlined the design differences between AODV and DYMO. Moreover, we have speculated on what those differences might imply w.r.t. overall performance. We now run exactly the same experiments as described in Sect. 3.1, this time for DYMO. The results averaged over all 4-node networks and all scenarios for both routing protocols are presented in Fig. 4; in these diagrams we also indicate the average times by vertical bars.

To our surprise, the variation in performance between the two is marginal: DYMO appears to be more reliable in that it can establish more routes than does AODV in some cases (Fig. 4(b,c)). DYMO takes on average longer to complete (Fig. 4(a)) but the average time to find routes is almost exactly the same as for AODV (Fig. 4(b)).

A first analysis of the circumstances behind the observed non-establishment of routes in DYMO is presented in [6], indicating that problems occur when messages can overtake others. The reason why DYMO needs longer running times is the additional RREP-message sent to the destination of a route request (cf. Page 325).

3.3   Quantitative Measurements

So far we have looked at running times and route discovery. In this section we illustrate how to the use Value-Estimation-Feature (E) of SMC-Uppaal to explore the quality and quantity of the routes established by AODV and DYMO.

One side effect of broadcasting route requests is that intermediate nodes, which handle those requests, are able to establish routes to the originator. Whilst this certainly represents an increase in "knowledge" across the network, there is no guarantee that the routes established are optimal. In [13] it is shown that non-optimal paths can impact overall performance of packet delivery dramatically.

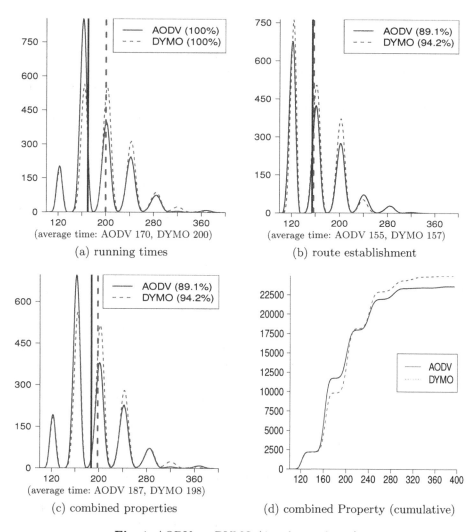

Fig. 4. AODV vs. DYMO (4-node topologies)

We examine two properties: the total number of routes established over all routing tables, averaged over all network topologies for up to 5 nodes; and the average difference between the length of the route established and the length of the optimal route.

Route Quantity. Routing tables are updated whenever control messages are received. In case of RREQ and RREP messages, AODV does so only for the originator/destination and for the sender of the message, whereas DYMO uses path accumulation (cf. Page 325). This difference in design implies that DYMO could potentially establish more routes than AODV. We check whether this is indeed the case for all topologies and all scenarios described earlier using the property

$$E[<=10000;26492](max:total\_knowledge())$$

(4)

Here, the function `total_knowledge()` counts the number of entries in all routing tables along a run (path); `max` takes the largest of these values. Since value estimation does not determine the number of runs, we set it to the same number as determined previously (26492); the time bound is again set to 10000.

Table 1. Average number of routes found

	3 nodes	4 nodes	5 nodes
AODV	5.28	8.83	13.99
DYMO	5.25	7.87	11.94
max	6	12	20

Table 1 presents the results, grouped by network size. Note that the last row shows the maximal number of possible routing table entries: this is $n \cdot (n-1)$ since each node can hold $n-1$ entries in an n-node network.

To our surprise, DYMO establishes fewer routes on average than does AODV. (Although it does establish more of the *requested* routes Fig. 4.) A possible explanation is the following: when DYMO floods the network with the first RREQ, many nodes establish many routes (more than with AODV), due to path accumulation. When the second RREQ is sent, the chance of an intermediate route reply is now greater (than for AODV)—an intermediate route reply means that the RREQ is not forwarded, thus additional opportunities to create routes in receiving nodes are suppressed.[10]

Route Quality. In almost all routing protocols based on RREQ-broadcast, non-optimal routes can be established [13]. This can happen when the destination does not forward the RREQ message, as the example in Fig. 5 shows. The scenario depicts node S searching for a route to node T. As soon as T receives the RREQ message, it generates a route reply, and suppresses the RREQ. Node A receives the same RREQ via B and establishes a non-optimal path to S via B.

In our second experiment we check the extent of establishing non-optimal routes. We use the query `E[<=10000;26492](max:quality())`, which is similar to (4), but instead uses a function `quality` that compares the length of established routes with the length of the corresponding optimal routes.[11]

The results in Table 2 show that the average deviation from the optimal length (in ‰) is small; which is to be expected in small networks. More interesting is that again DYMO performs less well than AODV. Again a potential explanation for this is the implication of path accumulation in DYMO. In the example, node A establishes a (non-optimal) route to S, but because of path accumulation node A will also establish a non-optimal path to B (as well as all the other nodes on this non-optimal path).

3.4   Networks of Realistic Size

In complex protocols used for routing, analysis by "classical" model checking is limited to around 8 nodes. WMNs usually consist of more than 50 nodes placing them far beyond the capabilities of systematic logical analysis. In this section we explore the scalability of SMC for such networks.

---

[10] An example is found at the website—it requires detailed knowledge of the protocols.
[11] The length of optimal routes can be calculated from the static network topology.

Table 2. Average deviation from the optimal

	3 nodes	4 nodes	5 nodes
AODV	0.00‰	0.50‰	2.31‰
DYMO	0.00‰	2.00‰	9.68‰

Fig. 5. Node A "accidentally" creates a non-optimal route to S

Our first task is to generate a sample realistic topology. We use the *Node Placement Algorithm for Realistic Topologies* (NPART) [12]. This tool allows the specification of arbitrary-sized topologies and transmission ranges, and it has been shown that generated topologies have graph characteristics similar to realistic wireless multihop ones.

We analyse NPART topologies consisting of 25, 50, 75 and 100 nodes. Fig. 6 depicts the 100-node topology used for our analysis. The links between nodes are determined by the distance between nodes; rather than displaying the actual 201 links, we instead indicate the link distance by scale. The node labelled A is the originator of two packets with destinations B and C, both of which are connected to A albeit at several hops distance. We check Property (3), which confirms that both routes are found and that the protocols terminates. More significant are the resources required to perform the experiments for large networks which we report next.

transmission range: ⊢——⊣

Fig. 6. A topology with 100 nodes

A network with 25 nodes is easily checked with a standard desktop machine in less than half an hour with a confidence level of 95% (which means 738 runs). However the memory consumption grows with the number of nodes. A summary of our observations is given in Table 3.

Table 3. Memory Consumption[12]

#nodes	50	75	100
memory (Gb)	14	30	80
run time (m)	270	328	1777

Fig. 7 shows that the protocol finishes on average within $24 \times 40\,ms$[13] for the given scenario. This also suggests that there is little interference between the

---

[13] The average time for sending a single message.

two requests for B and C, since the number of hops between A and C is roughly 10, and so at least 20 messages are required to establish that route alone.

4   Related Work

Traditionally, protocols for WMNs are evaluated using test-bed experiments and simulation, e.g., [10]. Test-bed experiments evaluate protocols under realistic circumstances, whereas simulation is performed on a single machine, thus is closely related to our work. Simulation-based studies show that AODV performs better than DYMO in some scenarios and vice versa in others [1,11]. Under packet delivery ratio (PDR) as measure Saleem et al. [17] imply that DYMO compares unfavourably to AODV (consistent with our results), but this analysis does not help to diagnose the reasons for this conclusion.

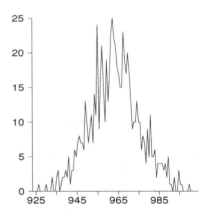

Fig. 7. Property (3) with 100 nodes

More recently formal analysis has been used to investigate the behaviour of complex protocols [2,5]. Although formal analysis is often more detailed than test bed analysis, with the result that only small samples can be investigated, the outcome is often a more penetrating understanding of protocol behaviour. For example a study using the Spin model checker showed that an early draft of AODV could create routing loops [2]; Zave [21] uses the Alloy analyser in combination with the Spin model checker to show that no published version of the Chord ring-maintenance protocol is correct, and Schuts et al. establish an impossibility result for clock synchronisation in the Chess gMAC WSN protocol [18]. Other specific formal analyses of AODV include that of Chiyangwa and Kwiatkowska [5] who investigate the relation between protocol parameters and performance, such as time outs in AODV, and Espensen et al. [7] use coloured Petri nets to perform test runs to confirm specified behaviour.

5   Conclusion and Outlook

Our aim in this study was twofold: (i) We developed timed models for AODV and DYMO in order to carry out a systematic analysis across all small networks. In comparison to simulation and test bed studies, our analysis based on quality and quantity enabled us to examine reasons for observed differences in performance between AODV and DYMO, which was an open question before (cf. studies in [1,11]). (ii) We examined the feasibility of SMC w.r.t. scalability. None of the formal studies above analysed routing protocols for networks containing more than 10 nodes, whereas our results imply that networks of realistic size can be analysed. Finally we draw some general conclusions about SMC critical analysis.

5.1 Statistical Model Checking: Lessons Learned

Resourcing. One of the main bottlenecks in the analysis was time—to analyse a 100 node network takes about 30 hours. One of the next steps is to determine whether the most recent distributed release [3] is able to reduce that overhead.

Choosing the Right Scenario. For small networks it is possible to analyse all topologies for given scenarios. This gives a good overall view of the performance and behaviour in any situation. For large networks this is not feasible, and so the selection of topologies in combination with the right scenarios becomes something of a "stab in the dark".For our study we used the comparison of AODV and DYMO to observe that odd behaviour occur in the setting of two requests, thus we chose that scenario for our large networks. In general, a systematic analysis of small networks can be used as a preliminary phase for selecting the most informative scenarios.

Interpreting the Results. The results are frequently hard to interpret, particularly when they indicate odd behaviour. Unfortunately SMC-Uppaal does not store traces during analysis, thus it is not possible to recover counterexamples to explain the observations. We tried to diagnose odd observations by formulating more probing queries beyond looking at overall performance. This suggests that more powerful statistical analysis such as "rare event simulation" in combination with multiple queries could be used to compile better evidence.

5.2 Future Work

The models for AODV and DYMO are general enough to allow for the study of more complex scenarios, in particular mobility. In future work we will develop a number of mobility models for understanding the behaviour of these and other routing protocols.

Acknowledgement. We are grateful to David Jansen and Frits Vaandrager for helpful discussions, and to the NWO grant 040.11.302 for financial support. NICTA is funded by the Australian Government as represented by the Department of Broadband, Communications and the Digital Economy and the Australian Research Council through the ICT Centre of Excellence program.

References

1. Amin, M., Abrar, M., Khan, Z.U., Andusalam, Rizwan, S.: Comparison of OLSR & DYMO routing protocols on the basis of different performance metrics in mobile ad-hoc networks. American Journal of Scientific Research (2011)
2. Bhargavan, K., Obradovic, D., Gunter, C.: Formal verification of standards for distance vector routing protocols. J. ACM 49(4), 538–576 (2002)
3. Bulychev, P., David, A., Larsen, K.G., Legay, A., Mikučionis, M., Bøgsted Poulsen, D.: Checking and distributing statistical model checking. In: Goodloe, A.E., Person, S. (eds.) NFM 2012. LNCS, vol. 7226, pp. 449–463. Springer, Heidelberg (2012)

4. Bulychev, P., David, A., Larsen, K., Mikučionis, M., Bøgsted Poulsen, D., Legay, A., Wang, Z.: UPPAAL-SMC: Statistical model checking for priced timed automata. In: Wiklicky, H., Massink, M. (eds.) Quantitative Aspects of Programming Languages and Systems. EPTCS, vol. 85, pp. 1–16. Open Publishing Association (2012)
5. Chiyangwa, S., Kwiatkowska, M.: A timing analysis of AODV. In: Steffen, M., Zavattaro, G. (eds.) FMOODS 2005. LNCS, vol. 3535, pp. 306–321. Springer, Heidelberg (2005)
6. Edenhofer, S., Höfner, P.: Towards a rigorous analysis of AODVv2 (DYMO). In: Rigorous Protocol Engineering (W-RiPE 2012). IEEE Press (2012)
7. Espensen, K.L., Kjeldsen, M.K., Kristensen, L.M.: Modelling and initial validation of the DYMO routing protocol for mobile ad-hoc networks. In: van Hee, K.M., Valk, R. (eds.) PETRI NETS 2008. LNCS, vol. 5062, pp. 152–170. Springer, Heidelberg (2008)
8. Fehnker, A., van Glabbeek, R., Höfner, P., McIver, A., Portmann, M., Tan, W.L.: Automated analysis of AODV using UPPAAL. In: Flanagan, C., König, B. (eds.) TACAS 2012. LNCS, vol. 7214, pp. 173–187. Springer, Heidelberg (2012)
9. van Glabbeek, R.J., Höfner, P., Tan, W.L., Portmann, M.: Sequence numbers do not guarantee loop freedom—AODV can yield routing loops (2012), http://rvg.web.cse.unsw.edu.au/pub/AODVloop.pdf
10. Johnson, D., Lysko, A.: Comparison of MANET routing protocols using a scaled indoor wireless grid. Mob. Netw. Appl. 13(1-2), 82–96 (2008)
11. Kum, D.W., Park, J.S., Cho, Y.Z., Cheon, B.Y.: Performance evaluation of AODV and DYMO routing protocols in MANET. In: Consumer Communications and Networking Conference (CCNC 2010), pp. 1046–1047. IEEE Press (2010)
12. Milic, B., Malek, M.: NPART—node placement algorithm for realistic topologies in wireless multihop network simulation. In: Simulation Tools and Techniques (Simutools 2009), pp. 9:1–9:10. ICST (2009)
13. Miskovic, S., Knightly, E.: Routing primitives for wireless mesh networks: Design, analysis and experiments. In: Conference on Information communications (INFOCOM 2010), pp. 2793–2801. IEEE Press (2010)
14. Perkins, C., Belding-Royer, E., Das, S.: Ad hoc on-demand distance vector (AODV) routing. RFC 3561 (Experimental) (2003), http://www.ietf.org/rfc/rfc3561
15. Perkins, C., Chakeres, I.: Dynamic MANET on-demand (AODVv2) routing. IETF Internet Draft (Work in Progress) (March 2012), http://tools.ietf.org/html/draft-ietf-manet-dymo-22
16. R Core Team: R: A Language and Environment for Statistical Computing (2012), http://www.R-project.org
17. Saleem, M., Khayam, S.A., Farooq, M.: On performance modeling of ad hoc routing protocols. EURASIP J. Wirel. Commun. Netw. 2010, 31:1–31:13 (2010)
18. Schuts, M., Zhu, F., Heidarian, F., Vaandrager, F.: Modelling clock synchronization in the Chess gMAC WSN protocol. In: Andova, S., McIver, A., D'Argenio, P., Cuijpers, P., Markovski, J., Morgan, C., Núñez, M. (eds.) Quantitative Formal Methods: Theory and Applications (QFM 2009). EPTCS, vol. 13, pp. 41–54 (2009)
19. Sen, K., Viswanathan, M., Agha, G.A.: Vesta: A statistical model-checker and analyzer for probabilistic systems. In: Quantitative Evaluaiton of Systems (QEST 2005), pp. 251–252. IEEE Press (2005)
20. Younes, H.: Verification and Planning for Stochastic Processes with Asynchronous Events. Ph.D. thesis, Carnegie Mellon University (2004)
21. Zave, P.: Using lightweight modeling to understand CHORD. SIGCOMM Comput. Commun. Rev. 42(2), 49–57 (2012)

On-the-Fly Confluence Detection
for Statistical Model Checking*

Arnd Hartmanns[1] and Mark Timmer[2]

[1] Saarland University – Computer Science, Saarbrücken, Germany
[2] Formal Methods and Tools, University of Twente, The Netherlands

Abstract. Statistical model checking is an analysis method that circumvents the state space explosion problem in model-based verification by combining probabilistic simulation with statistical methods that provide clear error bounds. As a simulation-based technique, it can only provide sound results if the underlying model is a stochastic process. In verification, however, models are usually variations of nondeterministic transition systems. The notion of confluence allows the reduction of such transition systems in classical model checking by removing spurious nondeterministic choices. In this paper, we show that confluence can be adapted to detect and discard such choices on-the-fly during simulation, thus extending the applicability of statistical model checking to a subclass of Markov decision processes. In contrast to previous approaches that use partial order reduction, the confluence-based technique can handle additional kinds of nondeterminism. In particular, it is not restricted to interleavings. We evaluate our approach, which is implemented as part of the modes simulator for the MODEST modelling language, on a set of examples that highlight its strengths and limitations and show the improvements compared to the partial order-based method.

1 Introduction

Traditional and probabilistic model checking have grown to be useful techniques for finding inconsistencies in designs and computing quantitative aspects of systems and protocols. However, model checking is subject to the state space explosion problem, with probabilistic model checking being particularly affected due to its additional numerical complexity. Several techniques have been introduced to stretch the limits of model checking while preserving its basic nature of performing state space exploration to obtain results that unconditionally, certainly hold for the entire state space. Two of them, partial order reduction (POR) and confluence reduction, work by selecting a subset of the transitions of a model—and thus a subset of the reachable states—in a way that ensures that the reduced system is equivalent to the complete system. POR was first generalised to the probabilistic domain preserving linear time properties [2,10], with a

---

* This work has been supported by the DFG/NWO Bilateral Research Program ROCKS, by NWO under grant 612.063.817 (SYRUP), by the EU FP7-ICT project MEALS, contract no. 295261, and by the DFG as part of SFB/TR 14 AVACS.

G. Brat, N. Rungta, and A. Venet (Eds.): NFM 2013, LNCS 7871, pp. 337–351, 2013.
© Springer-Verlag Berlin Heidelberg 2013

later extension to preserve branching time properties [1]. Confluence reduction was generalised in [13,23], preserving branching time properties.

A much different approach for probabilistic models is statistical model checking (SMC) [18,21,26]: instead of exploring—and storing in memory—the entire state space, or even a reduced version of it, discrete-event simulation is used to generate traces through the state space. This comes at constant memory usage and thus circumvents state space explosion entirely, but cannot deliver results that hold with absolute certainty. Statistical methods such as sequential hypothesis testing are then used to make sure that the *probability* of returning the wrong result is below a certain threshold. As a simulation-based approach, however, SMC is limited to fully stochastic models such as Markov chains [14].

Previously, an approach based on POR was presented [6] to extend SMC and simulation to the nondeterministic model of Markov decision processes (MDPs). In that approach, simulation proceeds as usual until a nondeterministic choice is encountered; at that point, an on-the-fly check is performed to find a singleton subset of the available transitions that satisfies the *ample set* conditions of probabilistic POR [2,10]. If such an ample set is found, simulation can continue that way with the guarantee that ignoring the other transitions does not affect the verification results, i.e., the nondeterminism was *spurious*. Yet, the ample set conditions are based on the notion of *independence* of actions, which can in practice only feasibly be checked on a symbolic/syntactic level (using conditions such as J1 and J2 in [6]). This limits the approach to resolve spurious nondeterminism only when it results from the *interleaving* of behaviours of concurrently executing (deterministic) components.

In this paper, we present as an alternative to use confluence reduction, which has recently been shown theoretically to be more powerful than branching time POR [13]. It is absolutely vital for the search for a valid singleton subset to succeed in the approach discussed above: one choice that cannot be resolved means that the entire analysis fails and SMC cannot safely be applied to the given model at all. Therefore, any additional reduction power is highly welcome. Furthermore, in practice, confluence reduction is easily implemented on the level of the concrete state space alone, without any need to go back to the symbolic/syntactic level for an independence check. As opposed to the approach in [6], it thus allows even spurious nondeterminism that is internal to components to be ignored during simulation. Of course, models containing non-spurious nondeterminism can still not be dealt with.

Contributions and outline. After the introduction of the necessary preliminaries (Section 2), we present the three main contributions of this paper: (1) Since simulation works with a fully composed, closed system, we can relax the definition of confluence with respect to action labels compared to [13] (Section 3). We thus achieve more reduction/detection power at no computational cost; yet, we can prove that this adapted notion of confluence still preserves PCTL* formulae [3] without the *next* operator. (2) We then introduce an algorithm for detecting our new notion of probabilistic confluence on a concrete state space and state its correctness (Section 4). The algorithm is inspired by, but different

Table 1. SMC approaches for nondeterministic models (with n states)

approach	nondeterminism	probabilities	memory	error bounds
POR-based [6]	spurious interleavings	max = min	$s \ll n$	unchanged
confluence-based	spurious	max = min	$s \ll n$	unchanged
learning [17]	any	max only	$s \to n$	convergence

from, the one given in [12]; in particular, it does not require initial knowledge of the entire state space and can therefore be used on-the-fly during simulation. (3) Finally, we evaluate the new confluence-based approach to SMC on a set of three representative examples using our implementation within the modes statistical model checker [7] for the MODEST modelling language [8] (Section 5). We clearly identify its strengths and limitations. Since the previous POR-based approach is also implemented in modes, we compare the two in terms of reduction power and, on the one case that can actually be handled by the POR-based implementation as well, performance. Proofs for all our results can be found in [16].

Related work. Aside from [6] and an approach that focuses on planning problems and infinite-state models [20], the only other solution to the problem of nondeterminism in SMC that we are aware of is recent work by Henriques et al. [17]. They use reinforcement learning, a technique from artificial intelligence, to actually learn the resolutions of nondeterminism (by memoryless schedulers) that *maximise* probabilities for a given bounded LTL property. While this allows SMC for models with arbitrary nondeterministic choices (not only spurious ones), scheduling decisions need to be stored for every *explored* state. Memory usage can thus be as in traditional model checking, but is highly dependent on the structure of the model and the learning process. As the number of runs of the algorithm increases, the answer it returns will converge to the actual result, but definite error probabilities are not given. The approaches based on confluence and POR do not introduce any additional overapproximation and thus have no influence on the usual error bounds of SMC. Table 1 gives a condensed overview of the three approaches (where we measure memory usage in terms of the maximal number of states s stored at any time; see Section 5 for concrete values).

2   Preliminaries

Definition 1 (Basics). *A* probability distribution *over a countable set S is a function $\mu\colon S \to [0,1]$ such that $\sum_{s \in S} \mu(s) = 1$. We denote by* Distr$(S)$ *the set of all such functions. For $S' \subseteq S$, let $\mu(S') = \sum_{s \in S'} \mu(s)$. We let* support$(\mu) = \{s \in S \mid \mu(s) > 0\}$ *be the* support *of μ, and write $\mathbb{1}_s$ for the* Dirac distribution *for s, determined by $\mathbb{1}_s(s) = 1$.*

Given an equivalence relation $R \subseteq S \times S$, we write $[s]_R$ for the equivalence class induced by s, i.e. $[s]_R = \{s' \in S \mid (s, s') \in R\}$. We denote the set of all such equivalence classes by S/R. Given two probability distributions μ, μ' over S, we write $\mu \equiv_R \mu'$ to denote that $\mu([s]_R) = \mu'([s]_R)$ for every $s \in S$.

Our analyses are based on the model of Markov decision processes (MDPs, or equivalently probabilistic automata, PAs), which combines nondeterministic and probabilistic choices. In the variant we use states are labelled by a set of atomic propositions.

Definition 2 (MDPs). *A Markov decision process (MDP) is a tuple* $\mathcal{A} = (S, \Sigma, P, s^0, \mathsf{AP}, L)$, *where*

- *S is a countable set of* states, *of which $s^0 \in S$ is the* initial state;
- *Σ is a finite set of* action labels;
- *$P \subseteq S \times \Sigma \times \mathsf{Distr}(S)$ is the* probabilistic transition relation;
- *AP is the set of* atomic propositions;
- *$L\colon S \to \mathcal{P}(\mathsf{AP})$ is the* labelling function.

If $(s, a, \mu) \in P$, we write $s \xrightarrow{a} \mu$ and mean that it is possible to take an a-action from s and have a probability of $\mu(s')$ to go to s'. Given a state $s \in S$, we define its set of enabled *transitions $en(s) = \{(s, a, \mu) \in \{s\} \times \Sigma \times \mathsf{Distr}(S) \mid s \xrightarrow{a} \mu\}$.*

We will use $S_{\mathcal{A}}, \Sigma_{\mathcal{A}}, \ldots$, to refer to the components of an MDP $\mathcal{A}$. If the MDP is clear from the context, these subscripts are omitted.

We work in a state-based verification setting where properties only refer to the atomic propositions of states. The action labels are solely meant for synchronisation during parallel composition. Since we consider closed systems only, we can therefore ignore them. We do care about whether or not transitions change the observable behaviour of the system, i.e., the atomic propositions:

Definition 3 (Visibility and determinism). *A transition $s \xrightarrow{a} \mu$ in an MDP $\mathcal{A}$ is called* visible *if $\exists t \in \mathsf{support}(\mu)\colon L(s) \neq L(t)$. Otherwise, it is invisible. A transition $s \xrightarrow{a} \mu$ is* deterministic *if $\mu(t) = 1$ for some $t \in S$, i.e., $\mu = \mathbb{1}_t$.*

We write $s \xrightarrow{\tau} \mu$ to indicate that a transition is invisible. Transitions labelled by a letter different from τ can be either visible or invisible.

For a given MDP, a wide class of reductions can be defined using *reduction functions*. Informally, such a function F decides for each state which outgoing actions are enabled in the reduced MDP. This MDP's transition relation then consists of all transitions enabled according to F, and the set of states consists of all states that are still reachable using the reduced transition function.

Definition 4 (Reduction functions). *For an MDP $\mathcal{A} = (S_{\mathcal{A}}, \Sigma, P_{\mathcal{A}}, s^0, \mathsf{AP}, L_{\mathcal{A}})$, a* reduction function *is any function $F\colon S_{\mathcal{A}} \to \mathcal{P}(P_{\mathcal{A}})$ such that $F(s) \subseteq en(s)$ for every $s \in S_{\mathcal{A}}$. Given a reduction function F, the* reduced MDP for $\mathcal{A}$ *with respect to F is the minimal MDP $\mathcal{A}_F = (S_F, \Sigma, P_F, s^0, \mathsf{AP}, L_F)$ such that*

- *if $s \in S_F$ and $(s, a, \mu) \in F(s)$, then $(s, a, \mu) \in P_F$ and $\mathsf{support}(\mu) \subseteq S_F$;*
- *$L_F(s) = L_{\mathcal{A}}(s)$ for every $s \in S_F$,*

where minimal should be interpreted as having the smallest set of states and the smallest set of transitions.

Given a reduction function F and a state $s \in S_F$, we say that s is a reduced state *if $F(s) \neq en(s)$. All outgoing transitions of a reduced state are called* nontrivial transitions. *We say that a reduction function is* acyclic *if there are no cyclic paths when only nontrivial transitions are considered.*

3   Confluence for Statistical Model Checking

Confluence reduction is based on commutativity of invisible transitions. It works by denoting a subset of the invisible transitions of an MDP as *confluent*. Basic-ally, this means that they do not change the observable behaviour; everything that is possible before a confluent transition is still possible afterwards. There-fore, they can be given *priority*, omitting all their neighbouring transitions.

3.1   Confluent Sets of Transitions

Previous work defined conditions for a set of transitions to be confluent. In the non-probabilistic action-based setting, several variants were introduced, ranging from ultra weak confluence to strong confluence [4]. They are all given diagram-matically, and define in which way two outgoing transitions from the same state have to be able to join again. Basically, for a transition $s \xrightarrow{\tau} t$ to be confluent, every transition $s \xrightarrow{a} u$ has to be mimicked by a transition $t \xrightarrow{a} v$ such that u and v are bisimilar. This is ensured by requiring a confluent transition from u to v.

In the probabilistic action-based setting, a similar approach was taken [23]. For a transition $s \xrightarrow{\tau} \mathbb{1}_t$ to be confluent, every transition $s \xrightarrow{a} \mu$ has to be mimicked by a transition $t \xrightarrow{a} \nu$ such that μ and ν are equivalent; as usual in probabilistic model checking, this means that they should assign the same probability to each *equivalence class* of the state space in the bisimulation quotient. Bisimulation is again ensured using confluent transitions.

In this work we are dealing with a state-based context; only the atomic pro-positions that are assigned to each state are of interest. Therefore, we base our definition of confluence on the state-based probabilistic notions given in [13]. It is still parameterised in the way that distributions have to be connected by con-fluent transitions, denoted by $\mu \rightsquigarrow_\mathcal{T} \nu$. We instantiate this later, in Definition 6.

Definition 5 (Probabilistic confluence). *Let $\mathcal{A}$ be an MDP, then a subset $\mathcal{T}$ of transitions from $\mathcal{A}$ is probabilistically confluent if it only contains invisible deterministic transitions, and*

$$\forall s \xrightarrow{a} \mathbb{1}_t \in \mathcal{T} \colon \forall s \xrightarrow{b} \mu \colon (\mu = \mathbb{1}_t \lor \exists t \xrightarrow{c} \nu \colon \mu \rightsquigarrow_\mathcal{T} \nu)$$

Additionally, if $s \xrightarrow{b} \mu \in \mathcal{T}$, then so should $t \xrightarrow{c} \nu$ be.

A transition is probabilistically confluent *if there exists a probabilistically confluent set that contains it.*

Compared to [13], the definition is more liberal in two aspects. First, not ne-cessarily $b = c$ anymore. In [13] this was needed to preserve probabilistic visible bisimulation. Equivalent systems according to that notion preserve state-based as well as action-based properties. However, in our setting the actions are only for synchronisation of parallel components, and have no purpose anymore in the final model. Therefore, we can just as well rename them all to a single action. Then, if a transition is mimicked, the action will be the same by construction. Even easier, we chose to omit the required accordance of action names altogether.

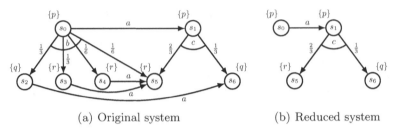

(a) Original system   (b) Reduced system

Fig. 1. An MDP to demonstrate confluence reduction

Second, we only require confluent transitions to be invisible and deterministic themselves. In [13], all transitions with the same label had to be so as well (for a more fair comparison with POR). Here, this is not an option, since during simulation we only know part of the state space. However, it is also not needed for correctness, as a local argument about mimicking behaviour until some joining point can clearly never be broken by transitions after this point.

In contrast to POR [2,10], confluence also allows mimicking by differently-labelled transitions, commutativity in triangles instead of diamonds, and local instead of global independence [13]. Additionally, its coinductive definition is well-suited for on-the-fly detection, as we show in this paper. However, as confluence preserves branching time properties, it cannot reduce probabilistic interleavings, a scenario that can be handled by the linear time notion of POR used in [6].

3.2   Equivalence of Probability Distributions

Confluent transitions are used to detect equivalent states. Hence, two distributions are equivalent if they assign the same probabilities to sets of states that are connected by confluent transitions. Given a confluent set $\mathcal{T}$, we denote this by $\mu \rightsquigarrow_{\mathcal{T}} \nu$. For ease of detection, we only consider confluent transitions from the support of μ to the support of ν. In principle, larger equivalence classes could be used when also considering transitions in the other direction and chains of confluent transitions. However, for efficiency reasons we chose not to be so liberal.

Definition 6 (Equivalence up-to $\mathcal{T}$-steps). *Let $\mathcal{A}$ be an MDP, $\mathcal{T}$ a set of deterministic transitions of $\mathcal{A}$ and $\mu, \nu \in \mathsf{Distr}(S)$ two probability distributions. Let R be the smallest equivalence relation containing the set*

$$R' = \{(s,t) \mid s \in \mathsf{support}(\mu), t \in \mathsf{support}(\nu), \exists a \colon s \xrightarrow{a} t \in \mathcal{T}\}$$

Then, μ and ν are equivalent up-to $\mathcal{T}$-steps, denoted by $\mu \rightsquigarrow_{\mathcal{T}} \nu$, if $\mu \equiv_R \nu$.

Example 1. As an example of Definition 6, consider Figure 1(a). Let $\mathcal{T}$ be the set consisting of all a-labelled transitions. Note that these transitions indeed are all deterministic. We denote by μ the probability distribution associated with the b-transition from s_0, and by ν the one associated with the c-transition from s_1.

We find $R' = \{(s_2, s_6), (s_3, s_5), (s_4, s_5)\}$, and so $R = Id \cup \{(s_2, s_6), (s_6, s_2), (s_3, s_4), (s_4, s_3), (s_3, s_5), (s_5, s_3), (s_4, s_5), (s_5, s_4)\}$ (with Id the identity relation).

Hence, R partitions the state space into $\{s_0\}$, $\{s_1\}$, $\{s_2, s_6\}$, and $\{s_3, s_4, s_5\}$. We find $\mu(\{s_0\}) = \nu(\{s_0\}) = 0$, $\mu(\{s_1\}) = \nu(\{s_1\}) = 0$, $\mu(\{s_2, s_6\}) = \nu(\{s_2, s_6\}) = \frac{1}{3}$ and $\mu(\{s_3, s_4, s_5\}) = \nu(\{s_3, s_4, s_5\}) = \frac{2}{3}$. Therefore, $\mu \equiv_R \nu$ and thus $\mu \rightsquigarrow_{\mathcal{T}} \nu$.

Also note that $\mathcal{T}$ is a valid confluent set according to Definition 5. First, all its transitions are indeed invisible and deterministic. Second, for the a-transitions from s_2, s_3 and s_4, nothing interesting has to be checked. After all, from their source states there are no other outgoing transitions, and every transition satisfies the condition $\mu = \mathbb{1}_t \vee \exists t \xrightarrow{c} \nu : \mu \rightsquigarrow_{\mathcal{T}} \nu$ for itself due to the clause $\mu = \mathbb{1}_t$. For $s_0 \xrightarrow{a} \mathbb{1}_{s_1}$, we do need to check if the condition holds for $s_0 \xrightarrow{b} \mu$. There is a mimicking transition $s_1 \xrightarrow{c} \nu$, and as we saw above $\mu \rightsquigarrow_{\mathcal{T}} \nu$, as required.   □

Our definition of equivalence up-to $\mathcal{T}$-steps is slightly more liberal than the one in [13]. There, the number of states in the support of μ was required to be at least as large as the number of states in the support of ν, since no nondeterministic choice between equally-labelled actions was allowed. Since we do allow this, we take the more liberal approach of just requiring the probability distributions to assign the same probabilities to the same classes of states with respect to confluent connectivity. The correctness arguments are not influenced by this, as the reasoning that confluent transitions connect bisimilar states does not break down if these support sets are potentially more distinct.

3.3   Confluence Reduction

We now define confluence reduction functions. Such a function always chooses to either fully explore a state, or only explore one outgoing confluent transition.

Definition 7 (Confluence reduction). *Given an MDP $\mathcal{A}$, a reduction function F is a* confluence reduction function *for $\mathcal{A}$ if there exists some confluent set $\mathcal{T} \subseteq P$ for which, for every $s \in S$ such that $F(s) \neq en(s)$, it holds that*

- $F(s) = \{(s, a, \mathbb{1}_t)\}$ *for some $a \in \Sigma$ and $t \in S$ such that $(s, a, \mathbb{1}_t) \in \mathcal{T}$.*

In such a case, we also say that F is a confluence reduction function under $\mathcal{T}$.

Confluent transitions might be taken indefinitely, ignoring the presence of other actions. This problem is well known as the *ignoring problem* [11], and is dealt with by the cycle condition of the ample set method of POR. We can just as easily deal with it in the context of confluence reduction by requiring the reduction function to be acyclic. Acyclicity can be checked in the same way as was done for POR in [6]: always check whether in the last l steps at least one state was fully explored (i.e., the state already contained only one outgoing transition).

Example 2. In the system of Figure 1(a), we already saw that the set of all a-labelled transitions is a valid confluent set. Based on this set, we can define the reduction function F given by $F(s_0) = \{(s_0, a, \mathbb{1}_{s_1})\}$ and $F(s) = en(s)$ for every other state s. That way, the reduced system is given by Figure 1(b).

Note that the two models indeed share the same properties, such as that the (minimum and maximum) probability of eventually observing r is $\frac{2}{3}$.   □

Confluence reduction preserves $\text{PCTL}^*_{\setminus X}$, and hence basically all interesting quantitative properties (including $\text{LTL}_{\setminus X}$, as was preserved in [6]).

Theorem 1. *Let $\mathcal{A}$ be an MDP, $\mathcal{T}$ a confluent set of its transitions and F an acyclic confluence reduction function under $\mathcal{T}$. Let $\mathcal{A}_F$ be the reduced MDP. Then, $\mathcal{A}$ and $\mathcal{A}_F$ satisfy the same $PCTL^*_{\backslash X}$ formulae.*

4   On-the-Fly Detection of Probabilistic Confluence

Non-probabilistic confluence was first detected directly on concrete state spaces to reduce them modulo branching bisimulation [12]. Although the complexity was linear in the size of the state space, the method was not very useful: it required the complete unreduced state space to be available, which could already be too large to generate. Therefore, two directions of improvements were pursued.

The first idea was to detect confluence on higher-level process-algebraic system descriptions [4,5]. Using this information from the symbolic level, the reduced state space could be generated directly without first constructing any part of the original state space. More recently, this technique was generalised to the probabilistic setting [23].

The other direction was to use the ideas from [12] to on-the-fly detect non-probabilistic weak or strong confluence [22,24] during state space generation. These techniques are based on Boolean equation systems and have not yet been generalised to the probabilistic setting.

We present a novel on-the-fly algorithm that works on concrete probabilistic states spaces and does not require the unreduced state space, making it perfectly applicable during simulation for statistical model checking of MDPs.

4.1   Detailed Description of the Algorithm

Our algorithm is presented on the next page. Given a deterministic transition $s \xrightarrow{a} \mathbb{1}_t$, the function call *checkConfluence*$(s \xrightarrow{a} \mathbb{1}_t)$ tells us whether or not this transition is confluent. We first discuss this function *checkConfluence*, and then the function *checkEquivalence* on which it relies (which determines whether or not two distributions are equivalent up-to confluent steps).

These functions do not yet fully take into account the fact that confluent transitions have to be mimicked by confluent transitions. Therefore, we have an additional function *checkConfluentMimicking* that is called after termination of *checkConfluence* to see if indeed no violations of this condition occur.

The function *checkConfluence* first checks if a transition is invisible and was not already detected to be confluent before. Then, it is added to the global set of confluent transitions $\mathcal{T}$. To check whether this is valid, a loop checks if indeed all outgoing transitions from s commute with $s \xrightarrow{a} \mathbb{1}_t$. If so, we return *true* and keep the transition in $\mathcal{T}$. Otherwise, all transitions that were added to $\mathcal{T}$ during these checks are removed again and we return *false*. Note that it would not be sufficient to only remove $s \xrightarrow{a} \mathbb{1}_t$ from $\mathcal{T}$, since during the loop some transitions might have been detected to be confluent (and hence added to $\mathcal{T}$) based on the fact that $s \xrightarrow{a} \mathbb{1}_t$ was in $\mathcal{T}$. As $s \xrightarrow{a} \mathbb{1}_t$ turned out not to be confluent, we can also not be sure anymore if these other transitions are indeed actually confluent.

Algorithm 1. Detecting confluence on a concrete state space

---

global $Set\langle Transition\rangle$ $\mathcal{T} := \varnothing$
global $Set\langle Transition, Transition\rangle$ $M := \varnothing$

bool $checkConfluence(s \xrightarrow{a} \mathbb{1}_t)$ {
  if $L(s) \neq L(t)$ **then**
    return *false*
  else if $s \xrightarrow{a} \mathbb{1}_t \in \mathcal{T}$ **then**
    return *true*

  $Set\langle Transition\rangle$ $\mathcal{T}_{\text{old}} := \mathcal{T}$
  $Set\langle Transition, Transition\rangle$ $M_{\text{old}} := M$
  $\mathcal{T} := \mathcal{T} \cup \{s \xrightarrow{a} \mathbb{1}_t\}$
  foreach $s \xrightarrow{b} \mu$ **do**
    if $\mu = \mathbb{1}_t$ **then continue**
    foreach $t \xrightarrow{c} \nu$ **do**
      if $checkEquivalence(\mu, \nu)$ **and**
      $(s \xrightarrow{b} \mu \notin \mathcal{T}$ **or** $(\exists u: \nu = \mathbb{1}_u$ **and** $checkConfluence(t \xrightarrow{c} \mathbb{1}_u)))$ **then**
        $M := M \cup \{(s \xrightarrow{b} \mu, t \xrightarrow{c} \nu)\}$
        continue outermost loop
    end
    $\mathcal{T} := \mathcal{T}_{\text{old}}$
    $M := M_{\text{old}}$
    return *false*
  return *true*
}

bool $checkEquivalence(\mu, \nu)$ {
  $Q := \{\{p\} \mid p \in \text{support}(\mu) \cup \text{support}(\nu)\}$
  foreach $u \xrightarrow{d} \mathbb{1}_v$ such that $u \in support(\mu)$, $v \in support(\nu)$ **do**
    if $checkConfluence(u \xrightarrow{d} \mathbb{1}_v)$ **then**
      $Q := \{q \in Q \mid u \notin q \wedge v \notin q\} \cup \{\bigcup_{\substack{q \in Q \\ u \in q \vee v \in q}} q\}$
  if $\mu(q) = \nu(q)$ *for every* $q \in Q$ **then**
    return *true*
  else
    return *false*
  end
}

bool $checkConfluentMimicking$ {
  foreach $(s \xrightarrow{b} \mu, t \xrightarrow{c} \nu) \in M$ **do**
    if $s \xrightarrow{b} \mu \in \mathcal{T}$ **and** $t \xrightarrow{c} \nu \notin \mathcal{T}$ **then**
      if $checkConfluence(t \xrightarrow{c} \nu)$ **then**
        return $checkConfluentMimicking$
      else
        return *false*
    end
  return *true*

The loop to check whether all outgoing transitions commute with s follows directly from the definition of confluent sets, which requires for every $s \xrightarrow{b} \mu$ that either $\mu = \mathbb{1}_t$, or that there exists a transition $t \xrightarrow{c} \nu$ such that $\mu \rightsquigarrow_{\mathcal{T}} \nu$, where $t \xrightarrow{c} \nu$ has to be in $\mathcal{T}$ if $s \xrightarrow{b} \mu$ is. Indeed, if $\mu = \mathbb{1}_t$ we immediately continue to the next transition (this includes the case that $s \xrightarrow{b} \mu = s \xrightarrow{a} \mathbb{1}_t$). Otherwise, we range over all transitions $t \xrightarrow{c} \nu$ to see if there is one such that $\mu \rightsquigarrow_{\mathcal{T}} \nu$. For this, we use the function $checkEquivalence(\mu, \nu)$, described below. Also, if $s \xrightarrow{b} \mu \in \mathcal{T}$, we have to check if also $t \xrightarrow{c} \nu \in \mathcal{T}$. We do this by checking it for confluence, which immediately returns if it is already in $\mathcal{T}$, and otherwise tries to add it.

If indeed we find a mimicking transition, we continue. If $s \xrightarrow{b} \mu$ cannot be mimicked, confluence of $s \xrightarrow{a} \mathbb{1}_t$ cannot be established. Hence, we reset $\mathcal{T}$ as discussed above, and return $false$. If this did not happen for any of the outgoing transitions of s, then $s \xrightarrow{a} \mathbb{1}_t$ is indeed confluent and we return $true$.

The function $checkEquivalence$ checks whether $\mu \rightsquigarrow_{\mathcal{T}} \nu$. Since $\mathcal{T}$ is constructed on-the-fly, during this check some of the transitions from the support of μ might have not been detected to be confluent yet, even though they are. Therefore, instead of checking for connecting transitions that are already in $\mathcal{T}$, we try to add possible connecting transitions to $\mathcal{T}$ using a recursive call.

In accordance to Definition 6, we first determine the smallest equivalence relation that relates states from the support of μ to states from the support of ν in case there is a confluent transition connecting them. We do so by constructing a set of equivalence classes Q, i.e., a partitioning of the state space according to this equivalence relation. We start with the smallest possible equivalence relation, in which each equivalence class is a singleton. Then, for each confluent transition $u \xrightarrow{d} \mathbb{1}_v$, with $u \in \text{support}(\mu)$ and $v \in \text{support}(\nu)$, we merge the equivalence classes containing u and v. Finally, we can easily compute the probability of reaching each equivalence class of Q by either μ or ν. If all of these probabilities coincide, indeed $\mu \equiv_R \nu$ and we return $true$; otherwise, we return $false$.

The function $checkConfluentMimicking$ is called after $checkConfluence$ designated a transition to be confluent, to verify if $\mathcal{T}$ satisfies the requirement that confluent transitions are mimicked by confluent transitions. After all, when a mimicking transition for some transition $s \xrightarrow{b} \mu$ was found, it might have been the case that $s \xrightarrow{b} \mu$ was not yet in $\mathcal{T}$ while in the end it is. Hence, $checkConfluence$ keeps track of the mimicking transitions in a global set M. If a transition $s \xrightarrow{a} \mathbb{1}_t$ is shown to be confluent, all pairs $(s \xrightarrow{b} \mu, t \xrightarrow{c} \nu)$ of other outgoing transitions from s and the transitions that were found to mimic them from t are added to M. If $s \xrightarrow{a} \mathbb{1}_t$ turns out not to be confluent after all, the mimicking transitions that were found in the process are removed again.

Based on M, $checkConfluentMimicking$ ranges over all pairs $(s \xrightarrow{b} \mu, t \xrightarrow{c} \nu)$, checking if one violates the requirement. If no such pair is found, we return $true$. Otherwise, the current set $\mathcal{T}$ is not valid yet. However, it could be the case that $t \xrightarrow{c} \nu$ is not in $\mathcal{T}$, while it is confluent (but since $s \xrightarrow{b} \mu$ was not in $\mathcal{T}$ at the moment the pair was added to M, this was not checked earlier). Therefore, we still try to denote $t \xrightarrow{c} \nu$ as confluent. If we fail, we return $false$. Otherwise, we check again for confluent mimicking using the new set $\mathcal{T}$.

4.2   Correctness

The following theorem states that the algorithm is sound. We assume that M and $\mathcal{T}$ are not reset to their initial value $\varnothing$ after termination of *checkConfluence*.

Theorem 2. *Given a transition $p \xrightarrow{l} \mathbb{1}_q$, checkConfluence($p \xrightarrow{l} \mathbb{1}_q$) and check-ConfluentMimicking together imply that $p \xrightarrow{l} \mathbb{1}_q$ is confluent.*

Note that the converse of this theorem does not always hold. To see why, consider the situation that *checkConfluentMimicking* fails because a transition $s \xrightarrow{b} \mu$ was mimicked by a transition $t \xrightarrow{c} \nu$ that is not confluent, and $s \xrightarrow{b} \mu$ was added to $\mathcal{T}$ later on. Although we then abort, there might have been another transition $t \xrightarrow{d} \rho$ that could also have been used to mimic $s \xrightarrow{b} \mu$ and that *is* confluent. We chose not to consider this due to the additional overhead of the implementation. Additionally, in none of our case studies this situation occurred.

5   Evaluation

The modes tool[1] provides SMC for models specified in the MODEST language [7]. It allowed SMC for MDPs using the POR-based approach of [6]. We have now implemented the confluence-based approach presented in this paper in modes as well. In this section, we apply it to three examples to evaluate its applicability and performance impact. They were selected so as to allow us to clearly identify its strengths and limitations. For each, we (1) give an overview of the model, (2) discuss, if POR fails, why it does and which, if any, modifications were needed to apply the confluence-based approach, and (3) evaluate memory use and runtime.

The performance results are summarised in Table 2. For the runtime assessment, we compare to simulation with uniformly-distributed probabilistic resolution of nondeterminism. Although such a hidden assumption cannot lead to trustworthy results in general (but is implemented in many tools), it is a good *baseline* to judge the *overhead* of confluence checking. We generated 10 000 runs per model instance to compute probabilities p_{smc} for case-specific properties. Using reasoning based on the Chernoff-Hoeffding bound [25], this guarantees the following probabilistic error bound: $\mathrm{Prob}(|p - p_{\mathrm{smc}}| > 0.01) < 0.017$, where p is the actual probability of the property under consideration.

We measure memory usage in terms of the maximum number of extra states kept in memory at any time during confluence (or POR) checking, denoted by s. We also report the maximum number of "lookahead" steps necessary in the confluence/POR checks as k, which is equivalent to $k_{\min} - 1$ in [6], as well as the average length t of a simulation trace and the average number c of nontrivial confluence checks, i.e., of nondeterministic choices encountered, per trace.

To get a sense for the size of the models considered, we also attempt model checking (using mcpta [15], which relies on PRISM [19]). Note that we do not intend to perform a rigorous comparison of SMC and traditional model checking in this paper and instead refer the interested reader to dedicated comparison

---

[1] modes is part of the MODEST TOOLSET, available at www.modestchecker.net.

Table 2. Confluence simulation runtime overhead and comparison

model	params	uniform: time	partial order: time	k	s	confluence: time	k	s	c	t	model checking: states	time
dining crypto-graphers (N)	(3)	1 s	–	–	–	3 s	4	9	4.0	8.0	609	1 s
	(4)	1 s	–	–	–	11 s	6	25	6.0	10.0	3 841	2 s
	(5)	1 s	–	–	–	44 s	8	67	8.0	12.0	23 809	7 s
	(6)	1 s	–	–	–	229 s	10	177	10.0	14.0	144 705	26 s
	(7)	1 s	–	–	–	– timeout –					864 257	80 s
CSMA/CD (RF, BC_{max})	(2, 1)	2 s	–	–	–	4 s	3	46	5.4	16.4	15 283	11 s
	(1, 1)	2 s	–	–	–	4 s	3	46	5.4	16.4	30 256	49 s
	(2, 2)	2 s	–	–	–	10 s	3	150	5.1	16.0	98 533	52 s
	(1, 2)	2 s	–	–	–	10 s	3	150	5.1	16.0	194 818	208 s
BEB (K, N, H)	(4, 3, 3)	1 s	3 s	3	4	1 s	3	7	3.3	11.6	$> 10^3$	> 0 s
	(8, 7, 4)	2 s	7 s	4	8	4 s	4	15	5.6	16.7	$> 10^7$	> 7 s
	(16,15,5)	3 s	18 s	5	16	11 s	5	31	8.3	21.5	– memout –	
	(16,15,6)	3 s	40 s	6	32	34 s	6	63	11.2	26.2	– memout –	

studies such as [27]. Model checking for the BEB example was performed on a machine with 120 GB of RAM [6]; all other measurements used a dual-core Intel Core i5 M450 system with 4 GB of RAM running 64-bit Windows 7.

5.1   Dining Cryptographers

As a first example, we consider the classical dining cryptographers problem [9]: N cryptographers use a protocol that has them toss coins and communicate the outcome with some of their neighbours at a restaurant table in order to find out whether their master or one of them just paid the bill, without revealing the payer's identity in the latter case. We model this problem as the parallel composition of N instances of a `Cryptographer` process that communicate via synchronisation on shared actions, and consider as properties the probabilities of (a) protocol termination and (b) correctness of the result.

The model is a nondeterministic MDP. In particular, the order of the synchronisations between the cryptographer processes is not specified, and could conceivably be relevant. It turns out that all nondeterminism can be discarded as spurious by the confluence-based approach though, allowing the application of SMC to this model. The computed probability p_{smc} is 1.0 for both properties, which coincides with the actual probabilities.

The POR-based approach does not work: Although the nondeterministic ordering of synchronisations between non-neighbouring cryptographers is due to interleaving, the choice of which neighbour to communicate with first for a given cryptographer process is a nondeterministic choice *within* that process.

Concerning performance, we see that runtime increases drastically with the number of cryptographers, N. An increase is expected, since the number of steps until independent paths from nondeterministic choices join again (k) depends directly on N. It is so drastic due to the sheer amount of branching that is present in this model. At the same time, the model is extremely symmetric and can thus be handled easily with a symbolic model checker like PRISM.

5.2   IEEE 802.3 CSMA/CD

As a second example, we take the MODEST model of the Ethernet (IEEE 802.3) CSMA/CD approach that was introduced in [15]. It consists of two identical stations attempting to send data at the same time, with collision detection and a randomised backoff procedure that tries to avoid collisions for subsequent retransmissions. We consider the probability that both stations eventually manage to send their data without collision. The model is a probabilistic timed automaton (PTA), but delays are fixed and deterministic, making it equivalent to an MDP (with real variables for clocks, updated on transitions that explicitly represent the delays; modes does this transformation automatically and on-the-fly). The model has two parameters: a time reduction factor RF (i.e., delays of t time units with $RF = 1$ correspond to delays of $\frac{t}{2}$ time units with $RF = 2$), and the maximum value used in the exponential backoff part of the protocol, BC_{max}.

Unfortunately, modes immediately reports nondeterminism that cannot be discarded as spurious. Inspection of the reported lines in the model quickly shows a nondeterministic choice between two probabilistic transitions—which confluence cannot handle. Fortunately, this problem can easily be eliminated through an additional synchronisation, leading to $p_{smc} = 1.0$ (which is the correct result). POR also fails, for reasons similar to the previous example: initially, both stations send at the same time, the order being determined nondeterministically. In the process representing the shared medium, this must be an *internal* nondeterministic choice. In contrast to the problem for confluence this cannot be fixed.

In terms of runtime, the confluence checks incur a moderate overhead for this example. Compared to the dining cryptographers, the slowdown is much less even where more states need to be explored in each check (s); performance appears to more directly depend on k, which stays low in this case.

5.3   Binary Exponential Backoff

The previous two examples clearly indicate that the added power of confluence reduction pays off, allowing SMC for models where it is not possible with POR. Still, we also need a comparison of the two approaches. For this purpose, we revisit the MDP model of the binary exponential backoff (BEB) procedure that was used to evaluate the POR-based approach in [6]. The probability we compute is that of some host eventually getting access to the shared medium, for different values of the model parameters K (maximum backoff counter value), N (number of tries per station before giving up) and H (number of stations/hosts involved).

Again, for the confluence check to succeed, we first need to minimally modify the model by making a probabilistic transition synchronise. This appears to be a recurring issue, yet the relevant model code could quite clearly be identified as a modelling artifact without semantic impact in both examples where it appears. We then obtain $p_{smc} = 0.91$ for model instance $(4, 3, 3)$, otherwise $p_{smc} = 1.0$.

The runtime overhead necessary to get trustworthy results by enabling either confluence or POR is again moderate. This is despite longer paths being explored in the confluence checks compared to the CSMA/CD example (k). The confluence-based approach is somewhat faster than POR in this implementation.

As noted in [6], large instances of this model cannot be solved with classical model checking due to the state space explosion problem.

6   Conclusion

We defined a more liberal variant of probabilistic confluence, tailored for the core simulation step of statistical model checking. It has more reduction potential than a previous variant at no extra computational cost, but still preserves $\text{PCTL}^*_{\backslash X}$. We provided an algorithm for on-the-fly detection of confluence during simulation and implemented this algorithm in the modes SMC tool. Compared to the previous approach based on partial order reduction [6], the use of confluence allows new kinds of nondeterministic choices to be handled, in particular lifting the limitation to spurious interleavings. In fact, for two of the three examples we presented, SMC is only possible using the new confluence-based technique, showing the additional power to be relevant. In terms of performance, it is somewhat faster than the POR-based approach, but the impact relative to (unsound) simulation using an arbitrary scheduler largely depends on the amount of lookahead that needs to be performed, for both approaches. Again, on two of our examples, the impact was moderate and should in general be acceptable to obtain trustworthy results. Most importantly, the memory overhead is negligible, and one of the central advantages of SMC over traditional model checking is thus retained.

As confluence preserves branching time properties, it cannot handle the interleaving of probabilistic choices. Although—as we showed—these can often be avoided, for some models POR might work while confluence does not. Hence, neither of the techniques subsumes the other, and it is best to combine them: if one cannot be used to resolve a nondeterministic choice, the SMC algorithm can still try to apply the other. Implementing this combination is trivial and yields a technique that handles the union of what confluence and POR can deal with.

Acknowledgments. We thank Luis María Ferrer Fioriti (Saarland University) for his help in analysing the behaviour of the partial order check on the case studies.

References

1. Baier, C., D'Argenio, P.R., Größer, M.: Partial order reduction for probabilistic branching time. ENTCS 153(2) (2006)
2. Baier, C., Größer, M., Ciesinski, F.: Partial order reduction for probabilistic systems. In: QEST, pp. 230–239. IEEE Computer Society (2004)
3. Baier, C., Katoen, J.P.: Principles of model checking. MIT Press (2008)
4. Blom, S.C.C.: Partial τ-confluence for efficient state space generation. Tech. Rep. SEN-R0123, CWI (2001)
5. Blom, S.C.C., van de Pol, J.: State space reduction by proving confluence. In: Brinksma, E., Larsen, K.G. (eds.) CAV 2002. LNCS, vol. 2404, pp. 596–609. Springer, Heidelberg (2002)
6. Bogdoll, J., Ferrer Fioriti, L.M., Hartmanns, A., Hermanns, H.: Partial order methods for statistical model checking and simulation. In: Bruni, R., Dingel, J. (eds.) FMOODS/FORTE 2011. LNCS, vol. 6722, pp. 59–74. Springer, Heidelberg (2011)
7. Bogdoll, J., Hartmanns, A., Hermanns, H.: Simulation and statistical model checking for Modestly nondeterministic models. In: Schmitt, J.B. (ed.) MMB & DFT 2012. LNCS, vol. 7201, pp. 249–252. Springer, Heidelberg (2012)

8. Bohnenkamp, H.C., D'Argenio, P.R., Hermanns, H., Katoen, J.P.: MoDeST: A compositional modeling formalism for hard and softly timed systems. IEEE Transactions on Software Engineering 32(10), 812–830 (2006)
9. Chaum, D.: The dining cryptographers problem: Unconditional sender and recipient untraceability. Journal of Cryptology 1(1), 65–75 (1988)
10. D'Argenio, P.R., Niebert, P.: Partial order reduction on concurrent probabilistic programs. In: QEST, pp. 240–249. IEEE Computer Society (2004)
11. Evangelista, S., Pajault, C.: Solving the ignoring problem for partial order reduction. Int. Journal on Software Tools for Technology Transfer 12(2), 155–170 (2010)
12. Groote, J.F., van de Pol, J.: State space reduction using partial τ-confluence. In: Nielsen, M., Rovan, B. (eds.) MFCS 2000. LNCS, vol. 1893, pp. 383–393. Springer, Heidelberg (2000)
13. Hansen, H., Timmer, M.: A comparison of confluence and ample sets in probabilistic and non-probabilistic branching time. To be published in TCS (2013)
14. Hartmanns, A.: Model-checking and simulation for stochastic timed systems. In: Aichernig, B.K., de Boer, F.S., Bonsangue, M.M. (eds.) FMCO 2010. LNCS, vol. 6957, pp. 372–391. Springer, Heidelberg (2011)
15. Hartmanns, A., Hermanns, H.: A Modest approach to checking probabilistic timed automata. In: QEST, pp. 187–196. IEEE Computer Society (2009)
16. Hartmanns, A., Timmer, M.: On-the-fly confluence detection for statistical model checking (extended version). Tech. Rep. TR-CTIT-13-04, CTIT, University of Twente (2013)
17. Henriques, D., Martins, J., Zuliani, P., Platzer, A., Clarke, E.M.: Statistical model checking for Markov decision processes. In: QEST, pp. 84–93. IEEE Computer Society (2012)
18. Hérault, T., Lassaigne, R., Magniette, F., Peyronnet, S.: Approximate probabilistic model checking. In: Steffen, B., Levi, G. (eds.) VMCAI 2004. LNCS, vol. 2937, pp. 73–84. Springer, Heidelberg (2004)
19. Kwiatkowska, M., Norman, G., Parker, D.: PRISM 4.0: Verification of probabilistic real-time systems. In: Gopalakrishnan, G., Qadeer, S. (eds.) CAV 2011. LNCS, vol. 6806, pp. 585–591. Springer, Heidelberg (2011)
20. Lassaigne, R., Peyronnet, S.: Approximate planning and verification for large Markov decision processes. In: SAC, pp. 1314–1319. ACM (2012)
21. Legay, A., Delahaye, B., Bensalem, S.: Statistical model checking: An overview. In: Barringer, H., Falcone, Y., Finkbeiner, B., Havelund, K., Lee, I., Pace, G., Roşu, G., Sokolsky, O., Tillmann, N. (eds.) RV 2010. LNCS, vol. 6418, pp. 122–135. Springer, Heidelberg (2010)
22. Mateescu, R., Wijs, A.: Sequential and distributed on-the-fly computation of weak tau-confluence. Science of Computer Programming 77(10-11), 1075–1094 (2012)
23. Timmer, M., Stoelinga, M., van de Pol, J.: Confluence reduction for probabilistic systems. In: Abdulla, P.A., Leino, K.R.M. (eds.) TACAS 2011. LNCS, vol. 6605, pp. 311–325. Springer, Heidelberg (2011)
24. Pace, G.J., Lang, F., Mateescu, R.: Calculating τ-confluence compositionally. In: Hunt Jr., W.A., Somenzi, F. (eds.) CAV 2003. LNCS, vol. 2725, pp. 446–459. Springer, Heidelberg (2003)
25. PRISM manual: The APMC method, http://www.prismmodelchecker.org/manual/RunningPRISM/ApproximateModelChecking
26. Younes, H.L.S., Simmons, R.G.: Probabilistic verification of discrete event systems using acceptance sampling. In: Brinksma, E., Larsen, K.G. (eds.) CAV 2002. LNCS, vol. 2404, pp. 223–235. Springer, Heidelberg (2002)
27. Younes, H.L.S., Kwiatkowska, M., Norman, G., Parker, D.: Numerical vs. Statistical probabilistic model checking: An empirical study. In: Jensen, K., Podelski, A. (eds.) TACAS 2004. LNCS, vol. 2988, pp. 46–60. Springer, Heidelberg (2004)

Optimizing Control Strategy Using Statistical Model Checking

Alexandre David[1], Dehui Du[2], Kim Guldstrand Larsen[1],
Axel Legay[3], and Marius Mikučionis[1]

[1] Computer Science, Aalborg University, Denmark
[2] Laboratory of Trustworthy Computing, East China Normal University, Shanghai,
China
[3] INRIA/IRISA, Rennes Cedex, France

This paper proposes a new efficient approach to optimize energy consumption
for energy aware buildings. Our approach relies on stochastic hybrid automata
for representing energy aware systems. The model is parameterized by several
cost values that need to be optimized in order to minimize energy consumption.
Our approach exploits a stochastic semantic together with simulation in order
to estimate the best value for such parameters. Contrary to existing techniques
that would estimate energy consumption for each value of the parameters, our
approach relies on a new statistical engine that exploits ANOVA, a technique
that can reduce the number of runs needed by the comparison algorithm to
perform the estimates. Our approach has been implemented and our experiments
show that we clearly outperform the naive approach.

1 Introduction

Cyber-Physical Systems. Cyber-physical systems are large-scale distributed systems, often viewed as networked embedded systems, where a large number of
computational components are deployed in a physical environment. Each component collects information about and offers services to its environment (e.g.,
environmental monitoring and control, health-care monitoring and traffic control). This information is processed either at the component, in the network or
at a remote location (e.g., the base station), or in any combination of these.

Characteristic for cyber-physical systems is that they have to meet a multitude
of quantitative constraints, e.g., timing constraints, power consumption, memory usage, communication bandwidth, QoS, and often under uncertainty of the
behavior of the environment. Existing model-driven methodologies for embedded
systems are rather sophisticated in handling functional requirements, and some
methods are good at handling special kinds of quantitative constraints. However,
there is a lack of a mathematical foundation and supporting tools allowing to
handle the combination of quantitative aspects concerning, for example, time,
stochastic behavior, hybrid behavior including energy consumption.

In our previous work [10,11] we have proposed to capture the behavior of
cyber-physical systems with Priced Timed Automata (PTA). Those models are
extensions of timed automata [2], where clocks may have different rates (even

G. Brat, N. Rungta, and A. Venet (Eds.): NFM 2013, LNCS 7871, pp. 352–367, 2013.

potentially negative) in different locations. Several projects at the EU level promoted PTA as an adequate model for energy-aware systems. PTAs are as expressive as linear hybrid automata [1] providing high expressive power useful for modeling complex cyber-physical systems, but also rendering most problems either undecidable or too complex to be solved with classical model checking approaches. To overcome these limitations, we proposed in [10] to give a stochastic semantics to PTAs and then apply Statistical Model Checking (SMC) techniques [17,24,21,14,13], which is a highly scalable simulation-based approach. SMC consists in randomly generating and monitoring simulation runs of the system and verify whether they satisfy a given property written in some temporal logic. The results are then used by statistical algorithms in order to compute an estimate of the probability for the system to satisfy the property with some level of significance. Our work has been implemented in UPPAAL SMC, that is, an extension of UPPAAL that relies on verifying metric interval temporal logic (MITL) properties using our stochastic semantic and statistical model checking algorithms. Our tool comes together with a friendly user interface that allows a user to specify complex problems in an efficient manner as well as to get feedback in the form of probability distributions and compare probabilities to analyze performance aspects of systems. UPPAAL SMC has been applied to a wide range of examples from networking and Nash equilibrium [5] to system biology [9], real-time scheduling [8], and energy-aware systems [7]. A major difference with classical MATLAB Simulink® approaches is that ours relies on formal models for both the system and the requirements, hence allowing to express eventually complex properties and behaviors in a straight-forward way.

As a main contribution we improve over the framework presented in [7] for modeling, analyzing and in particular optimizing control strategies for energy aware buildings. The framework consists of several parameterized components (rooms, building, heaters, weather, user, . . .) as well as a collection of properties for evaluating comfort, and energy profiles of various control strategies, i.e., various values for the parameters. The challenge is to find the best value of a parameter to optimize a given property.

We then propose a systematic approach to encode the problem via stochastic hybrid automata. Our approach relies on a new framework to optimize parameters of the controller given in the Hybrid Systems Verification Benchmark of [12] to control temperatures of rooms in a given building.

We address the problem by working with a refined technique called analysis of variance (ANOVA) to compare many distributions in one method potentially more efficient than many pair-wise Student's t-test [18] applications and thus generalizes t-test for many distributions. There can be many different arrangements of those distributions and in particular we are interested in a so called two-factor factorial experiment design [18], where our two parameters become the two factors (two orthogonal dimensions), the parameter values become factor levels (discrete values on those two dimensions), and a cost (discomfort or energy) is the measured outcome value. We can then reuse the data gathered by ANOVA to estimate the energy and discomfort for interesting values of parameters. "Discomfort" is interpreted as a distance between a desired range of temperature and the current temperature.

We have implemented our technique and show that it works faster than the naive statistical model checking approach.

2 Stochastic Hybrid Automata

In [11], we proposed UPPAAL SMC that is a new release of UPPAAL that supports verification of probabilistic timed automata via simulation-based approaches [22]. Details can be found in [10]. In [7] we generalized the model to stochastic hybrid automata (SHA) that are timed automata whose clock rates can be changed to be constants or expressions depending on other clocks, effectively defining ordinary differential equations (ODEs). UPPAAL SMC[1] supports fully hybrid automata with ODEs and a few built-in complex functions (such as sin, cos, log, exp and sqrt) since version 4.1.10. We only recall informally the modeling language of SHA through an example because it is not a contribution in this paper.

A Simple 2-Room Example. To illustrate the SHA model as supported by UP-PAAL SMC, we consider the case of two independent rooms that can be heated by a single heater shared by the two rooms, i.e., at most one room can be heated at a time. Figure 1a shows the automaton for the heater in UPPAAL notation where the circle inscribed means initial location and U inscribed means urgent location (no time delay is allowed). The heater starts in location OFF and turns itself on after picking a delay between $[0, 4]$ as there is no guard controlling lower bound and only an invariant $x \leq 4$ is setting the upper bound for time delay using clock x. The delay is chosen with a *uniform probability distribution* over that interval. Then one of the weighted transitions is taken: the plain edge transition from the location OFF is branched into either room 0 or room 1 (dashed edge). The dashed edges have probabilistic weights 1 and 3: the room 0 is chosen with probability $\frac{1}{1+3}$ and room 1 with probability $\frac{3}{1+3}$. The heater stays on (location ON_0 or ON_1) for some time, potentially forever. The delay in this case is picked with an *exponential probability distribution*, for which we have to define the rate. We use rate 2 for room 0 and rate 1 for room 1 and the interpretation is that the stochastic controller is more eager to initiate the heating of room 1 than room 0, as well as less eager to stop heating room 1. Both rooms are similar and are modeled by the same template instantiated twice. Figure 1b shows an automaton for room 0. The room is initialized to its initial temperature T=INIT[0] by leaving its initial location Init which is also a committed location (inscribed with C). Then the temperature T evolves by the derivatives $T' = -T/10$ or $T' = K - T/10$ depending on whether the heater is turned on or off. The equations are defined as part of invariant expressions. Furthermore, when the heater is turned on, its heating is not exact and is picked with a uniform distribution of $K \in [9, 12]$, realized by the update K=9+random(3). The variables T and K are clocks but

---

[1] http://www.uppaal.org/.

are used more generally as floating point numbers in the hybrid model. For this purpose we *stop* K with the derivative expression K'==0. Furthermore, the usage of ODEs, such as $T' = -T/10$, prompts the checker to integrate the value of T.

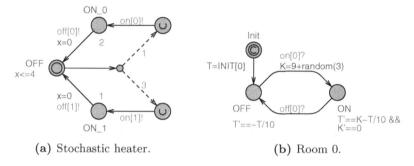

(a) Stochastic heater.   **(b)** Room 0.

Fig. 1. A simple two room example

Statistical Model Checking. We use SMC [16,21,23,3] to estimate and test on the probability that a random run of a network of SHAs will satisfy a given property. Given a model $\mathcal{H}$ and a trace property φ (e.g. expressed in LTL [19] or MTL [15]), SMC refers to a series of simulation-based techniques that can be used to answer two questions: (1) *Qualitative:* is the probability that a random run of $\mathcal{H}$ will satisfy φ greater or equal to a certain threshold θ (or greater or equal to the probability to satisfy another property φ')? and (2) *Quantitative:* what is the probability that a random run of $\mathcal{H}$ will satisfy φ? In both cases, the answer will be correct up to a user-specified level of significance or level of confidence that bounds the probability of making a wrong conclusion. Our UPPAAL SMC toolset implements a wide range of SMC algorithms for answering qualitative and quantitative questions on networks of SHAs. The tool supports not only classical reachability and safety properties, but also general weighted MTL properties [6,4]. One can exploit the quantitative engine of SMC to do parameter sweep in order to optimize some quantity. In this paper, we will rather exploit the statistical method called ANOVA that will ease the estimation of parameters in a single step.

SMC on the 2-Room Example. First we visualize the behaviour of our stochastic controller by checking the property simulate 1 [<=120] { Room(0).T, Room(1).T }. Figure 2 shows the evolution of both temperatures (shown with the short names T0 and T1). The results are in accordance with the controller automaton. Based on this plot we can now do some quantitative analysis by checking the query

$$Pr[<=120]([] \text{ Room(1).Init } || \text{ Room(1).T } >= 10)$$

This query asks for an estimate of the probability that the temperature of room 1 stays above 10 degrees for runs bounded by 120 time units. After 4239 runs the checker returns the interval [0.36, 0.42] with 99% confidence level. The tool can also test the hypothesis that this probability is greater or equal than 0.37. After 2523 runs, this is confirmed with a level of significance of 0.01 and an indifference region of size ±0.01.

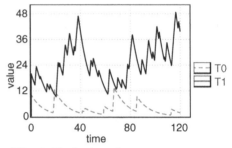

Fig. 2. Evolution of room temperatures

3   The Energy-Aware Building Challenge

We consider the case of an energy-aware building where rooms are modeled according to the layout shown in Fig. 3. A number of heaters are available and can be moved between rooms. The rooms can transfer heat between each other and an adjacency matrix gives the heat transfer coefficients (not shown here for brevity). The goal is to design a controller that will maintain the room temperatures within acceptable comfort ranges despite adverse weather conditions.

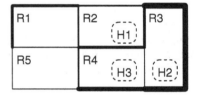

This case-study reproduces the model-checking challenge of hybrid systems proposed in HSCC [12]. In this paper, we focus on one

Fig. 3. Layout of the rooms R_i with the heaters H_k

type of controller for which we want to find good parameters to minimize energy consumption and maximize comfort. Furthermore, the weather model is fixed, though every run has an uncontrollable range of temperatures.

The room temperature dynamics is described by a differential equation:

$$T_i' = \sum_{j \neq i} a_{i,j}(T_j - T_i) + b_i(u - T_i) + c_i h_i$$

where T_i and T_j are the temperatures in room i and j respectively, u is the environment temperature, and h_i is equal to 1 when the heater is turned on in room i and 0 otherwise. The adjacency matrix a gives the heat exchange coefficients $a_{i,j}$ between rooms i and j. The heat exchange with the environment is encoded in a separate vector b, where b_i is a energy loss coefficient for room i. The power supply from heaters is encoded in a vector c, where c_i is a power coefficient for room i. The corresponding hybrid automaton is shown in Fig. 4a. The automaton is maintaining its own Boolean need[id] to inform the central controller that a heater is needed and cold[id] to keep track of uncomfortable rooms. This improves over the model of [7] since we can accumulate the discomfort over all the rooms with the (dynamic) rate in the (more compact) automaton of Fig. 5b.

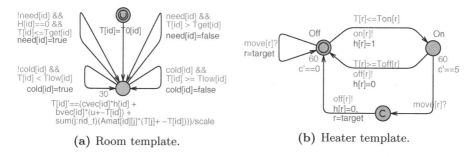

(a) Room template.

(b) Heater template.

Fig. 4. Stochastic hybrid automata model

The change in modeling discomfort allows us to avoid local optima when searching for good parameters (in the next section) where one room could be heated with low energy while another room would be cold. There are two levels of heater control: primary (local) controller at the individual heaters and secondary (central) controller which determines how the heaters are switched over from one room to another. The local controllers use a *bang-bang* strategy, i.e., when the controlled value (here the temperature T[r]) goes below or above a threshold, the controller changes action. In our case, when the temperature T[r] is below Ton[r], the heating is turned on (with h[r]=1), and when the temperature T[r] is above Toff[r], the heating is turned off (with h[r]=0). The hybrid automaton of the heater is shown in Fig. 4b. The central controller can switch over the heating from one room to another. The room is said to be needing a heater if the temperature drops below its Tget threshold and it is said to be outside the comfort zone if the temperature drops below Tlow. We used the thresholds according to [12], based on the heuristics that the temperature difference between rooms should not be too high. This controller is shown in Fig. 5a.

Whenever the heating is turned on, the heaters consume some energy whose rate is determined by the vector pow (power). The monitor automaton keeping track of discomfort (accumulated time spent when rooms are cold) and this energy consumption is shown in Fig. 5b.

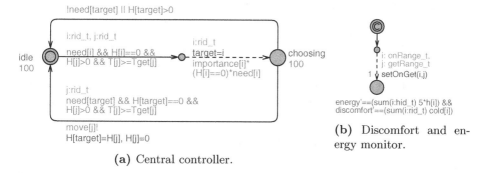

(a) Central controller.

(b) Discomfort and energy monitor.

Fig. 5. Stochastic hybrid model for controller and outcome monitor

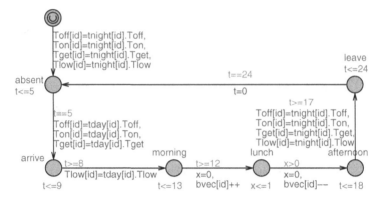

Fig. 6. Stochastic hybrid automaton of the user profile

Figure 6 shows the automaton used for the user profile: the room parameters are changed based on the time of the day and whether the room is occupied or not. For example, the room is preheated starting from 5o'clock in the morning and the user arrives between 8 and 9 which increases the Tlow threshold requirement. The energy leakage into environment is increased by bvec[id]++ when the user opens a window before entering location lunch and is decreased by bvec[id]−− when the user comes back and closes the window.

The weather model in this study is fixed to be a daily cycle of temperatures varying between $\pm A + B$ where the amplitude A is picked uniformly in $[0, 2]$ and the offset B in $[0, 1]$.

In order to optimize the energy consumption we also model a user profile which assumes that at night it is acceptable for the temperatures to drop to $8°C$. Furthermore, in the morning the rooms should be preheated to about $20°C$ and should not be lower than $17°C$ when the user arrives between 8 and 9 o'clock (with a uniform distribution).

Parameters. The goal of this study is to find optimal values for temperature thresholds Ton (primary controller) and Tget (secondary controller) with respect to energy consumption and user discomfort time. The method is simply to parameterize the model by varying the Ton and Tget between the values $[16, 22]°C$, and estimate energy consumption and comfort time for various configurations using UPPAAL SMC. The parameter value variation is modeled as a uniform choice during the first discrete stochastic transition in the automaton shown in Fig. 5b. Then the energy and discomfort time is computed using derivative expressions over all rooms by the same automaton.

4   Optimizing Control Strategies

First, we explain the methodology of our approach and then we present the empirical results following the methodology.

4.1   Methodology

We are interested in two aspects of the system: discomfort time and energy consumed – two notions of a cost that are in conflict if we try to optimize both of them, i.e. lowest energy might imply large discomfort and vice-versa, while some configurations are better compromises. Thus our goal is to identify the best configurations when preferring a lower discomfort for some energy ranges or a lower energy consumption for some ranges of discomfort – the so called Pareto-optimal frontier. But before we find the Pareto frontier, we need to estimate both costs for every configuration.

A simple approach would be to estimate confidence intervals (average ± standard error) for both costs with some given confidence level (say 95%) and for each configuration of the parameter values, and then compare them. The problem is that it can take a lot of measurements to achieve confidence for every configuration and even then the intervals may still overlap due to higher variance in some combinations. A better suited technique for comparisons is a pair-wise Student's t-test [18] which reduces the comparison of two distributions to checking that the mean of their differences is below, above or equal to zero. The improvement here is that if two distributions are significantly different then we would observe earlier with less samples that the confidence interval for the differences does not include zero and thus we could conclude with fewer measurements compared to estimating all the individual means. However, the Student's t-test is a pair-wise test but we have many more than just two configurations, thus we would need to apply this test at least $n \cdot log(n)$ times with the best sorting algorithm.

Statisticians developed a more refined technique called analysis of variance (ANOVA) to compare many distributions in one method potentially more efficient than many t-test applications and thus generalizes t-test for many configurations. There can be different arrangements, but we are interested in a so called two-factor factorial experiment design [18] in particular: our two parameters become the two factors (two orthogonal dimensions), the parameter values become factor levels (discrete values on those two dimensions) and the cost (discomfort or energy) is the measured outcome value. In such design, we are interested in all pair-wise combinations of parameter values, and those combinations can be arranged on a two dimensional grid. In this experiment design, ANOVA is based on estimating the parameters for a linear model[2] and computing how much influence each factor has on the outcome. The computed measure, called the F-statistic, is a ratio of a mean square for a particular factor and an error square. The F-statistic is then translated into a P-value by looking up the tables of F-distribution. P-value is called the factor significance: the probability of making an error by stating that the factor has influence on the outcome, thus the smaller the P-value the more confidence that the factor is significant.

An important assumption of this experiment design is that the measurements should be balanced (the amount of samples is the same across all configurations), therefore the minimum amount of data is one sample per each configuration, and

---

[2] A linear equation predicting the outcomes given the concrete factor values.

at least two samples per configuration if we are also interested in the interaction between factors. Our overall method is described by the following steps:

1. Using UPPAAL SMC, generate enough runs to provide enough measurements for each parameter configuration so that the data is balanced. At least two runs per configuration are required, but our parameter values are chosen stochastically by UPPAAL SMC, thus there might be some negligible balancing overhead.
2. Apply ANOVA on the gathered and balanced data so far. For this pilot study we use the implementation from the statistical tool R [20], but it is well known in textbooks and simple to implement in any other tool.
3. If our factors are significant then stop data generation and proceed to the next step, otherwise loop back to Step 1 and append more samples.
4. Reuse the gathered samples so far and compute the confidence intervals (average with standard error) for the means of cost (discomfort and energy) for each pair-wise parameter value combination.
5. Compute the Pareto frontier of discomfort and energy over configurations.
6. Present the Pareto frontier as a set of optimal parameter values the user can choose from as a compromise between energy consumption and discomfort.

Figure 7 shows a pipeline overview of operations performed with some steps marked where data is visualized by rectangles and operations as rounded rectangles. The dashed arrows indicate the change of control flow in Step 3. In general, Step 2 is not guaranteed to show factor significance so that Step 3 could proceed to Step 4, even if lots of data is presented. For example significance will not be reported if some factor/parameter has no influence on the measured outcome. Therefore an alternative test is needed to detect the independence in order to terminate the data generation (there can be several options to explore, thus we leave this generalization as a future work).

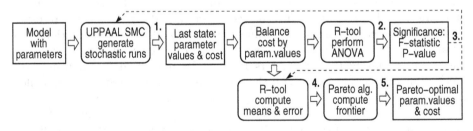

Fig. 7. Pipeline for finding the Pareto-optimal configurations of parameters

In addition, we pick out a few configurations, estimate means using UPPAAL SMC probabilistic query and compare them to validate some of the results. We also compare the performance of ANOVA based method with a simple mean value estimation method.

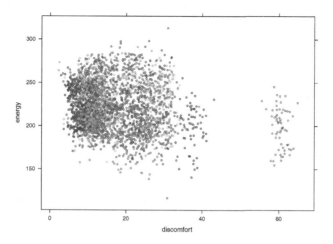

Fig. 8. Scatter plot of measurements colored by parameter value configuration

4.2   Results

We have parameterized the model with two parameters (factors in our experiment design) represented by temperature thresholds Ton and Tget each varying between 7 values (factor levels resp.), thus yielding 49 distinct pair-wise combinations to be tested. We instrumented UPPAAL SMC simulator to record the last values from a run. Consequently the query simulate 100 [<=2∗day] { Ton, Tget, discomfort, energy } generates 100 runs and stores the values of Ton, Tget, discomfort and energy as tuples. The gathered results can be plotted in terms of discomfort and energy. However, the individual data is scattered so much that it is impossible to distinguish individual clusters. An example plot of 3136 points is displayed in Fig. 8, where a different color used for every combination, but most configurations result in overlapping clusters (except one on the right), configurations are visually indistinguishable and thus the results need to be processed further.

In our setup the newly produced simulation results are streamed into a small C++ program which balances the data across parameter combinations, i.e. it outputs the data when all combinations have enough data. The balanced data is then analyzed using R scripts applying ANOVA. Table 1 shows an output from ANOVA performed on 98 measurements (two measurements per each combination, and there are $7 \cdot 7$ combinations): the first column shows factors, the fifth contains F-statistic and the sixth – P-value.

The coefficients of underlying linear model are appended at the bottom of the table, which means that the model predicts the mean discomfort with expression $60.82 - 2.29 \cdot \text{Ton} + 1.00 \cdot \text{Tget} - 0.05 \cdot \text{Ton} \cdot \text{Tget}$.

In our setup, we apply the ANOVA method each time new simulation data is appended. Table 2 displays a summary of ANOVA results for discomfort time

Table 1. ANOVA table with coefficients of the linear model provided by R [20]

```
Analysis of Variance Table
Response: discomfort
            Df Sum Sq Mean Sq F value    Pr(>F)
Ton          1 4159.3  4159.3 63.8874 3.303e-12 ***
Tget         1    0.4     0.4  0.0063    0.9369
Ton:Tget     1    4.1     4.1  0.0629    0.8026
Residuals 94 6119.7    65.1
---

(Intercept)          Ton        Tget    Ton:Tget
 60.8283113   -2.2867466   1.0029695  -0.0510851
```

and energy consumption when the amount of measurements is increased with each row. The first iteration with just one sample per configuration is not reliable to detect interactions, thus we start with two. The table shows that even in the first step Ton is significant for discomfort (since P<0.05) and get is significant for energy. Later more significance emerges as more data is supplied. We stop at iteration of 64 samples per configuration ($64 \cdot 49 = 3136$ simulations) where both factors Ton and Tget are significant (since P<0.05) in both outcomes. Their interaction (Ton:Tget) is still not significant in distinguishing outcomes (since P>0.05). Figures 9a and 9b show the planes of linear models learned by ANOVA: higher Ton and Tget values are preferred to lower the discomfort, but smaller

Table 2. Summary of sequential applications of ANOVA

Number of runs	Factor	Discomfort time F value	P-value	Energy consumption F value	P-value
$2 \cdot 49$	T_{on}	63.8874	**3.30e-12**	0.7147	0.4000
	T_{get}	0.0063	0.9369	17.5777	**6.24e-05**
	$T_{on} : T_{get}$	0.0629	0.8026	0.7181	0.3989
$4 \cdot 49$	T_{on}	136.1676	**<2e-16**	1.1647	0.2818
	T_{get}	0.1537	0.6955	17.9283	**3.55e-05**
	$T_{on} : T_{get}$	0.0003	0.9869	0.0582	0.8096
$8 \cdot 49$	T_{on}	315.7978	**<2e-16**	2.4425	0.1189
	T_{get}	0.1202	0.7290	35.8938	**4.76e-09**
	$T_{on} : T_{get}$	0.0096	0.9218	0.8253	0.3642
$16 \cdot 49$	T_{on}	629.1384	**<2e-16**	6.5909	0.01044
	T_{get}	0.5895	0.4429	90.9612	**<2e-16**
	$T_{on} : T_{get}$	0.2852	0.5935	5.3053	0.02152
$32 \cdot 49$	T_{on}	1263.5390	**<2e-16**	27.9527	**1.42e-07**
	T_{get}	1.0840	0.2980	172.3296	**<2.2e-16**
	$T_{on} : T_{get}$	0.5401	0.4625	3.2632	0.07104
$64 \cdot 49$	T_{on}	2575.3208	**<2e-16**	65.6245	**7.74e-16**
	T_{get}	4.6682	0.0308	405.4892	**<2.2e-16**
	$T_{on} : T_{get}$	0.5949	0.4406	0.1926	0.6608

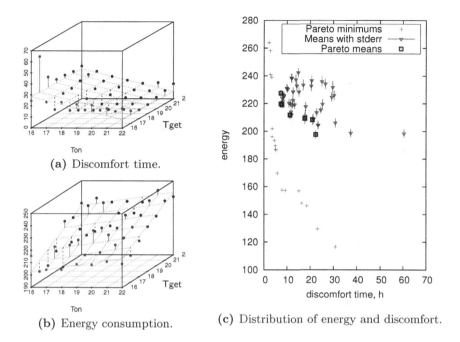

(a) Discomfort time.

(b) Energy consumption.

(c) Distribution of energy and discomfort.

Fig. 9. Estimated energy and discomfort for various parameter combinations

values are preferred for lower energy. Discomfort and energy are clearly in a conflict. Perhaps a compromise can be found in upper Ton and lower Tget levels as the plane seems more tilted in the opposite corner which should be avoided. Next, we look at the individual cost estimates.

Figure 9c shows estimated means with standard error bars (95% confidence intervals) aggregated by configurations. The plot shows Pareto-optimal frontier of mean values: points which dominate others by yielding smaller discomfort and energy values. We also plot the dominating minimum values to illustrate that original data is widely scattered.

Figure 10 shows level maps of averages as shades of gray and contours signifying equal levels. Discomfort is greatest on the bottom-left and there is a valley of small preferred values around (17;17) and (18;18) (discomfort=7.29, energy=219.6). The energy consumption is greatest on the top-right with a valley at around (17;18). Pareto-optimal means are marked by larger circles and it seems that configuration (22;18) (discomfort=7.83, energy=219.0) offers nice compromise between discomfort and energy, it is also further from steep slopes which might be at risk of yielding long discomfort time.

The plots show that four (more than half) of Pareto-optimal configurations are in the bottom-right corner as predicted by the ANOVA linear model and the other three are found closer to the center – the surface curving which could not be predicted by a linear model. Thus ANOVA can be used to detect the significant parameters and provide a linear model of overall tendencies.

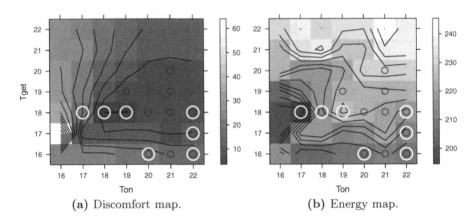

(a) Discomfort map.   (b) Energy map.

Fig. 10. Level maps of estimated mean values where Pareto-optimal configurations marked as: small circles for the minimum values and larger circles for mean

4.3   Comparison with Estimation

Next we evaluate the efficiency of ANOVA in discriminating the means of all the configurations in contrast to estimating simple costs (energy and discomfort). Two configurations are chosen for more detailed comparison: a Pareto-optimal configuration $(22; 18; 7.83 \pm 0.23; 218.99 \pm 2.32)$ and a non-optimal configuration worse than this optimal $(21; 18; 8.16 \pm 0.26; 221.38 \pm 2.33)$. To validate our results we would like to use our SMC technique in UPPAAL SMC to evaluate the means and compare them but we cannot directly do that. Instead we check the following queries Pr[discomfort<=100] (<> time>=2*day) and Pr[energy<=1000](<> time>=2*day). The actual probability is not interesting here (will be close to one), but rather the resulting distribution over discomfort and energy. We can then derive the mean that we want from this data as shown in Fig. 11.

The results for the Pareto-optimal configuration is in solid red lines. A summary of estimated means is described in a Table 3. The estimated means for combination (22;18) (discomfort 7.83 and energy 220.0) are smaller than in alternative configuration (21;18) (7.86 and 222.1 resp.), and thus (Ton=22; Tget=18) is a slightly better choice than (Ton=21; Tget=18). Another Pareto-optimal configuration (Ton=22;Tget=17) uses less energy, but the discomfort is noticeably

Table 3. Estimated means

Ton	Tget	discomfort	energy	Optimal?
22	18	7.83	220.0	Pareto
21	18	7.86	222.1	no
22	19	8.57	226.8	no
22	17	11.22	214.8	Pareto

larger, thus incomparable with (22;18).

UPPAAL SMC used 738 runs (80s) for each query to compute the cost with 95% confidence level (the confidence interval still needs to be computed). In principle it would take $7 \cdot 7$ such queries to estimate discomfort for each configuration (plus

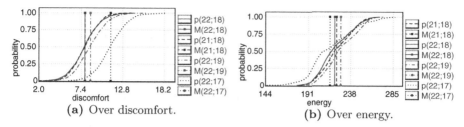

Fig. 11. Probability of reaching 2 days

the same amount for energy), thus in total 36162 simulation runs ($\approx 3920s \approx 1h\ 5min^3$). The ANOVA-based analysis required only 3136 simulation runs ($\approx 366s = 6min\ 6s$) – an improvement of 11.5 times. Thus we conclude that ANOVA method requires less measurements and consequently less simulations in order to differentiate and pick the optimal configurations.

5 Conclusion

The analysis of variance has been used in a sequential manner to decide if there is enough data for distinguishing the effects of two factors on two different costs in a two-factor factorial design. The ANOVA method can identify the significant factors by computing the F-statistic, however it can be problematic if the chosen factor has no influence on the outcomes (the P-value does not converge), thus an alternative test is needed to conclude independence to ensure termination.

We have demonstrated the technique on an energy aware buildings example and have identified Pareto-optimal configurations in terms of both discomfort and energy consumption. Thus SMC can be used to analyze complex models and determine cost-optimal parameter values using statistically efficient methods. The approach can also be distributed across a cluster of computers, but the load balancing algorithm need also to be fair with respect to parameter values as required by the analysis of variance.

There are many other experiment design variations including more factors and thus in the future it would be interesting to generalize the ANOVA method and implement the support for parametric SMC using general factorial designs inside the model checker.

References

1. Alur, R., Courcoubetis, C., Halbwachs, N., Henzinger, T.A., Ho, P.-H., Nicollin, X., Olivero, A., Sifakis, J., Yovine, S.: The algorithmic analysis of hybrid systems. Theor. Comput. Sci. 138(1), 3–34 (1995)
2. Alur, R., Dill, D.L.: A theory of timed automata. Theor. Comput. Sci. 126(2), 183–235 (1994)

---

[3] As measured on an Intel Core i7-2600 processor.

3. Legay, A., Delahaye, B., Bensalem, S.: Statistical model checking: An overview. In: Barringer, H., Falcone, Y., Finkbeiner, B., Havelund, K., Lee, I., Pace, G., Roşu, G., Sokolsky, O., Tillmann, N. (eds.) RV 2010. LNCS, vol. 6418, pp. 122–135. Springer, Heidelberg (2010)
4. Bulychev, P., David, A., Larsen, K.G., Legay, A., Li, G., Poulsen, D.B.: Rewrite-based statistical model checking of WMTL. In: Qadeer, S., Tasiran, S. (eds.) RV 2012. LNCS, vol. 7687, pp. 260–275. Springer, Heidelberg (2013)
5. Bulychev, P., David, A., Larsen, K.G., Legay, A., Mikučionis, M.: Computing nash equilibrium in wireless ad hoc networks: A simulation-based approach. In: Reich, J., Finkbeiner, B. (eds.) Second International Workshop on Interactions, Games and Protocols. EPTCS, vol. 78, pp. 1–14 (2012)
6. Bulychev, P., David, A., Guldstrand Larsen, K., Legay, A., Li, G., Bøgsted Poulsen, D., Stainer, A.: Monitor-based statistical model checking for weighted metric temporal logic. In: Bjørner, N., Voronkov, A. (eds.) LPAR-18. LNCS, vol. 7180, pp. 168–182. Springer, Heidelberg (2012)
7. David, A., Du, D., Larsen, K.G., Legay, A., Mikučionis, M., Poulsen, D.B., Sedwards, S.: Statistical model checking for stochastic hybrid systems. In: Bartocci, E., Bortolussi, L. (eds.) 1st International Workshop on Hybrid Systems and Biology. Electronic Proceedings in Theoretical Computer Science, vol. 92, pp. 122–136. Open Publishing Association (2012)
8. David, A., Larsen, K.G., Legay, A., Mikučionis, M.: Schedulability of herschel-planck revisited using statistical model checking. In: Margaria, T., Steffen, B. (eds.) ISoLA 2012, Part II. LNCS, vol. 7610, pp. 293–307. Springer, Heidelberg (2012)
9. David, A., Larsen, K.G., Legay, A., Mikučionis, M., Poulsen, D.B., Sedwards, S.: Runtime verification of biological systems. In: Margaria, T., Steffen, B. (eds.) ISoLA 2012, Part I. LNCS, vol. 7609, pp. 388–404. Springer, Heidelberg (2012)
10. David, A., Larsen, K.G., Legay, A., Mikučionis, M., Poulsen, D.B., van Vliet, J., Wang, Z.: Statistical model checking for networks of priced timed automata. In: Fahrenberg, U., Tripakis, S. (eds.) FORMATS 2011. LNCS, vol. 6919, pp. 80–96. Springer, Heidelberg (2011)
11. David, A., Larsen, K.G., Legay, A., Mikučionis, M., Wang, Z.: Time for statistical model checking of real-time systems. In: Gopalakrishnan, G., Qadeer, S. (eds.) CAV 2011. LNCS, vol. 6806, pp. 349–355. Springer, Heidelberg (2011)
12. Fehnker, A., Ivančić, F.: Benchmarks for hybrid systems verification. In: Alur, R., Pappas, G.J. (eds.) HSCC 2004. LNCS, vol. 2993, pp. 326–341. Springer, Heidelberg (2004)
13. Hartmanns, A., Hermanns, H.: A modest approach to checking probabilistic timed automata. In: Sixth International Conference on the Quantitative Evaluation of Systems, QEST 2009, pp. 187–196 (September 2009)
14. Katoen, J.-P., Zapreev, I.S., Hahn, E.M., Hermanns, H., Jansen, D.N.: The ins and outs of the probabilistic model checker MRMC. In: Proc. of 6th Int. Conference on the Quantitative Evaluation of Systems, QEST, pp. 167–176. IEEE Computer Society (2009)
15. Koymans, R.: Specifying real-time properties with metric temporal logic. Real-Time Systems 2(4), 255–299 (1990)
16. Larsen, K.G., Skou, A.: Bisimulation through probabilistic testing. Inf. Comput. 94(1), 1–28 (1991)
17. Legay, A., Delahaye, B., Bensalem, S.: Statistical model checking: An overview. In: Barringer, H., Falcone, Y., Finkbeiner, B., Havelund, K., Lee, I., Pace, G., Roşu, G., Sokolsky, O., Tillmann, N. (eds.) RV 2010. LNCS, vol. 6418, pp. 122–135. Springer, Heidelberg (2010)

18. Montgomery, D.C.: Design and Analysis of Experiments. John Wiley & Sons, Inc. (1997/2001) ISBN 0-471-31649-0
19. Pnueli, A.: The temporal logic of programs. In: FOCS, pp. 46–57 (1977)
20. R Core Team: R: A Language and Environment for Statistical Computing. R Foundation for Statistical Computing, Vienna, Austria (2012) ISBN 3-900051-07-0
21. Sen, K., Viswanathan, M., Agha, G.: Statistical model checking of black-box probabilistic systems. In: Alur, R., Peled, D.A. (eds.) CAV 2004. LNCS, vol. 3114, pp. 202–215. Springer, Heidelberg (2004)
22. Wald, A.: Sequential tests of statistical hypotheses. Annals of Mathematical Statistics 16(2), 117–186 (1945)
23. Younes, H.L.S., Simmons, R.G.: Probabilistic verification of discrete event systems using acceptance sampling. In: Brinksma, E., Larsen, K.G. (eds.) CAV 2002. LNCS, vol. 2404, pp. 223–235. Springer, Heidelberg (2002)
24. Younes, H.L.S., Simmons, R.G.: Statistical probabilistic model checking with a focus on time-bounded properties. Inf. Comput. 204(9), 1368–1409 (2006)

Formal Stability Analysis of Optical Resonators

Umair Siddique, Vincent Aravantinos, and Sofiène Tahar

Department of Electrical and Computer Engineering,
Concordia University, Montreal, Canada
{muh_sidd,vincent,tahar}@ece.concordia.ca

Abstract. An optical resonator usually consists of mirrors or lenses which are configured in such a way that the beam of light is confined in a closed path. Resonators are fundamental components used in many safety-critical optical and laser applications such as laser surgery, aerospace industry and nuclear reactors. Due to the complexity and sensitivity of optical resonators, their verification poses many challenges to optical engineers. Traditionally, the stability analysis of such resonators, which is the most critical design requirement, has been carried out by paper-and-pencil based proof methods and numerical computations. However, these techniques cannot provide accurate results due to the risk of human error and the inherent incompleteness of numerical algorithms. In this paper, we propose to use higher-order logic theorem proving for the stability analysis of optical resonators. Based on the multivariate analysis library of HOL Light, we formalize the notion of light ray and optical system (by defining medium interfaces, mirrors, lenses, etc.). This allows us to derive general theorems about the behaviour of light in such optical systems. In order to illustrate the practical effectiveness of our work, we present the formal analysis of a Fabry-Pérot resonator with fiber rod lens.

1 Introduction

In the last few decades, optical technology has revolutionized our daily life by providing new functionalities and resolving many bottlenecks in conventional electronic systems. The use of optics yields smaller components, high-speed communication and huge information capacity. This provides the basis of miniaturized complex engineering systems including digital cameras, high-speed internet links, telescopes and satellites. Optoelectronic and laser devices based on optical resonators [15] are fundamental building-blocks for new generation, reliable, high-speed and low-power optical systems. Typically, optical resonators are used in lasers [19], optical bio-sensors [1], refractometry [20] and reconfigurable wavelength division multiplexing-passive optical network (WDM-PON) systems [14].

An optical resonator usually consists of mirrors or lenses which are configured in such a way that the beam of light is confined in a closed path as shown in Figure 1. Optical resonators are usually designed to provide high quality-factor and little attenuation [15]. But the most important design requirement is the stability, which states that the beam of light remains within the optical

G. Brat, N. Rungta, and A. Venet (Eds.): NFM 2013, LNCS 7871, pp. 368–382, 2013.
© Springer-Verlag Berlin Heidelberg 2013

resonator even after N round-trips. The stability of a resonator depends on the properties and arrangement of its components, e.g., curvature of mirrors or lenses, and distance between them. For stability analysis, optical resonators are modelled using the principles of geometrical optics [15] which describes light as rays that obey geometrical rules. The theory of geometrical optics can be applied

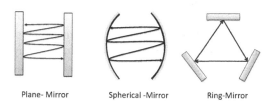

Plane- Mirror   Spherical -Mirror   Ring-Mirror

Fig. 1. Optical Resonators

for the modeling and analysis of physical objects with dimensions greater than the wavelength of light. It is based on a set of postulates which are used to derive the rules for the propagation of light through an optical medium. These postulates can be summed up as follows: Light travels in the form of rays emitted by a source; an optical medium is characterized by its refractive index and light rays follow Fermat's principle of least time [15].

Optical components, such as lenses and mirrors are usually centered about an optical axis, around which rays travel at small inclinations (angle with the optical axis). Such rays are called *paraxial rays* and this assumption provides the basis of *paraxial optics* which is the simplest framework of geometrical optics. The change in the position and inclination of a paraxial ray as it travels through an optical system can be described by the use of matrices called *ray-transfer matrices* [19]. This matrix formalism of geometrical optics allows for an accurate, scalable and systematic analysis of real-world complex optical and laser systems.

The widespread use of optical resonators in safety and mission-critical applications, such as astronomy [3] and medicine (e.g., refractive index measurement of cancer cells [20]), poses a real challenge to optical engineers for the modeling and verification of such resonators. Traditionally, the stability analysis of optical resonators has been done using paper-and-pencil based proof methods [10,15,19]. However, considering the complexity of present age optical and laser systems, such an analysis is very difficult if not impossible, and thus quite error-prone. Many examples of erroneous paper-and-pencil based proofs are available in the open literature, a recent one can be found in [2] and its identification and correction is reported in [11]. One of the most commonly used computer-based analysis techniques for stability analysis is numerical computation of complex ray-transfer matrices [13,21,8]. The stability analysis of optical and laser resonators involve complex and vector analysis along with transcendental functions and thus numerical computations cannot provide perfectly accurate results due to the heuristics and approximations of the underlying numerical algorithms. Another alternative is computer algebra systems [12], which are very efficient for computing mathematical solutions symbolically, but are not 100% reliable and sound due to their inability to deal with side conditions [5]. Another source of inaccuracy in computer algebra systems is the presence of unverified huge symbolic manipulation algorithms in their core, which are quite likely to contain bugs. Thus, these traditional techniques should not be relied upon for the analysis of optical resonators which are used in safety-critical applications (e.g., corneal surgery [23]), where inaccuracies in the analysis may even result in the loss of human lives.

In the past few years, higher-order logic theorem proving [4] has been successfully used for the precise analysis of a few continuous physical systems [18]. Developing a higher-order logic model for a physical system and analyzing this model formally is a very challenging task since it requires expertise in both mathematics and physics. However, it provides an effective way for identifying critical design errors that are often ignored by traditional analysis techniques like simulation and computer algebra systems. We believe that higher-order logic theorem proving offers a promising solution for conducting formal analysis of such critical optical resonators. Most of the classical mathematical theories behind geometrical optics, such as Euclidean spaces, multivariate analysis and complex numbers, have been formalized in the HOL Light theorem prover [6,7]. In this paper, we build on our formalization of geometrical optics [16] to provide a practical framework for the stability analysis of optical resonators. In order to illustrate the practical use of our work, we also present the formal analysis of a newly developed Fabry-Pérot resonator with fiber rod lens [10,9]. To the best of our knowledge, the present work is the first one of its kind.

The rest of the paper is organized as follows: Section 2 describes some fundamentals of geometrical optics, and its commonly used ray-transfer-matrix formalism. Section 3 presents the proposed framework for the formal stability analysis of optical resonators. Section 4 presents our HOL Light formalization of geometrical optics. Then, Section 5 describes the formalization of the stability of optical resonators. In order to demonstrate the practical effectiveness and the utilization of the proposed framework, we present the analysis of a real-world optical resonator i.e., Fabry-Pérot resonator with fiber rod lens in Section 6. Finally, Section 7 concludes the paper and highlights some future directions.

2 Geometrical Optics

When a ray passes through optical components, it undergoes *translation* or *refraction*. In translation, the ray simply travels in a straight line from one component to the next and we only need to know the thickness of the translation. On the other hand, refraction takes place at the boundary of two regions with different refractive indices and the ray obeys the law of refraction, i.e., the angle of refraction relates to the angle of incidence by the relation $n_0 \sin(\phi_0) = n_1 \sin(\phi_1)$, called *Snell's law* [15], where n_0, n_1 are the refractive indices of both regions and ϕ_0, ϕ_1 are the angles of the incident and refracted rays, respectively, with the normal to the surface. In order to model refraction, we thus need the normal to the refracting surface and the refractive indices of both regions.

In order to introduce the matrix formalism of geometrical optics, we consider the propagation of a ray through a spherical interface with radius of curvature R between two mediums of refractive indices n_0 and n_1, as shown in Figure 2. Our goal is to express the relationship between the incident and refracted rays. The trajectory of a ray as it passes through various optical components can be specified by two parameters: its distance from the optical axis and its angle with the optical axis. Here, the distances of the incident and refracted rays are r_1 and r_0, respectively, and $r_1 = r_0$ because the thickness of the surface is assumed to be very small. Here, ϕ_0 and ϕ_1 are the angles of the incident and refracted rays with the normal to the spherical surface, respectively. On the other hand, θ_0 and θ_1 are the angles of the incident and refracted rays with the optical axis. Applying Snell's law at the interface, we have $n_0 \sin(\phi_0) = n_1 \sin(\phi_1)$, which, in

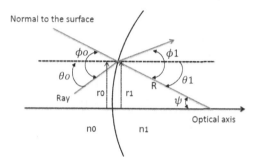

Fig. 2. Spherical Interface

the context of paraxial approximation (i.e., the assumption that light travels at small angles with respect to the normal, which is indeed the case in practice), reduces to the form $n_0\phi_0 = n_1\phi_1$ since $\sin(\phi) \simeq \phi$ if ϕ is small. We also have $\theta_0 = \phi_0 - \psi$ and $\theta_1 = \phi_1 - \psi$, where ψ is the angle between the surface normal and the optical axis. Since $\sin(\psi) = \frac{r_0}{R}$, then $\psi = \frac{r_0}{R}$ by paraxial approximation. We can deduce that:

$$\theta_1 = \left(\frac{n_0 - n_1}{n_1 R}\right) r_0 + \left(\frac{n_0}{n_1}\right) \theta_0 \tag{1}$$

So, for a spherical surface, we can relate the refracted ray with the incident ray by a matrix relationship using equation (1) as follows:

$$\begin{bmatrix} r_1 \\ \theta_1 \end{bmatrix} = \begin{bmatrix} 1 & 0 \\ \frac{n_0 - n_1}{n_1 R} & \frac{n_0}{n_1} \end{bmatrix} \begin{bmatrix} r_0 \\ \theta_0 \end{bmatrix}$$

Thus the propagation of a ray through a spherical interface can be described by a 2×2 matrix generally called, in the literature, *ABCD matrix*. This can be generalized to many optical components [15] and to the case of reflection as follows:

$$\begin{bmatrix} r_1 \\ \theta_1 \end{bmatrix} = \begin{bmatrix} A & B \\ C & D \end{bmatrix} \begin{bmatrix} r_0 \\ \theta_0 \end{bmatrix}$$

If we have an optical system consisting of k optical components, then we can trace the input ray R_i through all optical components using composition of matrices of each optical component as follows:

$$R_o = (M_k.M_{k-1}....M_1).R_i \qquad (2)$$

Simply, we can write $R_o = M_s R_i$ where $M_s = \prod_{i=k}^{1} M_i$. Here, R_o is the output ray and R_i is the input ray.

3 Formal Analysis Framework

The proposed framework, given in Figure 3, outlines the main idea behind the theorem-proving-based stability analysis of optical resonators. The grey shaded boxes in this figure show the key contributions of the paper that serve as the fundamental requirements for conducting formal stability analysis in a theorem prover. Like any system analysis tools, the inputs to this framework are the description of the optical resonator and geometric constraints, such as radius of curvature of mirrors and distance between different optical components. The

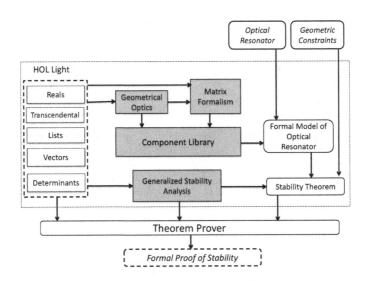

Fig. 3. Proposed Stability Analysis Framework for Optical Resonators

first step in conducting stability analysis of optical resonators using a theorem prover is to construct a formal model of the given resonator in higher-order logic.

For this purpose, the foremost requirement is the ability to formalize the underlying concepts of geometrical optics which includes the modeling of optical components and of the ray behaviour when it interacts with optical components. The second step in the proposed framework is to use the formalization of geometrical optics to formally derive the matrix formalism for geometrical components. This step requires the vector theory, which is already available as a part of multivariate analysis in HOL Light theorem prover. The third step to conduct formal stability analysis of optical resonators is to develop a library of frequently used optical components such as lenses, mirrors or crystals. Since such components are the basic blocks of optical systems, this library helps to formalize optical resonators. The next step is to formally define the stability of an optical resonator and verify some generalized stability theorems which are heavily dependent on matrix algebra within the HOL Light theorem prover. On top of that, one can finally state and prove the stability of an optical resonator in the theorem prover. The corresponding proof provides the output of the framework.

4   Formalization of Geometrical Optics

In order to fulfil the first requirement of the proposed stability analysis framework, we present the formalization of geometrical optics in this section. The formalization is two-fold: first, we model the geometry and physical parameters of an optical system; second, we model the physical behavior of a ray when it goes through an optical interface. Afterwards, we will be able to derive the ray-transfer matrices of the optical components, as explained in Section 2. We first define a type to describe optical systems:

Definition 1 (Optical Interface and System).
```
define_type "optical_interface = plane | spherical real"
define_type "interface_kind = transmitted | reflected"
new_type_abbrev("free_space",‘:real # real‘)
new_type_abbrev("optical_system",‘:(free_space # optical_interface #
                              interface_kind) list # free_space‘)
```

An optical system is a list of free spaces and interfaces between them. A free space is represented by one real number for its refractive index and one for its width. Optical interfaces are characterized both by their shape (plane or spherical, as shown in Figure 4) and by the behavior of the ray when it goes through it (transmitted or reflected), thus yielding the two above types ‘:optical_interface‘ and ‘:interface_kind‘. A spherical interface takes a real number representing its radius of curvature. A term of type ‘:free_space # optical_interface # interface_kind‘ is called an *optical component*. Note that this data type can easily be extended to many other optical components if needed.

A value of type ‘:free_space‘ does represent a real space only if the refractive index is greater than zero. In addition, in order to have a fixed order in the representation of an optical system, we impose that the distance of an optical interface relative to the previous interface is greater or equal to zero. We also need

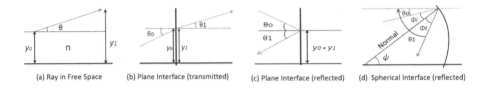

Fig. 4. Behavior of Ray at Different Interfaces

to assert the validity of a value of type `optical_interface` by ensuring that the radius of curvature of spherical interfaces is never equal to zero. These constraints are all packaged in a predicate `is_valid_optical_system os` which is true if and only if all the optical components of `os` satisfy the above requirements (the definition of this predicate is straightforward, see [16] for details).

We can now formalize the physical behaviour of a ray when it passes through an optical system. We only model the points where a ray hits an optical interface (instead of all the points constituting the ray). So it is sufficient to just provide the distance of the hitting point to the optical axis and the angle taken by the ray at that point. Consequently, we should have a list of such pairs $(distance, angle)$ for every component of a system. In addition, the same information should be provided for the source of the ray. For the sake of simplicity, we define a type for a pair $(distance, angle)$ as `ray_at_point`. This yields the following definition:

Definition 2 (Ray).
`new_type_abbrev ("ray_at_point", ':real # real')`
`new_type_abbrev ("ray", ':ray_at_point # ray_at_point #`
`                       (ray_at_point # ray_at_point) list')`

The first `ray_at_point` is the pair $(distance, angle)$ for the source of the ray, the second one is the one after the first free space, and the list of `ray_at_point` represents the same information for all hitting points of an optical system. It is not necessarily the case that every value of type `ray` constitutes a valid ray, we thus constrain this type by using a predicate `is_valid_ray_in_system ray sys` which asserts that the value `ray` indeed represents a ray travelling in the system `sys` [16]. For example, Figure 4 provides a couple of situations which are formalized by `is_valid_ray_in_system ray sys`.

Now, as explained in Section 2, the behavior of a ray through an optical system can be conveniently expressed by matrices. In our formalism, the matrix corresponding to an optical system `os` is given by the function `system_composition os`. For the sake of conciseness, we do not provide the detailed definition of this function, which can be found in [16]. We then obtain the following essential result:

Theorem 1 (Ray-Transfer-Matrix for Optical System).
$\vdash \forall$ sys ray. is_valid_optical_system sys $\wedge$
   is_valid_ray_in_system ray sys $\implies$
   let $(y_0, \theta_0), (y_1, \theta_1)$, rs = ray in

```
let yₙ,θₙ = last_ray_at_point ray in
```
$$\begin{bmatrix} y_n \\ \theta_n \end{bmatrix} = \text{system\_composition sys} * \begin{bmatrix} y_0 \\ \theta_0 \end{bmatrix}$$

where the function `last_ray_at_point` returns the last `ray_at_point` in system.

This concludes our formalization of geometrical optics and the verification of the generalized ray-transfer-matrix relationship (Theorem 1) of optical systems. The formal verification of the above important theorem reassures the correctness of our formal definitions related to optical systems. Now, we present the formalization of stability of an optical resonator and the verification of the generalized stability theorem in the following section.

5   Formalization of the Stability of Optical Resonators

Optical resonators are particular type of optical systems which are broadly classified as stable or unstable. One of the most interesting features of optical resonators is their diverse applications, e.g., stable resonators are used in the measurement of the refractive index of cancer cells [20], whereas unstable resonators are used in the laser oscillators for high energy applications [19]. Stability analysis identifies geometric constraints of the optical components which ensure that light remains inside the resonator (see Figure 5 (a)). In order to

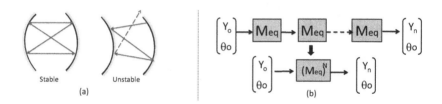

Fig. 5. (a) Types of Optical Resonators (b) ABCD Matrix After N Round-Trips

determine whether a given optical resonator is stable, we need to analyze the ray behaviour after many round trips. To model N round trips of light in the resonator, engineers usually "unfold" N times the resonator description, and compute the corresponding ray-transfer matrix. From the results presented in the previous section, it follows that it is equivalent to take the ray-transfer matrix corresponding to one round-trip and then raise it to the Nth power, as shown in Figure 5 (b). For an optical resonator to be stable, the distance of the ray from the optical axis and its orientation should remain bounded whatever the value of N. This is formalized as follows:

Definition 3 (Resonator Stability).
⊢ ∀ M. stable_optical_system M ⇔ (∀ X. ∃ Y. ∀ N.
abs((M mat_pow N) * X)$1 ≤ Y$1 ∧ abs((M mat_pow N) * X)$2 ≤ Y$2)

where X and Y are 2-dimensional vectors and M is a 2×2 matrix (intended to be the round-trip matrix of the resonator). The function mat_pow denotes the matrix power function and V$i denotes the ith component of a vector V.

Proving that a given resonator satisfies the abstract condition of Definition 3 does not seem trivial at first. However, if the determinant of M is 1 (It means that the refractive index is the same at the input and output of the system. This is generally the case for optical systems encountered in practice), optics engineers have known for a long time that having $-1 < \frac{M_{11}+M_{22}}{2} < 1$ is sufficient to ensure that the stability condition holds. The obvious advantage of this criterion is that it is immediate to check. In order to prove this result, we can use Sylvester's Theorem [22,24], which states that for a matrix $M = \begin{bmatrix} A & B \\ C & D \end{bmatrix}$ such that $| M | = 1$ and $-1 < \frac{A+D}{2} < 1$, the following holds:

$$\begin{bmatrix} A & B \\ C & D \end{bmatrix}^N = \frac{1}{\sin(\theta)} \begin{bmatrix} A\sin[N(\theta)] - \sin[(N-1)\theta] & B\sin[N(\theta)] \\ C\sin[N(\theta)] & D\sin[N(\theta)] - \sin[(N-1)\theta] \end{bmatrix}$$

where $\theta = cos^{-1}[\frac{(A+D)}{2}]$. This theorem ensures that stability holds under the considered assumptions: Indeed, N only occurs under a sine in the resulting matrix; since the sine itself is comprised between -1 and 1, it follows that the components of the matrix are obviously bounded, hence the stability. We formalize Sylvester's theorem as follows:

Theorem 2 (Sylvesters Theorem).

$\vdash \forall$ N A B C D. $\begin{vmatrix} A & B \\ C & D \end{vmatrix}$ = 1 $\wedge$ $-1 < \frac{(A+D)}{2}$ $\wedge$ $\frac{(A+D)}{2} < 1$ $\Longrightarrow$

let θ = acs($\frac{(A+D)}{2}$) in

$$\begin{bmatrix} A & B \\ C & D \end{bmatrix}^N = \frac{1}{\sin(\theta)} \begin{bmatrix} A * \sin[N(\theta)] - \sin[(N-1)\theta] & B * \sin[N(\theta)] \\ C * \sin[N(\theta)] & D * \sin[N(\theta)] - \sin[(N-1)\theta] \end{bmatrix}$$

We prove Theorem 2 by induction on N and using the fundamental properties of trigonometric functions, matrices and determinants. Now, we derive the generalized stability theorem for any ABCD matrix as follows:

Theorem 3 (Generalized Stability Theorem).

$\vdash \forall$ A B C D. $\begin{vmatrix} A & B \\ C & D \end{vmatrix}$ = 1 $\wedge$ $-1 < \frac{(A+D)}{2}$ $\wedge$ $\frac{(A+D)}{2} < 1$ $\Longrightarrow$

stable_optical_system $\begin{bmatrix} A & B \\ C & D \end{bmatrix}$

The formal verification of Theorem 3 requires the formal definition of stability (Definition 3) and Sylvester's theorem along with some fundamental properties of vectors. It is important to note that our stability theorem is quite general and can be applied to any ABCD matrix which satisfies the required assumptions. This completes our formalization of stability and we present its practical effectiveness by analyzing Fabry Pérot resonator in the next section.

6 Application: Stability Analysis of Fabry Pérot Resonator

Nowadays, optical systems are becoming more and more popular due to their huge potential of application. In order to bring this technology to the market, a lot of research has been done toward the integration of low cost, low power and portable building blocks in optical systems. One of the most important such building blocks is the Fabry Pérot (FP) resonator [15]. Originally, this resonator was used as a high resolution interferometer in astrophysical applications. Recently, the Fabry Pérot resonator has been realized as a microelectromechanical (MEMS) tuned optical filter for applications in reconfigurable Wavelength Division Multiplexing [14]. The other important applications are in the measurement of refractive index of cancer cells [20] and optical bio-sensing devices [1].

Due to diverse applications of the FP resonators, different architectures have been proposed in the open literature. The main limitation of traditional designs is the instability of the resonators which prevents their use in many practical applications (e.g., refractometry for cancer cells). Recently, a state-of-the-art FP core architecture has been proposed which overcomes the limitations of existing FP resonators [10,9]. In the new design, cylindrical mirrors are combined with a fiber rod lens (FRL) inside the cavity, to focus the beam of light in both transverse planes as shown in Figure 6 (a). The fiber rod lens is used as light pipe which allows the transmission of light from one end to the other with relatively small leakage. Building a stable FP resonator requires the geometric constraints to be determined in terms of the radius of curvature of mirrors R and the free space propagation distance (d_{free_space}) using the stability analysis.

As a direct application of the framework developed in the previous sections, we present the stability analysis of FP resonator with fiber rod lens as described above. It is important to note that the design shown in Figure 6 (a), has a 3-dimensional structure. We can still apply the ray-transfer-matrix approach to analyze the stability by dividing the given architecture into two planes, i.e., XZ and YZ planes. Now, the stability problem becomes a couple of planar problems which are still valid since the ray focusing behaviours in both directions (XZ and YZ) are decoupled. This is merely a consequence of the decomposition of Euclidean space vectors into a basis. This can be seen in Figure 6 (b) and (c), where the resonator is divided into two cross-sections. In the following, we focus only on the analysis of the XZ plane, since the analysis in the YZ plane is fairly similar (the complete analysis can be found in the source code [17]).

In the XZ cross-section (Figure 6 (b)), the focusing is done by the curved mirrors. The fiber rod lens acts as a refracting slab with width d_f and refractive index n_f. The first step in the stability analysis, as described in our proposed framework is to construct a formal model of the given resonator in higher-order logic. A ray that makes a round-trip in the cavity undergoes (from left to right) first reflection in a curved mirror of radius R, propagation through free space of length d_x and refractive index 1, refraction from free space to fiber rod lens, propagation within fiber rod lens of length d_f and refractive index n_f, refraction from fiber rod lens to free space and again the propagation through free space

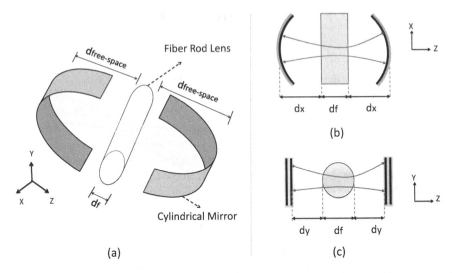

Fig. 6. Fabry Pérot (FP) Resonator with fiber rod lens (a) 3-Dimensional Resonator Design (b) Cross-Section view in the XZ Plane (c) Cross-Section view in the YZ Plane

of length d_x. Of course, the "return-trip" is symmetric. We formally model this system as follows:

Definition 4 (Formal Model of FP Resonator in XZ Plane).
⊢ ∀ R dx nf df. FP_XZ R dx df nf =
    ([(1,0),spherical R,reflected;(1,dx),plane,transmitted;
    (nf,df),plane,transmitted],1,dx)

Here, the pair (1,0) represents free space with refractive index 1 and null width. FP_XZ is a higher-order logic function which takes the parameters, radius of curvature of mirror (R), free space length (dx), length of fiber rod lens (df) and refractive index (nf). It returns an optical system (Definition 1) which corresponds to the formalization of a cavity with the corresponding input parameters. Next, we formally verify that the formal model of the cavity is valid under realistic geometric constraints, such as the fact that the refractive index (nf) and lengths of free space propagation (dx and df) should be greater than 0.

Theorem 4 (Validity of FP resonator in XZ Plane).
⊢ ∀ R dx df nf. R ≠ 0 ∧ 0 < dx ∧ 0 < df ∧ 0 < nf ⟹
    is_valid_optical_system (FP_XZ R dx df nf)

Next, we formally verify the equivalent matrix relationship of FP resonator in XZ plane using the formal definition of system composition.

Theorem 5 (Equivalent Matrix for FP resonator in XZ Plane).
⊢ ∀ R dx df nf. R ≠ 0 ∧ 0 < dx ∧ 0 < df ∧ 0 < nf ⟹

```
system_composition (FP_XZ R dx df nf) =
```

$$\begin{bmatrix} 1 - \dfrac{2 * (df + 2 * dx * nf)}{nf * R} & 2 * dx + \dfrac{df}{nf} \\ -\dfrac{2}{R} & 1 \end{bmatrix}$$

The verification of this theorem mainly involves the matrix algebra and some arithmetic reasoning. The following result is then easy to prove by making use of the results already obtained in our framework:

Theorem 6 (Ray-Transfer-Matrix Model in XZ plane).
$\vdash \forall$ R dx df nf . R $\neq$ 0 $\wedge$ 0 < dx $\wedge$ 0 < df $\wedge$ 0 < nf $\implies$
($\forall$ ray.is_valid_ray_in_system ray (FP_XZ R dx df nf)
$\implies$ (let (y$_0$,θ_0),(y1,theta1),rs = ray in
(y$_n$,θ_n) = last_single_ray ray in
vector [y$_n$;θ_n] = system_composition (FP_XZ R dx df nf) *
vector [y$_0$;θ_0]))

where last_single_ray is a function that takes a ray as input and returns the last pair (distance from the optical axis y and the orientation θ) of that ray.

To this point, we have formally developed the model of the FP resonator in the XZ plane and also verified important properties such as the validity of the model and the ray-transfer-matrix relationship. Now, we are in a position to formally verify the stability of the FP resonator in the XZ plane, which is the final step.

Theorem 7 (Stability in XZ plane).
$\vdash \forall$ R dx df nf . R $\neq$ 0 $\wedge$ 0 < dx $\wedge$ 0 < df $\wedge$ 0 < nf
$0 < \dfrac{2*dx+\frac{df}{nf}}{R} \wedge \dfrac{2*dx+\frac{df}{nf}}{R} < 2 \implies$ stable_optical_system
(system_composition (FP_XZ R dx df nf))

The first four assumptions just ensure the validity of the model description. The two following ones provide the intended stability criteria. The formal verification of Theorem 7 requires Theorem 5 and Theorem 3 along with some fundamental properties of matrices and arithmetic reasoning.

Similarly, we can model and verify the validity of the FP resonator in YZ plane by performing the above mentioned steps. For the sake of conciseness, we only present the stability theorem in YZ plane as follows:

Theorem 8 (Stability in YZ plane).
$\vdash \forall$ dy df nf . 0 < dy $\wedge$ 0 < df $\wedge$ 0 < nf
$0 < 1 - \frac{2}{nf} + \left(4 * \frac{dy}{df}\right) * \left(1 - \frac{1}{nf}\right) \wedge 1 - \frac{2}{nf} + \left(4 * \frac{dy}{df}\right) * \left(1 - \frac{1}{nf}\right) < 1$
$\implies$ stable_optical_system (system_composition (FP_YZ dy df nf))

The first three assumptions just ensure the validity of the model description. The two following ones provide the intended stability criteria.

It is important to note that for the FP resonator with fiber rod lens, we have two sets of stability constraints, i.e., in the XZ plane (Theorem 7) and in the YZ plane (Theorem 8). Consequently, the resonator can be stable in one plane and unstable in the other. Therefore, in practice, the criteria of Theorem 7 and 8 should both be satisfied.

This completes our formal stability analysis of the FP resonator with fiber rod lens, which clearly demonstrates the effectiveness of the proposed theorem proving based stability analysis framework. The above formal analysis allowed us to find some discrepancy in the paper-and-pencil based proof approach presented in [10]. Particularly, the order of matrix multiplication in Equations (16) and (24) in [10] should be reversed, so as to obtain correct stability constraints. Due to the formal nature of the model and inherent soundness of higher-order logic theorem proving, we have been able to verify the stability of Fabry Pérot (FP) resonator with fiber rod lens with an unrivaled accuracy. This improved accuracy comes at the cost of the time and effort spent, while formalizing the underlying theory of geometrical optics and resonator stability. But, the availability of such a formalized infrastructure significantly reduces the time required to analyze the Fabry Pérot (FP) resonator with fiber rod lens. Moreover, we automatized parts of the verification task by introducing new tactics, e.g., VALID_OPTICAL_SYSTEM_TAC, which automatically verifies the validity of a given optical system. We also formally analyzed a couple of other important resonator architectures such as FP resonator with curved mirrors and Z-shaped resonator. Our HOL Light developments of geometrical optics, Fabry Pérot (FP) resonators and Z-shaped resonator are available for download [17] and thus can be used by other researchers and optical engineers working in industry to conduct the formal stability analysis of their optical resonators.

7   Conclusion

In this paper, we report a novel application of formal methods in the stability analysis of optical resonators which is mainly based on geometrical optics. We provided a brief introduction of the current state-of-the-art and highlighted their limitations. Next, we presented an overview of geometrical optics followed by some highlights of our higher-order logic formalization. In order to show the practical effectiveness of our proposed framework, we presented the formal stability analysis of Fabry Pérot (FP) resonator with fiber rod lens. Note that this application is not a simple toy example but an advanced system which has been published only recently. In fact, we were able to identify some discrepancy in the paper-and-pencil based stability analysis presented in [10]. Catching this problem in paper-and-pencil based proofs clearly indicates the usefulness of using higher-order-logic theorem proving for the stability analysis of optical resonators. To the best of our knowledge, this is the first time that formal approach has been applied for the stability analysis of optical resonators.

The rigor of formal verification allows to go beyond what is traditionally done by optics engineers. For instance, during our formalization, we have identified that the paraxial approximation is not taken into account rigorously in traditional techniques. However, theorem proving provides the required mathematical background to tackle this precisely. This is one of our essential future work.

We also plan to automatize the verification of optical resonators' stability by developing dedicated conversions and tactics that would compute automatically the required matrix products and check that the resulting matrices indeed satisfy the conditions given by Sylvester's theorem. In the future, we also plan to extend this work in order to obtain an extensive library of verified optical components, along with the formalization of Gaussian beams, which would allow the formal analysis of resonator modes [19]. We also plan to package our HOL Light formalization in a GUI, so that it can be used by non-formal methods community in industry for the analysis of practical resonators and in academia for teaching and research purposes.

References

1. Baaske, M., Vollmer, F.: Optical Resonator Biosensors: Molecular Diagnostic and Nanoparticle Detection on an Integrated Platform. ChemPhysChem 13(2), 427–436 (2012)
2. Cheng, Q., Cui, T.J., Zhang, C.: Waves in Planar Waveguide Containing Chiral Nihility Metamaterial. Optics and Communication 274, 317–321 (2007)
3. Ellis, S.C., Crouzier, A., Bland-Hawthorn, J., Lawrence, J.: Potential Applications of Ring Resonators for Astronomical Instrumentation. In: Proceedings of the International Quantum Electronics and Lasers and Electro-Optics, pp. 986–988. Optical Society of America (2011)
4. Gordon, M.J.C., Melham, T.F.: Introduction to HOL: A Theorem Proving Environment for Higher-Order Logic. Cambridge University Press (1993)
5. Harrison, J.: Theorem Proving with the Real Numbers. Springer (1998)
6. Harrison, J.: A HOL Theory of Euclidean space. In: Hurd, J., Melham, T. (eds.) TPHOLs 2005. LNCS, vol. 3603, pp. 114–129. Springer, Heidelberg (2005)
7. Harrison, J.: Formalizing Basic Complex Analysis. In: From Insight to Proof: Festschrift in Honour of Andrzej Trybulec. Studies in Logic, Grammar and Rhetoric, vol. 10(23), pp. 151–165. University of Białystok (2007)
8. LASCAD (2013), http://www.las-cad.com/
9. Malak, M., Marty, F., Pavy, N., Peter, Y.-A., Liu, A.-Q., Bourouina, T.: Cylindrical Surfaces Enable Wavelength-Selective Extinction and Sub-0.2 nm Linewidth in 250 μm-Gap Silicon Fabry-Perot Cavities. IEEE Journal of Microelectromechanical Systems 21(1), 171–180 (2012)
10. Malak, M., Pavy, N., Marty, F., Richalot, E., Liu, A.Q., Bourouina, T.: Design, Modeling and Characterization of Stable, High Q-factor Curved Fabry Perot cavities. Microsyst. Technol. 17(4), 543–552 (2011)
11. Naqvi, A.: Comments on Waves in Planar Waveguide Containing Chiral Nihility Metamaterial. Optics and Communication 284, 215–216 (2011)
12. OpticaSoftware (2013), http://www.opticasoftware.com/
13. reZonator (2013), http://www.rezonator.orion-project.org/
14. Saadany, B., Malak, M., Kubota, M., Marty, F.M., Mita, Y., Khalil, D., Bourouina, T.: Free-Space Tunable and Drop Optical Filters Using Vertical Bragg Mirrors on Silicon. IEEE Journal of Selected Topics in Quantum Electronics 12(6), 1480–1488 (2006)
15. Saleh, B.E.A., Teich, M.C.: Fundamentals of Photonics. John Wiley & Sons, Inc. (1991)

16. Siddique, U., Aravantinos, V., Tahar, S.: Higher-Order Logic Formalization of Geometrical Optics. In: International Workshop on Automated Deduction in Geometry (ADG), pp. 185–196. Informatics Research Report, School of Informatics, University of Edinburgh, Edinburgh, UK (2012)
17. Siddique, U., Aravantinos, V., Tahar, S.: Formal Stability Analysis of Optical Resonators - HOL Light Script (2013),
    http://hvg.ece.concordia.ca/code/hol-light/opresonator/
18. Siddique, U., Hasan, O.: Formal Analysis of Fractional Order Systems in HOL. In: Proceedings of the IEEE International Conference on Formal Methods in Computer-Aided Design (FMCAD), Austin, TX, USA, pp. 163–170 (2011)
19. Siegman, A.E.: Lasers, 1st edn. University Science Books (1986)
20. Song, W.Z., Zhang, X.M., Liu, A.Q., Lim, C.S., Yap, P.H., Hosseini, H.M.M.: Refractive Index Measurement of Single Living Cells Using On-Chip Fabry-Perot Cavity. Applied Physics Letters 89(20), 203901 (2006)
21. Su, B., Xue, J., Sun, L., Zhao, H., Pei, X.: Generalised ABCD Matrix Treatment for Laser Resonators and Beam Propagation. Optics & Laser Technology 43(7), 1318–1320 (2011)
22. Sylvester, J.J.: The Collected Mathematical Papers of James Joseph Sylvester, vol. 4. Cambridge U. Press (1912)
23. Loesel, F.H., Kurtz, R.M., Horvath, C., Bille, J.F., Juhasz, T., Djotyan, G., Mourou, G.: Applications of Femtosecond Lasers in Corneal Surgery. Laser Physics 10(2), 495–500 (2011)
24. Tovar, A.A., Casperson, W.: Generalized Sylvester Theorems for Periodic Applications in Matrix Optics. J. Opt. Soc. Am. A 12(3), 578–590 (1995)

Formal Verification of Nonlinear Inequalities with Taylor Interval Approximations

Alexey Solovyev and Thomas C. Hales*

Department of Mathematics, University of Pittsburgh,
Pittsburgh, PA 15260, USA

Abstract. We present a formal tool for verification of multivariate nonlinear inequalities. Our verification method is based on interval arithmetic with Taylor approximations. Our tool is implemented in the HOL Light proof assistant and it is capable to verify multivariate nonlinear polynomial and non-polynomial inequalities on rectangular domains. One of the main features of our work is an efficient implementation of the verification procedure which can prove non-trivial high-dimensional inequalities in several seconds. We developed the verification tool as a part of the Flyspeck project (a formal proof of the Kepler conjecture). The Flyspeck project includes about 1000 nonlinear inequalities. We successfully tested our method on more than 100 Flyspeck inequalities and estimated that the formal verification procedure is about 3000 times slower than an informal verification method implemented in C++. We also describe future work and prospective optimizations for our method.

1 Introduction

In this paper, we present a tool for formal verification of nonlinear inequalities in HOL Light [1]. Our tool can verify multivariate polynomial and non-polynomial inequalities on rectangular domains. The verification technique is based on interval arithmetic with Taylor approximations. A short user manual describing our tool is available [2]. Solovyev's thesis [3] contains additional information about the verification tool and the corresponding formal techniques.

Our work is an integral part of the Flyspeck project [4, 5]. This project was launched in 2003 by T. Hales to produce a complete formal verification of Hales' proof of the Kepler conjecture [6, 7]. There are several major computationally extensive verification problems in the Flyspeck project. One of these problems is a formal verification of about 1000 multivariate nonlinear inequalities. We have successfully tested our formal verification tool on several simple Flyspeck nonlinear inequalities (we have verified 130 inequalities). In theory, almost all Flyspeck inequalities can be verified with our formal verification procedure. A rough estimate shows that the current formal procedure is about 3000 times slower than the corresponding informal verification algorithm in C++ [8]. With this estimate, it will take more than 4 years to verify all Flyspeck nonlinear

* Research supported by NSF grant 0804189 and a grant from the Benter Foundation.

G. Brat, N. Rungta, and A. Venet (Eds.): NFM 2013, LNCS 7871, pp. 383–397, 2013.
© Springer-Verlag Berlin Heidelberg 2013

inequalities formally on a single computer (the informal procedure requires about 9 hours).

Although the existing C++ program can verify all nonlinear inequalities in the Flyspeck project, it is still very important to have a complete formal verification of all these inequalities. The formal HOL Light tool is much more reliable than the original C++ program because all results produced by this tool are verified by a small (less than 700 lines of code) HOL Light kernel. It is very unlikely that the HOL Light tool will return a wrong result. On the other hand, even a subtle error in the C++ program could produce a wrong answer for some inequalities.

There exist other formal methods for verification of nonlinear inequalities. First of all, general quantifier elimination procedures may be used to solve some polynomial inequalities [9–11]. Another method for proving polynomial inequalities is known as the sums-of-squares (SOS) method [12].

A tool called MetiTarski [13, 14] is capable of verifying multivariate polynomial and non-polynomial inequalities on unbounded domains. It approximates non-polynomial functions by suitable polynomial bounds and then applies quantifier elimination procedures for resulting polynomials. The paper [15] describes a formal approximation method of univariate functions by polynomials.

The Bernstein polynomial technique [16] allows to verify multivariate polynomial inequalities. Each polynomial can be written as a sum of polynomials in the Bernstein polynomial basis. Coefficients of this representation give bounds of the polynomial itself. A complete formal implementation of this method is done in PVS [17]. Non-polynomial inequalities must be first converted into polynomial inequalities by finding polynomial bounds. One way to find polynomial bounds is to use Taylor model approximations [18]. R. Zumkeller's thesis describes this method in detail [16]. He also implemented an informal global optimization tool based on Bernstein polynomials [19] in Haskell.

There exists a tool in the PVS proof assistant which uses the same technique as our tool (interval arithmetic with Taylor approximations) [20] but this tool works only with univariate functions.

Methods based on quantifier elimination procedures do not scale well when the number of variables grows and when inequalities become more complicated. The Bernstein polynomial technique works well for polynomial inequalities but does not show very good results for inequalities involving special functions in high dimensions.

2   Verification of Nonlinear Inequalities

2.1   Nonlinear Inequalities and Interval Taylor Approximations

Consider the problem: Prove that

$$\forall \mathbf{x} \in \mathbb{R}^n, \mathbf{x} \in D \implies f(\mathbf{x}) < 0.$$

D is assumed to be a rectangle given by $D = \{(x_1, \ldots, x_n) \mid a_i \leq x_i \leq b_i\} = [\mathbf{a}, \mathbf{b}]$. We also assume that $f(\mathbf{x})$ is twice continuously differentiable in an open domain $U \supset D$.

One way to solve the problem is to consider a finite partition of $D = \bigcup_j D^j$ such that each D^j is rectangular. Also, we assume that $\bar{f}(D^j) < 0$ where $\bar{f}$ is an interval approximation of f (that is, $\bar{f}(D^j)$ is the interval corresponding to the interval evaluation of $f(x_1, \ldots, x_n)$ for input intervals $x_i \in [a_i^j, b_i^j]$; clearly, $\bar{f}(D) < 0 \implies f(D) < 0$). It is easy to see that such a partition always exists if f is continuous, $f(D) < 0$, and f can be arbitrary well approximated by $\bar{f}$ on sufficiently small domains. (It follows by the compactness argument: for each point $x \in D$ there is a small rectangle D^j such that $x \in \text{interior}(D^j)$ and $\bar{f}(D^j) < 0$; D is compact, so there are finitely many rectangles D^j such that $D = \bigcup_j D^j$.)

The main difficulty is finding a suitable partition $\{D^j\}$. The easiest way is the following. Let $D^0 = D$ and compute $\bar{f}(D^0)$. If this value is less than 0 (in the interval sense), then we are done. Otherwise divide D^0 into two regions $D^0 = D_1^1 \cup D_2^1$. Then repeat the procedure for regions with upper index 1. In general, either $\bar{f}(D_j^k) < 0$ or we get $D_j^k = D_{2j-1}^{k+1} \cup D_{2j}^{k+1}$. If we divide each region such that sizes of new regions become arbitrarily small in all dimensions, then the process will eventually stop and a suitable partition of D will be found. An easy way to achieve this goal is to divide each region in half along the coordinate for which its size is maximal, i.e., if $D_j^k = \{a_i \leq x_i \leq b_i\} = [\mathbf{a}, \mathbf{b}]$ and $b_m - a_m = \max_i\{b_i - a_i\}$, then set $D_{2j-1}^{(k+1)} = [\mathbf{a}, \mathbf{b}^{(m,y)}]$ and $D_{2j}^{(k+1)} = [\mathbf{a}^{(m,y))}, \mathbf{b}]$. Here, $y = (a_m + b_m)/2$ and $\mathbf{a}^{(m,y)}$ equals to $\mathbf{a}$ with the m-th component replaced by y.

As the result of the procedure above, we get a finite set of subregions $S = \{D_i^k\}$ with the property: for each $D_i^k \in S$ either $\bar{f}(D_i^k) < 0$ or $D_i^k = D_{i_1}^{k+1} \cup D_{i_2}^{k+1}$. In the last case, the verification relies on a trivial theorem

$$D = D_1 \cup D_2 \wedge f(D_1) < 0 \wedge f(D_2) < 0 \implies f(D) < 0.$$

Interval arithmetic works for any continuous function (at least in theory where numerical errors are not considered) but it is not very efficient in general. This is due to the dependency problem when even a simple function could require a lot of subdivisions in order to get the result on the full domain. For instance, consider $f(x) = x - \arctan(x)$. We have $\bar{f}([0,1]) = [0,1] - [0, \pi/4] = [-\pi/4, 1]$ and we don't get $f(x) < 1$. One way to decrease the dependency problem is to use Taylor approximations for computing bounds of f on a given domain D.

Fix $\mathbf{y} \in D = [\mathbf{a}, \mathbf{b}]$, then we can write

$$f(\mathbf{x}) = f(\mathbf{y}) + \sum_{i=1}^{n} \frac{\partial f}{\partial x_i}(\mathbf{y})(y_i - x_i) + \frac{1}{2} \sum_{i,j=1}^{n} \frac{\partial^2 f}{\partial x_i \partial x_j}(\mathbf{p})(y_i - x_i)(y_j - x_j)$$

where $\mathbf{p} \in [\mathbf{a}, \mathbf{b}]$. Let $\mathbf{w} = \max\{\mathbf{y} - \mathbf{a}, \mathbf{b} - \mathbf{y}\}$ (all operations are componentwise). Suppose we have interval bounds for $f(\mathbf{y}) \in [f_0^{lo}, f_0^{hi}]$, $\frac{\partial f}{\partial x_i}(\mathbf{y}) \in [f_i^{lo}, f_i^{hi}]$ and $\frac{\partial^2 f}{\partial x_i \partial x_j}(\mathbf{t}) \in [f_{ij}^{lo}, f_{ij}^{hi}]$ for all $\mathbf{t} \in D$. We can write

$$\forall \mathbf{x} \in D, \ f(\mathbf{x}) \le f(\mathbf{y}) + \sum_{i=1}^{n} \left| \frac{\partial f}{\partial x_i}(\mathbf{y}) \right| w_i + \frac{1}{2} \sum_{i,j=1}^{n} \left| \frac{\partial^2 f}{\partial x_i \partial x_j}(\xi) \right| w_i w_j$$

$$\le f_0^{hi} + \sum_{i=1}^{n} |[f_i^{lo}, f_i^{hi}]| \, w_i + \frac{1}{2} \sum_{i,j=1}^{n} |[f_{ij}^{lo}, f_{ij}^{hi}]| \, w_i w_j.$$

Absolute values of intervals are defined by $|[a, b]| = \max\{-a, b\}$.

Let's see how well this approximation works on an example. Again, take $f(x) = x - \arctan x$ and $D = [0, 1]$. We get $f'(x) = 1 - \frac{1}{1+x^2}$, $f''(x) = \frac{-2x}{(1+x^2)^2}$. If $x \in [0, 1]$, then $f''(x) \in [-2, 0] = [f_{11}^{lo}, f_{11}^{hi}]$ and hence $|f''(x)| \le 2$. We compute

$$\forall x \in [0, 1], \ f(x) \le 0.04 + 0.21 \times 0.5 + 2 \times 0.5^3 \le 0.4.$$

We see that interval arithmetic with Taylor approximations works much better. Moreover, we don't need to abandon direct interval approximations completely: every time when we have to verify whether $f(D_i) < 0$ we can first find an interval approximation $\bar{f}(D_i)$ and then compute a Taylor approximation. If we don't get the inequality in both cases, then we subdivide the domain.

One simple trick which can be done with both interval and Taylor interval approximations is estimation of partial derivatives on a given domain. If it happens that $f_j(D_k) = \frac{\partial f}{\partial x_j}(D_k) \le 0$ or $f_j(D_k) \ge 0$ then it will be immediately possible to restrict further verifications to the boundary of $D_k = [\mathbf{a}, \mathbf{b}]$. Indeed, if $f_j(D_k) \le 0$ and $f(D_k|_{x_j=a_j}) < 0$ then $f(D_k) < 0$ since the function is decreasing along the j-th coordinate and its maximal value is attained at $x_j = a_j$. The same is true for increasing functions (consider $D_k|_{x_j=b_j}$). Moreover, if $\{x_j = a_j\}$ ($\{x_j = b_j\}$) is not on the boundary of the original domain D_k, then it is possible to completely ignore any further verifications for the region D_k. Indeed, if the restriction of D_k is not on the boundary of the original domain, then there is another subdomain D_j such that the restriction of D_k is a subset of D_j and the inequality is true on D_j. However, we need to be careful. Consider an example. Suppose $f(x) = -x^2 - 1$ and $D = [-1, 1]$. Assume that we have $D_1 = [-1, 0]$ and $D_2 = [0, 1]$. We get $f'(x) = -2x \ge 0$ on $[-1, 0]$. Hence, the function is increasing and we can consider the restricted domain $\{0\}$ which is not on the boundary of $[-1, 1]$. Also, $f'(x) = -2x \le 0$ on $[0, 1]$ and we again get $\{0\}$ as the restriction of $[0, 1]$. If we don't continue verifications in both cases, then we will not be able to verify the inequality. In order to avoid this problem, we always check a strict inequality for decreasing functions, that is, we test if $f_j(\mathbf{x}) \ge 0$ or $f_j(\mathbf{x}) < 0$.

Another trick is to check convexity of a function before subdividing a domain D_k. If we need to subdivide D_k and find that $f_{jj}(D) = \frac{\partial^2 f}{\partial x_j \partial x_j}(D) \ge 0$, then it is enough to verify $f(D_k|_{x_j=a_j}) < 0$ and $f(D_k|_{x_j=b_j}) < 0$. By convexity of f (i.e., f attains its maximum on the boundary), we get $f(D_k) < 0$ from these two inequalities.

2.2   Solution Certificate Search Procedure

An informal verification procedure based on the ideas presented above has been developed in C++ for informal verification of Flyspeck nonlinear inequalities [8]. The starting point of our implementation of a formal procedure for verification of nonlinear inequalities is a port of this original C++ program into OCaml. This OCaml program informally verifies a given nonlinear inequality on a rectangular domain by finding Taylor interval approximations and subdividing domains if necessary. The result of this program is just a boolean value: yes or no, the inequality true or false (there is the third option: verification could fail due to numerical instability or when subdomains become very small without any definite results).

We have modified the OCaml informal verification procedure such that it returns a partition of the original domain in a special tree-like structure which also contains all necessary information about verification steps for each subdomain. We call this structure a solution certificate for a given nonlinear inequality. The informal procedure is called the solution certificate search procedure.

A solution certificate is defined with the following OCaml record

```
type result_tree =
  | Result_false
  | Result_pass
  | Result_mono of mono_status list * result_tree
  | Result_glue of (int * bool * result_tree * result_tree)
  | Result_pass_mono of mono_status
  | Result_pass_ref of int
```

The record `mono_status` contains monotonicity information (i.e., whether some first-order partial derivative is negative or positive).

A simplified solution certificate search algorithm is given below in OCaml-like pseudo code.

```
let search f dom =
  let taylor_inteval = {find Taylor approximation of f on dom}
  let bounds = {taylor_interval bounds}
  if bounds >= 0 then
    Result_false
  else if bounds < 0 then
    Result_pass
  else
    let d_bounds = {find bounds of partial derivatives}
    let mono = {list of negative and positive partial derivatives}
    if {mono is not empty} then
      let r_dom = {restrict dom using information from mono}
        Result_mono mono (search f r_dom)
    else
      let dd_bounds = {find bounds of second partial derivatives}
```

```
if {the j-th second partial derivative is non-negative} then
  let dom1, dom2 = {restrict dom along j}
  let c1 = search f dom1
  let c2 = search f dom2
    Result_glue (j, true, c1, c2)
else
  let j = {find j such that b_i - a_i is maximal}
  let dom1, dom2 = {split dom along j}
  let c1 = search f dom1
  let c2 = search f dom2
    Result_glue (j, false, c1, c2)
```

If the inequality $f(x) < 0$ holds on D, then the algorithm (applied to f and D) will return a solution certificate which does not contain `Result_false` nodes. Of course, the real algorithm could fail due to numerical instabilities and rounding errors. This failure never happens for existing Flyspeck inequalities but it could happen for inequalities which require more precise floating-point arithmetic. In any case, the verification procedure described below will detect any possible errors in a solution certificate. A solution certificate does not contain any explicit information about subdomains for which verification must be performed. All subdomains can be restored from a solution certificate and the initial domain D. For each `Result_glue(j, false, c1, c2)` node, it is necessary to split the domain in two halves along the j-th coordinate. The second argument is the convexity flag. If it is true, then the current domain must be restricted to its left and right boundaries along the j-th coordinate. For new subdomains, the node contains their solution certificates: `c1` and `c2`. The domain also has to be modified for `Result_mono` nodes. Each node of this type contains a list of indices and boolean parameters (packed in `mono_status` record) which indicate for which partial derivatives the monotonicity argument should be applied; boolean parameters determine if the corresponding partial derivatives are positive or negative.

The simplified algorithm never returns nodes of type `Result_pass_mono`. The real solution certificate search algorithm is a little more complicated. Every time monotonicity argument is applied, it checks if the restricted domain is on the boundary of the original domain or not (the original domain is a parameter of the algorithm). If the restricted domain is not on the boundary of the original domain, then `Result_pass_mono` will be returned.

If a solution certificate contains nodes of type `Result_pass_mono`, then it is necessary to transform such a certificate to get new certificates which can be formally verified. Indeed, suppose we have a `Result_pass_mono` node and the corresponding domain is D_k. `Result_pass_mono` requires to apply the monotonicity argument to D_k, that is, to restrict this domain to its boundary along some coordinate. But it doesn't contain any information on how to verify the inequality on the restricted subdomain. We can only claim that there is another subdomain D_j (corresponding to some other node of a solution certificate) such that the restriction of D_k is a subset of D_j. In other words, to verify the inequality on D_k, we first need to find D_j such that the restriction of D_k is a subset of D_j and such that the inequality can be verified on D_j. To solve this problem, we transform a given solution certificate into a list of solution certificates and subdomains for which these new solution certificates work. Each solution certificate in the list may refer to previous solution certificates with `Result_ref`. The last solution certificate in the list corresponds to the original domain. The transformation algorithm is the following

```
let transform certificate acc =
    let sub_certs = {find all maximal sub-certificates
                     which does not contain Result_pass_mono}
    if {sub_certs contains certificate} then
        {add certificate to acc and return acc}
    else
        let sub_certs = {remove certificates consisting of single
                         Result_ref from sub_certs}
        let paths = {find paths to sub-certificates in sub_cert}
        let _ = {add sub_certs and the corresponding paths to acc}
        let new_cert1 = {replace all sub_certs in certificate
                         with references}
        let new_cert2 = {replace Result_pass_mono nodes in new_cert1
                         if they can be verified using subdomains
                         defined by paths in acc}
            transform new_cert2 acc
```

This algorithm maintains a list `acc` of solution certificates which do not contain nodes of type `Result_pass_mono`. The list also contains paths to subdomains corresponding to certificates. Each path is a list of pairs and it can be used to construct the corresponding subdomain starting from the original domain. Each pair is one of `("l", i)`, `("r", i)`, `("ml", i)`, or `("mr", i)` where i is an index. The `"l"` and `"r"` labels correspond to left and right subdomains after splitting; `"ml"` and `"mr"` correspond to left and right restricted subdomains. The index i specifies the coordinate along which the operation must be performed. When a reference node `Result_ref` is generated for a sub-certificate at the j-th position in the accumulator list `acc`, then the argument of `Result_ref` is j.

3   Formal Verification

The first step of developing a formal verification procedure is formalization of all necessary theories involving the multivariate Taylor theorem and related topics. Standard HOL Light libraries contain a formalization of Euclidean vector spaces [21] and define general Frechet derivatives and Jacobian matrices for working with first-order partial derivatives. Also, HOL Light contains the general univariate Taylor theorem. We formalized all other important results including the theory of partial derivatives, the equality of second-order mixed partial derivatives, the multivariate Taylor formula with the second-order error term.

The main formal verification step is to compute a formal Taylor interval approximation for a function $f : \mathbb{R}^n \to \mathbb{R}$ on a given domain $D = [\mathbf{a}, \mathbf{b}]$. Each formal Taylor approximation includes the following data: a point $\mathbf{y} = (\mathbf{a} + \mathbf{b})/2 \in D$, a vector $\mathbf{w}$ which estimates the width of the domain and has the property $\mathbf{w} \geq \max\{\mathbf{b} - \mathbf{y}, \mathbf{y} - \mathbf{a}\}$ (all operations are componentwise), an interval bound of $f(\mathbf{y}) \in [f^{lo}, f^{hi}]$, interval bounds of partial derivatives $f_i(\mathbf{y}) \in [f_i^{lo}, f_i^{hi}] = d_i$ for all $i = 1, \ldots, n$, interval bounds of second-order partial derivatives on the full domain $f_{ij}(\mathbf{x}) \in [f_{ij}^{lo}, f_{ij}^{hi}] = d_{ij}$ for all $i = 1, \ldots, n$, $j \leq i$, and $\mathbf{x} \in D$. Based on this data, an interval approximation of $f(\mathbf{x})$ and its partial derivatives on D can be computed. For instance, the following theorem gives an interval approximation of $f(\mathbf{x})$ when $n = 2$

$$w_1|d_1| + w_2|d_2| \leq b \,\wedge\, w_1(w_1|d_{1,1}|) + w_2(w_2|d_{2,2}| + 2w_1|d_{2,1}|) \leq e$$

$$\wedge\, b + 2^{-1}e \leq a \,\wedge\, l \leq f^{lo} - a \,\wedge\, f^{hi} + a \leq h$$

$$\implies \big(\forall \mathbf{x}, \ \mathbf{x} \in [\mathbf{a}, \mathbf{b}] \implies f(\mathbf{x}) \in [l, h]\big).$$

(Here, $|d_i| = |[f_i^{lo}, f_i^{hi}]| = \max\{-f_i^{lo}, f_i^{hi}\}$.)

Formal computations of Taylor interval approximations require a lot of basic arithmetic operations. We implemented efficient procedures for working with natural numbers and real numbers in HOL Light. Our implementation of formal natural number arithmetic works with numerals in an arbitrary fixed base. Our implementation improves the performance of standard HOL Light arithmetic operations with natural numbers by the factor $\log_2 b$ (where b is a fixed base constant) for linear operations (in the size of input arguments) and by the factor $(\log_2 b)^2$ for quadratic operations. We approximate real numbers with floating-point numbers which have fixed precision of the mantissa. This precision is controlled by an informal parameter which specifies the maximal number of digits in results of formal floating-point operations. All formal floating-point operations yield inequality theorems which approximate real results from above or below. Formal verification procedures are based on our implementation of interval arithmetic which works with formal floating-point numbers. We also cache results of all basic arithmetic operations to improve the performance of formal computations.

A description of our formal verification procedure is technical and it can be found in [3]. Here we give an example which demonstrates how the formal verification procedure works. Let $f(x) = x - 2$ and we want to prove $f(x) < 0$ for $x \in [-1, 1]$. Suppose that we have the following solution certificate

```
Result_glue {1, false,
    Result_pass_mono {[1, incr]},
    Result_mono {[1, incr],
        Result_pass
    }
}
```

This certificate tells that the inequality may be verified by first splitting the domain into two subdomains along the first (and the only) variable; then the left branch follows from some other formal verification result by monotonicity (`Result_pass_mono`); the right branch follows by the monotonicity argument and by a direct verification. This certificate cannot be used directly for a formal verification since we don't know how the left branch is proved. The first step is to transform this certificate into a list of certificates such that each certificate can be verified on subdomains specified by the corresponding paths. We get the following list of certificates

```
[
  ["r", 1], Result_mono {[1], Result_pass};
  ["l", 1], Result_mono {[1], Result_ref {0}};
  [], Result_glue {1, false, Result_ref {1}, Result_ref {0}}
]
```

The first element corresponds to the right branch of the original `Result_glue` (hence, the path is `["r", 1]` which means subdivision along the first variable and taking the right subdomain). A formal verification of the first certificate yields $\vdash x \in [0,1] \implies f(x) < 0$. The second result is the transformed left branch of the original certificate. This transformed result explicitly refers to the first proved result (`Result_ref {0}`). Now it can be verified. Indeed, `Result_ref {0}` yields $\vdash x \in [0,0] \implies f(x) < 0$ (since $[0,0] \subset [0,1]$ and we have the theorem for $[0,1]$ which we use in the reference). Then the monotonicity argument

$$(\forall x, \ x \in [-1,0] \implies 0 \le f'(x)) \wedge (\forall x, x \in [0,0] \implies f(x) < 0)$$
$$\implies (\forall x, x \in [-1,0] \implies f(x) < 0)$$

yields $\vdash x \in [-1,0] \implies f(x) < 0$. The last entry of the list refers to two proved results and glues them together in the right order:

$$(\forall x, \ x \in [-1,0] \implies f(x) < 0) \wedge (\forall x, \ x \in [0,1] \implies f(x) < 0)$$
$$\implies (\forall x, \ x \in [-1,1] \implies f(x) < 0)$$

4   Optimization Techniques and Future Work

4.1   Implemented Optimization Techniques

There are several optimization techniques for formal verification of nonlinear inequalities. One of the basic ideas of optimization techniques is to compute extra information for solution certificates which helps to increase the performance of formal verification procedures.

The first optimization technique is to try direct interval evaluations without Taylor approximations. If a direct interval evaluation yields a desired result (verification of an inequality on a domain or verification of a monotonicity property), then a special flag is added to the corresponding certificate node.

This flag indicates that it is not necessary to compute full formal Taylor interval and it is enough to evaluate the function directly with interval arithmetic (which is faster). These flags are added to `Result_pass` and `Result_mono` nodes.

An important optimization procedure is to find the best (minimal) precision which is sufficient for verifying an inequality on each subdomain. We have a special informal implementation of all arithmetic, Taylor interval evaluation, and verification functions which compute results in the same way as the corresponding formal functions. This informal implementation is much simpler (because it does not prove anything) and faster (since it does not prove anything and all basic arithmetic is done by native machine arithmetic). For a given solution certificate, we run a modified informal verification procedure which tests different precision parameter values for each certificate node. It finds out the smallest value of the precision parameter for each certificate node such that the verification result is correct. Then a modified solution certificate is created where each node contains information about the best precision parameter. A special version of the formal verification procedure accepts this new certificate and verifies the inequality with computed precision parameters. This adaptive precision technique increases the performance of formal arithmetic computations.

4.2   Future Work

There are some optimization ideas which are not implemented yet. The first idea is to stop computations of bounds of second-order partial derivatives for Taylor intervals at some point and reuse bounds computed for larger domains. The error term in Taylor approximation depends quadratically on the size of a domain. When domains are sufficiently small, good approximations of bounds of second-order partial derivatives are not very important. This strategy could save quite a lot of verification time since formal evaluation of second-order partial derivative bounds is expensive for many functions.

Another unimplemented optimization is verification of sets of similar inequalities on the same domain. The idea is to reuse results of formal computations as much as possible for inequalities which have a similar structure and which are verified on the same domains. The basic strategy is to find a subdivision of the domain into subdomains such that each inequality in the set can be completely verified on each subdomain. If inequalities in the set share a lot of similar computations, then the verification of all inequalities in the set could be almost as fast as the verification of the most difficult inequality in the set. This approach should work well for Flyspeck inequalities where many inequalities share the same sub-expressions and domains.

An important unimplemented feature is verification of disjunctions of inequalities. That is, we want to verify inequalities in the form

$$\forall \mathbf{x} \in D \implies f_1(\mathbf{x}) < 0 \ \lor \ f_2(\mathbf{x}) < 0 \ \lor \ \ldots \ \lor \ f_k(\mathbf{x}) < 0.$$

This form is equivalent to an inequality on a non-rectangular domain since

$$(P(\mathbf{x}) \implies f(\mathbf{x}) < 0 \ \lor \ g(\mathbf{x}) < 0) \iff (P(\mathbf{x}) \land 0 \le g(\mathbf{x}) \implies f(\mathbf{x}) < 0).$$

Many Flyspeck inequalities are in this form. A formal verification of these inequalities is simple. It is enough to add indices of functions for which the inequality is satisfied to the corresponding nodes of solution certificates. Then it will be only necessary to modify the formal gluing procedure. It should be able to combine inequalities for different functions with disjunctions.

5 Results and Tests

This section briefly introduces the implemented verification tool and presents some test results for several polynomial and non-polynomial inequalities. We also compare the performance of the formal verification tool and the informal C++ verification procedure for Flyspeck nonlinear inequalities. All tests were performed on Intel Core i5, 2.67GHz running Ubuntu 9.10 inside Virtual Box 4.2.0 on a Windows 7 host; the Ocaml version was 3.09.3; the base of arithmetic was 200.

5.1 Overview of the Formal Verification Tool

A user manual which contains information about the tool and installation instructions is available at [2]. Here, we briefly describe how the tool can be used.

Suppose we want to verify a polynomial inequality

$$-\frac{1}{\sqrt{3}} \leq x \leq \sqrt{2} \ \wedge \ -\sqrt{\pi} \leq y \leq 1 \ \Longrightarrow \ x^2 y - xy^4 + y^6 + x^4 - 7 > -7.17995.$$

The following HOL Light script solves this problem

```
needs "verifier/m_verifier_main.hl";;
open M_verifier_main;;

let ineq = '-- &1 / sqrt(&3) <= x /\ x <= sqrt(&2)
           /\ -- sqrt(pi) <= y /\ y <= &1
           ==> x pow 2 * y - x * y pow 4 + y pow 6 - &7 + x pow 4
               > -- #7.17995';;

let th, stats = verify_ineq default_params 5 ineq;;
```

First two lines of the script load the verification tool. The main verification function is called `verify_ineq`. It takes 3 arguments. The first argument contains verification options. In most cases, it is enough to provide default options `default_params`. The second parameter specifies the precision of formal floating-point operations. The third parameter is the inequality itself given as a HOL Light term. The format of this term is simple: it is an implication with bounds of variables in the antecedent and an inequality in the consequent. The bounds of all variables should be in the form *a constant expression* $\leq x$ or $x \leq$ *a constant expression*. For each variable, upper and lower bounds must be given. The inequality must be a strict inequality ($<$ or $>$). The inequality may include `sqrt` ($\sqrt{\ }$), `atn` (arctan), and `acs` (arccos) functions. The constant `pi` (π) is also allowed.

The verification function returns a HOL Light theorem and a record with some verification information which includes verification time.

5.2   Polynomial Inequalities

Here is a list of test polynomial inequalities taken from [17].

– schwefel

$$\langle x_1, x_2, x_3 \rangle \in [\langle -10, -10, -10 \rangle, \langle 10, 10, 10 \rangle]$$
$$\implies -5.8806 \times 10^{-10} < (x_1 - x_2^2)^2 + (x_2 - 1)^2 + (x_1 - x_3^2)^2 + (x_3 - 1)^2.$$

– caprasse

$$\langle x_1, x_2, x_3, x_4 \rangle \in [\langle -0.5, -0.5, -0.5, -0.5 \rangle, \langle 0.5, 0.5, 0.5, 0.5 \rangle]$$
$$\implies -3.1801 < -x_1 x_3^3 + 4x_2 x_3^2 x_4 + 4x_1 x_3 x_4^2 + 2x_2 x_4^3$$
$$+ 4x_1 x_3 + 4x_3^2 - 10x_2 x_4 - 10x_4^2 + 2.$$

– magnetism

$$\langle x_1, x_2, x_3, x_4, x_5, x_6, x_7 \rangle \in [\langle -1, -1, -1, -1, -1, -1, -1 \rangle, \langle 1, 1, 1, 1, 1, 1, 1 \rangle]$$
$$\implies -0.25001 < x_1^2 + 2x_2^2 + 2x_3^2 + 2x_4^2 + 2x_5^2 + 2x_6^2 + 2x_7^2 - x_1.$$

– heart

$$\langle x_1, x_2, x_3, x_4, x_5, x_6, x_7, x_8 \rangle \in [\langle -0.1, 0.4, -0.7, -0.7, 0.1, -0.1, -0.3, -1.1 \rangle,$$
$$\langle 0.4, 1, -0.4, 0.4, 0.2, 0.2, 1.1, -0.3 \rangle]$$
$$\implies -1.7435 < -x_1 x_6^3 + 3x_1 x_6 x_7^2 - x_3 x_7^3 + 3x_3 x_7 x_6^2 - x_2 x_5^3$$
$$+ 3x_2 x_5 x_8^2 - x_4 x_8^3 + 3x_4 x_8 x_5^2 - 0.9563453.$$

Performance test results are given in Table 1. The column *total time* contains total verification time, the column *formal* contains time of the formal verification only. The formal verification excludes all preliminary processes: computations of partial derivatives, search of solution certificates, adaptive precision search procedures. The last two columns show the corresponding verification time for the PVS procedure which is based on the Bernstein polynomial technique and described in [17].

Test results show that our procedure is faster than the Bernstein polynomial procedure in PVS for most cases. On the other hand, there still exist cases where our tool is slower.

Table 1. Polynomial inequalities

Inequality ID	total time (s)	formal (s)	total PVS (s)	formal PVS (s)
schwefel	26.33	19.15	10.23	3.18
caprasse	8.06	1.29	11.44	1.25
magnetism	7.01	1.35	160.44	82.87
heart	17.30	1.28	79.68	26.14

5.3 Flyspeck Inequalities

The Flyspeck project contains 985 nonlinear inequalities. The informal verification program written in C++ can verify all these inequalities in about 10 hours. Most inequalities (683) can be informally verified in less than 10 seconds. Almost all inequalities (911) can be informally verified in less than 100 seconds.

We tested our formal verification procedure on several simple Flyspeck inequalities. Some of these inequalities are listed below. Table 2 contains performance test results for these inequalities. The column *total time* contains total formal verification time, the column *formal* contains time of the formal verification only (excluding all preliminary processes), the column *informal* contains informal verification time by the C++ program.

$$\Delta(x_1, \ldots, x_6) = x_1 x_4(-x_1 + x_2 + x_3 - x_4 + x_5 + x_6)$$
$$+ x_2 x_5(x_1 - x_2 + x_3 + x_4 - x_5 + x_6)$$
$$+ x_3 x_6(x_1 + x_2 - x_3 + x_4 + x_5 - x_6)$$
$$- x_2 x_3 x_4 - x_1 x_3 x_5 - x_1 x_2 x_6 - x_4 x_5 x_6,$$

$$\mathrm{dih}_x\,(x_1, \ldots, x_6) = \frac{\pi}{2} - \arctan\left(\frac{-\partial\Delta(x_1, \ldots, x_6)/\partial x_4}{\sqrt{4x_1\Delta(x_1, \ldots, x_6)}}\right),$$

$$\mathrm{dih}_y\,(y_1, \ldots, y_6) = \mathrm{dih}_x\,(y_1^2, \ldots, y_6^2).$$

– 4717061266

$$4 \le x_i \le 6.3504 \implies \Delta(x_1, x_2, x_3, x_4, x_5, x_6) > 0.$$

– 7067938795

$$4 \le x_{1,2,3} \le 6.3504, \; x_4 = 4, \; 3.01^2 \le x_{5,6} \le 3.24^2$$
$$\implies \mathrm{dih}_x\,(x_1, \ldots, x_6) - \pi/2 + 0.46 < 0.$$

– 3318775219

$$2 \le y_i \le 2.52 \implies 0 < \mathrm{dih}_y\,(y_1, \ldots, y_6) - 1.629 - 0.763(y_4 - 2.52)$$
$$- 0.315(y_1 - 2.0) + 0.414(y_2 + y_3 + y_5 + y_6 - 8.0).$$

Table 2. Flyspeck inequalities

Inequality ID	total time (s)	formal (s)	informal (s)
2485876245a	5.530	0.058	0
4559601669b	4.679	0.048	0
4717061266	27.1	0.250	0
5512912661	8.860	0.086	0.002
6096597438a	0.071	0.071	0
6843920790	2.824	0.076	0.002
SDCCMGA b	9.012	0.949	0.006
7067938795	431	387	0.070
5490182221	1726	1533	0.375
3318775219	17091	15226	8.000

Table 3. Flyspeck inequalities which can be informally verified in 1 second

time interval (ms)	# inequalities	total time (s)	formal (s)	informal (s)
0	57	423	2.159	0
1–100	35	5546	3854	1.134
101–500	11	12098	10451	3.944
501–700	14	32065	28705	8.423
701–1000	9	19040	16688	7.274

We also found formal verification time of all Flyspeck inequalities which can be verified in less than one second and which do not contain disjunctions of inequalities. Table 3 summarizes test results. The columns *total time* and *formal* show total formal verification time and formal verification time without preliminary processes for the corresponding sets of inequalities. The column *informal* contains informal verification time for the same sets of inequalities.

Test results show that our formal verification procedure is about 2000–4000 times slower than the informal verification program.

References

1. Harrison, J.: The HOL Light theorem prover (2010),
   http://www.cl.cam.ac.uk/~jrh13/hol-light/index.html
2. Solovyev, A.: A tool for formal verification of nonlinear inequalities (2012),
   http://flyspeck.googlecode.com/files/FormalVerifier.pdf
3. Solovyev, A.: Formal Computations and Methods. PhD thesis, University of Pittsburgh (2012), http://d-scholarship.pitt.edu/16721/
4. Hales, T.C.: Introduction to the Flyspeck project. In: Coquand, T., Lombardi, H., Roy, M.F. (eds.) Mathematics, Algorithms, Proofs. Dagstuhl Seminar Proceedings, vol. 05021, Internationales Begegnungs- und Forschungszentrum für Informatik (IBFI), Schloss Dagstuhl, Germany (2006),
   http://drops.dagstuhl.de/opus/volltexte/2006/432
5. Hales, T.C.: The Flyspeck Project (2012), http://code.google.com/p/flyspeck

6. Hales, T.C., Ferguson, S.P.: The Kepler conjecture. Discrete and Computational Geometry 36(1), 1–269 (2006)
7. Hales, T.C.: Dense Sphere Packings: a blueprint for formal proofs. London Math. Soc. Lecture Note Series, vol. 400. Cambridge University Press (2012)
8. Hales, T.C.: Some algorithms arising in the proof of the Kepler conjecture. Discrete and Computational Geometry 25, 489–507 (2003)
9. Tarski, A.: A decision method for elementary algebra and geometry, 2nd edn. University of California Press, Berkeley and Los Angeles (1951)
10. Collins, G.E.: Quantifier elimination for real closed fields by cylindrical algebraic decomposition. In: Brakhage, H. (ed.) GI-Fachtagung 1975. LNCS, vol. 33, pp. 134–183. Springer, Heidelberg (1975)
11. McLaughlin, S., Harrison, J.: A proof-producing decision procedure for real arithmetic. In: Nieuwenhuis, R. (ed.) CADE 2005. LNCS (LNAI), vol. 3632, pp. 295–314. Springer, Heidelberg (2005)
12. Harrison, J.: Verifying nonlinear real formulas via sums of squares. In: Schneider, K., Brandt, J. (eds.) TPHOLs 2007. LNCS, vol. 4732, pp. 102–118. Springer, Heidelberg (2007)
13. Akbarpour, B., Paulson, L.C.: MetiTarski: An automatic prover for the elementary functions. In: Autexier, S., Campbell, J., Rubio, J., Sorge, V., Suzuki, M., Wiedijk, F. (eds.) AISC/Calculemus/MKM 2008. LNCS (LNAI), vol. 5144, pp. 217–231. Springer, Heidelberg (2008)
14. Paulson, L.C.: MetiTarski: Past and future. In: Beringer, L., Felty, A. (eds.) ITP 2012. LNCS, vol. 7406, pp. 1–10. Springer, Heidelberg (2012)
15. Chevillard, S., Harrison, J., Jolde, M., Lauter, C.: Efficient and accurate computation of upper bounds of approximation errors. Theor. Comput. Sci. 412(16), 1523–1543 (2011)
16. Zumkeller, R.: Global Optimization in Type Theory. PhD thesis, École Polytechnique Paris (2008)
17. Muñoz, C., Narkawicz, A.: Formalization of a representation of Bernstein polynomials and applications to global optimization. Journal of Automated Reasoning (2012) (accepted for publication)
18. Zumkeller, R.: Formal global optimisation with Taylor models. In: Furbach, U., Shankar, N. (eds.) IJCAR 2006. LNCS (LNAI), vol. 4130, pp. 408–422. Springer, Heidelberg (2006)
19. Zumkeller, R.: Sergei. A Global Optimization Tool (2009), http://code.google.com/p/sergei/
20. Daumas, M., Lester, D., Muñoz, C.: Verified real number calculations: A library for interval arithmetic. IEEE Transactions on Computers 58(2), 226–237 (2009)
21. Harrison, J.V.: A HOL theory of Euclidean space. In: Hurd, J., Melham, T. (eds.) TPHOLs 2005. LNCS, vol. 3603, pp. 114–129. Springer, Heidelberg (2005)

Verifying a Privacy CA Remote Attestation Protocol*

Brigid Halling and Perry Alexander

Information and Telecommunication Technology Center
The University of Kansas
{bhalling,palexand}@ku.edu

Abstract. As the hardware root-of-trust in a trusted computing environment, the Trusted Platform Module (TPM) warrants formal specification and verification. This work presents results of an effort to specify and verify an abstract TPM 1.2 model using PVS that is useful for understanding the TPM and verifying protocols that utilize it. TPM commands are specified as state transformations and sequenced to represent protocols using a state monad. Postconditions and invariants are specified for individual commands and validated by verifying a Privacy CA attestation protocol. All specifications are written and verified automatically using the PVS decision procedures and rewriting system.

1   Introduction

At the heart of trusted computing [3] is the need to appraise a remote system in a trusted fashion. In this process – known as *remote attestation* [4,5,11] – an external appraiser sends an attestation request to an appraisal target and receives a quote used to assess the remote system's state. To achieve its goal, the appraiser must not only analyze the quote's contents, but also assess the trustworthiness of the information it contains.

The Trusted Platform Module (TPM) and its associated Trusted Software Stack (TSS) [1] provide core functionality for assembling and delivering a quote for appraisal with high integrity as well as binding confidential data to a specific platform. However, neither the TPM nor TSS have been formally specified or verified. Definitions of the over 90 current TPM commands as well as additional TSS commands are embedded in more than 700 pages of English documentation.

We formally specify and verify a remote attestation protocol – known as the Privacy CA Protocol – using commands from TPM version 1.2. Our objective is to capture an abstract specification from the TPM specification, validate it, and use it to verify the correctness of the Privacy CA Protocol. We are not making an argument for the protocol itself, we are merely verifying this protocol as a part of verifying the TPM. We use PVS [14] for our work, however the results and approach generalize to other tools.

---

* This work was sponsored in part by the Battelle Memorial Institute under PO US001-0000328568.

G. Brat, N. Rungta, and A. Venet (Eds.): NFM 2013, LNCS 7871, pp. 398–412, 2013.

1.1   Trusted Platform Module

The Trusted Platform Module (TPM) [1] is a hardware co-processor that provides cryptographic functions at the heart of establishing and maintaining a trusted computing infrastructure [3]. The TPM's functionality can be distilled into three major capabilities: (i) establishing, maintaining, and protecting a unique identifier; (ii) storing and securely reporting system measurements; and (iii) binding secrets to a specific platform.

The *endorsement key* (EK) and *storage root key* (SRK) are persistent asymmetric keys maintained by the TPM. EK uniquely identifies the TPM and EK^{-1} is maintained confidentially while EK encrypts secrets for use by TPM. EK^{-1} could theoretically sign TPM data, but is never used for this purpose to avoid unintended information aggregation. Instead, it provides a root-of-trust for reporting used in the attestation process. The SRK provides a root key for chaining *wrapped keys*. A wrapped key is an asymmetric key pair whose private key is encrypted by another asymmetric key. The resulting wrapped key can be safely stored outside the TPM and may only be installed and used if its wrapping key is installed. Using the SRK as the root of these chains binds information to its associated TPM.

A *platform configuration register* (PCR) is a special purpose register for storing and extending hashes within the TPM. As its name implies, a PCR records a platform's configuration during boot or at run time. The TPM ensures the integrity of PCRs and uses a quote mechanism to deliver them with integrity to an external appraiser. Rather than being set to a specific value, PCRs are extended using the formula $pcr \parallel h = SHA1(pcr + h)$. These hashes – called *measurements* – are gathered in PCRs at various points during system operation, but the most common use is to ensure trusted boot. As each system component boots, images and data are hashed, and each hash is used to extend a PCR. The nature of extension implies that at the conclusion of the boot process, the hashes in PCRs indicate whether the right parts were used in the right order during boot. Specifically, ideal PCR extension exhibits the property that $h_0 \parallel h_1 = h_1 \parallel h_0 \Leftrightarrow h_0 = h_1$. The only way to change a PCR value is with a platform reboot or by using the command TPM_Extend.

1.2   Privacy CA Protocol

Remote Attestation using a TPM is the process of gathering PCRs and delivering them to an external appraiser in a trusted fashion [9]. By examining the reported contents of PCRs, the appraiser can determine whether it trusts the system described. Using hashes guarantees the appraiser only learns whether the right system is running and nothing more. Our remote attestation method is to use a *Privacy Certificate Authority* (CA or Privacy CA) that produces an identity certificate verifying that an *attestation identity key* (AIK) public key belongs to a certain TPM using its EK. The Privacy CA is so named because it protects the EK while assuring the AIK belongs to the right EK. This protocol is shown in figure 1.

An AIK, wrapped by the SRK, is created using the TPM's `TPM_MakeIdentity` command and can only be used by the TPM that generated it. The command also returns a CA label digest identifying the CA certifying the AIK, and the public AIK signed with AIK^{-1}. The AIK signature tells us that the AIK came from the right TPM since the TPM that generated the AIK is the only entity with access to its private key. Using the public key embedded in the certificate, the CA can determine if the entire certificate did indeed come from the TPM associated with the AIK.

Although we are modeling the TPM, we also need to model the role of the Privacy CA. This interaction between the CA and the User is modeled by `CA_certify`. The CA returns a session key (identified as K with figure 1) encrypted by the public EK associated with the TPM that claims to have requested the certificate. `TPM_ActivateIdentity` attempts to decrypt K using the TPM's EK^{-1} and releases if it decrypts successfully. Finally, we are able to use the AIK to sign PCR values using the TPM command `TPM_Quote` [1]. This quote is returned to the User who can then send back to the appraiser the information that it needs. The command `CPU_BuildQuoteFromMemory` simulates this final step generating for the appraiser an evidence package of the form:

$$(\{|\{|AIK|\}_{CA^{-1}}|\}_{AIK^{-1}}, \{|n, PCR|\}_{AIK^{-1}}) \tag{1}$$

where: $\{|n, PCR|\}_{AIK^{-1}}$ is the nonce from the appraiser's request and desired PCR values; $\{|\{|AIK|\}_{CA^{-1}}|\}_{AIK^{-1}}$ is the certificate from a Privacy CA and public AIK; and both are signed by the AIK.

2   System Model

The overall approach we take for verifying the TPM is to establish a *weak bisimulation* [17] relation between an abstract requirements model and a concrete model derived from the TPM specification. Both the abstract and concrete models define transition systems in terms of system state and transitions over that system state. Here we address only the abstract model, useful in its own right for modeling protocols and verifying operations. Here we describe our abstract model of the TPM, including data structures and command execution.

2.1   Data Model

Our abstraction of data relevant to the TPM is defined in the PVS data type `tpmData`. Figure 2 shows a subset of this data that is relevant to verifying the remote attestation protocol. It may be noted that most elements of our `tpmData` data type include a tag that shows what cryptographic operations have been performed on data using the `CRYPTOSTATUS` type. These functions include encryption, signing, and sealing. For example, a symmetric key identified as `k:KVAL` and signed with the private key of `idKey:(tpmKey?)` is expressed as:

```
tpmSessKey(k, signed(private(idKey), clear))
```

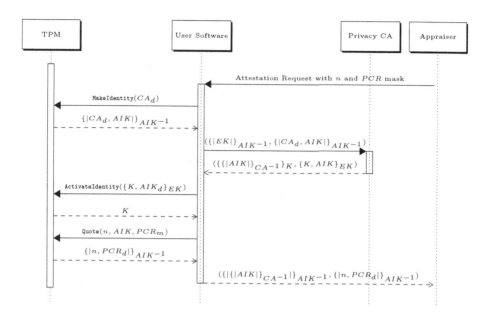

Fig. 1. Sequence diagram for the Privacy CA protocol

```
tpmData : DATATYPE
BEGIN
 tpmDigest(digest:list[tpmData],crs:CRYPTOSTATUS) : tpmDigest?
 tpmNonce : tpmNonce?
 tpmSessKey(skey:KVAL,crs:CRYPTOSTATUS) : tpmSessKey?
 tpmKey(key:KVAL,usage:KEY_USAGE,flags:KEY_FLAGS,PCRInfo:list[PCR],
    wrappingKey:KVAL,crs:CRYPTOSTATUS) : tpmKey?
 tpmQuote(digest:list[PCR],nonce:(tpmNonce?),crs:CRYPTOSTATUS) : tpmQuote?
 tpmIdContents(digest:(tpmDigest?),aik:(tpmKey?),
    crs:CRYPTOSTATUS) : tpmIdContents?
 tpmAsymCAContents(sessK:(tpmSessKey?),idDigest:(tpmDigest?),
    crs:CRYPTOSTATUS) : tpmAsymCAContents?
 ...
END tpmData;
```

Fig. 2. Data structure for abstract TPM data

A `tpmDigest` structure contains the list of things that are concatenated and then hashed to create the digest value – $SHA1(d_0 +\!\!+ d_1 +\!\!+ ... +\!\!+ d_n)$ while `tpmSessKey` is our representation of a symmetric key. Finally, the `tpmKey` structure represents an asymmetric key with additional properties used by the TPM. These include its usage, associated flags, and PCR information for wrapping. Virtually all asymmetric keys used by the TPM are created as wrapped keys. Thus, a reference to the wrapping key is part of the `tpmKey` structure. The type `KVAL` associated with all keys is an integer value that uniquely identifies the key.

2.2   Abstract State

The TPM manages state by maintaining several data fields and flags. We use a PVS record structure, referred to as `tpmAbsState` and shown in figure 3, to maintain an abstract view of this state as well as the memory associated with the environment where the TPM is being run. Elements key to the remote attestation protocol include `srk`, `ek`, `pcrs`, and `memory`.

```
tpmAbsState : TYPE =
  [# restore : restoreStateData, memory : mem, srk : (tpmKey?),
     ek : (tpmKey?), keyGenCnt : K, keys : KEYSET, pcrs : PCRS,
     locality : LOCALITY, permFlags : PermFlags, permData : PermData #];
```

Fig. 3. Abstract TPM and system state record data structure

The `srk` and the `ek` represent the asymmetric keys SRK and EK used by the TPM as roots of trust previously discussed in section 1.1. `memory` is not part of the actual TPM, but represents the memory used by the TPMs environment for storing values. This is necessary for our model due to our method of command sequencing discussed in section 2.6.

`pcrs` is an array of hash sequences that define the value of a PCR. Rather than calculate the hash, a sequence of values used to create the PCR value is maintained. One unusual feature of PCRs is they can have one of two initial values. Resettable PCRs initialize to -1 (all 1s) while non-resettable PCRs reset to 0. This feature along together with PCR locality is used by the appraiser determine if the `senter` command is called during boot.

2.3   Abstract Command Definitions

Figure 4 shows the PVS data type `tpmAbsInput` that represents the abstract syntax of the TPM command set. Each `TPM_Command` will have a corresponding `ABS_Command` in the `tpmAbsInput` data structure. This approach gives us an induction principle for the command set automatically usable by PVS to quantify over all possible TPM inputs.

```
tpmAbsInput : DATATYPE
BEGIN
 ABS_MakeIdentity(CADigest:(tpmDigest?),aikParams:(tpmKey?))
    : ABS_MakeIdentity?
 ABS_ActivateIdentity(aik:(tpmKey?),blob:(tpmAsymCAContents?))
    : ABS_ActivateIdentity?
 ABS_Extend(pcrNum:PCRINDEX,d:HV) : ABS_Extend?
 ABS_Quote(aik:(tpmKey?),nonce:(tpmNonce?),pm:PCRMASK) : ABS_Quote?
 ABS_certify(aik:(tpmKey?),certReq:(tpmIdContents?)) : ABS_certify?
 ABS_save(i:nat,v:tpmAbsOutput) : ABS_save?
 ABS_read(i:nat) : ABS_read?
 ...
END tpmAbsInput;
```

Fig. 4. Representative elements from the TPM command data type

Within the `tpmAbsInput` data structure, the arguments to each command are abstract representations of the actual TPM data formats and come from `tpmData` data type. This is appropriate for an abstract model such as ours where we are capturing functionality, not implementation. Some details are abstracted away when they do not contribute to verifying the basic functionality of the device.

2.4 Abstract Outputs

Like inputs to the TPM, outputs are modeled abstractly using an algebraic type. Again we avoid the complexity of bit-level representations specified in the TPM standard in favor of an abstract representation that captures the essence of TPM functionality. Figure 5 shows the representation of this type.

Each TPM command returns an output, often just to return the message that the command was successfully run. The `tpmAbsOutput` constructs allow for each command to return the correct output parameters as well as a return code. These return codes either indicate success or a non-fatal error. Fatal errors from TPM commands are generated using the `OUT_Error` construct, while non-TPM-related fatal errors are generated using `OUT_CPUError`.

2.5 Abstract Command Execution

The technique for specifying TPM command execution is to define state transition and output functions in the canonical fashion for transition systems. Specifically, we define the `executeCom` function as a transition from `tpmAbsState` (figure 3) and `tpmAbsInput` (figure 4) to `tpmAbsState`:

```
executeCom : tpmAbsState → tpmInput → tpmAbsState
```

and the function `outputCom` to transform `tmpAbsState` and `tpmAbsInput` into a `tpmAbsOutput` (figure 5) value:

```
tpmAbsOutput : DATATYPE
BEGIN
 OUT_MakeIdentity(aik:(tpmKey?),idc:(tpmIdContents?),m:ReturnCode)
   : OUT_MakeIdentity?
 OUT_ActivateIdentity(symmKey:(tpmSessKey?),m:ReturnCode)
   : OUT_ActivateIdentity?
 OUT_Extend(outDigest:PCR,m:ReturnCode) : OUT_Extend?
 OUT_Quote(pcrData:list[PCR],sig:(tpmQuote?),m:ReturnCode) : OUT_Quote?
 OUT_FullQuote(q:(tpmQuote?),idc:(tpmIdContents?),m:cpuReturn)
   : OUT_FullQuote?
 OUT_Certify(data:(tpmAsymCAContents?),m:cpuReturn) : OUT_Certify?
 OUT_Error(m:ReturnCode) : OUT_Error?
 OUT_CPUError(m:cpuReturn) : OUT_CPUError?
 ...
END tpmAbsOutput;
```

Fig. 5. Abstract TPM output record data structure

```
outputCom : tpmAbsState → tpmAbsInput → tpmAbsOutput
```

Given $s : tpmAbsState$ and $c : tpmAbsInput$, the output, state pair resulting from executing c is defined as:

$$(\text{outputCom}(s, c), \text{executeCom}(s, c))$$

As one would expect, executeCom and outputCom are defined by cases over tpmAbsInput. Specifically, for each command in tpmAbsInput a function is defined for generating the next state and for generating output. These commands are named within the specification using the suffix State and Out respectively for easy identification.

For example, consider the ABS_MakeIdentity input. At its core, the command TPM_MakeIdentity creates the AIK and returns the public AIK key for use in other operations as well as a tpmIdContents structure. This tpmIdContents structure, containing the identity of the privacy CA that the owner expects to certify the AIK and the AIK (see figure 5 for the OUT_MakeIdentity structure and figure 2 for the tpmIdContents structure), is signed by the private AIK [1].

The function makeIdentityState defines how the TPM state is modified (a new key value for the AIK is created):

```
makeIdentityState(s:tpmAbsState,CADigest:(tpmDigest?),
   aikParams:(tpmKey?)) : tpmAbsState =
 IF identity?(keyUsage(aikParams))
    AND not(migratable(keyFlags(aikParams)))
  THEN s WITH ['keyGenCnt := keyGenCnt(s)+1]
  ELSE s
  ENDIF;
```

while, the function `makeIdentityOut` defines the TPM output generated by the command:

```
makeIdentityOut(s:tpmAbsState,CADigest:(tpmDigest?),
     aikParams:(tpmKey?)) : tpmAbsOutput =
  IF identity?(keyUsage(aikParams))
     AND not(migratable(keyFlags(aikParams)))
   THEN LET aik:(tpmKey?) = tpmKey(keyGenCnt(s), keyUsage(aikParams),
                                   keyFlags(aikParams), pcrs(s),
                                   wrappingKey(srk(s)),clear) IN
         LET idBinding = tpmIdContents(CADigest, aik,
                                   signed(private(aik),clear)) IN
              OUT_MakeIdentity(aik,idBinding,TPM_SUCCESS)
   ELSE OUT_Error(TPM_INVALID_KEYUSAGE)
  ENDIF;
```

Functions like `makeIdentityState` and `makeIdentityOut` define the functionality associated with `ABS_MakeIdentity`. They are associated with the command in the `executeCom` and `outputCom` using a case structure defined over `tpmAbsInput`. Since all TPM commands return at least a success or error message, all abstract commands generate output, but not all commands modify state. In instances where the state is not modified, the `CASES` construct used to assemble the functions defaults to not modifying the state.

2.6   Sequencing Command Execution

TPM commands are executed in sequence like assembly commands in a traditional microprocessor. To validate the abstract model as well as verify TPM protocols, a mechanism must be chosen to sequence command execution. Such sequencing of TPM commands is a matter of using the output state from one command as the input to the next command. The classical mechanism for doing this involves executing a command and manually feeding its resulting state to the next command in sequence. Using a `LET` form, to execute `i;i'` would look like the following:

```
LET (o',s') = (outputCom(s,i),executeCom(s,i)) IN
   (outputCom(s',i'),executeCom(s',i'))
```

We choose to use an alternative approach that uses a state monad [13,18] to model sequential execution. The state monad threads the state through sequential execution in the background. The result is a modeling and execution pattern that closely resembles the execution pattern of TPM commands. Within PVS, we defined a state monad that gives us the traditional bind (`>>=`) and sequence (`>>`) operations. Examples of sequence and bind can be seen in figure 8.

3   Verification Results

To verify our requirements model we verify individual commands with respect to their postconditions and invariants. To provide a degree of validation, we use those commands to model protocols and verify execution results. Some aspects of attacks are considered, but there is no attempt to be comprehensive at this time. We also assume the hash function is perfect, giving the property $SHA1(b_0) = SHA1(b_1) \Leftrightarrow b_0 = b_1$. This and the constructive specification of the PCRS type gives us the important property that bad hashes or bad extension ordering is detectable in the PCR value.

3.1 Verifying Individual Commands

In order to prove the validity of our abstract TPM model, we define and verify postconditions and invariants for each TPM command and verify that our abstract specifications meet those properties. We consider only partial correctness in the abstract model, as termination is meaningless at this level.

For each command, we must show that given any value for all parameters of a command, running that command produces an output, state pair that satisfies the postcondition while not violating any invariant. Note that we do not address preconditions, as TPM output for every command and for each state must be defined, therefore preconditions are always trivial. Returning to our example of the TPM_MakeIdentity command, we verify the postconditions of command execution with the theorem shown in figure 6.

```
make_identity_post: THEOREM
  FORALL (state:(afterStartup?),CADigest:(tpmDigest?),aikParams:(tpmKey?)):
    LET (a,s)=runState(TPM_MakeIdentity(CADigest,aikParams))(state) IN
       LET waik:(tpmKey?)=tpmKey(state'keyGenCnt, keyUsage(aikParams),
                              keyFlags(aikParams), state'pcrs,
                              state'srk'wrappingKey, clear) IN
          LET idBind=tpmIdContents(CADigest,waik,
                              signed(private(waik),clear)) IN
  IF identity?(keyUsage(aikParams))
     AND not(migratable(keyFlags(aikParams)))
   THEN a=OUT_MakeIdentity(waik,idBind,TPM_SUCCESS) AND
       s=state WITH ['keyGenCnt := keyGenCnt(state)+1]
   ELSE a=OUT_Error(TPM_INVALID_KEYUSAGE) AND
       s=state
  ENDIF;
```

Fig. 6. Verifying postconditions of TPM_MakeIdentity

The LET form runs the command starting from any state in the predicate subtype (afterStartup?). This predicate ensures that the state is any valid tpmAbsState after the initialization commands have been run. The remainder of the theorem defines conditions on proper execution of TPM_MakeIdentity including both error and success cases.

In addition to defining and verifying postconditions of each TPM command, we also verify that properties that we want to remain invariant over command execution. Invariants in the model take two forms – those that are explicitly defined

Table 1. Invariant fields from `tpmAbsState`

State Field (Invariant)	Abstract Commands That Change Field
restore	ABS_Startup, ABS_Init, ABS_SaveState
memory	ABS_Startup, ABS_Init, ABS_save
srk	ABS_Startup, ABS_Init, ABS_TakeOwnership
ek	ABS_Startup, ABS_Init, ABS_CreateEndorsementKeyPair, ABS_CreateRevocableEK, ABS_RevokeTrust
keyGenCtr	ABS_Startup, ABS_Init, ABS_LoadKey2, ABS_CreateWrapKey ABS_MakeIdentity, ABS_certify
keys	ABS_Startup, ABS_Init, ABS_LoadKey2, ABS_ActivateIdentity ABS_OwnerClear, ABS_ForceClear, ABS_RevokeTrust
pcrs	ABS_Startup, ABS_Init, ABS_Extend ABS_sinit, ABS_senter
locality	ABS_Startup, ABS_Init
permFlags	ABS_Startup, ABS_Init, ABS_DisableOwnerClear, ABS_ForceClear, ABS_OwnerClear, ABS_TakeOwnership, ABS_CreateEndorsementKeyPair, ABS_CreateRevocableEK, ABS_RevokeTrust
permData	ABS_Startup, ABS_Init, ABS_CreateRevocableEK

and those that are captured in the abstract state type definitions. As was previously mentioned, the only way to change a PCR value is by rebooting the platform or using the `TPM_Extend` command. We can prove that this property holds in our model. With the following theorem, we show that along with `ABS_Extend`, the startup (after reboot) commands – `ABS_Startup` and `ABS_Init`, `ABS_sinit` and `ABS_senter` – are the only commands that change the state field `pcrs`:

```
pcrs_unchanged: THEOREM
  FORALL (s:tpmAbsState,c:tpmAbsInput) :
   not(ABS_Startup?(c) OR ABS_Init?(c) OR
       ABS_senter?(c) OR ABS_sinit?(c) OR
       ABS_Extend?(c)) =>
  pcrs(s) = pcrs(executeCom(s,c));
```

Note that while postconditions are associated with individual commands, invariants are typically proven over all commands simultaneously using the induction principle associated with the `tpmAbsInput` structure. The previous invariant is an example of one such theorem – note the universally quantified variable `c : tpmAbsInput` in the theorem signature.

The `ABS_Startup` and `ABS_Init` commands set up standard initial states following the startup command and hardware initialization, respectively. They reset all fields within `tpmAbsState` and are exceptions to most invariants. A list of invariants and the commands that modify them are shown in Table 1.

```
make_and_activate_identity: THEOREM
 FORALL (state:(afterStartup?),caDigest:(tpmDigest?),aikParams:(tpmKey?)):
  LET (a,s)=runState(
            TPM_MakeIdentity(caDigest,aikParams)
            >>= CPU_saveOutput(0)
            >>= (LAMBDA (a:tpmAbsOutput) :
                CASES a OF
                  OUT_MakeIdentity(aik,idBind,m) : CA_certify(aik,idBind)
                  ELSE TPM_Noop(a)
                ENDCASES)
            >>= CPU_saveOutput(1)
            >>= (LAMBDA (a:tpmAbsOutput) :
                CASES a OF
                  OUT_Certify(data,m) : TPM_ActivateIdentity(aikParams,data)
                  ELSE TPM_Noop(a)
                ENDCASES))
            (state) IN
    identity?(keyUsage(aikParams)) AND not(migratable(keyFlags(aikParams)))
     AND private(aikParams)=key(idKey(memory(s)(0)))
     AND caDigest=idBinding(memory(s)(0)) =>
    a=OUT_ActivateIdentity(sessK(data(memory(s)(1))),TPM_SUCCESS)
    AND s=state WITH ['keyGenCnt:=keyGenCnt(state)+2]
```

Fig. 7. Protocol used to verify AIK support

Possible invariants on the abstract state are captured in the subtype defined by the wellFormed? predicate. Specifically, the definition of instruction execution maps a state of type (wellFormed?) to another state of type (wellFormed?). Conditions in the wellFormed? predicate include basic structural properties such as the integrity of data for restoring TPM state that will automatically be checked during type checking.

Verifying protocols involves using the state monad to sequence command execution to perform more complex tasks. Before a quote can be generated, the TPM internally creates an AIK. The public AIK is certified by a trusted Certificate Authority (CA) [16] . The protocol for generating and certifying this AIK is shown in figure 7. The function runState runs the monad by calling it on the initial state.

The use of bind (>>=) and lambda constructs allows one instruction to consume the output of the previous instruction. For example, CA_Certify uses the output of TPM_MakeIdentity after it is stored in memory for later use. The use of CASE constructs accounts for the possibility that the previous output is not of the correct type. We are working on mechanisms for eliminating this, thereby cleaning up the protocol representation.

The conditions for proper execution of this sequence of commands involve conditions for proper execution of the commands individually. For example, notice the conditions that the key be non-migratable and an identity key were previously seen when discussing the verification of the single TPM_MakeIdentity command. The additional conditions in the antecedent are necessary to verify the memory was stored correctly within the tpmAbsState. In the consequent, we ensure that the output bound to a and the state bound to s correspond with the postconditions of `TPM_ActivateIdentity`, since it is the last command in the sequence. However, in doing so, we know that in order for these postconditions to be met, the previous commands were correctly executed.

3.2 Verifying Privacy CA Protocol

We are now ready to put all the moving parts together and verify the Privacy CA protocol. The PVS representation of the protocol from figure 1 that generates the output in equation 1 is shown in figure 8. To verify protocol execution, we first ensure that for all inputs the output bound by the LET form to a is the quote defined in equation 1 and that the state bound to s is the correct state following execution. This tells us the protocol generates the right output.

A collection of additional theorems verify detection of replay attacks, spoofed quotes and nonces, and bad signatures. For example, we can show that a bad nonce indicating potential replay is detectable in the quote:

```
bad_nonce: THEOREM
  FORALL (s:tpmAbsState,k:(tpmKey?), n1,n2:(tpmNonce?), pm:PCRMASK) :
    n1/=n2 =>
    runState(TPM_Quote(k,n1,pm))(s) /=
      runState(TPM_Quote(k,n2,pm))(s);
```

Additionally, we confirm that a bad AIK results in a bad quote recognizable in the quote returned by the protocol:

```
bad_signing_key: THEOREM
  FORALL (s:(afterStartup?),n:(tpmNonce?),pm:PCRMASK,k0,k1:(tpmKey?)) :
  LET (a0,s0)=runState(TPM_Quote(k0,n,pm))(s),
      (a1,s1)=runState(TPM_Quote(k1,n,pm))(s) IN
    private(k0)/=private(k1) =>
      a0/=a1;
```

These and similarly formed theorems verify that: (i) bad nonces, AIK signatures and PCR values are detectable; (ii) PCRs record measurement order as well as values; and (iii) **senter** was called to initiate the secure session. These are not properties of individual commands, but of the protocol run's output.

4 Related Work

Most verification work involving the TPM examines systems that use the TPM API [12,6], not the command set itself. Noteworthy exceptions are works by Delaune et. al. [8,7] and Gürgens et. al. [10]. Delaune's work examines properties of functions performed within the TPM using ProVerif for their analysis. While we are attempting to develop an abstract requirements model for the TPM, they focus on verifying cryptographic properties of TPM functions. Their work

```
cert_and_quote_with_prev_key : THEOREM
 FORALL (state:(afterStartup?),n:(tpmNonce?),pm:PCRMASK,idKey:(tpmKey?),
         caDig:(tpmDigest?)) :
   LET (a,s)=runState(
                 TPM_MakeIdentity(caDig,idKey)
                 >>= CPU_saveOutput(0)
                 >>= (LAMBDA (a:tpmAbsOutput) :
                     CASES a OF
                       OUT_MakeIdentity(aik,idBind,m) :
                         CA_certify(aik,idBind)
                       ELSE TPM_Noop(a)
                     ENDCASES)
                 >>= (LAMBDA (a:tpmAbsOutput) :
                     CASES a OF
                       OUT_Certify(data,m) :
                         TPM_ActivateIdentity(idKey,data)
                       ELSE TPM_Noop(a)
                     ENDCASES)
                 >> CPU_read(0)
                 >>= (LAMBDA (a:tpmAbsOutput) :
                     CASES a OF
                       OUT_MakeIdentity(aik,idBind,m) :
                         TPM_Quote(aik,n,pm)
                       ELSE TPM_Noop(a)
                     ENDCASES)
                 >>= CPU_saveOutput(2)
                 >> CPU_BuildQuoteFromMem(2,0))
                 (state) IN
             identity?(keyUsage(aikParams))
               AND not(migratable(keyFlags(aikParams)))
               AND OUT_MakeIdentity?(memory(s)(0))
               AND OUT_Quote?(memory(s)(2))
               AND private(idKey)=key(idKey(memory(s)(0)))
               AND caDig=idBinding(memory(s)(0)) =>
             LET pcrs=getPCRs(s`pcrs,pm) IN
               a=OUT_FullQuote(tpmQuote(pcrs,n,signed(private(idKey),clear)),
                     tpmIdContents(caDig,idKey,signed(private(idKey),clear)),
                     CPU_SUCCESS);
```

Fig. 8. Protocol used to generate full quote for an external appraiser

deals with verifying authentication [8] where they examine a command subset responsible for authentication. Two major differences are their inclusion of session management commands and their decision not to explicitly model state change. We have chosen to defer session management thus far and explicitly model state change using the state monad described earlier. In their analysis of Microsoft Bitlocker and the envelope protocol [7], they include an attacker while we are looking at functional correctness. These distinctions aside, the abstractions they choose are quite similar to ours even though we are working in higher-order logic in contrast to their use of horn clauses. This is encouraging and suggests that developing a common TPM requirements model may be feasible. It is also worth mentioning here that Ryan's unpublished work [15] is an excellent general introduction to the TPM and its use.

Gürgens and colleagues [10] develop a TPM model using asynchronous product automata (APA) and analyze models using the SH-Verification Tool (SHVT). Their work shares several protocols of interest with ours – secure boot, secure storage, remote attestation, and data migration – with only remote attestation being described in detail. Like our work they analyze interaction with a Privacy CA, but unlike our work and similar to Delaune, Gürgens includes various kinds of attackers in examining the protocol. Considering multiple attackers with multiple intents is the most interesting contribution of this work. By using a automata model, Gürgens also models state transition explicitly as we do, in contrast with Delaune.

5   Conclusions and Future Work

We have successfully verified about 40% of the TPM command set and the CA Protocol using TPM commands. As the TPM currently has no other formal verification, this is an important step to ensuring the validity of the TPM and its commands. Our CA Protocol steps through the role of the TPM in remote attestation and proves that the commands return what they are intended to return. Additional theorems verify invariants, postconditions, and detectability of various attacks. All models defined in this paper are available through the authors.

Immediate plans are continuing to specify the abstract TPM model while starting on the concrete model and bisimulation specification. In the abstract model, we are focusing now on data migration among TPMs and on direct anonymous attestation (DAA) [2] protocols while continuing to verify the full TPM command set. We also plan to extend our work to include virtual TPMs.

References

1. Trusted Computing Group, 3885 SW 153rd Drive, Beaverton, OR 97006: TCG TPM Specification, version 1.2 revision 103 edn. (July 2007), https://www.trustedcomputinggroup.org/resources/tpm_main_specification/
2. Brickell, E., Camenisch, J., Chen, L.: Direct anonymous attestation. In: Proceedings of the 11th ACM Conference on Computer and Communications Security, pp. 132–145. ACM (2004)

3. Challener, D., Yoder, K., Catherman, R., Stafford, D., Doorn, L.V.: A Practical Guide to Trusted Computing. IBM Press (2007)

4. Coker, G., Guttman, J., Loscocco, P., Herzog, A., Millen, J., O'Hanlon, B., Ramsdell, J., Segall, A., Sheehy, J., Sniffen, B.: Principles of remote attestation. International Journal of Information Security 10(2), 63–81 (2011)

5. Coker, G., Guttman, J., Loscocco, P., Sheehy, J., Sniffen, B.: Attestation: Evidence and trust. In: Chen, L., Ryan, M.D., Wang, G. (eds.) ICICS 2008. LNCS, vol. 5308, pp. 1–18. Springer, Heidelberg (2008)

6. Datta, A., Franklin, J., Garg, D., Kaynar, D.: A logic of secure systems and its application to trusted computing. In: 2009 30th IEEE Symposium on Security and Privacy, pp. 221–236. IEEE (2009)

7. Delaune, S., Kremer, S., Ryan, M., Steel, G.: Formal analysis of protocols based on tpm state registers. In: Proceedings of the 24th IEEE Computer Security Foundations Workshop, CSF 2011, pp. 66–82 (2011)

8. Delaune, S., Kremer, S., Ryan, M.D., Steel, G.: A formal analysis of authentication in the TPM. In: Degano, P., Etalle, S., Guttman, J. (eds.) FAST 2010. LNCS, vol. 6561, pp. 111–125. Springer, Heidelberg (2011)

9. Goldreich, O., Oren, Y.: Definitions and properties of zero-knowledge proof systems. Journal of Cryptology 7, 1–32 (1994), http://dx.doi.org/10.1007/BF00195207, doi:10.1007/BF00195207

10. Gürgens, S., Rudolph, C., Scheuermann, D., Atts, M., Plaga, R.: Security evaluation of scenarios based on the TCG's TPM specification. In: Biskup, J., López, J. (eds.) ESORICS 2007. LNCS, vol. 4734, pp. 438–453. Springer, Heidelberg (2007)

11. Haldar, V., Chandra, D., Franz, M.: Semantic remote attestation – a virtual machine directed approach to trusted computing. In: Proceedings of the Third Virtual Machine Research and Technology Symposium, San Jose, CA (May 2004)

12. Lin, A.H.: Automated analysis of security APIs. Ph.D. thesis, Massachusetts Institute of Technology (2005)

13. Moggi, E.: Notions of computation and monads. Information and Computation 93(1), 55–92 (1991), citeseer.nj.nec.com/moggi89notions.html

14. Owre, S., Rushby, J., Shankar, N.: PVS: A Prototype Verification System. In: Kapur, D. (ed.) CADE 1992. LNCS, vol. 607, pp. 748–752. Springer, Heidelberg (1992)

15. Ryan, M.: Introduction to the tpm 1.2 (March 2009), ftp://ftp.cs.bham.ac.uk/pub/authors/M.D.Ryan/08-intro-TPM.pdf (draft Report)

16. Sailer, R., Zhang, X., Jaeger, T., van Doorn, L.: Design and implementatation of a tcg-based integrity measurement architecture. In: Proceedings of the 13th USENIX Security Symposium. USENIX Association, Berkeley (2004)

17. Sangiorgi, D.: Introduction to Bisimulation and Coinduction. Cambridge University Press (2012)

18. Wadler, P.: The essence of functional programming. In: Conference Record of the Nineteenth Annual ACM SIGPLAN-SIGACT Symposium on Principles of Programming Languages, Albequerque, New Mexico, pp. 1–14 (1992), citeseer.nj.nec.com/wadler92essence.html

Formalization of Infinite Dimension Linear Spaces with Application to Quantum Theory

Mohamed Yousri Mahmoud, Vincent Aravantinos, and Sofiène Tahar

Electrical and Computer Engineering Dept., Concordia University,
1455 De Maisonneuve Blvd. W., Montreal, Canada
{mo_solim,vincent,tahar}@ece.concordia.ca

Abstract. Linear algebra is considered an essential mathematical theory that has many engineering applications. While many theorem provers support linear spaces, they only consider finite dimensional spaces. In addition, available libraries only deal with real vectors, whereas complex vectors are extremely useful in many fields of engineering. In this paper, we propose a new linear space formalization which covers both finite and infinite dimensional complex vector spaces, implemented in HOL-Light. We give the definition of a linear space and prove many properties about its operations, e.g., addition and scalar multiplication. We also formalize a number of related fundamental concepts such as linearity, hermitian operation, self-adjoint, and inner product space. Using the developed linear algebra library, we were able to implement basic definitions about quantum mechanics and use them to verify a quantum beam splitter, an optical device that has many applications in quantum computing.

1 Introduction

Linear algebra is a powerful mathematical tool which is widely used in different engineering areas: digital image processing (where images can be represented as eigenspaces [3]), bioinformatics (where DNA sequences form a vector space [19]), and control systems, e.g., robotics (where the system state is represented as a vector and each operational block as a matrix [2]). Consequently, there exist many computer tools allowing to deal with linear algebra: numerical tools (e.g., Matlab [18]), computer algebra systems (e.g., Maple [1]) and theorem provers (e.g., Coq [16]).

Classically, a *linear space* (or, equivalently *vector space*) is a set paired with two operations (called addition and scalar multiplications) which have to satisfy a particular set of axioms, e.g., closure of the set by these operations, commutativity of addition, or distributivity of scalar multiplication over addition (see, e.g., [4] for details). The concept of *dimension* of a vector space is extremely important: it is a cardinal, which can thus be finite or infinite. The properties of finite-dimension vector spaces can be very different from the ones of infinite-dimension ones. For instance, a finite-dimension linear space always has the same dimension as its dual space, whereas this is not the case in infinite dimension

G. Brat, N. Rungta, and A. Venet (Eds.): NFM 2013, LNCS 7871, pp. 413–427, 2013.
© Springer-Verlag Berlin Heidelberg 2013

(actually an infinite-dimension linear space always has a smaller dimension as its dual).

In this paper, we present a formalization, in HOL-Light, of complex-valued-function linear spaces. We define the basic types of such linear spaces and prove that they satisfy the axioms of linear spaces. We formalize many concepts such as (linear) operators, inner product, hermitian adjoints, eigenvectors. For all these concepts, we prove basic facts and provide tactics that allow to prove such basic facts in an automated way. We also prove non-basic results such as Pythagorean theorem, Cauchy-Schwarz inequality, or the fact that the eigenvalues of an auto-adjoint operator are real values. Then, we demonstrate the use of our library in practice by applying it to the formalization of basic quantum mechanics concepts. We use this to formalize a quantum beam splitter: a device with two optical inputs and two optical outputs which routes the incoming photons to the output ports [13]. We finally verify that this device preserves energy [14].

To the best of our knowledge, there currently exist only four significant formalizations of linear algebra: two in HOL-Light ([7] and [12]), one in PVS [9], and one in Coq [11]. The three former focus essentially on n-dimensional euclidean and complex spaces, whereas our work generalizes it to (possibly) infinite-dimension vector spaces of complex numbers (more precisely, complex-valued-function spaces). The work in [11] formalizes extensively a chapter of a classical textbook but, as far as we know, it does not handle many other useful concepts like operator algebra, linear operators, hermitian adjoints, eigenvectors or inner product. In a nutshell, the essential difference between this work and ours is that ours is oriented towards applications rather than a systematic formalization of a textbook. Consequently some theorems of purely theoretical interest are proved in [11] but not in ours. On the other hand, we formalized more notions and results that are useful for engineering applications.

The paper is organized as follows. Section 2 presents our HOL-Light formalization of linear algebra. Section 3 shows the usability of our framework by giving a brief summary about quantum mechanics and showing how it can be formalized using our development. It then introduces beam splitters, their formal definition, and the verification that they preserve energy. Finally, Section 4 concludes the paper.

2   Finite/Infinite Dimension Linear Space Formalization

In the following we present our formalization which is a collection of theories consisting in definitions (types, operations, predicates) and theorems over these definitions. This formalization is freely available at [15]. For practical use, most of these theories also come with a dedicated tactic allowing to prove automatically some basic but very useful facts. We believe that this makes our library a practical tool instead of just a set of theorems that can be difficult to manipulate in practice. Indeed, it allows the user to focus on the difficult tasks which involve some complex reasoning while getting rid easily of the simple tasks that are usually a burden to the user of interactive theorem proving.

2.1   Complex Functions Vector Space

In HOL-Light, the current formalization of linear spaces involves only finite real vectors represented by the type $\texttt{real}^N$ (i.e., a tuple of N real numbers). Extending this to complex linear spaces is achieved simply by considering the type $\texttt{complex}^N$. In order to consider infinite dimension, we take the *function space* of an arbitrary set to $\texttt{complex}$. This is expressed by the type $\texttt{cfun} = A \to \texttt{complex}$, where A is a type variable ($\texttt{cfun}$ stands for complex *function*). This representation allows both for infinite-dimension linear spaces (by taking, e.g., $\texttt{num}$ or $\texttt{real}$ for A) and finite-dimension ones (by taking for A any type with a finite extension). Note that a general formalization would be defined for any field, instead of $\texttt{complex}$ only, however this would require to parameterize the formalization with operations on the corresponding field. This would make the formalization much more complicated for no significant gain, since function spaces over the complex field already cover most of the engineering applications.

We define the linear space operations over the type $\texttt{cfun}$ as follows:

Definition 1.
$\texttt{cfun\_add} \ (v_1 : \texttt{cfun}) \ (v_2 : \texttt{cfun}) \ : \texttt{cfun} = \lambda x : A. \ v_1 \ x + v_2 \ x$
$\texttt{cfun\_smul} \ (a : \texttt{complex}) \ v = \lambda x : A. \ a * v \ x$

($\texttt{smul}$ stands for *scalar multiplication*). These functions just "lift" the corresponding operations over complex numbers to the type $\texttt{cfun}$. Note that, by convention, all operations dealing with a type $\texttt{t}$ are prefixed with this type (hence every operation dealing with the type $\texttt{cfun}$ starts with the prefix $\texttt{cfun\_}$). One can observe that these definitions match the finite case since, if A is finite, then the above operations correspond to the usual component-wise operations over vectors.

For convenience, we also define the commonly used operations of negation, subtraction and conjugation, as well as the null function:

Definition 2.
$\texttt{cfun\_neg} \ (v : \texttt{cfun}) \ : \texttt{cfun} = \texttt{cfun\_smul} \ (-\texttt{Cx}(\&1)) \ v$
$\texttt{cfun\_sub} \ (v_1 : \texttt{cfun}) \ (v_2 : \texttt{cfun}) \ : \texttt{cfun} = \texttt{cfun\_add} \ v_1 \ (\texttt{cfun\_neg} \ v_2)$
$\texttt{cfun\_cnj} \ (v : \texttt{cfun}) \ : \texttt{cfun} = \lambda x : A. \ \texttt{cnj} \ (v \ x)$
$\texttt{cfun\_zero} \ = \ \lambda x : A. \ \texttt{Cx}(\&0)$

where & is the HOL-Light function injecting natural numbers into reals, and $\texttt{Cx}$ injects real numbers into complex numbers.

We can then easily prove that the type $\texttt{cfun}$ with the above operations is a linear space by proving the usual axioms presented in Table 1 (we overload the usual symbols for multiplication, addition, etc. with the above operations for $\texttt{cfun}$; following HOL-Light notations, % denotes scalar multiplication).

Finally we define the notion of subspace as follows:

Definition 3.
$\texttt{is\_cfun\_subspace} \ (\texttt{spc} : \texttt{cfun} \to \texttt{bool}) \Leftrightarrow$
$\quad \forall x \ y. \ x \ \texttt{IN} \ \texttt{spc} \wedge y \ \texttt{IN} \ \texttt{spc} \Rightarrow$
$\qquad x + y \ \texttt{IN} \ \texttt{spc} \wedge (\forall \ a. \ a \ \% \ x \ \texttt{IN} \ \texttt{spc}) \wedge \texttt{cfun\_zero} \ \texttt{IN} \ \texttt{spc}$

Table 1. cfun_add and cfun_mul properties

Property	HOL Theorem
Addition commutativity	$\forall x\ y : \texttt{cfun}.\ x + y = y + x$
Addition Association	$\forall x\ y\ z : \texttt{cfun}.\ (x + y) + z = x + y + z$
Left Distributivity	$\forall (a : \texttt{complex})\ (x : \texttt{cfun})\ (y : \texttt{cfun}).\ a\ \%\ (x + y) = a\ \%\ x + a\ \%\ y$
Right Distributivity	$\forall (a\ b : \texttt{complex})\ (x : \texttt{cfun}).\ (a + b)\ \%\ x = a\ \%\ x + b\ \%\ x$
Compatibility	$\forall (a\ b : \texttt{complex})\ (x : \texttt{cfun}).\ a\ \%\ (b\ \%\ x) = (a * b)\ \%\ x$
Identity Element	$\forall (x : \texttt{cfun}).\ x + \texttt{cfun\_zero} = x$
Additive Inverse	$\forall (x : \texttt{cfun}).\ x - x = \texttt{cfun\_zero}$

Around 50 theorems have been proved about this theory. In order to make our formalization easier to use in practice we have developed a tactic CFUN_ARITH_TAC which allows to prove many simple facts about the above algebra. Indeed, the axioms of linear spaces are all proved automatically with this tactic, as well as many other theorems. This reduced our formalization from more than 300 lines of code to around 50, thus increasing readability and usability.

2.2   Operators

A very important notion is the one of transformation between vector spaces. Such a transformation is called an *operator*. The type of operators is thus $\texttt{cop} = (A \rightarrow \texttt{complex}) \rightarrow (B \rightarrow \texttt{complex})$, for which we define the following standard operations:

Definition 4.
$\texttt{cop\_add}\ (op_1 : \texttt{cop})\ (op_2 : \texttt{cop})\ : \texttt{cop} = \lambda x.\ op_1\ x + op_2\ x$
$\texttt{cop\_smul}\ (a : \texttt{complex})\ (op : \texttt{cop})\ : \texttt{cop} = \lambda x.\ a\ \%\ op\ x$

As well as negation, subtraction, conjugate and the null operator which are defined as above (note that the definitions for operators and for complex functions only differ by their type, so that higher-order logic and type polymorphism actually allows us to define general combinators which factorize these definitions; we expanded the use of these combinators for the sake of readability). Moreover, we proved that the set of operators with these operations satisfies all the axioms of a linear space.

The above is very similar to the linear space presented in the previous section, but an essential aspect of operators is the fact that we can also *multiply* them. This multiplication is simply the composition:

Definition 5.
$\texttt{cop\_mul}\ (op_1 : (A \rightarrow \texttt{complex}) \rightarrow (B \rightarrow \texttt{complex}))$
$\qquad\qquad (op_2 : (C \rightarrow \texttt{complex}) \rightarrow (A \rightarrow \texttt{complex})) = \lambda x.\ op_1\ (op_2\ x)$

Note that the types of op_1 and op_2 do not need to be the same. Following the conventions applied in HOL-Light for matrix multiplication, this operation is denoted with the infix $**$. Indeed, one can recognize that, when the operator is linear (see next section), then operators amount to matrices in finite dimension.

This multiplication has unusual properties, starting with the fact that it is not commutative. It follows that many results that are intuitively true in other contexts are actually false here. For instance, multiplication is only right-distributive over addition, i.e., the following holds:

Theorem 1. $\forall op_1 \; op_2 \; op_3. \; (op_1 + op_2) \; * * \; op_3 = op_1 \; * * \; op_3 + op_2 \; * * \; op_3$

But the following does not:

$$\forall op_1 \; op_2 \; op_3. \; op_3 \; * * \; (op_1 + op_2) = op_3 \; * * \; op_1 + op_3 \; * * \; op_2$$

Still, this multiplication has a lot of useful properties that we have proved in our library. The neutral element (both left and right) of this multiplication is the identity function. For convenience, exponentiation has also been defined (note that, here, the operator should have the same domain and range). In total, around 60 theorems have been proved, most of them automatically using our tactic COP_ARITH_TAC.

2.3   Linear Operators

Linear operators are of particular interest in our work. They correspond, in the finite-dimension case, to matrices. This notion is easily formalized as follows:

Definition 6.
is_linear_cop (op : cop) $\Leftrightarrow$
  $\forall x \; y. \; op \; (x + y) = op \; x + op \; y \; \wedge \forall a. \; op \; (a \; \% \; x) = a \; \% \; (op \; x)$

Linearity is a powerful property which allows to prove some new properties, in particular about multiplication. For instance, in the case of linear operators, left-distributivity now holds:

Theorem 2. $\forall op_1 \; op_2 \; op_3. \; \texttt{is\_linear\_cop} \; op_3 \Rightarrow$
  $op_3 \; * * \; (op_1 + op_2) = op_3 \; * * \; op_1 + op_3 \; * * \; op_2$

So does the associativity of scalar multiplication on the right of a multiplication:

Theorem 3. $\forall z \; op_1 \; op_2. \; \texttt{is\_linear\_cop} \; op_1 \Rightarrow$
  $op_1 \; * * \; (z \; \% \; op_2) = z \; \% \; (op_1 \; * * \; op_2)$

Around 10 additional theorems were proved that deal with the particular properties of linear operators.

In practice, one often has to prove that a given operator is linear. To do this, many congruence results are very useful and have indeed to be proved. We gathered the simplest ones in the following theorem:

Theorem 4.
$\forall op_1 \; op_2. \; \texttt{is\_linear\_cop} \; op_1 \wedge \texttt{is\_linear\_cop} \; op_2 \Rightarrow$
  $\texttt{is\_linear\_cop} \; (op_1 + op_2) \wedge \texttt{is\_linear\_cop} \; (op_1 * op_2) \wedge$
  $\texttt{is\_linear\_cop} \; (op_2 - op_1) \wedge \forall a. \; \texttt{is\_linear\_cop} \; (a \; \% \; op_1)$

The base cases for cop_zero and the identity function have also been proved. Together, these theorems allow to prove the most frequently seen situations dealing with linearity. Since the involved reasoning is often very similar, we have again developed a tactic to deal with such situations automatically: LINEARITY_TAC.

Finally, the notion of eigenvalues and eigenvectors are very important both in theory and in many applications:

Definition 7.
is_eigen_pair (op : cop) (f, v) ⟺
    is_linear_cop op ⟹ op f = v % f ∧ f ≠ zerofun

Here, f is called the *eigenfunction*, and v the *eigenvalue*. We then proved some useful properties, in particular, the set of all the eigenvectors of a given eigenvalue constitutes a linear space:

Theorem 5. ∀op. is_linear_cop op ⟹
    ∀z. is_cfun_subspace ({ f | is_eigen_pair op (f, z) } ∪ {cfun_zero})

2.4   Inner Product

The inner product is very useful both in theory and in practice, in particular in many engineering applications (e.g., digital communication or quantum optics). Since the type cfun depends on a type variable A, we cannot provide an implementation of the inner product which works with every possible instantiation of A. For instance, if A is substituted with num then we can provide a definition based on some infinite sum, but if it is substituted with real then a suitable notion of integration should be defined. This prevents a general definition of inner product. We thus introduce a predicate asserting whether a given function indeed satisfies the axioms of an inner product and then parameterize our formalization with this predicate:

Definition 8.
is_inprod (inprod : cfun → cfun → complex) ⟺
    ∀ x y z.
        cnj (inprod y x) = inprod x y ∧
        inprod (x + y) z = inprod x z + inprod y z ∧
        real (inprod x x) ∧ &0 ≤ real_of_complex (inprod x x) ∧
        (inprod x x = Cx(&0) ⟺ x = cfun_zero) ∧
        ∀a. inprod x (a % y) = a * (inprod x y)

where real x states that the complex value x has no imaginary part, and real_of_complex is a function casting such a complex number into a real one.

Around 20 theorems of the inner product have been proved in our formalization, e.g., distributivity with respect to addition, associativity with respect to scalar multiplication (modulo the conjugate when the scalar multiplication occurs on the left), etc. A particularly interesting property is the injectivity of the inner product seen as a curried function:

Theorem 6. ∀inprod. is_inprod inprod ⇒
    ∀x y. inprod x = inprod y ⇔ x = y

This is a powerful property which allows, in particular, to prove the uniqueness of a hermitian adjoint (see next section).

From the inner product, we can define orthogonality as follows:

Definition 9. are_orthogonal inprod u v ⇔
    is_inprod inprod ⇒ inprod u v = Cx(&0)

We proved some basic properties about orthogonality like the fact that it is symmetric or that scalar multiplication preserves orthogonality. However, we can prove some more difficult and interesting theorems like, e.g., the Pythagorean theorem:

Theorem 7 (Pythagorean).
∀ inprod u v. is_inprod inprod ∧ are_orthogonal inprod u v ⇒
    inprod (u + v) (u + v) = inprod u u + inprod v v

or the existence of an orthogonal decomposition of any vector with respect to another one:

Theorem 8 (Decomposition).
∀ inprod u v. is_inprod inprod ⇒
    let proj_v = $\frac{\text{inprod v u}}{\text{inprod v v}}$ in
    let orthogonal_component = u − proj_v % v in
        u = proj_v % v + orthogonal_component ∧
        are_orthogonal inprod v orthogonal_component

These two theorems play a crucial role in particular when proving the Cauchy-Schwarz Inequality, which has itself essential applications in the error analysis of many engineering systems:

Theorem 9 (Cauchy-Schwarz Inequality).
∀ x y inprod. is_inprod inprod ⇒
    norm (inprod x y) pow 2 ≤
        real_of_complex (inprod x x) ∗ real_of_complex (inprod y y)

where **norm** denotes the norm of a complex number. Note that, even without focusing on the infinite-dimension aspect, this theorem is still a not-so-trivial adaptation of the existing results in HOL-Light, since it extends it to *complex* linear spaces.

2.5   Hermitian Adjoint

A very useful notion of linear operators is the one of hermitian adjoint. It is very important theoretically and has many applications, e.g., in quantum mechanics. This operation generalizes the one of conjugate transpose in the finite-dimension case and we formalize it as follows:

Definition 10.
is_hermitian op_1 op_2 inprod $\Leftrightarrow$
  is_inprod inprod $\Rightarrow$
    is_linear_cop op_1 $\wedge$ is_linear_cop op_2 $\wedge$
    $\forall$ x y. inprod x $(op_1$ y$)$ = inprod $(op_2$ x$)$ y

The relation is_hermitian op_1 op_2 holds if and only if *op_2* is the hermitian adjoint of *op_1*. We use a relation instead of a function because the existence of a hermitian operator cannot be proved in a general way: it depends a lot on the underlying space. In particular, this highlights a big difference between the finite and the infinite dimension case: in finite dimension, one can just take the conjugate transpose of the underlying matrix to obtain the hermitian. But in infinite dimension, this is not as simple as that: there is indeed a notion of transpose operator, but it yields an operator in the *dual space* of the original vector space. If there is an isomorphism between this dual space and the original vector space, then one can obtain a satisfying definition of hermitian, however, in infinite dimension, there is not always such an isomorphism. However, in any case, if there is a hermitian operator, then it is unique, as proved by the following theorem:

Theorem 10.
$\forall op_1$ op_2 op_3 inprod.
  is_hermitian op_1 op_2 inprod $\wedge$ is_hermitian op_1 op_3 inprod
    $\Rightarrow$ $op_2 = op_3$

We also proved some other properties of the hermitian, such as for instance the symmetry of its relation:

Theorem 11.
$\forall$inprod op_1 op_2.
  is_hermitian op_1 op_2 inprod $\Leftrightarrow$ is_hermitian op_2 op_1 inprod

Seeing the hermitian as a function, this proves the usual property that taking the hermitian of the hermitian is the identity.

    Finally, we prove some congruence theorems which allow to prove, in many cases, that a given operator is the hermitian of another:

Theorem 12.
$\forall$inprod op_1 op_2 op_3 op_4 a.
  is_hermitian op_1 op_2 inprod $\wedge$ is_hermitian op_3 op_4 inprod $\Rightarrow$
    is_hermitian $(op_1 + op_3)$ $(op_2 + op_4)$ inprod $\wedge$
    is_hermitian $(op_1 - op_3)$ $(op_2 - op_4)$ inprod $\wedge$
    is_hermitian $(op_1 * op_3)$ $(op_4 * op_2)$ inprod $\wedge$
    is_hermitian $(a \% op_1)$ $(cnj a \% op_2)$ inprod

Finally, we also provide a more "computational" version of these congruence theorems:

Theorem 13.
$\forall$a b inprod op$_1$ op$_2$ op$_3$ op$_4$ op$_5$.
  is_hermitian op$_1$ op$_2$ inprod $\wedge$ is_hermitian op$_3$ op$_4$ inprod $\wedge$
  is_hermitian (a % op$_1$ + b % op$_3$) op$_5$ inprod $\Rightarrow$
    op$_5$ = cnj a % op$_2$ + cnj b % op$_4$

In total, around 10 theorems were proved about hermitian operators.

2.6 Self-adjoint Operators

We conclude the overview of our library by presenting the notion of self-adjoint operator, which simply denotes operators which are their own hermitian adjoint:

Definition 11. is_self_adjoint op inprod $\Leftrightarrow$ is_hermitian op op inprod

Once again, we have proved many congruence theorems allowing to deal with most self-adjoint operators that are encountered in proofs. Most of them are similar to the ones for the hermitians, only the case of scalar multiplication should be handled with a little bit of care, since we must require that the scalar is a real number:

Theorem 14.
$\forall$ inprod op a. is_inprod inprod $\wedge$ real a
  $\Rightarrow$ is_self_adjoint(a % op) inprod

Some other results are a less obvious and very useful, for instance:

Theorem 15.
$\forall$ inprod op x y.
  is_inprod inprod $\wedge$ is_linear_op op $\wedge$
  inprod (op x) y = $-$(inprod x (op y)))
    $\Rightarrow$ is_self_adjoint (ii % op) inprod

Proving that a given operator is self-adjoint using all these theorems is such a common task that we have developed a dedicated tactic for it: SELF_ADJOINT_TAC [15].

We finally give two examples of non-trivial theorems which involve many of the concepts presented until now. The first one states that any eigenvalue of a self-adjoint operator is real:

Theorem 16.
$\forall$ inprod op. is_inprod inprod $\wedge$ is_self_adjoint op inprod $\Rightarrow$
  $\forall$z. is_eigen_value op z $\Rightarrow$ real z

where is_eigen_value z is true if and only if there exists an eigenfunction such that z is its corresponding eigenvalue. Another result states that the eigenfunctions of a self-adjoint operator are orthogonal if the corresponding eigenvalues are different:

Theorem 17.
∀ inprod op f_1 f_2 z_1 z_2.
  is_inprod inprod ∧ is_self_adjoint op inprod ∧ $z_1 \neq z_2$ ∧
  is_eigen_pair op (f_1, z_1) ∧ is_eigen_pair op (f_2, z_2)
    ⇒ are_orthogonal inprod f_1 f_2

This concludes the presentation of our current formalization. In order to show its usefulness, we now give a sophisticated application by formalizing (basics of) Quantum Mechanics and applying this to the verification of a device called a *beam splitter*.

3   Application to Quantum Theory

In this section we briefly introduce quantum mechanics, how it can be mathematically represented using inner product spaces, and how we propose to formalize it using the results of the previous section.

3.1   Quantum Mechanics

It is assumed that the description of any physical system starts with a *state*. From this state, one can obtain the *coordinates* of the system: e.g., the position of a moving particle, or the temperature of a given system. Coordinates are the atomic pieces of information of the system. Being given the state of a system, one can also derive the values of other quantities called *observables*: e.g., the energy of the system. Observables are similar to coordinates except that they are not atomic, i.e., they can be derived from coordinates. In classical physics, the measurement of a system state (and thus observables) and its evolution are deterministic, whereas they are only probabilistic in quantum physics [6]. Consequently, whereas the state of the system is a set of real numbers in classical physics, it is a probability distribution in quantum mechanics. In both cases, coordinates and observables are functions which take the system state as input. However, in classical physics, the output of this function is a real number, but it is a probability distribution in quantum mechanics.

For our concern, the interesting aspect of quantum mechanics is that the involved probability distributions form an infinite-dimension (complex) inner product space: The state of a quantum system can be mathematically represented as a complex-valued function and coordinates (and observables) can be represented by (self-adjoint) operators. In practice, one is very often interested in the expected value of such an observable: This can be represented by the norm canonically associated with the inner product.

We thus have all the tools required to formalize these concepts. Note that we formalize only some basics of quantum mechanics. However, those definitions are sufficient to define formally the quantum system presented in the next section and to do simple verification tasks on it. We start by defining the type qstate as an abbreviation for cfun (note that this type contains a type variable: this variable can be instantiated differently depending on the considered system). The *space* of the possible values for states is defined as qspace = (qstate → bool) × (cfun → cfun → complex), where the first element of the pair is the considered set of possible states, and the second one is an inner product to be associated with this set. In order to ensure that a given value of type qspace indeed represents a valid quantum space, we define the following predicate:

Definition 12.
is_qspace ((vs, inprod) : qspace) ⇔
  is_cfun_subspace vs ∧ is_inprod inprod

Being given a space, we can define coordinates and observables: As mentioned above, these are mathematically represented by self-adjoint operators. They thus have the type qstate → qstate. Being given a quantum state space, we have to ensure that an observable (or coordinate) is self-adjoint and that the result of its application remains in the state space. This is achieved by the following predicate:

Definition 13.
is_observable (op : qstate → qstate) ((vs, inprod) : qspace) ⇔
  is_qspace (vs, inprod) ∧ is_self_adjoint op inprod ∧
  $\forall$ x. x ∈ vs ⇒ op x ∈ vs

Now, verifying a device requires that we formalize a model of it. Mathematically, a device is just a quantum system, we thus formalize this notion. A system is built of a state space, coordinates, and a function describing the evolution of the state. First of all, we should notice that coordinates depend on time, which we consider here to be a real number, so their type is actually coord = time → (qstate → qstate) (for readability, time is defined as an abbreviation of real). The evolution of the system is actually fully expressed by the expression of its total energy (called the "Hamiltonian"). Since the total energy is an observable, which also depends on time, it also has the type time → qstate → qstate. So, finally, the type of quantum systems is defined as:

$$qsys = qspace \times coord \ list \times (time \to qstate \to qstate)$$

To ensure that we have a valid system, we define again a predicate (qs stands for *q*uantum *s*ystem, cs for *c*oordinate*s*, and H for *H*amiltonian):

Definition 14.
is_qsys (qs, cs, H) ⇔
  is_qspace qs ∧ $\forall$t : time. is_observable (H t) qs ∧
  ALL (λc. is_observable (c t) qs) cs

where ALL P l is true if and only if every element of l satisfies the predicate P.

Using all these notions and our library, we could prove the famous uncertainty principle:

Theorem 18 (Uncertainty Principle).
$\forall$obs1 obs2 ((spc, inprod) : qspace) t qst.
  is_observable obs1 (spc, inprod) $\land$ is_observable obs2 (spc, inprod) $\land$
  qst $\in$ spc $\land$ qst $\neq$ cfun_zero $\Rightarrow$
  $\left(\dfrac{\text{expectation inprod qst (commutator op1 op2)}}{\text{Cx(\&2)}*\text{ii}} \right)$ pow 2
    $\leq$ real_of_complex (variance inprod qst op1)
      $*$ real_of_complex (variance inprod qst op2)

where `expectation inprod qst op` returns the expected value of an operator
op seen as a statistical measurement in a given state `qst`. This is classically
defined in quantum mechanics using the inner product as `inprod qst (op qst)`.
Similarly, the variance can be computed using the inner product, which yields
the function `variance`. Finally `commutator op₁ op₂ = op₁ * *op₂ − op₂ * *op₁`.
We refer the reader to [6] for detailed explanations about the uncertainty principle. Note that the proof of this result makes an essential use of the Cauchy-
Schwarz inequality (Theorem 9) and of our automation tactics `LINEARITY_TAC`
and `SELF_ADJOINT_TAC`.

This concludes our formalization of quantum mechanics basics. Note that this
could not have been done with the current library of linear algebra in HOL Light
[8], because of the lack of (complex-valued) function space formalization. Neither
could it be developed in Coq using [11] because it lacks many of the notions we
used here: operators, inner product, self-adjoint.

In the next section, we present the formalization of a quantum single-mode
electromagnetic field, i.e., the inputs and outputs of a beam splitter.

3.2   Single-Mode Electromagnetic Field

A single-mode field is an electromagnetic field with a single resonance frequency.
This is the simplest model of a light beam. Such a field constitutes a quantum
system according to the definition that we have given above. We should thus
specify its coordinates and Hamiltonian (we do not specify the state space in
order to keep our formalization general). The coordinates of an electromagnetic
field consists in its amount of charges $q(t)$ and the intensity of its flux $p(t)$.
In quantum mechanics, operators are usually written with a circumflex, so the
quantum versions of these coordinates are written $\hat{p}(t)$ and $\hat{q}(t)$. The Hamiltonian
is then defined as:

$$\hat{H}(t) = \frac{\omega^2}{2}\hat{q}(t)^2 + \frac{1}{2}\hat{p}(t)^2$$

where ω is the resonance frequency. In order to keep explicit the resonance
frequency, we define a type dedicated to single-mode fields by `sm = qsys × real`
(sm stands for *single-mode*) where the first component is the system itself and
the second one is the frequency. Once again we collect in a predicate all the
conditions required for a value of type `sm` to represent a valid single-mode field:

Definition 15.
is_sm $((qs, cs, H), \omega : sm) \Leftrightarrow$
   is_qsys $(qs, cs, H) \land 0 < omega \land$ LENGTH cords $= 2 \land$
   let p $=$ EL 0 cs and q $=$ EL 1 cs in
   $\forall t : time.$ H $t = Cx(\frac{\omega^2}{2})$ % $((q\ t)$ pow $2) + Cx(\frac{1}{2})$ % $((p\ t)$ pow $2)$

where EL i l is the ith element of a list l. Here, we assert that the system should indeed be a valid system, that the frequency should be positive and there should be two coordinates. We fix the first coordinate to be the charge and the second one to be the intensity.

Using our library, we can already prove a couple of useful theorems about single mode fields. For instance, we can prove that the Hamiltonian is linear:

Theorem 19.
$\forall$qs cs H ω t. is_sm $((qs, cs, H), \omega) \Rightarrow$ is_linear_cop (H t)

And even that it is self-adjoint:

Theorem 20.
$\forall$qs cs H ω t. is_sm $((qs, cs, H), \omega) \Rightarrow$ is_self_adjoint (H t)

Both theorems were proved automatically by using our tactics LINEARITY_TAC and SELF_ADJOINT_TAC.

3.3 Beam Splitter

A beam splitter is a generic name for an optical device which takes two input light beams and outputs two other beams. It can route the input beams towards the output in different ways, depending on the type of beam splitter which is considered. For instance, as its name suggests, a typical behavior is to "split" a single input beam, i.e., one can have a configuration where, if there is only one incident beam, then half of the photons are routed towards one output beam, and the other half is routed towards the other one. However other beam splitters can have other behaviors, e.g., beam phase shifting [5]. Note that beam splitters play an important role in some implementations of quantum computers [10], e.g., in [17]. In this section, we provide a general specification for a beam splitter and prove that any device satisfying this specification preserves the energy from the input to the output beams.

Again, we first define a dedicated type for beam splitters. The behavior of a beam splitter, which determines the route of photons, can be modeled by four parameters, given as complex numbers. This yields the following definition:

bmsp $=$ complex $\times$ complex $\times$ complex $\times$ complex $\times$ sm $\times$ sm $\times$ sm $\times$ sm

The four values of type sm represent the two input and two output single-mode fields, respectively. We then define a predicate ensuring that a value of type bmsp indeed represents a real beam splitter.

Definition 16.
$\text{is\_bmsp} (b_1, b_2, b_3, b_4, \text{in\_port}_1, \text{in\_port}_2, \text{out\_port}_1, \text{out\_port}_2) \Leftrightarrow$
$\quad \text{is\_sm in\_port}_1 \wedge \text{is\_sm in\_port}_2 \wedge \text{is\_sm out\_port}_1 \wedge \text{is\_sm out\_port}_2$
$\quad \wedge b_1 * \text{cnj } b_1 + b_2 * \text{cnj } b_2 = \text{Cx} (\&1) \wedge b_3 * \text{cnj } b_3 + b_4 * \text{cnj } b_4 = \text{Cx} (\&1)$
$\quad \wedge b_1 * \text{cnj } b_3 + b_2 * \text{cnj } b_4 = \text{Cx} (\&0) \wedge \text{cnj } b_1 * b_3 + \text{cnj } b_2 * b_4 = \text{Cx} (\&0)$
$\quad \wedge \forall t : \text{time}.$
$\qquad p_{\text{out}_1} t = b_1 \% p_{\text{in}_1} t + b_2 \% p_{\text{in}_2} t \wedge q_{\text{out}_1} t = b_1 \% q_{\text{in}_1} t + b_2 \% q_{\text{in}_2} t$
$\qquad \wedge p_{\text{out}_2} t = b_3 \% p_{\text{in}_1} t + b_4 \% p_{\text{in}_2} t \wedge q_{\text{out}_2} t = b_3 \% q_{\text{in}_1} t + b_4 \% q_{\text{in}_2} t$

where p_{in_x} and q_{in_x} denote the charge and flux intensity in the xth input beam, respectively, and the same holds with the out index for the output beams. The first line ensures that all the involved light beams are indeed single-mode fields. The four following lines impose general constraints on the configuration of the device. Finally, the last four lines provide the relation that holds between the light beams, according to the parameters.

Finally, using our formalization of linear algebra and quantum mechanics, we could prove that any beam splitter is an energy lossless device, i.e., the total energy of input ports is equal to the total energy of output ports. Formally:

Theorem 21.
$\forall \text{ bs. is\_bmsp bs} \Rightarrow H_{\text{in}_1} + H_{\text{in}_2} = H_{\text{out}_1} + H_{\text{out}_2}$

where H_b is the Hamiltonian of the light beam b. This result was proved in around 200 lines of HOL-Light proof script, which is quite small for an application requiring so many layers of formalization. P

4   Conclusion

Linear algebra is extremely useful in many engineering disciplines. However the developments currently available in theorem provers do not allow to tackle many of these fields due to the lack of support for the required concepts (function spaces, inner products, self-adjoints, etc.). In particular, in HOL-Light, only euclidean spaces are formalized thus preventing the application to many areas. In this paper, we presented a formalization of linear algebra which targets engineering applications rather than a purely theoretical development. Notably, we tried to emphasize the practical usability by providing tactics which allow to solve many small but commonly-encountered problems. Using this formalization, we were able to define some basic notions of quantum mechanics and to apply it to the verification that any beam splitter is an energy lossless device. In our opinion, this demonstrates that our library is general and practical enough to tackle complex problems that make use of linear algebra.

Furthermore, this work yields a lot of potential future research. We plan first to develop the linear algebra library even more by adding other useful notions of linear algebra: e.g., dual spaces or decomposition according to a basis. We also consider providing implementations of some specific instantiations of the theory presented here, depending on the value of the variable A in the type `cfun`. This would yield the development of some specific theories that could be especially useful to particular areas like, e.g., electromagnetic. Finally, our successful experiments with the formalization of quantum mechanics encourages to go further in this direction, by developing a theorem-proving framework that would allow easy but safe verification of quantum optics devices. This would have applications both in the verification of optics-related technologies, and in quantum computer engineering.

References

1. Aladev, V.Z.: Computer Algebra Systems: A New Software Toolbox For Maple. Computer Mathematics Series. Fultus Books (2004)
2. Bakshi, U.A., Bakshi, V.: Modern Control Theory. Technical Publications (2009)
3. Chandrasekaran, S., Manjunath, B.S., Wang, Y.F., Winkeler, J., Zhang, H.: An Eigenspace Update Algorithm for Image Analysis. Graphical Models and Image Processing 59(5), 321–332 (1997)
4. Dettman, J.W.: Introduction to Linear Algebra. Dover Books on Mathematics Series. Dover (1974)
5. Fox, M.: Quantum Optics: An Introduction. Oxford Master Series in Physics. Oxford University Press (2006)
6. Griffiths, D.J.: Introduction to Quantum Mechanics. Pearson Prentice Hall (2005)
7. Harrison, J.: HOL Light: A Tutorial Introduction. In: Srivas, M., Camilleri, A. (eds.) FMCAD 1996. LNCS, vol. 1166, pp. 265–269. Springer, Heidelberg (1996)
8. Harrison, J.: A HOL Theory of Euclidean Space. In: Hurd, J., Melham, T. (eds.) TPHOLs 2005. LNCS, vol. 3603, pp. 114–129. Springer, Heidelberg (2005)
9. Herencia-Zapana, H., Jobredeaux, R., Owre, S., Garoche, P.-L., Feron, E., Perez, G., Ascariz, P.: PVS linear algebra libraries for verification of control software algorithms in C/ACSL. In: Goodloe, A.E., Person, S. (eds.) NFM 2012. LNCS, vol. 7226, pp. 147–161. Springer, Heidelberg (2012)
10. Hirvensalo, M.: Quantum Computing. Natural Computing Series. Springer (2004)
11. Stein. J.: http://coq.inria.fr/pylons/contribs/view/LinAlg/trunk
12. Khan Afshar, S., Aravantinos, V.:
    http://hvg.ece.concordia.ca/code/hol-light/complex-vectors
13. Leonhardt, U.: Quantum Physics of Simple Optical Instruments. Reports on Progress in Physics 66(7), 1207 (2003)
14. Leonhardt, U.: Essential Quantum Optics: From Quantum Measurements to Black Holes. Cambridge University Press (2010)
15. Mahmoud, M.Y., Aravantinos, V.:
    http://hvg.ece.concordia.ca/code/hol-light/qoptics/qalgebra.ml
16. The Coq development team: The Coq Proof Assistant Reference Manual. LogiCal Project, Version 8.0 (2004)
17. Ralph, T.C., Gilchrist, A., Milburn, G.J., Munro, W.J., Glancy, S.: Quantum Computation with Optical Coherent States. Physical Review A 68, 042319 (2003)
18. Strang, G.: Introduction to Linear Algebra. Wellsley-Cambrige Press (2003)
19. Vinga, S., Almeida, J.: Alignment-Free Sequence Comparison – A Review. Bioinformatics 19(4), 513–523 (2003)

Formal Verification
of a Parameterized Data Aggregation Protocol

Sergio Feo-Arenis and Bernd Westphal

Albert-Ludwigs-Universität Freiburg, Germany

Abstract. We report on our experiences on the successful verification of a parameterized wireless fault-tolerant data aggregation protocol. We outline our verification method that involves automatic verification of a model of the node processing algorithm under system topology constraints. The presented work forms the basis for a generalization to verification rules for aggregation protocols that integrate automatic verification into an inductive framework.

1 Introduction

Data aggregation protocols are used in distributed systems to collect sensor data gathered by nodes of the system at dedicated *sink* nodes [5]. In case of unreliable wireless communication, a common correctness property of a data aggregation protocol is that, whenever there is a functioning communication path from a sensor node to its sink, then the data must be aggregated at the sink. One may, e.g., exploit the redundancy of radio communication, where more than one node may hear the transmissions of others, to provide multiple communication paths from a sensor to its sink. So-called *duplicate sensitive* data aggregation protocols have an additional correctness property which usually states that a sensor value should not be aggregated more than once at a sink node.

We consider the case of *parameterized* data aggregation protocols with a single sink and an arbitrary number of homogeneous nodes in a fixed *(network) topology*. For this case, we want to determine whether the correctness properties stated above are true of every configuration of the system by a semi-automatic, compositional approach. In general, this Parameterized Model Checking Problem is undecidable [1].

In this work, we report on the successful verification of the ridesharing protocol [6], that was proposed for use in DARPA's satellite cluster system F6 [4]. We applied a compositional approach that involves reasoning performed manually to derive verification conditions on the program running in the nodes. We were able to check those verification conditions fully automatically. We intend to generalize our experience from the ridesharing protocol into a general proof rule for a well-defined class of data aggregation systems which in particular comprises the ridesharing protocol.

Initially, we present an axiomatization of the system topology, the aggregation paths, and communication failures. Based on the axiomatization, we formalize

G. Brat, N. Rungta, and A. Venet (Eds.): NFM 2013, LNCS 7871, pp. 428–434, 2013.

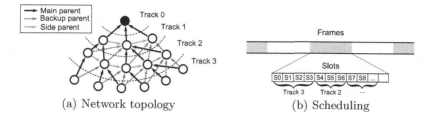

Fig. 1. Ridesharing Protocol

the correctness property of the protocol. We outline a compositional method to prove correctness that integrates the automatic verification of the program running in the nodes. We report on the automatic verification of a Boogie [2] model that integrates the axiomatization and the program, and on how we validated our axiomatization using an interactive theorem prover.

2   The Ridesharing Topology

The ridesharing protocol [6] was proposed for use in DARPA's satellite cluster system F6 [4] where satellites communicate over unreliable radio links. It is supposed to aggregate data from nodes that are logically organized in a tree structure by a *main parent* relation (cf. Figure 1(a)). Each node has a unique main parent and, in order to provide redundancy, a set of *backup parents* on the same depth level (called *track*) as the main parent. Nodes on the same track may have a *side links* as target of requests for correction if a message from a child was lost. Communication within one track is assumed to be reliable. Data is aggregated cyclically using *schedule* to avoid message collisions. Time is split into *frames* which is further partitioned into slots (cf. Figure 1(b)). Each node is assigned exactly one slot to send data.[1] Furthermore, nodes can be assumed to be *memoryless* wrt. frames, that is, they are initialized at the beginning of each frame. Therefore it is w.l.o.g. sufficient to consider a single frame in the correctness proof.

Ridesharing Network. Formally, a *ridesharing network* is a labeled graph (N, E, V) comprising a finite set of nodes N including the designated node n_0, called the *sink*, and a set of edges $E \subseteq N \times N$ which is the union of the three pairwise relations E_m, E_b, and E_s that represent the main and backup parents, and the side links, respectively. In a network, the main parent relation induces a tree with the sink as root, i.e. (N, E_m) is a tree, and the side link relation E_s is acyclic. The labeling function $V : N \to \mathcal{D}$ assigns each node the sensor reading in the considered frame, i.e. a value from the domain of the possible sensor values $\mathcal{D}$. Additionally, there is an *aggregation function* $(\cdot \oplus \cdot)$ such that $(\mathcal{D}, \oplus)$ form a *monoid*. When no sensor data is available, the neutral element of $\oplus$ is assumed.

---

[1] For simplicity, we assume that the side link relation is acyclic. In general, the ridesharing protocol [6] admits that nodes are assigned multiple slots under certain side conditions.

Node n' is called *main parent (backup parent, side link)* of n, denoted by $\longrightarrow_{E_m}$ ($\longrightarrow_{E_b}$, $\longrightarrow_{E_s}$) if and only if $(n, n') \in E_m$ (E_b, E_s). We use $E_p = E_m \cup E_b$ to denote the *parent* relation and say that nodes n and n' are *directly connected*, denoted by $n \longrightarrow_{E_p} n'$, if and only if n' is either main or backup parent of n. We use, e.g., $\longrightarrow_{E_p}^{*}$ to denote the reflexive, transitive closure of $\longrightarrow_{E_p}$. The *track* of a node n, denoted by $track(n)$, is 0 if n is the sink, and $track(n') + 1$ if there exists a parent node n' of n. We denote the set of all nodes at track k with N_k. Side parents of a node have to be of the same track as the node itself.

Unreliable Communication and Schedule. We model unreliable communication between parents and children by the *communication function* $f : E \to \mathbb{B}$. For an edge $e = (n, n') \in E$, we assume $f(e) = 1$ if and only if the communication was successful between nodes n and n'. We use $n \Longmapsto n'$ to denote that there was successful communication between connected nodes, i.e. that $n \longrightarrow_{E_p} n'$ and $f(n, n') = 1$. Its reflexive transitive closure $n \Longmapsto^* n'$ denotes that there is a *working path* between nodes n and n'. Note that working paths are in general not unique.

For the schedule we assume that the slots are assigned guaranteeing that for all nodes n, the input nodes according to the topology relations are scheduled before n.

Aggregation Paths. Two further concepts are useful to clarify the conditions that define a successful aggregation and under which correctness must be satisfied.

First, a sequence of successful transmissions $n_0 \Longmapsto n_1 \Longmapsto \ldots \Longmapsto n_k$ is called *aggregation path from n_0 to n_k* if and only if n_{i+1} is the first parent of n_i that successfully receives from n_i, i.e., if

$$\forall 0 \le i < k \,\forall n \in N_{i+1} \bullet \left(n_i \Longmapsto n \wedge n \longrightarrow_{E_s}^{*} n_{i+1} \right) \implies n = n_{i+1}$$

We say n_0 *has an aggregation path to* n_k, denoted by $n_0 \rightsquigarrow n_k$, if there exists an aggregation path from n_0 to n_k or if $n_0 = n_k$. Note that aggregation paths are unique in a ridesharing network for a given communication function.

Second, we introduce the term *responsible node*. A parent n' is *responsible* for aggregating the data of node n (and its children) if all preceding parents (by the side link relation) of n did not receive the transmission from n.

Correctness. Formally, a ridesharing protocol $\mathcal{P}$ can be described as a function that maps a ridesharing network with nodes N and edges E and a communication function f to a set of the nodes for which values were aggregated. I.e., $\mathcal{P} : (E \to \mathbb{B}) \to \mathbb{B}^N$. A ridesharing protocol is correct if and only if "If there is a working aggregation path between a node n and the sink then n's data is aggregated exactly once by the sink." I.e.

$$\mathcal{P} \text{ is correct} :\Longleftrightarrow \forall n \in N \bullet n \rightsquigarrow n_0 \implies \mathcal{P}(f)[n] = 1 \qquad (correctness)$$

where n_0 is the sink node.

Algorithm 1. Aggregation algorithm run by network nodes.

---

input : id, PC, BC, SP, v, rcv
$A := 0$; $P := \bar{0}$; $E := \bar{0}$;
if $v \neq NULL$ **then** { $A := A \oplus v$; $P[id] := 1$ } ;   // Aggregate local sensor reading
$E := rcv[SP]$;
foreach $c \in PC \cup BC$ **do**
    if $rcv[c] \neq$ *undefined* **then**
        if $c \in PC \vee (c \in BC \wedge E[c] = 1)$ **then**   // Aggregate received values
         | $(A_c, P_c) := rcv[c]$; $A := A \oplus A_c$; $P := P \mid P_c$; $E[c] := 0$;
        end
    else if $c \in PC$ **then**   // Request error correction
     | $E[c] := 1$;
    end
end
return (A, P, E);

---

3   A Ridesharing Protocol Algorithm

We seek an algorithm which, given a topology, realizes a correct protocol if executed on every node according to the schedule. We recall the aggregation algorithm as proposed in [6] (cf. Algorithm 1).

We assume that each node in the given topology has a unique identity. In order to abstract from communication and data gathering functionality, we assume that the algorithm is executed once per frame on each node. Input id gives the identity of the node and PC (BC, SP) the finite set of *primary children* (*backup children*, *side parents*) of the node, i.e. the inverse of E_m (E_b, E_s). Input v gives the current sensor reading and rcv the messages received by id in the current frame. The algorithm computes the message to be sent by id, given v and rcv.

The set of network messages M consists of triples (A, P, E) with the accumulated sensor value A and two control boolean vectors of length $|N|$. The *participation vector* P indicates for each node whether its value is included in A, the *error vector* E indicates at each position, whether correction is required for the node at that position.

Aggregation starts by initializing A with the neutral element of the aggregation function and P and E with all zeroes. If node id has sensor data, it is aggregated to A and P updated accordingly. We use $rcv[SP]$ to denote the bit-wise disjunction of the error vectors received from id's side parents. Then, E comprises all requests for corrections. In the loop, the received messages from id's children are processed as follows: if id received the message from c and if c is a primary child or a backup child with a pending request for correction in E then c's data is aggregated, i.e. A is updated and the P vector becomes the disjunction of the incoming P vectors. If id did not receive the message from primary child c, it flags a request for correction leaving A and P unchanged.

Executing Algorithm 1 once for each node in a network according to the schedule yields a history. A *history* h is a sequence of transmissions $\tau_1, \tau_2, \ldots, \tau_{|N|}$ where $\tau_j = (A_j, E_j, P_j)$ is the message transmitted by the node scheduled at slot j. Given the communication function f, that indicates which node received which transmission, there is the following relation between history h and the partial functions $rcv_n[\cdot] : N \nrightarrow M$: For each two connected nodes $n \longrightarrow_{E_p} n'$, $rcv_n[n'] = \tau_i$ if n'

is scheduled at slot i and $f(n, n')$. $rcv_n[n']$ is undefined otherwise. That is, rcv_{id} is passed as parameter rcv to the execution of Algorithm 1 on node id. The execution of Algorithm 1 once for each node in a network is a ridesharing protocol $\mathcal{P}$ as it maps a communication function f to the transmission of the sink, which is scheduled last, i.e., $\mathcal{P}(f) := P_{|N|}$.

4   Compositional Verification

In the formalizations presented in Sections 2 and 3, we have a formal model of all finite instances of Ridesharing, of which there are unboundedly many. We can model ridesharing networks for all numbers n of nodes (inducing length n for the vectors P and E) and all tree topologies (including all sizes up to n of PC and BC), each with $2^{|E_p|}$ failure scenarios. In general, correctness is, for this setting, undecidable.

Nonetheless, we have successfully verified the correctness of Algorithm 1 with respect to the correctness property of Section 2. Our approach focuses the verification efforts on any single node, due to the observation that the aggregation algorithm works symmetrically with respect to the id parameter. In principle, we verify whether, when a node in any given track receives *consistent* data from the subjacent track and its side parent, the track to which the node belongs also transmits *consistent* data.

In general, having correct data for an arbitrary node at its scheduled slot is a property of the complete earlier history, which again has an unbounded length. However, in this case, we can observe that for every node, only the exact structure of the network at the track immediately below and the own track is relevant. This observation allows us to produce an abstraction that partitions the history – and thus the input data for the node – in a finite manner according to whether the received data contains information for nodes on tracks below, on the same track, or on tracks above the node in question. We thus observed, that it is sufficient to assume that the nodes on a track aggregate data exclusively from the tracks below them, that no data is aggregated in a duplicate manner, and that the side parents do not transmit spurious correction messages. Formally, the data transmitted by track $N_k = \{n_1, \ldots, n_\ell\}$ in history h is the subsequence $\tau_1, \tau_2, \ldots, \tau_\ell$ where $\tau_i = (A_i, E_i, P_i)$ is the transmission of node n_i, $1 \leq i \leq \ell$. We call the data of track N_k consistent if and only if

$$\forall n_i \neq n_j \in N_k \; \forall n \in N \bullet (\neg(P_i[n] \wedge P_j[n]) \\ \wedge (P_i[n] \implies n = n_i \vee track(n) > k) \wedge (E_i[n] \implies track(n) = k + 1)) \tag{1}$$

This property allows us to give a specification for the aggregation algorithm, in the form of pre- and postconditions. The precondition is that the data in the rcv buffers of a node is consistent, in the sense of (1) and with respect to a communication function f. The algorithm should guarantee the postcondition that, for every possible role of a node, the bits in each position of the output vectors are set correctly with respect to the input data. That is, that no spurious aggregation occurred for nodes on the same track or tracks above, and that correction signals were correctly processed and generated such that no duplicate aggregation will occur. Satisfying that condition allows us to conclude that the data output by the track of the node being verified is consistent.

We utilized Boogie [2] to perform that verification task automatically. We used the axiomatization from Section 2 and added our pre- and postconditions. Due to the loop in Algorithm 1, an invariant was necessary. Framing conditions for the loop variables and the fact that consistency is preserved across iterations of the loop were sufficient.

We ensured the consistency of our model by checking that the axioms that describe the topology and the environment are consistent. We utilized a combination of smoke testing[2] and debugging by examination of counterexamples using BVD [7]. Boogie required approximately 1 second and 13MB of RAM to verify a total of 35 partial verification conditions.

To increase our confidence on the successful Boogie verification results, we checked whether our axiomatization was consistent, i.e., whether our axioms imply non-empty topologies and thus whether the verification conditions are not trivially satisfied. For that purpose, we used HOL-Boogie [3] to translate the model together with its verification conditions into Isabelle [9] and reconstructed the proof.[3] Only one manual lemma was necessary due to technicalities in the translation to Isabelle. The remaining proof was reconstructed automatically.

Having verified that tracks produce consistent output is sufficient to reason inductively and establish that for each topology of depth d, the messages of track 0 will be a correct aggregation of the nodes in the tracks below with respect to the communication function f. In our particular case, track 0 contains only the sink node.

Our induction proof is a double induction. Vertically, we consider ridesharing topologies of depth d and horizontally the width of tracks. The base case $d = 0$ is a track consisting of only leaf nodes. In the induction step, we inductively prove that for a depth $d + 1$ the chains of side links inside the track, starting at the leftmost node, preserve our consistency property where we can assume consistent data from track d.

5   Conclusions and Future Work

Applications of sensor networks for critical tasks commonly require robust data aggregation protocols. They represent an interesting instance of parameterized systems.

We presented the successful verification of the ridesharing protocol, a wireless aggregation protocol that employs redundant aggregation paths. The verification puts a "spotlight" [8] on a single node in a single track, while giving a finite abstraction of the data coming from the subjacent track. This allowed us to derive proof obligations on the aggregation algorithm which we discharged using automatic software model checking. We checked our axiomatization using interactive theorem proving. Overall we obtain a compositional approach which decouples

---

[2] In Boogie, adding `assert(false)` to each basic block to check for its reachability.
[3] Code available at: `http://www.informatik.uni-freiburg.de/~arenis/nfm13/`

the verification of the aggregation algorithm from the communication scheme. Using automatic software model checking increases the degree of automation and allows for an easy extension to a heterogeneous implementation: each implementation just needs to be verified to satisfy the proof obligations. To the extent of our knowledge, there are no previous works on the combination of deduction and automatic model checking for the verification of aggregation protocols.

In the future, we would like to generalize our approach. This amounts to a more general axiomatization of network topologies, e.g. lifting the restrictions on acyclicity and reliability of the side links, a deductive framework based on our inductive approach, and a simplification of the invariants required. Having narrowed down the conditions that are sufficient to ensure a finite case-split during verification, our generalization would then identify another decidable class of parameterized systems.

References

1. Apt, K.R., Kozen, D.: Limits for automatic verification of finite-state concurrent systems. Inf. Process. Lett. 22(6), 307–309 (1986)
2. Barnett, M., Chang, B.-Y.E., DeLine, R., Jacobs, B., Leino, K.R.M.: Boogie: A modular reusable verifier for object-oriented programs. In: de Boer, F.S., Bonsangue, M.M., Graf, S., de Roever, W.-P. (eds.) FMCO 2005. LNCS, vol. 4111, pp. 364–387. Springer, Heidelberg (2006)
3. Böhme, S., Moskal, M., Schulte, W., Wolff, B.: HOL-Boogie - an interactive prover-backend for the verifying C compiler. J. Autom. Reasoning 44(1-2), 111–144 (2010)
4. Brown, O., Eremenko, P.: The value proposition for Fractionated space architectures. In: AIAA Space 2006, No. 7506. AIAA (2006)
5. Feng, J., Eager, D.L., Makaroff, D.: Aggregation protocols for high rate, low delay data collection in sensor networks. In: Fratta, L., Schulzrinne, H., Takahashi, Y., Spaniol, O. (eds.) NETWORKING 2009. LNCS, vol. 5550, pp. 26–39. Springer, Heidelberg (2009)
6. Gobriel, S., Khattab, S., Mossé, D., Brustoloni, J., Melhem, R.: Ridesharing: Fault tolerant aggregation in sensor networks using corrective actions. In: IEEE Communications Society Conference on Sensor, Mesh and Ad Hoc Communications and Networks, pp. 595–604 (2006)
7. Le Goues, C., Leino, K.R.M., Moskal, M.: The boogie verification debugger (tool paper). In: Barthe, G., Pardo, A., Schneider, G. (eds.) SEFM 2011. LNCS, vol. 7041, pp. 407–414. Springer, Heidelberg (2011)
8. Wachter, B., Westphal, B.: The spotlight principle. On combining process-summarising state abstractions. In: Cook, B., Podelski, A. (eds.) VMCAI 2007. LNCS, vol. 4349, pp. 182–198. Springer, Heidelberg (2007)
9. Wenzel, M., Paulson, L.C., Nipkow, T.: The isabelle framework. In: Mohamed, O.A., Muñoz, C., Tahar, S. (eds.) TPHOLs 2008. LNCS, vol. 5170, pp. 33–38. Springer, Heidelberg (2008)

OnTrack: An Open Tooling Environment for Railway Verification

Phillip James[1], Matthew Trumble[2,*],
Helen Treharne[2], Markus Roggenbach[1], and Steve Schneider[2]

[1] Swansea University, UK
[2] University of Surrey, UK

Abstract. OnTrack automates workflows for railway verification, starting with graphical scheme plans and finishing with automatically generated formal models set up for verification. OnTrack is grounded on an established domain specification language (DSL) and is generic in the formal specification language used. Using a DSL allows the formulation of abstractions that work for verification in several formal specification languages. Here, we demonstrate the workflow using CSP||B and suggest how to extend the tool with further formal specification languages.

1 Introduction

It is becoming common industrial practice to utilize Domain Specific Languages (DSLs) for designing systems [10]. Such DSLs offer constructs native to the specific application area. Formal methods often fail to be easily accessible for engineers, but designs formulated in DSLs are open for systematic and, possibly, automated translation into formal models for verification. DSLs also allow abstractions to be formulated at the domain level.

Considering the railway industry, defining graphical descriptions is the de facto method of designing railway networks. This enables an engineer to visually represent the tracks and signals etc., within a railway network. This paper describes OnTrack[1], an open tool environment allowing graphical descriptions to be captured and supported by formal verification. Our work is inspired by the SafeCap toolset [5] which is a graphical editor tailored towards Event-B analysis. In OnTrack, we emphasise the use of a DSL and decoupling this DSL from the verification method. The novelty of this is that we define abstractions on the DSL in order to yield an optimised description prior to formal analysis. Importantly, these abstractions allow benefits for verification in different formal languages. Our graphical editor can be used as a basis for generating different formal specifications in different languages. Such automated generation eliminates errors introduced when hand-coding formal specifications, improving for instance, the hand-coded specifications in [6,8,9]. Finally, OnTrack is designed for the railway domain, but the clear separation of an editor with support for abstractions from the chosen formal language is a principle more widely applicable.

---

* The author was funded by an EPSRC vacation bursary, Summer 2012.

[1] OnTrack available for download from `http://www.csp-b.org`

G. Brat, N. Rungta, and A. Venet (Eds.): NFM 2013, LNCS 7871, pp. 435–440, 2013.
© Springer-Verlag Berlin Heidelberg 2013

2   Workflow

Figure 1 shows the workflow that we employ in OnTrack. Initially, a user draws a *Track Plan* using the graphical front end. Then the first transformation, *Generate Tables* leads to a *Scheme Plan*, which is a track plan and its associated control tables. Control tables contain information about when routes can be granted, see [9] for details. Track plans and scheme plans are models formulated relative to our railway DSL meta-model, see Section 3. A scheme plan is the basis for subsequent workflows that support its verification. Scheme plans can be captured as formal specifications. This is achieved following two transformations: (1) a *Represent* transformation translates a *Scheme Plan* into an equivalent *Formal Scheme Plan* over the meta-model of the formal specification language (FSL) - this is the core transformation within the toolset; (2) various *Generate for Verification* transformations turn a *Formal Scheme Plan* into a *Formal Specification Text* ready for verification using external tools. These *Generate for Verification* transformations can enrich the models appropriately for verification. These transformations are validated via manual review.

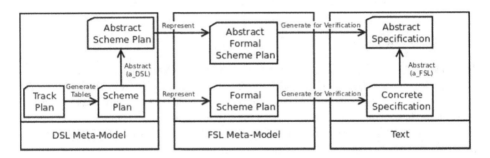

Fig. 1. OnTrack workflow

The horizontal workflow, described above, provides a validated transformation that yields a formal specification text that faithfully represents a scheme plan. In addition to this workflow, we are interested in abstractions to ease verification. Moller et al. [8] identify two abstractions: representing topological insights from the domain and reduction theorems over the language semantics. In OnTrack we define the topological abstractions with respect to the DSL, thus they are decoupled from the FSL. As any abstraction a_{DSL} w.r.t the DSL induces a corresponding abstraction a_{FSL} over specifications, it is possible to share them between different formal methods.

3   The OnTrack Editor

OnTrack implements the workflow from Section 2 in a typical EMF/GMF/Epsilon architecture [3,7]: a graphical editor realised in GMF is the front end for the user. As a basis for our tool, we have defined a modified version of the DSL developed by Bjørner [1]. The concepts of such a DSL can be easily captured within an ECORE meta-model which underlies our toolset. A small excerpt of topological concepts within our meta-model is given in Figure 2.

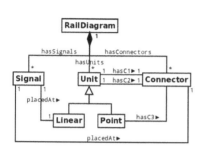

Fig. 2. Static concepts from Bjørner's DSL

A *Railway Diagram* is built from *Units, Connectors* and *Signals. Units* come in two forms: *Linear* representing straight tracks, or *Point* representing a splitting track. All *Unit(s)* are attached together via *Connector(s).* Finally, *Signals* can be placed on *Linear* units and at *Connectors.*

Implementing a GMF front-end for this meta-model involves selecting the concepts of the meta-model that should become graphical constructs within the editor and assigning graphical images to them. Figure 3 shows the OnTrack editor that consists of a drawing canvas and a palette. Graphical elements from the palette can be positioned onto the drawing canvas. Within the editor, the Epsilon Wizard Language (EWL) for model transformations has been used to implement calls to the various scripts realizing different transformations. The first EWL wizard, *Generate Tables*, automatically computes a control table for a track plan. We omit details of this transformation and focus instead on the *Abstraction, Represent* and *Generate for Verification* transformations.

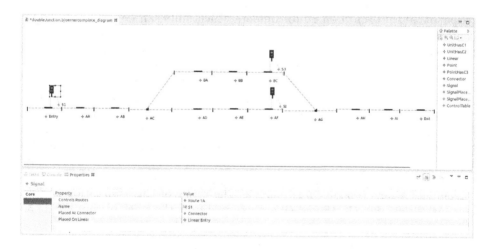

Fig. 3. A screenshot of "OnTrack" modelling a station

Listing 1.1. ETL rule for abstract model transformation

```
1   rule abs transform rd: Input!RailDiagram to rd2 : Target!RailDiagram {
2       rd.computeAbstractions();
3       for(ut:Unit in rd.hasUnits){
4           if(not (toDelete.contains(ut))){
5               if(consToBeMapped.contains(ut.hasC1)) {
6                   ut.hasC1 = ut.hasC1.getMapping(); }
7               if(consToBeMapped.contains(ut.hasC2)) {
8                   ut.hasC2 = ut.hasC2.getMapping(); }
9               rd2.hasUnits.add(ut); } }
10          //Omitted code: similar computation with connectors and signals//
11          rd2.computeTables(); }
```

4   Automatic DSL Abstractions

We have implemented a particular a_{DSL} abstraction based on the *simplifying scheme plan* abstraction by Moller et al. [8]. Various sequences of units are "collapsed" into single units. This abstraction has been shown correct, and to improve the feasibility of verification [8]. The abstraction is implemented using the Epsilon Transformation Language (ETL) [7] that is designed for model transformations. Listing 1.1 gives an excerpt of our transformation. The algorithm uses the following list structures: toDelete: storing units to be removed and consToBeMapped: storing which connectors require renaming.

The abs rule performs as follows: line 1 states that the rule translates the given rail diagram rd to another rd2. The second line simply calls an operation computeAbstraction() on rd to compute which units can be collapsed and to populate the lists with appropriate values. For example, considering Figure 3, toDelete = $[AA, AB, BA, BB, AD, AE, AH]$. Next, the algorithm will consider every unit ut within rd (line 3). If ut is not in the list toDelete (line 4), then the algorithm will perform analysis on the connectors of ut. If connector one of ut is within the set of connectors requiring renaming (line 5), then the first connector of ut is renamed using a call to the operation getMapping() (line 6). Lines 7 to 8 of the algorithm perform these steps for connector two of ut. After this computation, the modified unit ut is added as an element to rd2 (line 9). The algorithm continues in a similar manner, computing which connectors and signals should be added to rd2. Finally, an operation computeTables is called to compute a new control table for rd2. The result of this translation is that units AA, AB, BA, BB, AD, AE and AH are removed from the track plan in Figure 3.

5   Automatic Generation of CSP∥B Models

Here we describe the implementation of the *Represent* and *Generate for Verification* transformations for CSP∥B formal specifications. The use of CSP∥B specifications for railway modelling is presented in [8,9].

Listing 1.2. One of the ETL rules for unit to CSP datatype transformation

```
1   rule processUnits transform u : Bjoerner!Unit to d : CSP!DataTypeItem {
2       d.name = u.name;
3       d.type = pos;
4       if (pos_list.firstItem.isDefined()) {
5           d.preceeds = pos_list.firstItem; }
6       pos_list.size = pos_list.size + 1;
7       pos_list.firstItem = d; }
```

The goal of the *Represent* transformation is to iterate through a scheme plan, which is an instance of our DSL meta-model, in order to produce instances of the CSP||B meta-models. It is implemented using ETL. CSP||B meta-model instances contain collections of objects required to produce the final specification text. They do not include information on the structure of statements for the final formal specification. The Epsilon Validation Language (EVL) [7] can be used to validate all required objects are defined as expected. We achieve traceability between the meta-models by defining a structured ETL transformation, i.e., providing separate ETL scripts that reflect the final specification text architecture. Overall, our CSP||B model consists of six specifications [9], each generated by a separate ETL script. These scripts consist of 16 rules, 1 local operation and a 17 shared operations. Listing 1.2 gives an example rule that transforms units of a scheme plan to a CSP data type. For each unit, the **processUnits** rule constructs a corresponding **DataTypeItem** which is then added to the datatype (**pos_list**). For example, for Figure 3 **pos_list** = [AA,AB,AC,...].

The *Generate for Verification* transformation translates CSP||B meta-model instances into formal specification text. Interestingly, in CSP||B the formal specification text differs depending on the property to be proven, see [8] for details. Therefore, the *Generate for Verification* transformation produces a number of different specification texts. These transformations are implemented using the Epsilon Generation Language (EGL) [7] for generating text. For example, the **pos_list** datatype instance becomes the following fragment of CSP: **datatype ALLTRACK = AA | AB | AC | ...**. The transformations are novel as they apply pre-processing using Apache Velocity Java templates to avoid code repetition. These together with the EGL are used to generate models. Note that the CSP||B instance models produced from the *Represent* transformation only contain the information of a scheme plan. They do not include a model of the interlocking algorithm. This algorithm remains constant for all scheme plans and is therefore defined in a template file which is used in the *Generate for Verification* transformation to enrich the CSP||B specifications. Similarly, the behavioural description of a train remains constant and is again defined in a separate template file. Overall, we define six templates which reflect the final CSP||B architecture (1 CSP script and 5 B machines, see [9] for details). This gives a clear correspondence between the templates and formal specification structure.

6   Lessons Learnt and Discussion

The OnTrack toolset achieves the aim of automating the tedious production of formal specifications. The toolset allows for abstractions to be defined over the DSL in order to produce optimised railway models, from which transformations to formal specifications can be defined. Importantly, these abstractions are decoupled from the formal specifications. In building the tool, the encoding of the DSL into a meta-model is straightforward, however there needs to be a close relationship between the graphical artifacts and the meta-model. The benefit of using the toolset is that we can focus our efforts on understanding the impact of the verification results on the safety of a scheme plan.

Current work includes the development of a *Generate for Verification* transformation to the algebraic specification language CASL. Manual encoding has shown the abstractions over the DSL also aid verification for a CASL based railway modelling approach [6].

In order to extend the tool to produce formal specifications in languages other than CSP‖B, e.g., for railway verification based on NuSMV by [4], the following would be required: define a meta-model for the chosen formal language and then define the *Represent* and *Generate for Verification* transformations for that language.

Future improvements that would aid our understanding of the results is to visualise feedback of any counterexamples, produced during verification on the scheme plan itself. Similar visualisations have already been achieved in [2].

References

1. Bjørner, D.: Formal Software Techniques for Railway Systems. In: CTS 2000 (2000)
2. dos Santos, O.M., Woodcock, J., Paige, R.F.: Using model transformation to generate graphical counter-examples for the formal analysis of xUML models. In: ICECCS, pp. 117–126. IEEE Computer Society (2011)
3. Gronback, R.C.: Eclipse Modeling Project: A Domain-Specific Language (DSL) Toolkit. Addison-Wesley Professional (2009)
4. Haxthausen, A.E.: Automated generation of safety requirements from railway interlocking tables. In: Margaria, T., Steffen, B. (eds.) ISoLA 2012, Part II. LNCS, vol. 7610, pp. 261–275. Springer, Heidelberg (2012)
5. Iliasov, A., Romanovsky, A.: SafeCap domain language for reasoning about safety and capacity. In: Workshop on Dependable Transportation Systems. IEEE CS (2012)
6. James, P., Roggenbach, M.: Designing domain specific languages for verification: First steps. In: ATE 2011. CEUR (2011)
7. Kolovos, D., Rose, L., Paige, R., García-Domínguez, A.: The Epsilon Book. The Eclipse Foundation (2012)
8. Moller, F., Nguyen, H.N., Roggenbach, M., Schneider, S., Treharne, H.: Defining and Model Checking Abstractions of Complex Railway Models using CSP‖B. In: HVC 2012. LNCS (to be published)
9. Moller, F., Nguyen, H.N., Roggenbach, M., Schneider, S., Treharne, H.: Railway modelling in CSP‖B: the double junction case study. In: AVOCS 2012. EASST (2012)
10. Invensys Rail: Invensys Rail Data Model – Version 1A (2010)

Verification of Numerical Programs: From Real Numbers to Floating Point Numbers

Alwyn E. Goodloe[1], César Muñoz[1], Florent Kirchner[2], and Loïc Correnson[2]

[1] NASA Langley Research Center, USA
{a.goodloe,cesar.a.munoz}@nasa.gov
[2] CEA, LIST, France
{florent.kirchner,loic.correnson}@cea.fr

Abstract. Numerical algorithms lie at the heart of many safety-critical aerospace systems. The complexity and hybrid nature of these systems often requires the use of interactive theorem provers to verify that these algorithms are logically correct. Usually, proofs involving numerical computations are conducted in the infinitely precise realm of the field of real numbers. However, numerical computations in these algorithms are often implemented using floating point numbers. The use of a finite representation of real numbers introduces uncertainties as to whether the properties verified in the theoretical setting hold in practice. This short paper describes work in progress aimed at addressing these concerns. Given a formally proven algorithm, written in the Program Verification System (PVS), the Frama-C suite of tools is used to identify sufficient conditions and verify that under such conditions the rounding errors arising in a C implementation of the algorithm do not affect its correctness. The technique is illustrated using an algorithm for detecting loss of separation among aircraft.

1   Introduction

Virtually every aerospace application is composed of numerical algorithms. The mathematics in these algorithms is both continuous and discrete. The hybrid nature of aerospace applications often means that interactive theorem provers are required to reason about their logical correctness. As the models and algorithms are refined into an implementation, care must be taken so that assumptions made in the abstract models are not violated by the implementation. Of particular concern are the issues that arise when moving from the infinitely precise field of real numbers to an implementation using a floating point representation [4, 8] such as the IEEE 754 standard [5]. It is well-known that overflows, underflows, and accumulated rounding errors in floating point arithmetic can produce results that significantly differ from the ideal. Hence, properties that were demonstrated to hold in the abstract models may be violated in a concrete implementation. Therefore one cannot assert that theorems proven in the setting of the real numbers carry over to the implementation without additional arguments.

The domain of application of the case study in this paper is *air traffic management* (ATM). Advances in surveillance and communication systems allow for

G. Brat, N. Rungta, and A. Venet (Eds.): NFM 2013, LNCS 7871, pp. 441–446, 2013.
© Springer-Verlag Berlin Heidelberg 2013

ATM concepts where computer programs provide safety-critical functionality. For instance, the self-separation operational concept proposed by NASA [10] relies on airborne conflict detection and resolution (CD&R) systems that assist pilots and air traffic controllers to maintain safety in the airspace by keeping aircraft separated. Computer-based separation assurance systems are critical elements of air/ground distributed operational concepts for the next generation of air traffic management systems.

The Formal Methods group at NASA Langley has developed the Aiborne Coordinated Conflict Resolution and Detection (ACCoRD) formal framework for reasoning about aircraft separation assurance systems.[1] The framework, which is written in the Program Verification System (PVS) [9], consists of more than 1500 lemmas and includes formally verified algorithms for conflict detection, conflict resolution, conflict recovery, loss of separation recovery, and conflict prevention bands. This paper reports work in progress on a verification approach that is being applied to formally prove the correctness of the C implementations of some of these algorithms.

2   Conflict Detection

This paper concerns a conflict detection algorithm, namely CD2D, developed by NASA as part of the ACCoRD framework. CD2D is pairwise state-based 2-D conflict detection algorithm. Pairwise refers to the fact that CD2D only considers two aircraft called the *ownship* and the *intruder*. State-based refers to the use of an Euclidean airspace where the aircraft fly at constant velocity. In particular, in CD2D, the position and velocity of the ownship are represented by 2-D position $\mathbf{s}_o = (s_{ox}, s_{oy})$ and vector $\mathbf{v}_o = (v_{ox}, v_{oy})$, respectively, and the position and velocity of the intruder are represented by $\mathbf{s}_i = (s_{ix}, s_{iy})$ and $\mathbf{v}_i = (v_{ix}, v_{iy})$, respectively. As it simplifies the mathematical development, most definitions in ACCoRD use a relative coordinate system where the intruder is static at the center of the system. In this relative system, the ownship is located at $\mathbf{s} = \mathbf{s}_o - \mathbf{s}_i$ and moves at relative velocity $\mathbf{v} = \mathbf{v}_o - \mathbf{v}_i$.

In air traffic management, a *loss of separation* is a violation of the separation requirement between two aircraft. If the vertical dimension is ignored, the separation requirement is given by a minimum horizontal distance D. A *conflict* is a predicted loss of separation within a lookahead time T. In this paper, D and T are global constants. Loss of separation and conflict are formalized in ACCoRD as follows.

$$los?(\mathbf{s}) \equiv \sqrt{s_x^2 + s_y^2} < D, \quad conflict?(\mathbf{s}, \mathbf{v}) \equiv \exists\, 0 \leq t \leq T : los?(\mathbf{s} + t\mathbf{v}).$$

The PVS function *cd2d*, that models the CD2D algorithm, takes as parameters the state of the aircraft, i.e., $\mathbf{s}_o, \mathbf{v}_o, \mathbf{s}_i, \mathbf{v}_i$ and returns a Boolean value that indicates whether or not a loss of separation with respect to the minimum distance D is predicted to occur within the lookahead time T.

---

[1] http://shemesh.larc.nasa.gov/people/cam/ACCoRD

$cd2d(\mathbf{s}_o, \mathbf{v}_o, \mathbf{s}_i, \mathbf{v}_i) \equiv \texttt{let } \mathbf{s} = \mathbf{s}_o - \mathbf{s}_i, \mathbf{v} = \mathbf{v}_o - \mathbf{v}_i \texttt{ in } los?(\mathbf{s}) \texttt{ or } \omega(\mathbf{s}, \mathbf{v}) < 0,$

where ω is a continuous function that characterizes conflicts. It is defined as follows.

$$\omega(\mathbf{s}, \mathbf{v}) \equiv \begin{cases} \mathbf{s} \cdot \mathbf{v} & \text{if } \mathbf{s}^2 = D^2, \\ \mathbf{v}^2 \mathbf{s}^2 + 2\tau(\mathbf{s} \cdot \mathbf{v}) + \tau^2(\mathbf{s}, \mathbf{v}) - D^2 \mathbf{v}^2 & \text{otherwise,} \end{cases}$$

where $\tau(\mathbf{s}, \mathbf{v}) \equiv \min(\max(0, -(\mathbf{s} \cdot \mathbf{v})), T\mathbf{v}^2)$. When $\mathbf{v}^2 \neq 0$, $\frac{\tau(s, \mathbf{v})}{\mathbf{v}^2}$ denotes the time of closest approach for the aircraft and $\frac{\omega(\mathbf{s}, \mathbf{v})}{\mathbf{v}^2} + D$ denotes the minimum distance.

The ACCoRD development has a formal proof that the function $cd2d$ is sound and complete with respect to the predicate *conflict?*, i.e., that the following statement holds.

Proposition 1. *Given a distance $D > 0$ and a lookahead time $T > 0$, for all vectors $\mathbf{s} = \mathbf{s}_o - \mathbf{s}_i$ and $\mathbf{v} = \mathbf{v}_o - \mathbf{v}_i$,*

(soundness) *If conflict?$(\mathbf{s}, \mathbf{v})$ holds then $cd2d(\mathbf{s}_o, \mathbf{v}_o, \mathbf{s}_i, \mathbf{v}_i)$ returns true.*
(completeness) *If $cd2d(\mathbf{s}_o, \mathbf{v}_o, \mathbf{s}_i, \mathbf{v}_i)$ returns true then conflict?$(\mathbf{s}, \mathbf{v})$ holds.*

Soundness and completeness are closely related to the concepts of *missed-alerts* and *false-alerts*, respectively.

It should be noted that the theoretical development presented in this section assumes infinite precision real numbers and does not consider physical limitations of the aircraft. In a concrete implementation of the CD2D algorithm, those considerations become significant. In particular, arbitrary large/small numbers in the presence of floating point numbers and the use of floating point arithmetic introduce uncertainties as to whether properties verified in the ideal theoretical setting, such as Proposition 1, hold in practice.

3   Verification in Practice

In order to formally prove a stament such as Proposition 1 for a C program, it is necessary to have a verification environment that provides a specification language supporting both real numbers and floating point arithmetic and that easily integrates with automated and interactive theorem provers. Frama-C is an open-source framework developed at CEA comprising a suite of tools for static analysis of C programs in the form of plugins implementing abstract interpretation, slicing, and deductive verification engines. In particular, Frama-C uses the deductive verification plugin Jessie [6], which generates verification conditions for C programs. These verification conditions are submitted to different theorem provers via the Why3 back-end [2]. In particular, Why3 connects to the Gappa [7] tool, which specializes in verifying properties of numerical programs. Frama-C supports annotations written in the ANSI C Specification Language (ACSL) [1], an assertion language for specifying behavioral properties of C programs in a first-order logic. As PVS, ACSL supports mathematical expressions over the real numbers. Furthermore, ACSL has a built-in model of IEEE-754 arithmetic including the rounding modes, casts, and infinity. The analysis presented here assumes IEEE-754 in strict form, i.e., the generated verification conditions ensure no overflows or special values, and rounding to nearest with ties to even.

A straightforward C implementation of *cd2d* does not satisfy Proposition 1 due to the use of floating point arithmetic in C. Indeed, in the presence of computation errors, it is impossible to write a program that satisfies both correctness and completeness. In practice, there is a trade-off between soundness and completeness in any implementation of a conflict detection algorithm. From a safety point of view, soundness is usually considered the more desirable of the two properties since it eliminates the possibility for missed-alerts. Therefore, the target property for the verification presented here is soundness. However, it should be noted that completeness also has safety implications. For example, a program that always returns *true* would be trivially sound. Of course, such a program will have an unacceptable rate of false alerts and quickly erode the trust that a pilot may have on these kinds of systems.

This paper proposes a systematic construction of a C program, namely **cd2d**, from its PVS counterpart, namely *cd2d*, that is provably sound. The proof is conducted in the Frama-C environment and reuses Proposition 1 and other core geometric properties proved in PVS. The construction of **cd2d** starts by translating every real-valued function f involved in the definition of *cd2d* into an identical logical ACSL function f and into a C function f. Function f uses real number arithmetic, while function f uses floating point arithmetic. The specification of the function f states that the absolute error of the floating point computation is bounded by a given positive constant ϵ_f, i.e., $|f(x) - \mathtt{f}(x)| \le \epsilon_f$. Here only the C basic types **double** and **int** are used for the translation. Therefore, vectors are represented by their components. For instance, the function τ, used in Formula 2, is translated into ACSL-annotated C code as follows.[2]

```
/*@ logic real tauR(real s_x,real s_y,real v_x,real v_y,real t) =
  @    dmin(dmax(0.,-dotR(s_x,s_y,v_x,v_y)),t*sqvR(v_x,v_y)) ;
  @*/
```

```
/*@ requires -100. <= s_x <= 100. && ...;
  @ ensures \abs(\result - tauR(s_x,s_y,v_x,v_y,T)) <= E_tau;
  @*/
```

```
double tau(double s_x,double s_y,double v_x,double v_y) {
    return min(max(0,-dot(s_x,s_y,v_x,v_y)),T*sqv(v_x,v_y)); }
```

In ACSL, the precondition is denoted by the keyword **requires**, while the postcondition is denoted by the keyword **ensures**. By convention, real number

---

[2] Logical definitions in ACSL cannot refer to C constants. Hence, t has been added as a parameter to **tauR**.

functions are written with the postfix R. If function f is proven to satisfy its specification for a certain value of ϵ_f, this value is propagated into the specification of functions and Boolean conditions that depend on f. At the end of the process, the cd2d function is written as follows.

```
int cd2d(double so_x,double so_y,double vo_x,double vo_y,
        double si_x,double si_y,double vi_x,double vi_y) {
    double s_x = so_x - si_x; double s_y = si_x - si_y;
    double v_x = vo_x - vi_x; double v_y = vi_x - vi_y;
    return los(s_x,s_y) || omega(s_x,s_y,v_x,v_y) < E_cd2d; }
```

In order to appropriately bound the values of the input variables, a system of units needs to be chosen. As usual in air traffic management, distances are given in nautical miles, speeds are given in knots (nautical miles per hour), and, for unit consistency, times are given in hours. Typical bounds for state-based separation assurance algorithms such as CD2D are $|so\_x|, |so\_y|, |si\_x|, |si\_y| \leq$ 100 nautical miles and $|vo\_x|, |vo\_y|, |vi\_x|, |vi\_y| \leq 600$ knots. Furthermore, the constants D and T are set to 5 nautical miles and 0.083 hours (about 5 minutes), respectively.

An approach to verify that cd2d verifies soundness consists in replaying the soundness proof of *cd2d* and adapting, on this process, every proof step to deal with floating point inaccuracies. This paper takes a different approach. Since the PVS function *cd2d* is known to be sound *and* complete, soundness of cd2d is equivalent to the following proposition.

Proposition 2 (Soundness of cd2d). *Given the specified values of D and T, for all so_x, so_y, si_x, si_y, vo_x, vo_y, vi_x, vi_y that satisfy the specified bounds, if cd2d($so\_x, so\_y, vo\_x, vo\_y, si\_x, si\_y, vi\_x, vi\_y$) returns true, then cd2d($so\_x, so\_y, vo\_x, vo\_y, si\_x, si\_y, vi\_x, vi\_y$) returns 1.*

This leaves the question of how to find the error bounds for each f, i.e., ϵ_f. Sophisticated analytical techniques exist for estimating rounding errors [3] and while these are needed to analyze more complex computations, in many cases it is possible to exploit the capability of Frama-C to quickly and automatically prove assertions to discover an appropriate value for ϵ_f. The process implements a search by dichotomy, hinging on the provability of the proof assertions.

Beginning with an initial estimate for ϵ_f, the Frama-C/Jessie plugin is invoked generating a number of verification conditions. If the automated prover cannot show that ϵ_f is a good bound, the value of ϵ_f is increased. On the other hand, if the provers show that the bound holds, the value of ϵ_f is decreased. The process continues until convergence on a tight bound. In the case of tau, the initial value of E_tau was set to 2^{-30}, but the Gappa solver on the back-end could not prove the postcondition. Next, E_tau was set to 2^{-10}, which the solver easily discharged. The dichotomy process eventually reached a bound on an absolute error of 2^{-21}. Proposition 2 is formally verified in Frama-C for the value E_cd2d $= 2 \times 2^{-1}$.

4 Conclusion

This work in progress contributes a methodology for proving the correctness of implementations of numerical programs whose soundness and completeness have already been demonstrated in the ideal setting of real numbers. In particular, the approach proposed here focuses on discovering and proving the bounds on floating-point rounding errors that can invalidate in practice the theorems proven on reals. As a first case study, the technique was applied to candidate algorithms in the ACCoRD framework. These algorithms feature strong correctness conditions, use only bounded loops and conditionals, and employ well behaved mathematical operations. In addition, the algorithms have well defined bounded input, and units were chosen that kept the magnitude of the computed values from growing big enough to produce large rounding errors. Future work will apply the approach to more sophisticated programs and consider relative error in addition to the absolute error. Also, the task remains to validate the safety implications of the error bounds shown in the paper. As the methodology evolves, the Frama-C tool support is expected to evolve by incorporating new algorithms and plugins to aid in the verification of numerical programs.

References

1. Baudin, P., Cuoq, P., Filliâtre, J.-C., Marché, C., Monate, B., Moy, Y., Prevosto, V.: ACSL: ANSI/ISO C Specification Language, version 1.6 (2012)
2. Bobot, F., Filliâtre, J.-C., Marché, C., Paskevich, A.: Why3: Shepherd your herd of provers. In: Boogie 2011: First International Workshop on Intermediate Verification Languages, Wrocław, Poland, pp. 53–64 (August 2011)
3. Boldo, S., Nguyen, T.M.T.: Hardware-independent proofs of numerical programs. In: NASA Formal Methods, pp. 14–23 (2010)
4. Goldberg, D.: What every computer scientist should know about floating point arithmetic. ACM Computing Surveys 23(1), 5–48 (1991)
5. IEEE Task P754. ANSI/IEEE 754-1985, Standard for Binary Floating-Point Arithmetic. IEEE (1985)
6. Marhé, C., Moy, Y.: The Jessie Plugin for Deductive Verification in Frama-C. INRIA Saclay Île-de-France and LRI, CNRS UMR (2012)
7. Melquiond, G.: User's Guide for Gappa. INRIA (2012)
8. Muller, J.-M., Brisebarre, N., de Dinechin, F., Jeannerod, C.-P., Lefèvre, V., Melquiond, G., Revol, N., Stehlé, D., Torres, S.: Handbook of Floating-Point Arithmetic. Birkhäuser, Boston (2010)
9. Owre, S., Rushby, J.M., Shankar, N.: PVS: A prototype verification system. In: Kapur, D. (ed.) CADE 1992. LNCS, vol. 607, pp. 748–752. Springer, Heidelberg (1992)
10. Wing, D.J., Cotton, W.B.: Autonomous flight rules a concept for self-separation in U.S. domestic airspace. Technical Publication NASA/TP-2011-217174, NASA, Langley Research Center, Hampton VA 23681-2199, USA (November 2011)

Extracting Hybrid Automata from Control Code

Steven Lyde and Matthew Might

University of Utah, Salt Lake City, Utah, USA
{lyde,might}@cs.utah.edu

Abstract. Formal methods—and abstract interpretation in particular—can assist in the development of correct control code. However, current approaches to deploying formal methods do not always match the way practicing engineers develop real control code. Engineers tend to think in code first—not formal models. Standard practice is for engineers to develop their control code and *then* build a model like a hybrid automaton from which to verify properties. Since the construction of this model is manual, it leaves open the possibility of error. Existing formal approaches, on the other hand, tend to focus on synthesizing control code from a verified formal model. We propose a method for synthesizing a hybrid automaton from the control code directly. Specifically, we use abstract interpretation to create an abstract state transition system, and from this we systematically extract a hybrid automaton. Not only does this eliminate the introduction of error into the model based on the code, it fits with common practice in engineering cyberphysical systems. We test the technique on a couple examples—control code for a thermostat and a nuclear reactor. We then pass the generated automata to the HyTech model-checker to verify safety and liveness properties.

1 Introduction

Avionics, automobiles and medical equipment depend on complex control software. The proscribed approach to developing these systems is "model-first," with analysis, simulation, testing, verification and code generation to follow.

However, in practice, engineers often develop code first, and a model second, if ever. We propose an approach to formal analysis of cyber-physical systems more in line with practice: we demonstrate that a sound model—a hybrid automaton [9] in this case—can be inferred from the control code itself. This gives developers an efficient way to maintain and manipulate the model of a controller more naturally. To achieve our goal, we use abstract interpretation (a higher-order control flow analysis, in particular) to analyze control code, and from the result, we infer hybrid automata. We can then pass these hybrid automata on to model checkers and formally verify properties of program behavior. Source and examples for the tool described in this paper are available [15]. For examples and more details, we refer the reader to the companion technical report [11].

1.1 Contributions

We make the following contributions:

G. Brat, N. Rungta, and A. Venet (Eds.): NFM 2013, LNCS 7871, pp. 447–452, 2013.

1. We report preliminary work on a method to extract a hybrid automaton from an abstract transition system, which is in turn synthesized from abstract interpretation of control code.
2. We claim a core calculus for a subset of MATLAB as a secondary contribution, developed to facilitate our primary contribution.

2   Language: λ_M, a Core Calculus for MATLAB

We compile control code in MATLAB to an A-Normalized core calculus. A-Normal Form (ANF) [7] forces an order of evaluation and simplifies the transition rules of both the concrete and abstract semantics.

The grammar for the target language is an unsurprising subset of Scheme, except for perhaps the inclusion of `call/ec`, which we use to model exceptions. Another interesting inclusion is that the conditional expression allows a convex predicate cp in its test expression. A convex predicate cp is a finite conjunction of linear inequalities, e.g., $x_1 \geq 3 \land 3x_2 \leq x_3 + 5/2$ [8].

$$
\begin{array}{lll}
pr \in \mathsf{Prog} = \mathsf{Exp} & & \text{[programs]} \\
v \in \mathsf{Var} \text{ is a set of identifiers} & & \text{[variables]} \\
c \in \mathsf{Const} = \mathit{String} + \mathbb{Z} & & \text{[literals]} \\
lam \in \mathsf{Lam} ::= (\lambda\ (v_1 \ldots v_n)\ e) & & \text{[lambda terms]} \\
f, \ae \in \mathsf{AExp} ::= lam \mid v \mid c & & \text{[atomic expressions]} \\
\quad\quad \mid\ (op\ \ae_1 \ldots \ae_n) & & \text{[primitive operations]} \\
op \in \mathsf{Op} \supseteq \{\texttt{+}, \texttt{-}, \texttt{*}\} & & \text{[primitives]} \\
e \in \mathsf{Exp} ::= (\texttt{let}\ ((v\ ce))\ e) & & \text{[expressions]} \\
\quad\quad \mid\ \ae & & \text{[return]} \\
\quad\quad \mid\ ce & & \text{[tail]} \\
ce \in \mathsf{CExp} ::= (f\ \ae_1 \ldots \ae_n) & & \text{[complex expressions]} \\
\quad\quad \mid\ (\texttt{if}\ cp\ e_1\ e_2) & & \text{[physical branching]} \\
\quad\quad \mid\ (\texttt{if}\ ae\ e_1\ e_2) & & \text{[cyber branching]} \\
\quad\quad \mid\ (\texttt{set!}\ v\ \ae) & & \text{[variable mutation]} \\
\quad\quad \mid\ (\texttt{call/ec}\ \ae) & & \text{[first-class control]}
\end{array}
$$

Fig. 1. Syntax for λ_M—a core calculus for MATLAB

To model programs, we inject them into time-stamped CESK-machines [6], whose state-space has five components—the current expression, the current environment, the current store, the current continuation and the current time. The time component does not relate to physical time, but is a way to encode the history of the machine's execution to facilitate abstraction. It is a parameter used when allocating new addresses in the store. In a regular CESK machine there will be an infinite number of addresses that can be allocated in the store, but we can structurally abstract this machine by bounding the set of times available [14]. Bounding time forces the set of states $\hat{\Sigma}$ to be finite.

Figure 2 describes the concrete and abstract state-spaces for the analyzer. To save space, we omit the transition relations $(\Rightarrow) \subseteq \Sigma \times \Sigma$ and $(\leadsto) \subseteq \hat{\Sigma} \times \hat{\Sigma}$ and we also omit the abstraction map $\alpha : \Sigma \to \hat{\Sigma}$ that connects them. For examples of such transitions, we refer the reader to [14]. Computing the control-flow analysis consists of constructing the "abstract state transition graph" of reachable states under $(\leadsto)$.

$$\varsigma \in \Sigma = \mathsf{Exp} \times Env \times Store \times Kont \times Time$$
$$\rho \in Env = \mathsf{Var} \rightharpoonup Addr$$
$$\sigma \in Store = Addr \rightharpoonup D$$
$$d \in D = Clo + Kont + String + \mathbb{Z}$$
$$clo \in Clo = \mathsf{Lam} \times Env$$
$$\kappa \in Kont ::= \mathbf{letk}(v, e, \rho, \kappa)$$
$$\mid \mathbf{halt}$$
$$a \in Addr ::= \mathbf{bindaddr}(v, t)$$
$$t \in Time \text{ is an infinite, ordered set of times}$$

$$\hat{\varsigma} \in \hat{\Sigma} = \mathsf{Exp} \times \widehat{Env} \times \widehat{Store} \times \widehat{Kont} \times \widehat{Time}$$
$$\hat{\rho} \in \widehat{Env} = \mathsf{Var} \rightharpoonup \widehat{Addr}$$
$$\hat{\sigma} \in \widehat{Store} = \widehat{Addr} \rightharpoonup \hat{D}$$
$$\hat{d} \in \hat{D} = \mathcal{P}\left(\widehat{Clo} + \widehat{Kont} + \widehat{String} + \hat{\mathbb{Z}}\right)$$
$$\widehat{clo} \in \widehat{Clo} = \mathsf{Lam} \times \widehat{Env}$$
$$\hat{\kappa} \in \widehat{Kont} ::= \mathbf{letk}(v, e, \hat{\rho}, \hat{\kappa})$$
$$\mid \mathbf{halt}$$
$$\hat{a} \in \widehat{Addr} ::= \mathbf{bindaddr}(v, \hat{t})$$
$$\hat{t} \in \widehat{Time} \text{ is an finite set of abstract times}$$

Fig. 2. The concrete (left) and abstract (right) state-spaces

Since our ultimate goal is to extract hybrid automata, we make use of an alternate, labeled formulation of the abstract transition relation:

$$\hat{\varsigma} \overset{cp}{\leadsto} \hat{\varsigma}' \text{ iff } \hat{\varsigma} \leadsto \hat{\varsigma}' \text{ and the physical condition } cp \text{ holds after transition.}$$

Only physical branching expressions—(if cp ... ...)—acquire these labels. The label f indicates that the transition does not depend on a physical condition.

3 Extracting a Hybrid Automaton

Control-flow analysis leaves us with an abstract state transition graph. We now briefly describe how to compile this graph into a hybrid automaton.

First, we want to annotate the states with some kind of physical state-change equations, e.g., $\dot{x} = -3$, as well as invariants, e.g. $t < 10$, found in hybrid automata. To do so we require "physical" annotations in the source code. The annotations identify which procedures read physical quantities and which procedure calls initiate physical changes in the system.

3.1   Algorithm

To extract the hybrid automaton from the results of the abstract interpretation, we are going to define hybrid automaton locations as sets (really, partitions) of machine states:

$$p \in HyLocation = \mathcal{P}(\hat{\Sigma})$$

We can lift the transition relation from machine states to hybrid locations:

$$p \rightsquigarrow p' \text{ iff there exists } \hat{\varsigma} \in p, \hat{\varsigma}' \in p' \text{ such that } \hat{\varsigma} \rightsquigarrow \hat{\varsigma}'.$$

It's convenient to have a special form of the transition relation as well:

$$p \twoheadrightarrow p' \text{ iff } p \rightsquigarrow^{f} p' \text{ and } p'' \rightsquigarrow^{f} p' \text{ implies } p'' = p.$$

Next, we need a function, ∇, to extract governing differential equations:

$$\nabla(\hat{\varsigma}) = \begin{cases} [\dot{x} \mapsto [\![e]\!]] & \text{if } \hat{\varsigma} = ((\texttt{assertCPS } \dot{x} = e), \dots) \\ \emptyset & \text{otherwise.} \end{cases}$$

and, for partitions, it combines all equations in a partition:

$$\nabla\{\hat{\varsigma}_0, \dots, \hat{\varsigma}_n\} = \nabla(\hat{\varsigma}_0) \cup \cdots \cup \nabla(\hat{\varsigma}_n)$$

The procedure EXTRACT accepts an abstract state transition graph generated by the abstract interpretation; it returns a hybrid automaton over the state-space *HyLocation* whose transition relation is ($\rightsquigarrow^{cp}$) and whose governing differential equations are determined by the function ∇:

procedure EXTRACT(*G*):
    $P \leftarrow \{\{\hat{\varsigma}\} \mid \hat{\varsigma} \in G\}$
    do
        $P \leftarrow$ MERGE(P)
        $P \leftarrow$ SPLIT(P)
    until *P* does not change
    return *P*

The procedure MERGE coalesces partitions with compatible equations:

procedure MERGE(*P*):
    do
        for each partition *p* **in** *P*:
            if $p \twoheadrightarrow p'$ **and** $dom(\nabla(p)) \cap dom(\nabla(p')) = \emptyset$:
                merge partitions *p* and *p'* in *P*
            if $p' \rightsquigarrow^{f} p$ **and** $p'' \rightsquigarrow^{f} p$ **and** $\nabla(p) = \nabla(p')$:
                merge partitions *p'* and *p''* in *P*
    until *P* does not change
    return *P*

The procedure SPLIT duplicates nodes that are blocking a merge due to differential equations:

procedure SPLIT(P):
    for each partition pair p, p' **in** P:
        if $p' \rightsquigarrow p$ **and** $p'' \rightsquigarrow p$ **and** $dom(\nabla(p)) \cap dom(\nabla(p')) \neq \emptyset$:
            duplicate p as p^* in P
            replace the edge $p \rightsquigarrow p''$ with $p \rightsquigarrow p^*$
    return P

4 Preliminary Evaluation

All code and examples for our implementation are available [15]. We prototyped our technique using Octave (a superset of MATLAB) for the control code. We utilize MATLAB as the input language because in our interactions with practicing engineers, we have found substantial amounts of control code—some production, some prototype—written in MATLAB. We analyzed the control code for a simple thermostat and for a nuclear reactor with our tool. After producing hybrid automata, we verified properties of the control code using HyTech [10].

5 Related Work

To generate the abstract state transition graph, we used a small-step formulation of k-CFA [14], built upon the original formulation of k-CFA by Shivers [12] and the large body of abstract interpretation first started by the Cousots [4,5].

Our goal was to transform the abstract state-space into a model from which safety properties could be proved. For the model we chose hybrid automaton as formulated by Henzinger [9]. This choice was made not only for their ability to accurately model cyber-physical systems, but also because tools already exist that verify safety and liveness properties [10].

The idea of merging abstract interpretation and physical systems in not unique to our work. Cousot argues that static analysis of control software can be guided by knowledge of the physical system [3]. Our approach claims that given additional information of the physical system, in the form of annotations, abstract interpretation can be used to create a model of the entire system.

Similar work has been done to convert control code to hybrid automata by Bouissou [2]. He provides a semantics preserving transformation from H-SIMPLE to a sampled hybrid automata and then from sampled hybrid automata to a regular hybrid automata. H-SIMPLE is a simple imperative language that has statements to control sensors and actuators, very similar to the annotations provided in our framework. While our language is also simple, it provides first class functions, which allow powerful higher language constructs to be modeled.

Another similar work to ours is in transforming Simulink/Stateflow models into Hybrid Automata [1,13]. However, our work differs in that we start from the control code of the system, not another model of the system.

This research is partly supported by the National Science Foundation under Grant No. 1035658.

References

1. Agrawal, A., Simon, G., Karsai, G.: Semantic Translation of Simulink/Stateflow Models to Hybrid Automata Using Graph Transformations. Electron. Notes Theor. Comput. Sci. 109, 43–56 (2004)
2. Bouissou, O.: From control-command synchronous programs to hybrid automata. In: Analysis and Design of Hybrid Systems, pp. 291–298 (2012)
3. Cousot, P.: Integrating physical systems in the static analysis of embedded control software. In: Yi, K. (ed.) APLAS 2005. LNCS, vol. 3780, pp. 135–138. Springer, Heidelberg (2005)
4. Cousot, P., Cousot, R.: Abstract interpretation: A unified lattice model for static analysis of programs by construction or approximation of fixpoints. In: Conference Record of the Fourth ACM Symposium on Principles of Programming Languages, pp. 238–252. ACM Press, New York (1977)
5. Cousot, P., Cousot, R.: Systematic design of program analysis frameworks. In: POPL 1979: Proceedings of the 6th ACM SIGACT-SIGPLAN Symposium on Principles of Programming Languages, pp. 269–282. ACM Press, New York (1979)
6. Felleisen, M., Friedman, D.P.: A calculus for assignments in higher-order languages. In: POPL 1987: Proceedings of the 14th ACM SIGACT-SIGPLAN Symposium on Principles of Programming Languages, pp. 314–325. ACM, New York (1987)
7. Flanagan, C., Sabry, A., Duba, B.F., Felleisen, M.: The essence of compiling with continuations. In: PLDI 1993: Proceedings of the ACM SIGPLAN 1993 Conference on Programming Language Design and Implementation, pp. 237–247. ACM, New York (1993)
8. Henzinger, T.A., Ho, P.-H., Wong-Toi, H.: A user guide to hytech. In: Brinksma, E., Steffen, B., Cleaveland, W.R., Larsen, K.G., Margaria, T. (eds.) TACAS 1995. LNCS, vol. 1019, pp. 41–71. Springer, Heidelberg (1995)
9. Henzinger, T.A.: The theory of hybrid automata. In: Proceedings of the Eleventh Annual IEEE Symposium on Logic in Computer Science, LICS 1996, pp. 278–292. IEEE (July 1996)
10. Henzinger, T.A., Ho, P.H., Toi, H.W.: HYTECH: A model checker for hybrid systems. International Journal on Software Tools for Technology Transfer 1(1-2), 110–122 (1997)
11. Lyde, S., Might, M.: Extracting hybrid automata from control code. Tech. rep., University of Utah (2013), http://matt.might.net/a/2013/03/03/ha-extract/lyde2013hybrid.pdf
12. Shivers, O.G.: Control-Flow Analysis of Higher-Order Languages. PhD thesis, Carnegie Mellon University, Pittsburgh, PA, USA (1991)
13. Silva, B.I., Richeson, K., Krogh, B., Chutinan, A.: Modeling and verifying hybrid dynamic systems using checkmate. In: Proceedings of 4th International Conference on Automation of Mixed Processes, pp. 323–328 (2000)
14. Van Horn, D., Might, M.: Abstracting abstract machines. In: ICFP 2010: Proceedings of the 15th ACM SIGPLAN International Conference on Functional Programming, pp. 51–62. ACM Press (2010)
15. Hybrid Automata Extraction, https://github.com/stevenlyde/ha-extraction

PyNuSMV: NuSMV as a Python Library

Simon Busard* and Charles Pecheur

ICTEAM Institute, Université catholique de Louvain, Louvain-la-Neuve, Belgium
{simon.busard,charles.pecheur}@uclouvain.be

Abstract. NuSMV is a state-of-the-art model checker providing BDD-based and SAT-based techniques and a rich modeling language. While the tool is powerful, it is hard to customize it because of the size and complexity of its code base (more than 200K LOC). This paper presents PyNuSMV, a Python framework for prototyping and experimenting with BDD-based model-checking algorithms based on NuSMV.

PyNuSMV provides a rich and flexible programmable platform to implement new logics and experiment with custom model-checking algorithms. Thanks to PyNuSMV, it is possible to use NuSMV functionalities without understanding its whole code base or struggling with implementation details such as memory management. PyNuSMV has already been used to implement model-checking algorithms for rich logics such as ARCTL and CTLK.

This paper describes the structure and usage of PyNuSMV, illustrates its use by re-implementing CTL model checking, and reports initial performance results showing negligible impact compared to native NuSMV.

Keywords: Symbolic Model Checking, NuSMV, Python Interface, Binary Decision Diagrams.

1 Introduction

NuSMV is a state-of-the-art BDD-based and SAT-based model checker for temporal logics providing additional features such as model simulation [4]. While it is a very powerful tool, its (open-source) code base adds up to more than 200K lines of C code, making it difficult to extend or customize to implement new logics or new model-checking algorithms.

PyNuSMV is a Python framework for prototyping and experimenting with BDD-based model-checking algorithms based on NuSMV. It gives access to some of NuSMV's main functionalities, such as source model parsing and BDD manipulation, while hiding NuSMV implementation details by providing wrappers to NuSMV functions and data structures. In particular, NuSMV models can be read, parsed and compiled, giving full access to SMV's rich modeling language and vast collection of existing models. It makes it easy to implement new BDD-based model-checking algorithms and has already been

---

* This work is supported by the European Fund for Regional Development and by the Walloon Region.

G. Brat, N. Rungta, and A. Venet (Eds.): NFM 2013, LNCS 7871, pp. 453–458, 2013.
© Springer-Verlag Berlin Heidelberg 2013

used to implement (1) rich counter-examples for CTL, (2) ARCTL model checking, an extension of CTL reasoning about the actions of a model, and (3) CTLK model checking, an extension of CTL reasoning about knowledge of the agents of a system [3,6,7]. The tool, including implementations for rich counter-examples, ARCTL and CTLK model checking, is available at `http://lvl.info.ucl.ac.be/Tools/PyNuSMV`.

Python has been retained to implement PyNuSMV because it comes with a full standard library and a full-fledged programming language supporting high-level programming (garbage collection, functional closures). PyNuSMV uses SWIG [1], a wrapper generator for C code, to wrap all NuSMV functions. On top of this wrapper, PyNuSMV provides a library of classes and modules reflecting NuSMV's main data structures (BDDs, expressions) at the Python level. Thanks to these classes and modules, it is easy to use NuSMV functionalities in Python, without struggling with implementation details such as memory management.

Note that SWIG has already been used in the RATSY tool to provide a wrapper of NuSMV functions at Python level [2]. But the goal of the tool was to support RATSY features by implementing them in NuSMV, not to provide a library of NuSMV functionalities.

The remainder of this paper is structured as follows: Section 2 presents the structure of PyNuSMV, Section 3 demonstrates its uses and reports initial evaluation results, and Section 4 describes future work.

2   PyNuSMV

The architecture of PyNuSMV, depicted in Figure 1, consists of three layers. The first one consists in the original **code of NuSMV** written in C. On this layer is the **lower interface**, composed of all modules generated by SWIG. Finally, the **upper interface**, built upon the lower one, consists of additional classes and modules providing access to some NuSMV main functionalities with Python capabilities such as garbage collection.

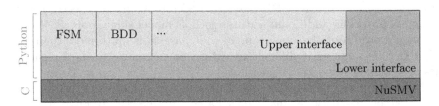

Fig. 1. PyNuSMV three-layer architecture

The lower interface is composed of a set of Python modules generated by SWIG. For every NuSMV package there is a SWIG interface generating a Python module that provides wrappers for functions and data structures of the package.

The upper interface is composed of classes wrapping data structures of NuSMV, and modules giving access to main functionalities such as CTL model checking and model parsing. The classes of the upper interface give access to:

- BDDs, states and inputs (i.e. actions) of the model and standard operations on BDDs provided as built-in operators: & (conjunction), | (disjunction), ~ (negation);
- the model itself, encoded as BDDs, and basic functionalities like computing the pre- or post-image of a set of states through the transition relation of the model;
- CTL formulae expressing properties of the model;
- functions acting on the global environment of NuSMV: intializing and finalizing NuSMV, reading the model and encoding it into BDDs;
- the parser of NuSMV to get, for example, the AST of a given simple expression;
- the CTL model-checking algorithms implemented in NuSMV.

Both interfaces have their advantages. The lower interface, fully generated by SWIG, allows the user to directly access NuSMV functions and data structures from the Python level, but the user has to manage all the implementation details he would manage at C level, memory in particular. On the other hand, the upper interface abstracts implementation details such as memory management and allows the user to focus on design and algorithmic concerns, at the cost of an additional level of indirection. While PyNuSMV gives access to both interfaces, most PyNuSMV applications are expected to rely only on the upper interface.

3   Evaluation

This section provides an initial evaluation of the tool. Section 3.1 shows how to re-implement CTL model checking with PyNuSMV and Section 3.2 presents some performance measures on small models.

3.1   Re-implementing CTL Model Checking

In order to illustrate how PyNuSMV allows to quickly and concisely experiment with new logics and custom model-checking algorithms while abstracting away from implementation details, this section presents an implementation of CTL model-checking algorithms [5]. The full code (about 175 LOC), of which only some pieces are presented here, is provided with the PyNuSMV distribution.

Figure 2 presents the main function of the program. It encodes the system into BDDs (line 3) and, for each CTL formula identified in the model file, computes the set of states of fsm satisfying the formula (line 8, eval_ctl(fsm, spec)) and the set of initial states violating the specification. Finally, the specification is reported as true if and only if this set is empty (lines 9 and 10).

Figure 3 shows parts of the eval_ctl function. Dedicated functions are implemented to evaluate basic Boolean operators and EX, EU and EG operators while the other operators are computed by standard reduction to these operators.[1]

---

[1] $f \rightarrow g \equiv \neg f \vee g$ and $A[f\ U\ g] \equiv \neg(E[\neg g\ U\ \neg g \wedge \neg f] \vee EG \neg g)$ are shown.

```
1  def main(modelPath):
2    init_nusmv()
3    fsm = BddFsm.from_filename(modelPath)
4    propDb = glob.prop_database()
5    for prop in propDb:
6      if prop.type == propTypes['CTL']:
7        spec = prop.exprcore
8        violating = fsm.init & ~eval_ctl(fsm, spec)
9        print('Specification',str(spec),
10              'is',str(violating.is_false()))
11       # We could generate counter-examples here
12   deinit_nusmv()
```

Fig. 2. The main function of the CTL model checking algorithm

```
1  def eval_ctl(fsm, spec):
2    ...
3    elif spec.type == parser.IMPLIES:
4      left = eval_ctl(fsm, spec.car, context)
5      right = eval_ctl(fsm, spec.cdr, context)
6      return ~left | right
7    elif spec.type == parser.AU:
8      left = eval_ctl(fsm, spec.car, context)
9      right = eval_ctl(fsm, spec.cdr, context)
10     return ~(eu(fsm,~right,~left & ~right) | eg(fsm,~right))
11   ...
```

Fig. 3. CTL evaluation: implication and `AU` operator cases

Figure 4 presents the implementation dedicated to the `EU` operator. Note how Python's lambda-abstractions allow to express this in an abstract, declarative style reflecting the mathematical definition, $\mathrm{E}[\phi\mathsf{U}\psi] = \mu Z.\psi \vee (\phi \wedge \mathbf{EX}Z)$, using a generic higher-level `fixpoint` function.

3.2 Performance Comparisons

As an initial performance assessment, we verified a sample of NuSMV models both with native NuSMV and with CTL model checking implemented in PyNuSMV. Note that the PyNuSMV version used here, provided with the tool, has been adjusted to reproduce exactly the algorithms implemented in NuSMV and is not the version presented in the previous section. The main difference is that it takes reachable states into account.

The results are summarized in Table 1. Eight models, taken from the NuSMV distribution, have been processed by the two tools; the first four are very small (up to 6000 states), the last four are a bit larger (from 10^6 to 10^{16} states). Each model features up to three CTL formulae. The measured time is the time needed to check the specifications only; the time needed to initialize NuSMV and to build the model is not taken into account and is very similar in both cases.

```
1  def eu(fsm, phi, psi):
2      return fixpoint(lambda Z: psi | (phi & fsm.pre(Z)),
3                      BDD.false(fsm.bddEnc.DDmanager))
4  def fixpoint(funct, start):
5      old = start
6      new = funct(start)
7      while old != new:
8          old = new
9          new = funct(old)
10         return old
```

Fig. 4. CTL evaluation: EU operator implementation

Table 1. NuSMV and PyNuSMV times to evaluate model specifications (in seconds)

Model	NuSMV	PyNuSMV
counter	0	0
mutex	0.001	0.009
dme1	0.275	0.288
gas-nq7	8.913	11.027

Model	NuSMV	PyNuSMV
msi_wtrans	23.285	23.652
dme1-16	61.246	64.733
ftp3	75.607	78.771
key10	100.614	103.606

These results are very promising: the overhead caused by the two Python layers of PyNuSMV remains very low. This was expected, as most of the time needed to evaluate the CTL formulae is spent in computing BDDs operations, and these operations take place within NuSMV in both cases.

4 Future Work

While PyNuSMV's lower interface is automatically generated by SWIG, the upper interface is hand-crafted and needs more work to be developed. A number of NuSMV features remain to be supported: only CTL- and BDD-related functionalities are provided. For now, SAT-based and LTL model checking, and simulation-related features, are not exposed at the Python level. Note that there should be no additional difficulties to expose them in the upper interface, but a significant amount of engineering work.

Second, NuSMV can react in various ways when an error occurs. It can output a message on stderr, or in other cases return an error value. It also integrates a try/fail mechanism using longjmp functionalities. Some additional work should be provided to hide these different behaviors and provide a homogeneous error management in the upper interface, based on Python exceptions.

5 Conclusion

This paper presents PyNuSMV, a framework for experimenting BDD-based model-checking algorithms for new logics based on NuSMV. It allows the user to use some NuSMV main functionalities such as model building, BDD manipulation and model-checking algorithms without having to understand the NuSMV code base and to struggle with implementation details such as memory management. Model checkers for rich logics such as CTLK have been re-implemented in a matter of days and a few thousands lines of Python code. Models can be written using the rich NuSMV modeling language and existing NuSMV models can be directly processed. Initial evaluation shows very little loss of efficiency compared to native NuSMV. While no performance tests have been performed yet on ARCTL and CTLK implementations, the overhead of PyNuSMV Python layers should remain low in these cases, too.

On the other hand, because NuSMV is primarily a standalone program, its developers made some implementation choices that make it not ideal to use as a library. For example, a lot of data structures are global, such as the parsing abstract syntax tree of the model, the main flat hierarchy or the proposition database. This imposes some limitations to PyNuSMV users that could be avoided if the platform was developed from scratch.

References

1. Beazley, D.M.: SWIG: an easy to use tool for integrating scripting languages with C and C++. In: Proceedings of the 4th Conference on USENIX Tcl/Tk Workshop, TCLTK 1996, vol. 4, p. 15. USENIX Association, Berkeley (1996)
2. Bloem, R., Cimatti, A., Greimel, K., Hofferek, G., Könighofer, R., Roveri, M., Schuppan, V., Seeber, R.: RATSY – A new requirements analysis tool with synthesis. In: Touili, T., Cook, B., Jackson, P. (eds.) CAV 2010. LNCS, vol. 6174, pp. 425–429. Springer, Heidelberg (2010)
3. Busard, S., Pecheur, C.: Rich counter-examples for temporal-epistemic logic model checking. In: Reich, J., Finkbeiner, B. (eds.) Proceedings Second International Workshop on Interactions, Games and Protocols, Tallinn, Estonia, March 25. Electronic Proceedings in Theoretical Computer Science, vol. 78, pp. 39–53. Open Publishing Association (2012)
4. Cimatti, A., Clarke, E., Giunchiglia, E., Giunchiglia, F., Pistore, M., Roveri, M., Sebastiani, R., Tacchella, A.: NuSMV 2: An opensource tool for symbolic model checking. In: Brinksma, E., Larsen, K.G. (eds.) CAV 2002. LNCS, vol. 2404, pp. 359–364. Springer, Heidelberg (2002)
5. Clarke, E.M., Grumberg, O., Peled, D.: Model Checking. MIT Press (1999)
6. Pecheur, C., Raimondi, F.: Symbolic model checking of logics with actions. In: Edelkamp, S., Lomuscio, A. (eds.) MoChArt IV. LNCS (LNAI), vol. 4428, pp. 113–128. Springer, Heidelberg (2007)
7. Penczek, W., Lomuscio, A.: Verifying epistemic properties of multi-agent systems via bounded model checking. Fundamenta Informaticae 55(2), 167–185 (2003)

jUnit^{RV}—Adding Runtime Verification to jUnit

Normann Decker, Martin Leucker, and Daniel Thoma

Institute for Software Engineering and Programming Languages
Universität zu Lübeck, Germany
{decker,leucker,thoma}@isp.uni-luebeck.de

Abstract. This paper presents jUnit^{RV} as a tool extending the unit testing framework jUnit by runtime verification capabilities. Roughly, jUnit^{RV} provides a new annotation @Monitors listing monitors that are synthesized from temporal specifications. The monitors check whether the currently executed tests satisfy the correctness properties underlying the monitors. As such, jUnit's concept of plain assert-based verification limited to checking properties of single states of a program is extended significantly towards checking properties of complete execution paths.

1 Introduction

Testing is the verification technique that is most applied in practice. Yet, testing is still quite ad-hoc, time consuming and as such, expensive. Easily, testing of software systems consumes up-to 50% of total development costs in safety-critical systems.

One of the most popular testing approaches to Java code is unit testing based on the jUnit framework [1]. Unit testing is essential in test-driven development such as extreme programming but also common when following classical development models.

Runtime verification is still a rather new verification technique in which a formal correctness property is checked on the actual execution of a system under scrutiny. Typically, monitor code checking the property at hand is synthesized and interweaved with the underlying program. Then, any execution of the resulting program is checked with respect to this property.

In this paper, we present jUnit^{RV} as a tool combining the ideas of unit testing and runtime verification.[1] It allows for high-level specifications of monitors for temporal assertions within the jUnit framework. Testing temporal properties commonly leads to complicated test cases and may require modifications to the application code. In jUnit^{RV}, monitors can be annotated to single test cases to automatically check the corresponding properties during execution.

While there are several runtime verification frameworks (see [2] for a recent overview), none of the available tools provides a close integration into jUnit.

In the next section, we give a brief overview on how to use jUnit and jUnit^{RV}. Afterwards, we discuss technical issues of our tool. Section 3 details how temporal

---

[1] jUnit^{RV} is freely available at http://www.isp.uni-luebeck.de/junitrv

G. Brat, N. Rungta, and A. Venet (Eds.): NFM 2013, LNCS 7871, pp. 459–464, 2013.

specifications are related to program executions and Section 4 describes how monitoring is integrated into the jUnit framework.

2   jUnit^{RV}—A Quick Starting Guide

In this section, we introduce jUnit^{RV} by means of an example. We recall the ideas of jUnit, explain current limitations and show how jUnit^{RV} can simplify testing of so-called *temporal assertions* by means of runtime verification.

Testing and jUnit. The aim of unit testing is to check simple, individual units of a program. While jUnit is originally developed to support unit testing, it allows, in principle, for complex test scenarios and it is often used for integration testing and system testing in practice as well.

Let us explain the main ideas about jUnit based on the following, exemplifying hospital application: For every patient, the hospital personnel takes the necessary data and submits it to the central hospital information system. The information may be queried and modified later on. For this, the hospital personnel uses terminals which may be shared by different users by switching between the respective accounts.

The terminal runs a Java application which takes care of user management and modification of patient data. To access and modify patient data in the hospital information system, it uses the following (simplified) interface.

```
public interface DataService {
    void connect(String userID) throws UnknownUserException;
    void disconnect();
    Data readData(String field);
    void modifyData(String field, Data data);
    void commit() throws CommitException;
}
```

The terminal application, called client in the following, is to be tested whether it meets the following requirement: If data was modified through the interface, the client must instruct the data service to commit the changes before the user logs out since local changes would be lost otherwise. A user is logged out from the system, e.g. when the client is shut down or the user is switched, and, as such, the requirement has to be tested at different functions of the application.

Within Java's unit testing framework jUnit, test cases are specified in dedicated test classes. A test case in jUnit is a method comprising the annotation @Test and a sequence of method calls to be executed. Additionally, assertions are used to specify expectations to the program state at certain steps. jUnit loads a specified test class and consecutively invokes all included test cases. A typical test case for the requirement mentioned above looks as follows.

```
@Test
public void test1() {
    DataService service = new MyDataService("http://myserver.net");
    MyDataClient client = new MyDataClient(service);

    client.authenticate("daniel");
    client.addPatient("Mr. Smith");
```

```
    client.switchToUser("ruth");
    assertTrue(service.debug_committed()); // switching means logout

    client.getPatientFile("miller-2143-1");
    client.setPhone("miller-2143-1", "012345678");
    client.exit();
    assertTrue(service.debug_committed());
}
```

The difficulty of using jUnit in this example is twofold: (i) for executing the test case above the implementation must be refactored to provide enough information to indicate whether a commit has happened. Moreover, (ii) the tester needs the information which methods actually perform a logout (`switch()` and `exit()` in our example).

Clearly, the need for complete knowledge of such information as well as the need for refactoring e.g. an interface in late development phases makes testing labor-intensive and error prone. In essence, the problem in the example above is that a requirement on the execution trace should be checked while jUnit only supports assertions to be checked in individual states of the system.

Runtime Verification and jUnit^{RV}. Runtime verification (see [3] for a survey) aims at verifying properties on individual execution traces. To this end, *temporal assertions* may be specified, typically in terms of temporal logic formulae, and are automatically translated into a so-called monitoring code. A monitor is a program that observes the current execution and yields a verdict whether the property is fulfilled or violated.

The requirement in the example above can be stated as

$$\text{Always (modify} \Rightarrow \neg\text{disconnect Until committed)}$$

meaning it is always the case, that whenever the method `DataService.modify()` is invoked, the client does not disconnect until a call to `DataService.commit()` returned successfully. The link between formal events and method calls are made explicit in jUnit^{RV} as follows:

```
String dataService = "myPackage.DataService";

private static Event modify = called(dataService, "modify");
private static Event committed = returned(dataService, "commit");
private static Event disconnect = called(dataService, "disconnect");
```

Note that, besides *events*, jUnit^{RV} also supports *propositions*. The distinction is made precise in the next section. A corresponding monitor definition within the jUnit^{RV} framework can be given as follows.

```
private static Monitor commitBeforeDisconnect = new FLTL4Monitor(
    Always(implies(
        modify,
        Until(not(disconnect), committed)
    )
));
```

jUnit^{RV} is in general capable to deal with different logic plug-ins but comes with a DSL for specifying temporal assertions in the temporal logic FLTL$_4$, which follows [4] and is defined formally in [2].

Individual test cases can now be monitored by just adding an annotation @Monitors together with a list of monitor names that have been defined before. For our example, we get:

```
@Test
@Monitors({"commitBeforeDisconnect"})
public void test1() {
    DataService service = new MyDataService("http://myserver.net");
    MyDataClient client = new MyDataClient(service);

    client.authenticate("daniel");
    client.addPatient("Mr. Smith");
    client.switchToUser("ruth");
    client.getPatientFile("miller-2143-1");
    client.setPhone("miller-2143-1", "012345678");
    client.exit();
}
```

3   Execution Traces and Formal Runs

jUnit^{RV} allows for specifying temporal assertions in jUnit. Such specifications can be annotated to test cases and are monitored during test execution. At every execution step, the monitor reports a (possibly preliminary) verdict. The test case fails, if the monitor reports a violation of the property during the execution.

The monitor specifications are based on temporal logic, which describes discrete sequences of observations, i.e. individual steps in time. At every such time step, atomic propositions are assumed to evaluate to either true or false. However, the actual observation that is made and the user intends to describe is the *execution trace* or run of a program.

Such a run includes e.g. method invocations and returns, variable access and variable evaluations. To use temporal logic as a tool to describe program runs, the mapping between formal semantics and program traces must be clear, intuitively as well as formally. We therefore introduce our notion of *events* and *propositions*. In first place, events serve as clock triggers to the monitors, thereby defining the discrete steps in time. Additionally, propositions characterize the current program state within such a discrete time unit. They are evaluated within the scope of an event, i.e. a specific time instant.

Events. In jUnit^{RV}, events are specified explicitly and are automatically triggered. The temporal assertion in our example above uses the events modify, committed and disconnect. Such events, mark specific actions of the program. The events modify and disconnect trigger as soon as the methods modify() and disconnect(), respectively, are invoked on an object of type DataService. The event committed occurs when the method commit() returned successfully, i.e. without throwing an exception. Each monitor is associated with a set of events and whenever one of them occurs, a time step is indicated to it.

Propositions. Within the context of a particular time step, propositions are evaluated and define the *current* observation. This evaluation defines which transition a monitor takes in the current step. In jUnit^{RV}, propositions are defined explicitly as follows:

```
private static Proposition auth =
    new Proposition(eq(invoke($this, "getStatus"),AUTH);
```

The proposition `auth` evaluates to true if the method `getStatus()` returns the value `AUTH`. The method is invoked on the *current* object (denoted `$this`), which is the object on which the method was invoked that *caused the current event*, i.e. the current time step.

Additional propositions are defined implicitly in terms of events: For each event there is a proposition with the same name that can be used in the temporal specification. Note that in any time step, only a single event can occur and thus the propositions implicitly defined by events exclude each other. For example, the property `modify` ∧ `committed`, meaning that the events `modify` and `committed` occur at the same time, can never be true. In the data service example, the specified property only uses propositions that are defined implicitly by the corresponding events.

4 jUnit Integration

The jUnit testing framework comes with sophisticated default test case execution capabilities. Moreover, it provides the possibility to change the test execution behavior with the help of annotation `@RunWith`, which takes as argument a suitable test runner class. As jUnit^{RV} has to take care of event injection and monitor execution, it provides the class `RVRunner`. To reuse most of jUnit's standard test runner, like its reporting facilities etc., `RVRunner` inherits from jUnit's test runner.

The notion of events is bound to the access of fields and invocation or return of methods in the program under test. That means that the program must be interleaved with code being executed whenever a respective method is invoked. As the classes to be tested are compiled and already loaded by jUnit, when they are about to be tested with `RVRunner`, monitoring code cannot be added to the byte code directly. For code injection, `RVRunner` uses the following idea: It creates a customized class loader that will inject corresponding code when loading classes. It then reloads all involved classes using this custom class loader, which now adds the monitoring code into the program under test. Our framework uses the Javassist library [5] that provides the functionality to manipulate the Java bytecode at load-time of Java classes. For test execution, `RVRunner` delegates to jUnit's the default implementation preserving the standard functionality.

While jUnit^{RV} maintains the monitor state, recognizes events and evaluates propositions, the behavior of monitors is provided by the implementation of a single interface `Mealy` which basically represents the transition function and output labeling of some deterministic (possibly infinite-state) Mealy machine. That is, jUnit^{RV} provides the current state and proposition evaluations and expects the subsequent monitor state. The implementation of a monitor construction remains independent of the state and event management. This easily allows for the integration of custom monitoring approaches.

Since all required classes are loaded by the jUnit framework, jUnit^{RV} can be deployed as a standard jar-archive and integrated into any common testing environment, it suffices to make jUnit^{RV} available through the Java class path. The tool works with common IDEs, e.g. Eclipse or Netbeans as it leverages the jUnit test integration.

A major advantage of manipulation of byte code runtime verification is, that it allows to insert event generation routines even into third party code where the sources are not available. jUnit^{RV} is hence also independent of the programming language of the target program as long as it is run on the JVM. Testing Scala applications or libraries, for example, is thus also possible.

Note that, in principle, manipulation of byte code must be treated with care as the tested and deployed byte code differ. However, we consider this uncritical in most practical cases. Additionally, jUnit^{RV} allows for deploying the instrumented application, i.e. including all modifications.

5   Conclusion

In this paper, we introduced jUnit^{RV} as a tool extending the unit testing framework jUnit by runtime verification capabilities. Within jUnit, test cases are specified manually together with assertions that are evaluated in the corresponding states of the system under scrutiny. Using jUnit^{RV}, it is now possible to specify temporal assertions that specify correctness properties for complete test runs. As such, test case specification is simplified significantly in many situations. In the near future, we plan a case study with a larger number of users to investigate jUnit^{RV}'s usability in practical applications, including scalability under larger test suites and the practical overhead.

References

1. Beck, K., Gamma, E.: Test-infected: programmers love writing tests. In: Deugo, D. (ed.) More Java Gems. SIGS Reference Library, pp. 357–376. Cambridge University Press (2000)
2. Leucker, M.: Teaching runtime verification. In: Khurshid, S., Sen, K. (eds.) RV 2011. LNCS, vol. 7186, pp. 34–48. Springer, Heidelberg (2012)
3. Leucker, M., Schallhart, C.: A brief account of runtime verification. J. Log. Algebr. Program. 78(5), 293–303 (2009)
4. Lichtenstein, O., Pnueli, A., Zuck, L.: The glory of the past. In: Parikh, R. (ed.) Logic of Programs 1985. LNCS, vol. 193, pp. 196–218. Springer, Heidelberg (1985)
5. Chiba, S.: Load-time structural reflection in java. In: Bertino, E. (ed.) ECOOP 2000. LNCS, vol. 1850, pp. 313–336. Springer, Heidelberg (2000)

Using Language Engineering to Lift Languages and Analyses at the Domain Level

Daniel Ratiu[1], Markus Voelter[2], Bernd Kolb[3], and Bernhard Schaetz[1]

[1] Fortiss
{ratiu,schaetz}@fortiss.org
[2] Independent/itemis
voelter@acm.org
[3] Itemis
kolb@itemis.de

Abstract. Developers who use C model checkers have to overcome three usability challenges: First, it is difficult to express application level properties as C-level verification conditions, due to the abstraction gap. Second, without advanced IDE support, it is difficult to interpret the counterexamples produced by the model checker and understand what went wrong in terms of application level properties. Third, most C model checkers support only a subset of C and it is easy for developers to inadvertently use C constructs outside this subset. In this paper we report on our preliminary experience with using the MPS language workbench to integrate the CBMC model checker with a set of domain-specific extensions of C for developing embedded software. Higher level language constructs such as components and decision tables makes it easier for end users to bridge the abstraction gap, to write verification conditions and to interpret the analysis results. Furthermore, the use of language workbenches allows the definition of analyzable language subsets, making the implementation of analyses simpler and their use more predictable.

1 Introduction

Current C model checkers have reached a level of scalability that makes them useful for real-world projects. However, their adoption in practice is much lower than it could be. There are three categories of challenges in using C model checkers [1,2]: First, it is difficult to formalize the to-be-verified application-level properties at the level of C, so model checkers are used only to verify implicit C-level properties (e.g., program does no crash, no overflow occurs). However, this is often not enough for end users. Second, once the result is obtained (at the abstraction level of C) it is difficult for a user to interpret it at the application level. Third, due to the complexity of C itself, many model checkers support only a subset of C and/or are simply buggy when certain C features are used. All these challenges are due to the gap between the abstractions relevant at the application level and how they are reflected in programs on the one hand, and the abstractions of the analysis tool on the other hand.

G. Brat, N. Rungta, and A. Venet (Eds.): NFM 2013, LNCS 7871, pp. 465–471, 2013.
© Springer-Verlag Berlin Heidelberg 2013

In this paper we propose a method to simplify the use of C model checkers that is based on the following three pillars: 1) we describe how various extensions of C encode higher level abstractions and their (explicit or implicit) properties; 2) we lift the analysis results to the application level, making them more understandable to the user; and 3) we define language restrictions that reflect limitations of C model checkers, making them evident to the user. We have implemented this method in mbeddr, an extensible version of C. As examples for C extensions we use components and decision tables. As analyses examples we show completeness and consistency of decision tables, and checking of interface contracts and protocols for components by using the CBMC model checker [3].

2   mbeddr: An Extensible C Language

mbeddr ([4] and `http://mbeddr.com`) is an extensible set of languages for embedded software development based on C, supporting the incremental, modular domain-specific extension of C. mbeddr also supports language restriction, in order to create subsets of existing languages. mbeddr is based on the JetBrains MPS language workbench (`http://jetbrains.com/mps`) and exploits its capabilities for language modularization and composition [5].

Out of the box, mbeddr comes with a set of extensions for interfaces and components, state machines, physical units and decision tables. Some of them lend themselves to formal analysis: currently we have integrated the Yices SMT solver (e.g. to verify decision table consistency) and the NuSMV model checker (for verifying state machines) [4,6,7]. In this paper we illustrate how language extension mechanisms allow a deep integration of the CBMC model checker.

```
exported cs interface SpeedComputer {        instances comp {
  void activate()                              instance PlauzibilizedSpeedComputer sp
    protocol init(0) -> new Active(1)          adapt comp -> sp.speedComputer }
  float computeSpeed(int16 distance, int16 time)
    pre(0) time > 0                          float emitCurrentSpeed() {
    pre(1) distance > 0                        int16 time = readTime();
    post(2) result > 0                         int16 dist = readDistance();
    protocol Active -> Active                  if (dist >= 1 && time >= 0) {
  void deactivate()                              return comp.computeSpeed(dist, time); }
    protocol Active -> init(0)                 return 0; } emitCurrentSpeed (function)
}
                                             exported int32 main(int32 argc, int8*[] argv) {
                                               initialize comp;
                                               emitCurrentSpeed();
                                               return 0; } main (function)
```

Fig. 1. Interface definition (left); Use of the interface in client code (right)

Interfaces, Components, Contracts. An interface defines a set of operations. In addition to the signature, each operation can define preconditions and postconditions. In addition, a protocol state machine defines the valid call sequences of the operations in an interface. The left part of Fig. 1 shows an example interface definition. `computeSpeed` has two preconditions, one postcondition and a protocol specification that specifies that `activate` must be called before calling `computeSpeed` (when `computeSpeed` is called, the interface must be in the `Active` state, which can be reached by calling `activate`). Fig. 2 shows a

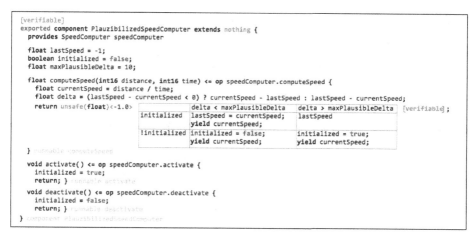

```
[verifiable]
exported component PlauzibilizedSpeedComputer extends nothing {
  provides SpeedComputer speedComputer

  float lastSpeed = -1;
  boolean initialized = false;
  float maxPlausibleDelta = 10;

  float computeSpeed(int16 distance, int16 time) <= op speedComputer.computeSpeed {
    float currentSpeed = distance / time;
    float delta = (lastSpeed - currentSpeed < 0) ? currentSpeed - lastSpeed : lastSpeed - currentSpeed;
    return unsafe(float)<-1.0>
```

	delta < maxPlausibleDelta	delta > maxPlausibleDelta	[verifiable];
initialized	lastSpeed = currentSpeed; yield currentSpeed;	lastSpeed	
!initialized	initialized = false; yield currentSpeed;	initialized = true; yield currentSpeed;	

```
  } runnable computeSpeed

  void activate() <= op speedComputer.activate {
    initialized = true;
    return; } runnable activate
  void deactivate() <= op speedComputer.deactivate {
    initialized = false;
    return; } runnable deactivate
} component PlauzibilizedSpeedComputer
```

Fig. 2. Components implement each function of their provided interfaces. The users of a component must comply with the preconditions and use protocol defined in the interface. The implementation of each interface functions should comply with the defined post-conditions. In **computeSpeed** we show an example of decision tables.

component that provides the **SpeedComputer** interface. The right part of Fig. 1 shows an example of client code of the component. Using model checking, we can verify whether a clients conforms to the preconditions and the protocol, and whether the implementation of the interface satisfies the postconditions.

Decision Tables. Decision tables [8] exploit JetBrains MPS' projectional editor in order to represent two-level nested if statements as a table (Fig. 2). The tabular notations makes it easier for developers to write and understand sets of input conditions. Decision tables suggest two verifications: completeness (check whether all possible input value combinations are covered), and determinism (checks that for any given set of input values only one option is valid).

3   Integrating CBMC into mbeddr

Fig. 3 shows the integration of CBMC: from programs written with higher-level constructs we generate C that includes a set of labels that represent higher-level verification properties (see next paragraph). The C code is then analyzed with CBMC and the analysis results are parsed and lifted back to the abstraction level of the higher-level constructs to make them easy to interpret.

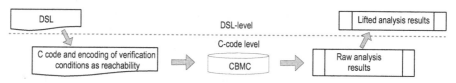

Fig. 3. Approach at a glance: generate C code, run CBMC and lift the raw results

```
1  float computeSpeed(int16_t distance, int16_t time, void* ___inst) {
2    PlauzibilizedSpeedComputer* ___ci = ((PlauzibilizedSpeedComputer*)(___inst));
3    switch (___ci->___protocolState) {
4      case 2: { ___ci->___speedComputer_protocolState = 2; break; }
5      default: { protocolViolationForRunnable_2161187783549496741: break; }
6    }
7    if (!(time > 0)) { pre_2161187783549496724__2161187783549496741: ... }
8    float currentSpeed = distance / time;
9    float delta = ...
10   float ___result = decTabExp(delta, ___ci, delta, currentSpeed);
11   if (!(___result > 0)) { post_2161187783549496732__8053687140971342992: ...
12     return ___result;
13   }
14 static float decTabExp(float delta, struct PlauzibilizedSpeedComputer* ___inst,
15                        float delta, float currentSpeed) {
16   if (/* no case covered */) { label_dectab_completeness_8053687140971342993: ... }
17   if ((delta < ___inst->field_maxPlausibleDelta) && (___inst->field_initialized) &&
18       (delta < ___inst->field_maxPlausibleDelta) && !(___ci->field_initialized)) {
19     label_dectab_nondeterminism_0_8053687140971342993: ... } ... }
```

Fig. 4. Generated C code from the implementation of the interface

Encoding Verification Conditions as Reachability. We verify pre- and postconditions, protocols and decision tables with the help of reachability analysis. As shown in Fig. 4, we generate labels (the things with the long numbers) to annotate locations in the code which represent violations of the high level properties. For example, operation implementations in components have if statements at the beginning that check the preconditions. The label is placed inside the body of the if. The body is only executed if the precondition fails. We maintain a mapping between each label and the higher-level construct whose property the label represents. We then use CBMC to check whether the labels can be reached.

Lifting the Result. Running the reachability analysis with CBMC on the generated C provides a raw analysis result at the abstraction level of C. It specifies for each label whether it can be reached or not (if it can be reached the result includes a trace through the C code). This raw result needs to be interpreted with respect to the higher-level verification condition that is encoded by the label. In addition, the counterexample must be related to the program that includes the higher-level constructs. In Fig. 5 we illustrate examples for lifted results for checking contracts, protocol of components and the completeness of decision tables. Lifting the counterexample involves several abstraction steps:

1. *Eliminate the generation noise from the C code.* Part of the generated C code represents encodings of higher level concepts. For example, additional functions are generated that implement decision tables. In these cases, the corresponding sections of the counterexample are irrelevant in terms of the higher-level construct; they should not be visible in the lifted result.

2. *Interpret the C-level counterexample.* Higher-level constructs are encoded in C through generation with the help of variables or function calls. These encodings need to be traced back. For example, the components are initialized in a function. If this function shows up in a C-level counterexample, it means that the components were initialized.

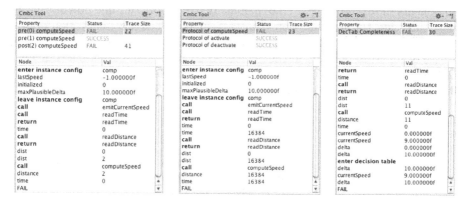

Fig. 5. Examples of lifted analyses results. In the case when an analysis fails, a lifted counterexample at the DSL-level is provided.

3. *Restore original names.* Since mbeddr supports namespaces, the names of the high-level program elements are mingled with module names in the C code. During lifting, we must recover the names of the higher-level abstractions.

Making Users Aware about the Analyzability of Their Code. Due to the *model construction problem* [2], building robust verification tools for large and complex languages is challenging. In the case when the underlying verification tool does not support a language feature (intentionally, or because it has bugs), we inform the user about the non-analyzability of the code by showing a warning in the IDE. This way, unpleasant surprises are avoided and end user acceptance can be increased. For example, Fig. 6 (above the line) shows a program fragment that cannot be analyzed with CBMC 4.2 (there is a problem with function pointers that has since been fixed). The part below the line shows CBMC's error message if that code is used as input. Code like this is generated when the

```
1  struct PlauzibilizedSpeedComputer {        struct PlauzibilizedSpeedComputer anSC;
2    char (*activate)();                       void initializeComponents() {
3    int (*computeSpeed)(int, int);              anSC.activate = &activateImpl;
4  };                                            anSC.computeSpeed = &computeSpeedImpl;
5  char activateImpl() { return 0; }          }
6  int computeSpeedImpl(int d, int t) {       int main() {
7    return 0;                                  initializeComponents();
8  }                                            int x = (*(snSC.computeSpeed))(2, 3);... }
9  -----------------------------------------------------------------------------
10 Assertion failed (base_type_eq(assignment.lhs().type().assignment.rhs().type().ns)),
11    function return_assignment, file symex_function_call.cpp, line 483
```

Fig. 6. Example of a code fragment that is generated from mbeddr but is not supported by CBMC (top) and the error message provided by CBMC when this program is analyzed (bottom). We explicitly inform mbeddr users when they use a high-level construct that leads to a non-supported language fragment in the generated code. In this manner, we make the usage of analysis more predictible to the developers.

components in mbeddr are wired dynamically to support runtime polymorphism (via indirection through function pointers). mbeddr has a configuration option that forces static wiring of components (by using a language restriction), avoiding the use of function pointers in the generated C code. This makes the code analyzable, but it also limits the flexibility of the user. Making this tradeoff explicit allows users to make an informed decision regarding flexibility vs. analyzability.

4   Related Work

In this paper we extend our previous work on using language workbenches to enable more user-friendly and high-level formal verification [4,6,7] by integrating a general purpose C-level model checker. There is significant related work on integrating C model checkers into development environments [9,10]. There is also already work on generating verification properties from higher level models [11] and to trace the analyses results at a code level back at the model level [12].

Our work is different mainly in that instead of using models to generate verification properties, we use language extensions. This way we retain the benefits of generating verification conditions from higer-level abstractions: deriving the verification conditions is straight forward, and lifting the counterexample to the higher abstraction level eliminates a significant amount of noise and thereby improve usability. In addition, we avoid the semantic and tool integration issues that arise when (verifiable) parts of programs are expressed with different formalisms than the regular C code: the extensions have clearly defined semantics in terms of C, and the tool integration is seamless.

5   Conclusions and Future Work

We see domain-specific languages, language engineering and language workbenches as key enablers to increase the usability of formal verification. In the future, we will generate invariants from high level constructs and we will support to set different entry points in the analysis. A challenge that we foresee is that the semantics at DSL level ("big step") might miss many C-level errors ("small-step") and make the interpretation of the high-level counterexample unsound.

Acknowledgement. This work is developed in the LWES project, supported by the German BMBF, FKZ 01/S11014.

References

1. Loer, K., Harrison, M.: Towards Usable and Relevant Model Checking Techniques for the Analysis of Dependable Interactive Systems. In: ASE (2002)
2. Corbett, J., Dwyer, M., Hatcliff, J., Laubach, S., Păsăreanu, C., Zheng, H.: Bandera: extracting finite-state models from Java source code. In: ICSE 2000 (2000)
3. Clarke, E., Kroening, D., Lerda, F.: A tool for checking ANSI-C programs. In: Jensen, K., Podelski, A. (eds.) TACAS 2004. LNCS, vol. 2988, pp. 168–176. Springer, Heidelberg (2004)

4. Voelter, M., Ratiu, D., Schätz, B., Kolb, B.: mbeddr: an extensible c-based programming language and ide for embedded systems. In: SPLASH 2012 (2012)
5. Voelter, M.: Language and IDE Modularization and Composition with MPS. In: Lämmel, R., Saraiva, J., Visser, J. (eds.) GTTSE 2011. LNCS, vol. 7680, pp. 383–430. Springer, Heidelberg (2013)
6. Ratiu, D., Voelter, M., Schaetz, B., Kolb, B.: Language Engineering as Enabler for Incrementally Defined Formal Analyses. In: FORMSERA 2012 (2012)
7. Ratiu, D., Markus Voelter, Z.M., Schaetz, B.: Implementing modular domain specific languages and analyses. In: MoDEVVa 2012 (2012)
8. Janicki, R., Parnas, D.L., Zucker, J.: Tabular representations in relational documents. In: Relational Methods in Computer Science (1997)
9. Beyer, D., Henzinger, T., Jhala, R., Majumdar, R.: An eclipse plug-in for model checking. In: IWPC 2004 (2004)
10. Ball, T., Cook, B., Levin, V., Rajamani, S.K.: SLAM and static driver verifier: Technology transfer of formal methods inside microsoft. In: Boiten, E.A., Derrick, J., Smith, G.P. (eds.) IFM 2004. LNCS, vol. 2999, pp. 1–20. Springer, Heidelberg (2004)
11. Zalila, F., Crégut, X., Pantel, M.: Leveraging formal verification tools for DSML users: A process modeling case study. In: Margaria, T., Steffen, B. (eds.) ISoLA 2012, Part II. LNCS, vol. 7610, pp. 329–343. Springer, Heidelberg (2012)
12. Combemale, B., Gonnord, L., Rusu, V.: A Generic Tool for Tracing Executions Back to a DSML's Operational Semantics. In: France, R.B., Kuester, J.M., Bordbar, B., Paige, R.F. (eds.) ECMFA 2011. LNCS, vol. 6698, pp. 35–51. Springer, Heidelberg (2011)

On Designing an ACL2-Based
C Integer Type Safety Checking Tool

Kevin Krause and Jim Alves-Foss

Center for Secure and Dependable Systems
University of Idaho, Moscow, ID 83844, USA
krau1931@vandals.uidaho.edu, jimaf@uidaho.edu

Abstract. The C integer types are prone to errors due to unchecked casting that can leave programs vulnerable to a host of security exploits. These errors manifest themselves when there is a semantic disconnect between the programmer's view of the language and the actual implementation of the programming language. To help detect these errors, we are developing a C integer type safety checking tool written in ACL2. This paper presents the justification and fundamental logic behind the tool, the basic operations of the tool, and discussion of future plans.

1 Introduction

Even with its latest standardization [1], the programming language C remains weakly typed and, except for a select few of its operators that can only be applied to integer type operands, the majority of its operators can be applied to operands of different data types by the means of its wholesale explicit or implicit type casting. While cast operations involving C floating point types have the support of runtime checks to ensure proper representation of real numbers, casting of C integer types do not; leaving c integers subject to ***overflow/underflow***, ***signage***, and ***truncation*** errors during both runtime and compilation. According to Seacord [2], these integer errors are the most overlooked and least understood C memory errors.

For a runtime example, suppose a variable x is holding the value 10 and x is used in a conditional statement, such as

$$\text{if(x > -10)\{ // do something important... \}.}$$

Semantically, if x is greater than -10, the code's execution path branches into "do something important". In C, the literal value -10 is typed as an int. If x was declared as an int or unsigned short, then the "do something important" branch would be taken as expected. However, if x was declared as an unsigned int, "do something important" would not be executed. This is due to the compiler casting the literal -10, according to C's ***integer promotion*** rules, to an unsigned int type, and its resulting value is interpreted as a very large positive number. Although the different integer types of x can produce different outcomes in the above conditional example, each are correct according to the C casting rules.

G. Brat, N. Rungta, and A. Venet (Eds.): NFM 2013, LNCS 7871, pp. 472–477, 2013.
© Springer-Verlag Berlin Heidelberg 2013

By being weakly typed, C is not type safe because of its potential integer errors. Integer errors corrupt data and data corruption becomes a fault leaving a system vulnerable to attacks including denial of service (DoS), escalation of privilege (EoP), and execution of arbitrary code attacks. Since type safety is defined as a characteristic of a program that indicates that it is free from unintended behaviors, the goal of the ACL2 C integer type safety analysis tool introduced in this paper is to identify all existing and potential integer errors contained in any given C source code. While other C type safety analysis tools have been introduced, such as Astree [3], with claims they can show an absence of integer bugs, we believe the ACL2 proof generating capacity of our tool can insure an absence of integer bugs. The logic behind the tool is based on C's static typing semantics derived from its casting rules and the typing constraints placed on expressions and statements as stated in the C standard and discussed in Sect. 2. The basic tool design is discussed in Sect. 3 before concluding remarks.

2   Notes on Deriving the C Static Typing Semantics

Programs written in weakly typed languages, such as C, can be type safe, if programmers undertake the responsibility to do so. Most programmers understand the operational semantics of C operators such as the binary +. However, many programmers make the wrong assumption that if an operation is allowed on mixed operand types, the operation is type safe. Even Ritchie [4] said, C's typing rules with respect to operations are quirky and flawed.

C's typing system is defined in §6.2.5 of the standard[1]. Accordingly, type gives a value meaning and a value's type is determined by the expression accessing a memory object or function return. For all C types, each belongs to one of three general type categories: **object types** that fully describe memory objects; **function types**, that describe the return type of a function; and **incomplete types** that are either a void pointer or a declared object that is not fully defined, such as an array with an unknown size.

To formalize C's typing system, we begin with a syntax of types. The syntax is extracted from the 26 rules outlined in §6.2.5 of the standard and expressed in Backus-Naur Form (BNF). For example, all C types and the three general type categories are expressed as:

$$\langle \texttt{c\_type} \rangle := \langle \texttt{object\_type} \rangle | \langle \texttt{function\_type} \rangle | \langle \texttt{incomplete\_type} \rangle$$

Each general type can be further reduced until the terminal or base types are revealed. For example, $\langle \texttt{object\_type} \rangle$ can be reduced to $\langle \texttt{scalar-type} \rangle$, $\langle \texttt{aggregate-type} \rangle$, and $\langle \texttt{union-type} \rangle$. In $\langle \texttt{scalar-type} \rangle$, the $\langle \texttt{arithmetic-type} \rangle$ is held, and in $\langle \texttt{arithmetic-type} \rangle$, the base types such as int and float reside.

According to Mitchell [6], casting implies sub-typing and the syntax of C types expressed in BNF shows sub-type relationships used by the C casting

---

[1] Any reference to C refers to the standard ISO/IEC 9899:1999 [5](C99), since work on this project started in advance of the C11 standard roll out.

$$\frac{\begin{array}{cc} \Gamma \vdash e_1 : exp[\tau_1] & \Gamma \vdash e_2 : exp[\tau_2] \\ isArithmetic(\tau_1) & isArithmetic(\tau_2) \\ arithConv(\tau_1, \tau_2) \rightsquigarrow \tau' \end{array}}{\Gamma \vdash e_1/e_2 : exp[\tau']} \ (Division)$$

Fig. 1. Partial typing inference rules for the division operator

rules defined in §6.3 of the standard, such as ***integer conversion rank, integer promotions***, and ***usual arithmetic conversions***. A sub-type relation, written $\tau_1 \subseteq \tau_2$, means that any value held in type τ_1 may also be held in τ_2. Sub-type relationships are reflexive ($\tau \subseteq \tau$), transitive (if $\tau_1 \subseteq \tau_2$ and $\tau_2 \subseteq \tau_3$, then $\tau_1 \subseteq \tau_3$), and antisymmetric (if $\tau_1 \subseteq \tau_2$ and $\tau_2 \subseteq \tau_1$, then $\tau_1 = \tau_2$).

With C's type syntax in hand, C's static typing semantics can be constructed and expressed (1) as typing judgments of the form

$$\Gamma \vdash E : \theta \tag{1}$$

where E is an expression, Γ is the expression's type environment, and θ is the type *attributed* to E. If a typing derivation using this judgment reaches a conclusion, then E is a well typed expression of type θ as it complies to the standard's typing rules. The typing semantics of a programming language is typically defined as a consistent set of *axioms* and *inference rules*. The complete collection of typing rules for a language is called a (*formal*) *type system* [7].

The major components of a C program are a collection of declarations (§6.7) with or without initializations, expressions (§6.5), statements (§6.8), and functions (§6.9.1). The type inference rules are drawn from the standard that provides a combination of syntax, constraints, and semantics for each component. Constraints state the type restrictions; while the semantics, in addition to giving operational meaning, specify the casting method.

Let the division / multiplicative operator be an example (Fig. 1); where the conclusion (under the bar) is true if the premises (above the bar) are true. The premises state that the operand expressions of **/** are constrained to be of arithmetic type and according to the semantics, the usual arithmetic conversions are performed on the operands. If the premises hold, the conclusion is that the result has the type of the promoted type and its value contains the quotient derived by dividing the first operand by the second operand.

To complete the division type safety analysis, it must be shown that operand $e_2 \neq 0$ and the result value belongs to the range of legal values that can be held by the promoted type. That is, if the *result* of expression e_1/e_2 is of type τ and if $\tau_{min_{value}} \leq result \leq \tau_{max_{value}}$, then the operation is type safe.

3   Notes on Designing the Static Analysis Tool

The type safety analysis tool is being coded in ACL2 [8]. There were four factors behind the choice of ACL2. ACL2 is 1) executable and 2) uses the **bignums** data type. 3) ACL2 supports formal proofs and our intent is to use the theorem prover to prove properties of the tool. That is, we can evaluate the formal semantics of the language as encoded in the tool, to ensure that is it correct; and, we can use that formalism to reason about limitations or completeness of the tool. 4) The tool leverages another suite of ACL2 based tools, starting with the **c2acl2** [9] translator, that models C source code (Listing 1.1), in a lisp style abstract parse tree (AST) and generates a symbol table (symtab).

At a black box level, the analysis tool inputs the .lisp AST and the .symtab symtab generated by c2acl2 and outputs a final report (Listing 1.2). Usefulness of the final report depends on what happens inside the black box. For example, a naïve approach would have the tool flag and issue a warning on every type mismatch contained in every expression or statement. However, taking this approach on C programs, where implicit coercions are standard and routine would produce too many *false positives* (i.e., false alarms) and too many *false negatives* (i.e., misses).

Arriving with a false positive is straightforward. For example, the positive value 1 belongs to all integer types. Suppose unsigned int x with the value 1 is being added to long int y also with a value 1. The naïve approach would flag the expression x + y as a type mismatch (a type safety false positive) even though the result 2 belongs to all integer types. On the other hand, suppose that there is an expression containing three signed char variables named result, x, and y where result is being assigned the addition of x with value 10 and y with value 120. The naïve approach would not raise an alarm (a type safety false negative) even though result is in an overflow condition. In the two scenarios just enumerated, the naïve approach fails because it does not evaluate and test values with respect to the valid ranges of C types.

Because of the potentially large number of false positives and false negatives, a better tool design takes into consideration how a C program executes through its components. According to Liskov [10], program execution can be modeled as a series of states and transitions (2). Let σ represent a state, σ_0 the initial state, σ_n the final state, and Tr represent a transition, then the execution of a program is modeled as:

$$\sigma_0 Tr_1 \sigma_1 \ldots \sigma_{n-1} Tr_n \sigma_n \tag{2}$$

```
1  int main()
   {
3    char c1;
     unsigned short s2 = 12;
5    int i1 = 123;

7    c1 = s2 + s2; // unsigned short + unsigned short
     c1 = i1 + c1; // int + char
9    c1 = c1 + i1; // char + int
   }
```

Listing 1.1. Simple C program that adds mixed integer types

```
 (C2ACL2 (FILE "expAddVV")
2    (
     ";***************************************************"
4    ";␣Function␣Definition␣for␣function:␣main"
     ";***************************************************"
6    (FUNC (INT )(ID "main" 1 ) NIL
        (BLOCK
8         (DECL (CHAR )(ID "c1" 2 )NIL)
          (DECL (UNSIGNED CHAR )(ID "c2" 3 ) (INIT (LIT "'a'")))
10        (DECL (UNSIGNED SHORT )(ID "s2" 5 ) (INIT (LIT 12)))
          (DECL (INT )(ID "i1" 6 ) (INIT (LIT 123)))
12        (EXPSTMT (ASSN (ID "c1" 2) (ADD (ID "s2" 5) (ID "s2" 5))))
          (EXPSTMT (ASSN (ID "c1" 2) (ADD (ID "i1" 6) (ID "c1" 2))))
14        (EXPSTMT (ASSN (ID "c1" 2) (ADD (ID "c1" 2) (ID "i1" 6))))
          ))"␣;␣End␣of␣function␣main"
16   (TYPE-SAFETY-ANALYSIS
         ... "removed␣repeat␣of␣code␣for␣brevity"
18       (DECLARATIONS ((2 ("c1")((CHAR) (NOQUAL) (NOSTORE))(NIL))
                        (3 ("c2")((UCHAR) (NOQUAL) (NOSTORE))(97))
20                      (5 ("s2")((USHORT) (NOQUAL) (NOSTORE))(12))
                        (6 ("i1")((INT) (NOQUAL) (NOSTORE))(123))))
22       (EXP-STMTS (((EXPSTMT (ASSN (ID "c1" 2)
                                     (ADD (ID "s2" 5) (ID "s2" 5)))
24                            (LINE 6))
                      (2 ("c1")((CHAR) (NOQUAL) (NOSTORE))(24)))
26                  ((EXPSTMT (ASSN (ID "c1" 2)
                                    (ADD (ID "i1" 6) (ID "c1" 2)))
28                           (LINE 7))
                     (2 ("c1")((CHAR) (NOQUAL) (NOSTORE))
30                       (147 "Error:␣exceeds␣value␣range␣of␣type" CHAR)))
                  ((EXPSTMT (ASSN (ID "c1" 2)
32                                (ADD (ID "c1" 2) (ID "i1" 6)))
                           (LINE 8))
34                  (2 ("c1")((CHAR) (NOQUAL) (NOSTORE))
                       (270 "Error:␣exceeds␣value␣range␣of␣type"
36                           CHAR))))))
```

Listing 1.2. Type-Safety analysis tool output for Listing 1.1

While it is impossible to statically determine the state of all C programs because of unknown input and externally defined functions, the tool should evaluate and track expression and statement results whenever operand values are known. Once evaluated, the result values are checked to see if they fall within the valid range of values representable by the result type. If the value falls outside the valid range or if any of the checks based on the static typing rules fail, the tool issues an error statement. If any operand value is not known, such as a point of unknown input data, a warning should be issued about the unknown value and display the range of acceptable values. The intent is to make this warning into a verification condition for the tool.

The process behind this design starts with listing the declaration statements. Once the declarations have been verified, the tool uses the declaration table and the code's AST to validate all expressions, statements and their execution branches, and function calls. As each is evaluated, value changes, if any, are updated in the declaration table. For example, the analysis report for Listings 1.1 appears in Listing 1.2. In this example, lines 6–15 show the lisp model of the code, lines 18–21 show program state after execution, with final variable values, or ranges of values, as the last item in the list for each variable. Lines 22–36 show the full output of the analysis, with detected integer errors listed on lines 30 and 35.

4   Conclusions

An ACL2 C integer type safety analysis tool is being constructed. To date, a formal type system has been constructed and the final functions for the declaration statements for the tool are being coded. Unlike some static type-checking tools, we support dynamic analysis over the type ranges of possible values of the variables whenever a variable value is known; thus detecting some potentially overlooked errors, while reducing the number of false positives.

The tool in its present form does not adequately handle floats, ACL2 readily handles rational numbers such as $\frac{1}{2}$ but rejects floating point numbers such as 0.5. We are examining approaches to handling floats. In addition, proofs of correctness of the analysis are being developed. With the support of ACL2 we will be able to verify properties of the type inference rules, and to validate if certain errors can always be detected in all code (or a subset of programs).

References

1. ISO/IEC: Programming Language—C. International Committee for Information Technology Standards. Iso/iec 9899:2011 edn. (October 2011)
2. Seacord, R.C.: Secure Coding in C and C++. Pearson Education (2006)
3. Cousot, P., Cousot, R., Feret, J., Mauborgne, L., Miné, A., Monniaux, D., Rival, X.: The ASTREÉ analyzer. In: Sagiv, M. (ed.) ESOP 2005. LNCS, vol. 3444, pp. 21–30. Springer, Heidelberg (2005)
4. Ritichie, D.M.: The development of the C language. ACM SIGPLAN Notices 4, 201–208 (March 1993); Reprints of the Second ACM SIGPLAN History of Programming Language (HOPL II)
5. ISO/IEC: C Programming Language. International Committee for Information Technology Standards. Iso/iec 9899:1999 edn. (1999)
6. Mitchell, J.C.: Type inference with simple subtypes. Journal of Functional Programming 1(3), 245–285 (1991)
7. Cardelli, L.: Type systems. In: Handbook of Computer Science and Engineering. CRC Press (1997)
8. Kaufmann, M., Manolios, P., Moore, J.S.: Computer-Aided Reasoning: An Approach. Kluwer Academic Publishers, USA (2002)
9. Alves-Foss, J.: C2acl2 translator design document. Technical report, Computer Science Department, University of Idaho (2010)
10. Liskov, B.H., Wing, J.M.: A behavioral notion of subtyping. ACM Transactions on Programming Languages and Systems 16, 1811–1841 (1994)

Hierarchical Safety Cases

Ewen Denney[1], Ganesh Pai[1], and Iain Whiteside[2]

[1] SGT / NASA Ames Research Center
Moffett Field, CA 94035, USA
{ewen.denney,ganesh.pai}@nasa.gov
[2] School of Informatics, University of Edinburgh
Edinburgh, EH8 9AB, Scotland
i.whiteside@sms.ed.ac.uk

Abstract. The development of a safety case has become common practice for the certification of systems in many safety-critical domains, but large safety cases still remain difficult to develop, evaluate and maintain. We propose hierarchical safety cases (*hicases*) as a technique to overcome some of the difficulties that arise in manipulating industrial-size safety arguments. This paper introduces and motivates hicases, lays their formal foundations and relates them to other safety case concepts. Our approach extends the existing Goal Structuring Notation (GSN) with abstraction mechanisms that allow viewing the safety case at different levels of detail.

Keywords: Abstraction, Automation, Formal methods, Hierarchy, Safety assurance, Safety cases.

1 Introduction

A *safety case*, or more generally an assurance case, is a structured argument supported by a body of evidence, which provides a convincing and valid justification that a system meets its (safety) assurance requirements, for a given application in a given operating environment. The development of a safety case is increasingly becoming an accepted practice for the certification of safety-critical systems in the nuclear, defense, oil and gas, and transportation domains. Indeed, the development and acceptance of a safety case is a key element of safety regulation in many safety-critical sectors [1].

At present, safety cases are manually constructed often using patterns; they also have some natural higher-level structure, but this can become obscured by lower-level details during their evolution. Furthermore, due to the volume of information aggregated, safety cases remain difficult to develop, evaluate (or understand), and maintain. As an anecdotal example, the size of the *preliminary* safety case for surveillance on airport surfaces with ADS-B [9] is about 200 pages, and is expected to grow as the operational safety case is created. Tools such as AdvoCATE [5] can assist in and, to an extent, automate the construction of assurance argument structures from external verification tools [6], and artifacts such as requirements tables [3]. Often, these have inherent structure that can be exploited to help comprehension.

These observations, and our own prior experience [2], suggest a need for abstraction and structuring mechanisms in creating, and when communicating, a safety argument.

G. Brat, N. Rungta, and A. Venet (Eds.): NFM 2013, LNCS 7871, pp. 478–483, 2013.
© Springer-Verlag Berlin Heidelberg 2013

The motivation for our work is the ongoing construction of a safety case [4] for the Swift unmanned aircraft system (UAS), being developed at NASA Ames. We have used the goal structuring notation (GSN) [10] to document the Swift UAS safety case. In brief, GSN is an effective graphical notation for representing the structure of an argument from its premises to its conclusions. Using GSN (e.g., as illustrated in Fig. 1), we can express the *goals* or claims made (rectangle), the *strategies* (parallelogram) to develop goals, *solutions* (circle) that justify the claims, together with the appropriate associated *context* (rounded rectangle), *assumptions*, and/or *justifications* (ovals). GSN also provides a graphical annotation ('◊') to indicate *undeveloped* elements. There are, additionally, two link types with which to connect the notational elements: *in-context-of* and *is-solved-by*.

In this paper, we extend GSN to include hierarchical structuring mechanisms, motivating and illustrating our ideas with a simple, but real, example argument structure fragment. The resulting structures, *hicases*, better clarify the structure of a safety case and, we believe, improve the quality and comprehensibility of the argument. Our specific contributions are a formalization of the notion of a *partial safety case (argument structure)*, its extension to include hierarchy, and relating the unfolding of a hicase to an (ordinary) safety case argument structure.

2   Types of Hierarchy and Their Restrictions

Fig. 1 shows part of a chain of claims, strategies and evidence, from the top level of the auto-generated fragment of the Swift UAS safety case (see [4] for details). The top-level claim AC1 concerns the correct computation of aileron control variable values, during descent, by the relevant PID control loop in the Swift UAS autopilot. The chain of argumentation shown represents a *direct* proof of a verification condition. Some of the details of the proof have been transformed into the safety case, such as the theorem prover used as context, the proof objects, i.e., verification conditions, as claims, etc. This is an instance of a sub-structure that we may abstract away in a hierarchical presentation.

In general, we define three types of hierarchical abstractions, i.e., *hinodes*:

(1) *Hierarchical evidence* abstracts a *fully developed* chain of related strategy applications, e.g., in Fig. 1, since the argument structure starting from the strategy AC10 downwards is complete (has no undeveloped elements), we can construct a hierarchical evidence node, H1: Proof using Vampire–0.6 Prover, that abstracts and encapsulates it. As there are many such verification conditions (in the auto-generated safety case fragment of the Swift UAS), we have many instances of this structure. We can iterate this procedure up the proof tree which offers opportunities for nesting hierarchies. Thus, iterated abstraction can greatly reduce the size of the argument structure when viewed.

(2) *Hierarchical goals*, or *higoals*, are an abstraction to hide a chain of goals; one of their main purposes is to provide a high-level view of an argument structure. In Fig. 1, we can abstract the argument structure starting from (but not including) the strategy AC2 downwards, into the higoal H2: Decomposed correctness properties hold.

(3) *Hierarchical strategies* aggregate a meaningful chain of (one or more) related strategy applications, e.g., in Fig. 1, we can abstract the strategy AC30, along with its sub-goals (AC76 and AC86), and its context elements (AC32 and AC34), into a single

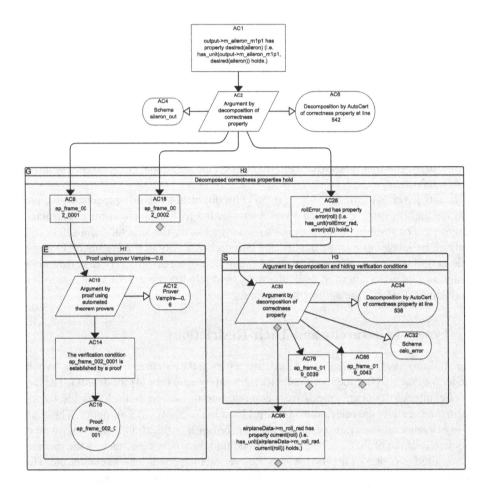

Fig. 1. Fragment of an auto-generated part of the Swift UAS safety case [4], showing *hinodes* annotated as G (goal), S (strategy) and E (evidence)

hierarchical strategy H3: Argument by decomposition and hiding verification conditions. Thus, hierarchical strategies can hide side-conditions (or trivial subgoals) by fully enclosing particular paths of the safety case argument structure. This gives us the flexibility to concentrate an inspection on specific *important* paths through the safety argument, e.g., those paths addressing claims having 'high-risk'.

There are restrictions on what can be abstracted inside a hinode: firstly, to preserve well-formedness, input and output node types should be consistent, e.g., a hierarchical strategy would have a goal as an incoming node and goals as outgoing nodes, in the same way as an ordinary strategy. Next, we cannot abstract disconnected fragments as there would be no path from the input goal to all the outputs. It is important to note that this restriction does not force each hinode to have only one input. Rather, the restriction applies to the input, so multiple connections can enter a hinode. A design decision was to place any context, justification, and assumption nodes inside a hinode; thus, we may not link two (or more) hinodes, using a link of type *in-context-of*. Finally, we permit encapsulation of both hierarchical evidence and strategies by higoals (e.g., as shown in Fig. 1), or of both hierarchical goals and evidence by hierarchical strategies. This gives us a notion of *nesting* of hierarchies as a way to manage the size of an argument structure.

3 Formalization

To formalize standard safety case argument structures and hierarchical argument structures, we represent them as a labeled tree. The labeling function distinguishes the types of nodes subject to some intuitive well-formedness conditions.

Definition 1. *Let* $\{s, g, e, a, j, c\}$ *be the node types* strategy, goal, evidence, assumption, justification, *and* context *respectively. A partial safety case (argument structure) is a triple* $\langle N, l, \rightarrow \rangle$, *comprising nodes* N, *the labeling function* $l : N \rightarrow \{s, g, e, a, j, c\}$ *that gives the node type, and the connector relation,* $\rightarrow: \langle N, N \rangle$, *which is defined on nodes. We define the transitive closure,* $\rightarrow^*: \langle N, N \rangle$, *in the usual way. We require the connector relation to form a finite forest with the operation* $isroot_N(r)$ *checking if the node* r *is a root in some tree[1]. Furthermore, the following conditions must be met:*
(1) Each part of the partial safety case has a root goal: $isroot_N(r) \Rightarrow l(r) = g$
(2) Connectors only leave strategies or goals: $n \rightarrow m \Rightarrow l(n) \in \{s, g\}$
(3) Goals cannot connect to other goals: $(n \rightarrow m) \wedge [l(n) = g] \Rightarrow l(m) \in \{s, e, a, j, c\}$
(4) Strategies cannot connect to other strategies or evidence:
$\quad (n \rightarrow m) \wedge [l(n) = s] \Rightarrow l(m) \in \{g, a, j, c\}$

By virtue of forming a tree, we ensure that nodes cannot connect to themselves, that there are no cycles and, finally, that two nodes cannot connect to the same child node. Additionally, we see that the two link types (*is-solved-by* and *in-context-of*) have no semantic content, but rather provide an informational role.

Now, we extend Definition 1 with an additional partial order relation $\leq$ representing hierarchical structure, where $n < n'$ means that the node n is encapsulated in n'. We define a partial hierarchical safety case, i.e., hicase, such that we can always *unfold* all the hierarchy to regain an ordinary safety case argument structure.

Definition 2. *A partial hierarchical safety case is a tuple* $\langle N, l, \rightarrow, \leq \rangle$. *The set of nodes* N *and labeling function* l *are as in Definition 1. The forest* $\langle N, \rightarrow \rangle$ *is subject to the same conditions as in Definition 1. The hierarchical relation* $\leq$ *fulfils the axioms of a partial order and can thus also be viewed alongside* N *as a forest. Finally, we impose the following conditions on the interaction between the two relations* $\rightarrow$ *and* $\leq$:
(1) If v *is a local root (using* $\rightarrow$*) of a higher-level node* w *(i.e.* $v < w$*), then* $l(w) =$

$$
\begin{cases}
g, \text{ if } l(v) = g \wedge \forall v' \, v''. \, (v' < w \wedge v' \rightarrow v'' \wedge v'' \not< w) \Rightarrow l(v'') = s \\
s, \text{ if } l(v) = s \wedge [\forall v' \, v''. \, (v' < w \wedge v' \rightarrow v'' \wedge v'' \not< w) \Rightarrow l(v') = g \\
\qquad \vee \text{ subtree rooted at } v \text{ is not fully developed}] \\
e, \text{ if } l(v) = s \wedge [\nexists v' \, v''. \, (v' < w \wedge v'' \not< w \wedge v' \rightarrow v'') \\
\qquad \wedge \text{ subtree rooted at } v \text{ is fully developed}]
\end{cases}
$$

---

[1] A safety case argument structure has a single root.

(2) *Connectors will target the outer nodes:* $(v \to w_1) \wedge (w_1 < w_2) \Rightarrow v < w_2$

(3) *Connectors come from inner nodes:* $(v \to w_1) \wedge (w_1 \leq w_2) \Rightarrow v = w_1$

(4) *Hierarchy and connection are mutually exclusive:* $(v \leq w) \wedge (v \to^* w) \Rightarrow v = w$

(5) *Two nodes which are both at the top level, or immediately included in some node, means that at most one node has no incoming $\to$ edge:*
$siblings_i(v_1, v_2) \wedge isroot_s(v_1) \wedge isroot_s(v_2) \Rightarrow v_1 = v_2$

Condition (1) formalizes our intuition that (a) a higoal must have a goal as root and any nodes immediately outside the higoal must be strategy nodes, (b) a hierarchical strategy must have a strategy as root, and either any nodes immediately outside the hierarchical strategy must be goals, or the subtree rooted at v inside is not fully developed. The latter accounts for the possibility that there are no outgoing goals, but the node is not evidence; and (c) a hierarchical evidence node is the special case of a hierarchical strategy with no outgoing goals, but where the subtree with root at v is fully developed. That is, we can view hierarchical evidence as a hierarchical strategy without outgoing goals just as evidence is an axiomatic strategy. Conditions (2) through (5) are designed to produce a mapping from a hierarchical argument structure to its ordinary argument structure unfolding, i.e., its *skeleton*.

We note that a safety case argument structure $\langle N, l, \to \rangle$ can be mapped to a hicase $\langle N, l, \to, id_V \rangle$ where id_V is the trivial partial order with only reflexive pairs. This ordering trivially satisfies all the well-formedness properties of a hicase. Conversely, we define a *skeleton* operation (sk), which maps hicases to ordinary safety case argument structures, such that the tuple it constructs is well-formed with respect to the safety case argument structure conditions (of Definition 1).

Theorem 1. *The skeleton operation (sk) which maps a hicase $\langle N, l, \to, \leq \rangle$ to a safety case argument structure $\langle N', l', \to' \rangle$, where N' is the set of leaves of $\leq$, l' is the restriction of the labeling function l, and $v_1 \to' v_2$ iff $\exists w \in N \mid v_2 \leq w$ and $v_1 \to w$ maps a well-formed hicase to a safety case argument structure.*

Proof Sketch. The relationship between *hiproofs* [7] and hicases (as well as the corresponding relationship between safety cases and proofs) allows us to claim that the mapping constructs the appropriate forest structure on $\langle N', \to' \rangle$. We simply need to show the well-formedness conditions (2) through (4) of Definition 1. For instance, condition (2), i.e., $(v_1 \to v_2) \Rightarrow l(v_1) \in \{s, g\}$, comes for free since if $v_1 \to w$ then it already has this property for $v_1 \to' v_2$.

4   Related Work and Conclusions

Hierarchy in safety cases has been proposed as a basic (hierarchical) decomposition represented as indentations in a spreadsheet-based argument structure [11]. This work creates the equivalent of hierarchical evidence, but cannot hierarchically abstract strategies, as in our approach. Our notion of hierarchy considers ways in which to combine nodes for meaningful abstraction, unlike the notion of argument structure *depth*. GSN supplies a concept for *modules* and references to *away* nodes [10] that are complementary to hicases, though neither modules nor hicases subsume each other's functionality. Whereas *away* objects are simply references to a separate safety case fragment, *higoals* are an additional node enclosing an existing argument structure. GSN modules do not have an equivalent notion of a hierarchical strategy as an enclosure of (possibly) a complex (unfinished) safety case fragment. Modules can be seen as a large segment of a safety case, typically applied at a higher level, whereas we view hinodes as being viable at all scales. Modules also have informal *contracts* that they must fulfill to be well-formed, but hinodes do not enforce any semantic properties.

We have implemented hicases in our assurance case toolset, AdvoCATE [5], providing basic features for constructing, modifying, and viewing hinodes, e.g., we can modify existing argument structures to add hinodes with *open* (white-box) or *closed* (black-box) views. We can also generate a tree representation of a hicase and modify its contents [8]. Our current definition for safety cases and hicases only accounts for core GSN and potential meta-data extensions. In practice, most safety case argument structures make use of either (or all) of the GSN modular extensions and pattern mechanisms; we would like to give an account for each of these within our model, with careful thought about the module language to ensure that no inconsistencies are introduced.

We would also like to investigate the formal notions of *hicase view* (a slice through the hierarchy giving a safety case fragment), and *hicase refinement* (providing a mathematical meaning for well-formed changes to the hicase); although both exist informally in our tool implementation, we believe it is important to formalize these concepts.

Acknowledgement. This work has been funded by the AFCS element of the SSAT project in the Aviation Safety Program of the NASA Aeronautics Mission Directorate.

References

1. Bloomfield, R., Bishop, P.: Safety and Assurance Cases: Past, Present and Possible Future – An Adelard Perspective. In: Proc. 18th Safety-Critical Sys. Symp. (February 2010)
2. Denney, E., Habli, I., Pai, G.: Perspectives on Software Safety Case Development for Unmanned Aircraft. In: Proc. 42nd Intl. Conf. Dependable Sys. and Networks (June 2012)
3. Denney, E., Pai, G.: A lightweight methodology for safety case assembly. In: Ortmeier, F., Daniel, P. (eds.) SAFECOMP 2012. LNCS, vol. 7612, pp. 1–12. Springer, Heidelberg (2012)
4. Denney, E., Pai, G., Pohl, J.: Automating the generation of heterogeneous aviation safety cases. Tech. Rep. NASA/CR-2011-215983, NASA Ames Research Center (August 2011)
5. Denney, E., Pai, G., Pohl, J.: AdvoCATE: An Assurance Case Automation Toolset. In: Ortmeier, F., Daniel, P. (eds.) SAFECOMP 2012 Workshops. LNCS, vol. 7613, pp. 8–21. Springer, Heidelberg (2012)
6. Denney, E., Pai, G., Pohl, J.: Heterogeneous aviation safety cases: Integrating the formal and the non-formal. In: 17th IEEE Intl. Conf. Eng. of Complex Comp. Sys. (July 2012)
7. Denney, E., Power, J., Tourlas, K.: Hiproofs: A hierarchical notion of proof tree. Electr. Notes on Theoretical Comp. Sci. 155, 341–359 (2006)
8. Denney, E., Whiteside, I.: Hierarchical safety cases. Tech. Rep. NASA/TM-2012-216481, NASA Ames Research Center (December 2012)
9. European Organisation for the Safety of Air Navigation: Preliminary safety case for ADS-B airport surface surveillance application. PSC ADS-B-APT (November 2011)
10. Goal Structuring Notation Working Group: GSN Community Standard v.1 (November 2011), http://www.goalstructuringnotation.info/
11. Stone, G.: On arguing the safety of large systems. In: 10th Australian Workshop on Safety-Related Programmable Sys. ACM Intl. Conf. Proc. Series, vol. 162, pp. 69–75 (2006)

Author Index